SECOND EDITION

Programming Scala

Dean Wampler and Alex Payne

öln · Sebastopol · Tokyo  O'REILLY®

Programming Scala, Second Edition

by Dean Wampler and Alex Payne

Printed in the United States of America.

Published by O'Reilly Media, Inc., 1005 Gravenstein Highway North, Sebastopol, CA 95472.

O'Reilly books may be purchased for educational, business, or sales promotional use. Online editions are also available for most titles (*http://safaribooksonline.com*). For more information, contact our corporate/institutional sales department: 800-998-9938 or *corporate@oreilly.com*.

Editor: Meghan Blanchette		**Indexer:** Wendy Catalano
Production Editor: Nicole Shelby		**Cover Designer:** Ellie Volckhausen
Copyeditor: Kim Cofer		**Interior Designer:** David Futato
Proofreader: Charles Roumeliotis		**Illustrator:** Rebecca Demarest

September 2009:   First Edition

November 2014:   Second Edition

Revision History for the First Edition:

2014-11-25:   First release

See *http://oreilly.com/catalog/errata.csp?isbn=9781491949856* for release details.

ISBN: 978-1-491-94985-6

[LSI]

To Everette Lawrence Wampler, August 28, 1931 - May 9, 2013.

— Dean

Table of Contents

Foreword

If there has been a common theme throughout my career as a programmer, it has been the quest for better abstractions and better tools to support the craft of writing software. Over the years, I have come to value one trait more than any other: composability. If one can write code with good composability, it usually means that other traits we software developers value—such as orthogonality, loose coupling, and high cohesion—are already present. It is all connected.

When I discovered Scala some years ago, the thing that made the biggest impression on me was its composability.

Through some very elegant design choices and simple yet powerful abstractions that were taken from the object-oriented and functional programming worlds, Martin Odersky has managed to create a language with high cohesion and orthogonal, deep abstractions that invites composability in all dimensions of software design. Scala is truly a SCAlable LAnguage that scales with usage, from scripting all the way up to large-scale enterprise applications and middleware.

Scala was born out of academia, but it has grown into a pragmatic and practical language that is very much ready for real-world production use.

What excites me most about this book is that it's so practical. Dean has done a fantastic job, not only by explaining the language through interesting discussions and samples, but also by putting it in the context of the real world. It's written for the programmer who wants to get things done.

I had the pleasure of getting to know Dean some years ago when we were both part of the aspect-oriented programming community. Dean holds a rare mix of deep analytical academic thinking and a pragmatic, get-things-done kind of mentality.

You are about to learn how to write reusable components using mixin and function composition; how to write Reactive applications using Akka; how to make effective use of advanced features in Scala such as macros and higher kinded types; how to utilize Scala's rich, flexible, and expressive syntax to build domain-specific languages; how to effectively test your Scala code; how to let Scala simplify your Big Data problems; and much, much more.

Enjoy the ride. I sure did.

—Jonas Bonér
CTO & cofounder Typesafe, August 2014

Preface

Programming Scala introduces an exciting and powerful language that offers all the benefits of a modern object model, *functional programming* (FP), and an advanced type system, while leveraging the industry's investment in the Java Virtual Machine (JVM). Packed with code examples, this comprehensive book teaches you how to be productive with Scala quickly, and explains what makes this language ideal for today's scalable, distributed, component-based applications that support concurrency and distribution. You'll also learn how Scala takes advantage of the advanced JVM as a platform for programming languages.

Learn more at *http://programming-scala.org* or at the book's catalog page (*http://bit.ly/programmingScala_2E*).

Welcome to Programming Scala, Second Edition

Programming Scala, First Edition was published five years ago, in the fall of 2009. At the time, it was only the third book dedicated to Scala, and it just missed being the second by a few months. Scala version 2.7.5 was the official release, with version 2.8.0 nearing completion.

A lot has changed since then. At the time of this writing, the Scala version is 2.11.2. Martin Odersky, the creator of Scala, and Jonas Bonér, the creator of Akka, an actor-based concurrency framework, cofounded Typesafe (*http://typesafe.com*) to promote the language and tools built on it.

There are also a lot more books about Scala. So, do we really need a second edition of this book? Many excellent beginner's guides to Scala are now available. A few advanced books have emerged. The encyclopedic reference remains *Programming in Scala*, Second Edition, by Odersky et al. (Artima Press).

Yet, I believe *Programming Scala, Second Edition* remains unique because it is a *comprehensive* guide to the Scala language and ecosystem, a guide for beginners to advanced users, and it retains the focus on the pragmatic concerns of working professionals. These characteristics made the first edition popular.

Scala is now used by many more organizations than in 2009 and most Java developers have now heard of Scala. Several persistent questions have emerged. Isn't Scala complex? Since Java 8 added significant new features found in Scala, why should I switch to Scala?

I'll tackle these and other, real-world concerns. I have often said that I was *seduced by Scala*, warts and all. I hope you'll feel the same way after reading *Programming Scala, Second Edition*.

How to Read This Book

Because this is a comprehensive book, beginning readers don't need to read the whole thing to be productive with Scala. The first three chapters, *Zero to Sixty: Introducing Scala, Type Less, Do More*, and *Rounding Out the Basics*, provide a quick summary of core language features. The fourth and fifth chapters, *Pattern Matching* and *Implicits*, begin the more in-depth coverage with two fundamental tools that you'll use every day in your Scala code.

If you're new to functional programming (FP), Chapter 6 provides an introduction to this important approach to software development, as implemented in Scala. Next is Chapter 7, which explains Scala's extensions to the venerable for loop and how it provides a succinct syntax for sophisticated, idiomatic functional code.

Then we turn to Scala's support for *object-oriented programming* (OOP) in Chapter 8. I put the FP chapter before the OOP chapters to emphasize the importance of FP in solving many software development problems of our time. It would be easy to use Scala as a "better object-oriented Java," but that would ignore its most powerful tools! Most of this chapter will be conceptually easy to understand, as you learn how Scala defines classes, constructors, etc. that are familiar in Java.

Chapter 9 explores Scala's ability to compose behaviors using *traits*. Java 8 adds a subset of this functionality through its enhancements to interfaces, partially inspired by Scala traits. Even experienced Java programmers will need to understand this material.

The next four chapters, 10 through 13, *The Scala Object System, Part I, The Scala Object System, Part II, The Scala Collections Library*, and *Visibility Rules*, walk through Scala's object model and library types in detail. You should read Chapter 10 carefully, because it contains essential information to master early on. However, Chapter 11 goes into less critical information, the details of properly implementing nontrivial type hierarchies. You might skim that chapter the first time through the book. Chapter 12 discusses the design of the collections and some useful information about using them wisely. Again, skim this chapter if you're new to Scala and come back to it when you're trying to master the details of the collections API. Finally, Chapter 13 explains in detail Scala's fine-grained extensions to Java's notions of public, protected, and private visibility. Skim this chapter.

Next we move into more advanced territory, starting with Chapter 14 and Chapter 15, which cover Scala's sophisticated type system. I've divided the coverage into two chapters: the first chapter covers concepts that new Scala programmers will need to learn relatively quickly, while the second chapter covers more advanced material that can be deferred until later.

Similarly, Chapter 16, *Advanced Functional Programming*, covers more advanced mathematical concepts that the average Scala developer won't need initially, such as *Monad* and *Functor* from *Category Theory*.

Chapter 17, *Tools for Concurrency*, will be useful for developers of large-scale services that require concurrency for resiliency and scalability (most of us, actually). It discusses Akka (*http://akka.io*), a rich actor-based concurrency model, and library types such as Futures for writing asynchronous code.

Chapter 18, *Scala for Big Data*, makes the case that a *killer app* for Scala, and functional programming in general, is *Big Data*, or any data-centric computation.

Chapters 19 and 20, *Dynamic Invocation in Scala* and *Domain-Specific Languages in Scala*, go together. They are somewhat advanced topics, discussing tools for construction of rich *domain-specific languages*.

Chapter 21, *Scala Tools and Libraries*, discusses tools like IDEs and third-party libraries. If you're new to Scala, read about IDE and editor support, and the section on *SBT*, the de facto build tool for Scala projects. Use the library lists for reference later on. Chapter 22, *Java Interoperability*, will be useful for teams that need to interoperate between Java and Scala code.

I wrote Chapter 23, *Application Design*, for architects and software leads to share my thoughts about good application design. I believe the traditional model of relatively fat JAR files with complex object graphs is a broken model and needs to go.

Finally, the most advanced topic in the book is covered in Chapter 24, *Metaprogramming: Macros and Reflection*. You can definitely skip this chapter if you're a beginner.

The book concludes with Appendix A, *References* for further reading.

What Isn't Covered?

A focus of the latest 2.11 release is modularizing the library to decompose it into smaller JAR files, so it's easier to exclude unneeded code from deployment in space-sensitive environments (e.g., mobile devices). Some previously deprecated packages and types of the library were also removed. Other parts are deprecated in the 2.11 release, often because they are no longer maintained and there are better, third-party alternatives.

Hence, we won't discuss the following packages that are deprecated in 2.11:

scala.actors *(http://bit.ly/1tIem7W)*
> An actor library. Use Akka actors instead (which we'll discuss in "Robust, Scalable Concurrency with Actors" on page 429).

scala.collection.script *(http://bit.ly/13p3wKl)*
> A library for writing collection observations and update "scripts."

scala.text *(http://bit.ly/1s0PvrR)*
> A "pretty-printing" library.

The following were deprecated in Scala 2.10 and removed in 2.11:

scala.util.automata *(http://bit.ly/1DDinM1)*
> For building deterministic, finite automatons (DFAs) from regular expressions.

scala.util.grammar *(http://bit.ly/1tIeunQ)*
> Part of a parsing library.

scala.util.logging *(http://bit.ly/1E8xNKn)*
> The recommendation is to use one of the many third-party, actively maintained logging libraries for the JVM.

scala.util.regexp *(http://bit.ly/10akU3j)*
> Regular expression parsing. The scala.util.matching *(http://bit.ly/13p4Lcm)* package with regular expression support has been enhanced instead.

The .NET compiler backend
> For a while, the Scala team worked on a compiler backend and library for the .NET runtime environment, but interest in this port has waned, so it was discontinued.

We won't discuss *every* package and type in the library. Here is a partial list of omissions for space and other reasons:

scala.swing *(http://bit.ly/13p4LcD)*
> Wrapper around the Java Swing library. While still maintained, it is rarely used.

scala.util.continuations *(http://bit.ly/13p4LJp)*
> Compiler plug-in for continuation-passing style (CPS) code generation. It is a specialized tool with limited adoption.

The App (http://bit.ly/108gMRJ) and DelayedInit (http://bit.ly/1E8xQpF) traits
> This pair of types was meant to conveniently implement main (entry-point) types, the analog of static main methods in Java classes. However, they sometimes cause surprising behavior, so I don't recommend using them. Instead, I'll write main routines in the normal, idiomatic Scala way.

`scala.ref` *(http://bit.ly/1tIeMv5)*

> Wrappers around Java types such as `WeakReference` *(http://bit.ly/1wO9WfM)*, which corresponds to `java.lang.ref.WeakReference` *(http://bit.ly/1OFvyjC)*.

`scala.runtime` *(http://bit.ly/13p4RB0)*

> Types used as part of the library implementation.

`scala.util.hashing` *(http://bit.ly/1zmu0cL)*

> Hashing algorithms.

Welcome to Programming Scala, First Edition

Programming languages become popular for many reasons. Sometimes, programmers on a given platform prefer a particular language, or one is institutionalized by a vendor. Most Mac OS programmers use Objective-C. Most Windows programmers use C++ and .NET languages. Most embedded-systems developers use C and C++.

Sometimes, popularity derived from technical merit gives way to fashion and fanaticism. C++, Java, and Ruby have been the objects of fanatical devotion among programmers.

Sometimes, a language becomes popular because it fits the needs of its era. Java was initially seen as a perfect fit for browser-based, rich client applications. Smalltalk captured the essence of object-oriented programming as that model of programming entered the mainstream.

Today, concurrency, heterogeneity, always-on services, and ever-shrinking development schedules are driving interest in functional programming. It appears that the dominance of object-oriented programming may be over. Mixing paradigms is becoming popular, even necessary.

We gravitated to Scala from other languages because Scala embodies many of the optimal qualities we want in a general-purpose programming language for the kinds of applications we build today: reliable, high-performance, highly concurrent Internet and enterprise applications.

Scala is a multiparadigm language, supporting both object-oriented and functional programming approaches. Scala is scalable, suitable for everything from short scripts up to large-scale, component-based applications. Scala is sophisticated, incorporating state-of-the-art ideas from the halls of computer science departments worldwide. Yet Scala is practical. Its creator, Martin Odersky, participated in the development of Java for years and understands the needs of professional developers.

Both of us were seduced by Scala, by its concise, elegant, and expressive syntax and by the breadth of tools it put at our disposal. In this book, we strive to demonstrate why all these qualities make Scala a compelling and indispensable programming language.

If you are an experienced developer who wants a fast, thorough introduction to Scala, this book is for you. You may be evaluating Scala as a replacement for or complement to your current languages. Maybe you have already decided to use Scala, and you need to learn its features and how to use it well. Either way, we hope to illuminate this powerful language for you in an accessible way.

We assume that you are well versed in object-oriented programming, but we don't assume that you have prior exposure to functional programming. We assume that you are experienced in one or more other programming languages. We draw parallels to features in Java, C#, Ruby, and other languages. If you know any of these languages, we'll point out similar features in Scala, as well as many features that are new.

Whether you come from an object-oriented or functional programming background, you will see how Scala elegantly combines both paradigms, demonstrating their complementary nature. Based on many examples, you will understand how and when to apply OOP and FP techniques to many different design problems.

In the end, we hope that you too will be seduced by Scala. Even if Scala does not end up becoming your day-to-day language, we hope you will gain insights that you can apply regardless of which language you are using.

Conventions Used in This Book

The following typographical conventions are used in this book:

Italic
> Indicates new terms, URLs, email addresses, filenames, and file extensions.

`Constant width`
> Used for program listings, as well as within paragraphs to refer to program elements such as variable or function names, databases, data types, environment variables, statements, and keywords.

`Constant width bold`
> Shows commands or other text that should be typed literally by the user.

`Constant width italic`
> Shows text that should be replaced with user-supplied values or by values determined by context.

 This element signifies a tip or suggestion.

This element signifies a general note.

This element indicates a warning or caution.

Using Code Examples

This book is here to help you get your job done. In general, you may use the code in this book in your programs and documentation. You do not need to contact us for permission unless you're reproducing a significant portion of the code. For example, writing a program that uses several chunks of code from this book does not require permission. Selling or distributing a CD-ROM of examples from O'Reilly books does require permission. Answering a question by citing this book and quoting example code does not require permission. Incorporating a significant amount of example code from this book into your product's documentation does require permission.

We appreciate, but do not require, attribution. An attribution usually includes the title, author, publisher, and ISBN. For example: "*Programming Scala, Second Edition* by Dean Wampler and Alex Payne. Copyright 2015 Kevin Dean Wampler and Alex Payne, 978-1-491-94985-6."

If you feel your use of code examples falls outside fair use or the permission given above, feel free to contact us at *permissions@oreilly.com*.

Getting the Code Examples

You can download the code examples from GitHub (*http://bit.ly/prog-scala-code*). Unzip the files to a convenient location. See the *README* file in the distribution for instructions on building and using the examples. (I'll summarize those instructions in the first chapter.)

Some of the example files can be run as scripts using the `scala` command. Others must be compiled into class files. Some files contain deliberate errors and won't compile. I have adopted a filenaming convention to indicate each of these cases, although as you learn Scala it should become obvious from the contents of the files, in most cases:

*.scala

The standard Scala file extension is *.scala*, but that doesn't distinguish between source files that must be compiled using `scalac`, script files you run directly with `scala`, or deliberately invalid code files used at times in this book. So, in the example code, any file with the *.scala* extension must be compiled separately, like you would compile Java code.

*.sc

Files that end in *.sc* can be run as scripts on a command line using `scala`, e.g., `scala foo.sc`. You can also start `scala` in the interpreter mode and load any script file in the interpreter using the `:load filename` command. Note that this naming convention is *not* a standard convention in the Scala community, but it's used here because the *SBT* build will ignore these files. Also, this file extension is used by the new IDE *worksheet* feature we will discuss in the next chapter. So, it's a convenient hack. To be clear, you will normally use *.scala* as the extension of scripts and code files alike.

*.scalaX and *.scX

Some example files contain deliberate errors that will cause compilation errors. Rather than break the build for the examples, those files will use the extension *.scalaX* for code files or *.scX* for scripts. Again, this is not an industry convention. These files will also have embedded comments to explain what's wrong with them.

Safari® Books Online

 *Safari Books Online* is an on-demand digital library that delivers expert content in both book and video form from the world's leading authors in technology and business.

Technology professionals, software developers, web designers, and business and creative professionals use Safari Books Online as their primary resource for research, problem solving, learning, and certification training.

Safari Books Online offers a range of plans and pricing for enterprise, government, education, and individuals.

Members have access to thousands of books, training videos, and prepublication manuscripts in one fully searchable database from publishers like O'Reilly Media, Prentice Hall Professional, Addison-Wesley Professional, Microsoft Press, Sams, Que, Peachpit Press, Focal Press, Cisco Press, John Wiley & Sons, Syngress, Morgan Kaufmann, IBM Redbooks, Packt, Adobe Press, FT Press, Apress, Manning, New Riders, McGraw-Hill, Jones & Bartlett, Course Technology, and hundreds more. For more information about Safari Books Online, please visit us online.

How to Contact Us

Please address comments and questions concerning this book to the publisher:

O'Reilly Media, Inc.
1005 Gravenstein Highway North
Sebastopol, CA 95472
800-998-9938 (in the United States or Canada)
707-829-0515 (international or local)
707-829-0104 (fax)

We have a web page for this book, where we list errata, examples, and any additional information. You can access this page at *http://bit.ly/programmingScala_2E*.

To comment or ask technical questions about this book, send email to *bookques tions@oreilly.com*.

For more information about our books, courses, conferences, and news, see our website at *http://www.oreilly.com*.

Find us on Facebook: *http://facebook.com/oreilly*

Follow us on Twitter: *http://twitter.com/oreillymedia*

Watch us on YouTube: *http://www.youtube.com/oreillymedia*

Acknowledgments for the Second Edition

As I, Dean Wampler, worked on this edition of the book, I continued to enjoy the mentoring and feedback from many of my Typesafe colleagues, plus the valuable feedback from people who reviewed the early-access releases. I'm especially grateful to Ramnivas Laddad, Kevin Kilroy, Lutz Huehnken, and Thomas Lockney, who reviewed drafts of the manuscript. Thanks to my long-time colleague and friend, Jonas Bonér, for writing an updated Foreword for the book.

And special thanks to Ann who allowed me to consume so much of our personal time with this project. I love you!

Acknowledgments for the First Edition

As we developed this book, many people read early drafts and suggested numerous improvements to the text, for which we are eternally grateful. We are especially grateful to Steve Jensen, Ramnivas Laddad, Marcel Molina, Bill Venners, and Jonas Bonér for their extensive feedback.

Much of the feedback we received came through the Safari Rough Cuts releases and the online edition available at *http://programmingscala.com.* We are grateful for the feedback provided by (in no particular order) Iulian Dragos, Nikolaj Lindberg, Matt Hellige, David Vydra, Ricky Clarkson, Alex Cruise, Josh Cronemeyer, Tyler Jennings, Alan Supynuk, Tony Hillerson, Roger Vaughn, Arbi Sookazian, Bruce Leidl, Daniel Sobral, Eder Andres Avila, Marek Kubica, Henrik Huttunen, Bhaskar Maddala, Ged Byrne, Derek Mahar, Geoffrey Wiseman, Peter Rawsthorne, Geoffrey Wiseman, Joe Bowbeer, Alexander Battisti, Rob Dickens, Tim MacEachern, Jason Harris, Steven Grady, Bob Follek, Ariel Ortiz, Parth Malwankar, Reid Hochstedler, Jason Zaugg, Jon Hanson, Mario Gleichmann, David Gates, Zef Hemel, Michael Yee, Marius Kreis, Martin Süsskraut, Javier Vegas, Tobias Hauth, Francesco Bochicchio, Stephen Duncan Jr., Patrik Dudits, Jan Niehusmann, Bill Burdick, David Holbrook, Shalom Deitch, Jesper Nordenberg, Esa Laine, Gleb Frank, Simon Andersson, Patrik Dudits, Chris Lewis, Julian Howarth, Dirk Kuzemczak, Henri Gerrits, John Heintz, Stuart Roebuck, and Jungho Kim. Many other readers for whom we only have usernames also provided feedback. We wish to thank Zack, JoshG, ewilligers, abcoates, brad, teto, pjcj, mkleint, dandoyon, Arek, rue, acangiano, vkelman, bryanl, Jeff, mbaxter, pjb3, kxen, hipertracker, ctran, Ram R., cody, Nolan, Joshua, Ajay, Joe, and anonymous contributors. We apologize if we have overlooked anyone!

Our editor, Mike Loukides, knows how to push and prod gently. He's been a great help throughout this crazy process. Many other people at O'Reilly were always there to answer our questions and help us move forward.

We thank Jonas Bonér for writing the Foreword for the book. Jonas is a longtime friend and collaborator from the aspect-oriented programming (AOP) community. For years, he has done pioneering work in the Java community. Now he is applying his energies to promoting Scala and growing that community.

Bill Venners graciously provided the quote on the back cover. The first published book on Scala, *Programming in Scala* (Artima), that he cowrote with Martin Odersky and Lex Spoon, is indispensable for the Scala developer. Bill has also created the wonderful ScalaTest library.

We have learned a lot from fellow developers around the world. Besides Jonas and Bill, Debasish Ghosh, James Iry, Daniel Spiewak, David Pollack, Paul Snively, Ola Bini, Daniel Sobral, Josh Suereth, Robey Pointer, Nathan Hamblen, Jorge Ortiz, and others have illuminated dark corners with their blog entries, forum discussions, and personal conversations.

Dean thanks his colleagues at Object Mentor and several developers at client sites for many stimulating discussions on languages, software design, and the pragmatic issues facing developers in industry. The members of the Chicago Area Scala Enthusiasts (CASE) group have also been a source of valuable feedback and inspiration.

Alex thanks his colleagues at Twitter for their encouragement and superb work in demonstrating Scala's effectiveness as a language. He also thanks the Bay Area Scala Enthusiasts (BASE) for their motivation and community.

Most of all, we thank Martin Odersky and his team for creating Scala.

## CHAPTER 1

Zero to Sixty: Introducing Scala

Let's start with a brief look at why you should give Scala a serious look. Then we'll dive in and write some code.

Why Scala?

Scala is a language that addresses the needs of the modern software developer. It is a statically typed, mixed-paradigm, JVM language with a succinct, elegant, and flexible syntax, a sophisticated type system, and idioms that promote scalability from small, interpreted scripts to large, sophisticated applications. That's a mouthful, so let's look at each of those ideas in more detail:

A JVM and JavaScript language
> Scala exploits the performance and optimizations of the JVM, as well as the rich ecosystem of tools and libraries built around Java. But it's not limited to the JVM! *Scala.js* (*http://www.scala-js.org*) is an experimental port to JavaScript.

Statically typed
> Scala embraces *static typing* as a tool for creating robust applications. It fixes many of the flaws of Java's type system and it uses type inference to eliminate much of the typing boilerplate.

Mixed paradigm—object-oriented programming
> Scala fully supports *object-oriented programming* (OOP). Scala improves Java's object model with the addition of *traits*, a clean way of implementing types using *mixin composition*. In Scala, everything *really* is an object, even numeric types.

Mixed paradigm—functional programming
> Scala fully supports *functional programming* (FP). FP has emerged as the best tool for thinking about problems of concurrency, *Big Data*, and general code correctness. Immutable values, first-class functions, functions without side effects,

"higher-order" functions, and function collections all contribute to concise, powerful, correct code.

A sophisticated type system
> Scala extends the type system of Java with more flexible generics and other enhancements to improve code correctness. With type inference, Scala code is often as concise as code in dynamically typed languages.

A succinct, elegant, and flexible syntax
> Verbose expressions in Java become concise idioms in Scala. Scala provides several facilities for building *domain-specific languages* (DSLs), APIs that feel "native" to users.

Scalable—architectures
> You can write small, interpreted scripts to large, distributed applications in Scala. Four language mechanisms promote scalable composition of systems: 1) *mixin* composition using *traits*; 2) abstract type members and generics; 3) nested classes; and 4) explicit *self types*.

The name *Scala* is a contraction of the words *scalable language*. It is pronounced *scahlah*, like the Italian word for "staircase." Hence, the two "a"s are pronounced the same.

Scala was started by Martin Odersky in 2001. The first public release was January 20th, 2004 (see *http://bit.ly/1toEmFE*). Martin is a professor in the School of Computer and Communication Sciences at the Ecole Polytechnique Fédérale de Lausanne (EPFL). He spent his graduate years working in the group headed by Niklaus Wirth, of Pascal fame. Martin worked on Pizza, an early functional language on the JVM. He later worked on GJ, a prototype of what later became Generics in Java, along with Philip Wadler, one of the designers of Haskell. Martin was hired by Sun Microsystems to produce the reference implementation of `javac`, the descendant of which is the Java compiler that ships with the Java Developer Kit (JDK) today.

The Seductions of Scala

The rapid growth of Scala users since the first edition of this book confirms my view that Scala is a language for our time. You can leverage the maturity of the JVM, libraries, and production tools, while enjoying state-of-the-art language features with a concise, yet expressive syntax for addressing today's challenges, such as Big Data, scaling through concurrency, and providing highly available and robust services.

In any field of endeavor, the professionals need sophisticated, powerful tools and techniques. It may take a while to master them, but you make the effort because mastery is the key to your success.

I believe Scala is a language for *professional* developers. Not all users are professionals, of course, but Scala is the kind of language a professional in our field needs, rich in features, highly performant, expressive for a wide class of problems. It will take you a while to master Scala, but once you do, you won't feel constrained by your programming language.

What About Java 8?

Java 8 is the most significant update to Java since Java 5 introduced generics. Now we have real anonymous functions, called *lambdas*. You'll see why they are so useful in this book. Interfaces have been extended to allow "default" implementations of the methods they declare, making them more usable as *composable mixins*, like Scala's *traits*. These features are arguably the two most valuable improvements that Scala brought to the JVM compared to Java before version 8. So, is there any point in switching?

Scala adds many improvements that Java may never have, due to backward compatibility limitations, or Java may eventually have them but not until years from now. For example, Scala has richer type inference than Java can provide. Scala has powerful *pattern matching* and *for comprehensions* that dramatically reduce code size and coupling between types. You'll see why they are so valuable as we go.

Also, many organizations are understandably cautious about upgrading their JVM infrastructure. For them deploying the Java 8 JVM may not be an option for a while. At least those organizations can use Scala now with the Java 6 and 7 JVMs.

Still, if you can use Java 8 you might decide it's the best path forward for your team. Reading this book will still teach you many useful techniques that you can apply to Java 8 applications. However, I suspect you'll still find all the additional features of Scala worth the switch.

Okay, let's get started.

Installing Scala

To get up and running as quickly as possible, this section describes how to install some command-line tools that are all you need to work with the examples in the book.[1] The examples used in this book were written and compiled using Scala version 2.11.2, the latest release at the time of this writing. Most also work unmodified with the previous release, Scala version 2.10.4, because many teams are still using that version.

---

1. For more details on these tools, see Chapter 21.

Scala 2.11 introduced some new features compared to 2.10, but the release mostly focused on general performance improvements and library refactoring. Scala 2.10 introduced a number of new features compared to 2.9. Because your organization may be using any of these versions, we'll discuss the most important differences as we go. (See an overview of 2.11 here (*http://bit.ly/1DDlYtH*) and an an overview of 2.10 here (*http://bit.ly/1toEt3R*).)

Here are the steps:

Install Java

Until Scala 2.12 comes along, Java 6, 7, or 8 can be used and it must be installed on your computer (Scala 2.12, which is planned for early 2016, will support Java 8 only). If you need to install Java, go to the Oracle website (*http://bit.ly/TEA7iC*) and follow the instructions to install the full Java Development Kit (JDK).

Install SBT

Install the de facto build tool for Scala, *SBT* by following the instructions at *scala-sbt.org* (*http://bit.ly/1toEO6H*). When you are finished, you will have an `sbt` command that you can run from a Linux or OS X terminal or Windows command window. (Other build tools can be used, as we'll see in "Other Build Tools" on page 490.)

Get the book's code examples

Download the code examples as described in "Getting the Code Examples" on page xxiii. Expand the archive somewhere convenient on your computer.

Start SBT

Open a shell or command window and move to the directory where you expanded the code examples. Type the command `sbt test`, which will download all the dependencies you need, including the Scala compiler and third-party libraries. This will take a while and you'll need an Internet connection. Then `sbt` will compile the code and run the unit tests. You'll see lots of output, ending with a "success" message. If you run the command again, it should finish very quickly because it won't need to do anything again.

Congratulations! You're ready to get started. However, you might want to install a few more things that are useful.

For most of the book, we'll use these tools indirectly through SBT, which downloads the Scala compiler version we want, the standard library, and the required third-party dependencies automatically.

It's handy to download the Scala tools separately, for those times when you aren't working in SBT. We'll run a few of our examples using Scala outside SBT.

Follow the links on the official Scala website (*http://www.scala-lang.org*) to install Scala and optionally, the *Scaladocs*, the analog of *Javadocs* for Scala (in Scala 2.11, the Scala library and Scaladocs have been split into several, smaller libraries). You can also read the Scaladocs online (*http://bit.ly/1u1pv56*). For your convenience, most mentions of a type in the Scala library will be a link corresponding to a Scaladocs page.

A handy feature of the Scaladocs is a search field above the list of types on the lefthand side. It is very handy for finding a type quickly. Also, the entry for each type has a link to view the corresponding source code in Scala's GitHub repository (*http://bit.ly/1wOjJU0*), which is a good way to learn how the library was implemented. Look for the link on the line labeled "Source." It will be near the bottom of the overview discussion for the type.

Any text editor or IDE (integrated development environment) will suffice for working with the examples. You can find Scala support plug-ins for all the major editors and IDEs. For more details, see "Integration with IDEs and Text Editors" on page 491. In general, the community for your favorite editor is your best source of up-to-the-minute information on Scala support.

Using SBT

We'll learn how SBT works in "SBT, the Standard Build Tool for Scala" on page 488. For now, let's cover the basics we need to get started.

When you start the `sbt` command, if you don't specify a task to run, SBT starts an interactive REPL (*Read, Eval, Print, Loop*). Let's try that now and see a few of the available "tasks."

In the listing that follows, the `$` is the shell command prompt (e.g., `bash`), where you start the `sbt` command, the `>` is the default SBT interactive prompt, and the `#` starts an sbt comment. You can type most of these commands in any order:

```
$ sbt
> help      # Describe commands.
> tasks     # Show the most commonly-used, available tasks.
> tasks -V  # Show ALL the available tasks.
> compile   # Incrementally compile the code.
> test      # Incrementally compile the code and run the tests.
> clean     # Delete all build artifacts.
> ~test     # Run incr. compiles and tests whenever files are saved.
            # This works for any command prefixed by "~".
> console   # Start the Scala REPL.
> run       # Run one of the "main" routines in the project.
> show x    # Show the definition of variable "x".
```

```
> eclipse    # Generate Eclipse project files.
> exit       # Quit the REPL (also control-d works).
```

I run ~test all the time to keep compiling changes and running the corresponding tests. SBT uses an incremental compiler and test runner, so I don't have to wait for a full rebuild every time. When you want to run a different task or exit sbt, just hit Return.

The eclipse task is handy if you use Eclipse with its Scala plug-in. It generates the appropriate project files so you can import the code as an Eclipse project. If you'll use Eclipse to work with the example code, run the eclipse task now.

If you use a recent release of IntelliJ IDEA with its Scala plug-in, you can simply import the SBT project directly.

Scala has its own REPL. You can invoke it using the console command. Most of the time in this book when you try the examples yourself in the REPL, you'll do so by first running console:

```
$ sbt
> console
[info] Updating {file:/.../prog-scala-2nd-ed/}prog-scala-2nd-ed...
[info] ...
[info] Done updating.
[info] Compiling ...
[info] Starting scala interpreter...
[info]
Welcome to Scala version 2.11.2 (Java HotSpot(TM) 64-Bit Server VM, Java ...).
Type in expressions to have them evaluated.
Type :help for more information.

scala> 1 + 2
res0: Int = 3

scala> :quit
```

I've elided some of the output here. Like the SBT REPL, you can also exit with *Ctrl-D*.

When you run console, SBT builds your project first and makes the build products available on the CLASSPATH. Hence, you can experiment with your code using the REPL.

Using the Scala REPL is a very effective way to experiment with code idioms and to learn an API, even Java APIs. Invoking it from SBT using the console task conveniently adds project dependencies and the compiled project code to the classpath for the REPL.

Running the Scala Command-Line Tools

If you installed the Scala command-line tools separately, the Scala compiler is called `scalac`, analogous to the Java compiler `javac`. We won't use it directly, relying instead on SBT to invoke it for us, but the command syntax is straightforward if you've ever run `javac`.

In your command window, try these commands to see what version you are running and to see help on the command-line arguments. As before, you type the text after the $ prompt. The rest of the text is the command output:

```
$ scalac -version
Scala compiler version 2.11.2 -- Copyright 2002-2013, LAMP/EPFL
$ scalac -help
Usage: scalac <options> <source files>
where possible standard options include:
  -Dproperty=value      Pass -Dproperty=value directly to the runtime system.
  -J<flag>              Pass <flag> directly to the runtime system.
  -P:<plugin>:<opt>     Pass an option to a plugin
  ...
```

Similarly, the `scala` command, which is similar to `java`, is used to run programs:

```
$ scala -version
Scala code runner version 2.11.2 -- Copyright 2002-2013, LAMP/EPFL
$ scala -help
Usage: scala <options> [<script|class|object|jar> <arguments>]
   or  scala -help

All options to scalac (see scalac -help) are also allowed.
...
```

We will also occasionally run `scala` to invoke Scala "script" files, something that the `java` command doesn't support. Consider this example script from the code examples:

```
// src/main/scala/progscala2/introscala/upper1.sc

class Upper {
  def upper(strings: String*): Seq[String] = {
    strings.map((s:String) => s.toUpperCase())
  }
}

val up = new Upper
println(up.upper("Hello", "World!"))
```

Let's run it with the `scala` command. Try this example, where the Linux and Mac OS X paths are shown. I'm assuming your current working directory is the root of the code examples. For Windows, use backslashes instead:

```
$ scala src/main/scala/progscala2/introscala/upper1.sc
ArrayBuffer(HELLO, WORLD!)
```

And thus we have have satisfied the requirement of the Programming Book Guild that our first program must print "Hello World!"

Finally, if you invoke scala without a compiled main routine to run or a script file, scala enters the REPL mode, like running console in sbt. (However, it won't have the same classpath you get when running the console tasks in sbt.) Here is a REPL session illustrating some useful commands (if you didn't install Scala separately, just start console in sbt to play with the Scala REPL). The REPL prompt is now scala> (some output elided):

```
$ scala
Welcome to Scala version 2.11.2 (Java HotSpot(TM)...).
Type in expressions to have them evaluated.
Type :help for more information.

scala> :help
All commands can be abbreviated, e.g. :he instead of :help.
:cp <path>              add a jar or directory to the classpath
:edit <id>|<line>       edit history
:help [command]         print this summary or command-specific help
:history [num]          show the history (optional num is commands to show)
...   Other messages

scala> val s = "Hello, World!"
s: String = Hello, World!

scala> println("Hello, World!")
Hello, World!

scala> 1 + 2
res3: Int = 3

scala> s.con<tab>
concat    contains    contentEquals

scala> s.contains("el")
res4: Boolean = true

scala> :quit
$     # back at the shell prompt.
```

We assigned a string, "Hello, World!", to a variable named s, which we declared as an immutable value using the val keyword. The println (*http://bit.ly/1aLWLEh*) function prints a string to the console, followed by a line feed.

This println is effectively the same thing as Java's System.out.println (*http://bit.ly/1s0NQ5n*). Also, Scala uses Java Strings (*http://bit.ly/1wl7Bdg*).

Next, note that when we added two numbers, we didn't assign the result to a variable, so the REPL made up a name for us, `res3`, which we could have used in subsequent expressions.

The REPL supports tab completion. The input command shown as `s.con<tab>` is used to indicate that a tab was typed after the `s.con`. The REPL responded with a list of methods on `String` that could be called. The expression was completed with a call to the `contains` method.

Finally, we used `:quit` to exit the REPL. Ctrl-D can also be used.

We'll see additional REPL commands as we go and we'll explore the REPL commands in depth in "Command-Line Tools" on page 479.

Running the Scala REPL in IDEs

Let's quickly discuss one other way to run the REPL that's handy if you use Eclipse, IntelliJ IDEA, or NetBeans. Eclipse and IDEA support a *worksheet* feature that let's you edit Scala code as you would normally edit code for compilation or scripting, but the code is interpreted immediately whenever you save the file. Hence, it's more convenient than using the REPL when you need to modify and rerun nontrivial code fragments. NetBeans has a similar *Interactive Console* feature.

If you use one of these IDEs, see "Integration with IDEs and Text Editors" on page 491 for information on the Scala plug-ins and how to use the *worksheet* or *Interactive Console* feature.

A Taste of Scala

In the rest of this chapter and the two chapters that follow, we'll do a rapid tour of many of Scala's features. As we go, we'll discuss just enough of the details to understand what's going on, but many of the deeper background details will have to wait for later chapters. Think of it as a primer on Scala syntax and a taste of what programming in Scala is like day to day.

 When we mention a type in the Scala library, you might find it useful to read more in the Scaladocs about it. The Scaladocs for the current release of Scala can be found here (*http://bit.ly/1u1pv56*). Note that a search field is shown above the list of types on the lefthand side. It is very handy for finding a type quickly, because the Scaladocs segregate types by package, rather than list them all alphabetically, as in Javadocs.

We will use the Scala REPL most of the time in this book. Recall that you can run it one of three ways, either directly using the `scala` command with no script or "main" argument, using one of the SBT `console` commands, or using the worksheet feature in the popular IDEs.

If you don't use an IDE, I recommend using SBT most of the time, especially when you're working with a particular project. That's what we'll do here, but once you've started `scala` directly or created a worksheet in an IDE, the steps will be the same. Take your pick. Actually, even if you *prefer* IDEs, give SBT in a command window a try, just to see what it's like. I personally rarely use IDEs, but that's just my personal preference.

In a shell window, change to the root directory of the code examples and start `sbt`. At the > prompt, type **console**. From now on, we'll omit some of the "boilerplate" in the `sbt` and `scala` output.

Type in the following two lines of code at the `scala>` prompts:

```
scala> val book = "Programming Scala"
book: java.lang.String = Programming Scala

scala> println(book)
Programming Scala
```

The first line uses the `val` keyword to declare an *immutable* variable named book. Using immutable values is recommended, because mutable data is a common source of bugs.

Note that the output returned from the interpreter shows you the type and value of book. Scala infers from the *literal* value `"Programming Scala"` that book is of type `java.lang.String` (*http://bit.ly/1wl7Bdg*).

When type information is shown or explicit type information is added to declarations, these *type annotations* follow a colon after the item name. Why doesn't Scala follow Java conventions? Type information is often *inferred* in Scala. Hence, we don't always show type annotations explicitly in code. Compared to Java's `type item` convention, the `item: type` convention is easier for the compiler to analyze unambiguously when you omit the colon and the type annotation and just write `item`.

As a general rule, when Scala deviates from Java syntax, it is usually for a good reason, like supporting a new feature that would be difficult using Java syntax.

 Showing the types in the REPL is very handy for learning the types that Scala infers for particular expressions. It's one example of exploration that the REPL enables.

Larger examples can be tedious to edit and resubmit using only the REPL. Hence, it's convenient to write Scala scripts in a text editor or IDE. You can then execute the script or copy and paste blocks of code.

Let's look again at the *upper1.sc* we ran earlier:

```
// src/main/scala/progscala2/introscala/upper1.sc

class Upper {
  def upper(strings: String*): Seq[String] = {
    strings.map((s:String) => s.toUpperCase())
  }
}

val up = new Upper
println(up.upper("Hello", "World!"))
```

Throughout the book, if a code example is part of the downloadable archive of examples, the first line will be a comment with the path to the file in the archive. Scala follows the same comment conventions as Java, C#, C, etc. A *// comment* goes to the end of a line, while a */* comment */* can cross line boundaries.

Also, recall from "Getting the Code Examples" on page xxiii in the Preface that the script files use the *.sc* extension as a naming convention, while compiled files use the normal *.scala* extension. *This is the book's convention only*. Normally, script files are also named with the *.scala* extension. However, SBT will attempt to compile these scripts when it builds the project and script files cannot be compiled (as we'll discuss in a moment).

First, let's run this script, then discuss the code in detail. Start sbt and then run con sole to start Scala. Then use the :load command to load (compile and run) the file:

```
scala> :load src/main/scala/progscala2/introscala/upper1.sc
Loading src/main/scala/progscala2/introscala/upper1.sc...
defined class Upper
up: Upper = Upper@4ef506bf      // Used Java's Object.toString.
ArrayBuffer(HELLO, WORLD!)
```

The last line is the actual println output in the script. The other lines are feedback the REPL provides.

So, why can't scripts be compiled? Scripts are designed to be simple and one simplification is that you don't have to wrap declarations (variables and functions) in objects like you would for compiled Java *and* Scala code (a requirement for valid JVM byte code). The scala command uses a clever hack to reconcile these conflicting requirements; it wraps your script in an anonymous object that you don't see.

If you really want to compile your script into JVM byte code (a set of **.class* files), you can pass the -Xscript <object> arguments to scalac, where <object> is a name of your choosing. It will be the name of the "main" class that is the entry point for the generated Java application:

```
$ scalac -Xscript Upper1 src/main/scala/progscala2/introscala/upper1.sc
$ scala Upper1
ArrayBuffer(HELLO, WORLD!)
```

Look in your current directory and you will see several *.class* files with funny names. (Hint: some are *anonymous functions* turned into objects!) We'll come back to those names later, but *Upper1.class* has the main routine. Let's reverse engineer it with javap and the Scala analog, scalap:

```
$ javap -cp . Upper1
Compiled from "upper1.sc"
public final class Upper1 {
  public static void main(java.lang.String[]);
}
$ scalap -cp . Upper1
object Upper1 extends scala.AnyRef {
  def this() = { /* compiled code */ }
  def main(argv : scala.Array[scala.Predef.String]) : scala.Unit =
    { /* compiled code */ }
}
```

OK, let's finally discuss the code itself. Here it is again:

```
// src/main/scala/progscala2/introscala/upper1.sc

class Upper {
  def upper(strings: String*): Seq[String] = {
    strings.map((s:String) => s.toUpperCase())
  }
}

val up = new Upper
println(up.upper("Hello", "World!"))
```

The upper method in the Upper class (no pun intended) converts the input strings to uppercase and returns them in a Seq (*http://bit.ly/1E8xLCt*) (for "sequence"). The last two lines create an instance of Upper and use it to convert two strings, "Hello" and "World!" to uppercase and finally print the resulting Seq.

In Scala, a class begins with the class keyword and the entire class body is inside the outermost curly braces ({...}). In fact, the body is also the *primary constructor* for the class. If we needed to pass arguments to this constructor, we would put an argument list after the class name, Upper.

This bit of code starts the definition of a method:

```
def upper(strings: String*): Seq[String] = ...
```

Method definitions begin with the def keyword, followed by the method name and an optional argument list. Next comes an optional return type (it can be inferred in many cases), indicated by a colon and a type. Finally, an equals sign (=) separates the method signature from the method body.

The argument list in parentheses is actually a *variable-length argument list* of Strings, indicated by the * after the String type for the strings argument. That is, you can pass in as many comma-separated strings as you want (including an empty list). Inside the method, the type of the strings parameter is actually WrappedArray (*http://bit.ly/1OFtpV6*), which wraps Java arrays.

The method return type appears after the argument list. In this case, the return type is Seq[String], where Seq ("sequence") is an abstraction for collections that you can iterate through in a fixed order (as opposed to random or undefined order, like Sets and Maps, where no order is guaranteed). The actual type returned by this method will be scala.collection.mutable.ArrayBuffer (*http://bit.ly/1voKn1H*), but callers don't really need to know that most of the time.

Note that Seq is a *parameterized type*, like a *generic* type in Java. It's a "sequence of something," in this case a sequence of strings. Note that Scala uses square brackets ([...]) for parameterized types, whereas Java uses angle brackets (<...>).

Scala allows angle brackets to be used in *identifiers*, like method and variable names. For example, defining a "less than" method and naming it < is common and allowed by Scala, whereas Java doesn't allow characters like that in *identifiers*. So, to avoid ambiguity, Scala uses square brackets instead for parameterized types and disallows them in identifiers.

The body of the upper method comes after the equals sign (=). Why an equals sign? Why not just use curly braces ({...}) to indicate the method body, as in Java?

One reason is to reduce ambiguity. Scala infers semicolons when you omit them. It infers the method's return type in most cases. It lets you omit the argument list in the definition if the method takes no arguments.

The equals sign also emphasizes the principle in *functional programming* that values and functions are more closely aligned concepts. As we'll see, functions are passed as arguments to other functions, returned from functions, and assigned to variables, just like with objects.

Finally, Scala lets you omit the curly braces if the method body has a single expression. So, using an equals sign prevents several possible parsing ambiguities.

The method body calls the `map` (*http://bit.ly/1yMk4pK*) method on the `strings` collection, which takes a *function literal* as an argument. Function literals are "anonymous" functions. In other languages, they are variously called *lambdas, closures, blocks*, or *procs*. Java 8 finally added true anonymous functions, called *lambdas*. Before Java 8, you would implement an interface, usually with an anonymous inner class, that declares a method to do the work. So, even before Java 8 you could sort of do the same thing, "parameterize" some outer behavior by passing in some nested behavior, but the bloated syntax really undermined and obscured the power of this technique.

In this case, we passed in the following function literal:

```
(s:String) => s.toUpperCase()
```

It takes an argument list with a single `String` argument named `s`. The body of the function literal is after the "arrow," `=>`. (UTF8 ⇒ is also allowed.) The body calls `toUpperCase()` on `s`. The result of this call is automatically returned by the function literal. In Scala, the last *expression* in a function or method is the return value. The `return` keyword exists in Scala, but it can only be used in methods, not in anonymous functions like this one. In fact, it is rarely used in methods.

Methods Versus Functions

Following the convention in most *object-oriented programming* languages, the term *method* is used to refer to a function defined within a class or object. Methods have an implicit `this` reference to the object as an additional argument when they are called. Of course, in most OO languages, the syntax used is `this.method_name(other_args)`. We'll use the term *method* in the usual way. We'll use the term *function* to refer to non-methods, but also use it generically to include methods, in some cases. The context will indicate the distinction.

The expression `(s:String) => s.toUpperCase()` in *upper1.sc* is an example of a *function* that is not a method.

So, the `map` method we call on the sequence `strings` passes each `String` to the function literal and builds up a new collection with the results returned by the function literal. If there were five elements in the original list, for example, the new list will also have five elements.

Continuing with the example, to exercise the code, we create a new `Upper` instance and assign it to a variable named `up`. As in Java, C#, and similar languages, the syntax `new Upper` creates a new instance. No argument list is required because the primary constructor doesn't take any arguments. The `up` variable is declared as a read-only "value" using the `val` keyword. It behaves like a `final` variable in Java.

Finally, we call the `upper` method on a list of strings, and print out the result with `println(…)`.

We can actually simplify our script even further. Consider this simplified version:

```
// src/main/scala/progscala2/introscala/upper2.sc

object Upper {
  def upper(strings: String*) = strings.map(_.toUpperCase())
}

println(Upper.upper("Hello", "World!"))
```

This code does exactly the same thing, but with a third fewer characters.

On the first line, `Upper` is now declared as an `object`, which is a *singleton*. Scala makes the *Singleton Design Pattern* a first-class member of the language. We are declaring a class, but the Scala runtime will only create one instance of `Upper`. You can't write `new Upper`, for example. Scala uses `objects` for situations where other languages would use "class-level" members, like `statics` in Java. We don't really need more than one *instance* here, because `Upper` carries no state information, so a singleton is fine.

The Singleton Pattern is often criticized for its drawbacks. For example, it's hard to replace a singleton instance with a *test double* in unit tests, and forcing all computation through a single instance raises concerns about thread safety and performance. However, just as there are times when a `static` method or value is appropriate in languages like Java, there are times when singletons make sense, as in this example where no state is maintained and the object doesn't interact with the outside world. Hence, we have no reason to ever need a test double nor worry about thread safety when using `Upper`.

 Why doesn't Scala support `statics`? Compared to languages that allow static members (or equivalent constructs), Scala is more true to the vision that *everything* should be an object. The `object` construct keeps this policy more consistent than in languages that mix static and *instance* class members. Recall Java's `static` methods and fields are not tied to an actual instance of some type, whereas Scala `objects` are single instances of a type.

The implementation of `upper` on the second line is also simpler. Scala can usually infer the return type of the method, but not the types of the method arguments, so we drop the explicit declaration. Also, because there is only one expression in the method body, we can drop the braces and put the entire method definition on one line. The equals sign before the method body tells the compiler, as well as the human reader, where the method body begins.

Why can't Scala infer the method argument types? Technically, the type inference algorithm does *local type inference*, which means it doesn't work globally over your whole program, but locally within certain scopes. Hence, it can't tell what types the arguments must have, but it is able to infer the type of the method's returned value in most cases, because it sees the whole function body. Recursive functions are one exception where the execution scope extends beyond the scope of the body, so the return type must be declared.

In any event, the types in the argument lists do provide useful documentation for the reader. Just because Scala can infer the return type of a function, should you let it? For simple functions, where the return type is obvious to the reader, perhaps it's not that important to show it explicitly. However, sometimes the inferred type won't be what's expected, perhaps due to a bug or some subtle behavior triggered by certain input argument values or expressions in the function body. Explicit return types express what you *think* should be returned. They also provide useful documentation for the reader. Hence, I recommend erring on the side of adding return types rather than omitting them, especially in public APIs.

We have also exploited a shorthand for the function literal. Previously we wrote it as follows:

```
(s:String) => s.toUpperCase()
```

We have now shortened it to the following expression:

```
_.toUpperCase()
```

The `map` method takes a single function argument, where the function itself takes a single argument. In this case, the function body only uses the argument once, so we can use the "placeholder" indicator _ instead of a named parameter. That is, the _ acts like an anonymous variable, to which the string will be assigned before `toUpperCase` is called. The `String` type is inferred for us, too.

On the last line, using an `object` rather than a `class` simplifies the invocation. Instead of creating an instance with `new Upper`, we can just call the `upper` method on the `Upper` object directly. This is the same syntax you would use when calling static methods in a Java class.

Finally, Scala automatically imports many methods for I/O, like `println` (*http://bit.ly/1aLWLEh*), which is actually a method on the `Console` (*http://bit.ly/1aLWLEh*) object in the `scala` (*http://bit.ly/1sRxo6F*) package. Packages provide a "namespace" for scoping like they do in Java.

So, we don't need to call `scala.Console.println` (*http://bit.ly/1aLWLEh*). We can just use `println` by itself. This method is one of many methods and types imported automatically that are defined in a library object called `Predef` (*http://bit.ly/1086O2z*).

Let's do one more *refactoring*; convert the script into a compiled, command-line tool. That is, let's create a more traditional JVM application with a `main` method:

```scala
// src/main/scala/progscala2/introscala/upper1.scala
package progscala2.introscala

object Upper {
  def main(args: Array[String]) = {
    args.map(_.toUpperCase()).foreach(printf("%s ",_))
    println("")
  }
}
```

Recall that we use the *.scala* extension for code that we compile with `scalac`. Now the upper method has been renamed `main`. Because `Upper` is an `object`, this `main` method works exactly like a `static main` method in a Java class. It is the entry point to the `Upper` *application*.

 In Scala, `main` must be a method in an `object`. (In Java, `main` must be a `static` method in a `class`.) The command-line arguments for the application are passed to `main` in an array of strings, e.g., `args: Array[String]`.

The first code line in the file defines the `package` for the type, named `intro`. Inside the `Upper.main` method, the expression uses the same shorthand notation for `map` (*http://bit.ly/1yMk4pK*) that we just examined:

```scala
args.map(_.toUpperCase())...
```

The call to `map` returns a new collection. We iterate through it with `foreach`. We use a `_` placeholder shortcut again in another *function literal* that we pass to `foreach`. In this case, each string in the collection is passed as an argument to `scala.Console.printf` (*http://bit.ly/1aLWLEh*), another function imported from `Predef`, which takes a format string followed by arguments to stuff into the string:

```scala
args.map(_.toUpperCase()).foreach(printf("%s ",_))
```

To be clear, these two uses of `_` are completely independent of each other, because they are in different scopes.

Function chaining and function-literal shorthands like these can take some getting used to, but once you are comfortable with them, they yield very readable, yet concise and powerful code that minimizes use of temporary variables and other boilerplate. If you are a Java programmer, imagine writing the same logic in pre-Java 8 code using anonymous inner classes.

The last line in `main` adds a final line feed to the output.

This time, you must first compile the code to a JVM *.class* file using `scalac` (the $ is the command prompt):

```
$ scalac src/main/scala/progscala2/introscala/upper1.scala
```

You should now have a new directory named *progscala2/introscala* that contains several *.class* files, including a file named *Upper.class*. Scala must generate valid JVM byte code. One requirement is that the directory structure must match the package structure. Java enforces this at the source code level, too, but Scala is more flexible. Note that the source file in our downloaded code examples is actually in a directory called *IntroScala*, but we use a different name for the package. Java also requires a separate file for each top-level class, but in Scala you can have as many types in each file as you want. While you don't have to follow Java conventions for organizing your source code into directories that match the package structure and one file per top-level class, many teams follow this convention anyway because it's familiar and helps keep track of where code is defined.

Now, you can execute this command for any list of strings. Here is an example:

```
$ scala -cp . progscala2.introscala.Upper Hello World!
HELLO WORLD!
```

The `-cp .` option adds the current directory to the search classpath, although this isn't actually required in this case.

Try running the program with other arguments. Also, see what other class files are in the *progscala2/introscala* directory and use `javap` or `scalap`, as before, to see what definitions they contain.

Finally, we didn't really need to compile the file, because the SBT build does that for us. We could run it at the SBT prompt using this command:

```
> run-main progscala2.introscala.Upper Hello World!
```

Using the `scala` command, we need to point to the correct directory where SBT writes class files:

```
$ scala -cp target/scala-2.11/classes progscala2.introscala.Upper Hello World!
HELLO WORLD!
```

Interpreting Versus Compiling and Running Scala Code

To summarize, if you type `scala` on the command line without a file argument, the REPL is started. You type in commands, expressions, and statements that are evaluated on the fly. If you give the `scala` command a Scala source file argument, it compiles and runs the file as a script. Otherwise, if you provide a JAR file or the name of class with a `main` routine, `scala` executes it just like the `java` command.

Let's do one last refactoring of this code:

```scala
// src/main/scala/progscala2/introscala/upper2.scala
package progscala2.introscala

object Upper2 {
  def main(args: Array[String]) = {
    val output = args.map(_.toUpperCase()).mkString(" ")
    println(output)
  }
}
```

After mapping over the input arguments, instead of iterating through them with `foreach` to print each word, we call a convenience method on the iterable collections to make a string from them. The `mkString` (*http://bit.ly/1tpsKAD*) method that takes a single argument lets us specify the delimiter between the collection elements. There is another `mkString` method that takes three arguments, a leftmost prefix string, the delimiter, and a rightmost suffix string. Try changing the code to use `mkString("[", " ", ", "]")`. What's the output look like?

We saved the output of `mkString` to a variable and then used `println` to print it. We could have simply wrapped `println` around the whole `map` followed by `mkString`, but using a variable here makes the code easier to read.

A Taste of Concurrency

There are many reasons to be seduced by Scala. One reason is the Akka API for building robust concurrent applications using an intuitive model called *actors* (see *http://akka.io*).

This next example is a bit ambitious to tackle so soon, but it gives us a taste for how the power and elegance of Scala, combined with an intuitive concurrency API, can yield elegant and concise implementations of concurrent software. One of the reasons you might be investigating Scala is because you're looking for better ways to scale your applications by exploiting concurrency across the cores in your CPUs and the servers in your clusters. Here's one way to do it.

In the *Actor Model of Concurrency*, independent software entities called *actors* share no mutable state information with each other. Instead, they communicate by exchanging messages. By eliminating the need to synchronize access to shared, mutable state, it is far easier to write robust, concurrent applications. Each actor might mutate state as needed, but if it has exclusive access to that state and the actor framework guarantees that invocations of actor code are thread-safe, then the programmer doesn't have to use tedious and error-prone synchronization primitives.

In this simple example, instances in a geometric `Shape` hierarchy are sent to an actor for drawing on a display. Imagine a scenario where a rendering farm generates scenes for an animation. As the rendering of a scene is completed, the geometric shapes that are part of the scene are sent to an actor for a display subsystem.

To begin, we define a Shape class hierarchy:

```scala
// src/main/scala/progscala2/introscala/shapes/Shapes.scala
package progscala2.introscala.shapes

case class Point(x: Double = 0.0, y: Double = 0.0)                // ❶

abstract class Shape() {                                          // ❷
  /**
   * Draw takes a function argument. Each shape will pass a stringized
   * version of itself to this function, which does the "drawing".
   */
  def draw(f: String => Unit): Unit = f(s"draw: ${this.toString}")  // ❸
}

case class Circle(center: Point, radius: Double) extends Shape    // ❹

case class Rectangle(lowerLeft: Point, height: Double, width: Double) // ❺
    extends Shape

case class Triangle(point1: Point, point2: Point, point3: Point)  // ❻
    extends Shape
```

❶ Declare a class for two-dimensional points.

❷ Declare an abstract class for geometric shapes.

❸ Implement a draw method for "rendering" the shapes. We just write a formatted string.

❹ A circle with a center and radius.

❺ A rectangle with a lower-left point, height, and width. We assume for simplicity that the sides are are parallel to the horizontal and vertical axes.

❻ A triangle defined by three points.

The argument list after the Point class name is the list of constructor parameters. In Scala, the *whole* class body is the constructor, so you list the arguments for the *primary* constructor after the class name and before the class body. In this case, there is no class body. Because we put the **case** keyword before the class declaration, each constructor parameter is automatically converted to a read-only (immutable) field of Point instances. That is, if you instantiate a Point instance named point, you can read the fields using point.x and point.y, but you *can't change their values*. Attempting to use point.y = 3.0 triggers a compilation error.

You can also provide default values for the arguments. The = 0.0 after each argument definition specifies 0.0 as the default. Hence, the user doesn't have to provide them explicitly, but they are inferred left to right. Let's use our SBT project to explore:

```
$ sbt
...
> compile
Compiling ...
[success] Total time: 15 s, completed ...
> console
[info] Starting scala interpreter...

scala> import progscala2.intro.shapes._
import progscala2.intro.shapes._

scala> val p00 = new Point
p00: intro.shapes.Point = Point(0.0,0.0)

scala> val p20 = new Point(2.0)
p20: intro.shapes.Point = Point(2.0,0.0)

scala> val p20b = new Point(2.0)
p20b: intro.shapes.Point = Point(2.0,0.0)

scala> val p02 = new Point(y = 2.0)
p02: intro.shapes.Point = Point(0.0,2.0)

scala> p00 == p20
res0: Boolean = false

scala> p20 == p20b
res1: Boolean = true
```

So, when we specified no arguments, Scala used 0.0 for both. When we specified one argument, Scala applied it to the leftmost argument, x, and used the default value for the remaining argument. We can even reference the arguments by name. For p02, we wanted to use the default value for x, but specify the value for y, so we used Point(y = 2.0).

While there is no class body for Point, another feature of the case keyword is the compiler automatically generates several methods for us, including the familiar to String, equals, and hashCode methods in Java. The output shown for each point, e.g., Point(2.0,0.0), is the toString output. The equals and hashCode methods are difficult for most developers to implement correctly, so autogeneration is a real benefit.

When we asked if p00 == p20 and p20 == p20b, Scala invoked the generated equals method. This is in contrast with Java, where == just compares *references*. You have to call equals explicitly to do a *logical* comparison.

A final feature of case classes we'll mention now is that the compiler also generates a *companion object*, a singleton of the same name, for each case class (in this case, `object Point`).

 You can define companions yourself. Any time an `object` and a `class` have the same name *and* they are defined in the same file, they are *companions*.

You can add methods to the companion object; we'll see how later on. However, it will have several methods added automatically, one of which is named `apply`. It takes the same argument list as the constructor.

Any time you write an object followed by an argument list, Scala looks for an `apply` method to call. That is to say, the following two lines are equivalent:

```
val p1 = Point.apply(1.0, 2.0)
val p2 = Point(1.0, 2.0)
```

It's a compilation error if no `apply` method exists for the object. The arguments must conform to the expected argument list, as well.

The `Point.apply` method is effectively a *factory* for constructing `Point`s. The behavior is simple here; it's just like calling the constructor without the `new` keyword. The companion object generated is equivalent to this:

```
object Point {
  def apply(x: Double = 0.0, y: Double = 0.0) = new Point(x, y)
  ...
}
```

However, a more sophisticated use of the companion object `apply` methods is possible for class hierarchies. A parent class object could choose to instantiate a particular subtype that works best for the argument list. For example, a data structure must have an implementation that is optimal for a small number of elements and a different implementation that is optimal for a large number of elements. A factory can hide this logic, giving the user a single uniform interface.

When an argument list is put after an object, Scala looks for an ap
ply method to call that matches the argument list. Put another way,
apply is *inferred*. Syntacticly, any object with an apply method behave like a function.

Putting an apply method on a companion object is the conventional idiom for defining a factory method for the class. An apply method on a class that isn't an object has whatever meaning is appropriate for instances of that class. For example, Seq.apply(index: Int)
retrieves the element at position index for sequences (counting from
zero).

Shape is an abstract class. As in Java, we can't instantiate an abstract class, even if none
of the members is abstract. Shape.draw is defined, but we only want to instantiate concrete shapes: Circle, Rectangle, and Triangle.

Note the argument passed to draw. It is a *function* of type String => Unit. That is, f
takes a String argument and returns Unit, which is a real type, but it behaves roughly
like void in Java. The name is a common convention in functional programming.

The idea is that callers of draw will pass a function that does the actual drawing when
given a string representation of the shape.

When a function returns Unit it is *totally side-effecting*. There's nothing useful that can be done with Unit, so the function can only perform side effects on some state, either globally, like performing input or output (I/O), or locally in some object.

Normally in functional programming, we prefer *pure* functions that have no side effects
and return all their work as their return value. These functions are far easier to reason
about, test, and reuse. Side effects are a common source of bugs. However, real-world
programs require I/O, at least.

Shape.draw demonstrates the idea that functions are *first-class values*, just like Strings,
Ints, Points, and other objects. Like other values, we can assign functions to variables,
pass them to other functions as arguments, as in draw, and return them from functions.
We'll use this feature as a powerful tool for building composable, yet flexible software.

When a function accepts other functions as arguments or returns functions as values,
it is called a *higher-order function* (HOF).

You could say that draw defines a *protocol* that all shapes have to support, but users can
customize. It's up to each shape to serialize its state to a string representation through

its `toString` method. The `f` method is called by `draw` and it constructs the final string using an *interpolated string*, a feature introduced in Scala 2.10.

 If you forget the `s` before the interpolated string, you'll get the literal output `draw: ${this.toString}`, i.e., with no interpolation.

`Circle`, `Rectangle`, and `Triangle` are concrete subclasses of `Shape`. They have no class bodies, because the `case` keyword defines all the methods we need, such as the `to String` methods required by `Shape.draw`.

For simplicity, we assume that `Rectangles` are not rotated relative to the *x* and *y* axes. Hence, all we need is one point, the lower lefthand point will do, and the height and width of the rectangle. `Triangle` takes three `Points` as its constructor arguments.

In our simple program, the `f` we will pass to `draw` will just write the string to the console, but you could build a real graphics application that uses an `f` to render the shape to a display.

Now that we have defined our shapes types, let's return to actors. We'll use the Akka library (*http://akka.io*) distributed by Typesafe (*http://typesafe.com*). We have already defined it as a dependency in our project *build.sbt* file.

Here is the code for our `ShapesDrawingActor`:

```
// src/main/scala/progscala2/introscala/shapes/ShapesDrawingActor.scala
package progscala2.introscala.shapes

object Messages {                                        // ❶
  object Exit                                            // ❷
  object Finished
  case class Response(message: String)                  // ❸
}

import akka.actor.Actor                                  // ❹

class ShapesDrawingActor extends Actor {                 // ❺
  import Messages._                                      // ❻

  def receive = {                                        // ❼
    case s: Shape =>
      s.draw(str => println(s"ShapesDrawingActor: $str"))
      sender ! Response(s"ShapesDrawingActor: $s drawn")
    case Exit =>
      println(s"ShapesDrawingActor: exiting...")
      sender ! Finished
    case unexpected =>  // default. Equivalent to "unexpected: Any"
```

```
        val response = Response(s"ERROR: Unknown message: $unexpected")
        println(s"ShapesDrawingActor: $response")
        sender ! response
    }
  }
```

❶ Declare an object `Messages` that defines most of the messages we'll send between actors. They work like "signals" to trigger behavior. Putting them in an object is a common encapsulation idiom.

❷ `Exit` and `Finished` have no state of their own, so they function like "flags."

❸ The case class `Response` is used to send an arbitrary string message to a sender in response to a message received from the sender.

❹ Import the `akka.actor.Actor` (*http://bit.ly/1wNOjMI*) type, an abstract base class, which we'll subclass to define our actors.

❺ Define an actor for drawing shapes.

❻ Import the three messages defined in `Messages` here. Nesting imports, which is permitted in Scala, scopes these values to where they are used.

❼ Implement the one abstract method, `Actor.receive`, that we have to implement, which defines how to handle incoming messages.

In most actor systems, including Akka, there is a *mailbox* associated with each actor where messages are stored until they can be processed by the actor. Akka guarantees that messages are processed in the order in which they are received, and it guarantees that while each message is being processed, the code won't be preempted by another thread, so the handler code is inherently thread-safe.

Note that the `receive` method has a curious form. It takes no arguments and the body is just a sequence of expressions starting with the `case` keyword:

```
def receive = {
  case first_pattern =>
    first_pattern_expressions
  case second_pattern =>
    second_pattern_expressions
}
```

This body is the *literal* syntax for a special kind of function called a `PartialFunction` (*http://bit.ly/1yMpzEP*). The actual type is `PartialFunction[Any,Unit]`, which means it takes an argument of type `Any` and returns `Unit`. `Any` is the root class of the type hierarchy in Scala, so the function accepts any argument. Because it returns `Unit`, the body must be *purely side-effecting*. This is necessary for actor systems, because the messaging is asynchronous. There is nothing to "return" to, in the usual sense. So, our code blocks will usually send other messages, including replies to the sender.

A `PartialFunction` consists only of `case` clauses, which do *pattern matching* on the message that will be passed to the function. There is no function argument shown for the message. It's handled internally by the implementation.

When one of the patterns matches, the expressions after the arrow (=>) up to the next `case` keyword (or the end of the function) are evaluated. The expressions don't need to be wrapped in curly braces, because the arrow and the next `case` keyword (or the end of the function) provide unambiguous boundaries. Also, if there is just one short expression, it can go on the same line after the arrow.

A *partial function* sounds complicated, but it's actually a simple idea. Recall that a one-argument function takes a value of some type and returns a value of another or the same type. A partial function explicitly says, "I might not be able to do anything with every value you give me." A classic example from mathematics is division, x/y, which is undefined when the denominator y is 0. Hence, division is a *partial function*.

So, each message is tried against the three pattern match expressions and the first one that matches wins. Let's break down the details of `receive`:

```scala
def receive = {
  case s: Shape =>                                      // ❶
    ...
  case Exit =>                                          // ❷
    ...
  case unexpected =>                                    // ❸
    ...
}
```

❶ If the message is a `Shape` instance, the first `case` clause matches. The variable `s` is assigned to refer to the shape; i.e., `s` will be of type `Shape`, while the input message has the type `Any`.

❷ The message equals `Exit`. This will be a signal that we're done.

❸ This is the "default" clause that matches anything. It is equivalent to `unexpec ted: Any`, so it matches anything passed in that didn't match the preceding pattern matches. The message is assigned to the variable `unexpected`.

Because the last match works for all messages, it must be the last one. If you tried moving it before the others you would get an error message about "unreachable code" for the subsequent `case` clause.

Note that because we have a default clause, it means that our "partial" function is actually "total"; it successfully handles all inputs.

Now let's look at the expressions invoked for each match:

```scala
def receive = {
  case s: Shape =>
```

```
    s.draw(str => println(s"ShapesDrawingActor: $str"))        // ❶
    sender ! Response(s"ShapesDrawingActor: $s drawn")          // ❷
  case Exit =>
    println(s"ShapesDrawingActor: exiting...")                 // ❸
    sender ! Finished                                          // ❹
  case unexpected =>
    val response = Response(s"ERROR: Unknown message: $unexpected")  // ❺
    println(s"ShapesDrawingActor: $response")
    sender ! response                                          // ❻
}
```

❶ Call `draw` on the shape `s`, passing it an anonymous function that knows what to do with the string generated by `draw`. In this case, it just prints the string.

❷ Send a message to the "sender" with a response.

❸ Print a message that we're quitting.

❹ Send the `Finished` message to the "sender."

❺ Create an error message as a `Response`, then print it.

❻ Send a message to the "sender" with the response.

Lines like `sender ! Response(s"ShapesDrawingActor: $s drawn")` construct a reply and send it to the sender of the shape. `Actor.sender` is a function that returns a reference to whichever actor sent the message and the `!` is a method for sending *asynchronous* messages. Yes, `!` is a method name. The choice of `!` is a convention adopted from *Erlang*, a language that popularized the actor model.

We are also using a bit of syntactic sugar that Scala allows. The following two lines of code are equivalent:

```
sender ! Response(s"ShapesDrawingActor: $s drawn")
sender.!(Response(s"ShapesDrawingActor: $s drawn"))
```

When a method takes a single argument, you can drop the period after the object and drop the parentheses around the argument. Note that the first line has a cleaner appearance, which is why this syntax is supported. This notation is called *infix notation*, because the "operator" `!` is between the object and argument.

 Scala method names can use operator symbols. When methods are called that take a single argument, the period after the object and the parentheses around the argument can be dropped. However, there will sometimes be expressions with parsing ambiguities that require you to keep the period or the parentheses or both.

One last note before we move on to the last actor. One of the commonly taught tenets of object-oriented programming is that you should never use case statements that match on instance type, because inheritance hierarchies evolve, which breaks these case statements. Instead, polymorphic functions should be used. So, is the pattern-matching code just discussed an *antipattern*?

Recall that we defined Shape.draw to call the toString method on the Shape, which is implemented in each concrete subclass because they are case classes. Hence, the code in the first case statement invokes a polymorphic toString operation and we don't match on specific subtypes of Shape. This means our code won't break if we change the Shape class hierarchy. The other case clauses match on unrelated conditions that also won't change frequently, if at all.

Hence, we have combined polymorphic dispatch from object-oriented programming with pattern matching, a workhorse of functional programming. This is one way that Scala elegantly integrates these two programming paradigms.

Pattern Matching Versus Subtype Polymorphism

Pattern matching plays a central role in functional programming just as *subtype polymorphism* (i.e., overriding methods in subtypes) plays a central role in object-oriented programming. Functional pattern matching is much more important and sophisticated than the corresponding switch/case statements found in most *imperative* languages, as we'll explore in Chapter 4. In our example here, we can begin to see that joining functional-style pattern matching with polymorphic dispatch is a powerful combination that is a benefit of mixed paradigm languages like Scala.

Finally, here is the ShapesDrawingDriver that runs the example:

```scala
// src/main/scala/progscala2/introscala/shapes/ShapesActorDriver.scala
package progscala2.introscala.shapes
import akka.actor.{Props, Actor, ActorRef, ActorSystem}
import com.typesafe.config.ConfigFactory

// Message used only in this file:
private object Start                                          // ❶

object ShapesDrawingDriver {                                  // ❷
  def main(args: Array[String]) {                             // ❸
    val system = ActorSystem("DrawingActorSystem", ConfigFactory.load())
    val drawer = system.actorOf(
      Props(new ShapesDrawingActor), "drawingActor")
    val driver = system.actorOf(
       Props(new ShapesDrawingDriver(drawer)), "drawingService")
    driver ! Start                                            // ❹
  }
}

class ShapesDrawingDriver(drawerActor: ActorRef) extends Actor {   // ❺
```

```scala
import Messages._

def receive = {
  case Start =>                                           // ❻
    drawerActor ! Circle(Point(0.0,0.0), 1.0)
    drawerActor ! Rectangle(Point(0.0,0.0), 2, 5)
    drawerActor ! 3.14159
    drawerActor ! Triangle(Point(0.0,0.0), Point(2.0,0.0), Point(1.0,2.0))
    drawerActor ! Exit
  case Finished =>                                        // ❼
    println(s"ShapesDrawingDriver: cleaning up...")
    context.system.shutdown()
  case response: Response =>                              // ❽
    println("ShapesDrawingDriver: Response = " + response)
  case unexpected =>                                      // ❾
    println("ShapesDrawingDriver: ERROR: Received an unexpected message = "
      + unexpected)
  }
}
```

❶ A message used only in this file (`private`) is used to start everything. Using a special start message is a common idiom.

❷ The "driver" actor.

❸ The `main` method that is run to drive the application. It constructs an `akka.ac tor.ActorSystem` (*http://bit.ly/1pbk2rd*) and then builds the two actors, the `ShapesDrawingActor` we discussed earlier and the `ShapesDrawingDriver` we'll discuss shortly. We'll defer discussing the details of Akka setup logic until "Robust, Scalable Concurrency with Actors" on page 429. For now, note that we need to pass `ShapesDrawingActor` to `ShapesDrawingDriver`. Actually, we pass an `akka.actor.ActorRef` (*http://bit.ly/1tI2GSy*) ("actor reference") that points to the actual instance.

❹ Send `Start` to the driver to begin!

❺ The `ShapesDrawingDriver` actor.

❻ When its `receive` handler gets the `Start` message, it fires off five asynchronous messages to `ShapesDrawingActor`: three shapes, the value of Pi (which will be considered an error), and `Exit`. So, this will be a short-lived actor system!

❼ When `Finished` is received as a reply to `Exit` (recall what `ShapesDrawingDriv er` does with `Exit`), we shut down the actor system, accessed through a `con text` field in `Actor`.

❽ Simply print any other expected responses.

❾ A similar default clause for unexpected messages as we used previously.

Let's try it! At the sbt prompt, type **run**, which will compile the code if necessary and then present you with a list of all the code examples that have a main method:

```
> run
[info] Compiling ...

Multiple main classes detected, select one to run:

 [1] progscala2.introscala.shapes.ShapesDrawingDriver
 ...

Enter number:
```

Enter **1** and you should see output similar to the following (output wrapped to fit):

```
...
Enter number: 1

[info] Running progscala2.introscala.shapes.ShapesDrawingDriver
ShapesDrawingActor: draw: Circle(Point(0.0,0.0),1.0)
ShapesDrawingActor: draw: Rectangle(Point(0.0,0.0),2.0,5.0)
ShapesDrawingActor: Response(ERROR: Unknown message: 3.14159)
ShapesDrawingActor: draw: Triangle(
  Point(0.0,0.0),Point(2.0,0.0),Point(1.0,2.0))
ShapesDrawingActor: exiting...
ShapesDrawingDriver: Response = Response(
  ShapesDrawingActor: Circle(Point(0.0,0.0),1.0) drawn)
ShapesDrawingDriver: Response = Response(
  ShapesDrawingActor: Rectangle(Point(0.0,0.0),2.0,5.0) drawn)
ShapesDrawingDriver: Response = Response(ERROR: Unknown message: 3.14159)
ShapesDrawingDriver: Response = Response(
  ShapesDrawingActor: Triangle(
    Point(0.0,0.0),Point(2.0,0.0),Point(1.0,2.0)) drawn)
ShapesDrawingDriver: cleaning up...
[success] Total time: 10 s, completed Aug 2, 2014 7:45:07 PM
>
```

Because all the messages are sent asynchronously, note how responses printed by the driver are interleaved with output from the drawing actor, but messages were handled in the order sent. The output will vary from run to run.

So now you have a taste of actor-based concurrency and a few more powerful Scala features.

Recap and What's Next

We introduced Scala, then dove into some nontrivial Scala code, including a taste of Akka's actor library for concurrency.

As you explore Scala, you will find other useful resources that are available on *http://scala-lang.org*. You will find links for libraries, tutorials, and various papers that describe features of the language.

Typesafe, Inc. is the commercial company that supports Scala and several JVM-based development tools and frameworks, including Akka (*http://akka.io*), Play (*http://www.playframework.com*), and others. You'll find many useful resources on the company's website (*http://typesafe.com*). In particular, the Typesafe Activator (*http://typesafe.com/activator*) is a tool for exploring, downloading, and building from templates for different kinds of applications using Scala and Java tools. Finally, Typesafe offers support subscriptions, consulting, and training.

Next we'll continue our introduction to Scala features, emphasizing the various concise and efficient ways of getting lots of work done.

## CHAPTER 2

Type Less, Do More

We ended the first chapter with a "teaser" example of an Akka actor application. This chapter continues our tour of Scala features, focusing on features that promote succinct, flexible code. We'll discuss organization of files and packages, importing other types, variable and method declarations, a few particularly useful types, and miscellaneous syntax conventions.

Semicolons

Semicolons are expression delimiters and they are inferred. Scala treats the end of a line as the end of an expression, except when it can infer that the expression continues to the next line, as in this example:

```
// src/main/scala/progscala2/typelessdomore/semicolon-example.sc

// Trailing equals sign indicates more code on the next line.
def equalsign(s: String) =
  println("equalsign: " + s)

// Trailing opening curly brace indicates more code on the next line.
def equalsign2(s: String) = {
  println("equalsign2: " + s)
}

// Trailing commas, periods, and operators indicate more code on the next line.
def commas(s1: String,
           s2: String) = Console.
  println("comma: " + s1 +
          ", " + s2)
```

Compared to the compiler, the REPL is more aggressive at interpreting the end of a line as the end of an expression, so when entering a multiline expression, it's safest to end each line (except for the last) with one of the indicators shown in the previous script.

Conversely, you can put multiple expressions on the same line, separated by semicolons.

 Use the REPL's :paste mode when semicolon inference is too aggressive or multiple expressions need to be parsed as a whole, not individually. Enter :paste, followed by the code you want to enter, then finish with Ctrl-D.

Variable Declarations

Scala allows you to decide whether a variable is immutable (read-only) or not (read-write) when you declare it. We've already seen that an immutable "variable" is declared with the keyword val (think *value object*):

```
val array: Array[String] = new Array(5)
```

Scala is like Java in that most variables are actually references to heap-allocated objects. Hence, the array reference cannot be changed to point to a different Array, but the array elements themselves are mutable, so the elements can be modified:

```
scala> val array: Array[String] = new Array(5)
array: Array[String] = Array(null, null, null, null, null)

scala> array = new Array(2)
<console>:8: error: reassignment to val
       array = new Array(2)

scala> array(0) = "Hello"

scala> array
res1: Array[String] = Array(Hello, null, null, null, null)
```

A val must be initialized when it is declared.

Similarly, a mutable variable is declared with the keyword var and it must also be initialized immediately, even though it can be changed later, because it is mutable:

```
scala> var stockPrice: Double = 100.0
stockPrice: Double = 100.0

scala> stockPrice = 200.0
stockPrice: Double = 200.0
```

To be clear, we changed the *value* of stockPrice itself. However, the "object" that stockPrice refers to can't be changed, because Doubles in Scala are immutable.

In Java, so-called *primitive* types, char, byte, short, int, long, float, double, and boolean, are fundamentally different than reference objects. Indeed, there is no object and no reference, just the "raw" value. Scala tries to be consistently more object-oriented, so these types *are* actually objects with methods, like reference types (see "Reference

Versus Value Types" on page 248). However, Scala compiles to primitives where possible, giving you the performance benefit they provide (we'll discuss this in depth in "Specialization for Value Types" on page 345).

There are a few exceptions to the rule that you must initialize `val`s and `var`s when they are declared. For example, either keyword can be used with a constructor parameter, turning it into a field of the type. It will be immutable if `val` is used and mutable if `var` is used.

Consider the following REPL session, where we define a `Person` class with immutable first and last names, but a mutable age (because people age, I guess):

```
// src/main/scala/progscala2/typelessdomore/person.sc
scala> class Person(val name: String, var age: Int)
defined class Person

scala> val p = new Person("Dean Wampler", 29)
p: Person = Person@165a128d

scala> p.name
res0: String = Dean Wampler        // Show the value of firstName.

scala> p.age
res2: Int = 29                     // Show the value of age.

scala> p.name = "Buck Trends"
<console>:9: error: reassignment to val     // Disallowed!
       p.name = "Buck Trends"
             ^

scala> p.age = 30
p.age: Int = 30                    // Okay!
```

> The `var` and `val` keywords only specify whether the reference can be changed to refer to a different object (`var`) or not (`val`). They don't specify whether or not the object they reference is mutable.

Use immutable values whenever possible to eliminate a class of bugs caused by mutability.

For example, a mutable object is dangerous as a key in hash-based maps. If the object is mutated, the output of the `hashCode` method will change, so the corresponding value won't be found at the original location.

More common is unexpected behavior when an object you are using is being changed by someone else. Borrowing a phrase from Quantum Physics, these bugs are *spooky action at a distance*, because nothing you are doing locally accounts for the unexpected behavior; it's coming from somewhere else.

These are the most pernicious bugs in multithreaded programs, where synchronized access to shared, mutable state is required, but difficult to get right.

Using immutable values eliminates these issues.

Ranges

We're going to discuss method declarations next, but some of our examples will use the concept of a Range (*http://bit.ly/1wNfl5V*), so let's discuss that first.

Sometimes we need a sequence of numbers from some start to finish. A Range literal is just what we need. The following examples show how to create ranges for the types that support them, Int, Long, Float, Double, Char, BigInt (*http://bit.ly/13FUtUH*) (which represents integers of arbitrary size), and BigDecimal (*http://bit.ly/1b7tLWP*) (which represents floating-point numbers of arbitrary size).

You can create ranges with an inclusive or exclusive upper bound, and you can specify an interval not equal to one:

```
scala> 1 to 10              // Int range inclusive, interval of 1, (1 to 10)
res0: scala.collection.immutable.Range.Inclusive =
  Range(1, 2, 3, 4, 5, 6, 7, 8, 9, 10)

scala> 1 until 10           // Int range exclusive, interval of 1, (1 to 9)
res1: scala.collection.immutable.Range = Range(1, 2, 3, 4, 5, 6, 7, 8, 9)

scala> 1 to 10 by 3         // Int range inclusive, every third.
res2: scala.collection.immutable.Range = Range(1, 4, 7, 10)

scala> 10 to 1 by -3        // Int range inclusive, every third, counting down.
res2: scala.collection.immutable.Range = Range(10, 7, 4, 1)

scala> 1L to 10L by 3       // Long
res3: scala.collection.immutable.NumericRange[Long] = NumericRange(1, 4, 7, 10)

scala> 1.1f to 10.3f by 3.1f   // Float with an interval != 1
res4: scala.collection.immutable.NumericRange[Float] =
  NumericRange(1.1, 4.2, 7.2999997)

scala> 1.1f to 10.3f by 0.5f   // Float with an interval < 1
res5: scala.collection.immutable.NumericRange[Float] =
  NumericRange(1.1, 1.6, 2.1, 2.6, 3.1, 3.6, 4.1, 4.6, 5.1, 5.6, 6.1, 6.6,
    7.1, 7.6, 8.1, 8.6, 9.1, 9.6, 10.1)

scala> 1.1 to 10.3 by 3.1       // Double
res6: scala.collection.immutable.NumericRange[Double] =
```

```
    NumericRange(1.1, 4.2, 7.300000000000001)

scala> 'a' to 'g' by 3            // Char
res7: scala.collection.immutable.NumericRange[Char] = NumericRange(a, d, g)

scala> BigInt(1) to BigInt(10) by 3
res8: scala.collection.immutable.NumericRange[BigInt] =
    NumericRange(1, 4, 7, 10)

scala> BigDecimal(1.1) to BigDecimal(10.3) by 3.1
res9: scala.collection.immutable.NumericRange.Inclusive[scala.math.BigDecimal]
    = NumericRange(1.1, 4.2, 7.3)
```

I wrapped some of the output lines to fit the page.

Partial Functions

Let's discuss the properties of PartialFunction (*http://bit.ly/1yMpzEP*). We learned that partial functions are *partial* in the sense that they aren't defined for all possible inputs, only those inputs that match at least one of the specified case clauses.

Only case clauses can be specified in a partial function and the entire function must be enclosed in curly braces. In contrast, "regular" function literals can be wrapped in parentheses or curly braces.

If the function is called with an input that doesn't match one of the case clauses, a MatchError (*http://bit.ly/1DDkcsB*) is thrown at runtime.

You can test if a PartialFunction will match an input using the isDefinedAt method. This function avoids the risk of throwing a MathError exception.

You can "chain" PartialFunctions together: pf1 orElse pf2 orElse pf3 …. If pf1 doesn't match, then pf2 is tried, then pf3, etc. A MathError is only thrown if none of them matches.

The following example illustrates these points:

```
// src/main/scala/progscala2/typelessdomore/partial-functions.sc

val pf1: PartialFunction[Any,String] = { case s:String => "YES" }    // ❶
val pf2: PartialFunction[Any,String] = { case d:Double => "YES" }    // ❷

val pf = pf1 orElse pf2                                              // ❸

def tryPF(x: Any, f: PartialFunction[Any,String]): String =         // ❹
  try { f(x).toString } catch { case _: MatchError => "ERROR!" }

def d(x: Any, f: PartialFunction[Any,String]) =                     // ❺
  f.isDefinedAt(x).toString
```

```
println("      |  pf1 - String |  pf2 - Double |    pf - All")   // ❻
println("x     | def? | pf1(x) | def? |  pf2(x) | def? |  pf(x)")
println("+++++++++++++++++++++++++++++++++++++++++++++++++++++++++++")
List("str", 3.14, 10) foreach { x =>
  printf("%-5s | %-5s | %-6s  | %-5s | %-6s  | %-5s | %-6s\n", x.toString,
    d(x,pf1), tryPF(x,pf1), d(x,pf2), tryPF(x,pf2), d(x,pf), tryPF(x,pf))
}
```

❶   A partial function that only matches on strings.

❷   A partial function that only matches on doubles.

❸   Combine the two functions to construct a new partial function that matches on strings *and* doubles.

❹   A helper function to try the partial function and catch possible MatchError exceptions. With either success or failure, a string is returned.

❺   A helper function to try isDefinedAt and return a string result.

❻   Try the combinations and output a table of results!

The rest of the code tries different values with the three partial functions, first calling isDefinedAt (the def? column in the output) and then trying the function itself:

```
      |  pf1 - String |  pf2 - Double |    pf - All
x     | def? | pf1(x) | def? |  pf2(x) | def? |  pf(x)
++++++++++++++++++++++++++++++++++++++++++++++++++++++++++
str   | true  | YES    | false | ERROR! | true  | YES
3.14  | false | ERROR! | true  | YES    | true  | YES
10    | false | ERROR! | false | ERROR! | false | ERROR!
```

Note that pf1 fails unless a string is given, while pf2 fails unless a double is given. Both fail if an integer is given. The combined function pf succeeds for both doubles and strings, but also fails for integers.

Method Declarations

Let's continue our examination of method definitions, using a modified version of our Shapes hierarchy from before. (We'll drop Triangle for simplicity.)

Method Default and Named Arguments

Here is an updated Point case class:

```
// src/main/scala/progscala2/typelessdomore/shapes/Shapes.scala
package progscala2.typelessdomore.shapes

case class Point(x: Double = 0.0, y: Double = 0.0) {          // ❶

  def shift(deltax: Double = 0.0, deltay: Double = 0.0) =      // ❷
```

```
    copy (x + deltax, y + deltay)
}
```

❶   Define `Point` with default initialization values (as before).

❷   A new `shift` method for creating a new `Point` offset from the existing `Point`. It uses the `copy` method that is also created automatically for case classes.

The `copy` method allows you to construct new instances of a case class while specifying just the fields that are changing. This is very useful for larger case classes:

```
scala> val p1 = new Point(x = 3.3, y = 4.4)     // Used named arguments explicitly.
p1: Point = Point(3.3,4.4)

scala> val p2 = p1.copy(y = 6.6)   // Copied with a new y value.
p2: Point = Point(3.3,6.6)
```

Named arguments make client code more readable. They also help avoid bugs when a long argument list has several fields of the same type. It's easy to pass values in the wrong order. Of course, it's better to avoid long argument lists in the first place.

Methods with Multiple Argument Lists

Next, consider the changes to `Shape`, specifically the changes to the `draw` method:

```
abstract class Shape() {
  /**
   * Draw takes TWO argument LISTS, one list with an offset for drawing,
   * and the other list that is the function argument we used previously.
   */
  def draw(offset: Point = Point(0.0, 0.0))(f: String => Unit): Unit =
    f(s"draw(offset = $offset), ${this.toString}")
}

case class Circle(center: Point, radius: Double) extends Shape

case class Rectangle(lowerLeft: Point, height: Double, width: Double)
  extends Shape
```

Yes, `draw` now has *two* argument *lists*, each of which has a single argument, rather than a single argument list with two arguments. The first argument list lets you specify an offset point where the shape will be drawn. It has a default value of `Point(0.0, 0.0)`, meaning no offset. The second argument list is the same as in the original version of `draw`, a function that does the drawing.

You can have as many argument lists as you want, but it's rare to use more than two.

So, why allow more than one argument list? Multiple lists promote a very nice block-structure syntax when the last argument list takes a single function. Here's how we might invoke this new `draw` method:

```
s.draw(Point(1.0, 2.0))(str => println(s"ShapesDrawingActor: $str"))
```

Scala lets us replace parentheses with curly braces around an argument list. So, this line can also be written this way:

```
s.draw(Point(1.0, 2.0)){str => println(s"ShapesDrawingActor: $str")}
```

Suppose the function literal is too long for one line? We might rewrite it this way:

```
s.draw(Point(1.0, 2.0)) { str =>
  println(s"ShapesDrawingActor: $str")
}
```

Or equivalently:

```
s.draw(Point(1.0, 2.0)) {
  str => println(s"ShapesDrawingActor: $str")
}
```

It looks like a typical block of code we're used to writing with constructs like `if` and `for` expressions, method bodies, etc. However, the {…} block is still a function we're passing to `draw`.

So, this "syntactic sugar" of using {…} instead of (…) looks better with longer function literals; they look more like the block structure syntax we know and love.

If we use the default offset, the first set of parentheses is still required:

```
s.draw() {
  str => println(s"ShapesDrawingActor: $str")
}
```

To be clear, `draw` could just have a single argument list with two values, like Java methods. If so, the client code would look like this:

```
s.draw(Point(1.0, 2.0),
  str => println(s"ShapesDrawingActor: $str")
)
```

That's not nearly as clear and elegant. It's also less convenient to use the default value for the `offset`. We would have to name the function argument:

```
s.draw(f = str => println(s"ShapesDrawingActor: $str"))
```

A second advantage is type inference in the subsequent argument lists. Consider the following example:

```
scala> def m1[A](a: A, f: A => String) = f(a)
m1: [A](a: A, f: A => String)String

scala> def m2[A](a: A)(f: A => String) = f(a)
m2: [A](a: A)(f: A => String)String

scala> m1(100, i => s"$i + $i")
<console>:12: error: missing parameter type
```

```
    m1(100, i => s"$i + $i")
           ^
```

```
scala> m2(100)(i => s"$i + $i")
res0: String = 100 + 100
```

The functions m1 and m2 look almost identical, but notice what happens when we call each one with the same arguments, an Int and a function Int => String. For m1, Scala can't infer the type of the i argument for the function. For m2, it can.

A third advantage of allowing extra argument lists is that we can use the *last* argument list for *implicit* arguments. These are arguments declared with the implicit keyword. When the methods are called, we can either explicitly specify these arguments, or we can let the compiler fill them in using a suitable value that's in scope. Implicit arguments are a more flexible alternative to arguments with default values. Let's explore an example from the Scala library that uses implicit arguments, Futures.

A Taste of Futures

The scala.concurrent.Future (*http://bit.ly/1xIkpsr*) API uses implicit arguments to reduce boilerplate in your code. They are another tool for concurrency provided by Scala. Akka uses Futures, but you can use them separately when you don't need the full capabilities of actors.

When you wrap some work in a Future, the work is executed asynchronously and the Future API provides various ways to process the results, such as providing callbacks that will be invoked when the result is ready. Let's use callbacks here and defer discussion of the rest of the API until Chapter 17.

The following example fires off five work items concurrently and handles the results as they finish:

```
// src/main/scala/progscala2/typelessdomore/futures.sc
import scala.concurrent.Future
import scala.concurrent.ExecutionContext.Implicits.global

def sleep(millis: Long) = {
  Thread.sleep(millis)
}

// Busy work ;)
def doWork(index: Int) = {
  sleep((math.random * 1000).toLong)
  index
}

(1 to 5) foreach { index =>
  val future = Future {
    doWork(index)
```

```
  }
  future onSuccess {
    case answer: Int => println(s"Success! returned: $answer")
  }
  future onFailure {
    case th: Throwable => println(s"FAILURE! returned: $th")
  }
}

sleep(1000)  // Wait long enough for the "work" to finish.
println("Finito!")
```

After the imports, we use a `sleep` method to simulate staying busy for an arbitrary amount of time. The `doWork` method simply calls it with a randomly generated number of milliseconds between 0 and 1000.

The interesting bit comes next. We iterate through a `Range` (*http://bit.ly/1wNfl5V*) of integers from 1 to 5, inclusive, with `foreach` and call `scala.concurrent.Future.ap ply` (*http://bit.ly/1xIkpsr*), the "factory" method on the singleton object `Future`. In this case `Future.apply` is passed an anonymous function of work to do. We use curly braces instead of parentheses to wrap the no-argument anonymous function we pass to it:

```
val future = Future {
  doWork(index)
}
```

`Future.apply` returns a new `Future` object, which executes the `doWork(index)` body on another thread; control then immediately returns to the loop. We then use `onSuc cess` to register a callback to be invoked if the `future` completes successfully. This callback function is a `PartialFunction` (*http://bit.ly/1yMpzEP*).

Similarly, we use `onFailure` to register a callback for failure handling, where the failure will be encapsulated in a `Throwable` (*http://bit.ly/1zmtxad*).

A final `sleep` call waits before exiting to allow the work to finish.

A sample run might go like this, where the results come out in arbitrary order, as you would expect:

```
$ scala src/main/scala/progscala2/typelessdomore/futures.sc
Success! returned: 1
Success! returned: 3
Success! returned: 4
Success! returned: 5
Success! returned: 2
Finito!
```

Okay, what does all this have to do with implicit arguments? A clue is the second import statement:

```
import scala.concurrent.ExecutionContext.Implicits.global
```

I've been cavalier when I said that each future runs on its own thread. In fact, the Future API lets us configure how these concurrent operations are performed by specifying an ExecutionContext (*http://bit.ly/1s0FtqF*). That import brings in a default Execution Context that uses Java's ForkJoinPool (*http://bit.ly/1DDlp2U*) facilities for managing pools of Java threads. Our example calls *three* methods that have a second argument list where an implicit ExecutionContext is expected. We aren't specifying those three argument lists explicitly, so the default ExecutionContext is used.

Here is the declaration for one of the methods, apply, in the Future.apply Scaladocs (*http://bit.ly/1pbjSQR*):

```
apply[T](body: => T)(implicit executor: ExecutionContext): Future[T]
```

Note the implicit keyword in the second argument list.

Here are their declarations from the Future.onSuccess (*http://bit.ly/1sR3rnc*) and Future.onFailure (*http://bit.ly/1sR3rnc*) Scaladocs.

```
def onSuccess[U](func: (Try[T]) => U)(
  implicit executor: ExecutionContext): Unit
def onFailure[U](callback: PartialFunction[Throwable, U])(
  implicit executor: ExecutionContext): Unit
```

The Try construct is a tool for handling try {…} catch {…} clauses, which we'll discuss later.

So how do you declare a value to be implicit? The import, scala.concurrent.ExecutionContext.Implicits.global, is the default ExecutionContext typically used with Futures. It is declared with the implicit keyword, so the compiler will use it when these methods are called without an ExecutionContext specified explicitly, as in our example. Only objects declared implicit *and* visible in the current scope will be considered for use, and only function arguments declared implicit are allowed to be unspecified and subject to this substitution.

Here is the actual declaration of Implicits.global in the Scala source code for scala.concurrent.ExecutionContext. It demonstrates using the implicit keyword to declare an implicit value (some details omitted):

```
object Implicits {
  implicit val global: ExecutionContextExecutor =
    impl.ExecutionContextImpl.fromExecutor(null: Executor)
}
```

We'll create our own implicit values in other examples later on.

Nesting Method Definitions and Recursion

Method definitions can also be nested. This is useful when you want to refactor a lengthy method body into smaller methods, but the "helper" methods aren't needed outside the original method. Nesting them inside the original method means they are invisible to the rest of the code base, including other methods in the type.

Here is an implementation of a factorial calculator, where we call a second, nested method to do the work:

```
// src/main/scala/progscala2/typelessdomore/factorial.sc

def factorial(i: Int): Long = {
  def fact(i: Int, accumulator: Int): Long = {
    if (i <= 1) accumulator
    else fact(i - 1, i * accumulator)
  }

  fact(i, 1)
}

(0 to 5) foreach ( i => println(factorial(i)) )
```

This is the output it produces:

```
1
1
2
6
24
120
```

The second method calls itself recursively, passing an `accumulator` parameter, where the result of the calculation is "accumulated." Note that we return the accumulated value when the counter i reaches 1. (We're ignoring negative integer arguments, which would be invalid. The function just returns 1 for i <= 1.) After the definition of the nested method, `factorial` calls it with the passed-in value i and the initial accumulator "seed" value of 1.

 It's easy to forget to call the nested function! If you get a compiler error that `Unit` is found, but `Long` is required, you probably forgot to call the function.

Did you notice that we use i as a parameter name twice, first in the `factorial` method and again in the nested `fact` method? The use of i as a parameter name for `fact` "shadows" the outer use of i as a parameter name for `factorial`. This is fine, because we don't need the outer value of i inside `fact`. We only use it the first time we call `fact`, at the end of `factorial`.

Like a local variable declaration in a method, a nested method is also only visible inside the enclosing method.

Look at the return types for the two functions. We used `Long` because factorials grow in size quickly. So, we didn't want Scala to infer `Int` as the return type. Otherwise, we don't need the type annotation on `factorial`. However, we *must* declare the return type for `fact`, because it is recursive and Scala's local-scope type inference can't infer the return type of recursive functions.

You might be a little nervous about a recursive function. Aren't we at risk of blowing up the stack? The JVM and many other language environments don't do *tail-call optimizations*, which would convert a tail-recursive function into a loop. (The term *tail-call* means that the recursive call is the last thing done in the expression. The return value of the expression is the value returned by the call.)

Recursion is a hallmark of functional programming and a powerful tool for writing elegant implementations of many algorithms. Hence, the Scala compiler does limited tail-call optimizations itself. It will handle functions that call themselves, but not so-called "trampoline" calls, i.e., "a calls b calls a calls b," etc.

Still, you want to know if you got it right and the compiler did in fact perform the optimization. No one wants a blown stack in production. Fortunately, the compiler can tell you if you got it wrong, if you add an *annotation*, `tailrec` (*http://bit.ly/1wl47Y9*), as shown in this refined version of `factorial`:

```
// src/main/scala/progscala2/typelessdomore/factorial-tailrec.sc
import scala.annotation.tailrec

def factorial(i: Int): Long = {
  @tailrec
  def fact(i: Int, accumulator: Int): Long = {
    if (i <= 1) accumulator
    else fact(i - 1, i * accumulator)
  }

  fact(i, 1)
}

(0 to 5) foreach ( i => println(factorial(i)) )
```

If `fact` is not actually tail recursive, the compiler will throw an error. Consider this attempt to write a recursive Fibonacci function in the REPL:

```
scala> import scala.annotation.tailrec

scala> @tailrec
     | def fibonacci(i: Int): Long = {
     |   if (i <= 1) 1L
     |   else fibonacci(i - 2) + fibonacci(i - 1)
     | }

<console>:16: error: could not optimize @tailrec annotated method fibonacci:
        it contains a recursive call not in tail position
```

```
    else fibonacci(i - 2) + fibonacci(i - 1)
                 ^
```

That is, we make not one, but two recursive calls and *then* do something with the returned values, so this function is not tail recursive.

Finally, the nested function can see anything in scope, including arguments passed to the outer function. Note the use of n in count:

```
// src/main/scala/progscala2/typelessdomore/count-to.sc

def countTo(n: Int): Unit = {
  def count(i: Int): Unit = {
    if (i <= n) { println(i); count(i + 1) }
  }
  count(1)
}
```

Inferring Type Information

Statically typed languages can be very verbose. Consider this typical declaration in Java, before Java 7:

```
import java.util.HashMap;
...
HashMap<Integer, String> intToStringMap = new HashMap<Integer, String>();
```

We have to specify the type parameters <Integer, String> twice. Scala uses the term *type annotations* for explicit type declarations like HashMap<Integer, String>.

Java 7 introduced the *diamond operator* to infer the generic types on the righthand side, reducing the verbosity a bit:

```
HashMap<Integer, String> intToStringMap = new HashMap<>();
```

We've already seen some examples of Scala's support for type inference. The compiler can discern quite a bit of type information from the context, without explicit type annotations. Here's the same declaration rewritten in Scala, with inferred type information:

```
val intToStringMap: HashMap[Integer, String] = new HashMap
```

If we specify HashMap[Integer, String] on the righthand side of the equals sign, it's even more concise:

```
val intToStringMap2 = new HashMap[Integer, String]
```

Some functional programming languages, like Haskell, can infer almost all types, because they can perform global type inference. Scala can't do this, in part because Scala has to support *subtype polymorphism* (inheritance), which makes type inference much harder.

Here is a summary of the rules for when explicit type annotations are required in Scala.

The last case is somewhat rare, fortunately.

The Any type is the root of the Scala type hierarchy (we'll explore Scala's types in "The Scala Type Hierarchy" on page 294). If a block of code returns a value of type Any unexpectedly, chances are good that the code is more general than you intended so that only the Any type can fit all possible values.

Let's look at a few examples of cases we haven't seen yet where explicit types are required.

Overloaded methods require an explicit return type when one such method calls another, as in this example:

```
// src/main/scala/progscala2/typelessdomore/method-overloaded-return-v1.scX
// Version 1 of "StringUtil" (with a compilation error).
// ERROR: Won't compile: needs a String return type on the second "joiner".

object StringUtilV1 {
  def joiner(strings: String*): String = strings.mkString("-")

  def joiner(strings: List[String]) = joiner(strings :_*)   // COMPILATION ERROR
}

println( StringUtilV1.joiner(List("Programming", "Scala")) )
```

In this contrived example, the two `joiner` methods concatenate a `List` of strings together, separated by `"-"`, but the code won't compile. They also illustrate a few useful idioms, but let's fix the compilation error first.

If you run this script, you get the following error:

```
...
<console>:10: error: overloaded method joiner needs result type
       def joiner(strings: List[String]) = joiner(strings :_*)    // ERROR
                                                  ^
...
```

Because the *second* `joiner` method calls the first, it requires an explicit `String` return type. It should look like this:

```
def joiner(strings: List[String]): String = joiner(strings :_*)
```

Now let's return to the implementation idioms this script demonstrates. Scala supports methods that take *variable argument lists* (sometimes just called *variadic methods*). The first `joiner` method has this signature:

```
def joiner(strings: String*): String = strings.mkString("-")
```

The "*" after the `String` in the argument list says "zero or more Strings." A method can have other arguments, but they would have to come before the variable argument and only one variable argument is allowed.

However, sometimes a user might already have a list of strings ready to pass to `join er`. The second method is a convenience method for this case. It simply calls the first `joiner` method, but it uses a special syntax to tell the compiler to convert the input `List` into the variable argument list expected by the first `joiner` method:

```
def joiner(strings: List[String]): String = joiner(strings :_*)
```

The way I read this curious expression, `strings :_*`, is to think of it as a hint to the compiler that you want the list `strings` to be treated as a variable argument list ("*") of some unspecified, but inferred type (":_"). Scala doesn't let you write `strings :String*`, even though that's the actual type we need for the other `joiner` method.

We don't actually need this convenience version of `joiner`. The user could also pass a list to the first `joiner` method, the one that takes a variable argument list, and use this same syntax to do the conversion.

The final scenario for return types can be subtle, especially when a more general return type is inferred than what you expected. You usually see this issue when you assign a value returned from a function to a variable with a more specific type. For example, you were expecting a `String`, but the function inferred an `Any` for the return type. Let's see a contrived example that reflects a bug where this scenario can occur:

```
// src/main/scala/progscala2/typelessdomore/method-broad-inference-return.scX
// ERROR: Won't compile. Method actually returns List[Any], which is too "broad".

def makeList(strings: String*) = {
  if (strings.length == 0)
    List(0)  // #1
  else
    strings.toList
}

val list: List[String] = makeList()  // COMPILATION ERROR
```

Running this script triggers the following error:

```
...8: error: type mismatch;
 found    : List[Any]
 required: List[String]
val list: List[String] = makeList()   // ERROR
                         ^
```

We intended for `makeList` to return a `List[String]`, but when `strings.length` equals zero, we return `List(0)`, incorrectly "assuming" that this expression is the correct way to create an empty list. In fact, we are returning a `List[Int]` with one element, `0`.

Instead, we should return `List.empty[String]` or the special "marker" type for empty lists, `Nil`. Either choice results in the correct inference for the return type.

When the `if` clause returns `List[Int]` and the `else` clause returns `List[String]` (the result of `strings.toList`), the only possible inferred return type for the method is the closest common supertype of `List[Int]` and `List[String]`, which is `List[Any]`.

It's important to note that the code *compiled* without error. We only noticed the problem at runtime because we cautiously declared the value `list` to have the type `List[String]`.

In this case, adding an explicit return type of `List[String]` to the method would have triggered the compiler to catch the bug. Of course, a return type annotation also provides documentation for readers.

There are two other scenarios to watch for if you omit a return type annotation where you might get an unexpected inferred type. First, it could be that a function called by your function is triggering the unexpected inference. Perhaps that function was modified recently in a way that changed its return type, triggering a change in your function's inferred type on recompilation.

A second, related scenario is more often seen as a project grows and different modules are built at different times. If you see a `java.lang.NoSuchMethodError` during integration testing—or worse, production runs—for a method call that you *know* exists in another module, it could be that the return type of that function has been changed, either explicitly or through type inference, and the calling module is out of date and expecting the obsolete return type.

 When developing APIs that are built separately from their clients, declare method return types explicitly and use the most general return type you can. This is especially important when APIs declare *abstract* methods (see, e.g., Chapter 9).

Let's finish this section by looking at a common typing mistake that is easy to make, especially when you're new to Scala. Consider the following REPL session:

```scala
scala> def double(i: Int) { 2 * i }
double: (i: Int)Unit

scala> println(double(2))
()
```

Why did the second command print () instead of 4? Look carefully at what the scala interpreter said about the method signature: double (Int)Unit. We thought we defined a method named double that takes an Int argument and returns a new Int with the value "doubled," but it actually returns Unit. Why?

The cause of this unexpected behavior is a missing equals sign in the method definition. Here is the definition we actually intended:

```scala
scala> def double(i: Int) = { 2 * i }
double: (i: Int)Int

scala> println(double(2))
4
```

Note the equals sign before the body of double. Now, the output says we have defined double to return an Int and the second command does what we expect it to do.

There is a reason for this behavior. Scala regards a method with the equals sign before the body as a function definition and a function always returns a value in functional programming. On the other hand, when Scala sees a method body without the leading equals sign, it assumes the programmer intended the method to be a "procedure" definition, meant for performing side effects only with the return value Unit. In practice, it is more likely that the programmer simply forgot to insert the equals sign!

When the return type of a method is inferred and you don't use an equals sign before the opening curly brace for the method body, Scala infers a Unit return type, even when the last expression in the method is a value of another type.

However, this behavior is too subtle and the mistake is easy to make. Because it is easy enough to define a function that returns Unit, the "procedure" syntax is now deprecated as of Scala 2.11. Don't use it!

I didn't tell you where the () came from that was printed before we fixed the bug. It is actually the real name of the *single* instance of the Unit type! We said before that Unit behaves like void in other languages. However, unlike void, Unit is actually a type with a single value, named (), which is a historical convention in functional languages—we'll explain why in "Sum Types Versus Product Types" on page 407.

Reserved Words

Table 2-1 lists the reserved keywords in Scala. Some of them we've seen already. Many are found in Java and they usually have the same meanings in both languages. For the keywords that we haven't encountered already, we'll learn about them as we proceed.

Table 2-1. Reserved words

Word	Description	See ...
abstract	Makes a declaration abstract.	"Class and Object Basics" on page 246
case	Start a case clause in a match expression. Define a "case class."	Chapter 4
catch	Start a clause for catching thrown exceptions.	"Using try, catch, and finally Clauses" on page 84
class	Start a class declaration.	"Class and Object Basics" on page 246
def	Start a method declaration.	"Method Declarations" on page 38
do	Start a do...while loop.	"Other Looping Constructs" on page 83
else	Start an else clause for an if clause.	"Scala if Statements" on page 77
extends	Indicates that the class or trait that follows is the parent type of the class or trait being declared.	"Parent Types" on page 253
false	Boolean *false*.	"Boolean Literals" on page 55
final	Applied to a class or trait to prohibit deriving child types from it. Applied to a member to prohibit overriding it in a derived class or trait.	"Attempting to Override final Declarations" on page 314
finally	Start a clause that is executed after the corresponding try clause, whether or not an exception is thrown by the try clause.	"Using try, catch, and finally Clauses" on page 84
for	Start a for comprehension (loop).	"Scala for Comprehensions" on page 78

Word	Description	See ...
forSome	Used in *existential type* declarations to constrain the allowed concrete types that can be used.	"Existential Types" on page 386
if	Start an if clause.	"Scala if Statements" on page 77
implicit	Marks a method or value as eligible to be used as an *implicit* type converter or value. Marks a method parameter as optional, as long as a type-compatible substitute object is in the scope where the method is called.	"Implicit Conversions" on page 149
import	Import one or more types or members of types into the current scope.	"Importing Types and Their Members" on page 65
lazy	Defer evaluation of a val.	"lazy val" on page 91
match	Start a pattern-matching clause.	Chapter 4
new	Create a new instance of a class.	"Class and Object Basics" on page 246
null	Value of a reference variable that has not been assigned a value.	"The Scala Type Hierarchy" on page 294
object	Start a *singleton* declaration: a class with only one instance.	"A Taste of Scala" on page 9
override	Override a *concrete* member of a type, as long as the original is not marked final.	"Overriding Members of Classes and Traits" on page 311
package	Start a package scope declaration.	"Organizing Code in Files and Namespaces" on page 63
private	Restrict visibility of a declaration.	Chapter 13
protected	Restrict visibility of a declaration.	Chapter 13
requires	Deprecated. Was used for *self-typing*.	"Self-Type Annotations" on page 376
return	Return from a function.	"A Taste of Scala" on page 9
sealed	Applied to a parent type. Requires all derived types to be declared in the same source file.	"Sealed Class Hierarchies" on page 62
super	Analogous to this, but binds to the parent type.	"Overriding Abstract and Concrete Methods" on page 315
this	How an object refers to itself. The method name for *auxiliary constructors*.	"Class and Object Basics" on page 246
throw	Throw an exception.	"Using try, catch, and finally Clauses" on page 84
trait	A *mixin module* that adds additional state and behavior to an instance of a class. Can also be used to just declare methods, but not define them, like a Java interface.	Chapter 9
try	Start a block that may throw an exception.	"Using try, catch, and finally Clauses" on page 84
true	Boolean *true*.	"Boolean Literals" on page 55
type	Start a *type* declaration.	"Abstract Types Versus Parameterized Types" on page 67
val	Start a read-only "variable" declaration.	"Variable Declarations" on page 34
var	Start a read-write variable declaration.	"Variable Declarations" on page 34

Word	Description	See ...
while	Start a `while` loop.	"Other Looping Constructs" on page 83
with	Include the trait that follows in the class being declared or the object being instantiated.	Chapter 9
yield	Return an element in a `for` comprehension that becomes part of a sequence.	"Yielding" on page 80
_	A placeholder, used in imports, function literals, etc.	Many
:	Separator between identifiers and type annotations.	"A Taste of Scala" on page 9
=	Assignment.	"A Taste of Scala" on page 9
=>	Used in *function literals* to separate the argument list from the function body.	"Anonymous Functions, Lambdas, and Closures" on page 175
<-	Used in `for` comprehensions in *generator* expressions.	"Scala for Comprehensions" on page 78
<:	Used in *parameterized* and *abstract type* declarations to constrain the allowed types.	"Type Bounds" on page 365
<%	Used in *parameterized* and *abstract type* "view bounds" declarations.	"View Bounds" on page 371
>:	Used in *parameterized* and *abstract type* declarations to constrain the allowed types.	"Type Bounds" on page 365
#	Used in *type projections*.	"Type Projections" on page 393
@	Marks an *annotation*.	"Annotations" on page 504
⇒	(Unicode \u21D2) Same as =>.	"Anonymous Functions, Lambdas, and Closures" on page 175
→	(Unicode \u2192) Same as ->.	"Implicit Conversions" on page 149
←	(Unicode \u2190) Same as <-.	"Scala for Comprehensions" on page 78

Notice that `break` and `continue` are not listed. These control keywords don't exist in Scala. Instead, Scala encourages you to use functional programming idioms that are usually more succinct and less error-prone, as we'll see.

Some Java methods use names that are reserved words by Scala, for example, `java.util.Scanner.match`. To avoid a compilation error, surround the name with single back quotes ("back ticks"), e.g., `java.util.Scanner.`match`.

Literal Values

We've seen a few *literal values* already, such as `val book = "Programming Scala"`, where we initialized a `val book` with a `String` literal, and `(s: String) => s.toUpperCase`, an example of a function literal. Let's discuss all the literals supported by Scala.

Integer Literals

Integer literals can be expressed in decimal, hexadecimal, or octal. The details are summarized in Table 2-2.

Table 2-2. Integer literals

Kind	Format	Examples
Decimal	0 *or* a nonzero digit followed by zero or more digits (0–9)	0, 1, 321
Hexadecimal	0x followed by one or more hexadecimal digits (0–9, A–F, a–f)	0xFF, 0x1a3b
Octal	0 followed by one or more octal digits (0–7)[a]	013, 077

[a] Octal literals are deprecated as of Scala 2.10.

You indicate a negative number by prefixing the literal with a – sign.

For Long literals, it is necessary to append the L or l character at the end of the literal, unless you are assigning the value to a variable declared to be Long. Otherwise, Int is inferred. The valid values for an integer literal are bounded by the type of the variable to which the value will be assigned. Table 2-3 defines the limits, which are inclusive.

Table 2-3. Ranges of allowed values for integer literals (boundaries are inclusive)

Target type	Minimum (inclusive)	Maximum (inclusive)
Long	-2^{63}	$2^{63} - 1$
Int	-2^{31}	$2^{31} - 1$
Short	-2^{15}	$2^{15} - 1$
Char	0	$2^{16} - 1$
Byte	-2^7	$2^7 - 1$

A compile-time error occurs if an integer literal number is specified that is outside these ranges, as in the following examples:

```
scala> val i = 1234567890123
<console>:1: error: integer number too large
       val i = 12345678901234567890
                  ^

scala> val i = 1234567890123L
i: Long = 1234567890123

scala> val b: Byte = 128
<console>:19: error: type mismatch;
 found   : Int(128)
 required: Byte
       val b: Byte = 128
                     ^
```

```
scala> val b: Byte = 127
b: Byte = 127
```

Floating-Point Literals

Floating-point literals are expressions with an optional minus sign, zero or more digits, followed by a period (.), followed by *one* or more digits. For Float literals, append the F or f character at the end of the literal. Otherwise, a Double is assumed. You can optionally append a D or d for a Double.

Floating-point literals can be expressed with or without exponentials. The format of the exponential part is e or E, followed by an optional + or -, followed by one or more digits.

Here are some example floating-point literals, where Double is inferred unless the declared variable is Float or an f or F suffix is used:

```
.14
3.14
3.14f
3.14F
3.14d
3.14D
3e5
3E5
3.14e+5
3.14e-5
3.14e-5
3.14e-5f
3.14e-5F
3.14e-5d
3.14e-5D
```

Float consists of all IEEE 754 32-bit, single-precision binary floating-point values. Double consists of all IEEE 754 64-bit, double-precision binary floating-point values.

Before Scala 2.10, floating-point literals without a digit after the period were allowed, e.g., 3. and 3.e5. This syntax leads to some ambiguities, where it can be interpreted as the period before a method name. How should 1.toString be parsed? Is it 1 the Int or 1.0 the Double? Hence, literals without at least one digit after the period are deprecated in 2.10 and disallowed in 2.11.

Boolean Literals

The Boolean literals are true and false. The type of the variable to which they are assigned will be inferred to be Boolean:

```
scala> val b1 = true
b1: Boolean = true
```

```
scala> val b2 = false
b2: Boolean = false
```

Character Literals

A character literal is either a *printable* Unicode character or an escape sequence, written between single quotes. A character with a Unicode value between 0 and 255 may also be represented by an octal escape, i.e., a backslash (\) followed by a sequence of up to three octal characters. It is a compile-time error if a backslash character in a character or string literal does not start a valid escape sequence.

Here are some examples:

```
'A'
'\u0041'   // 'A' in Unicode
'\n'
'\012'     // '\n' in octal
'\t'
```

The valid escape sequences are shown in Table 2-4.

Table 2-4. Character escape sequences

Sequence	Meaning
\b	Backspace (BS)
\t	Horizontal tab (HT)
\n	Line feed (LF)
\f	Form feed (FF)
\r	Carriage return (CR)
\"	Double quote (")
\'	Single quote (')
\\	Backslash (\)

Note that *nonprintable* Unicode characters like \u0009 (tab) are not allowed. Use the equivalents like \t. Recall that three Unicode characters were mentioned in Table 2-1 as valid replacements for corresponding ASCII sequences, ⇒ for =>, → for ->, and ← for <-.

String Literals

A string literal is a sequence of characters enclosed in double quotes or *triples* of double quotes, i.e., """..."""".

For string literals in double quotes, the allowed characters are the same as the character literals. However, if a double quote (") character appears in the string, it must be "escaped" with a \ character. Here are some examples:

```
"Programming\nScala"
"He exclaimed, \"Scala is great!\""
"First\tSecond"
```

The string literals bounded by triples of double quotes are also called *multiline* string literals. These strings can cover several lines; the line feeds will be part of the string. They can include any characters, including one or two double quotes together, but not three together. They are useful for strings with \ characters that don't form valid Unicode or escape sequences, like the valid sequences listed in Table 2-4. Regular expressions are a good example, which use lots of escaped characters with special meanings. Conversely, if escape sequences appear, they aren't interpreted.

Here are three example strings:

```
"""Programming\nScala"""
"""He exclaimed, "Scala is great!" """
"""First line\n
Second line\t

Fourth line"""
```

Note that we had to add a space before the trailing """ in the second example to prevent a parse error. Trying to escape the second " that ends the "Scala is great!" quote, i.e., "Scala is great!\", doesn't work.

When using multiline strings in code, you'll want to indent the substrings for proper code formatting, yet you probably don't want that extra whitespace in the actual string output. String.stripMargin solves this problem. It removes all whitespace in the substrings up to and including the first occurrence of a vertical bar, |. If you want some whitespace indentation, put the whitespace you want after the |. Consider this example:

```
// src/main/scala/progscala2/typelessdomore/multiline-strings.sc

def hello(name: String) = s"""Welcome!
  Hello, $name!
  * (Gratuitous Star!!)
  |We're glad you're here.
  |  Have some extra whitespace.""".stripMargin

hello("Programming Scala")
```

It prints the following:

```
Welcome!
  Hello, Programming Scala!
  * (Gratuitous Star!!)
```

```
We're glad you're here.
  Have some extra whitespace.
```

Note where leading whitespace is removed and where it isn't.

If you want to use a different leading character than |, use the overloaded version of stripMargin that takes a Char (character) argument. If the whole string has a prefix or suffix you want to remove (but not on individual lines), there are corresponding strip Prefix and stripSuffix methods:

```
// src/main/scala/progscala2/typelessdomore/multiline-strings2.sc

def goodbye(name: String) =
  s"""xxxGoodbye, ${name}yyy
xxxCome again!yyy""".stripPrefix("xxx").stripSuffix("yyy")

goodbye("Programming Scala")
```

This example prints the following:

```
Goodbye, Programming Scalayyy
  xxxCome again!
```

Symbol Literals

Scala supports symbols, which are *interned* strings, meaning that two symbols with the same "name" (i.e., the same character sequence) will actually refer to the same object in memory. Symbols are used less often in Scala compared to some other languages, like Ruby and Lisp.

A symbol literal is a single quote ('), followed by one or more digits, letters, or under-scores ("_"), except the first character can't be a digit. So, an expression like '1symbol is invalid.

A symbol literal '*id* is a shorthand for the expression scala.Symbol("id"). If you want to create a symbol that contains whitespace, use Symbol.apply, e.g., Symbol(" Pro gramming Scala "). All the whitespace is preserved.

Function Literals

We've seen function literals already, but to recap, (i: Int, s: String) => s+i is a function literal of type Function2[Int,String,String] (String is returned).

You can even use the literal syntax for a type declaration. The following declarations are equivalent:

```
val f1: (Int,String) => String     = (i, s) => s+i
val f2: Function2[Int,String,String] = (i, s) => s+i
```

Tuple Literals

How many times have you wanted to return *two* or more values from a method? In many languages, like Java, you only have a few options, none of which is very appealing. You could pass in parameters to the method that will be modified for use as the "return" values, which is ugly. (Some languages even use keywords to indicate which parameters are input versus output.) You could declare some small "structural" class that holds the two or more values, then return an instance of that class.

The Scala library includes `TupleN` classes (e.g., `Tuple2` (*http://bit.ly/1rGMP1q*)), for grouping *N* items, with the literal syntax of a comma-separated list of the items inside parentheses. There are separate `TupleN` classes for N between 1 and 22, inclusive (though this upper bound may be eliminated eventually in a future version of Scala).

For example, `val tup = ("Programming Scala", 2014)` defines a `Tuple2` instance with `String` inferred for the first element and `Int` inferred for the second element. Tuple instances are immutable, *first-class* values (because they are objects like any custom type you define), so you can assign them to variables, pass them as values, and return them from methods.

You can also use the literal syntax for `Tuple` type declarations:

```
val t1: (Int,String)        = (1, "two")
val t2: Tuple2[Int,String]  = (1, "two")
```

The following example demonstrates working with tuples:

```
// src/main/scala/progscala2/typelessdomore/tuple-example.sc

val t = ("Hello", 1, 2.3)                                // ❶
println( "Print the whole tuple: " + t )
println( "Print the first item:  " + t._1 )              // ❷
println( "Print the second item: " + t._2 )
println( "Print the third item:  " + t._3 )

val (t1, t2, t3) = ("World", '!', 0x22)                  // ❸
println( t1 + ", " + t2 + ", " + t3 )

val (t4, t5, t6) = Tuple3("World", '!', 0x22)            // ❹
println( t4 + ", " + t5 + ", " + t6 )
```

❶   Use the literal syntax to construct a three-element tuple of type `Tuple3`.

❷   Extract the first element of the tuple (counting from 1, not 0). The next two lines extract the second and third elements.

❸   On the fly declare three values, `t1`, `t2`, and `t3`, that are assigned the three corresponding fields from the tuple.

❹   Use the `Tuple3` "factory" method to construct a tuple.

Running this script produces the following output:

```
Print the whole tuple: (Hello,1,2.3)
Print the first item:  Hello
Print the second item: 1
Print the third item:  2.3
World, !, 34
World, !, 34
```

The expression t._n retrieves the nth item from tuple t, starting at one, *not* zero, following historical conventions.

There are several ways to define a two-element tuple, which is sometimes called a *pair* for short. In addition to the syntax that uses a parenthesized list of values, you can also use the "arrow operator" between two values, as well as special factory methods on the tuple-related classes:

```
(1, "one")
1 -> "one"
1 → "one"          // Using → character instead of ->
Tuple2(1, "one")
```

The arrow operator is only available for two-element tuples.

Option, Some, and None: Avoiding nulls

Let's discuss three useful types that express a very useful concept, when we may or may not have a value.

Most languages have a special keyword or type instance that's assigned to reference variables when there's nothing else for them to refer to. In Java, it's null, which is a keyword, not an instance of a type. Thus, it's illegal to call any methods on it. But this is a confusing choice on the language designer's part. Why return a keyword when the programmer expects an instance of a type?

Of course, the real problem is that null is a giant source of nasty bugs. What null really signals is that we don't have a value in a given situation. If the value is not null, we do have a value. Why not express this situation explicitly with the type system and exploit type checking to avoid NullPointerExceptions (*http://bit.ly/1pbzh3C*)?

Option (*http://bit.ly/1wl8KBy*) lets us express this situation explicitly without the null "hack." Option is an abstract class and its two concrete subclasses are Some (*http://bit.ly/10aqvGK*), for when we have a value, and None (*http://bit.ly/1tpxZjN*), when we don't.

You can see Option, Some, and None in action in the following example, where we create a map of state capitals in the United States:

```
// src/main/scala/progscala2/typelessdomore/state-capitals-subset.sc
```

```
val stateCapitals = Map(
  "Alabama" -> "Montgomery",
  "Alaska"  -> "Juneau",
  // ...
  "Wyoming" -> "Cheyenne")

println( "Get the capitals wrapped in Options:" )
println( "Alabama: " + stateCapitals.get("Alabama") )
println( "Wyoming: " + stateCapitals.get("Wyoming") )
println( "Unknown: " + stateCapitals.get("Unknown") )

println( "Get the capitals themselves out of the Options:" )
println( "Alabama: " + stateCapitals.get("Alabama").get )
println( "Wyoming: " + stateCapitals.get("Wyoming").getOrElse("Oops!") )
println( "Unknown: " + stateCapitals.get("Unknown").getOrElse("Oops2!") )
```

Notice what happens when we run the script:

```
Get the capitals wrapped in Options:
Alabama: Some(Montgomery)
Wyoming: Some(Cheyenne)
Unknown: None
Get the capitals themselves out of the Options:
Alabama: Montgomery
Wyoming: Cheyenne
Unknown: Oops2!
```

The `Map.get` method returns an `Option[T]`, where `T` is `String` in this case. In contrast, Java's `Map.get` returns `T`, where `null` or a real value will be returned. By returning an `Option`, we can't "forget" that we have to verify that something was returned. In other words, the fact that a value may not exist for a given key is enshrined in the return type for the method declaration.

The first group of `println` statements invoke `toString` implicitly on the instances returned by `get`. We are calling `toString` on `Some` or `None` instances because the values returned by `Map.get` are automatically wrapped in a `Some`, when there is a value in the map for the specified key. Conversely, when we ask for a map entry that doesn't exist, the `None` object is returned, rather than `null`. This occurred in the last `println` of the three.

The second group of `println` statements goes a step further. After calling `Map.get`, they call `get` or `getOrElse` on each `Option` instance to retrieve the value it contains.

`Option.get` is a bit dangerous. If the `Option` is a `Some`, `Some.get` returns the value. However, if the `Option` is actually `None`, then `None.get` throws a `NoSuchElementException` (*http://bit.ly/1xIwEVV*).

We also see the alternative, safer method, `getOrElse`, in the last two `println` statements. This method returns either the value in the `Option`, if it is a `Some` instance, or it returns the argument passed to getOrElse, if it is a None instance. In other words, the getOr Else argument behaves as the default return value.

So, getOrElse is the more defensive of the two methods. It avoids a potential thrown exception.

To reiterate, because the Map.get method returns an Option, it automatically documents for the reader that there may not be an item matching the specified key. The map handles this situation by returning a None. Most languages would return null (or the equivalent). It's true that you learn from experience to expect a possible null in these languages, but using Option makes the behavior more explicit in the method signature and more self-documenting.

Also, thanks to Scala's static typing, you can't make the mistake of "forgetting" that an Option is returned and attempting to call a method supported by the type of the value inside the Option (if there is a value). In Java, when a method returns a value, it's easy to forget to check for null before calling a method on the value. When a Scala method returns Option, the type checking done by the compiler forces you to extract the value from the Option first before calling a method on it. That "reminds" you to check if the Option is actually None. So, the use of Option strongly encourages more resilient programming.

Because Scala runs on the JVM and it must interoperate with other libraries, Scala has to support null. Some devious soul could hand you a Some(null), too. Still, you now have an alternative and you should avoid using null in your code, except for interoperating with Java libraries that require it. Tony Hoare (*http://bit.ly/null-refs-th*), who invented the null reference in 1965 while working on a language called ALGOL W, called its invention his "billion dollar" mistake. Use Option instead.

Sealed Class Hierarchies

While we're discussing Option, let's discuss a useful design feature it uses. A key point about Option is that there are really only two valid subtypes. Either we have a value, the Some case, or we don't, the None case. There are *no* other subtypes of Option that would be valid. So, we would really like to prevent users from creating their own.

Scala has a keyword sealed for this purpose. Option is declared like this (eliding some details):

```
sealed abstract class Option[+A] ... { ... }
```

The sealed keyword tells the compiler that all subclasses must be declared *in the same source file*. Some and None are declared in the same file with Option in the Scala library. This technique effectively prevents additional subtypes of Option.

You can also declare a type final if you want to prevent users from subtyping it.

Organizing Code in Files and Namespaces

Scala adopts the package concept that Java uses for namespaces, but Scala offers more flexibility. Filenames don't have to match the type names and the package structure does not have to match the directory structure. So, you can define packages in files independent of their "physical" location.

The following example defines a class MyClass in a package com.example.mypkg using the conventional Java syntax:

```
// src/main/scala/progscala2/typelessdomore/package-example1.scala
package com.example.mypkg

class MyClass {
  // ...
}
```

Scala also supports a block-structured syntax for declaring package scope, which is similar to the namespace syntax in C# and the use of modules as namespaces in Ruby:

```
// src/main/scala/progscala2/typelessdomore/package-example2.scala
package com {
  package example {
    package pkg1 {
      class Class11 {
        def m = "m11"
      }
      class Class12 {
        def m = "m12"
      }
    }

    package pkg2 {
      class Class21 {
        def m = "m21"
        def makeClass11 = {
          new pkg1.Class11
        }
        def makeClass12 = {
          new pkg1.Class12
        }
      }
    }

    package pkg3.pkg31.pkg311 {
      class Class311 {
        def m = "m21"
      }
    }
```

```
    }
  }
```

Two packages, pkg1 and pkg2, are defined under the com.example package. A total of three classes are defined between the two packages. The makeClass11 and make Class12 methods in Class21 illustrate how to reference a type in the "sibling" package, pkg1. You can also reference these classes by their full paths, com.exam ple.pkg1.Class11 and com.example.pkg1.Class12, respectively.

The package pkg3.pkg31.pkg311 shows that you can "chain" several packages together in one statement. It is not necessary to use a separate package statement for each package.

However, there is one situation where you might use separate statements. Let's call it the *successive package statement idiom*:

```
// src/main/scala/progscala2/typelessdomore/package-example3.scala
// Bring into scope all package level declarations in "example".
package com.example
// Bring into scope all package level declarations in "mypkg".
package mypkg

class MyPkgClass {
  // ...
}
```

If you have package-level declarations, like types, in each of several parent packages that you want to bring into scope, use separate package statements as shown for each level of the package hierarchy with these declarations. Each subsequent package statement is interpreted as a subpackage of the previously specified package, as if we used the block-structure syntax shown previously. The first statement is interpreted as an absolete path.

Following the convention used by Java, the root package for Scala's library classes is named scala.

Although the package declaration syntax is flexible, one limitation is that packages cannot be defined within classes and objects, which wouldn't make much sense anyway.

 Scala does not allow package declarations in scripts, which are implicitly wrapped in an object, where package declarations are not permitted.

Importing Types and Their Members

To use declarations in packages, you have to import them, just as you do in Java. However, Scala offers additional options, as shown in the following examples that import Java types:

```
import java.awt._
import java.io.File
import java.io.File._
import java.util.{Map, HashMap}
```

You can import all types in a package, using the underscore (_) as a wildcard, as shown on the first line. You can also import individual Scala or Java types, as shown on the second line.

 Java uses the "star" character (*) as the wildcard for imports. In Scala, this character is allowed as a method name, so _ is used instead to avoid ambiguity. For example, if object Foo defined a * method, as well as other methods, then what should import Foo.* mean?

The third line imports all the static methods and fields in `java.io.File`. The equivalent Java import statement would be `import static java.io.File.*;`. Scala doesn't have an `import static` construct because it treats `object` types uniformly like other types.

Selective importing has a very handy syntax, as shown on the fourth line, where we import just `java.util.Map` and `java.util.HashMap`.

Finally, you can put import statements almost anywhere, so you can scope their visibility to just where they are needed, you can rename types as you import them, and you can suppress the visibility of unwanted types:

```
def stuffWithBigInteger() = {

  import java.math.BigInteger.{
    ONE => _,
    TEN,
    ZERO => JAVAZERO }

  // println( "ONE: "+ONE )      // ONE is effectively undefined
  println( "TEN: "+TEN )
  println( "ZERO: "+JAVAZERO )
}
```

Because this import statement is inside `stuffWithBigInteger`, the imported types and values are not visible outside the function.

Renaming the `java.math.BigInteger.ONE` constant to underscore (_) makes it invisible and unavailable. Use this technique when you want to import everything except a few items.

Next, the `java.math.BigInteger.TEN` constant is imported without renaming, so it can be referenced simply as `TEN`.

Finally, the `java.math.BigInteger.ZERO` constant is given the "alias" `JAVAZERO`.

Aliasing is useful if you want to give an item a more convenient name or you want to avoid ambiguities with other items in scope that have the same name. It is used a lot to rename imported Java types so they don't conflict with Scala types of the same name, e.g., `java.util.List` (*http://bit.ly/1sRezAw*) and `java.util.Map` (*http://bit.ly/13p7wdL*), for which we have Scala library types with the same names.

Imports Are Relative

Another important difference compared to Java imports is that Scala imports are *relative*. Note the comments for the following imports:

```
// src/main/scala/progscala2/typelessdomore/relative-imports.scala
import scala.collection.mutable._
import collection.immutable._          // Since "scala" is already imported
import _root_.scala.collection.parallel._  // full path from real "root"
```

It's fairly rare that you'll have problems with relative imports, but sometimes surprises occur. If you get a mystifying compiler error that a package wasn't found, verify that you are using relative versus absolute import statements correctly. On rare occasions, you'll need the _root_ prefix. Usually the top-level package, like `com`, `org`, or `scala` will suffice. Also, be sure that the library in question is visible on the CLASSPATH.

Package Objects

A design decision for library writers is where to expose public entry points for APIs that clients will import and use. As for Java libraries, it's common to import some or all of the types defined within a package. For example, the Java statement `import java.io.*;` imports all the types in the `io` package. Java 5 added "static imports" to allow individual static members of classes to be imported. Though convenient, it still presents a slightly inconvenient syntax. Consider a fictitious JSON parsing library you might use with a top-level package `json` and static API access methods in a class named JSON:

```
static import com.example.json.JSON.*;
```

In Scala, you can at least omit the `static` keyword, but wouldn't it be nice to write something like the following, which can expose with a single import statement all the types, methods, and values needed by the API user:

```
import com.example.json._
```

Scala supports *package objects*, a special kind of `object` scoped at the level of the package, `json` in this case. It is declared just like a normal `object`, but with with the differences illustrated by the following example:

```
// src/com/example/json/package.scala        ❶

package com.example                           // ❷

package object json {                         // ❸
  class JSONObject {...}                       // ❹
  def fromString(string: String): JSONObject = {...}
  ...
}
```

❶   The name of the file must be `package.scala`. By convention, it is located in the same package directory as the package object it is defining, `com/example/json` in this case.

❷   The parent package scope.

❸   Use the `package` keyword and name the object after the package, `json` in this case.

❹   Appropriate members to expose to clients.

Now the client can import all these definitions with `import com.example.json._` or import individual elements in the usual way.

Abstract Types Versus Parameterized Types

We mentioned in "A Taste of Scala" on page 9 that Scala supports *parameterized types*, which are very similar to *generics* in Java. (We could use the two terms *parameterized types* and *generics* interchangeably, but it's more common to use *parameterized types* in the Scala community and *generics* in the Java community.) Java uses angle brackets (<...>), while Scala uses square brackets ([...]), because < and > are often used for method names.

For example, here is a declaration of a list of strings:

```
val strings: List[String] = List("one", "two", "three")
```

Because we can plug in almost any type for a type parameter A in a collection like `List[A]`, this feature is called *parametric polymorphism*, because generic implementations of the `List` methods can be used with instances of any type A.

Let's discuss the most important details to learn about parameterized types, especially when you're trying to understand type signatures in Scaladocs, such as the entry for

List (*http://bit.ly/10FrqQC*), where you'll see that the declaration is written as `sealed abstract class List[+A]`.

The + in front of the A means that `List[B]` is a *subtype* of `List[A]` for any B that is a subtype of A. This is called *covariant typing*. It is a reasonably intuitive idea. If we have a function `f(list: List[Any])`, it makes sense that passing a `List[String]` to it should work fine.

If there is a – in front of a type parameter, the relationship goes the other way; `Foo[B]` would be a *supertype* of `Foo[A]`, if B is a *subtype* of A and the declaration is `Foo[-A]` (called *contravariant typing*). This is less intuitive, but we'll wait until "Parameterized Types" on page 364 to explain it along with the other details of parameterized types.

Scala supports another type abstraction mechanism called *abstract types*, which can be applied to many of the same design problems for which parameterized types are used. However, while the two mechanisms overlap, they are not redundant. Each has strengths and weaknesses for certain design problems.

These types are declared as members of other types, just like methods and fields. Here is an example that uses an abstract type in a parent class, then makes the type member concrete in child classes:

```
// src/main/scala/progscala2/typelessdomore/abstract-types.sc
import java.io._

abstract class BulkReader {
  type In
  val source: In
  def read: String  // Read source and return a String
}

class StringBulkReader(val source: String) extends BulkReader {
  type In = String
  def read: String = source
}

class FileBulkReader(val source: File) extends BulkReader {
  type In = File
  def read: String = {
    val in = new BufferedInputStream(new FileInputStream(source))
    val numBytes = in.available()
    val bytes = new Array[Byte](numBytes)
    in.read(bytes, 0, numBytes)
    new String(bytes)
  }
}

println(new StringBulkReader("Hello Scala!").read)
// Assumes the current directory is src/main/scala:
```

```
println(new FileBulkReader(
  new File("TypeLessDoMore/abstract-types.sc")).read)
```

It produces the following output:

```
Hello Scala!
// src/main/scala/progscala2/typelessdomore/abstract-types.sc

import java.io._

abstract class BulkReader {
...
```

The BulkReader *abstract* class declares three abstract members: a type named In, a val field source of type In, and a read method.

The derived classes, StringBulkReader and FileBulkReader, provide concrete definitions for these abstract members.

Note that the type field works very much like a type parameter in a parameterized type. In fact, we could rewrite this example as follows, where we show only what would be different:

```
abstract class BulkReader[In] {
  val source: In
  ...
}

class StringBulkReader(val source: String) extends BulkReader[String] {...}

class FileBulkReader(val source: File) extends BulkReader[File] {...}
```

Just as for parameterized types, if we define the In type to be String, the source field must also be defined as a String. Note that the StringBulkReader's read method simply returns the source field, while the FileBulkReader's read method reads the contents of the file.

So what's the advantage here of using type members instead of parameterized types? The latter are best for the case where the type parameter has no relationship with the parameterized type, like List[A] when A is Int, String, Person, etc. A type member works best when it "evolves" in parallel with the enclosing type, as in our BulkReader example, where the type member needed to match the "behaviors" expressed by the enclosing type. Sometimes this characteristic is called *family polymorphism* or *covariant specialization*.

Recap and What's Next

We covered a lot of practical ground, such as literals, keywords, file organization, and imports. We learned how to declare variables, methods, and classes. We learned about `Option` as a better tool than `null`, plus other useful techniques. In the next chapter, we will finish our fast tour of the Scala "basics" before we dive into more detailed explanations of Scala's features.

## CHAPTER 3

Rounding Out the Basics

Let's finish our survey of essential "basics" in Scala.

Operator Overloading?

Almost all "operators" are actually methods. Consider this most basic of examples:

```
1 + 2
```

That plus sign between the numbers? It's a method.

First, note that all the types that are special "primitives" in Java are actually regular objects in Scala, meaning they can have methods: `Float`, `Double`, `Int`, `Long`, `Short`, `Byte`, `Char`, and `Boolean`.

As we've seen, Scala identifiers can have nonalphanumeric characters, with a few exceptions that we'll go over in a moment.

So, `1 + 2` is the same as `1.+(2)`, because of the "infix" notation where we can drop the period and parentheses for single-argument methods.[1]

Similarly, a method with no arguments can be invoked without the period. This is called "postfix" notation. However, use of this postfix convention can sometimes be confusing, so Scala 2.10 made it an *optional* feature. We set up the SBT build to trigger a warning if we use this feature without explicitly telling the compiler we want to use it. We do that with an import statement. Consider the following REPL session using the `scala` command (versus SBT `console`):

---

1. Actually, they don't always behave identically, due to operator precedence rules. Here, `1 + 2 * 3 = 7`, while `1.+(2)*3 = 9`. The period, when present, binds before the star. Also, when using pre-2.11 versions of Scala, put a space after the `1`, because `1.` will be interpreted as a `Double` otherwise!

```
$ scala
...
scala> 1 toString
warning: there were 1 feature warning(s); re-run with -feature for details
res0: String = 1
```

Well, that's not helpful. Let's restart REPL with the -feature flag to produce a more informative warning:

```
$ scala -feature
...
scala> 1.toString    // normal invocation
res0: String = 1

scala> 1 toString    // postfix invocation
<console>:8: warning: postfix operator toString should be enabled
by making the implicit value scala.language.postfixOps visible.
This can ... adding the import clause 'import scala.language.postfixOps'
or by setting the compiler option -language:postfixOps.
See the Scala docs for value scala.language.postfixOps for a discussion
why the feature should be explicitly enabled.
             1 toString
               ^
res1: String = 1

scala> import scala.language.postfixOps
import scala.language.postfixOps

scala> 1 toString
res2: String = 1
```

Because I prefer to have this longer warning turned on all the time, I configured the SBT project to use the -feature flag. So running the REPL using the console task in SBT has this compler flag enabled already.

We can resolve the warning in one of two ways. We showed one way, which is to use import scala.language.postfixOps. We can also pass another flag to the compiler to enable the feature globally, -language:postfixOps. I tend to prefer case-by-case import statements, to remind the reader which optional features I'm using (we'll list all the optional features in "scalac Command-Line Tool" on page 479).

Dropping the punctuation, when it isn't confusing or ambiguous for the compiler, makes the code cleaner and can help create elegant programs that read more naturally.

So, what characters can you use in identifiers? Here is a summary of the rules for identifiers, used for method and type names, variables, etc:

Characters
   Scala allows all the printable ASCII characters, such as letters, digits, the underscore (_), and the dollar sign ($), with the exceptions of the "parenthetical" characters,

(,), [,], {, and }, and the "delimiter" characters, `` ` ``, ', ', ", ., ;, and ,. Scala allows the other characters between \u0020 and \u007F that are not in the sets just shown, such as mathematical symbols, the so-called *operator characters* like / and <, and some other symbols.

Reserved words can't be used

As in most languages, you can't reuse reserved words for identifiers. We listed the reserved words in "Reserved Words" on page 51. Recall that some of them are combinations of operator and punctuation characters. For example, a single underscore (_) is a reserved word!

Plain identifiers—combinations of letters, digits, $, _, and operators

A *plain identifier* can begin with a letter or underscore, followed by more letters, digits, underscores, and dollar signs. Unicode-equivalent characters are also allowed. Scala reserves the dollar sign for internal use, so you shouldn't use it in your own identifiers, although this isn't prevented by the compiler. After an underscore, you can have either letters and digits, *or* a sequence of operator characters. The underscore is important. It tells the compiler to treat all the characters up to the next whitespace as part of the identifier. For example, `val xyz_++= = 1` assigns the variable `xyz_++=` the value 1, while the expression `val xyz++= = 1` won't compile because the "identifier" could also be interpreted as `xyz ++=`, which looks like an attempt to append something to `xyz`. Similarly, if you have operator characters after the underscore, you can't mix them with letters and digits. This restriction prevents ambiguous expressions like this: `abc_-123`. Is that an identifier `abc_-123` or an attempt to subtract 123 from `abc_`?

Plain identifiers—operators

If an identifier begins with an operator character, the rest of the characters must be operator characters.

"Back-quote" literals

An identifier can also be an arbitrary string between two back quote characters, e.g., ``def `test that addition works` = assert(1 + 1 == 2)``. (Using this trick for literate test names is the one use of this otherwise-questionable technique you'll see occasionally in production code.) We also saw back quotes used previously to invoke a method or variable in a Java class when the name is identical to a Scala reserved word, e.g., ``java.net.Proxy.`type`()``.

Pattern-matching identifiers

In pattern-matching expressions (recall the actor example in "A Taste of Concurrency" on page 19), tokens that begin with a lowercase letter are parsed as *variable identifiers*, while tokens that begin with an uppercase letter are parsed as *constant identifiers* (such as class names). This restriction prevents some ambiguities because of the very succinct variable syntax that is used, e.g., no `val` keyword is present.

Syntactic Sugar

Once you know that all operators are methods, it's easier to reason about unfamiliar Scala code. You don't have to worry about special cases when you see new operators. Our actors in "A Taste of Concurrency" on page 19 sent asynchronous messages to each other with an exclamation point, !, which is actually just an ordinary method.

This flexible method naming gives you the power to write libraries that feel like a natural extension of Scala itself. You can write a new math library with numeric types that accept all the usual mathematical operators. You can write a new concurrent messaging layer that behaves just like actors. The possibilities are constrained by just a few limitations for method names.

 Just because you *can* make up operator symbols doesn't mean you *should*. When designing your own APIs, keep in mind that obscure punctuational operators are hard for users to read, learn, and remember. Overuse of them contributes a "line noise" quality of unreadability to your code. So, stick to established conventions for operators and err on the side of readable method names when an operator shortcut isn't obvious.

Methods with Empty Argument Lists

Along with the infix and postfix invocation options, Scala is flexible about the use of parentheses in methods with no arguments.

If a method takes no parameters, you can define it without parentheses. Callers must invoke the method without parentheses. Conversely, if you add empty parentheses to your definition, callers have the option of adding parentheses or not.

For example, `List.size` has no parentheses, so you write `List(1, 2, 3).size`. If you try `List(1, 2, 3).size()`, you'll get an error.

However, the `length` method for `java.lang.String` does have parentheses in its definition (because Java requires them), but Scala lets you write both `"hello".length()` and `"hello".length`. That's also true for Scala-defined methods with empty parentheses.

It's because of Java interoperability that the rules are not consistent for the two cases where empty parentheses are part of the definition or not. Scala would prefer that definition and usage remain consistent, but it's more flexible when the definition has empty parentheses, so that calling Java no-argument methods can be consistent with calling Scala no-argument methods.

A convention in the Scala community is to omit parentheses for no-argument methods that have no side effects, like the size of a collection. When the method performs side effects, parentheses are usually added, offering a small "caution signal" to the reader that mutation might occur, requiring extra care. If you use the option -Xlint when you invoke `scala` or `scalac`, it will issue a warning if you define a method with no parentheses that performs side effects (e.g., I/O). I've added that flag to our SBT build.

Why bother with optional parentheses in the first place? They make some method call chains read better as expressive, self-explanatory "sentences" of code:

```
// src/main/scala/progscala2/rounding/no-dot-better.sc

def isEven(n: Int) = (n % 2) == 0

List(1, 2, 3, 4) filter isEven foreach println
```

It prints the following output:

```
2
4
```

Now, if you're not accustomed to this syntax, it can take a while to understand what's going on, even though it is quite "clean." So here is the last line repeated four times with progressively less of the details filled in. The last line is the original:

```
List(1, 2, 3, 4).filter((i: Int) => isEven(i)).foreach((i: Int) => println(i))
List(1, 2, 3, 4).filter(i => isEven(i)).foreach(i => println(i))
List(1, 2, 3, 4).filter(isEven).foreach(println)
List(1, 2, 3, 4) filter isEven foreach println
```

The first three versions are more explicit and hence better for the beginning reader to understand. However, once you're familiar with the fact that `filter` is a method on collections that takes a single argument, `foreach` is an implicit loop over a collection, and so forth, the last, "Spartan" implementation is much faster to read and understand. The other two versions have more visual noise that just get in the way, once you're more experienced. Keep that in mind as you learn to read Scala code.

To be clear, this expression works because each method we used took a single argument. If you tried to use a method in the chain that takes zero or more than one argument, it would confuse the compiler. In those cases, put some or all of the punctuation back in.

Precedence Rules

So, if an expression like `2.0 * 4.0 / 3.0 * 5.0` is actually a series of method calls on `Doubles`, what are the *operator precedence* rules? Here they are in order from lowest to highest precedence:

1. *All letters*

2. |

3. ^

4. &

5. < >

6. = !

7. :

8. + -

9. * / %

10. *All other special characters*

Characters on the same line have the same precedence. An exception is = when it's used for assignment, in which case it has the lowest precedence.

Because * and / have the same precedence, the two lines in the following scala session behave the same:

```
scala> 2.0 * 4.0 / 3.0 * 5.0
res0: Double = 13.333333333333332

scala> (((2.0 * 4.0) / 3.0) * 5.0)
res1: Double = 13.333333333333332
```

In a sequence of left-associative method invocations, they simply bind in left-to-right order. Aren't all methods "left-associative"? No. In Scala, any method with a name that ends with a colon (:) binds to the *right*, while all other methods bind to the *left*. For example, you can prepend an element to a List using the :: method, called "cons," which is short for "constructor," a term introduced by Lisp:

```
scala> val list = List('b', 'c', 'd')
list: List[Char] = List(b, c, d)

scala> 'a' :: list
res4: List[Char] = List(a, b, c, d)
```

The second expression is equivalent to list.::('a').

 Any method whose name ends with a : binds to the *right*, not the *left*.

Domain-Specific Languages

Domain-specific languages, or DSLs, are languages written for a specific problem domain, with the goal of making it easy to express the concepts in that domain in a concise and intuitive manner. For example, SQL could be considered a DSL, because it is programming language to express an interpretation of the Relational Model.

However, the term DSL is usually reserved for ad hoc languages that are *embedded* in a host language or parsed with a custom parser. The term *embedded* means that you write code in the host language using idiomatic conventions that express the DSL. Embedded DSLs are also called *internal* DSLs, as distinct from *external* DSLs that require a custom parser.

Internal DSLs allow the developer to leverage the entirety of the host language for edge cases that the DSL does not cover (or from a negative point of view, the DSL can be a "leaky abstraction"). Internal DSLs also save the work of writing lexers, parsers, and the other tools for a custom language.

Scala provides excellent support for both kinds of DSLs. Scala's flexible rules for identifiers, such as operator names, and the support for infix and postfix method calling syntax, provide building blocks for writing embedded DSLs using normal Scala syntax.

Consider this example of a style of test writing called *Behavior-Driven Development* using the ScalaTest (*http://www.scalatest.org/*) library. The Specs2 (*http://bit.ly/ 1tpceR3*) library is similar.

```
// src/main/scala/progscala2/rounding/scalatest.scX
// Example fragment of a ScalaTest. Doesn't run standalone.

import org.scalatest.{ FunSpec, ShouldMatchers }

class NerdFinderSpec extends FunSpec with ShouldMatchers {

  describe ("nerd finder") {
    it ("identify nerds from a List") {
      val actors = List("Rick Moranis", "James Dean", "Woody Allen")
      val finder = new NerdFinder(actors)
      finder.findNerds shouldEqual List("Rick Moranis", "Woody Allen")
    }
  }
}
```

This is just a taste of the power of Scala for writing DSLs. We'll see more examples in Chapter 20 and learn how to write our own.

Scala if Statements

Superficially, Scala's if statement looks like Java's. The if conditional expression is evaluated. If it's true, then the corresponding block is evaluated. Otherwise, the next branches are tested and so forth. A simple example:

```
// src/main/scala/progscala2/rounding/if.sc
```

```
if (2 + 2 == 5) {
  println("Hello from 1984.")
} else if (2 + 2 == 3) {
    println("Hello from Remedial Math class?")
} else {
  println("Hello from a non-Orwellian future.")
}
```

What's different in Scala is that `if` statements and almost all other statements in Scala are actually expressions that return values. So, we can assign the result of an `if` expression, as shown here:

```
// src/main/scala/progscala2/rounding/assigned-if.sc

val configFile = new java.io.File("somefile.txt")

val configFilePath = if (configFile.exists()) {
  configFile.getAbsolutePath()
} else {
  configFile.createNewFile()
  configFile.getAbsolutePath()
}
```

The type of the value will be the so-called *least upper bound* of all the branches, the closest parent type that matches all the potential values from each clause. In this example, the value `configFilePath` is the result of an `if` expression that handles the case of a configuration file not existing internally, then returns the absolute path to that file. This value can now be reused throughout an application. Its type will be `String`.

Because `if` statements are expressions, the ternary conditional expression that exists in C-derived languages, e.g., `predicate ? trueHandler() : falseHandler()`, isn't supported, because it would be redundant.

Scala for Comprehensions

Another familiar control structure that's particularly feature-rich in Scala is the `for` loop, called the `for` *comprehension* or `for` *expression*.

Actually, the term *comprehension* comes from functional programming. It expresses the idea that we are traversing one or more collections of some kind, "comprehending" what we find, and computing something new from it, often another collection.

for Loops

Let's start with a basic `for` expression:

```
// src/main/scala/progscala2/rounding/basic-for.sc

val dogBreeds = List("Doberman", "Yorkshire Terrier", "Dachshund",
```

```
                    "Scottish Terrier", "Great Dane", "Portuguese Water Dog")
for (breed <- dogBreeds)
  println(breed)
```

As you might guess, this code says, "For every element in the list dogBreeds, create a temporary variable called breed with the value of that element, then print it." The output is the following:

```
Doberman
Yorkshire Terrier
Dachshund
Scottish Terrier
Great Dane
Portuguese Water Dog
```

Because this form doesn't return anything, it only performs side effects. These kinds of for comprehensions are sometimes called for *loops*, analogous to Java for loops.

Generator Expressions

The expression breed <- dogBreeds is called a *generator expression*, so named because it's *generating* individual values from a collection. The left arrow operator (<-) is used to iterate through a collection, such as a List.

We can also use it with a Range to write a more traditional-looking for loop:

```
// src/main/scala/progscala2/rounding/generator.sc

for (i <- 1 to 10) println(i)
```

Guards: Filtering Values

What if we want to get more granular? We can add if expressions to filter for just elements we want to keep. These expressions are called *guards*. To find all terriers in our list of dog breeds, we modify the previous example to the following:

```
// src/main/scala/progscala2/rounding/guard-for.sc

val dogBreeds = List("Doberman", "Yorkshire Terrier", "Dachshund",
                     "Scottish Terrier", "Great Dane", "Portuguese Water Dog")
for (breed <- dogBreeds
  if breed.contains("Terrier")
) println(breed)
```

Now the output is this:

```
Yorkshire Terrier
Scottish Terrier
```

You can have more than one guard:

```
// src/main/scala/progscala2/rounding/double-guard-for.sc

val dogBreeds = List("Doberman", "Yorkshire Terrier", "Dachshund",
                     "Scottish Terrier", "Great Dane", "Portuguese Water Dog")

for (breed <- dogBreeds
  if breed.contains("Terrier")
  if !breed.startsWith("Yorkshire")
) println(breed)

for (breed <- dogBreeds
  if breed.contains("Terrier") && !breed.startsWith("Yorkshire")
) println(breed)
```

The second `for` comprehension combines the two `if` statements into one. The combined output of both `for` comprehensions is this:

```
Scottish Terrier
Scottish Terrier
```

Yielding

What if, rather than printing your filtered collection, you needed to hand it off to another part of your program? The `yield` keyword is your ticket to generating new collections with `for` expressions.

Also, we're going to switch to curly braces, which can be used instead of parentheses, in much the same way that method argument lists can be wrapped in curly braces when a block-structure format is more visually appealing:

```
// src/main/scala/progscala2/rounding/yielding-for.sc

val dogBreeds = List("Doberman", "Yorkshire Terrier", "Dachshund",
                     "Scottish Terrier", "Great Dane", "Portuguese Water Dog")
val filteredBreeds = for {
  breed <- dogBreeds
  if breed.contains("Terrier") && !breed.startsWith("Yorkshire")
} yield breed
```

Every time through the `for` expression, the filtered result is yielded as a value named `breed`. These results accumulate with every run, and the resulting collection is assigned to the value `filteredBreeds`. The type of the collection resulting from a `for-yield` expression is inferred from the type of the collection being iterated over. In this case, `filteredBreeds` is of type `List[String]`, because it is derived from the original dog Breeds list, which is of type `List[String]`.

An informal convention is to use parentheses when the `for` comprehension has a single expression and curly braces when multiple expressions are used. Note that older versions of Scala required semicolons between expressions when parentheses were used.

When a `for` comprehension doesn't use `yield`, but performs side effects like printing instead, the comprehension is called a `for` *loop*, because this behavior is more like the `for` loops you know from Java and other languages.

Expanded Scope and Value Definitions

Another useful feature of Scala's `for` comprehensions is the ability to define values inside the first part of your `for` expressions that can be used in the later expressions, as in this example:

```
// src/main/scala/progscala2/rounding/scoped-for.sc

val dogBreeds = List("Doberman", "Yorkshire Terrier", "Dachshund",
                     "Scottish Terrier", "Great Dane", "Portuguese Water Dog")
for {
  breed <- dogBreeds
  upcasedBreed = breed.toUpperCase()
} println(upcasedBreed)
```

Note that `upcasedBreed` is an immutable value, but the `val` keyword isn't required.[2] The result is:

```
DOBERMAN
YORKSHIRE TERRIER
DACHSHUND
SCOTTISH TERRIER
GREAT DANE
PORTUGUESE WATER DOG
```

If you recall `Option`, which we discussed as a better alternative to using `null`, it's useful to recognize that it is a special kind of collection, limited to zero or one elements. We can "comprehend" it too:

```
// src/main/scala/progscala2/patternmatching/scoped-option-for.sc

val dogBreeds = List(Some("Doberman"), None, Some("Yorkshire Terrier"),
                     Some("Dachshund"), None, Some("Scottish Terrier"),
                     None, Some("Great Dane"), Some("Portuguese Water Dog"))
println("first pass:")
for {
```

---

2. The `val` keyword was optional in early versions of Scala. It is now deprecated.

```
    breedOption <- dogBreeds
    breed <- breedOption
    upcasedBreed = breed.toUpperCase()
} println(upcasedBreed)

println("second pass:")
for {
  Some(breed) <- dogBreeds
  upcasedBreed = breed.toUpperCase()
} println(upcasedBreed)
```

Imagine that we called some services to return various breed names. The services returned Options, because some of the services couldn't return anything, so they returned None. In the first expression of the first for comprehension, each element extracted is an Option this time. The next line uses the arrow to extract the value in the option.

But wait! Doesn't None throw an exception if you try to extract an object from it? Yes, but the comprehension effectively checks for this case and skips the Nones. It's as if we added an explicit if breedOption != None before the second line.

The second for comprehension makes this even cleaner, using *pattern matching*. The expression Some(breed) <- dogBreeds only succeeds when the breedOption is a Some and it extracts the breed, all in one step. None elements are not processed further.

When do you use the left arrow (<-) versus the equals sign (=)? You use the arrow when you're iterating through a collection or other "container," like an Option, and extracting values. You use the equals sign when you're assigning a value that doesn't involve iteration. A limitation is that the first expression in a for comprehension has to be an extraction/iteration using the arrow.

When working with loops in most languages, you can break out of a loop or contin ue the iterations. Scala doesn't have either of these statements, but when writing idiomatic Scala code, they are rarely necessary. Use conditional expressions to test if a loop should continue, or make use of recursion. Better yet, filter your collections ahead of time to eliminate complex conditions within your loops.[3]

Scala for comprehensions do not offer a break or contin ue feature. Other features make them unnecessary.

---

3. However, because of demand for it, Scala does provide a scala.util.control.Breaks (*http://bit.ly/ 1zmwKGO*) object that can be used to implement break functionality. I've never used it and neither should you.

Other Looping Constructs

Scala provides several other looping constructs, although they are not widely used, because for comprehensions are so flexible and powerful. Still, sometimes a while loop is just what you need.

Scala while Loops

The while loop executes a block of code as long as a condition is true. For example, the following code prints out a complaint once a day until the next Friday the 13th has arrived:

```
// src/main/scala/progscala2/rounding/while.sc
// WARNING: This script runs for a LOOOONG time!
import java.util.Calendar

def isFridayThirteen(cal: Calendar): Boolean = {
  val dayOfWeek = cal.get(Calendar.DAY_OF_WEEK)
  val dayOfMonth = cal.get(Calendar.DAY_OF_MONTH)

  // Scala returns the result of the last expression in a method
  (dayOfWeek == Calendar.FRIDAY) && (dayOfMonth == 13)
}

while (!isFridayThirteen(Calendar.getInstance())) {
  println("Today isn't Friday the 13th. Lame.")
  // sleep for a day
  Thread.sleep(86400000)
}
```

Scala do-while Loops

Like the while loop, a do-while loop executes some code while a conditional expression is true. That is, the do-while checks to see if the condition is true *after* running the block. To count up to 10, we could write this:

```
// src/main/scala/progscala2/rounding/do-while.sc

var count = 0

do {
  count += 1
  println(count)
} while (count < 10)
```

Conditional Operators

Scala borrows most of the conditional operators from Java and its predecessors. You'll find the ones listed in Table 3-1 in `if` statements, `while` loops, and everywhere else conditions apply.

Table 3-1. Conditional operators

Operator	Operation	Description
&&	and	The values on the left and right of the operator are true. The righthand side is *only* evaluated if the lefthand side is *true*.
||	or	At least one of the values on the left or right is true. The righthand side is *only* evaluated if the lefthand side is *false*.
>	greater than	The value on the left is greater than the value on the right.
>=	greater than or equals	The value on the left is greater than or equal to the value on the right.
<	less than	The value on the left is less than the value on the right.
<=	less than or equals	The value on the left is less than or equal to the value on the right.
==	equals	The value on the left is the same as the value on the right.
!=	not equals	The value on the left is not the same as the value on the right.

Note that && and || are "short-circuiting" operators. They stop evaluating expressions as soon as the answer is known.

Most of the operators behave as they do in Java and other languages. An exception is the behavior of == and its negation, !=. In Java, == compares object references only. It doesn't perform a logical equality check, i.e., comparing field values. You use the `equals` method for that purpose. So, if two *different* objects are of the same type and have the same field values (that is, the same state), == will still return false in Java.

In contrast, Scala uses == for logical equality, but it calls the `equals` method. A new method, `eq`, is available when you want to compare references, but not test for logical equality (we'll discuss the details of object equality in "Equality of Objects" on page 308).

Using try, catch, and finally Clauses

Through its use of functional constructs and strong typing, Scala encourages a coding style that lessens the need for exceptions and exception handling. But exceptions are still used, especially where Scala interacts with Java code, where use of exceptions is more prevalent.

Unlike Java, Scala does not have checked exceptions, which are now regarded as an unsuccessful design. Java's checked exceptions are treated as unchecked by Scala. There is also no throws clause on method declarations. However, there is a @throws (*http://bit.ly/1rGL04n*) annotation that is useful for Java interoperability. See the section "Annotations" on page 504.

Scala treats exception handling as just another pattern match, allowing us to implement concise handling of many different kinds of exceptions.

Let's see this in action in a common application scenario, resource management. We want to open files and process them in some way. In this case, we'll just count the lines. However, we must handle a few error scenarios. The file might not exist, especially since we'll ask the user to specify the filenames. Also, something might go wrong while processing the file. (We'll trigger an arbitrary failure to test what happens.) We need to ensure that we close all open file handles, whether or not the we process the files successfully:

```scala
// src/main/scala/progscala2/rounding/TryCatch.scala
package progscala2.rounding

object TryCatch {
  /** Usage: scala rounding.TryCatch filename1 filename2 ... */
  def main(args: Array[String]) = {
    args foreach (arg => countLines(arg))             // ❶
  }

  import scala.io.Source                               // ❷
  import scala.util.control.NonFatal

  def countLines(fileName: String) = {                 // ❸
    println()  // Add a blank line for legibility
    var source: Option[Source] = None                  // ❹
    try {                                              // ❺
      source = Some(Source.fromFile(fileName))         // ❻
      val size = source.get.getLines.size
      println(s"file $fileName has $size lines")
    } catch {
      case NonFatal(ex) => println(s"Non fatal exception! $ex")  // ❼
    } finally {
      for (s <- source) {                              // ❽
        println(s"Closing $fileName...")
        s.close
      }
    }
  }
}
```

❶ Use `foreach` to loop through the list of arguments and operate on each. `Unit` is returned by each pass and by `foreach` as the final result of the expression.

❷ Import `scala.io.Source` (*http://bit.ly/1toCEnE*) for reading input and `sca la.util.control.NonFatal` (*http://bit.ly/1tI2D9y*) for matching on "nonfatal" exceptions.

❸ For each filename, count the lines.

❹ Declare the `source` to be an `Option`, so we can tell in the `finally` clause if we have an actual instance or not.

❺ Start of `try` clause.

❻ `Source.fromFile` will throw a `java.io.FileNotFoundException` (*http://bit.ly/1G2Hr34*) if the file doesn't exist. Otherwise, wrap the returned `Source` instance in a `Some`. Calling `get` on the next line is safe, because if we're here, we know we have a `Some`.

❼ Catch nonfatal errors. For example, out of memory would be fatal.

❽ Use a `for` comprehension to extract the `Source` instance from the `Some` and close it. If `source` is `None`, then nothing happens!

Note the `catch` clause. Scala uses pattern matches to pick the exceptions you want to catch. This is more compact and more flexible than Java's use of separate `catch` clauses for each exception. In this case, the clause `case NonFatal(ex) => …` uses `sca la.util.control.NonFatal` to match any exception that isn't considered fatal.

The `finally` clause is used to ensure proper resource cleanup in one place. Without it, we would have to repeat the logic at the end of the `try` clause and the `catch` clause, to ensure our file handles are closed. Here we use a `for` comprehension to extract the `Source` from the option. If the option is actually a `None`, nothing happens; the block with the `close` call is not invoked.

 This is a widely used idiom; use a `for` comprehension when you need to test whether an `Option` is a `Some`, in which case you do some work, or is a `None`, in which case you ignore it.

This program is already compiled by `sbt` and we can run it from the `sbt` prompt using the `run-main` task, which lets us pass arguments. I've wrapped some lines to fit the page, using a \ to indicate line continuations, and elided some text:

```
> run-main progscala2.rounding.TryCatch foo/bar \
  src/main/scala/progscala2/rounding/TryCatch.scala
[info] Running rounding.TryCatch foo/bar .../rounding/TryCatch.scala
```

```
... java.io.FileNotFoundException: foo/bar (No such file or directory)

file src/main/scala/progscala2/rounding/TryCatch.scala has 30 lines
Closing src/main/scala/progscala2/rounding/TryCatch.scala...
[success] ...
```

The first file doesn't exist. The second file is the source for the program itself. The
`scala.io.Source` API is a convenient way to process a stream of data from a file and
other sources. Like many such APIs, it throws an exception if the file doesn't exist. So,
the exception for `foo/bar` is expected.

 When resources need to be cleaned up, whether or not the resource
is used successfully, put the cleanup logic in a `finally` clause.

Pattern matching aside, Scala's treatment of exception handling is similar to the approaches used in most popular languages. You throw an exception by writing `throw
new MyBadException(...)`, as in Java. If your custom exception is a `case` class, you can
omit the `new`. That's all there is to it.

Automatic resource management is a common pattern. There is a separate Scala project
by Joshua Suereth called *ScalaARM* (*http://jsuereth.com/scala-arm/*) for this purpose.
Let's try writing our own.

Call by Name, Call by Value

Here is our implementation of a reusable *application resource manager*:

```
// src/main/scala/progscala2/rounding/TryCatchArm.scala
package progscala2.rounding
import scala.language.reflectiveCalls
import scala.util.control.NonFatal

object manage {
  def apply[R <: { def close():Unit }, T](resource: => R)(f: R => T) = {
    var res: Option[R] = None
    try {
      res = Some(resource)        // Only reference "resource" once!!
      f(res.get)
    } catch {
      case NonFatal(ex) => println(s"Non fatal exception! $ex")
    } finally {
      if (res != None) {
        println(s"Closing resource...")
        res.get.close
```

```
        }
      }
    }
  }

  object TryCatchARM {
    /** Usage: scala rounding.TryCatch filename1 filename2 ... */
    def main(args: Array[String]) = {
      args foreach (arg => countLines(arg))
    }

    import scala.io.Source

    def countLines(fileName: String) = {
      println()  // Add a blank line for legibility
      manage(Source.fromFile(fileName)) { source =>
        val size = source.getLines.size
        println(s"file $fileName has $size lines")
        if (size > 20) throw new RuntimeException("Big file!")
      }
    }
  }
```

You can run it like the previous example, substituting TryCatchARM for TryCatch. The output will be similar.

This is a lovely little bit of *separation of concerns*, but to implement it, we used a few new power tools.

First, we named our object manage rather than Manage. Normally, you follow the convention of using a leading uppercase letter for type names, but in this case we will use manage like a function. We want client code to look like we're using a built-in operator, similar to a while loop. See how it's used in countLines. This is another example of Scala's tools for building little *domain-specific languages* (DSLs).

That manage.apply method declaration is hairy looking. Let's deconstruct it. Here is the signature again, spread over several lines and annotated:

```
def apply[
  R <: { def close():Unit },    ❶
  T ]                           ❷
  (resource: => R)              ❸
  (f: R => T) = {...}           ❹
```

❶ Two new things are shown here. R is the type of the resource we'll manage. The <: means R is a subclass of something else, in this case *structural type* with a close():Unit method. What would be more intuitive, especially if you haven't seen structural types before, would be for all resources to implement a Closable interface that defines a close():Unit method. Then we could say R <: Closable. Instead, structural types let us use reflection and plug in any type that has a close():Unit method (like Source). Reflection has a lot of overhead and structural types are a bit scary, so reflection is another *optional feature*, like postfix expressions, which we saw earlier. So we add the import statement to tell the compiler we know what we're doing.

❷ T will be the type returned by the anonymous function passed in to do work with the resource.

❸ It looks like resource is a function with an unusual declaration. Actually, re source is a *by-name* parameter. For the moment, think of this as a function that we call without parentheses.

❹ Finally we pass a second argument list containing the work to do with the resource, an anonymous function that will take the resource as an argument and return a result of type T.

Recapping point 1, here is how the apply method declaration would look if we could assume that all resources implement a Closable abstraction:

```
object manage {
  def apply[R <: Closable, T](resource: => R)(f: R => T) = {...}
  ...
}
```

The line, val res = Some(resource), is the *only* place resource is evaluated, which is essential. Because resource behaves like a function, it is evaluated every time it's referenced, just like a function would be evaluated repeatedly. We don't want to evaluate Source.fromFile(fileName) every time we reference resource, because we would re-open new Source instances each time!

Next, this res value is passed to the work function f.

See how manage is used in TryCatchARM.countLines. It looks like a built-in control structure with one argument list that creates the Source and a second argument list that is a block of code that works with the Source. So, manage looks something like a conventional while statement, for example.

To recap a bit, the first expression that creates the Source is not evaluated immediately, *before* execution moves to manage. The evaluation of the expression is delayed until the line val res = Some(resource) within manage. This is what the *by-name* parameter resource gives us. We can write a function `manage.apply` that accepts as a parameter an arbitrary expression, but we defer evaluation until later.

Scala, like most languages, normally uses *call-by-value* semantics. If we write `man age(Source.fromFile(fileName))` in a call-by-value context, the `Source.fromFile` method is called and the value it returns is passed to `manage`.

By deferring evaluation until the line `val res = Some(resource)` within `apply`, this line is effectively the following:

```
val res = Some(Source.fromFile(fileName))
```

Supporting idioms like this is the reason that Scala offers *by-name* parameters.

What if we didn't have *by-name* parameters? We could use an anonymous function, but it would be a bit uglier.

The call to `manage` would now look like this:

```
manage(() => Source.fromFile(fileName)) { source =>
```

Within `apply`, our reference to `resource` would now be an "obvious" function call:

```
val res = Some(resource())
```

Okay, that's not a terrible burden, but *call by name* enables a syntax for building our own control structures, like our `manage` utility.

Remember that by-name parameters behave like functions; the expression is evaluated every time it is used. In our ARM example, we only wanted to evaluate it *once*, but that's not the general case.

Here is a simple implementation of a while-like loop construct, called `continue`:

```
// src/main/scala/progscala2/rounding/call-by-name.sc

@annotation.tailrec                                         // ❶
def continue(conditional: => Boolean)(body: => Unit) {      // ❷
  if (conditional) {                                        // ❸
    body                                                    // ❹
    continue(conditional)(body)
  }
}

var count = 0                                               // ❺
continue(count < 5) {
  println(s"at $count")
  count += 1
}
```

❶ Ensure the implementation is tail recursive.

❷   Define a `continue` function that accepts two argument lists. The first list takes a single, by-name parameter that is the conditional. The second list takes a single, by-name value that is the body to be evaluated for each iteration.

❸   Test the condition.

❹   If still true, evaluate the body, then call the `continue` recursively.

❺   Try it!

It's important to note that the by-name parameters are evaluated every time they are referenced. (By the way, this implementation shows how "loop" constructs can be replaced with recursion). So, by-name parameters are in a sense *lazy*, because evaluation is deferred, but possibly repeated over and over again. Scala also provides lazy values.

lazy val

A related scenario to *by-name* parameters is the case where you want to evaluate an expression *once* to initialize a value, not repeatedly, but you want to defer that invocation. There are some common scenarios where this is useful:

- The expression is expensive (e.g., opening a database connection) and we want to avoid the overhead until the value is actually needed.

- Improve startup times for modules by deferring work that isn't needed immediately.

- Sometimes a field in an object needs to be initialized lazily so that other initializations can happen first. We'll explore these scenarios when we discuss Scala's object model in "Overriding fields in traits" on page 317.

Here is an example using a `lazy val`:

```
// src/main/scala/progscala2/rounding/lazy-init-val.sc

object ExpensiveResource {
  lazy val resource: Int = init()
  def init(): Int = {
    // do something expensive
    0
  }
}
```

The `lazy` keyword indicates that evaluation should be deferred until the value is needed.

So, how is a `lazy val` different from a method call? In a method call, the body is executed *every* time the method is invoked. For a `lazy val`, the initialization "body" is evaluated only once, when the value is used for the first time. This one-time evaluation makes little sense for a mutable field. Therefore, the `lazy` keyword is not allowed on `var`s.

So, why not mark object field values `lazy` all the time, so that creating objects is always faster? Actually, it may not be faster except for truly expensive operations.

Lazy values are implemented with a *guard*. When client code references a lazy value, the reference is intercepted by the guard to check if initialization is required. This guard step is really only essential the *first* time the value is referenced, so that the value is initialized first before the access is allowed to proceed. Unfortunately, there is no easy way to eliminate these checks for subsequent calls. So, lazy values incur overhead that "eager" values don't. Therefore, you should only use them when the guard overhead is outweighed by the expense of initialization or in certain circumstances where careful ordering of initialization dependencies is most easily implemented by making some values lazy (see "Overriding fields in traits" on page 317).

Enumerations

Remember our examples involving various dog breeds? In thinking about the types in these programs, we might want a top-level `Breed` type that keeps track of a number of breeds. Such a type is called an *enumerated type*, and the values it contains are called *enumerations*.

While enumerations are a built-in part of many programming languages, Scala takes a different route and implements them as an `Enumeration` (*http://bit.ly/1rGL2Jy*) class in its standard library. This means there is no special syntax for enumerations baked into Scala's grammar, as there is for Java. Instead, you just define an object that extends the `Enumeration` class and follow its idioms. So, at the byte code level, there is no connection between Scala enumerations and the `enum` constructs in Java.

Here is an example:

```
// src/main/scala/progscala2/rounding/enumeration.sc

object Breed extends Enumeration {
  type Breed = Value
  val doberman = Value("Doberman Pinscher")
  val yorkie   = Value("Yorkshire Terrier")
  val scottie  = Value("Scottish Terrier")
  val dane     = Value("Great Dane")
  val portie   = Value("Portuguese Water Dog")
}
import Breed._

// print a list of breeds and their IDs
println("ID\tBreed")
for (breed <- Breed.values) println(s"${breed.id}\t$breed")

// print a list of Terrier breeds
println("\nJust Terriers:")
Breed.values filter (_.toString.endsWith("Terrier")) foreach println
```

```
def isTerrier(b: Breed) = b.toString.endsWith("Terrier")

println("\nTerriers Again??")
Breed.values filter isTerrier foreach println
```

It prints the following:

```
ID      Breed
0       Doberman Pinscher
1       Yorkshire Terrier
2       Scottish Terrier
3       Great Dane
4       Portuguese Water Dog

Just Terriers:
Yorkshire Terrier
Scottish Terrier

Terriers Again??
Yorkshire Terrier
Scottish Terrier
```

We can see that our `Breed` enumerated type contains several values of type `Value`, as in the following example:

```
val doberman = Value("Doberman Pinscher")
```

Each declaration is actually calling a method named `Value` that takes a string argument. We use this method to assign a long-form breed name to each enumeration value, which is what the `Value.toString` method returned in the output.

The type `Breed` is an alias that lets us reference `Breed` instead of `Value`. The only place we actually use this is the argument to the `isTerrier` method. If you comment out the `type` definition, this function won't compile.

There is no namespace collision between the type and method that both have the name `Value`. The compiler maintains separate namespaces for values and methods.

There are other overloaded versions of the `Value` method. We're using the one that takes a `String`. Another one takes no arguments, so the string will just be the name of the value, e.g., "doberman." Another `Value` method takes an `Int` ID value, so the default string is used and the integer `id` is a value we assign explicitly. Finally, the last `Value` method takes both an `Int` and `String`.

Because we're not calling one of the methods that takes an explicit ID value, the values are incremented and assigned automatically starting at 0, in declaration order. These `Value` methods return a `Value` object, and they add the value to the enumeration's collection of values.

To work with the values as a collection, we call the `values` method. So, we can easily iterate through the breeds with a `for` comprehension and `filter` them by name or see the `ids` that are automatically assigned if we don't explicitly specify a number.

You'll often want to give your enumeration values human-readable names, as we did here. However, sometimes you may not need them. Here's another enumeration example adapted from the Scaladoc entry for `Enumeration` (*http://bit.ly/14U04n2*):

```
// src/main/scala/progscala2/rounding/days-enumeration.sc

object WeekDay extends Enumeration {
  type WeekDay = Value
  val Mon, Tue, Wed, Thu, Fri, Sat, Sun = Value
}
import WeekDay._

def isWorkingDay(d: WeekDay) = ! (d == Sat || d == Sun)

WeekDay.values filter isWorkingDay foreach println
```

Running this script yields the following output (v2.7):

```
Mon
Tue
Wed
Thu
Fri
```

Note that we imported `WeekDay._`. This made each enumeration value (`Mon`, `Tues`, etc.) in scope. Otherwise, you would have to write `WeekDay.Mon`, `WeekDay.Tues`, etc. We can iterate through the values by calling the `values` method. In this case, we filter the values for "working days" (weekdays).

You don't actually see enumerations used a lot in Scala code, especially compared to Java code. They are lightweight, but they are also limited to the case where you know in advance the exact set of values to define. Clients can't add more values.

Instead, case classes are often used when an "enumeration of values" is needed. They are a bit more heavyweight, but they have two advantages. First, they offer greater flexibility to add methods and fields, and to use pattern matching on them. The second advantage is that they aren't limited to a fixed set of known values. Client code can add more case classes to a base set that your library defines, when useful.

Interpolated Strings

We introduced *interpolated* strings in "A Taste of Concurrency" on page 19. Let's explore them further.

A `String` of the form `s"foo ${bar}"` will have the value of expression `bar`, converted to a `String` and inserted in place of `${bar}`. If the expression `bar` returns an instance of a type other than `String`, a `toString` method will be invoked, if one exists. It is an error if it can't be converted to a `String`.

If `bar` is just a variable reference, the curly braces can be omitted. For example:

```
val name = "Buck Trends"
println(s"Hello, $name")
```

When using interpolated strings, to write a literal dollar sign $, use two of them, $$.

There are two other kinds of interpolated strings. The first kind provides *printf* formatting and uses the prefix `f`. The second kind is called "raw" interpolated strings. It doesn't expand escape characters, like `\n`.

Suppose we're generating financial reports and we want to show floating-point numbers to two decimal places.[4] Here's an example:

```
val gross   = 100000F
val net     = 64000F
val percent = (net / gross) * 100
println(f"$$${gross}%.2f vs. $$${net}%.2f or ${percent}%.1f%%")
```

The output of the last line is the following:

```
$100000.00 vs. $64000.00 or 64.0%
```

Scala uses Java's `Formatter` (*http://bit.ly/1wl7yOL*) class for `printf` formatting. The embedded references to expressions use the same `${...}` syntax as before, but `printf` formatting directives trail them with no spaces.

In this example, we use two dollar signs, $$, to print a literal US dollar sign, and two percent signs, %%, to print a literal percent sign. The expression `${gross}%.2f` formats the value of `gross` as a floating-point number with two digits after the decimal point.

The types of the variables used must match the format expressions, but some implicit conversions are performed. The following attempt to use an `Int` expression in a `Float` context is allowed. It just pads with zeros. However, the second expression, which attempts to render a `Double` as an `Int`, causes a compilation error:

```
scala> val i = 200
i: Int = 200

scala> f"${i}%.2f"
res4: String = 200.00
```

---

4. Raw floats and doubles are not typically used in financial applications for representing money, because of the requirement to handle various accounting rules correctly (e.g., rounding). However, we'll use them for simplicity.

```
scala> val d = 100.22
d: Double = 100.22

scala> f"${d}%2d"
<console>:9: error: type mismatch;
 found    : Double
 required: Int
               f"${d}%2d"
                ^
```

As an aside, you can still format strings using printf-style formatting with Java's static method String.format (*http://bit.ly/1wl7Bdg*). It takes as arguments a format string and a variable argument list of values to substitute into the final string. There is a second version of this method where the first argument is the locale.

While Scala uses Java strings, in certain contexts the Scala compiler will wrap a Java String with extra methods defined in scala.collection.immutable.StringLike (*http://bit.ly/18bCByX*). One of those extra methods is an *instance* method called format. You call it on the format string itself, then pass as arguments the values to be incorporated into the string. For example:

```
scala> val s = "%02d: name = %s".format(5, "Dean Wampler")
s: String = "05: name = Dean Wampler"
```

In this example, we asked for a two-digit integer, padded with leading zeros.

The final version of the built-in string interpolation capabilities is the "raw" format that doesn't expand control characters. Consider these two examples:

```
scala> val name = "Dean Wampler"
name: String = "Dean Wampler"

scala> s"123\n$name\n456"
res0: String =
123
Dean Wampler
456

scala> raw"123\n$name\n456"
res1: String = 123\nDean Wampler\n456
```

Finally, we can actually define our own string interpolators, but we'll need to learn more about *implicits* first. See "Build Your Own String Interpolator" on page 153 for details.

Traits: Interfaces and "Mixins" in Scala

Here we are, about 100 pages in and we haven't discussed one of the most basic features of any object-oriented language: how abstractions are defined, the equivalent of Java's *interfaces*. What about inheritance of classes, too?

I put this off deliberately to emphasize the powerful capabilities that functional programming brings to Scala, but now is a good time to provide an overview of this important topic.

I've used vague terms like abstractions before. Some of our examples used abstract classes as "parent" classes already. I didn't dwell on them, assuming that you've seen similar constructs in other languages before.

Java has interfaces, which let you *declare*, but not *define* methods, at least you couldn't define them before Java 8. You can also declare and define static variables and nested types.

Scala replaces interfaces with *traits*. We'll explore them in glorious detail in Chapter 9, but for now, think of them of interfaces that also give you the option of defining the methods you declare. Traits can also declare and optionally define *instance* fields (not just *static* fields, as in Java interfaces), and you can declare and optionally define *type* values, like the types we just saw in our enumeration examples.

It turns out that these extensions fix many limitations of Java's object model, where only classes can define methods and fields. Traits enable true composition of behavior ("mixins") that simply isn't possible in Java before Java 8.

Let's see an example that every enterprise Java developer has faced; mixing in logging. First, let's start with a service:

```
// src/main/scala/progscala2/rounding/traits.sc

class ServiceImportante(name: String) {
  def work(i: Int): Int = {
    println(s"ServiceImportante: Doing important work! $i")
    i + 1
  }
}

val service1 = new ServiceImportante("uno")
(1 to 3) foreach (i => println(s"Result: ${service1.work(i)}"))
```

We ask the service to do some work and get this output:

```
ServiceImportante: Doing important work! 1
Result: 2
ServiceImportante: Doing important work! 2
Result: 3
ServiceImportante: Doing important work! 3
Result: 4
```

Now we want to mix in a standard logging library. For simplicity, we'll just use println.

Here are two traits, one that defines the abstraction (that has no concrete members) and the other that implements the abstraction for "logging" to standard output:

```
trait Logging {
  def info   (message: String): Unit
  def warning(message: String): Unit
  def error  (message: String): Unit
}

trait StdoutLogging extends Logging {
  def info   (message: String) = println(s"INFO:    $message")
  def warning(message: String) = println(s"WARNING: $message")
  def error  (message: String) = println(s"ERROR:   $message")
}
```

Note that Logging is *exactly* like a Java interface. It is even implemented the same way in JVM byte code.

Finally, let's declare a service that "mixes in" logging:

```
val service2 = new ServiceImportante("dos") with StdoutLogging {
  override def work(i: Int): Int = {
    info(s"Starting work: i = $i")
    val result = super.work(i)
    info(s"Ending work: i = $i, result = $result")
    result
  }
}
(1 to 3) foreach (i => println(s"Result: ${service2.work(i)}"))

INFO:    Starting work: i = 1
ServiceImportante: Doing important work! 1
INFO:    Ending work: i = 1, result = 2
Result: 2
INFO:    Starting work: i = 2
ServiceImportante: Doing important work! 2
INFO:    Ending work: i = 2, result = 3
Result: 3
INFO:    Starting work: i = 3
ServiceImportante: Doing important work! 3
INFO:    Ending work: i = 3, result = 4
Result: 4
```

Now we log when we enter and leave work.

To mix in traits, we use the with keyword. We can mix in as many as we want. Some traits might not modify existing behavior at all, and just add new useful, but independent methods.

In this example, we're actually *modifying* the behavior of work, in order to inject logging, but we are not changing its "contract" with clients, that is, its external behavior.[5]

---

5. That's not strictly true, in the sense that the extra I/O has changed the code's interaction with the "world."

If we needed multiple instances of ServiceImportante with StdoutLogging, we could declare a class:

```scala
class LoggedServiceImportante(name: String)
  extends ServiceImportante(name) with StdoutLogging {...}
```

Note how we pass the name argument to the parent class ServiceImportante. To create instances, new LoggedServiceImportante("tres") works as you would expect it to work.

However, if we need just one instance, we can mix in StdoutLogging as we define the variable.

To use the logging enhancment, we have to override the work method. Scala requires the override keyword when you override a concrete method in a parent class. Note how we access the parent class work method, using super.work, as in Java and many other languages.

There is a lot more to discuss about traits and object composition, as we'll see.

Recap and What's Next

We've covered a lot of ground in these first chapters. We learned how flexible and concise Scala code can be. In this chapter, we learned some powerful constructs for defining DSLs and for manipulating data, such as for comprehensions. Finally, we learned how to encapsulate values in enumerations and the basic capabilities of traits.

You should now be able to read quite a bit of Scala code, but there's plenty more about the language to learn. Now we'll begin a deeper dive into Scala features.

## CHAPTER 4

Pattern Matching

At first glance, *pattern-matching* expressions look like the familiar `case` statements from your favorite C-like language. In the typical C-like `case` statement you're limited to matching against values of ordinal types and triggering trivial expressions for matches. For example, "In the case that `i` is 5, print a message; in the case that `i` is 6, exit the program."

With Scala's pattern matching, your cases can include types, wildcards, sequences, regular expressions, and even deep inspections of an object's state. This deep inspection follows a protocol that allows the type implementer to control the visibility of internal state. Finally, the exposed state is easy to capture to variables for use. Hence, the terms "extraction" or "destructuring" are sometimes used for this capability.

Pattern matching can be used in several code contexts. We'll start with the most common usage, within `match` clauses. Afterwards, we'll show other uses. We saw two relatively simple examples of `match` clauses in our actor example in "A Taste of Concurrency" on page 19. We also discussed additional uses in "Partial Functions" on page 37.

A Simple Match

To begin with, let's simulate flipping a coin by matching the value of a Boolean:

```
// src/main/scala/progscala2/patternmatching/match-boolean.sc

val bools = Seq(true, false)

for (bool <- bools) {
  bool match {
    case true => println("Got heads")
    case false => println("Got tails")
  }
}
```

It looks just like a C-style `case` statement. As an experiment, try commenting out the second `case false` clause and run the script again. You get a warning and then an error:

```
<console>:12: warning: match may not be exhaustive.
It would fail on the following input: false
                bool match {
                     ^
Got heads
scala.MatchError: false (of class java.lang.Boolean)
  at .<init>(<console>:11)
  at .<clinit>(<console>)
  ...
```

From the type of the list, the compiler knows that there are two possible cases, `true` and `false`. So, it warns that the match isn't exhaustive. Then we see what happens when we try to match on a value for which there is no matching `case` clause. A `MatchError` (*http://bit.ly/1udfTVy*) is thrown.

I should mention that a simpler alternative is an old-fashioned `if` expression in this case:

```
for (bool <- bools) {
  val which = if (bool) "head" else "tails"
  println("Got " + which)
}
```

Values, Variables, and Types in Matches

Let's cover several kinds of matches. The following example matches on specific values, all values of specific types, and it shows one way of writing a "default" clause that matches anything:

```
// src/main/scala/progscala2/patternmatching/match-variable.sc

for {
  x <- Seq(1, 2, 2.7, "one", "two", 'four)          // ❶
} {
  val str = x match {                                // ❷
    case 1           => "int 1"                      // ❸
    case i: Int      => "other int: "+i              // ❹
    case d: Double   => "a double: "+x               // ❺
    case "one"       => "string one"                 // ❻
    case s: String   => "other string: "+s           // ❼
    case unexpected  => "unexpected value: " + unexpected  // ❽
  }
  println(str)                                       // ❾
}
```

❶   Because of the mix of values, the list is of type `Seq[Any]`.

❷   The `x` is of type `Any`.

❸ Match if x equals 1.

❹ Match any *other* Int value. Safely cast the value of x to an Int and assign to i.

❺ Match any Double, where the value of x is assigned to the Double variable d.

❻ Match the String "one".

❼ Match any other String, where the value of x is assigned to the String variable s.

❽ Match all other inputs, where unexpected is the variable to which the value of x is assigned. Because no type annotation is given, Any is inferred. This functions as the "default" clause.

❾ Print the returned String.

I lined up the => ("arrows") to make things a bit clearer. Here is the output:

```
int 1
other int: 2
a double 2.7
string one
other string: two
unexpected value: 'four
```

Matches, like all expressions, return a value. In this case, all clauses return strings, so the return type of the whole clause is String. The compiler infers the closest supertype (also called the *least upper bound*) for types of values returned by all the case clauses.

Because x is of type Any, we need enough clauses to cover all possible values. (Compare with our first example that matched on Boolean values.). That's why the "default" clause (with unexpected) is needed. However, when writing PartialFunctions, we *aren't* required to match all possible values, because they are intentionally *partial*.

Matches are eager, so more specific clauses must appear before less specific clauses. Otherwise, the more specific clauses will never get the chance to match. So, the default clause shown must be the last one. The compiler will catch the error, fortunately.

I didn't include a clause with a floating-point literal, because matching on floating-point literals is a bad idea, as rounding errors mean two values that appear to be the same often differ in the least significant digits.

Here is a slight variation of the previous example:

```
// src/main/scala/progscala2/patternmatching/match-variable2.sc

for {
  x <- Seq(1, 2, 2.7, "one", "two", 'four)
} {
  val str = x match {
    case 1          => "int 1"
```

```
    case _: Int      => "other int: "+x
    case _: Double   => "a double: "+x
    case "one"       => "string one"
    case _: String   => "other string: "+x
    case _           => "unexpected value: " + x
  }
  println(str)
}
```

We replaced the variables i, d, s, and unexpected with the placeholder _. We don't actually need variables of the specific types, because we're just going to generate strings. So, we can use x for all cases.

 Except for PartialFunctions, matches must be exhaustive. When the input is of type Any, end with a default match clause, case _ or case some_name.

There are a few rules and gotchas to keep in mind when writing case clauses. The compiler assumes that a term that starts with a capital letter is a type name, while a term that begins with a lowercase letter is assumed to be the name of a variable that will hold an extracted or matched value.

This rule can cause surprises, as shown in the following example:

```
// src/main/scala/progscala2/patternmatching/match-surprise.sc

def checkY(y: Int) = {
  for {
    x <- Seq(99, 100, 101)
  } {
    val str = x match {
      case y => "found y!"
      case i: Int => "int: "+i
    }
    println(str)
  }
}

checkY(100)
```

We want the ability to pass in a specific value for the first case clause, rather than hard-code it. So, we might expect the first case clause to match when x equals y, which holds the value of 100, producing the following output when we run the script:

```
int: 99
found y!
int: 101
```

This is what we actually get:

```
<console>:12: warning: patterns after a variable pattern cannot match (SLS 8.1.1)
If you intended to match against parameter y of method checkY, you must use
backticks, like: case `y` =>
              case y => "found y!"
                   ^
<console>:13: warning: unreachable code due to variable pattern 'y' on line 12
              case i: Int => "int: "+i
                        ^
<console>:13: warning: unreachable code
              case i: Int => "int: "+i
                        ^
checkY: (y: Int)Unit
found y!
found y!
found y!
```

The `case` y actually means, "match anything (because there is no type annotation) and assign it to this *new* variable named y." The y here is not interpreted as a reference to the method argument y. So, we actually wrote a default, match-all clause first, triggering the three warnings that this "variable pattern" will capture everything and so we won't reach the second `case` expression. Then we get two warnings about unreachable code. The "SLS 8.1.1" refers to Section 8.1.1 in the *Scala Language Specification* (*http://bit.ly/1wNBOR8*).

The first error message tells us what to do: use "back ticks" to indicate we really want to match against the value held by y:

```
// src/main/scala/progscala2/patternmatching/match-surprise-fix.sc

def checkY(y: Int) = {
  for {
    x <- Seq(99, 100, 101)
  } {
    val str = x match {
      case `y` => "found y!"          // The only change: `y`
      case i: Int => "int: "+i
    }
    println(str)
  }
}
checkY(100)
```

Now the output is what we want.

In `case` clauses, a term that begins with a lowercase letter is assumed to be the name of a new variable that will hold an extracted value. To refer to a previously defined variable, enclose it in back ticks. Conversely, a term that begins with an uppercase letter is assumed to be a type name.

Finally, sometimes we want to handle several different matches with the same code body. To avoid duplication, we could refactor the code body into a method, but `case` clauses also support an "or" construct, using a | method:

```
// src/main/scala/progscala2/patternmatching/match-variable2.sc

for {
  x <- Seq(1, 2, 2.7, "one", "two", 'four)
} {
  val str = x match {
    case _: Int | _: Double => "a number: "+x
    case "one"              => "string one"
    case _: String          => "other string: "+x
    case _                  => "unexpected value: " + x
  }
  println(str)
}
```

Now, both `Int` and `Double` values are matched by the first `case` clause.

Matching on Sequences

Seq (*http://bit.ly/1wQxJyd*) (for "sequence") is a parent type for the concrete collection types that support iteration over the elements in a deterministic order, such as `List` (*http://bit.ly/1toub3N*) and `Vector` (*http://bit.ly/1tozAI0*).

Let's examine the classic idiom for iterating through a `Seq` using pattern matching and recursion, and along the way, learn some useful fundamentals about sequences:

```
// src/main/scala/progscala2/patternmatching/match-seq.sc

val nonEmptySeq    = Seq(1, 2, 3, 4, 5)                      // ❶
val emptySeq       = Seq.empty[Int]
val nonEmptyList   = List(1, 2, 3, 4, 5)                     // ❷
val emptyList      = Nil
val nonEmptyVector = Vector(1, 2, 3, 4, 5)                   // ❸
val emptyVector    = Vector.empty[Int]
val nonEmptyMap    = Map("one" -> 1, "two" -> 2, "three" -> 3)  // ❹
val emptyMap       = Map.empty[String,Int]

def seqToString[T](seq: Seq[T]): String = seq match {       // ❺
  case head +: tail => s"$head +: " + seqToString(tail)      // ❻
  case Nil => "Nil"                                          // ❼
```

```
  }

  for (seq <- Seq(                                          // ❽
      nonEmptySeq, emptySeq, nonEmptyList, emptyList,
      nonEmptyVector, emptyVector, nonEmptyMap.toSeq, emptyMap.toSeq)) {
    println(seqToString(seq))
  }
```

❶   Construct a nonempty Seq[Int] (*http://bit.ly/1E8xLCt*) (a List (*http://bit.ly/ 15iqGNE*) is actually returned), followed by the idiomatic way of constructing an empty Seq[Int].

❷   Construct a nonempty List[Int] (a subtype of Seq), followed by the special object in the library, Nil (*http://bit.ly/1wQuIOs*), that represents an empty List of any type parameter.

❸   Construct a nonempty Vectors[Int] (*http://bit.ly/1bgKyXi*) (a subtype of Seq), followed by an empty Vector[Int].

❹   Construct a nonempty Map[String,Int] (*http://bit.ly/13MzP5e*), which *isn't* a subtype of Seq. We'll come back to this point in the discussion that follows. The keys are Strings and the values are Ints. Then construct an empty Map[String,Int].

❺   Define a recursive method that constructs a String from a Seq[T] for some type T. The body is one four-line expression that matches on the input Seq[T].

❻   There are two match clauses and they are exhaustive. The first matches on any nonempty Seq, extracting the head, the first element, and the tail, which is the rest of the Seq. (Seq has head and tail methods, but here these terms are interpreted as variable names as usual for case clauses.) The body of the clause constructs a String with the head followed by +: followed by the result of calling seqToString on the tail.

❼   The only other possible case is an empty Seq. We can use the special object for empty Lists, Nil, to match all the empty cases. Note that any Seq can always be interpreted as terminating with an empty instance of the same type, although only some types, like List, are actually implemented that way.

❽   Put the Seqs in another Seq (calling toSeq on the Maps to convert them to a sequence of key-value pairs), then iterate through it and print the results of calling seqToString on each one.

Here is the output:

```
1 +: 2 +: 3 +: 4 +: 5 +: Nil
Nil
1 +: 2 +: 3 +: 4 +: 5 +: Nil
Nil
```

```
1 +: 2 +: 3 +: 4 +: 5 +: Nil
Nil
(one,1) +: (two,2) +: (three,3) +: Nil
Nil
```

Map is not a subtype of Seq, because it doesn't guarantee a particular order when you iterate over it. Hence, we called Map.toSeq to create sequences of key-value tuples. Still, the resulting Seq has the pairs in the insert order. That's a side effect of the implementation for small Maps, but not a general guarantee. The empty collections show that seqToString works correctly for empty collections.

There are two new kinds of case clauses. The first, head +: tail, matches the head element and the tail Seq (the remainder) of a sequence. The operator +: is the "cons" (construction) operator for sequences. It is similar to the :: operator we saw in "Precedence Rules" on page 75 for Lists. Recall that methods that end with a colon (:) bind to the *right*, toward the Seq tail.

I'm calling them "operators" and "methods," but actually that's not quite right in this context; we'll come back to this expression a bit later and really examine what's going on. For now, let's note a few key points.

First, this case clause only matches a nonempty sequence, one with at least a head element, and it extracts that head element and the rest of the sequence into immutable variables named head and tail, respectively.

Second, to reiterate, the terms head and tail are arbitrary variable names. However, there are also head and tail methods on Seq for returning the head and tail of a sequence, respectively. Normally, it's clear from the context when the methods are being used. By the way, calling either method on an empty sequence results in a thrown exception.

Because Seq behaves conceptually like a linked list, where each head node holds an element and it points to the tail (the rest of the sequence), creating a hierarchical structure that looks schematically like the following for a four-node sequence, an empty sequence is the most natural marker at the end:

```
(node1, (node2, (node3, (node4, (end)))))
```

The Scala library has an object called Nil for lists and it matches all empty sequences, which is why we used it. We can use Nil even for collections that aren't a List because of the way equality for sequences is implemented. The types don't have to match exactly.

This variant adds the parentheses. We'll just use a few of the collections this time:

```
// src/main/scala/progscala2/patternmatching/match-seq-parens.sc

val nonEmptySeq   = Seq(1, 2, 3, 4, 5)
val emptySeq      = Seq.empty[Int]
val nonEmptyMap   = Map("one" -> 1, "two" -> 2, "three" -> 3)
```

```
def seqToString2[T](seq: Seq[T]): String = seq match {
  case head +: tail => s"($head +: ${seqToString2(tail)})"           // ❶
  case Nil => "(Nil)"
}

for (seq <- Seq(nonEmptySeq, emptySeq, nonEmptyMap.toSeq)) {
  println(seqToString2(seq))
}
```

❶   Reformatted to add outer parentheses, (…).

The output of this script is the following, which shows the hierarchical structure explicitly, where each "sublist" is surrounded by parentheses:

```
(1 +: (2 +: (3 +: (4 +: (5 +: (Nil))))))
(Nil)
((one,1) +: ((two,2) +: ((three,3) +: (Nil))))
```

So, we process sequences with just two `case` clauses and recursion. Note that this implies something fundamental about all sequences; they are either empty or not. That sounds trite, but once you recognize simple patterns like this, it gives you a surprisingly general tool for "divide and conquer." The idiom used by `processSeq` is widely reusable.

Before Scala 2.10, it was common to use a closely related idiom for `List`s instead:

```
// src/main/scala/progscala2/patternmatching/match-list.sc

val nonEmptyList = List(1, 2, 3, 4, 5)
val emptyList    = Nil

def listToString[T](list: List[T]): String = list match {
  case head :: tail => s"($head :: ${listToString(tail)})"          // ❶
  case Nil => "(Nil)"
}

for (l <- List(nonEmptyList, emptyList)) { println(listToString(l)) }
```

❶   Replaced +: with ::.

The output is similar:

```
(1 :: (2 :: (3 :: (4 :: (5 :: (Nil))))))
(Nil)
```

It's more conventional now to write code that uses `Seq`, so it can be applied to all subclasses, including `List` and `Vector`.

We can copy and paste the output of the previous examples to reconstruct the original objects:

```
scala> val s1 = (1 +: (2 +: (3 +: (4 +: (5 +: Nil)))))
s1: List[Int] = List(1, 2, 3, 4, 5)

scala> val l  = (1 :: (2 :: (3 :: (4 :: (5 :: Nil)))))
l: List[Int] = List(1, 2, 3, 4, 5)

scala> val s2 = (("one",1) +: (("two",2) +: (("three",3) +: Nil)))
s2: List[(String, Int)] = List((one,1), (two,2), (three,3), (four,4))

scala> val m  = Map(s2 :_*)
m: scala.collection.immutable.Map[String,Int] =
   Map(one -> 1, two -> 2, three -> 3, four -> 4)
```

Note that the Map.apply factory method expects a variable argument list of two-element tuples. So, in order to use the sequence s2 to construct a Map, we had to use the :_* idiom for the compiler to convert it to a variable-argument list.

So, there's an elegant symmetry between construction and pattern matching ("deconstruction") when using +: and ::. We'll explore the implementation and see other examples later in this chapter.

Matching on Tuples

Tuples are also easy to match on, using their literal syntax:

```
// src/main/scala/progscala2/patternmatching/match-tuple.sc

val langs = Seq(
  ("Scala",    "Martin", "Odersky"),
  ("Clojure", "Rich",    "Hickey"),
  ("Lisp",     "John",   "McCarthy"))

for (tuple <- langs) {
  tuple match {
    case ("Scala", _, _) => println("Found Scala")            // ❶
    case (lang, first, last) =>                               // ❷
      println(s"Found other language: $lang ($first, $last)")
  }
}
```

❶   Match a three-element tuple where the first element is the string "Scala" and we ignore the second and third arguments.

❷   Match any three-element tuple, where the elements could be any type, but they are inferred to be Strings due to the input langs. Extract the elements into variables lang, first, and last.

The output is this:

```
Found Scala
Found other language: Clojure (Rich, Hickey)
Found other language: Lisp (John, McCarthy)
```

A tuple can be taken apart into its constituent elements. We can match on literal values within the tuple, at any positions we want, and we can ignore elements we don't care about.

Guards in case Clauses

Matching on literal values is very useful, but sometimes you need a little additional logic:

```
// src/main/scala/progscala2/patternmatching/match-guard.sc

for (i <- Seq(1,2,3,4)) {
  i match {
    case _ if i%2 == 0 => println(s"even: $i")      // ❶
    case _             => println(s"odd:  $i")      // ❷
  }
}
```

❶ Match only if i is even. We use _ instead of a variable, because we already have i.

❷ Match the only other possibility, that i is odd.

The output is this:

```
odd:  1
even: 2
odd:  3
even: 4
```

Note that we didn't need parentheses around the condition in the if expression, just as we don't need them in for comprehensions.

Matching on case Classes

Let's see more examples of *deep matching*, where we examine the contents of instances of case classes:

```
// src/main/scala/progscala2/patternmatching/match-deep.sc

// Simplistic address type. Using all strings is questionable, too.
case class Address(street: String, city: String, country: String)
case class Person(name: String, age: Int, address: Address)

val alice   = Person("Alice",   25, Address("1 Scala Lane", "Chicago", "USA"))
val bob     = Person("Bob",     29, Address("2 Java Ave.",  "Miami",   "USA"))
val charlie = Person("Charlie", 32, Address("3 Python Ct.", "Boston",  "USA"))
```

```
for (person <- Seq(alice, bob, charlie)) {
  person match {
    case Person("Alice", 25, Address(_, "Chicago", _)) => println("Hi Alice!")
    case Person("Bob", 29, Address("2 Java Ave.", "Miami", "USA")) =>
      println("Hi Bob!")
    case Person(name, age, _) =>
      println(s"Who are you, $age year-old person named $name?")
  }
}
```

The output is this:

```
Hi Alice!
Hi Bob!
Who are you, 32 year-old person named Charlie?
```

Note that we could match into nested types. Here's a more real-world example with tuples. Imagine we have a sequence of (String, Double) tuples for the names and prices of items in a store and we want to print them with their index. The Seq.zipWithIn dex method is handy here:

```
// src/main/scala/progscala2/patternmatching/match-deep-tuple.sc

val itemsCosts = Seq(("Pencil", 0.52), ("Paper", 1.35), ("Notebook", 2.43))
val itemsCostsIndices = itemsCosts.zipWithIndex
for (itemCostIndex <- itemsCostsIndices) {
  itemCostIndex match {
    case ((item, cost), index) => println(s"$index: $item costs $cost each")
  }
}
```

Let's run it in the REPL using the :load command to see the types, as well as the output (reformatted slightly):

```
scala> :load src/main/scala/progscala2/patternmatching/match-deep-tuple.sc
Loading src/main/scala/progscala2/patternmatching/match-deep-tuple.sc...
itemsCosts: Seq[(String, Double)] =
  List((Pencil,0.52), (Paper,1.35), (Notebook,2.43))
itemsCostsIndices: Seq[((String, Double), Int)] =
  List(((Pencil,0.52),0), ((Paper,1.35),1), ((Notebook,2.43),2))
0: Pencil costs 0.52 each
1: Paper costs 1.35 each
2: Notebook costs 2.43 each
```

Note that the call to zipWithIndex returned tuples of the form ((name,cost),index). We matched on this form to extract the three elements and print them. I write code like this *a lot*.

unapply Method

So, not only the Scala library types, but also our own case classes can exploit pattern matching and extraction, even with deep nesting.

How does this work? We learned already in "A Taste of Concurrency" on page 19 that a case class gets a *companion object* that has a factory method named `apply`, which is used for construction. Using "symmetry" arguments, we might infer that there must be another method generated called `unapply`, which is used for extraction or "deconstruction." Indeed there is such an *extractor* method and it is invoked when a pattern-match expression like this is encountered:

```
person match {
  case Person("Alice", 25, Address(_, "Chicago", _)) => ...
  ...
}
```

Scala looks for `Person.unapply(…)` and `Address.unapply(…)` and calls them. All `unapply` methods return an `Option[TupleN[…]]`, where N is the number of values that can be extracted from the object, three for the `Person` case class, and the types that parameterize the tuple match the values that can be extracted, `String`, `Int`, and `Address`, in this case. So, the `Person` companion object that the compiler generates looks like this:

```
object Person {
  def apply(name: String, age: Int, address: Address) =
    new Person(name, age, address)
  def unapply(p: Person): Option[Tuple3[String,Int,Address]] =
    Some((p.name, p.age, p.address))
  ...
}
```

Why is an `Option` used, if the compiler already knows that the object is a `Person`? Scala allows an implementation of `unapply` to "veto" the match for some reason and return `None`, in which case Scala will attempt to use the next `case` clause. Also, we don't have to expose all fields of the instance if we don't want to. We could suppress our `age`, if we're embarrassed by it. We'll explore the details in "unapplySeq Method" on page 117, but for now, just note that the extracted fields are returned in a `Some` wrapping a `Tuple3`. The compiler then extracts those tuple elements for comparison with literal values, like our first clause that looks for "Alice," or it assigns them to variables we've named, or it drops the ones we don't care about when we use `_`.

 To gain some performance benefits, Scala 2.11.1 relaxed the requirement that `unapply` return an `Option[T]`. It can now return any type as long as it has the following methods:

```
def isEmpty: Boolean
def get: T
```

The unapply methods are invoked recursively, if necessary, as in this case where we have a nested Address object in the Person. Similarly, our tuple example invoked the corresponding unapply methods recursively.

It's no coincidence that the same case keyword is used for declaring "special" classes and for case expressions in match expressions. The features of case classes were designed to enable convenient pattern matching.

Before we move on, note that the return type signature, Option[Tuple3[String,Int,Address]], is a bit wordy. Scala lets us use the tuple literal syntax for the types, too! The following type declarations are all equivalent:

```
val t1: Option[Tuple3[String,Int,Address]] = ...
val t2: Option[(String,Int,Address)] = ...
val t3: Option[ (String, Int, Address) ] = ...
```

The tuple literal syntax is easier to read. Extra whitespace helps, too.

Now let's return to that mysterious head +: tail expression and really understand what it means. We saw that the +: (cons) operator can be used to construct a new sequence by prepending an element to an existing sequence, and we can construct an entire sequence from scratch this way:

```
val list = 1 +: 2 +: 3 +: 4 +: Nil
```

Because +: is a method that binds to the right, we first prepend 4 to Nil, then prepend 3 to that list, etc.

Scala wants to support uniform syntax for *construction* and *destruction/extraction*, when possible. We've seen this at work for sequences, lists, and tuples. These operations are *dual*, inverses of each other.

If the construction of sequences is done with a method named +:, how is extraction done with the same syntax? We just looked at unapply methods, but they could cheat; Person.unapply and TupleN.unapply already know now many "things" are in their instances, three and N, respectively. Now we want to support nonempty collections of arbitrary length.

To do that, the Scala library defines a special singleton object named +: (*http://bit.ly/ 1nWFE9W*). Yes, the name is "+:". Like methods, types can have names with a wide variety of characters.

It has just one method, the unapply method the compiler needs for our extraction case statement. The declaration of unapply is schematically like this (I've simplified the actual declaration a bit, because we haven't yet covered details about the type system that we need to understand the full signature):

```
def unapply[T, Coll](collection: Coll): Option[(T, Coll)]
```

The head is of type T, which is inferred, and some collection type Coll, which represents the type of the input collection and the output tail collection. So, an Option of a two-element tuple with the head and tail is returned.

How can the compiler see the expression case head +: tail => … and use a method +:.unapply(collection)? We might expect that the case clause would have to be written case +:(head, tail) => … to work consistently with the behavior we just examined for pattern matching with Person, Address, and tuples.

As a matter of fact, we can write it that way:

```scala
scala> def processSeq2[T](l: Seq[T]): Unit = l match {
     |   case +:(head, tail) =>
     |     printf("%s +: ", head)
     |     processSeq2(tail)
     |   case Nil => print("Nil")
     | }

scala> processSeq2(List(1,2,3,4,5))
1 +: 2 +: 3 +: 4 +: 5 +: Nil
```

But we can also use *infix* notation, head +: tail, because the compiler exploits another bit of syntactic sugar. Types with two type parameters can be written with infix notation and so can case clauses. Consider this REPL session:

```scala
// src/main/scala/progscala2/patternmatching/infix.sc
scala> case class With[A,B](a: A, b: B)
defined class With

scala> val with1: With[String,Int] = With("Foo", 1)
with1: With[String,Int] = With(Foo,1)

scala> val with2: String With Int  = With("Bar", 2)
with2: With[String,Int] = With(Bar,2)

scala> Seq(with1, with2) foreach { w =>
     |   w match {
     |     case s With i => println(s"$s with $i")
     |     case _        => println(s"Unknown: $w")
     |   }
     | }
Foo with 1
Bar with 2
```

So we can write the type signature one of two ways, With[String,Int] or String With Int. The latter reads nicely, but it might confuse less experienced Scala programmers. However, note that trying to initialize a value in a similar way doesn't work:

```scala
// src/main/scala/progscala2/patternmatching/infix.sc
scala> val w = "one" With 2
<console>:7: error: value With is not a member of String
```

```
        val w = "one" With 2
                  ^
```

There is also a similar object for Lists, :: (*http://bit.ly/1udnOm3*) What if you want to process the sequence elements in reverse? There's an app... err... object for that! The library object :+ (*http://bit.ly/1voWs6S*) allows you to match on the end elements and work backward:

```
// src/main/scala/progscala2/patternmatching/match-reverse-seq.sc
// Compare to match-seq.sc

val nonEmptyList    = List(1, 2, 3, 4, 5)
val nonEmptyVector  = Vector(1, 2, 3, 4, 5)
val nonEmptyMap     = Map("one" -> 1, "two" -> 2, "three" -> 3)

def reverseSeqToString[T](l: Seq[T]): String = l match {
  case prefix :+ end => reverseSeqToString(prefix) + s" :+ $end"
  case Nil => "Nil"
}

for (seq <- Seq(nonEmptyList, nonEmptyVector, nonEmptyMap.toSeq)) {
  println(reverseSeqToString(seq))
}
```

The output is this:

```
Nil :+ 1 :+ 2 :+ 3 :+ 4 :+ 5
Nil :+ 1 :+ 2 :+ 3 :+ 4 :+ 5
Nil :+ (one,1) :+ (two,2) :+ (three,3)
```

Note that the Nils come first and the methods bind to the left. Also, the same output was generated for the first two inputs, a List and a Vector.

You should compare the implementations of seqToString and reverseSeqToString, which implement the recursion differently. Make sure you understand how they work.

As before, you could use this output to reconstruct collections (skipping the duplicate second line of the previous output):

```
scala> Nil :+ 1 :+ 2 :+ 3 :+ 4 :+ 5
res0: List[Int] = List(1, 2, 3, 4, 5)
```

For List, the :+ method for appending elements and the :+ object for pattern matching both require *O(n)* time, because they have to traverse the list from the head. However, some other sequences, such as Vector, are *O(1)*.

unapplySeq Method

What if you want a bit more flexibility to return a sequence of extracted items, rather than a fixed number of them? The unapplySeq method lets you do this. It turns out the Seq (*http://bit.ly/1s0SvV7*) companion object implements apply and unapplySeq, but not unapply:

```
def apply[A](elems: A*): Seq[A]
def unapplySeq[A](x: Seq[A]): Some[Seq[A]]
```

Recall that A* means that elems is a variable argument list. Matching with unapply Seq is invoked in this variation of our previous example for +:, where we examine a "sliding window" of pairs of elements at a time:

```
// src/main/scala/progscala2/patternmatching/match-seq-unapplySeq.sc

val nonEmptyList    = List(1, 2, 3, 4, 5)                              // ❶
val emptyList       = Nil
val nonEmptyMap     = Map("one" -> 1, "two" -> 2, "three" -> 3)

// Process pairs
def windows[T](seq: Seq[T]): String = seq match {
  case Seq(head1, head2, _*) =>                                       // ❷
    s"($head1, $head2), " + windows(seq.tail)                        // ❸
  case Seq(head, _*) =>
    s"($head, _), " + windows(seq.tail)                             // ❹
  case Nil => "Nil"
}

for (seq <- Seq(nonEmptyList, emptyList, nonEmptyMap.toSeq)) {
  println(windows(seq))
}
```

❶ Use a nonempty List, Nil, and a Map.

❷ It looks like we're calling Seq.apply(…), but in a match clause, we're actually calling Seq.unapplySeq. We grab the first two elements and ignore the rest of the variable arguments with _*. Think of the * as matching zero to many, like in regular expressions.

❸ Format a string with the first two elements, then move the "window" one over by calling seq.tail. Note that we didn't capture this tail in the match.

❹ We also need a match for a one-element sequence or we won't have exhaustive matching. Use _ for the nonexistent "second" element. We actually know that this call to windows(seq.tail) will simply return Nil, but rather than duplicate the string, we take the extra performance hit by calling the method again.

Note the *sliding window* output:

```
(1, 2), (2, 3), (3, 4), (4, 5), (5, _), Nil
Nil
((one,1), (two,2)), ((two,2), (three,3)), ((three,3), _), Nil
```

We could still use the +: matching we saw before, which is more elegant:

```
// src/main/scala/progscala2/patternmatching/match-seq-without-unapplySeq.sc

val nonEmptyList    = List(1, 2, 3, 4, 5)
val emptyList       = Nil
val nonEmptyMap     = Map("one" -> 1, "two" -> 2, "three" -> 3)

// Process pairs
def windows2[T](seq: Seq[T]): String = seq match {
  case head1 +: head2 +: tail => s"($head1, $head2), " + windows2(seq.tail)
  case head +: tail => s"($head, _), " + windows2(tail)
  case Nil => "Nil"
}

for (seq <- Seq(nonEmptyList, emptyList, nonEmptyMap.toSeq)) {
  println(windows2(seq))
}
```

Working with sliding windows is actually so useful that Seq gives us two methods to create them:

```
scala> val seq = Seq(1,2,3,4,5)
seq: Seq[Int] = List(1, 2, 3, 4, 5)

scala> val slide2 = seq.sliding(2)
slide2: Iterator[Seq[Int]] = non-empty iterator

scala> slide2.toSeq
res0: Seq[Seq[Int]] = res56: Seq[Seq[Int]] = Stream(List(1, 2), ?)

scala> slide2.toList
res1: List[Seq[Int]] = List(List(1, 2), List(2, 3), List(3, 4), List(4, 5))

scala> seq.sliding(3,2).toList
res2: List[Seq[Int]] = List(List(1, 2, 3), List(3, 4, 5))
```

Both sliding methods return an iterator, meaning they are "lazy" and don't immediately make a copy of the list, which would be expensive for large sequences. Calling toSeq converts the iterator into a collection.immutable.Stream (*http://bit.ly/1q8XiTI*), a lazy list that evaluates its head eagerly, but only evaluates the tail elements on demand. In contrast, calling toList evaluates the whole iterator eagerly, creating a List.

Note there is a slight difference in the results. We don't end with (5, _), for example.

Matching on Variable Argument Lists

In "Inferring Type Information" on page 46, we described how Scala supports variable argument lists for methods. For example, suppose I'm writing a tool for interoperating with SQL and I want a case class to represent the WHERE foo IN (val1, val2, ...) SQL clause (this example is inspired by a real project, not open source). Here's an example case class with a variable argument list to handle the list of values in this clause. I've also included some other definitions for the WHERE x OP y clauses, where OP is one of the SQL comparison operators:

```
// src/main/scala/progscala2/patternmatching/match-vararglist.sc

// Operators for WHERE clauses
object Op extends Enumeration {                              // ❶
  type Op = Value

  val EQ   = Value("=")
  val NE   = Value("!=")
  val LTGT = Value("<>")
  val LT   = Value("<")
  val LE   = Value("<=")
  val GT   = Value(">")
  val GE   = Value(">=")
}
import Op._

// Represent a SQL "WHERE x op value" clause, where +op+ is a
// comparison operator: =, !=, <>, <, <=, >, or >=.
case class WhereOp[T](columnName: String, op: Op, value: T)  // ❷

// Represent a SQL "WHERE x IN (a, b, c, ...)" clause.
case class WhereIn[T](columnName: String, val1: T, vals: T*) // ❸

val wheres = Seq(                                            // ❹
  WhereIn("state", "IL", "CA", "VA"),
  WhereOp("state", EQ, "IL"),
  WhereOp("name", EQ, "Buck Trends"),
  WhereOp("age", GT, 29))

for (where <- wheres) {
  where match {
    case WhereIn(col, val1, vals @ _*) =>                    // ❺
      val valStr = (val1 +: vals).mkString(", ")
      println (s"WHERE $col IN ($valStr)")
    case WhereOp(col, op, value) => println (s"WHERE $col $op $value")
    case _ => println (s"ERROR: Unknown expression: $where")
  }
}
```

❶ An enumeration for the comparison operators, where we assign a "name" that's the string representation of the operator in SQL.

❷ A case class for WHERE x OP y clauses.

❸ A case class for WHERE x IN (val1, val2, …) clauses.

❹ Some example objects to parse.

❺ Note the syntax for matching on a variable argument: name @ _*.

The syntax for pattern matching on a variable argument list, name @ _*, is not that intuitive. Occasionally, you'll need it. Here is the output:

```
WHERE state IN (IL, CA, VA)
WHERE state = IL
WHERE name = Buck Trends
WHERE age > 29
```

Matching on Regular Expressions

Regular expressions (or *regexes*) are convenient for extracting data from strings that have a particular structure.

Scala wraps Java's regular expressions.[1] Here is an example:

```
// src/main/scala/progscala2/patternmatching/match-regex.sc

val BookExtractorRE = """Book: title=([^,]+),\s+author=(.+)""".r      // ❶
val MagazineExtractorRE = """Magazine: title=([^,]+),\s+issue=(.+)""".r

val catalog = Seq(
  "Book: title=Programming Scala Second Edition, author=Dean Wampler",
  "Magazine: title=The New Yorker, issue=January 2014",
  "Unknown: text=Who put this here??"
)

for (item <- catalog) {
  item match {
    case BookExtractorRE(title, author) =>                            // ❷
      println(s"""Book "$title", written by $author""")
    case MagazineExtractorRE(title, issue) =>
      println(s"""Magazine "title", issue $issue""")
    case entry => println(s"Unrecognized entry: $entry")
  }
}
```

---

1. See *The Java Tutorials. Lesson: Regular Expressions* (*http://bit.ly/1xIv4mO*).

❶ Match a book string, with two *capture groups* (note the parentheses), one for the title and one for the author. Calling the r method on a string creates a regex from it. Match a magazine string, with *capture groups* for the title and issue (date).

❷ Use them like case classes, where the string matched by each capture group is assigned to a variable.

The output is:

```
Book "Programming Scala Second Edition", written by Dean Wampler
Magazine "The New Yorker", issue January 2014
Unrecognized entry: Unknown: text=Who put this here??
```

We use triple-quoted strings for the regexes. Otherwise, we would have to escape the regex "backslash" constructs, e.g, \\s instead of \s. You can also define regular expressions by creating new instances of the Regex class, as in new Regex("""\W"""), but this isn't very common.

> Using interpolation in triple-quoted strings doesn't work cleanly for the regex escape sequences. You still need to escape these sequences, e.g., s"""$first\\s+$second""".r instead of s"""$first\s+$second""".r. If you aren't using interpolation, escaping isn't necessary.

scala.util.matching.Regex (*http://bit.ly/1E8xZcO*) defines several methods for other manipulations, such as finding and replacing matches.

More on Binding Variables in case Clauses

Suppose you want to extract values from an object, but you also want to assign a variable to the whole object itself.

Let's modify our previous example matching on fields in Person instances:

```
// src/main/scala/progscala2/patternmatching/match-deep2.sc

case class Address(street: String, city: String, country: String)
case class Person(name: String, age: Int, address: Address)

val alice   = Person("Alice",   25, Address("1 Scala Lane", "Chicago", "USA"))
val bob     = Person("Bob",     29, Address("2 Java Ave.",  "Miami",   "USA"))
val charlie = Person("Charlie", 32, Address("3 Python Ct.", "Boston",  "USA"))

for (person <- Seq(alice, bob, charlie)) {
  person match {
    case p @ Person("Alice", 25, address) => println(s"Hi Alice! $p")
    case p @ Person("Bob", 29, a @ Address(street, city, country)) =>
```

```
      println(s"Hi ${p.name}! age ${p.age}, in ${a.city}")
    case p @ Person(name, age, _) =>
      println(s"Who are you, $age year-old person named $name? $p")
  }
}
```

The p @ … syntax assigns to p the whole Person instance and similarly for a @ … and an Address. Here is the output now (reformatted to fit the page):

```
Hi Alice! Person(Alice,25,Address(1 Scala Lane,Chicago,USA))
Hi Bob! age 29, in Miami
Who are you, 32 year-old person named Charlie? Person(Charlie,32,
  Address(3 Python Ct.,Boston,USA))
```

Keep in mind that if we aren't extracting fields from the Person instance, we can just write p: Person => ….

More on Type Matching

Consider the following example, where we attempt to discriminate between List[Dou ble] and List[String] inputs:

```
// src/main/scala/progscala2/patternmatching/match-types.sc
scala> for {
     |   x <- Seq(List(5.5,5.6,5.7), List("a", "b"))
     | } yield (x match {
     |   case seqd: Seq[Double] => ("seq double", seqd)
     |   case seqs: Seq[String] => ("seq string", seqs)
     |   case _                 => ("unknown!", x)
     | })
<console>:12: warning: non-variable type argument Double in type pattern
Seq[Double] (the underlying of Seq[Double]) is unchecked since it is
eliminated by erasure
              case seqd: Seq[Double] => ("seq double", seqd)
                    ^
<console>:13: warning: non-variable type argument String in type pattern
Seq[String] (the underlying of Seq[String]) is unchecked since it is
eliminated by erasure
              case seqs: Seq[String] => ("seq string", seqs)
                    ^
<console>:13: warning: unreachable code
              case seqs: Seq[String] => ("seq string", seqs)
                                      ^
res0: List[(String, List[Any])] =
  List((seq double,List(5.5, 5.6, 5.7)),(seq double,List(a, b)))
```

What do the warnings mean? Scala runs on the JVM and these warnings result from the JVM's *type erasure*, a historical legacy of Java's introduction of *generics* in Java 5. In order to avoid breaking older code, the JVM byte code doesn't retain information about the actual type parameters that were used for instances of generic (parameterized) types, like List.

So, the compiler is warning us that, while it can check that a given object is a `List`, it can't check at *runtime* that it's a `List[Double]` or a `List[String]`. In fact, it considers the second `case` clause for `List[String]` to be unreachable code, meaning the previous `case` clause for `List[Double]` will match *any* `List`. Note the output, which shows that "seq double" was written for both inputs.

One ugly, but effective workaround is to match on the collection first, then use a nested match on the head element to determine the type. We now have to handle an empty sequence, too:

```
// src/main/scala/progscala2/patternmatching/match-types2.sc

def doSeqMatch[T](seq: Seq[T]): String = seq match {
  case Nil => "Nothing"
  case head +: _ => head match {
    case _ : Double => "Double"
    case _ : String => "String"
    case _ => "Unmatched seq element"
  }
}

for {
  x <- Seq(List(5.5,5.6,5.7), List("a", "b"), Nil)
} yield {
  x match {
    case seq: Seq[_] => (s"seq ${doSeqMatch(seq)}", seq)
    case _           => ("unknown!", x)
  }
}
```

This script returns the desired result, `Seq((seq Double,List(5.5, 5.6, 5.7)), (seq String,List(a, b)), (seq Nothing,List()))`.

Sealed Hierarchies and Exhaustive Matches

Let's revisit the need for exhaustive matches and consider the situation where we have a `sealed` class hierarchy, which we discussed in "Sealed Class Hierarchies" on page 62. As an example, suppose we define the following code to represent the allowed message types or "methods" for HTTP:

```
// src/main/scala/progscala2/patternmatching/http.sc

sealed abstract class HttpMethod() {                    // ❶
  def body: String                                      // ❷
  def bodyLength = body.length
}

case class Connect(body: String) extends HttpMethod     // ❸
case class Delete (body: String) extends HttpMethod
```

```
case class Get     (body: String) extends HttpMethod
case class Head    (body: String) extends HttpMethod
case class Options(body: String) extends HttpMethod
case class Post    (body: String) extends HttpMethod
case class Put     (body: String) extends HttpMethod
case class Trace   (body: String) extends HttpMethod

def handle (method: HttpMethod) = method match {              // ❹
  case Connect (body) => s"connect: (length: ${method.bodyLength}) $body"
  case Delete  (body) => s"delete:  (length: ${method.bodyLength}) $body"
  case Get     (body) => s"get:     (length: ${method.bodyLength}) $body"
  case Head    (body) => s"head:    (length: ${method.bodyLength}) $body"
  case Options (body) => s"options: (length: ${method.bodyLength}) $body"
  case Post    (body) => s"post:    (length: ${method.bodyLength}) $body"
  case Put     (body) => s"put:     (length: ${method.bodyLength}) $body"
  case Trace   (body) => s"trace:   (length: ${method.bodyLength}) $body"
}

val methods = Seq(
  Connect("connect body..."),
  Delete ("delete body..."),
  Get    ("get body..."),
  Head   ("head body..."),
  Options("options body..."),
  Post   ("post body..."),
  Put    ("put body..."),
  Trace  ("trace body..."))

methods foreach (method => println(handle(method)))
```

❶ Define a sealed, abstract base class `HttpMethod`. Because it is declared `sealed`, the only allowed subtypes must be defined in this file.

❷ Define a method for the body of the HTTP message.

❸ Define eight case classes that extend `HttpMethod`. Note that each declares a constructor argument `body: String`, which is a `val` because each of these types is a case class. This `val` *implements* the abstract `def` method in `HttpMethod`.

❹ An *exhaustive* pattern-match expression, even though we don't have a default clause, because the `method` argument can only be an instance of one of the eight case classes we've defined.

 When pattern matching on an instance of a sealed base class, the match is exhaustive if the `case` clauses cover all the derived types defined in the same source file. Because no user-defined derived types are allowed, the match can never become nonexhaustive as the project evolves, since users are prevented from defining new types.

A corollary is to avoid using `sealed` if the type hierarchy is at all likely to change. Instead, rely on your traditional object-oriented inheritance principles, including polymorphic methods. What if you added a new derived type, either in this file or in another file, and you removed the `sealed` keyword on `HttpMethod`? You would have to find and fix all pattern-match clauses in your code base *and* your client's code bases that match on `HttpMethod` instances.

As a side note, we are exploiting a useful feature for implementing certain methods. An abstract, no-argument method declaration in a parent type can be implemented by a `val` in a subtype. This is because a `val` has a single, fixed value (of course), whereas a no-argument method returning the same type can return any value of the type. Hence, the `val` implementation is more restrictive in the return type, which means using it where the method is "called" is always just as safe as calling a method. In fact, this is an application of *referential transparency*, where we are substituting a value for an expression that *should* always return the same value!

An abstract, no-argument method declaration in a parent type can be implemented by a `val` in a subtype. A recommended practice is to declare abstract, no-argument methods instead of `val`s in abstract parent types, leaving subtype implementers greater freedom to implement the member with either a method or a `val`.

Running this script yields the following output:

```
connect: (length: 15) connect body...
delete:  (length: 14) delete body...
get:     (length: 11) get body...
head:    (length: 12) head body...
options: (length: 15) options body...
post:    (length: 12) post body...
put:     (length: 11) put body...
trace:   (length: 13) trace body...
```

The `HTTPMethod` case classes are small, so we could in principle also use an `Enumera tion` for them, but there's a big drawback. The compiler can't tell whether or not the match clauses on `Enumeration` values are exhaustive. If we converted this example to use `Enumeration` and forgot a match clause for `Trace`, we would only know at runtime when a `MatchError` is thrown.

Avoid enumerations when pattern matching is required. The compiler can't tell if the matches are exhaustive.

Other Uses of Pattern Matching

Fortunately, this powerful feature is not limited to case clauses. You can use pattern matching when defining values, including in for comprehensions:

```scala
scala> case class Address(street: String, city: String, country: String)
defined class Address

scala> case class Person(name: String, age: Int, address: Address)
defined class Person

scala> val Person(name, age, Address(_, state, _)) =
     |    Person("Dean", 29, Address("1 Scala Way", "CA", "USA"))
name: String = Dean
age: Int = 29
state: String = CA
```

Yes, in one step we extracted all those fields from the Person object, and skipped a few of them. It works for Lists, too:

```scala
scala> val head +: tail = List(1,2,3)
head: Int = 1
tail: List[Int] = List(2, 3)

scala> val head1 +: head2 +: tail = Vector(1,2,3)
head1: Int = 1
head2: Int = 2
tail: scala.collection.immutable.Vector[Int] = Vector(3)

scala> val Seq(a,b,c) = List(1,2,3)
a: Int = 1
b: Int = 2
c: Int = 3

scala> val Seq(a,b,c) = List(1,2,3,4)
scala.MatchError: List(1, 2, 3, 4) (of class collection.immutable.$colon$colon)
   ... 43 elided
```

Very handy. Try some of your own examples.

We can use pattern matching in if expressions:

```scala
scala> val p = Person("Dean", 29, Address("1 Scala Way", "CA", "USA"))
p: Person = Person(Dean,29,Address(1 Scala Way,CA,USA))

scala> if (p == Person("Dean", 29,
     |    Address("1 Scala Way", "CA", "USA"))) "yes" else "no"
res0: String = yes

scala> if (p == Person("Dean", 29,
     |    Address("1 Scala Way", "CA", "USSR"))) "yes" else "no"
res1: String = no
```

However, the _ placeholders don't work here:

```scala
scala> if (p == Person(_, 29, Address(_, _, "USA"))) "yes" else "no"
<console>:13: error: missing parameter type for expanded function
((x$1) => p.$eq$eq(Person(x$1,29,((x$2,x$3) => Address(x$2,x$3,"USA")))))
            if (p == Person(_, 29, Address(_, _, "USA"))) "yes" else "no"
                 ^
...
```

There's an internal function called eqeq that's used for the == test. We've opened the magic kimono a bit. Because the JVM specification only allows alphanumeric characters, _, and $ in identifiers, Scala "mangles" nonalphanumeric characters to something acceptable to the JVM. In this case, = becomes $eq. All these mappings are listed in Table 22-1 in Chapter 22.

Suppose we have a function that takes a sequence of integers and returns the sum and count of the elements in a tuple:

```scala
scala> def sum_count(ints: Seq[Int]) = (ints.sum, ints.size)

scala> val (sum, count) = sum_count(List(1,2,3,4,5))
sum: Int = 15
count: Int = 5
```

I use this idiom frequently. We saw a teaser example in "Expanded Scope and Value Definitions" on page 81 that used pattern matching in a for comprehension. Here's the relevant part from that example again:

```scala
// src/main/scala/progscala2/patternmatching/scoped-option-for.sc

val dogBreeds = Seq(Some("Doberman"), None, Some("Yorkshire Terrier"),
                    Some("Dachshund"), None, Some("Scottish Terrier"),
                    None, Some("Great Dane"), Some("Portuguese Water Dog"))

println("second pass:")
for {
  Some(breed) <- dogBreeds
  upcasedBreed = breed.toUpperCase()
} println(upcasedBreed)
```

As before, the output is the following:

```
DOBERMAN
YORKSHIRE TERRIER
DACHSHUND
SCOTTISH TERRIER
GREAT DANE
PORTUGUESE WATER DOG
```

A particularly convenient use of pattern matching and case clauses is to make function literals of complex arguments easier to use:

```
// src/main/scala/progscala2/patternmatching/match-fun-args.sc

case class Address(street: String, city: String, country: String)
case class Person(name: String, age: Int)

val as = Seq(
  Address("1 Scala Lane", "Anytown", "USA"),
  Address("2 Clojure Lane", "Othertown", "USA"))
val ps = Seq(
  Person("Buck Trends", 29),
  Person("Clo Jure", 28))

val pas = ps zip as

// Ugly way:
pas map { tup =>
  val Person(name, age) = tup._1
  val Address(street, city, country) = tup._2
  s"$name (age: $age) lives at $street, $city, in $country"
}

// Nicer way:
pas map {
  case (Person(name, age), Address(street, city, country)) =>
    s"$name (age: $age) lives at $street, $city, in $country"
}
```

Note that the type of the zipped list is Seq[(Person,Address)]. So, the function we pass to map must have the type (Person,Address) => String. We show two functions. The first is a "regular" function that takes a tuple argument, then pattern matches to extract the fields from the two elements of the tuple.

The second function is a *partial function*, as discussed in "Partial Functions" on page 37. The syntax is more concise, especially for extracting values from tuples and more complex structures. Just remember that because the function given is actually a PartialFunction (*http://bit.ly/1yMpzEP*), the case expressions must match the inputs exactly or a MatchError (*http://bit.ly/1DDkcsB*) will be thrown at runtime.

In both cases, the resulting sequence of strings is the following:

```
List(
  "Buck Trends (age: 29) lives at 1 Scala Lane, Anytown, in USA",
  "Clo Jure (age: 28) lives at 2 Clojure Lane, Othertown, in USA")
```

Finally, we can use pattern matching on a regular expression to decompose a string. Here's an example extracted from tests I once wrote for parsing (simple!) SQL strings:

```
// src/main/scala/progscala2/patternmatching/regex-assignments.sc
scala> val cols = """\*|[\w, ]+""" // for columns
cols: String = \*|[\w, ]+
```

```
scala> val table = """\w+"""          // for table names
table: String = \w+

scala> val tail = """.*"""            // for other clauses
tail: String = .*

scala> val selectRE =
     | s"""SELECT\\s*(DISTINCT)?\\s+($cols)\\s*FROM\\s+($table)\\s*($tail)?;""".r
selectRE: scala.util.matching.Regex = \
  SELECT\s*(DISTINCT)?\s+(\*|[\w, ]+)\s*FROM\s+(\w+)\s*(.*)?;

scala> val selectRE(distinct1, cols1, table1, otherClauses) =
     |     "SELECT DISTINCT * FROM atable;"
distinct1: String = DISTINCT
cols1: String = *
table1: String = atable
otherClauses: String = ""

scala> val selectRE(distinct2, cols2, table2, otherClauses) =
     |     "SELECT col1, col2 FROM atable;"
distinct2: String = null
cols2: String = "col1, col2 "
table2: String = atable
otherClauses: String = ""

scala> val selectRE(distinct3, cols3, table3, otherClauses) =
     |     "SELECT DISTINCT col1, col2 FROM atable;"
distinct3: String = DISTINCT
cols3: String = "col1, col2 "
table3: String = atable
otherClauses: String = ""

scala> val selectRE(distinct4, cols4, table4, otherClauses) =
     |     "SELECT DISTINCT col1, col2 FROM atable WHERE col1 = 'foo';"
distinct4: String = DISTINCT
cols4: String = "col1, col2 "
table4: String = atable
otherClauses: String = WHERE col1 = 'foo'
```

Note that we had to add extra backslashes, e.g., \\s instead of \s, in the regular expression string, because we used interpolation.

Obviously, using regular expressions to parse complex text, like XML or programming languages, has its limits. Beyond simple cases, consider a parser library, like the ones we'll discuss in Chapter 20.

Concluding Remarks on Pattern Matching

Pattern matching is a powerful "protocol" for extracting data inside data structures. One of the unintended consequences of the *JavaBeans* model (*http://bit.ly/1wNbg1E*) was that it encouraged developers to expose fields in their objects through getters and setters, often ignoring concerns that state should be encapsulated and only exposed as appropriate, especially for mutable fields. Access to state information should be carefully designed to reflect the abstraction exposed.

Consider using pattern matching for those times when you need to extract information in a controlled way. You can customize `unapply` methods, as we saw in "unapply Method" on page 113, to control the state exposed. These methods let you extract that information while hiding the implementation details. In fact, the information returned by `unapply` might be a transformation of the actual fields in the type.

Finally, when designing pattern-matching statements, be wary of relying on a default `case` clause. Under what circumstances would "none of the above" be the correct answer? It may indicate that the design should be refined so you know more precisely all the possible matches that might occur.

Along with `for` comprehensions, pattern matching makes idiomatic Scala code concise, yet powerful. It's not unusual for Scala programs to have 10 times fewer lines of code than comparable programs written in Java.

So, even though Java 8 added anonymous functions ("lambdas"), which was an enormous improvement, tools like pattern matching and `for` comprehensions are compelling reasons to switch to Scala.

Recap and What's Next

Pattern matching is a hallmark of many functional languages. It is a flexible and concise technique for extracting data from data structures. We saw examples of pattern matching in `case` clauses and how to use pattern matching in other expressions.

The next chapter discusses a unique, powerful, but controversial feature in Scala, *implicits*, which are a set of tools for building intuitive DSLs (domain-specific languages), reducing boilerplate, and making APIs both easier to use and more amenable to customization.

## CHAPTER 5

Implicits

Implicits are a powerful, if controversial feature in Scala. They are used to reduce boilerplate, to simulate adding new methods to existing types, and to support the creation of *domain-specific languages* (DSLs).

Implicits are controversial because they are "nonlocal" in the source code. You import implicit values and methods into the local scope, except for those that are imported automatically through `Predef` (*http://bit.ly/1086O2z*). Once in scope, an implicit might be invoked by the compiler to populate a method argument or to convert a provided argument to the expected type. However, when reading the source code, it's not obvious when an implicit value or method is being used, which can be confusing to the reader. Fortunately, you learn from experience to be aware when implicits might be invoked, and you learn the APIs that exploit them. Nevertheless, surprises await the beginner.

Understanding how implicits work is fairly straightforward. Most of this long chapter is devoted to example design problems that implicits solve.

Implicit Arguments

In "A Taste of Futures" on page 41, we saw one use of the `implicit` keyword, to label method arguments that the user does not have to provide explicitly. When an implicit argument is omitted, a type-compatible value will be used from the enclosing scope, if available. Otherwise, a compiler error occurs.

Suppose we have a method to compute sales tax where the rate is implicit:

```
def calcTax(amount: Float)(implicit rate: Float): Float = amount * rate
```

In code that uses this method, an implicit value in the local scope will be used:

```
implicit val currentTaxRate = 0.08F
...
val tax = calcTax(50000F)  // 4000.0
```

For simple cases, a fixed Float value might be sufficient. However, an application might need to know the location where the transaction takes place, to add on city taxes, for example. Some jurisdictions might offer "tax holidays" to promote shopping during the end of the year holidays.

Fortunately, an implicit method can also be used. To function as an implicit value, it must not take arguments itself, *unless* the arguments are also implicit. Here is a complete example for calculating sales tax:

```
// src/main/scala/progscala2/implicits/implicit-args.sc

// Never use Floats for money:
def calcTax(amount: Float)(implicit rate: Float): Float = amount * rate

object SimpleStateSalesTax {
  implicit val rate: Float = 0.05F
}

case class ComplicatedSalesTaxData(
  baseRate: Float,
  isTaxHoliday: Boolean,
  storeId: Int)

object ComplicatedSalesTax {
  private def extraTaxRateForStore(id: Int): Float = {
    // From id, determine location, then extra taxes...
    0.0F
  }

  implicit def rate(implicit cstd: ComplicatedSalesTaxData): Float =
    if (cstd.isTaxHoliday) 0.0F
    else cstd.baseRate + extraTaxRateForStore(cstd.storeId)
}

{
  import SimpleStateSalesTax.rate

  val amount = 100F
  println(s"Tax on $amount = ${calcTax(amount)}")
}

{
  import ComplicatedSalesTax.rate
  implicit val myStore = ComplicatedSalesTaxData(0.06F, false, 1010)

  val amount = 100F
  println(s"Tax on $amount = ${calcTax(amount)}")
}
```

It doesn't matter that we call calcTax inside an interpolated string. The implicit values are still used for the rate argument.

For the "complicated" case, we use an implicit method, which itself takes an implicit argument with the data it needs.

Running the script produces this output:

```
Tax on 100.0 = 5.0
Tax on 100.0 = 6.0
```

Using implicitly

Predef (*http://bit.ly/1086O2z*) defines a method called implicitly. Combined with a type signature addition, it provides a useful shorthand way of defining method signatures that take a single implicit argument, where that argument is a parameterized type.

Consider the following example, which wraps the List (*http://bit.ly/15iqGNE*) method sortBy:

```
// src/main/scala/progscala2/implicits/implicitly-args.sc
import math.Ordering

case class MyList[A](list: List[A]) {
  def sortBy1[B](f: A => B)(implicit ord: Ordering[B]): List[A] =
    list.sortBy(f)(ord)

  def sortBy2[B : Ordering](f: A => B): List[A] =
    list.sortBy(f)(implicitly[Ordering[B]])
}

val list = MyList(List(1,3,5,2,4))

list sortBy1 (i => -i)
list sortBy2 (i => -i)
```

List.sortBy is one of several sorting methods available for many of the collections. It takes a function that transforms the arguments into something that satisfies math.Ordering, which is analogous to Java's Comparable (*http://bit.ly/1u1hDR8*) abstraction. An implicit argument is required that knows how to order instances of type B.

MyList shows two alternative ways of writing a method like sortBy. The first implementation, sortBy1, uses the syntax we already know. The method takes an additional implicit value of type Ordering[B]. For sortBy1 to be used, there must be an instance in scope that knows how to "order" instances of the desired type B. We say that B is bound by a "context," in this case, the ability to order instances.

This idiom is so common that Scala provides a shorthand syntax, which is used by the second implementation, sortBy2. The type parameter B : Ordering is called a *context bound*. It implies the second, implicit argument list that takes an Ordering[B] instance.

However, we need to access this `Ordering` instance in the method, but we no longer have a name for it, because it's no longer explicitly declared in the source code. That's what `Predef.implicitly` does for us. Whatever instance is passed to the method for the implicit argument is resolved by `implicitly`. Note the type signature that it requires, `Ordering[B]` in this case.

 The combination of a *context bound* and the `implicitly` method is a shorthand for the special case where we need an implicit argument of a parameterized type, where the type parameter is one of the other types in scope (for example, [B : Ordering] for an implicit `Ordering[B]` parameter).

Scenarios for Implicit Arguments

It's important to use implicits wisely and sparingly. Excessive use makes it difficult for the reader to understand what the code is actually doing.

Why use implicit arguments in the first place, especially if they have drawbacks? There are several common idioms implemented with implicit arguments whose benefits fall into two broad categories. The first category is boilerplate elimination, such as providing context information implicitly rather than explicitly. The second category includes constraints that reduce bugs or limit the allowed types that can be used with certain methods with parameterized types. Let's explore these idioms.

Execution Contexts

We saw in the `Future` example in "A Taste of Futures" on page 41 that a second, implicit argument list was used to pass an `ExecutionContext` (*http://bit.ly/1s0FtqF*) to the `Future.apply` (*http://bit.ly/1pbjSQR*) method:

```
apply[T](body: => T)(implicit executor: ExecutionContext): Future[T]
```

Several other methods also have this implicit argument.

We didn't specify an `ExecutionContext` when we called these methods, but we imported a global default that the compiler used:

```
import scala.concurrent.ExecutionContext.Implicits.global
```

Passing an "execution context" is one recommended use of implicit arguments. Other example contexts include transactions, database connections, thread pools, and user sessions. Using a method argument permits composition of behavior. Making that argument implicit creates a cleaner API for users.

Capabilities

Besides passing contexts, implicit arguments can be used to control *capabilities*.

For example, an implicit user session argument might contain authorization tokens that control whether or not certain API operations can be invoked on behalf of the user or to limit data visibility.

Suppose you are constructing a menu for a user interface and some menu items are shown only if the user is logged in, while others are shown only if the user isn't logged in:

```
def createMenu(implicit session: Session): Menu = {
  val defaultItems = List(helpItem, searchItem)
  val accountItems =
    if (session.loggedin()) List(viewAccountItem, editAccountItem)
    else List(loginItem)
  Menu(defaultItems ++ accountItems)
}
```

Constraining Allowed Instances

Suppose we have a method with parameterized types and we want to constrain the allowed types that can be used for the type parameters.

If the types we want to permit are all subtypes of a common supertype, we can use object-oriented techniques and avoid implicits. Let's consider that approach first.

We saw an example in "Call by Name, Call by Value" on page 87, where we implemented a resource manager:

```
object manage {
  def apply[R <: { def close():Unit }, T](resource: => R)(f: R => T) = {...}
  ...
}
```

The type parameter R must be a subtype of any type with the close():Unit method. Or, if we can assume that all resources we'll manage implement a Closable trait (recall that traits replace and extend Java interfaces; see "Traits: Interfaces and "Mixins" in Scala" on page 96):

```
trait Closable {
  def close(): Unit
}
...
object manage {
  def apply[R <: Closable, T](resource: => R)(f: R => T) = {...}
  ...
}
```

This technique doesn't help when there is no common superclass. For that situation, we can use an implicit argument to limit the allowed types. The Scala collections API does this to solve a design problem.

Many of the methods supported by the concrete collections classes are implemented by parent types. For example, `List[A].map(f: A ⇒ B): List[B]` creates a new list after applying the function `f` to each element. The `map` method is supported by most collections. Therefore, it makes sense to implement `map` once in a generic trait, then mix that trait into all the collections that need it (we discussed "mixins" using traits in "Traits: Interfaces and "Mixins" in Scala" on page 96). However, we want to return the same collection type we started with, so how can we tell the one `map` method to do that?

The Scala API uses a convention of passing a "builder" as an implicit argument to `map`. The builder knows how to construct a new collection of the same type. This is what the actual signature of `map` looks like in `TraversableLike` (*http://bit.ly/1yMk4pK*), a trait that is mixed into the collection types that are "traversable":

```
trait TraversableLike[+A, +Repr] extends ... {
  ...
  def map[B, That](f: A => B)(
    implicit bf: CanBuildFrom[Repr, B, That]): That = {...}
  ...
}
```

Recall that `+A` means that `TraversableLike[A]` is *covariant* in `A`; if `B` is a subtype of `A`, then `TraversableLike[B]` is a subtype of `TraversableLike[A]`.

`CanBuildFrom` (*http://bit.ly/1zRqZC9*) is our builder. It's named that way to emphasize the idea that you can build any new collection you want, as long as an implicit builder object exists.

`Repr` is the type of the actual collection used internally to hold the items. `B` is the type of elements created by the function `f`.

`That` is the type parameter of the target collection we want to create. Normally, we want to construct a new collection of the same input kind, perhaps with a different type parameter. That is, `B` may or may not be the same type as `A`. The Scala API defines implicit `CanBuildFroms` for all the built-in collection types.

So, the allowed output collections of a `map` operation are constrained by the existence of corresponding instances of `CanBuildFrom`, declared in scope as `implicit`. If you implement your own collections, you'll want to reuse method implementations like `TraversableLike.map`, so you'll need to create your own `CanBuildFrom` types and import `implicit` instances of them in code that uses your collections.

Let's look at another example. Suppose you're writing a Scala wrapper for a Java database API. Here is an example inspired by Cassandra's API (*http://bit.ly/10aucwc*):

```scala
// src/main/scala/progscala2/implicits/java-database-api.scala

// A Java-like Database API, written in Scala for convenience.
package progscala2.implicits {
  package database_api {

    case class InvalidColumnName(name: String)
      extends RuntimeException(s"Invalid column name $name")

    trait Row {
      def getInt    (colName: String): Int
      def getDouble(colName: String): Double
      def getText   (colName: String): String
    }
  }

  package javadb {
    import database_api._

    case class JRow(representation: Map[String,Any]) extends Row {
      private def get(colName: String): Any =
        representation.getOrElse(colName, throw InvalidColumnName(colName))

      def getInt    (colName: String): Int    = get(colName).asInstanceOf[Int]
      def getDouble(colName: String): Double = get(colName).asInstanceOf[Double]
      def getText   (colName: String): String = get(colName).asInstanceOf[String]
    }

    object JRow {
      def apply(pairs: (String,Any)*) = new JRow(Map(pairs :_*))
    }
  }
}
```

I wrote it in Scala for convenience. I used a Map as the representation of a row in a result set, but for efficiency, a real implementation would probably use byte arrays.

The key feature is the set of methods named getInt, getDouble, getText, and others that we might have implemented. They handle conversion of the "raw" data for a column into a value of the appropriate type. They will throw a ClassCastException (*http://bit.ly/1toAB2S*) if you use the wrong type method for a given column.

Wouldn't it be nice to have a single get[T] method, where T is one of the allowed types? That would promote more uniform invocation, where we wouldn't need a case statement to pick the correct method to call, and we could exploit type inference in many cases.

One of the distinctions Java makes between primitive types and reference types is that we can't use primitives in parameterized methods like get[T]. We would have to use boxed types, like java.lang.Integer instead of int, but we don't want the boxing overhead for a high-performance data application!

However, we can do this in Scala:

```scala
// src/main/scala/progscala2/implicits/scala-database-api.scala

// A Scala wrapper for the Java-like Database API.
package progscala2.implicits {
    package scaladb {
    object implicits {
      import javadb.JRow

      implicit class SRow(jrow: JRow) {
        def get[T](colName: String)(implicit toT: (JRow,String) => T): T =
          toT(jrow, colName)
      }

      implicit val jrowToInt: (JRow,String) => Int =
        (jrow: JRow, colName: String) => jrow.getInt(colName)
      implicit val jrowToDouble: (JRow,String) => Double =
        (jrow: JRow, colName: String) => jrow.getDouble(colName)
      implicit val jrowToString: (JRow,String) => String =
        (jrow: JRow, colName: String) => jrow.getText(colName)
    }

    object DB {
      import implicits._

      def main(args: Array[String]) = {
        val row = javadb.JRow("one" -> 1, "two" -> 2.2, "three" -> "THREE!")

        val oneValue1: Int    = row.get("one")
        val twoValue1: Double  = row.get("two")
        val threeValue1: String = row.get("three")
        // val fourValue1: Byte    = row.get("four")  // won't compile

        println(s"one1   -> $oneValue1")
        println(s"two1   -> $twoValue1")
        println(s"three1 -> $threeValue1")

        val oneValue2   = row.get[Int]("one")
        val twoValue2   = row.get[Double]("two")
        val threeValue2 = row.get[String]("three")
        // val fourValue2    = row.get[Byte]("four")  // won't compile

        println(s"one2   -> $oneValue2")
        println(s"two2   -> $twoValue2")
        println(s"three2 -> $threeValue2")
      }
    }
  }
}
```

In the `Implicits` object, we add an implicit class to wrap the Java `JRow` in a type that has the `get[T]` method we want. We call these classes *implicit conversions* and we'll discuss them later in this chapter. For now, just note that our implicit conversion allows the source code to call `get[T]` on a `JRow` instance, as if that method was defined for it.

The `get[T]` method takes two argument lists. The first is the column name to retrieve from the row and the second is an implicit function argument. This function is used to extract the data for the column from a row and convert it to the correct type.

If you read `get[T]` carefully, you'll notice that it references the `jrow` instance that was passed to the constructor for `SRow`. However, that value isn't declared a `val`, so it's not a field of the class. So, how can `get[T]` reference it? Simply because `jrow` is in the scope of the class body.

 Sometimes a constructor argument is not declared to be a field (using `val` or `var`), because it doesn't hold state information the type should expose to clients. However, the argument can still be referenced by other members of the type, because it is in the scope of the entire body of the type.

Next we have three implicit values, functions that take a `JRow` and a `String`, where the latter is the column name, and returns a column value of the appropriate type. These functions will be used implicitly in calls to `get[T]`.

Finally, we define an object `DB` to test it. It creates a `JRow`, then calls `get[T]` on it for the three columns. It does this twice. The first time, the `T` is inferred from the types of the variables, such as `oneValue1`. The second time, we omit variable type annotations and use explicit parameter values for `T` in `get[T]`. I actually like the second style better.

To run the code, start **sbt** and type **run-main progscala2.implicits.scaladb.DB**. It will compile the code first, if necessary:

```
> run-main progscala2.implicits.scaladb.DB
[info] Running scaladb.DB
one1    -> 1
two1    -> 2.2
three1 -> THREE!
one2    -> 1
two2    -> 2.2
three2 -> THREE!
[success] Total time: 0 s, ...
```

Note that the source code has commented lines for extracting `Byte` values. If you remove the `//` characters on these lines, you'll get compilation errors. Here is the error for the first line (wrapped to fit):

```
[error] .../implicits/scala-database-api.scala:31: ambiguous implicit values:
[error]   both value jrowToInt in object Implicits of type =>
          (javadb.JRow, String) => Int
[error]   and value jrowToDouble in object Implicits of type =>
          (javadb.JRow, String) => Double
[error]   match expected type (javadb.JRow, String) => T
[error]       val fourValue1: Byte    = row.get("four")  // won't compile
```

We get one of two possible errors. In this case, because there are implicit conversions in scope and `Byte` is a number like `Int` and `Double`, the compiler could try to use either one, but it disallows the ambiguity. It would be an error anyway, because both functions extract too many bytes!

If no implicits are in scope at all, you'll get a different error. If you temporarily comment out all three implicit values defined in object `Implicits`, you'll get an error like this for each call to `get`:

```
[error] .../implicits/scala-database-api.scala:28:
  could not find implicit value for parameter toT: (javadb.JRow, String) => T
[error]       val oneValue1: Int     = row.get("one")
```

To recap, we limited the allowed types that can be used for a parameterized method by passing an implicit argument and only defining corresponding implicit values that match the types we want to allow.

By the way, the API I once wrote that inspired this example made the equivalent of `JRow` and the implicit functions more generic so I could plug in "fake" and real representations of Cassandra data, where the fakes were used for testing.

Implicit Evidence

The previous section discussed using implicit objects to constrain the allowed types that don't all conform to a common supertype, and the objects were also used to help do the work of the API.

Sometimes, we just need to constrain the allowed types and not provide additional processing capability. Put another way, we need "evidence" that the proposed types satisfy our requirements. Now we'll discuss another technique called *implicit evidence* that constrains the allowed types, but doesn't require them to conform to a common supertype.

A nice example of this technique is the `toMap` method available for all traversable collections. Recall that the `Map` constructor wants key-value pairs, i.e., two-tuples, as arguments. If we have a sequence of pairs, wouldn't it be nice to create a `Map` out of them in one step? That's what `toMap` does, but we have a dilemma. We can't allow the user to call `toMap` if the sequence is *not* a sequence of pairs.

The `toMap` method is defined in `TraversableOnce` (*http://bit.ly/1tpsKAD*):

```
trait TraversableOnce[+A] ... {
  ...
  def toMap[T, U](implicit ev: <:<[A, (T, U)]): immutable.Map[T, U]
  ...
}
```

The implicit argument ev is the "evidence" we need to enforce our constraint. It uses a type defined in Predef (*http://bit.ly/1086O2z*) called <:<, named to resemble the type parameter constraint <:, e.g., A <: B.

Recall we said that types with two type parameters can be written in "infix" notation. So, the following two expressions are equivalent:

```
<:<(A, B)
A <:< B
```

In toMap, the B is really a pair:

```
<:<(A, (T, U))
A <:< (T, U)
```

Now, when we have a traversable collection that we want to convert to a Map, the implicit evidence ev value we need will be synthesized by the compiler, but only if A <: (T,U); that is, if A is actually a pair. If true, then toMap can be called and it simply passes the elements of the traversable to the Map constructor. However, if A is not a pair type, a compiler error is thrown:

```
scala> val l1 = List(1, 2, 3)
l1: List[Int] = List(1, 2, 3)

scala> l1.toMap
<console>:9: error: Cannot prove that Int <:< (T, U).
              l1.toMap
                 ^

scala> val l2 = List("one" -> 1, "two" -> 2, "three" -> 3)
l2: List[(String, Int)] = List((one,1), (two,2), (three,3))

scala> l2.toMap
res3: scala.collection.immutable.Map[String,Int] =
  Map(one -> 1, two -> 2, three -> 3)
```

Hence, "evidence" only has to exist to enforce a type constraint. We don't have to define an implicit value ourselves to do extra, custom work.

There is a related type in Predef for providing evidence that two types are equivalent, called =:=. It is less widely used.

Working Around Erasure

With implicit evidence, we didn't use the implicit object in the computation. Rather, we only used its existence as confirmation that certain type constraints were satisfied.

Another example where the implicit object only provides evidence is a technique for working around limitations due to *type erasure*.

For historical reasons, the JVM "forgets" the type arguments for parameterized types. For example, consider the following definitions for an *overloaded* method, which is a set of methods with the same name, but unique type signatures:

```
object C {
  def m(seq: Seq[Int]): Unit = println(s"Seq[Int]: $seq")
  def m(seq: Seq[String]): Unit = println(s"Seq[String]: $seq")
}
```

Let's see what happens in a REPL session:

```
scala> :paste
// Entering paste mode (ctrl-D to finish)

object M {
  def m(seq: Seq[Int]): Unit = println(s"Seq[Int]: $seq")
  def m(seq: Seq[String]): Unit = println(s"Seq[String]: $seq")
}
<ctrl-d>

// Exiting paste mode, now interpreting.

<console>:8: error: double definition:
method m:(seq: Seq[String])Unit and
method m:(seq: Seq[Int])Unit at line 7
have same type after erasure: (seq: Seq)Unit
        def m(seq: Seq[String]): Unit = println(s"Seq[String]: $seq")
            ^
```

The `<ctrl-d>` indicates where I entered the Ctrl-D character, which is not echoed to the console, of course.

By the way, try inputting these two method definitions without the `object M` and without using `:paste` mode. You'll see no complaints. That's because the REPL lets you *redefine* types, values, and methods, for your convenience, while the compiler doesn't allow it when compiling regular code. If you forget about this "convenience," you might think you successfully defined two versions of `m`. Using `:paste` mode makes the compiler process the entire input up to the Ctrl-D as it would compile a normal file.

So, the compiler disallows the definitions because they are effectively the same in byte code.

However, we can add an implicit argument to disambiguate the methods:

```
// src/main/scala/progscala2/implicits/implicit-erasure.sc
object M {
  implicit object IntMarker                                      // ❶
  implicit object StringMarker

  def m(seq: Seq[Int])(implicit i: IntMarker.type): Unit =       // ❷
    println(s"Seq[Int]: $seq")

  def m(seq: Seq[String])(implicit s: StringMarker.type): Unit = // ❸
    println(s"Seq[String]: $seq")
}

import M._                                                       // ❹
m(List(1,2,3))
m(List("one", "two", "three"))
```

❶ Define two special-purpose implicit objects that will be used to disambiguate the methods affected by type erasure.

❷ Redefinition of the method that takes `Seq[Int]`. It now has a second argument list expecting an implicit `IntMarker`. Note the type, `IntMarker.type`. This is how to reference the *type* of a singleton object!

❸ The method for `Seq[String]`.

❹ Import the implicit values and the methods, then use them. The code compiles and prints the correct output.

Now the compiler considers the two m methods to be distinct after type erasure. You might wonder why I didn't just use implicit `Int` and `String` values, rather than invent new types. Using implicit values for such common types is not recommended. To see why, suppose that one module in the current scope defines an implicit argument of type `String`, for example, and a "default" implicit `String` value. Then another module in scope defines its own implicit `String` argument. Two things can go wrong. First, suppose the second module doesn't define a "default" implicit value, but expects the user to define an implicit value that's meaningful for the application. If the user doesn't define this value, the other module's implicit value will be used, probably causing unexpected behavior. If the user does define a second implicit value, the two values in scope will be ambiguous and the compiler will throw an error.

At least the second scenario triggers an immediate error rather than allowing unintentional behavior to occur.

The safer bet is to limit your use of implicit arguments and values to very specific, purpose-built types.

Avoid using implicit arguments and corresponding values of common types like Int and String. It's more likely that implicits of such types will be defined in multiple places and cause confusing bugs or compilation errors when they are imported into the same scope.

We'll discuss type erasure in more detail in Chapter 14.

Improving Error Messages

Let's return to the collections API and CanBuildFrom for a moment. What happens if we attempt to use map for a a custom target type that doesn't have a corresponding CanBuildFrom defined for it?

```scala
scala> case class ListWrapper(list: List[Int])
defined class ListWrapper

scala> List(1,2,3).map[Int,ListWrapper](_ * 2)
<console>:10: error: Cannot construct a collection of type ListWrapper
with elements of type Int based on a collection of type List[Int].
              List(1,2,3).map[Int,ListWrapper](_*2)
                                               ^
```

The explicit type annotations on map, map[Int,ListWrapper], ensured that an output object of type ListWrapper is what we wanted, rather than the default List[Int]. It also triggered the error we wanted. Note the descriptive error message, "Cannot construct a collection of type ListWrapper with elements of type Int based on a collection of type List[Int]." This is *not* the usual default message the compiler emits when it can't find an implicit value for an implicit argument. Instead, CanBuildFrom is declared with an *annotation* (like Java annotations), called scala.annotation.implicitNotFound (*http://bit.ly/1zmvcwJ*), which is used to specify a format string for these error messages (see "Annotations" on page 504 for more on Scala annotations). The CanBuildFrom declaration looks like this:

```scala
@implicitNotFound(msg =
  "Cannot construct a collection of type ${To} with elements of type ${Elem}" +
  " based on a collection of type ${From}.")
trait CanBuildFrom[-From, -Elem, +To] {...}
```

You can only use this annotation on types intended for use as implicit values for satisfying implicit arguments. You can't use it to annotate methods that take implicit arguments, like our SRow.get[T] method.

This is a second reason for creating custom types for implicits, rather than using more common types, like Int or String, or even function types like the (JRow,String) => T used in our SRow example. With custom types, you can provide helpful error messages for your users.

Phantom Types

We saw the use of implicit arguments that add behavior, such as `CanBuildFrom`, and the use of the existence of an implicit value that allows an API call to be used, such as `toMap` on collections and implicit instances of the `<:<` type.

The next logical step in the progression is the removal of instances altogether, where just the *existence* of a type is all that's required. When such types are defined that have no instances at all, they are called *phantom types*. That's a fancy name, but it just means that we only care that the type exists. It functions as a "marker." We won't actually use any instances of it.

The use of phantom types we're about to discuss has nothing to do with implicits, but it fits nicely in the discussion of design problems that we've been solving.

Phantom types are very useful for defining work flows that must proceed in a particular order. As an example, consider a simplified payroll calculator. In US tax law, payroll deductions for insurance premiums and contributions to certain retirement savings (401k) accounts can be subtracted before calculating payroll taxes. So, a payroll calculator must process these so-called "pre-tax" deductions first, then calculate the tax deductions, then calculate post-tax deductions, if any, to determine the net pay.

Here is one possible implementation:

```scala
// src/main/scala/progscala2/implicits/phantom-types.scala

// A workflow for payroll calculations.

package progscala.implicits.payroll

sealed trait PreTaxDeductions
sealed trait PostTaxDeductions
sealed trait Final

// For simplicity, use Float for money. Not recommended...
case class Employee(
  name: String,
  annualSalary: Float,
  taxRate: Float,  // For simplicity, just 1 rate covering all taxes.
  insurancePremiumsPerPayPeriod: Float,
  _401kDeductionRate: Float,  // A pretax, retirement savings plan in the USA.
  postTaxDeductions: Float)

case class Pay[Step](employee: Employee, netPay: Float)

object Payroll {
  // Biweekly paychecks. Assume exactly 52 weeks/year for simplicity.
  def start(employee: Employee): Pay[PreTaxDeductions] =
    Pay[PreTaxDeductions](employee, employee.annualSalary / 26.0F)
```

```scala
    def minusInsurance(pay: Pay[PreTaxDeductions]): Pay[PreTaxDeductions] = {
      val newNet = pay.netPay - pay.employee.insurancePremiumsPerPayPeriod
      pay copy (netPay = newNet)
    }

    def minus401k(pay: Pay[PreTaxDeductions]): Pay[PreTaxDeductions] = {
      val newNet = pay.netPay - (pay.employee._401kDeductionRate * pay.netPay)
      pay copy (netPay = newNet)
    }

    def minusTax(pay: Pay[PreTaxDeductions]): Pay[PostTaxDeductions] = {
      val newNet = pay.netPay - (pay.employee.taxRate * pay.netPay)
      pay copy (netPay = newNet)
    }

    def minusFinalDeductions(pay: Pay[PostTaxDeductions]): Pay[Final] = {
      val newNet = pay.netPay - pay.employee.postTaxDeductions
      pay copy (netPay = newNet)
    }
  }

  object CalculatePayroll {
    def main(args: Array[String]) = {
      val e = Employee("Buck Trends", 100000.0F, 0.25F, 200F, 0.10F, 0.05F)
      val pay1 = Payroll start e
      // 401K and insurance can be calculated in either order.
      val pay2 = Payroll minus401k pay1
      val pay3 = Payroll minusInsurance pay2
      val pay4 = Payroll minusTax pay3
      val pay  = Payroll minusFinalDeductions pay4
      val twoWeekGross = e.annualSalary / 26.0F
      val twoWeekNet   = pay.netPay
      val percent      = (twoWeekNet / twoWeekGross) * 100
      println(s"For ${e.name}, the gross vs. net pay every 2 weeks is:")
      println(
        f"   $$$${twoWeekGross}%.2f vs. $$$${twoWeekNet}%.2f or ${percent}%.1f%%")
    }
  }
```

This code is already compiled by sbt, so we can run it at the sbt prompt:

```
> run-main progscala.implicits.payroll.CalculatePayroll
[info] Running progscala.implicits.payroll.CalculatePayroll
For Buck Trends, the gross vs. net pay every 2 weeks is:
   $3846.15 vs. $2446.10 or 63.6%
```

Note the sealed traits with no data and no classes that implement them. Because they are "sealed," they can't be implemented in other files. Hence, they only serve as "markers."

These markers are used as type parameters for the Pay type, which is a token passed through the Payroll calculator object. Each method in Payroll takes a Pay[Step] object with a particular type for the Step parameter. So, we can't call minus401k with a Pay[PostTaxDeductions] object. Hence, the tax rules are enforced by the API.

The CalculatePayroll object demonstrates the use of the API. If you try reordering some of the steps, for example, moving the Payroll.minusFinalDeductions call before the Payroll.minusTax call (and fixing the variable names), you get a compiler error.

Note that the example ends with a *printf* interpolated string very similar to the example we discussed in "Interpolated Strings" on page 94.

Actually, this main routine is not very elegant, undermining the virtue of this approach. Let's fix that, borrowing a "pipelining" operator in F#, Microsoft's functional programming language. This example is adapted from James Iry's blog (*http://bit.ly/1tHUsdb*):

```
// src/main/scala/progscala2/implicits/phantom-types-pipeline.scala
package progscala.implicits.payroll
import scala.language.implicitConversions

object Pipeline {
  implicit class toPiped[V](value:V) {
    def |>[R] (f : V => R) = f(value)
  }
}

object CalculatePayroll2 {
  def main(args: Array[String]) = {
    import Pipeline._
    import Payroll._

    val e = Employee("Buck Trends", 100000.0F, 0.25F, 200F, 0.10F, 0.05F)
    val pay = start(e) |>
      minus401k          |>
      minusInsurance     |>
      minusTax           |>
      minusFinalDeductions
    val twoWeekGross = e.annualSalary / 26.0F
    val twoWeekNet   = pay.netPay
    val percent      = (twoWeekNet / twoWeekGross) * 100
    println(s"For ${e.name}, the gross vs. net pay every 2 weeks is:")
    println(
      f"  $$$${twoWeekGross}%.2f vs. $$$${twoWeekNet}%.2f or ${percent}%.1f%%")
  }
}
```

Now the main routine is a more elegant sequencing of steps, the calls to Payroll methods. Note that the pipeline *operator* |> looks fancy, but all it really does is reorder tokens. For example, it turns an expression like this:

```
pay1 |> Payroll.minus401k
```

into this expression:

```
Payroll.minus401k(pay1)
```

Rules for Implicit Arguments

Returning to implicit arguments, the following sidebar lists the general rules for implicit arguments.

Rules for Implicit Arguments

1. Only the last argument list, including the only list for a single-list method, can have implicit arguments.
2. The `implicit` keyword must appear first and only once in the argument list. The list can't have "nonimplicit" arguments followed by implicit arguments.
3. All the arguments are implicit when the list starts with the `implicit` keyword.

Note the errors reported in these examples, which break the rules:

```
scala> class Bad1 {
     |   def m(i: Int, implicit s: String) = "boo"
<console>:2: error: identifier expected but 'implicit' found.
       def m(i: Int, implicit s: String) = "boo"
                     ^

scala> }
<console>:1: error: eof expected but '}' found.
       }
       ^

scala> class Bad2 {
     |   def m(i: Int)(implicit s: String)(implicit d: Double) = "boo"
<console>:2: error: '=' expected but '(' found.
       def m(i: Int)(implicit s: String)(implicit d: Double) = "boo"
                                        ^

scala> }
<console>:1: error: eof expected but '}' found.
       }
       ^

scala> class Good1 {
     |   def m(i: Int)(implicit s: String, d: Double) = "boo"
     | }
```

```
defined class Good1

scala> class Good2 {
     |    def m(implicit i: Int, s: String, d: Double) = "boo"
     | }
defined class Good2
```

Implicit Conversions

We saw in "Tuple Literals" on page 59 that there are several ways to create a pair:

```
(1, "one")
1 -> "one"
1 → "one"          // Using → instead of ->
Tuple2(1, "one")
Pair(1, "one")     // Deprecated as of Scala 2.11
```

It seems a bit wasteful to bake into the Scala grammar two literal forms: (a, b) and a -> b.

The a -> b (or equivalently, a → b) idiom for pair creation is popular for initializing a Map:

```
scala> Map("one" -> 1, "two" -> 2)
res0: scala.collection.immutable.Map[String,Int] = Map(one -> 1, two -> 2)
```

The Map.apply (*http://bit.ly/1zmvd3K*) method being called expects a variable argument list of pairs:

```
def apply[A, B](elems: (A, B)*): Map[A, B]
```

In fact, Scala knows nothing about a -> b, so it's not "wasteful." This "literal" form is actually a method -> and a special Scala feature, *implicit conversions*, which allows us to use this method between two values of any type. Also, because a -> b is not a literal syntax for tuples, we must somehow convert that expression to (a, b).

The obvious first step is to define a method ->, but where? We want the ability to call this method for all possible objects that might be the first element in a pair. Even if we could edit the code for all the types where we want this method, it wouldn't be practical nor wise to do so.

The trick is to use a "wrapper" object that has -> defined. Scala has one in Predef (*http://bit.ly/1pbvaVd*) already:

```
implicit final class ArrowAssoc[A](val self: A) {
  def -> [B](y: B): Tuple2[A, B] = Tuple2(self, y)
}
```

(I omitted a few unimportant details of the actual declaration for clarity.) Like for Java, the final keyword prevents subclasses of ArrowAssoc from being declared.

We could use it like this to create a `Map`:

```
scala> Map(new ArrowAssoc("one") -> 1, new ArrowAssoc("two") -> 2)
res0: scala.collection.immutable.Map[String,Int] = Map(one -> 1, two -> 2)
```

That's way worse than just using `Map( ("one", 1), ("two", 2) )`. However, it does take us partly there. `ArrowAssoc` accepts an object of any type, then when `->` is called, a pair is returned.

This is where the `implicit` keyword comes into play again. Because `ArrowAssoc` is declared implicit, the compiler goes through the following logical steps:

1. It sees that we're trying to call a `->` method on `String` (e.g., `"one" -> 1`).

2. Because `String` has no `->` method, it looks for an *implicit conversion* in scope to a type that has this method.

3. It finds `ArrowAssoc`.

4. It constructs an `ArrowAssoc`, passing it the `"one"` string.

5. It then resolves the `-> 1` part of the expression and confirms the whole expression's type matches the expectation of `Map.apply`, which is a pair instance.

For something to be considered an *implicit conversion*, it must be declared with the `implicit` keyword and it must either be a class that takes a single constructor argument or it must be a method that takes a single argument.

Before Scala 2.10, it was necessary to define a wrapper class without the `implicit` keyword, and an `implicit` method that performed the conversion to the wrapper class. That "two-step" seemed pointless, so you can now mark the class `implicit` and eliminate the method. So, for example, `ArrowAssoc` looked like this before Scala 2.10 (`any2Arro wAssoc` still exists, but it's deprecated):

```
final class ArrowAssoc[A](val self: A) {
  def -> [B](y: B): Tuple2[A, B] = Tuple2(self, y)
}
...
implicit def any2ArrowAssoc[A](x: A): ArrowAssoc[A] = new ArrowAssoc(x)
```

Implicit methods can still be used, but now they are only necessary when converting to a type that already exists for other purposes and it isn't declared implicit.

Another example is the pipeline operator we defined earlier in "Phantom Types" on page 145:

```
... pay1 |> Payroll.minus401k ...
```

Indiscriminate use of implicit methods can lead to mysterious behavior that is hard to debug. For this reason, implicit methods are considered an optional feature as of Scala 2.10, so you should enable the feature explicitly with the import statement, `import`

scala.language.implicitConversions, or with the global -language:implicitCon
versions compiler option.

Here is a summary of the lookup rules used by the compiler to find and apply conversions methods:

1. No conversion will be attempted if the object and method combination type check
   successfully.
2. Only classes and methods with the implicit keyword are considered.
3. Only implicit classes and methods in the current scope are considered, as well as
   implicit methods defined in the *companion object* of the *target* type (see the following discussion).
4. Implicit methods aren't chained to get from the available type, through intermediate
   types, to the target type. Only a method that takes a single available type instance
   and returns a target type instance will be considered.
5. No conversion is attempted if more than one possible conversion method could be
   applied. There must be one and only one, unambiguous possibility.

The third point that mentions implicit methods in companion objects has the following
meaning. First, no implicit conversion is used unless it's already in the current scope,
either because it's declared in an enclosing scope or it was imported from another scope,
such as a separate object that defines some implicit conversions.

However, another scope automatically searched *last* is the companion object of the type
to which a conversion is needed, if there is one. Consider the following example:

```
// src/main/scala/progscala2/implicits/implicit-conversions-resolution.sc
import scala.language.implicitConversions

case class Foo(s: String)
object Foo {
  implicit def fromString(s: String): Foo = Foo(s)
}

class O {
  def m1(foo: Foo) = println(foo)
  def m(s: String) = m1(s)
}
```

The Foo companion object defines a conversion from String. The O.m method attempts
to call O.m1 with a String, but it expects a Foo. The compiler finds the Foo.from
String conversion method, even though we didn't import it explicitly into the scope
of O.

However, if there is another Foo conversion in scope, it will override the Foo.from
String conversion:

```
// src/main/scala/progscala2/implicits/implicit-conversions-resolution.sc
import scala.language.implicitConversions

case class Foo(s: String)
object Foo {
  implicit def fromString(s: String): Foo = Foo(s)
}

class O {
  def m1(foo: Foo) = println(foo)
  def m(s: String) = m1(s)
}
```

Now, `overridingConversion` will be used instead.

We mentioned before that a recommended convention is to put implicit values and conversions into a special package named `implicits` or an object named `Implicits`, except for those defined in companion objects, as we just discussed. The resulting import statements make it clear to the reader that custom implicits are being used.

To finish, note that Scala has several implicit wrapper types for Java types like `String` and `Array`. For example, the following methods appear to be `String` methods, but they are actually implemented by `WrappedString` (*http://bit.ly/1wO9UFE*):

```
scala> val s = "Programming Scala"
s: String = Programming Scala

scala> s.reverse
res0: String = alacS gnimmargorP

scala> s.capitalize
res1: String = Programming Scala

scala> s.foreach(c => print(s"$c-"))
P-r-o-g-r-a-m-m-i-n-g- -S-c-a-l-a-
```

The implicit conversions for the built-in "Wrapped" types are always in scope. They are defined in `Predef` (*http://bit.ly/11QI0fF*).

Another example is the `Range` (*http://bit.ly/1wNfl5V*) type we saw earlier. For example, `1 to 100 by 3` represents every third integer from 1 to 100. You can now guess that the words to, by, and the exclusive range `until` are actually methods on wrapper types, not language keywords. For example, `scala.runtime.RichInt` (*http://bit.ly/179yv9F*) wraps `Int` and it has these methods. Similar wrapper types exist for the other numeric types in the same package: `RichLong` (*http://bit.ly/10anzKl*), `RichFloat` (*http://bit.ly/1voUaEU*), `RichDouble` (*http://bit.ly/14O87Sn*), and `RichChar` (*http://bit.ly/1voUcNd*). The types `scala.math.BigInt` (*http://bit.ly/13FUtUH*) and `scala.math.BigDecimal` (*http://bit.ly/1b7tLWP*) are already wrapper types for the Java equivalents, so they don't have their own wrapper types. They just implement the methods `to`, `until`, and `by` themselves.

Build Your Own String Interpolator

Let's look at a final example of an implicit conversion, one that lets us define our own string interpolation capability. Recall from "Interpolated Strings" on page 94 that Scala has several built-in ways to format strings through interpolation. For example:

```
val name = ("Buck", "Trends")
println(s"Hello, ${name._1} ${name._2}")
```

When the compiler sees an expression like `x"foo bar"`, it looks for an `x` method in `scala.StringContext` (*http://bit.ly/1tIhAIv*). The last line in the previous example is translated to this:

```
StringContext("Hello, ", " ", "").s(name._1, name._2)
```

The arguments passed to `StringContext.apply` are the "parts" around the `${…}` expressions that were extracted. The arguments passed to `s` are the extracted expressions. (Try experimenting with variations of this example.) There are also `StringContext` methods named `f` and `raw` for those forms of interpolation.

We can define our own interpolator using an implicit conversion in the usual way to "extend" `StringContext` with new methods. Let's flesh out the example shown on the `StringContext` Scaladoc (*http://bit.ly/1tIhAIv*) page, an interpolator that converts a simple JSON string to a `scala.util.parsing.json.JSONObject` (*http://bit.ly/108joiw*) object.[1]

We'll make a few simplifying assumptions. First, we won't handle arrays or nested objects, just "flat" JSON expressions like `{"a": "A", "b": 123, "c": 3.14159}`. Second, we'll require that the keys are hardcoded in the string and the values are all specified as interpolation parameters, e.g., `{"a": $a, "b": $b, "c": $c}`. This second restriction would be reasonable if we were using the implementation as a *template* mechanism for generating similar JSON objects with different values. Here it is:

```
// src/main/scala/progscala2/implicits/custom-string-interpolator.sc
import scala.util.parsing.json._

object Interpolators {
  implicit class jsonForStringContext(val sc: StringContext) {    // ❶
    def json(values: Any*): JSONObject = {                        // ❷
      val keyRE = """^\s{,]*(\S+):\s*""".r                        // ❸
      val keys = sc.parts map {                                   // ❹
```

---

1. In Scala 2.11, this `json` package is in the separate parser-combinators library discussed in "Examples: XML and JSON DSLs for Scala" on page 466.

```
        case keyRE(key) => key
        case str => str
      }
      val kvs = keys zip values                              // ❺
      JSONObject(kvs.toMap)                                   // ❻
    }
  }
}

import Interpolators._

val name = "Dean Wampler"
val book = "Programming Scala, Second Edition"

val jsonobj = json"{name: $name, book: $book}"             // ❼
println(jsonobj)
```

❶ Implicit classes must be defined inside objects to limit their scope. (This is a "safety measure.") The import statement after the class brings the implementation class into the scope of the code that needs it.

❷ A `json` method. It takes a variable argument list, the parameters embedded in the string, and it returns a constructed `scala.util.parsing.json.JSONObject` (*http://bit.ly/1O8joiw*).

❸ Regular expression to extract the key name from a string fragment.

❹ Extract the key names from the `parts` (string fragments), using the regular expression. If the regular expression doesn't match, just use the whole string, but it might be better to throw an exception to avoid using an invalid key string.

❺ "Zip" the keys and values together into a collection of key-value pairs. We'll discuss the `zip` method further after this list.

❻ Construct a `Map` using the key-value pairs and use it to construct the `JSONObject`.

❼ Use our string interpolator, just like the built-in versions.

Custom string interpolators don't have to return a `String`, like s, f, and raw return. We return a `JSONObject` instead. Hence, they can function as instance factories that are driven by data encapsulated in strings.

The `zip` method on collections is a handy way to line up the values between two collections, like a zipper. Here's an example:

```
scala> val keys = List("a", "b", "c", "d")
keys: List[String] = List(a, b, c, d)

scala> val values = List("A", 123, 3.14159)
values: List[Any] = List(A, 123, 3.14159)
```

```
scala> val keysValues = keys zip values
keysValues: List[(String, Any)] = List((a,A), (b,123), (c,3.14159))
```

The elements of the zipped collection are two-element tuples, (key1, value1), etc. Note that because one list is longer than the other, the extra elements at the end are simply dropped. That's actually what we want in json, because there is one more string fragment than there are value parameters. It's the trailing fragment at the end of the string and we don't need it.

Here's the output from the last two lines in a REPL session:

```
scala> val jsonobj = json"{name: $name, book: $book}"
jsonobj: scala.util.parsing.json.JSONObject = \
  {"name" : "Dean Wampler", "book" : "Programming Scala, Second Edition"}

scala> println(jsonobj)
{"name" : "Dean Wampler", "book" : "Programming Scala, Second Edition"}
```

The Expression Problem

Let's step back for a moment and ponder what we've just accomplished: we've effectively added a new method to all types without editing the source code for any of them!

This desire to extend modules without modifying their source code is called the *Expression Problem*, a term coined by Philip Wadler (*http://bit.ly/1ucWnbN*).

Object-oriented programming solves this problem with subtyping, more precisely called *subtype polymorphism*. We program to abstractions and use derived classes when we need changed behavior. Bertrand Meyer coined the term *Open/Closed Principle* to describe the OOP approach, where base types declare behavior in an abstraction and subtypes implement appropriate variations of the behavior, without modifying the base types.

Scala certainly supports this technique, but it has drawbacks. What if it's questionable that we should have that behavior defined in the type hierarchy in the first place? What if the behavior is only needed in a few contexts, while for most contexts, it's just a burden that the client code carries around?

It can be a burden for several reasons. First, the extra, unused code takes up system resources. A few cases don't matter much, but inevitably a mature code base will have a lot of this baggage. Second, it's also inevitable that most defined behaviors will be refined over time. Every change to an unused behavior forces unwanted changes on client code that doesn't use that behavior.

This problem led to the *Single Responsibility Principle*, a classic design principle that encourages us to define abstractions and implementing types with just a single behavior.

Still, in realistic scenarios, it's sometimes necessary for an object to combine several behaviors. For example, a service often needs to "mix in" the ability to log messages. Scala makes these *mixin* features relatively easy to implement, as we saw in "Traits: Interfaces and "Mixins" in Scala" on page 96. We can even declare objects that combine traits on the fly.

Dynamically typed languages typically provide *metaprogramming* facilities that allow you to modify classes in the runtime environment without modifying source code. This approach can partially solve the problem of types with rarely used behavior. Unfortunately, for most dynamic languages, any runtime modifications to a type are global, so all users are affected.

The implicit conversion feature of Scala lets us implement a statically typed alternative approach, called *type classes*, which was pioneered in Haskell—see, for example, *A Gentle Introduction to Haskell* (*http://bit.ly/1zRCMQX*). The name comes from Haskell and it shouldn't be confused with Scala's usual notion of classes.

Type Class Pattern

Type classes help us avoid the temptation of creating "kitchen-sink" abstractions, like Java's `Object`, because we can add behavior on an ad hoc basis. Scala's `->` pair-construction idiom is one example. Recall that we aren't modifying these types; we are using the implicit mechanism to wrap objects with types that provide the behaviors we need. It only appears that we are modifying the types, as seen in the source code.

Consider the ubiquitous `Object.toString` in Java, which Scala inherits as a JVM language. Note that Java's default `toString` is of little value, because it just shows the type name and its address in the JVM's heap. The syntax used by Scala for case classes is more useful and human readable. There are times when a machine-readable format like JSON or XML would also be very useful. With implicit conversions, it's feasible to "add" `toJSON` and `toXML` methods to any type. If `toString` weren't already present, we could use implicit conversions for it, as well.

Type classes in Haskell define the equivalent of an interface, then concrete implementations of it for specific types. The *Type Class Pattern* in Scala adds the missing interface piece that our example implementations of implicit conversions so far didn't provide.

Let's look at a possible `toJSON` type class:

```
// src/main/scala/progscala2/implicits/toJSON-type-class.sc

case class Address(street: String, city: String)
case class Person(name: String, address: Address)

trait ToJSON {
  def toJSON(level: Int = 0): String
```

```scala
  val INDENTATION = "  "
  def indentation(level: Int = 0): (String,String) =
    (INDENTATION * level, INDENTATION * (level+1))
}

implicit class AddressToJSON(address: Address) extends ToJSON {
  def toJSON(level: Int = 0): String = {
    val (outdent, indent) = indentation(level)
    s"""{
      |${indent}"street": "${address.street}",
      |${indent}"city":   "${address.city}"
      |$outdent}""".stripMargin
  }
}

implicit class PersonToJSON(person: Person) extends ToJSON {
  def toJSON(level: Int = 0): String = {
    val (outdent, indent) = indentation(level)
    s"""{
      |${indent}"name":    "${person.name}",
      |${indent}"address": ${person.address.toJSON(level + 1)}
      |$outdent}""".stripMargin
  }
}

val a = Address("1 Scala Lane", "Anytown")
val p = Person("Buck Trends", a)

println(a.toJSON())
println()
println(p.toJSON())
```

For simplicity, our `Person` and `Address` types have just a few fields and we'll format multiline JSON strings rather than objects in the `scala.util.parsing.json` (*http://bit.ly/1wNfXID*) package (see "Examples: XML and JSON DSLs for Scala" on page 466 for details).

We define a default indentation string in the `ToJSON` trait and a method that calculates the actual indentation for fields and for the closing brace of a JSON object {...}. The `toJSON` method takes an argument that specifies the indentation level; that is, how many units of `INDENTATION` to indent. Because of this argument for `toJSON`, clients must provide empty parentheses or an alternative indentation level. Note that we put double quotes around string values, but not integer values.

Running this script produces the following output:

```
{
  "street": "1 Scala Lane",
  "city":   "Anytown"
}
```

```
{
  "name":     "Buck Trends",
  "address": {
    "street": "1 Scala Lane",
    "city":    "Anytown"
  }
}
```

Scala doesn't allow the implicit and case keywords together. That is, an implicit class can't also be a case class. It wouldn't make much sense anyway, because the extra, auto-generated code for the case class would never be used. Implicit classes have a very narrow purpose.

Note that we used this mechanism to add methods to existing classes. Hence, another term for this capability is *extension methods*. Languages like C# and F# support a different mechanism for extension methods (see, for example, the Extension Methods page on the Microsoft Developer Network (*http://bit.ly/1xIhCj0*)). This term is perhaps more obvious than *type classes*, but the latter term is more widely used.

From another perspective, this capability is called *ad hoc polymorphism*, because the polymorphic behavior of toJSON is not tied to the type system, as in *subtype polymorphism*, the conventional object-oriented inheritance. Recall that we discussed a third kind, *paremetric polymorphism*, in "Abstract Types Versus Parameterized Types" on page 67, where containers like Seq[A] behave uniformly for any A type.

The Type Class Pattern is ideal for situations where certain clients will benefit from the "illusion" that a set of classes provide a particular behavior that isn't useful for the majority of clients. Used wisely, it helps balance the needs of various clients while maintaining the Single Responsibility Principle.

Technical Issues with Implicits

So what's not to like? Why not define types with very little behavior that are little more than "bags" of fields (sometimes called *anemic* types), then add all behaviors using type classes?

First, the extra code involved in defining implicits is extra work you have to do and the compiler must work harder to process implicits. Therefore, a project that uses implicits heavily is a project that is slow to build.

Implicit conversions also incur extra runtime overhead, due to the extra layers of indirection from the wrapper types. It's true that the compiler will inline some method calls and the JVM will do additional optimizations, but the extra overhead needs to be justified. In Chapter 14 we'll discuss *value types* where the extra runtime overhead is eliminated during compilation.

There are some technical issues involving the intersection with other Scala features, specifically subtyping (for a more complete discussion, see the thread (*http://bit.ly/1wOrmce*) from the *scala-debate* email group).

Let's use a simple example to demonstrate the point:

```
// src/main/scala/progscala2/implicits/type-classes-subtyping.sc

trait Stringizer[+T] {
  def stringize: String
}

implicit class AnyStringizer(a: Any) extends Stringizer[Any] {
  def stringize: String = a match {
    case s: String => s
    case i: Int => (i*10).toString
    case f: Float => (f*10.1).toString
    case other =>
      throw new UnsupportedOperationException(s"Can't stringize $other")
  }
}

val list: List[Any] = List(1, 2.2F, "three", 'symbol)

list foreach { (x:Any) =>
  try {
    println(s"$x: ${x.stringize}")
  } catch {
    case e: java.lang.UnsupportedOperationException => println(e)
  }
}
```

We define a contrived `Stringizer` abstraction. If we followed the example of `ToJSON` previously, we would create implicit classes for all the types we want to "stringize." There's a problem, though. If we want to process a list of instances with heterogeneous types, we can only pass *one* `Stringizer` instance implicitly in the `list map …` code. Therefore, we're forced to define an `AnyStringerize` class that embeds all knowledge of all types we know about. It even includes a default clause to throw an exception.

This is quite ugly and it violates a core rule in object-oriented programming that you should not write *switch* statements that make decisions based on types that might change. Instead, you're supposed to use polymorphic dispatch, such as the way `to String` works in both Scala and Java.

For a more involved attempt to make `ToJSON` work with a list of objects, see the example in the code distribution, *Implicits/type-classes-subtyping2.sc*.

To finish, here are a few other tips that can help you avoid potential problems.

Always specify the return type of an implicit conversion method. Allowing type inference to determine the return type sometimes yields unexpected results.

Also, the compiler does a few "convenient" conversions for you that are now considered more troublesome than beneficial (future releases of Scala will probably change these behaviors).

First, if you define a + method on a type and attempt to use it on an instance that actually isn't of the correct type, the compiler will instead call `toString` on the instance so it can then call the `String` + (concatenation) operation. So, if you get a mysterious error about a `String` being the wrong type in the particular context, it's probably for this reason.

Also, the compiler will "auto-tuple" arguments to a method when needed. Sometimes this is very confusing. Fortunately, Scala 2.11 now warns you:

```
scala> def m(pair:Tuple2[Int,String]) = println(pair)

scala> m(1, "two")
<console>:9: warning: Adapting argument list by creating a 2-tuple:
  this may not be what you want.
        signature: m(pair: (Int, String)): Unit
  given arguments: 1, "two"
 after adaptation: m((1, "two"): (Int, String))
                m(1,"two")
                  ^
(1,two)
```

It's okay if your head is spinning a bit at this point, but hopefully it's clear that implicits are a powerful tool in Scala, but they have to be used wisely.

Implicit Resolution Rules

When Scala looks for implicits, it follows a sequence of fairly sophisticated rules for the search, some of which are designed to resolve potential ambiguities.[2]

I'll just use the term "value" in the following discussion, although methods, values, or classes can be used, depending on the implicit scenario:

- Any type-compatible implicit value that doesn't require a prefix path. In other words, it is defined in the same scope, such as within the same block of code, within the same type, within its companion object (if any), and within a parent type.

- An implicit value that was imported into the current scope. (It also doesn't require a prefix path to use it.)

---

2. For a precise definition of the rules, see *The Scala Language Specification* (*http://bit.ly/1wNBOR8*), Chapter 7.

Imported values, the second bullet point, take precedence over the already-in-scope values.

In some cases, several possible matches are type compatible. The most specific match wins. For example, if the type of an implicit argument is Foo, then an implicit value in scope of type Foo will be chosen over an implicit value of type AnyRef, if both are in scope.

If two or more implicit values are ambiguous, such as they have the same specific type, it triggers a compiler error.

The compiler always puts some library implicits in scope, while other library implicits require an import statement. Let's discuss these implicits now.

Scala's Built-in Implicits

The source code for the Scala 2.11 library has more than 300 implicit methods, values, and types. Most of them are methods, and most of those are used to convert from one type to another. Because it's important to know what implicits might affect your code, let's discuss them as groups, without listing every single one of them. It's definitely not important to learn every detail, but developing a "sense" of what implicits exist will be beneficial. So, skim this section as you see fit.

We've already discussed CanBuildFrom for collections. There is a similar CanCombine From used by various operations for combining instances, as the name implies. We won't list these definitions.

All of the companion objects for AnyVal types have widening conversions, such as converting an Int to a Long. Most actually just call toX methods on the type. For example:

```
object Int {
  ...
  implicit def int2long(x: Int): Long = x.toLong
  ...
}
```

The following code snippits list these AnyVal implicit conversions. Note that because of the implicit conversion feature, the Scala grammar doesn't need to implement the most common type conversions that other language grammars have to implement.

From the Byte (*http://bit.ly/1sOS3Gk*) companion object:

```
implicit def byte2short(x: Byte): Short = x.toShort
implicit def byte2int(x: Byte): Int = x.toInt
implicit def byte2long(x: Byte): Long = x.toLong
implicit def byte2float(x: Byte): Float = x.toFloat
implicit def byte2double(x: Byte): Double = x.toDouble
```

From the Char (*http://bit.ly/1wOfGWV*) companion object:

```
// From the scala.Char companion object:
implicit def char2int(x: Char): Int = x.toInt
implicit def char2long(x: Char): Long = x.toLong
implicit def char2float(x: Char): Float = x.toFloat
implicit def char2double(x: Char): Double = x.toDouble
```

From the `Short` (*http://bit.ly/1E8xY8y*) companion object:

```
implicit def short2int(x: Short): Int = x.toInt
implicit def short2long(x: Short): Long = x.toLong
implicit def short2float(x: Short): Float = x.toFloat
implicit def short2double(x: Short): Double = x.toDouble
```

From the `Int` (*http://bit.ly/1wOaKCf*) companion object:

```
implicit def int2long(x: Int): Long = x.toLong
implicit def int2float(x: Int): Float = x.toFloat
implicit def int2double(x: Int): Double = x.toDouble
```

From the `Long` (*http://bit.ly/1yMo2P4*) companion object:

```
implicit def long2float(x: Long): Float = x.toFloat
implicit def long2double(x: Long): Double = x.toDouble
```

From the `Float` (*http://bit.ly/1toBg4x*) companion object:

```
implicit def float2double(x: Float): Double = x.toDouble
```

The `scala.math` types `BigInt` and `BigDecimal` have converters from many of the Any
Val types and from the corresponding Java implementations. From the `BigDecimal`
(*http://bit.ly/13p5R89*) companion object:

```
implicit def int2bigDecimal(i: Int): BigDecimal = apply(i)
implicit def long2bigDecimal(l: Long): BigDecimal = apply(l)
implicit def double2bigDecimal(d: Double): BigDecimal = ...
implicit def javaBigDecimal2bigDecimal(x: BigDec): BigDecimal = apply(x)
```

The calls to `apply` are invocations of the `BigDecimal.apply` factory methods. These
implicits are a convenient, alternative way of invoking these methods.

From the `BigInt` (*http://bit.ly/10ao7jo*) companion object:

```
implicit def int2bigInt(i: Int): BigInt = apply(i)
implicit def long2bigInt(l: Long): BigInt = apply(l)
implicit def javaBigInteger2bigInt(x: BigInteger): BigInt = apply(x)
```

`Option` (*http://bit.ly/1G2G30k*) can be converted to a list of zero or one items:

```
implicit def option2Iterable[A](xo: Option[A]): Iterable[A] = xo.toList
```

Scala uses many of Java's types, including `Array[T]` and `String`. There are corresponding `ArrayOps[T]` and `StringOps` types that provide the operations commonly defined
for all Scala collections. So, implicit conversions to and from these wrapper types are
useful. Other operations are defined on types with the word `Wrapper` in their name.

Most are defined in Predef (*http://bit.ly/11QI0fF*). Some of these definitions have the @inline (*http://bit.ly/1u1jIMU*) annotation, which encourages the compiler to try especially hard to inline the method call, eliminating the stack frame overhead. There is a corresponding @noinline (*http://bit.ly/10aoavB*) annotation that prevents the compiler from attempting to inline the method call, even if it can.

Several methods convert one type to another, such as wrapping a type in a new type that provides additional methods:

```scala
@inline implicit def augmentString(x: String): StringOps = new StringOps(x)
@inline implicit def unaugmentString(x: StringOps): String = x.repr
implicit def tuple2ToZippedOps[T1, T2](x: (T1, T2))
  = new runtime.Tuple2Zipped.Ops(x)
implicit def tuple3ToZippedOps[T1, T2, T3](x: (T1, T2, T3))
  = new runtime.Tuple3Zipped.Ops(x)
implicit def genericArrayOps[T](xs: Array[T]): ArrayOps[T] = ...

implicit def booleanArrayOps(xs: Array[Boolean]): ArrayOps[Boolean] =
  = new ArrayOps.ofBoolean(xs)
...       // Similar functions for the other AnyVal types.
implicit def refArrayOps[T <: AnyRef](xs: Array[T]): ArrayOps[T]
  = new ArrayOps.ofRef[T](xs)

@inline implicit def byteWrapper(x: Byte) = new runtime.RichByte(x)
...       // Similar functions for the other AnyVal types.

implicit def genericWrapArray[T](xs: Array[T]): WrappedArray[T] = ...
implicit def wrapRefArray[T <: AnyRef](xs: Array[T]): WrappedArray[T] = ...
implicit def wrapIntArray(xs: Array[Int]): WrappedArray[Int] = ...
...       // Similar functions for the other AnyVal types.

implicit def wrapString(s: String): WrappedString = ...
implicit def unwrapString(ws: WrappedString): String = ...
```

To understand the purpose of runtime.Tuple2Zipped.Ops, first note that most of the collections have a zip method for joining two collections paired by elements, like closing a zipper:

```scala
scala> val zipped = List(1,2,3) zip List(4,5,6)
zipped: List[(Int, Int)] = List((1,4), (2,5), (3,6))
```

Such zipped collections are useful for pair-wise operations, for example:

```scala
scala> val products = zipped map { case (x,y) => x * y }
products: List[Int] = List(4, 10, 18)
```

Note that we used the pattern-matching trick for anonymous functions that take tuple arguments, because each Int pair is passed to the anonymous function that multiplies the pair elements.

`Tuple2Zipper.Ops` and `Tuple3Zipper.Ops` provide an `invert` method to convert a two- and three-element tuple of collections, respectively, into collections of tuples. In other words, they zip collections that are already held in a tuple. For example:

```scala
scala> val pair = (List(1,2,3), List(4,5,6))
pair: (List[Int], List[Int]) = (List(1, 2, 3),List(4, 5, 6))

scala> val unpair = pair.invert
unpair: List[(Int, Int)] = List((1,4), (2,5), (3,6))

val pair = (List(1,2,3), List("one", "two", "three"))
tuple2ToZippedOps(pair) map {case (int, string) => (int*2, string.toUpperCase)}

val pair = (List(1,2,3), List(4,5,6))
pair map { case (int1, int2) => int1 + int2 }
```

Next, there are a lot of conversions to and from other Java types. Again, from `Predef` (*http://bit.ly/11QI0fF*):

```scala
implicit def byte2Byte(x: Byte) = java.lang.Byte.valueOf(x)
implicit def Byte2byte(x: java.lang.Byte): Byte = x.byteValue
...       // Similar functions for the other AnyVal types.
```

For completeness, recall these definitions from `Predef` that we used earlier in the chapter:

```scala
implicit def conforms[A]: A <:< A = ...
implicit def tpEquals[A]: A =:= A = ...
```

To convert between `java.util.Random` (*http://bit.ly/1s0SdNX*) and `scala.util.Random` (*http://bit.ly/12wYbIE*):

```scala
implicit def javaRandomToRandom(r: java.util.Random): Random = new Random(r)
```

The `scala.collection.convert` (*http://bit.ly/1tpuHx4*) package has several traits that add conversion methods between Java and Scala collections, which are very handy for Java interopability. Actually, where possible, no conversion is done for efficiency, but the abstractions of the target collection are layered on top of the underlying collection.

Here are the "decorations" of Scala collections as Java collections defined in `DecorateAsJava` (*http://bit.ly/1u1k3zb*). The return type annotations are wrapped to fit the page and the `ju` and `jl` are import aliases for `java.lang` and `java.util` in the actual source code for `DecorateAsJava`. The `AsJava*` types are helpers for exposing operations:

```scala
implicit def asJavaIteratorConverter[A](i : Iterator[A]):
  AsJava[ju.Iterator[A]] = ...
implicit def asJavaEnumerationConverter[A](i : Iterator[A]):
  AsJavaEnumeration[A] = ...
implicit def asJavaIterableConverter[A](i : Iterable[A]):
  AsJava[jl.Iterable[A]] = ...
implicit def asJavaCollectionConverter[A](i : Iterable[A]):
```

```
AsJavaCollection[A] = ...
implicit def bufferAsJavaListConverter[A](b : mutable.Buffer[A]):
  AsJava[ju.List[A]] = ...
implicit def mutableSeqAsJavaListConverter[A](b : mutable.Seq[A]):
  AsJava[ju.List[A]] = ...
implicit def seqAsJavaListConverter[A](b : Seq[A]):
  AsJava[ju.List[A]] = ...
implicit def mutableSetAsJavaSetConverter[A](s : mutable.Set[A]):
  AsJava[ju.Set[A]] = ...
implicit def setAsJavaSetConverter[A](s : Set[A]):
  AsJava[ju.Set[A]] = ...
implicit def mutableMapAsJavaMapConverter[A, B](m : mutable.Map[A, B]):
  AsJava[ju.Map[A, B]] = ...
implicit def asJavaDictionaryConverter[A, B](m : mutable.Map[A, B]):
  AsJavaDictionary[A, B] = ...
implicit def mapAsJavaMapConverter[A, B](m : Map[A, B]):
  AsJava[ju.Map[A, B]] = ...
implicit def mapAsJavaConcurrentMapConverter[A, B](m: concurrent.Map[A, B]):
  AsJava[juc.ConcurrentMap[A, B]] = ...
```

We can decorate Java collections as Scala collections using implicits defined in `Decora`
`teAsScala` (*http://bit.ly/1yMouNm*):

```
implicit def asScalaIteratorConverter[A](i : ju.Iterator[A]):
  AsScala[Iterator[A]] = ...
implicit def enumerationAsScalaIteratorConverter[A](i : ju.Enumeration[A]):
  AsScala[Iterator[A]] = ...
implicit def iterableAsScalaIterableConverter[A](i : jl.Iterable[A]):
  AsScala[Iterable[A]] = ...
implicit def collectionAsScalaIterableConverter[A](i : ju.Collection[A]):
  AsScala[Iterable[A]] = ...
implicit def asScalaBufferConverter[A](l : ju.List[A]):
  AsScala[mutable.Buffer[A]] = ...
implicit def asScalaSetConverter[A](s : ju.Set[A]):
  AsScala[mutable.Set[A]] = ...
implicit def mapAsScalaMapConverter[A, B](m : ju.Map[A, B]):
  AsScala[mutable.Map[A, B]] = ...
implicit def mapAsScalaConcurrentMapConverter[A, B](m: juc.ConcurrentMap[A, B]):
  AsScala[concurrent.Map[A, B]] = ...
implicit def dictionaryAsScalaMapConverter[A, B](p: ju.Dictionary[A, B]):
  AsScala[mutable.Map[A, B]] = ...
implicit def propertiesAsScalaMapConverter(p: ju.Properties):
  AsScala[mutable.Map[String, String]] = ...
```

While the methods are defined in these `traits`, the object `JavaConverters` (*http://bit.ly/
1sRrYIR*) gives you the hook to bring them in scope with an important statement:

```
import scala.collection.JavaConverters._
```

The purpose of these converters is to allow you to call `asJava` on a Scala collection to
create a corresponding Java collection, and call `asScala` on a Java collection to go the

other way. These methods effectively define a one-to-one correspondence between one Scala collection type and one Java collection type.

For the more general case, where you want to choose the output collection type, rather than accept the one choice asScala or asJava offer, there are additional conversion methods defined in WrapAsJava (*http://bit.ly/1toBFUs*) and WrapAsScala (*http://bit.ly/1wNgUAB*).

Here are the WrapAsJava (*http://bit.ly/1toBFUs*) methods:

```scala
implicit def asJavaIterator[A](it: Iterator[A]): ju.Iterator[A] = ...
implicit def asJavaEnumeration[A](it: Iterator[A]): ju.Enumeration[A] = ...
implicit def asJavaIterable[A](i: Iterable[A]): jl.Iterable[A] = ...
implicit def asJavaCollection[A](it: Iterable[A]): ju.Collection[A] = ...
implicit def bufferAsJavaList[A](b: mutable.Buffer[A]): ju.List[A] = ...
implicit def mutableSeqAsJavaList[A](seq: mutable.Seq[A]): ju.List[A] = ...
implicit def seqAsJavaList[A](seq: Seq[A]): ju.List[A] = ...
implicit def mutableSetAsJavaSet[A](s: mutable.Set[A]): ju.Set[A] = ...
implicit def setAsJavaSet[A](s: Set[A]): ju.Set[A] = ...
implicit def mutableMapAsJavaMap[A, B](m: mutable.Map[A, B]): ju.Map[A, B] =...
implicit def asJavaDictionary[A, B](m: mutable.Map[A, B]): ju.Dictionary[A, B]
implicit def mapAsJavaMap[A, B](m: Map[A, B]): ju.Map[A, B] = ...
implicit def mapAsJavaConcurrentMap[A, B](m: concurrent.Map[A, B]):
    juc.ConcurrentMap[A, B] = ...
```

Here are the WrapAsScala (*http://bit.ly/1wNgUAB*) methods:

```scala
implicit def asScalaIterator[A](it: ju.Iterator[A]): Iterator[A] = ...
implicit def enumerationAsScalaIterator[A](i: ju.Enumeration[A]):
    Iterator[A] = ...
implicit def iterableAsScalaIterable[A](i: jl.Iterable[A]): Iterable[A] = ...
implicit def collectionAsScalaIterable[A](i: ju.Collection[A]): Iterable[A]=...
implicit def asScalaBuffer[A](l: ju.List[A]): mutable.Buffer[A] = ...
implicit def asScalaSet[A](s: ju.Set[A]): mutable.Set[A] = ...
implicit def mapAsScalaMap[A, B](m: ju.Map[A, B]): mutable.Map[A, B] = ...
implicit def mapAsScalaConcurrentMap[A, B](m: juc.ConcurrentMap[A, B]):
    concurrent.Map[A, B] = ...
implicit def dictionaryAsScalaMap[A, B](p: ju.Dictionary[A, B]):
    mutable.Map[A, B] = ...
implicit def propertiesAsScalaMap(p: ju.Properties):
    mutable.Map[String, String] = ...
[source,scala]
```

Similar to JavaConverters, the methods defined in these traits can be imported into the current scope using the object JavaConversions (*http://bit.ly/1toBMiX*):

```scala
import scala.collection.JavaConversions._
```

Because sorting of collections is so commonly done, there are many implicits for Ordering[T] (*http://bit.ly/1O8kxqm*), where T is a String, one of the AnyVal types that can be converted to Numeric (*http://bit.ly/1Oan8zL*), or a user-defined ordering. (Numeric is an abstraction for typical operations on numbers.) See also Ordered[T].

We won't list the implicit `Orderings` defined in many collection types, but here are the definitions in `Ordering[T]`:

```
implicit def ordered[A <% Comparable[A]]: Ordering[A] = ...
implicit def comparatorToOrdering[A](implicit c: Comparator[A]):Ordering[A]=...
implicit def seqDerivedOrdering[CC[X] <: scala.collection.Seq[X], T](
  implicit ord: Ordering[T]): Ordering[CC[T]] = ...
implicit def infixOrderingOps[T](x: T)(implicit ord: Ordering[T]):
  Ordering[T]#Ops = ...
implicit def Option[T](implicit ord: Ordering[T]): Ordering[Option[T]] = ...
implicit def Iterable[T](implicit ord: Ordering[T]): Ordering[Iterable[T]] =...
implicit def Tuple2[T1, T2](implicit ord1: Ordering[T1], ord2: Ordering[T2]):
  Ordering[(T1, T2)] = ...
...         // Similar functions for Tuple3 through Tuple9.
```

Finally, there are several conversions that support "mini-DSLs" for concurrency and process management.

First, the `scala.concurrent.duration` (*http://bit.ly/1rGK9km*) package provides useful ways of defining time durations (we'll see them and the other types mentioned next for concurrency in use in Chapter 17):

```
implicit def pairIntToDuration(p: (Int, TimeUnit)): Duration = ...
implicit def pairLongToDuration(p: (Long, TimeUnit)): FiniteDuration = ...
implicit def durationToPair(d: Duration): (Long, TimeUnit) = ...
```

Here are miscellaneous conversions in several files in the `scala.concurrent` (*http://bit.ly/1OFzktw*) package:

```
// scala.concurrent.FutureTaskRunner:
implicit def futureAsFunction[S](x: Future[S]): () => S

// scala.concurrent.JavaConversions:
implicit def asExecutionContext(exec: ExecutorService):
  ExecutionContextExecutorService = ...
implicit def asExecutionContext(exec: Executor): ExecutionContextExecutor = ...

// scala.concurrent.Promise:
private implicit def internalExecutor: ExecutionContext = ...

// scala.concurrent.TaskRunner:
implicit def functionAsTask[S](fun: () => S): Task[S] = ...

// scala.concurrent.ThreadPoolRunner:
implicit def functionAsTask[S](fun: () => S): Task[S] = ...
implicit def futureAsFunction[S](x: Future[S]): () => S = ...
```

Lastly, `Process` (*http://bit.ly/1tIj4mh*) supports operating systems processes, analogous to running UNIX shell commands:

```
implicit def buildersToProcess[T](builders: Seq[T])(
  implicit convert: T => Source): Seq[Source] = ...
implicit def builderToProcess(builder: JProcessBuilder): ProcessBuilder = ...
```

```
implicit def fileToProcess(file: File): FileBuilder = ...
implicit def urlToProcess(url: URL): URLBuilder = ...
implicit def stringToProcess(command: String): ProcessBuilder = ...
implicit def stringSeqToProcess(command: Seq[String]): ProcessBuilder = ...
```

Whew! This is a long list, but hopefully skimming the list gives you a sense of how the Scala library supports and uses implicits.

Wise Use of Implicits

The implicit argument mechanism is quite powerful for building DSLs (domain-specific languages) and other APIs that minimize boilerplate. However, because the implicit arguments and values passed for them are almost invisible, code comprehension is harder. So, they should be used wisely.

One way to improve their visibility is to adopt the practice of putting implicit values in a special package named `implicits` or an object named `Implicits`. That way, readers of code see the word "implicit" in the imports and know to be aware of their presence, in addition to Scala's ubiquitous, built-in implicits. Fortunately, IDEs can now show when implicits are being invoked, too.

Recap and What's Next

We dove into the details of implicits in Scala. I hope you can appreciate their power and utility, but also their drawbacks.

Now we're ready to dive into the principles of functional programming. We'll start with a discussion of the core concepts and why they are important. Then we'll look at the powerful functions provided by most container types in the library. We'll see how we can use those functions to construct concise, yet powerful programs.

## CHAPTER 6

Functional Programming in Scala

It is better to have 100 functions operate on one data structure than 10 functions on 10 data structures.

— Alan J. Perlis

Every decade or two, a major computing idea goes mainstream. The idea may have lurked in the background of academic Computer Science research or in obscure corners of industry, perhaps for decades. The transition to mainstream acceptance comes in response to a perceived problem for which the idea is well suited. Object-oriented programming (OOP), which was invented in the 1960s, went mainstream in the 1980s, arguably in response to the emergence of graphical user interfaces, for which the OOP paradigm is a natural fit.

Functional programming (FP) is going through a similar breakout. Long the topic of research and actually much older than OOP, FP offers effective techniques for three major challenges of our time:

1. The need for pervasive concurrency, so we can scale our applications horizontally and improve their resiliency against service disruptions. Hence, concurrent programming is now an essential skill for every developer to master.

2. The need to write data-centric (e.g., "Big Data") applications. Of course, at some level all programs are about data, but the recent Big Data trend has highlighted the importance of effective techniques for working with large data sets.

3. The need to write bug-free applications. Of course, this is a challenge as old as programming itself, but FP gives us new tools, from mathematics, that move us further in the direction of *provably bug-free* programs.

Immutability eliminates the hardest problem in concurrency, coordinating access to shared, mutable state. Hence, writing immutable code is an essential tool for writing robust, concurrent programs and embracing FP is the best way to write immutable code.

Immutability and the rigor of functional thinking in general, based on its mathematical roots, also lead to programs with fewer logic flaws.

The benefits of FP for data-centric applications will become apparent as we master the functional operations discussed in this and subsequent chapters. We'll explore the connection in depth in Chapter 18. Many of the topics we discuss in this book help minimize programming bugs. We'll highlight particular benefits as we go.

In the book so far, I've assumed that you know at least the basics of OOP, but because FP is less widely understood, we'll spend some time going over basic concepts. We'll see that FP is not only a very effective way to approach concurrent programming, which we'll explore in depth in Chapter 17 and "Robust, Scalable Concurrency with Actors" on page 429, but FP also improves our OO code, as well.

We'll begin our discussion of functional programming ignoring Scala for a moment. As a mixed-paradigm language, it doesn't *require* the rules of functional programming to be followed, but it recommends that you do so whenever possible.

What Is Functional Programming?

Don't all programming languages have functions of some sort? Whether they are called methods, procedures, or GOTOs, programmers are always writing functions.

Functional programming is based on the rules of mathematics for the behavior of functions and values. This starting point has far-reaching implications for software.

Functions in Mathematics

In mathematics, functions have no *side effects*. Consider the classic function $sin(x)$:

$$y = sin(x)$$

No matter how much work $sin(x)$ does, all the results are returned and assigned to y. No global state of any kind is modified internally by $sin(x)$. Hence, we say that such a function is free of *side effects*, or *pure*.

Purity drastically simplifies the challenge of analyzing, testing, and debugging a function. You can do all these things without having to know anything about the context in which the function is invoked, subject to the behavior of other functions it might call.

This obliviousness to the surrounding context provides *referential transparency*, which has two implications. First, you can call such a function anywhere and be confident that it will always behave the same way, independent of the calling context. Because no global state is modified, concurrent invocation of the function is also straightforward and reliable. No tricky thread-safe coding is required.

The second sense of the term is that you can substitute the value computed by an expression for subsequent invocations of the expression. Consider, for example, the equation `sin(pi/2)` = 1. A code analyzer, such as the compiler or the runtime virtual machine, could replace repeated calls to `sin(pi/2)` with 1 with no loss of correctness, as long as `sin` is truly pure.

 A function that returns `Unit` can only perform side effects. It can only modify mutable state somewhere. A simple example is a function that just calls `println` or `printf`, where I/O modifies "the world."

Note that there is a natural uniformity between values and functions, due to the way we can substitute one for the other. What about substituting functions for values, or treating functions as values?

In fact, functions are *first-class* values in functional programming, just like data values. You can compose functions from other functions (for example, $tan(x) = sin(x) / cos(x)$). You can assign functions to variables. You can pass functions to other functions as arguments. You can return functions as values from functions.

When a function takes other functions as arguments or returns a function, it is called a *higher-order function*. In mathematics, two examples of higher-order functions from calculus are derivation and integration. We pass an expression, like a function, to the derivation "operation," which returns a new function, the derivative.

We've seen many examples of higher-order functions already, such as the `map` methods on the collection types, which take a single function argument that is applied to each element.

Variables That Aren't

The word "variable" takes on a new meaning in functional programming. If you come from a *procedural-oriented programming* background, of which traditional object-oriented programming is a subset, you are accustomed to variables that are *mutable*. In functional programming, variables are *immutable*.

This is another consequence of the mathematical orientation. In the expression $y = sin(x)$, once you pick x, then y is fixed. Similarly, values are immutable; if you increment the integer 3 by 1, you don't "modify the 3 object," you create a new value to represent 4. We've already been using the term "value" as a synonym for immutable instances.

Immutability is difficult to work with at first when you're not used to it. If you can't change a variable, then you can't have loop counters, you can't have objects that change their state when methods are called on them, and you can't do input and output, which changes the state of the world! Learning to think in immutable terms takes some effort.

Obviously you can't be pure always. Without input and output, your computer would just heat the room. Practical functional programming makes principled decisions about where code should perform mutation and where code should be pure.

Why Aren't Input and Output Pure?

It's easy to grasp that idea that sin(x) is a pure function without side effects. Why are input and output considered side effects and therefore not pure? They modify the state of the world around us, such as the contents of files or what we see on the screen. They aren't referentially transparent either. Every time I call readline (defined in Predef (*http://bit.ly/11QI0fF*)), I get a different result. Every time I call println (also defined in Predef), I pass a different argument, but Unit is always returned.

This does not mean that functional programming is stateless. If so, it would also be useless. You can always represent state changes with new instances or new stack frames, i.e., calling functions and returning values.

Recall this example from Chapter 2:

```
// src/main/scala/progscala2/typelessdomore/factorial.sc

def factorial(i: Int): Long = {
  def fact(i: Int, accumulator: Int): Long = {
    if (i <= 1) accumulator
    else fact(i - 1, i * accumulator)
  }

  fact(i, 1)
}

(0 to 5) foreach ( i => println(factorial(i)) )
```

We calculate factorials using recursion. Updates to the accumulator are pushed on the stack. We don't modify a running value in place.

At the end of the example, we "mutate" the world by printing the results. All functional languages provide such mechanisms to escape purity for doing I/O and other necessary mutations. In hybrid languages like Scala that provide greater flexibility, the art is learning how to use mutation when you must in a deliberate, principled way. The rest of your code should be as pure as possible.

Immutability has enormous benefits for writing code that scales through concurrency. Almost all the difficulty of multithreaded programming lies in synchronizing access to shared, mutable state. If you remove mutability, the problems vanish. It is the

---

combination of referentially transparent functions and immutable values that make functional programming compelling as a better way to write concurrent software. The growing need to scale applications through concurrency has been a major driver in the growing interest in functional programming.

These qualities benefit programs in other ways, too. Almost all the constructs we have invented in 60-odd years of computer programming have been attempts to manage complexity. Higher-order, pure functions are called *combinators*, because they compose together very well as flexible, fine-grained building blocks for constructing larger, more complex programs. We've already seen examples of collection methods chained together to implement nontrivial logic with a minimum of code.

Pure functions and immutability drastically reduce the occurrence of bugs. Mutable state is the source of the most pernicious bugs, the ones that are hardest to detect with testing before deploying to production, and often the hardest bugs to fix.

Mutable state means that state changes made by one module are *unexpected* by other modules, causing a "spooky action at a distance" phenomenon.

Purity simplifies designs by eliminating a lot of the defensive boilerplate required in object-oriented code. It's common to encapsulate access to data structures in objects, because if they are mutable, we can't simply share them with clients. Instead, we add special accessor methods to control access, so clients can't modify the data outside our control. These accessors increase code size and therefore they increase the testing and maintenance burden. They also broaden the footprint of APIs, which increases the learning burden for clients.

In contrast, when we have immutable data structures, most of these problems simply vanish. We can make internal data public without fear of data loss or corruption. Of course, the general principles of minimal coupling and exposing coherent abstractions still apply. Hiding implementation details is still important for minimizing the API footprint.

A paradox of immutability is that performance can actually be faster than with mutable data. If you can't mutate an object, then you must copy it when the state changes, right? Fortunately, *functional data structures* minimize the overhead of making copies by sharing the unmodified parts of the data structures between the two copies.

In contrast, the data structures often used in object-oriented languages don't support efficient copying. A defensive client is forced to make expensive copies of mutable data structures when it's necessary to share the internal state stored in those data structures without risking corruption of them by unwanted mutation.

Another source of potential performance gains is the use of data structures with *lazy evaluation*, such as Scala's `Stream` (*http://bit.ly/1toy0G5*) type. A few functional languages, like Haskell, are lazy by default. What this means is that evaluation is delayed until an answer is required.[1]

Scala uses *eager* or *strict* evaluation by default, but the advantage of lazy evaluation is the ability to avoid work that won't be necessary. For example, when processing a very large stream of data, if only a tiny leading subset of the data is actually needed, processing all of it is wasteful. Even if all of it will eventually be needed, a lazy strategy can yield preliminary answers earlier, rather than forcing the client to wait until all the data has been processed.

So why isn't Scala lazy by default? There are many scenarios where lazy evaluation is less efficient and it is harder to predict the performance of lazy evaluation. Hence, most functional languages use eager evaluation, but most also provide lazy data structures when that model is best, such as handling a stream of data.

It's time to dive into the practicalities of functional programming in Scala. We'll discuss other aspects and benefits as we proceed. We're diving into Scala's functional programming support before its object-oriented support to encourage you to really understand its benefits. The path of least resistance for the Java developer is to adopt Scala as "a better Java," an improved object-oriented language with some strange, dark functional corners best avoided. I want to bring those corners into the light, so you can appreciate their beauty and power.

This chapter covers what I consider to be the essentials that every new Scala programmer needs to know. Functional programming is a large and rich field. We'll cover some of the more advanced topics that are less essential for new programmers in Chapter 16.

Functional Programming in Scala

As a hybrid object-functional language, Scala does not require functions to be pure, nor does it require variables to be immutable. It does encourage you to write your code this way whenever possible.

Let's quickly recap a few things we've seen already.

Here are several higher-order functions that we compose together to iterate through a list of integers, filter for the even ones, map each one to its value multiplied by two, and finally multiply them together using reduce:

```
// src/main/scala/progscala2/fp/basics/hofs-example.sc

(1 to 10) filter (_ % 2 == 0) map (_ * 2) reduce (_ * _)
```

The result is 122880.

---

1. There's a joke in the Haskell community that they have delayed success until the last possible minute.

Recall that `_ % 2 == 0`, `_ * 2`, and `_ * _` are *function literals*. The first two functions take a single argument assigned to the placeholder `_`. The last function, which is passed to `reduce`, takes two arguments.

The `reduce` function is used to multiply the elements together. That is, it "reduces" the collection of integers to a single value. The function passed to `reduce` takes two arguments, where each is assigned to a `_` placeholder. One of the arguments is the current element from the input collection. The other argument is the "accumulator," which will be one of the collection elements for the first call to `reduce` or the result returned by the last call to `reduce`. (Whether the accumulator is the first or the second argument depends on the implementation.) A requirement of the function passed to `reduce` is that the operation performed must be *associative*, like multiplication or addition, because we are not guaranteed that the collection elements will be processed in a particular order!

So, with a single line of code, we successfully "looped" through the list without the use of a mutable counter to track iterations, nor did we require mutable accumulators for the reduction work in progress.

Anonymous Functions, Lambdas, and Closures

Consider the following modification of the previous example:

```
// src/main/scala/progscala2/fp/basics/hofs-closure-example.sc

var factor = 2
val multiplier = (i: Int) => i * factor

(1 to 10) filter (_ % 2 == 0) map multiplier reduce (_ * _)

factor = 3
(1 to 10) filter (_ % 2 == 0) map multiplier reduce (_ * _)
```

We define a variable, `factor`, to use as the multiplication factor, and we extract the previous anonymous function `_ * 2` into a value called `multiplier` that now uses `factor`. Note that `multiplier` is a *function*. Because functions are first-class in Scala, we can define values that are functions. However, `multiplier` references `factor`, rather than a hardcoded value of 2.

Note what happens when we run the same code over the collection with two different values of `factor`. First, we get 122880 as before, but then we get 933120.

Even though `multiplier` was an immutable function value, its behavior changed when `factor` changed.

There are two variables in `multiplier`: `i` and `factor`. One of them, `i`, is a *formal parameter* to the function. Hence, it is *bound* to a new value each time `multiplier` is called.

However, `factor` is not a formal parameter, but a *free variable*, a reference to a variable in the enclosing scope. Hence, the compiler creates a *closure* that encompasses (or "closes over") `multiplier` and the external context of the unbound variables that `multiplier` references, thereby binding those variables as well.

This is why the behavior of `multiplier` changed after changing `factor`. It references `factor` and reads its current value each time. If a function has no external references, it is trivially closed over itself. No external context is required.

This would work even if `factor` were a local variable in some scope, like a method, and we passed `multiplier` to another scope, like another method. The free variable `factor` would be carried along for the ride:

```
// src/main/scala/progscala2/fp/basics/hofs-closure2-example.sc

def m1 (multiplier: Int => Int) = {
  (1 to 10) filter (_ % 2 == 0) map multiplier reduce (_ * _)
}

def m2: Int => Int = {
  val factor = 2
  val multiplier = (i: Int) => i * factor
  multiplier
}

m1(m2)
```

We call m2 to return a function value of type `Int => Int`. It returns the internal value `multiplier`. But m2 also defines a `factor` value that is out of scope once m2 returns.

We then call m1, passing it the function value returned by m2. Yet, even though `factor` is out of scope inside m1, the output is the same as before, 122880. The function returned by m2 is actually a *closure* that encapsulates a reference to `factor`.

There are a few partially overlapping terms that are used a lot:

Function
    An operation that is named or anonymous. Its code is not evaluated until the function is called. It may or may not have free (unbound) variables in its definition.

Lambda
    An anonymous (unnamed) function. It may or may not have free (unbound) variables in its definition.

Closure
    A function, anonymous *or* named, that closes over its environment to bind variables in scope to free variables within the function.

Different programming languages use these and other terms to mean slightly different things. In Scala, we typically just say *anonymous function* or *function literal* for lambdas and we don't distinguish closures from other functions unless it's important for the discussion.

Methods as Functions

While discussing variable capture in the preceding section, we defined an anonymous function `multiplier` as a value:

```scala
val multiplier = (i: Int) => i * factor
```

However, you can also use a method:

```scala
// src/main/scala/progscala2/fp/basics/hofs-closure3-example.sc

object Multiplier {
  var factor = 2
  // Compare: val multiplier = (i: Int) => i * factor
  def multiplier(i: Int) = i * factor
}

(1 to 10) filter (_ % 2 == 0) map Multiplier.multiplier reduce (_ * _)

Multiplier.factor = 3
(1 to 10) filter (_ % 2 == 0) map Multiplier.multiplier reduce (_ * _)
```

Note that `multiplier` is now a method. Compare the syntax of a method versus a function definition. Despite the fact `multiplier` is now a method, we use it just like a function, because it doesn't reference `this`. When a method is used where a function is required, we say that Scala *lifts* the method to be a function. We'll see other uses for the term *lift* later on.

Purity Inside Versus Outside

If we called *sin(x)* thousands of times with the same value of *x*, it would be wasteful if it calculated the same value every single time. Even in "pure" functional libraries, it is common to perform internal optimizations like caching previously computed values (sometimes called *memoization*). Caching introduces side effects, as the state of the cache is modified.

However, this lack of purity should be invisible to the user (except perhaps in terms of the performance impact). The implementer is responsible for preserving the "contract," namely thread-safety and referential transparency.

Recursion

Recursion plays a larger role in pure functional programming than in imperative programming. Recursion is the pure way to implement "looping," because you can't have mutable loop counters.

Calculating factorials provides a good example. Here is a Java implementation with an imperative loop:

```java
// src/main/java/progscala2/fp/loops/Factorial.java
package progscala2.fp.loops;

public class Factorial {
  public static long factorial(long l) {
    long result = 1L;
    for (long j = 2L; j <= l; j++) {
      result *= j;
    }
    return result;
  }

  public static void main(String args[]) {
    for (long l = 1L; l <= 10; l++)
      System.out.printf("%d:\t%d\n", l, factorial(l));
  }
}
```

Both the loop counter j and the `result` are mutable variables. (For simplicity, we're ignoring input numbers that are less than or equal to zero.) The code is built by sbt, so we can run it from the sbt prompt as follows:

```
> run-main progscala2.fp.loops.Factorial
[info] Running FP.loops.Factorial
1:   1
2:   2
3:   6
4:   24
5:   120
```

```
 6:    720
 7:    5040
 8:    40320
 9:    362880
10:    3628800
[success] Total time: 0 s, completed Feb 12, 2014 6:12:18 PM
```

Here's a first pass at a recursive implementation:

```
// src/main/scala/progscala2/fp/recursion/factorial-recur1.sc
import scala.annotation.tailrec

// What happens if you uncomment the annotation??
// @tailrec
def factorial(i: BigInt): BigInt =
  if (i == 1) i
  else i * factorial(i - 1)
}

for (i <- 1 to 10)
  println(s"$i:\t${factorial(i)}")
```

The output is the same, but now there are no mutable variables. (You might think the i is mutable in the last for comprehension that tests the function. It isn't, as we'll see in Chapter 7.) Recursion is also the most natural way to express some functions.

However, there are two disadvantages with recursion: the performance overhead of repeated function invocations and the risk of a stack overflow.

It would be nice if we could write our pure functional, recursive implementation and the compiler or runtime would optimize it into a loop. Let's explore that option next.

Tail Calls and Tail-Call Optimization

A particular kind of recursion is called *tail-call* self-recursion, which occurs when a function calls itself and the call is the final ("tail") operation it does. Tail-call self-recursion is very important because it is the easiest kind of recursion to optimize by conversion into a loop. Loops eliminate the potential of a stack overflow, and they improve performance by eliminating the recursive function call overhead. Although tail-call self-recursion optimizations are not yet supported natively by the JVM, scalac will attempt them.

However, our factorial example is not a tail recursion, because factorial calls itself and *then* does a multiplication with the results. Recall from Chapter 2 that Scala has an annotation, @tailrec (*http://bit.ly/1wl47Y9*), you can add to recursive functions that you think are tail-call recursive. If the compiler can't optimize them, it will throw an exception.

Try removing the `//` in front of the `@tailrec` in the previous example and see what happens.

Fortunately, there is a tail-recursive implementation, which we saw in "Nesting Method Definitions and Recursion" on page 43. Here is a refined version of that implementation:

```
// src/main/scala/progscala2/fp/recursion/factorial-recur2.sc
import scala.annotation.tailrec

def factorial(i: BigInt): BigInt = {
  @tailrec
  def fact(i: BigInt, accumulator: BigInt): BigInt =
    if (i == 1) accumulator
    else fact(i - 1, i * accumulator)

  fact(i, 1)
}

for (i <- 1 to 10)
  println(s"$i:\t${factorial(i)}")
```

This script produces the same output as before. Now, `factorial` does all the work with a nested method, `fact`, that is tail recursive because it passes an `accumulator` argument to hold the computation in progress. This argument is computed with a multiplication *before* the recursive call to `fact` in the tail position. Also, the `@tailrec` annotation no longer triggers a compilation error, because the compiler can successfully convert the recursion to a loop.

If you call our original non-tail-recursive implementation of `factorial` with a large number—say 10,000—you'll cause a stack overflow on a typical desktop computer. The tail-recursive implementation works successfully, returning a very large number.

This idiom of nesting a tail-recursive function that uses an accumulator is a very useful technique for converting many recursive algorithms into tail-call recursions.

 The tail-call optimization *won't* be applied when a method that calls itself might be overridden in a derived type. Hence, the recursive method must be defined with the `private` or `final` keyword, or it must be nested in another method.

Trampoline for Tail Calls

A *trampoline* is a loop that works through a list of functions, calling each one in turn. The metaphor of bouncing the functions back and forth off a trampoline is the source of the name.

Consider a kind of recursion where a function A doesn't call itself recursively, but instead it calls another function B, which then calls A, which calls B, etc. This kind of back-and-forth recursion can also be converted into a loop using a *trampoline*, a data structure that makes it easier to perform the back-and-forth calculation without recursive function calls.

The Scala library has a `TailCalls` (*http://bit.ly/1q95Jyn*) object for this purpose.

The following code provides a somewhat inefficient way of determining if a number is even (because `isEven` and `isOdd` refer to each other, use the REPL's `:paste` mode to enter this example code):

```
// src/main/scala/progscala2/fp/recursion/trampoline.sc
// From: scala-lang.org/api/current/index.html#scala.util.control.TailCalls$
import scala.util.control.TailCalls._

def isEven(xs: List[Int]): TailRec[Boolean] =
  if (xs.isEmpty) done(true) else tailcall(isOdd(xs.tail))

def isOdd(xs: List[Int]): TailRec[Boolean] =
 if (xs.isEmpty) done(false) else tailcall(isEven(xs.tail))

for (i <- 1 to 5) {
  val even = isEven((1 to i).toList).result
  println(s"$i is even? $even")
}
```

The code bounces back and forth for each list element until the end of the list. If it hits the end of the list while it's in `isEven`, it returns `true`. If it's in `isOdd`, it returns `false`.

Running this script produces the following expected output:

```
1 is even? false
2 is even? true
3 is even? false
4 is even? true
5 is even? false
```

Partially Applied Functions Versus Partial Functions

Consider this simple method with two argument lists:

```
// src/main/scala/progscala2/fp/datastructs/curried-func.sc
```

```
scala> def cat1(s1: String)(s2: String) = s1 + s2
cat1: (s1: String)(s2: String)String
```

Suppose we want a special version that always uses "Hello" as the first string. We can define such a function using *partial application*:

```
scala> val hello = cat1("Hello ") _
hello: String => String = <function1>
```

```
scala> hello("World!")
res0: String = Hello World!

scala> cat1("Hello ")("World!")
res1: String = Hello World!
```

The REPL tells us that hello is a <function1>, a function of one argument.

We defined hello by calling cat1 with the *first* argument list, followed by an underscore (_). Try entering that expression *without* the underscore:

```
scala> val hello = cat1("Hello ")
>console<:8: error: missing arguments for method cat1;
follow this method with `_' if you want to treat it as a
partially applied function
        val hello = cat1("Hello ")
                  ^
```

The key phrase is *partially applied function*. For a function with more than one argument list, you can define a new function if you omit one or more of the *trailing* argument lists. That is, if you *partially apply* the arguments required. To avoid the potential of an ambiguous expression, Scala requires the trailing underscore to tell the compiler that you really meant to do this. Note that you're not allowed to omit trailing arguments within a single argument list and then apply them later. This feature only works for argument lists.

When we wrote cat1("Hello ")("World"), it's as if we start with a partial application, cat1("Hello ") _, but then we complete the application with the second argument list.

Let's clarify some confusing terminology. We've been discussing *partially applied functions* here, where we used a function in an expression, but we didn't provide all the argument lists it requires. Hence, a new function was returned that will expect the remaining argument lists to be applied either partially or fully later on.

We have also seen *partial functions*, described in "Partial Functions" on page 37. Recall that a partial function takes a single argument of some type, but it is not defined for all values of that type. Consider this example:

```
scala> val inverse: PartialFunction[Double,Double] = {
     |    case d if d != 0.0 => 1.0 / d
     | }
inverse: PartialFunction[Double,Double] = <function1>

scala> inverse(1.0)
res128: Double = 1.0

scala> inverse(2.0)
res129: Double = 0.5
```

```
scala> inverse(0.0)
scala.MatchError: 0.0 (of class java.lang.Double)
  at scala.PartialFunction$$anon$1.apply(PartialFunction.scala:248)
  at scala.PartialFunction$$anon$1.apply(PartialFunction.scala:246)
  ...
```

This isn't a very robust "inverse" function, because 1/d can blow up for very small, but nonzero d! Of course the real point is that `inverse` is "partial" for all `Doubles` except for `0.0`.

 A *partially applied function* is an expression with some, but not all of a function's argument lists applied (or provided), returning a new function that takes the remaining argument lists. A *partial function* is a single-argument function that is not defined for all values of the type of its argument. The literal syntax for a partial function is one or more `case` match clauses enclosed in curly braces.

Currying and Other Transformations on Functions

In "Methods with Multiple Argument Lists" on page 39, we introduced the idea that methods can have multiple argument lists. We discussed their practical uses, but there's also a fundamental property of functions that supports this idea, called *currying*, which is named after the mathematician Haskell Curry (for whom the Haskell language is named). Actually, Curry's work was based on an original idea of Moses Schönfinkel, but *Schönfinkeling* or maybe *Schönfinkelization* is harder to say…

Currying transforms a function that takes multiple arguments into a chain of functions, each taking a single argument.

In Scala, curried functions are defined with multiple argument lists, each with a *single* argument. Recall the `cat1` method we just looked at in the previous section:

```
// src/main/scala/progscala2/fp/datastructs/curried-func.sc

def cat1(s1: String)(s2: String) = s1 + s2
```

We can also use the following syntax to define a curried function:

```
def cat2(s1: String) = (s2: String) => s1 + s2
```

While the first syntax is more readable, the second syntax eliminates the requirement to add a trailing underscore when treating the curried function as a partially applied function:

```
scala> def cat2(s1: String) = (s2: String) => s1 + s2
cat2: (s1: String)String => String

scala> val cat2hello = cat2("Hello ")  // No _
cat2hello: String => String = <function1>
```

```
scala> cat2hello("World!")
res0: String = Hello World!
```

Calling both functions looks the same and returns the same result:

```
scala> cat1("foo")("bar")
res0: String = foobar

scala> cat2("foo")("bar")
res1: String = foobar
```

We can also convert methods that take multiple arguments into a curried form with the
curried method (notice how it has to be invoked, with partial-application syntax):

```
scala> def cat3(s1: String, s2: String) = s1 + s2
cat3: (s1: String, s2: String)String

scala> cat3("hello", "world")
res2: String = helloworld

scala> val cat3Curried = (cat3 _).curried
cat3Curried: String => (String => String) = <function1>

scala> cat3Curried("hello")("world")
res3: String = helloworld
```

In this example, we transform a function that takes two arguments, cat3, into its curried
equivalent that takes multiple argument lists. If cat3 had taken three parameters, its
curried equivalent would take three lists of arguments, and so on.

Note the type signature shown for cat3Curried, String => (String => String). Let's
explore this a bit more, using function values instead:

```
// src/main/scala/progscala2/fp/datastructs/curried-func2.sc

scala> val f1: String =>  String => String  =
    (s1: String) => (s2: String) => s1+s2
f1: String => (String => String) = <function1>

scala> val f2: String => (String => String) =
    (s1: String) => (s2: String) => s1 + s2
f2: String => (String => String) = <function1>

scala> f1("hello")("world")
res4: String = helloworld

scala> f2("hello")("world")
res5: String = helloworld
```

The type signature String => String => String is equivalent to String => (String
=> String). Calling f1 or f2 with an argument binds the first argument and returns a
new function of type String => String.

We can "uncurry" a function, too, using a method in the Function (*http://bit.ly/1zmu8ce*) object:

```scala
scala> val cat3Uncurried = Function.uncurried(cat3Curried)
cat3Uncurried: (String, String) => String = <function2>

scala> cat3Uncurried("hello", "world")
res6: String = helloworld

scala> val ff1 = Function.uncurried(f1)
ff1: (String, String) => String = <function2>

scala> ff1("hello", "world")
res7: String = helloworld
```

A practical use for currying is to specialize functions for particular types of data. You can start with an extremely general case, and use the curried form of a function to narrow down to particular cases.

As a simple example of this approach, the following code provides specialized forms of a base function that handles multiplication:

```scala
scala> def multiplier(i: Int)(factor: Int) = i * factor
multiplier: (i: Int)(factor: Int)Int

scala> val byFive = multiplier(5) _
byFive: Int => Int = <function1>

scala> val byTen = multiplier(10) _
byTen: Int => Int = <function1>

scala> byFive(2)
res8: Int = 10

scala> byTen(2)
res9: Int = 20
```

We start with multiplier, which takes two parameters: an integer, and another integer to multiply the first one by. We then curry two special cases of multiplier into function values. Don't forget the trailing underscores, as shown. We then use these two functions.

As you can see, currying and partially applied functions are closely related concepts. You may see them referred to almost interchangeably, but what's important is their application (no pun intended).

There are a few other function transformations worth knowing.

One scenario you'll encounter occasionally is when you have data in a tuple, let's say a three-element tuple, and you need to call a three-argument function:

```scala
scala> def mult(d1: Double, d2: Double, d3: Double) = d1 * d2 * d3
mult: (d1: Double, d2: Double, d3: Double)Double
```

```
scala> val d3 = (2.2, 3.3, 4.4)
d3: (Double, Double, Double) = (2.2,3.3,4.4)

scala> mult(d3._1, d3._2, d3._3)
res10: Double = 31.944000000000003
```

Ugly. Because of the literal syntax for tuples, e.g., (2.2, 3.3, 4.4), there seems to be a natural symmetry between tuples and function argument lists. We would love to have a new version of mult that takes the tuple itself as a single argument. Fortunately, the Function (*http://bit.ly/1zmu8ce*) object provides tupled and untupled methods for us:

```
scala> val multTupled = Function.tupled(mult _)
multTupled: ((Double, Double, Double)) => Double = <function1>

scala> multTupled(d3)
res11: Double = 31.944000000000003

scala> val multUntupled = Function.untupled(multTupled)
multUntupled: (Double, Double, Double) => Double = <function3>

scala> multUntupled(d3._1, d3._2, d3._3)
res12: Double = 31.944000000000003
```

Note how we needed to use partial application when we passed the mult *method* to Function.tupled, but when we passed *function* values to other Function methods, we didn't need to do this. This syntactic wart is a consequence of mixing object-oriented methods with function composition from functional programming. Fortunately, we can treat methods and functions uniformly, most of the time.

Finally, there are transformations between partial functions and functions that return options:

```
// src/main/scala/progscala2/fp/datastructs/lifted-func.sc

scala> val finicky: PartialFunction[String,String] = {
     |    case "finicky" => "FINICKY"
     | }
finicky: PartialFunction[String,String] = <function1>

scala> finicky("finicky")
res13: String = FINICKY

scala> finicky("other")
scala.MatchError: other (of class java.lang.String)
    ...

scala> val finickyOption = finicky.lift
finickyOption: String => Option[String] = <function1>

scala> finickyOption("finicky")
```

```
res14: Option[String] = Some(FINICKY)

scala> finickyOption("other")
res15: Option[String] = None

scala> val finicky2 = Function.unlift(finickyOption)
finicky2: PartialFunction[String,String] = <function1>

scala> finicky2("finicky")
res16: String = FINICKY

scala> finicky2("other")
scala.MatchError: other (of class java.lang.String)
  ...
```

Here is another use for the concept of *lifting* a function. If we have a partial function and we don't like the idea of an exception being thrown, we can lift the function into one that returns an Option instead. We can also "unlift" a function that returns an option to create a partial function.

Functional Data Structures

Functional programs put greater emphasis on the use of a core set of data structures and algorithms, compared to object languages, where it's more common to invent ad hoc classes that map to domain concepts. Even though code reuse was a promise of object-oriented programming, the proliferation of ad hoc classes undermines this goal. Hence, perhaps paradoxically, functional programs tend to be more concise and achieve better code reuse compared to comparable object programs, because there is less re-invention and more emphasis on implementing logic using the core data structures and algorithms.

What's in this core set depends on the language, but the minimum set typically includes sequential collections like lists, vectors, and arrays, plus maps and sets. Each collection supports the same higher-order, side effect–free functions, called *combinators*, such as map, filter, fold, etc. Once you learn these combinators, you can pick the appropriate collection to meet your requirements for data access and performance, then apply the same familiar combinators to manipulate that data. These collections are the most successful tools for code reuse and composition that we have in all of software development.

Sequences

Let's look at a few of the most common data structures used in Scala programs.

Many data structures are *sequential*, where the elements can be traversed in a predictable order, which might be the order of insertion or sorted in some way. The collection.Seq (*http://bit.ly/1voJwOs*) trait is the abstraction for all mutable and immutable sequential types. Child traits collection.mutable.Seq (*http://bit.ly/1tpocKD*) and col `lection.immutable.Seq` (*http://bit.ly/1wO3Ih1*) represent mutable and immutable sequences, respectively.

Linked lists are sequences and they are the most commonly used data structure in functional programs, beginning with the very first functional programming language, Lisp.

By convention, when adding an element to a list, it is prepended to the existing list, becoming the "head" of the new list. The existing list remains unchanged and it becomes the "tail" of the new list. Figure 6-1 shows two lists, `List(1,2,3,4,5)` and `List(2,3,4,5)`, where the latter is the tail of the former.

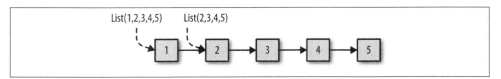

Figure 6-1. Two linked lists

Note that we created a new list from an existing list using an *O(1)* operation. We shared the tail with the original list and just constructed a new link from the new head element to the old list. This is our first example of an important idea in functional data structures, sharing a structure to minimize the cost of making copies. To support immutability, we need the ability to make copies with minimal cost.

Note that any other code using the original list is oblivious to the existence of the new list. Lists are immutable, so there's no risk that the other code will be surprised by unexpected mutations happening on another thread in the code that created the new list.

It should be clear from the way linked lists are constructed that computing the size of a list is *O(N)*, as are all other operations involving a traversal past the head of the list.

The following REPL session demonstrates constructing `Lists` (*http://bit.ly/1toub3N*) in Scala:

```
// src/main/scala/progscala2/fp/datastructs/list.sc

scala> val list1 = List("Programming", "Scala")
list1: Seq[String] = List(Programming, Scala)

scala> val list2 = "People" :: "should" :: "read" :: list1
list2: Seq[String] = List(People, should, read, Programming, Scala)
```

You can construct a list with the `List.apply` (*http://bit.ly/10FrqQC*) method, then prepend additional elements with the `::` method, called "cons" (for "construct"), creating new lists. Here we used the infix notation that drops the periods and parentheses. Recall that a method name that ends with a colon (:) binds to the *right*. Hence x :: list is actually list.::(x).

We can also use the :: method to construct a list by prepending elements to the Nil (*http://bit.ly/1wQuIOs*) empty list:

```scala
scala> val list3 = "Programming" :: "Scala" :: Nil
list3: Seq[String] = List(Programming, Scala)

scala> val list4 = "People" :: "should" :: "read" :: Nil
list4: Seq[String] = List(People, should, read)
```

Nil is equivalent to List.empty[Nothing], where Nothing (*http://bit.ly/1wObBSq*) is the subtype of *all* other types in Scala. See "The Scala Type Hierarchy" on page 294 for much ado about Nothing and why you can use it in this context.

Finally, you can concatenate two lists (or any sequence) together using the ++ method:

```scala
scala> val list5 = list4 ++ list3
list5: Seq[String] = List(People, should, read, Programming, Scala)
```

While it's still common to construct lists when appropriate, it is not recommended that methods be defined to take List arguments or return List values. Instead, use Seq (*http://bit.ly/1wQxJyd*), so that an instance of any subtype of Seq can be used, including List (*http://bit.ly/1toub3N*) and Vector (*http://bit.ly/1tozAI0*).

For Seq, the "cons" operator is +: instead of ::. Here is the previous session rewritten to use Seq. Note that when you use the Seq.apply (*http://bit.ly/1s0QyI0*) method on the companion object, it constructs a List, because Seq is a trait, not a concrete class:

```scala
// src/main/scala/progscala2/fp/datastructs/seq.sc

scala> val seq1 = Seq("Programming", "Scala")
seq1: Seq[String] = List(Programming, Scala)

scala> val seq2 = "People" +: "should" +: "read" +: seq1
seq2: Seq[String] = List(People, should, read, Programming, Scala)

scala> val seq3 = "Programming" +: "Scala" +: Seq.empty
seq3: Seq[String] = List(Programming, Scala)

scala> val seq4 = "People" +: "should" +: "read" +: Seq.empty
seq4: Seq[String] = List(People, should, read)

scala> val seq5 = seq4 ++ seq3
seq5: Seq[String] = List(People, should, read, Programming, Scala)
```

Note that we defined an empty tail for seq3 and seq4 using Seq.empty. Most of the Scala collections have companion objects with an empty method for creating an empty instance of the collection, analogous to Nil for lists.

The sequential collections define :+ and +:. How are they different and how do you remember which is which? Just recall that the : will always be on the side of the collection, e.g., list :+ x and x +: list. So, you *append* an element with :+ and *prepend* an element with +:.

```scala
scala> val seq1 = Seq("Programming", "Scala")
seq1: Seq[String] = List(Programming, Scala)

scala> val seq2 = seq1 :+ "Rocks!"
seq2: Seq[String] = List(Programming, Scala, Rocks!)
```

Scala only defines an immutable List. However, it also defines some mutable list types, such as ListBuffer (*http://bit.ly/108hxKt*) and MutableList (*http://bit.ly/1tIfQPr*), when there are good reasons to use a mutable alternative.

While List is a venerable choice for a sequence, consider using immutable.Vector (*http://bit.ly/1tozAI0*) instead, because it provides *O(1)* (constant time) performance for *all* operations, while List is *O(n)* for all operations that don't just involve accessing the head element.

Here is the previous Seq example rewritten to use Vector. Except for replacing the words Seq with Vector and changing variable names, the code is identical:

```scala
// src/main/scala/progscala2/fp/datastructs/vector.sc

scala> val vect1 = Vector("Programming", "Scala")
vect1: scala.collection.immutable.Vector[String] = Vector(Programming, Scala)

scala> val vect2 = "People" +: "should" +: "read" +: vect1
vect2: ...Vector[String] = Vector(People, should, read, Programming, Scala)

scala> val vect3 = "Programming" +: "Scala" +: Vector.empty
vect3: ...Vector[String] = Vector(Programming, Scala)

scala> val vect4 = "People" +: "should" +: "read" +: Vector.empty
vect4: ...Vector[String] = Vector(People, should, read)

scala> val vect5 = vect4 ++ vect3
vect5: ...Vector[String] = Vector(People, should, read, Programming, Scala)
```

However, we also get constant-time indexing.

```scala
scala> vect5(3)
res0: String = Programming
```

To finish our discussion of Seq, there is an important implementation issue you should know. To encourage the use of immutable collections, Predef (*http://bit.ly/1086O2z*) and several other types it uses expose several immutable collection types without requiring explicit import statements or fully qualified paths in your code. Examples include List (*http://bit.ly/1toub3N*) and Map (*http://bit.ly/15y3BGn*).

However, `Predef` also brings `scala.collection.Seq` (*http://bit.ly/1E8xLCt*) into scope, an exception to the rule of only exposing immutable collections. The types in `scala.collection` (*http://bit.ly/1DDiLKu*) are abstractions shared by both `immutable` (*http://bit.ly/1wQxSBO*) collections and by `mutable` (*http://bit.ly/1wl4TEy*) collections.

Although there is a `scala.collection.immutable.Seq` (*http://bit.ly/1wQxTWe*) (which subclasses `scala.collection.Seq`), the primary reason for exposing `scala.collection.Seq` instead is to make it easy to treat Java `Arrays` (*http://bit.ly/13p3phR*) as a `Seq` uniformly with other collections, but they are mutable. Most other mutable collections also implement `scala.collection.Seq`.

Now, `scala.collection.Seq` does not expose any methods for mutation, but using this "default" `Seq` does expose a potential concurrency risk to your code, because mutable collections are not thread-safe by default, so special handling of them is required.

For example, suppose your highly concurrent library has methods that take `Seq` arguments, but you really only want immutable collections passed in. Using `Seq` opens a hole, because a client could pass you an `Array` (*http://bit.ly/13p3phR*), for example.

 Keep in mind that the default `Seq` type is actually `scala.collection.Seq`. So, an instance of `Seq` passed to your code could be mutable and therefore thread-unsafe.

The current plan for the Scala 2.12 release or a subsequent release is to change the `scala.Seq` alias to point to `scala.collection.immutable.Seq`.

Until then, if you really want to enforce usage of `scala.collection.immutable.Seq` instead, use the following technique (adapted from Heiko Seeberger's blog (*http://bit.ly/1u1foNE*)).

We'll use a *package object*, which we introduced in "Package Objects" on page 66. We'll use it to define a new type alias for `Seq` that overrides the default definition. In fact, the `scala` package object is where `Seq` is defined to be an alias for `scala.collection.Seq`. We have been using the convention `fp.datastructs` in this section, so let's define a package object for this package:

```
// src/main/scala/progscala2/fp/datastructs/package.scala
package progscala2.fp
package object datastructs {
  type Seq[+A] = scala.collection.immutable.Seq[A]
  val Seq = scala.collection.immutable.Seq
}
```

Note that we specify the `package fp` first, not `package fp.datastructs`, followed by the `package object datastructs {…}` definition. The `package` keyword is part of the object definition. There can be only one package object per package. Finally, note the path to this file and the naming convention `package.scala` that are shown in the comment.

We declare a `type` alias and a `val`. Recall we discussed `type` declarations in "Abstract Types Versus Parameterized Types" on page 67. If user code includes the import statement `import fp.datastructs._`, then when `Seq` instances are declared (without a package qualifier) they will now use `scala.collection.immutable.Seq` instead of Scala's default `scala.collection.Seq`.

The `val Seq` declaration puts the companion object in scope, so statements like `Seq(1,2,3,4)` invoke the `scala.collection.immutable.Seq.apply` method.

What about packages underneath `fp.datastructs`? If you're implementing a package in this hierarchy, use the idiom for successive package statements we discussed in "Organizing Code in Files and Namespaces" on page 63:

```
package fp.datastructs    // Make Seq refer to immutable.Seq
package asubpackage       // Stuff in this package
package asubsubpackage    // The package I'm working on...
```

Consider using this idiom of defining type aliases in package objects for exposing the most important types in your own APIs.

Maps

Another common data structure is the `Map` (*http://bit.ly/15y3BGn*), sometimes referred to as a *hash*, *hash map*, or *dictionary* in various languages. Maps are used to hold pairs of keys and values and they shouldn't be confused with the `map` function on many data structures, although the names reflect a similar idea, associating a key with a value, or an input element with an output element.

Scala supports the special initialization syntax we saw previously:

```
// src/main/scala/progscala2/fp/datastructs/map.sc

scala> val stateCapitals = Map(
     |    "Alabama" -> "Montgomery",
     |    "Alaska"  -> "Juneau",
     |    "Wyoming" -> "Cheyenne")
stateCapitals: scala.collection.immutable.Map[String,String] =
  Map(Alabama -> Montgomery, Alaska -> Juneau, Wyoming -> Cheyenne)

scala> val lengths = stateCapitals map {
     |    kv => (kv._1, kv._2.length)
     | }
lengths: scala.collection.immutable.Map[String,Int] =
  Map(Alabama -> 10, Alaska -> 6, Wyoming -> 8)
```

```
scala> val caps = stateCapitals map {
    |    case (k, v) => (k, v.toUpperCase)
    | }

caps: scala.collection.immutable.Map[String,String] =
  Map(Alabama -> MONTGOMERY, Alaska -> JUNEAU, Wyoming -> CHEYENNE)

scala> val stateCapitals2 = stateCapitals + (
    |    "Virginia" -> "Richmond")
stateCapitals2: scala.collection.immutable.Map[String,String] =
  Map(Alabama -> Montgomery, Alaska -> Juneau,
  Wyoming -> Cheyenne, Virginia -> Richmond)

scala> val stateCapitals3 = stateCapitals2 + (
    |    "New York" -> "Albany", "Illinois" -> "Springfield")
stateCapitals3: scala.collection.immutable.Map[String,String] =
  Map(Alaska -> Juneau, Virginia -> Richmond, Alabama -> Montgomery,
  New York -> Albany, Illinois -> Springfield, Wyoming -> Cheyenne)
```

We learned previously that the key -> value idiom is actually implemented with an implicit conversion in the library. The Map.apply method expects a variable argument list of two-element tuples (pairs).

The example demonstrates two ways to define the function passed to map. Each key-value pair (tuple) is passed to this function. We can define it to take a single tuple argument or use the case match syntax discussed in Chapter 4 to decompose the tuple into a key and a value.

Finally, we see that we can add one or more new key-value pairs to the Map (creating new Maps), using +.

By the way, notice what happens if we drop the parentheses in the stateCapitals + ("Virginia" -> "Richmond") expression:

```
scala> stateCapitals + "Virginia" -> "Richmond"
res2: (String, String) = (Map(Alabama -> Montgomery, Alaska -> Juneau,
  Wyoming -> Cheyenne)Virginia,Richmond)
```

Wait, what? We end up with a pair of strings, (String,String). Unfortunately, we encountered Scala's eagerness to convert something to a String so the + method can be used if no suitable alternative exists. The compiler first evaluated this subexpression, stateCapitals.toString + "Virginia". Then the -> was applied to create the tuple with "Richmond" as the second element in the tuple. That is, the resulting tuple is ("Map(Alabama -> … -> Cheyenne)Virginia", "Richmond").

 If an expression involving a + turns into a String when you don't expect it, you probably encountered a situation where the compiler decided that the only viable way to parse the expression is to convert subexpressions to strings and add them together.

You can't actually call new Map("Alabama" -> "Montgomery", …); it is a trait. Instead, Map.apply constructs an instance of a class that is optimal for the data set, usually based on size. For example, there are concrete maps for one, two, three, and four key-value pairs.

Unlike List, there are immutable and mutable implementations of Map: scala.collection.immutable.Map[A,B] and scala.collection.mutable.Map[A,B], respectively. You have to import the mutable version explicitly, while the immutable version is already exposed by Predef. Both implementations define + and - operators for adding and removing elements, and ++ and - - operators for adding and removing elements defined in Iterators (which could be other sets, lists, etc.).

Sets

Sets are an example of unordered collections, so they aren't sequences. They also require each element to be unique:

```
// src/main/scala/progscala2/fp/datastructs/set.sc
scala> val states = Set("Alabama", "Alaska", "Wyoming")
states: scala.collection.immutable.Set[String] = Set(Alabama, Alaska, Wyoming)

scala> val lengths = states map (st => st.length)
lengths: scala.collection.immutable.Set[Int] = Set(7, 6)

scala> val states2 = states + "Virginia"
states2: scala.collection.immutable.Set[String] =
  Set(Alabama, Alaska, Wyoming, Virginia)

scala> val states3 = states2 + ("New York", "Illinois")
states3: scala.collection.immutable.Set[String] =
  Set(Alaska, Virginia, Alabama, New York, Illinois, Wyoming)
```

Just as for Map, the scala.collection.Set (*http://bit.ly/1tprGN8*) trait only defines methods for immutable operations. There are derived traits for immutable and mutable sets: scala.collection.immutable.Set (*http://bit.ly/1u1fTHy*) and scala.collection.mutable.Set (*http://bit.ly/1wl5arf*), respectively. You have to import the mutable version explicitly, while the immutable version is already imported by Predef. Both define + and - operators for adding and removing elements, and ++ and - - operators for adding and removing elements defined in Iterators (which could be other sets, lists, etc.).

Traversing, Mapping, Filtering, Folding, and Reducing

The common functional collections—sequences, lists, maps, sets, as well as arrays, trees, and others—all support several common operations based on read-only traversal. In fact, this uniformity can be exploited if any "container" type you implement also supports these operations. For example, an `Option` is a container with zero or one elements, for `None` or `Some`, respectively.

Traversal

The standard traversal method for Scala containers is `foreach`, which is defined in `scala.collection.IterableLike` (*http://bit.ly/1E8xVd5*) and has the following signature:

```scala
trait IterableLike[A] {  // Some details omitted.
  ...
  def foreach[U](f: A => U): Unit = {...}
  ...
}
```

Some subclasses of `IterableLike` may redefine the method to exploit local knowledge for better performance.

It actually doesn't matter what the `U` is, the return type of the function. The output of `foreach` is `Unit`, so it's a totally side-effecting function. Because it takes a function argument, `foreach` is a higher-order function, as are all the operations we'll discuss here.

Foreach is *O(N)* in the number of elements. Here is an example of its use for lists and maps:

```scala
// code-examples/progscala2/fp/datastructs/foreach.sc

scala> List(1, 2, 3, 4, 5) foreach { i => println("Int: " + i) }
Int: 1
Int: 2
Int: 3
Int: 4
Int: 5

scala> val stateCapitals = Map(
     |     "Alabama" -> "Montgomery",
     |     "Alaska"  -> "Juneau",
     |     "Wyoming" -> "Cheyenne")
stateCapitals: scala.collection.immutable.Map[String,String] =
  Map(Alabama -> Montgomery, Alaska -> Juneau, Wyoming -> Cheyenne)

// stateCapitals foreach { kv => println(kv._1 + ": " + kv._2) }

scala> stateCapitals foreach { case (k, v) => println(k + ": " + v) }
Alabama: Montgomery
Alaska: Juneau
Wyoming: Cheyenne
```

Note that for the Map example, the A type for the function passed to foreach is actually a pair (K,V) for the key and value types. We use a pattern-match expression to extract the key and value. The alternative tuple syntax is shown in the comment.[2]

foreach is not a pure function, because it can only perform side effects. However, once we have foreach, we can implement all the other, pure operations we'll discuss next, which are hallmarks of functional programming: mapping, filtering, folding, and reducing.

Mapping

We've encountered the map method before. It returns a new collection of the same size as the original collection, where each element of the original collection is transformed by a function. It is defined in **scala.collection.TraversableLike** (*http://bit.ly/1yMk4pK*) and inherited by most of the collections. Its signature is the following:

```scala
trait TraversableLike[A] {  // Some details omitted.
  ...
  def map[B](f: (A) ⇒ B): Traversable[B]
  ...
}
```

We saw examples of map earlier in this chapter.

Actually, this signature for map is not the one that's in the source code. Rather, it's the signature shown in the Scaladocs (*http://bit.ly/1yMk4pK*). If you look at the Scaladocs entry, you'll see a "full signature" part at the end, which you can expand by clicking the arrow next to it. It shows the actual signature, which is this:

```scala
def map[B, That](f: A => B)(implicit bf: CanBuildFrom[Repr, B, That]): That
```

Recent versions of Scaladocs show simplified method signatures for some methods, in order to convey the "essence" of the method without overwhelming the reader with implementation details. The essence of a map method is to transform one collection into a new collection of the same size and kind, where the elements of type A in the original collection are transformed into elements of type B by the function.

The actual signature carries additional implementation information. That is the output kind of collection, which is usually the same as the input collection. We discussed the purpose of the implicit argument bf: CanBuildFrom in "Capabilities" on page 135. Its existence means we can construct a That from the output of map and the function f. It also does the building for us. Repr is the internal "representation" used to hold the elements.

---

2. The anonymous function with the case clause is actually defining a PartialFunction, but it's really *total* because it will successfully match on all the inputs in this case.

Although the implicit `CanBuildFrom` complicates the method's real signature (and triggers complaints on mailing lists...), without it, we would not be able to create a new `Map`, `List`, or other collection that inherits from `TraversableLike`. This is a consequence of using an object-oriented type hierarchy to implement the collections API. All the concrete collection types could reimplement `map` and return new instances of themselves, but the lack of reuse would undermine the whole purpose of using an object-oriented hierarchy.

In fact, when the first edition of *Programming Scala* came out, Scala v2.7.X ruled the land, and the collections API didn't attempt to do this at all. Instead, `map` and similar methods just declared that they returned an `Iterable` or a similar abstraction and often it was just an `Array` or a similar low-level type that was returned.

From now on, I'll show the simplified signatures, to focus on the behaviors of the methods, but I encourage you to pick a collection, say `List` (*http://bit.ly/1toub3N*) or `Map` (*http://bit.ly/15y3BGn*), and look at the full signature for each method. Learning how to read these signatures can be a bit daunting at first, but it is essential for using the collections effectively.

There's another interesting fact about `map` worth understanding. Look again at its simplified signature. I'll just use `List` for convenience. The collection choice doesn't matter for the point I'm making:

```
trait List[A] {
  ...
  def map[B](f: (A) ⇒ B): List[B]
  ...
}
```

The argument is a function `A => B`. The behavior of `map` is actually `List[A] => List[B]`. This fact is obscured by the object syntax, e.g., `list map f`. If instead we had a separate module of functions that take `List` instances as arguments, it would look something like this:

```
// src/main/scala/progscala2/fp/combinators/combinators.sc

object Combinators1 {
  def map[A,B](list: List[A])(f: (A) ⇒ B): List[B] = list map f
}
```

(I'm cheating and using `List.map` to implement the function...)

What if we exchanged the argument lists?

```
object Combinators {
  def map[A,B](f: (A) ⇒ B)(list: List[A]): List[B] = list map f
}
```

Finally, let's use this function in a REPL session:

```scala
scala> object Combinators {
     |    def map[A,B](f: (A) ⇒ B)(list: List[A]): List[B] = list map f
     | }
defined module Combinators

scala> val intToString = (i:Int) => s"N=$i"
intToString: Int => String = <function1>

scala> val flist = Combinators.map(intToString) _
flist: List[Int] => List[String] = <function1>

scala> val list = flist(List(1,2,3,4))
list: List[String] = List(N=1, N=2, N=3, N=4)
```

The crucial point is the second and third steps. In the second step, we defined a function intToString of type Int => String. It knows nothing about Lists. In the third step, we defined a new function by *partial application* of Combinators.map. The type of flist is List[Int] => List[String]. Therefore, we used map to *lift* a function of type Int => String to a function of type List[Int] => List[String].

We normally think of map as transforming a collection with elements of type A into a collection of the same size with elements of type B, using some function f: A => B that knows nothing about the collection. Now we know that we can also view map as a tool to *lift* an ordinary function f: A => B to a new function flist: List[A] => List[B]. We used lists, but this is true for any container type with map.

Well, unfortunately, we can't quite do this with the ordinary map methods in the Scala library, because they are instance methods, so we can't partially apply them to create a lifted function that works for all instances of List, for example.

Maybe this is a limitation, a consequence of Scala's hybrid OOP-FP nature, but we're really talking about a corner case. Most of the time, you'll have a collection and you'll call map on it with a function argument to create a new collection. It won't be that often that you'll want to lift an ordinary function into one that transforms an arbitrary instance of a collection into another instance of the collection.

Flat Mapping

A generalization of the Map operation is flatMap, where we generate zero to many new elements for each element in the original collection. We pass a function that returns a collection, instead of a single element, and flatMap "flattens" the generated collections into one collection.

Here is the simplified signature for flatMap in TraversableLike, along with the signature for map again, for comparison:

```scala
def flatMap[B](f: A => GenTraversableOnce[B]): Traversable[B]
def map[B](f: (A) => B): Traversable[B]
```

Note that for map, the function f had the signature A => B. Now we return a collection, where GenTraversableOnce is an interface for anything that can be traversed at least once.

Consider this example:

```
// src/main/scala/progscala2/fp/datastructs/flatmap.sc

scala> val list = List("now", "is", "", "the", "time")
list: List[String] = List(now, is, "", the, time)

scala> list flatMap (s => s.toList)
res0: List[Char] = List(n, o, w, i, s, t, h, e, t, i, m, e)
```

Calling toList on each string creates a List[Char]. These nested lists are then flattened into the final List[Char]. Note that the empty string in list resulted in no contribution to the final list, while each of the other strings contributed two or more characters.

In fact, flatMap behaves exactly like calling map, followed by another method, flatten:

```
// src/main/scala/progscala2/fp/datastructs/flatmap.sc

scala> val list2 = List("now", "is", "", "the", "time") map (s => s.toList)
list2: List[List[Char]] =
  List(List(n, o, w), List(i, s), List(), List(t, h, e), List(t, i, m, e))

scala> list2.flatten
res1: List[Char] = List(n, o, w, i, s, t, h, e, t, i, m, e)
```

Note that the intermediate collection is a List[List[Char]]. However, flatMap is more efficient than making two method calls, because flatMap doesn't create the intermediate collection.

Note that flatMap won't flatten elements beyond one level. If our function literal returned deeply nested trees, they would be flattened only one level.

Filtering

It is common to traverse a collection and extract a new collection from it with elements that match certain criteria:

```
// src/main/scala/progscala2/fp/datastructs/filter.sc

scala> val stateCapitals = Map(
     |    "Alabama" -> "Montgomery",
     |    "Alaska"  -> "Juneau",
     |    "Wyoming" -> "Cheyenne")
stateCapitals: scala.collection.immutable.Map[String,String] =
  Map(Alabama -> Montgomery, Alaska -> Juneau, Wyoming -> Cheyenne)

scala> val map2 = stateCapitals filter { kv => kv._1 startsWith "A" }
```

```
map2: scala.collection.immutable.Map[String,String] =
    Map(Alabama -> Montgomery, Alaska -> Juneau)
```

There are several different methods defined in scala.collection.TraversableLike
(*http://bit.ly/1yMk4pK*) for filtering or otherwise returning part of the original collection. Note that some of these methods won't return for infinite collections and some
might return different results for different invocations unless the collection type is ordered. The descriptions are adapted from the Scaladocs:

def drop (n : Int) : TraversableLike.Repr
> Selects all elements except the first n elements. Returns a new traversable collection,
> which will be empty if this traversable collection has less than n elements.

def dropWhile (p : (A) => Boolean) : TraversableLike.Repr
> Drops the longest prefix of elements that satisfy a predicate. Returns the longest
> suffix of this traversable collection whose first element does not satisfy the
> predicate p.

def exists (p : (A) => Boolean) : Boolean
> Tests whether a predicate holds for at least one of the elements of this traversable
> collection. Returns true if so or false, otherwise.

def filter (p : (A) => Boolean) : TraversableLike.Repr
> Selects all elements of this traversable collection that satisfy a predicate. Returns a
> new traversable collection consisting of all elements of this traversable collection
> that satisfy the given predicate p. The order of the elements is preserved.

def filterNot (p : (A) => Boolean) : TraversableLike.Repr
> The "negation" of filter; selects all elements of this traversable collection that do
> not satisfy the predicate p...

def find (p : (A) => Boolean) : Option[A]
> Finds the first element of the traversable collection satisfying a predicate, if any.
> Returns an Option containing the first element in the traversable collection that
> satisfies p, or None if none exists.

def forall (p : (A) => Boolean) : Boolean
> Tests whether a predicate holds for all elements of this traversable collection. Re-
> turns true if the given predicate p holds for all elements, or false if it doesn't.

def partition (p : (A) => Boolean): (TraversableLike.Repr, Traversable
Like.Repr)
> Partitions this traversable collection in two traversable collections according to a
> predicate. Returns a pair of traversable collections: the first traversable collection
> consists of all elements that satisfy the predicate p and the second traversable
> collection consists of all elements that don't. The relative order of the elements in

the resulting traversable collections is the same as in the original traversable collection.

```
def take (n : Int) : TraversableLike.Repr
```
Selects the first n elements. Returns a traversable collection consisting only of the first n elements of this traversable collection, or else the whole traversable collection, if it has less than n elements.

```
def takeWhile (p : (A) => Boolean) : TraversableLike.Repr
```
Takes the longest prefix of elements that satisfy a predicate. Returns the longest prefix of this traversable collection whose elements all satisfy the predicate p.

Many collection types have additional methods related to filtering.

Folding and Reducing

Let's discuss folding and reducing together, because they're similar. Both are operations for "shrinking" a collection down to a smaller collection or a single value.

Folding starts with an initial "seed" value and processes each element in the context of that value. In contrast, reducing doesn't start with a user-supplied initial value. Rather, it uses one of the elements as the initial value, usually the first or last element:

```
// src/main/scala/progscala2/fp/datastructs/foldreduce.sc

scala> val list = List(1,2,3,4,5,6)
list: List[Int] = List(1, 2, 3, 4, 5, 6)

scala> list reduce (_ + _)
res0: Int = 21

scala> list.fold (10) (_ * _)
res1: Int = 7200

scala> (list fold 10) (_ * _)
res1: Int = 7200
```

This script reduces the list of integers by adding them together, returning 21. It then folds the same list using multiplication with a seed of 10, returning 7,200.

Like reduce, the function passed to fold takes two arguments, an accumulator and an element in the initial collection. The new value for the accumulator must be returned by the function. Note that our examples either add or multiply the accumulator with the element to produce the new accumulator.

The example shows two common ways to write a fold expression, which requires two argument lists: the seed value and the function to compute the results. So, we can't just use infix notation like we can for reduce.

However, if we really like infix notation, we can use parentheses as in the last example (list fold 10), followed by the function argument list. I've come to prefer this syntax myself.

It isn't obvious why we can use parentheses in this way. To explain why it works, consider the following code:

```
scala> val fold1 = (list fold 10) _
fold1: ((Int, Int) => Int) => Int = <function1>

scala> fold1(_ * _)
res10: Int = 7200
```

Note that we created fold1 using *partial application*. Then we called it, applying the remaining argument list, (_ * _). You can think of (list fold 10) as starting a partial application, then the application is completed with the function that follows, (_ * _).

If we fold an empty collection it simply returns the seed value. In contrast, reduce can't work on an empty collection, because there would be nothing to return. In this case, an exception is thrown:

```
scala> (List.empty[Int] fold 10) (_ + _)
res0: Int = 10

scala> List.empty[Int] reduce (_ + _)
java.lang.UnsupportedOperationException: empty.reduceLeft
...
```

However, if you're not sure that a collection is empty, for example because it was passed into your function as an argument, you can use optionReduce:

```
scala> List.empty[Int] optionReduce (_ + _)
res1: Option[Int] = None

scala> List(1,2,3,4,5) optionReduce (_ + _)
res2: Option[Int] = Some(15)
```

If you think about it, reducing can only return the closest, common parent type[3] of the elements. If the elements all have the same type, the final output will have that type. In contrast, because folding takes a seed value, it offers more options for the final result. Here is a "fold" operation that is really a map operation:

```
// src/main/scala/progscala2/fp/datastructs/fold-map.sc

scala> (List(1, 2, 3, 4, 5, 6) foldRight List.empty[String]) {
     |    (x, list) => ("[" + x + "]") :: list
     | }
res0: List[String] = List([1], [2], [3], [4], [5], [6])
```

---

3. Also called the *least upper bound* or LUB.

First, we used a variation of fold called foldRight, which traverses the collection from right to left, so that we construct the new list with the elements in the correct order. That is, the 6 is processed first and prepended to the empty list, then the 5 is prepended to that list, etc. Here, the accumulator is the *second* argument in the anonymous function.

In fact, all the other operations can be implemented with fold, as well as foreach. If you could only have *one* of the powerful functions we're discussing, you could choose fold and reimplement the others with it.

Here are the signatures and descriptions for the various fold and reduce operations declared in scala.collection.TraversableOnce (*http://bit.ly/1tpsKAD*) and sca la.collection.TraversableLike (*http://bit.ly/1yMk4pK*). The descriptions are adapted from the Scaladocs:

def fold[A1 >: A](z: A1)(op: (A1, A1) ⇒ A1): A1
 Folds the elements of this traversable or iterator using the specified associative binary operator op. The order in which operations are performed on elements is unspecified and may be nondeterministic. However, for most ordered collections like Lists, fold is equivalent to foldLeft.

def foldLeft[B](z: B)(op: (B, A) ⇒ B): B
 Applies a binary operator op to a start value and all elements of this traversable or iterator, going left to right.

def foldRight[B](z: B)(op: (A, B) ⇒ B): B
 Applies a binary operator op to all elements of this traversable or iterator and a start value, going right to left.

def /:[B](z: B)(op: (B, A) ⇒ B): B = foldLeft(z)(op)
 A synonym for foldLeft. Example: (0 /: List(1,2,3))(_ + _). Most people consider the operator form /: for foldLeft to be too obscure and hard to remember. Don't forget the importance of communicating with your readers when writing code.

def :\[B](z: B)(op: (A, B) ⇒ B): B = foldRight(z)(op)
 A synonym for foldRight. Example: (List(1,2,3) :\ 0)(_ + _). Most people consider the operator form :\ for foldRight to be too obscure and hard to remember.

def reduce[A1 >: A](op: (A1, A1) ⇒ A1): A1
 Reduces the elements of this traversable or iterator using the specified associative binary operator op. The order in which operations are performed on elements is unspecified and may be nondeterministic. However, for most ordered collections like Lists, reduce is equivalent to reduceLeft. An exception is thrown if the collection is empty.

```
def reduceLeft[A1 >: A](op: (A1, A1) ⇒ A1): A1
```
Applies a binary operator op to all elements of this traversable or iterator, going left to right. An exception is thrown if the collection is empty.

```
def reduceRight[A1 >: A](op: (A1, A1) ⇒ A1): A1
```
Applies a binary operator op to all elements of this traversable or iterator going right to left. An exception is thrown if the collection is empty.

```
def optionReduce[A1 >: A](op: (A1, A1) ⇒ A1): Option[A1]
```
Like reduce, but returns None if the collection is empty or Some(…) if not.

```
def reduceLeftOption[B >: A](op: (B, A) ⇒ B): Option[B]
```
Like reduceLeft, but returns None if the collection is empty or Some(…) if not.

```
def reduceRightOption[B >: A](op: (A, B) ⇒ B): Option[B]
```
Like reduceRight, but returns None if the collection is empty or Some(…) if not.

```
def aggregate[B](z: B)(seqop: (B, A) ⇒ B, combop: (B, B) ⇒ B): B
```
Aggregates the results of applying an operator to subsequent elements. This is a more general form of fold and reduce. It has similar semantics, but does not require the result to be a parent type of the element type. It traverses the elements in different partitions sequentially, using seqop to update the result, and then applies combop to results from different partitions. The implementation of this operation may operate on an arbitrary number of collection partitions, so combop may be invoked an arbitrary number of times.

```
def scan[B >: A](z: B)(op: (B, B) ⇒ B): TraversableOnce[B]
```
Computes a prefix scan of the elements of the collection. Note that the neutral element z may be applied more than once. (I'll show you an example at the end of this section.)

```
def scanLeft[B >: A](z: B)(op: (B, B) ⇒ B): TraversableOnce[B]
```
Produces a collection containing cumulative results of applying the operator op going left to right.

```
def scanRight[B >: A](z: B)(op: (B, B) ⇒ B): TraversableOnce[B]
```
Produces a collection containing cumulative results of applying the operator op going right to left.

```
def product: A
```
Multiplies the elements of this collection. Returns the product of all elements in the collection, as long as the elements have an implicit conversion to type Numer ic[A] (*http://bit.ly/10an8zL*) (for example, Int, Long, Float, Double, and BigInt). The full signature of this method is actually def product[B >: A](implicit num: Numeric[B]): B. See "Constraining Allowed Instances" on page 135 for more on using implicit conversions to constrain the use of methods to allowed types.

```
def mkString: String
```
Displays all elements of this traversable or iterator in a string. This is a custom implementation of fold used for conveniently generating a custom string from the collection. There will be no delimiter between elements in the string.

```
def mkString(sep: String): String
```
Displays all elements of this traversable or iterator in a string using the specified separator (sep) string.

```
def mkString(start: String, sep: String, end: String): String
```
Displays all elements of this traversable or iterator in a string using the specified start (prefix), sep (separator), and end (suffix) strings.

Pay careful attention to the arguments passed to the anonymous functions for various reduce, fold, and aggregate methods. For the Left methods, e.g., foldLeft, the *first* argument is the accumulator and the collection is traversed left to right. For the Right functions, e.g., foldRight, the *second* argument is the accumulator and the collection is traversed right to left. For the methods like fold and reduce that aren't left- or right-biased, the traversal order and which argument is the accumulator are *undefined* (but typically they delegate to the left-biased methods).

The reduce and fold methods can output a completely different type, based on the seed value, while the reduce methods always return the same element type or a supertype.

None of these functions will terminate for infinite collections. Also, they might return different results for different runs if the collection is not a sequence (i.e., the elements are not stored in a defined order) or the operation isn't associative.

The aggregate method is not widely used. Because it has several "moving parts," it is harder to understand.

The scan methods are useful for processing successive subsets of a collection. Consider the following example:

```
scala> val list = List(1, 2, 3, 4, 5)
list: List[Int] = List(1, 2, 3, 4, 5)

scala> (list scan 10) (_ + _)
res0: List[Int] = List(10, 11, 13, 16, 20, 25)
```

First the seed value 10 is emitted, followed by the first element plus the seed, 11, followed by the second element plus the previous value, 11 + 2 = 13, and so on.

Finally, the three mkString methods are mentioned here because they are actually special-case versions of fold and reduce for generating a String. They are also quite handy when the default toString for a collection isn't what you want.

Left Versus Right Traversals

Note from our listing that fold and reduce do not guarantee a particular traversal order. In contrast, foldLeft and reduceLeft traverse the element left to right, while fold Right and reduceRight traverse the elements from right to left.

Hence, any operation that must preserve the order, such as our example that converted a list of integers to a list of formatted strings, must use either foldLeft or foldRight, as appropriate.

Let's examine the left and right forms of fold and reduce. They have important differences in behavior.

Let's repeat a few of the examples we saw before, but now using fold, foldLeft, fold Right, reduce, reduceLeft, and reduceRight, for comparison. First, the fold examples:

```scala
scala> (List(1,2,3,4,5) fold 10) (_ * _)
res0: Int = 1200

scala> (List(1,2,3,4,5) foldLeft 10) (_ * _)
res1: Int = 1200

scala> (List(1,2,3,4,5) foldRight 10) (_ * _)
res2: Int = 1200
```

Now the reduce examples:

```scala
scala> List(1,2,3,4,5) reduce (_ + _)
res3: Int = 15

scala> List(1,2,3,4,5) reduceLeft (_ + _)
res4: Int = 15

scala> List(1,2,3,4,5) reduceRight (_ + _)
res5: Int = 15
```

OK, not too exciting because the choice of method doesn't seem to matter. The reason is the anonymous functions used, _ * _ and _ + _. They are *associative* and *commutative*.

Let's explore this further. First, for Lists, fold just calls foldLeft; they do the same thing. That's true for most, but not all collections. So, we'll focus on foldLeft and foldRight. Second, the same anonymous function is used for foldLeft and fold Right, but in each case the arguments are actually reversed. For foldLeft, the first argument is the accumulator, while for foldRight, the second argument is the accumulator.

Let's compare foldLeft and foldRight, starting with *associative* and *commutative* functions that make the purpose of the arguments explicit:

```
// src/main/scala/progscala2/fp/datastructs/fold-assoc-funcs.sc

scala> val facLeft  = (accum: Int, x: Int) => accum + x
facLeft: (Int, Int) => Int = <function2>

scala> val facRight = (x: Int, accum: Int) => accum + x
facRight: (Int, Int) => Int = <function2>

scala> val list1 = List(1,2,3,4,5)
list1: List[Int] = List(1, 2, 3, 4, 5)

scala> list1 reduceLeft  facLeft
res0: Int = 15

scala> list1 reduceRight facRight
res1: Int = 15
```

The facLeft and facRight functions are associative and commutative. They differ only in how they interpret their arguments, but both have the body accum + x. To be clear, we can define a function *value* and pass it as an argument to a higher-order function, like reduceLeft or reduceRight.

Finally, when reduceLeft is called on list1 with facLeft passed as the anonymous function, we get the same result we get when calling reduceRight with facRight. Actually, using either anonymous function would yield the same result, because they are associative and commutative.

Let's sketch out the actual computation that's done in these cases. When we call reduceLeft for list1, we first pass 1 to facLeft as the accum argument (i.e., the initial seed value) and 2 as the value of x. The anonymous function facLeft then returns 1 + 2 as the next accum value, 3. The next call to facLeft passes 3 as accum and 3 as x, which then returns 3 + 3 or 6. Working through the remaining steps shows us that the following computation is performed:

```
((((1 + 2) + 3) + 4) + 5)   // = 15
```

In contrast, when reduceRight is used, 5 is the seed value and we process values from right to left. If you work through the steps, the computation is the following:

```
((((5 + 4) + 3) + 2) + 1)   // = 15
```

Let's reorder this expression to put the elements back in their original order. We'll repeat the reduceLeft expression first for comparison. Note the parentheses:

```
((((1 + 2) + 3) + 4) + 5)   // = 15 (reduceLeft case)
(1 + (2 + (3 + (4 + 5))))   // = 15 (reduceRight case)
```

Note how the parentheses reflect the direction of traversal. We'll come back to these expressions shortly.

What if we use a function that is still associative, but not commutative?

```scala
scala> val fncLeft  = (accum: Int, x: Int) => accum - x
fncLeft: (Int, Int) => Int = <function2>

scala> val fncRight = (x: Int, accum: Int) => accum - x
fncRight: (Int, Int) => Int = <function2>

scala> list1 reduceLeft  fncLeft
res0: Int = -13

scala> list1 reduceRight fncRight
res1: Int = -5
```

To see why we get different results, let's consider the actual computation that these functions construct.

If we repeat the preceding exercise to construct parenthesized lists of arithmetic expressions, we get the following for this example:

```scala
((((1 - 2) - 3) - 4) - 5)          // = -13 (foldLeft)
((((5 - 4) - 3) - 2) - 1)          // = -5  (foldRight)
(-1 + (-2 + (-3 + (-4 + 5))))      // = -5  (foldRight, rearranged)
```

Hence, as before, the parentheses indicate explicitly that reduceLeft processes the list elements from the left, while reduceRight processes the list elements from the right.

To be clear that the functions fncLeft and fncRight are associative, recall that x - y is equivalent to x + -y, which can be written -y + x without changing the results:

```scala
((((1 - 2) - 3) - 4) - 5)          // original
((((1 + -2) + -3) + -4) + -5)      // changing x - y to x + -y
(1 + (-2 + (-3 + (-4 + -5))))      // demonstrating associativity
```

Finally, let's consider what happens when we use functions that are neither associative nor commutative. We'll use functions that construct Strings:

```scala
scala> val fnacLeft  = (x: String, y: String) => s"($x)-($y)"

scala> val fnacRight = (x: String, y: String) => s"($y)-($x)"

scala> val list2 = list1 map (_.toString)   // Make a list of Strings

scala> list2 reduceLeft  fnacLeft
res2: String = (((((1)-(2))-(3))-(4))-(5)

scala> list2 reduceRight fnacRight
res3: String = ((((5)-(4))-(3))-(2))-(1)

scala> list2 reduceRight fnacLeft
res4: String = (1)-((2)-((3)-((4)-(5))))
```

Note again the different results from using fnacLeft and fnacRight. Be sure you understand how the resulting strings are produced.

Tail Recursion Versus Traversals of Infinite Collections

It turns out that `foldLeft` and `reduceLeft` have an important advantage over `fold Right` and `reduceRight`: the left traversals are tail-call recursive, so they can benefit from Scala's tail-call optimization.

To see this, recall the expressions we constructed previously for adding the elements of a list:

```
((((1 + 2) + 3) + 4) + 5)   // = 15 (reduceLeft case)
(1 + (2 + (3 + (4 + 5))))   // = 15 (reduceRight case)
```

Recall that a tail call must be the last operation in an iteration. For each line in the `reduceRight` sequence, the outermost addition (1 + …) can't be performed until all of the nested additions finish, so the operation can't be converted to a loop and it isn't tail recursive. Recall that for lists we have to process the elements from head to tail, because of the way lists are constructed. In contrast, for the `reduceLeft` case, we can add the first two elements, then the third, then the fourth, etc. In other words, we can convert it to a loop, because it's tail recursive.

Another way to see this is to implement our own `foldLeft` and `foldRight` for Seqs:

```scala
// src/main/scala/progscala2/fp/datastructs/fold-impl.sc

// Simplified implementation. Does not output the actual collection type
// that was input as Seq[A].
def reduceLeft[A,B](s: Seq[A])(f: A => B): Seq[B] = {
  @annotation.tailrec
  def rl(accum: Seq[B], s2: Seq[A]): Seq[B] = s2 match {
    case head +: tail => rl(f(head) +: accum, tail)
    case _ => accum
  }
  rl(Seq.empty[B], s)
}

def reduceRight[A,B](s: Seq[A])(f: A => B): Seq[B] = s match {
  case head +: tail => f(head) +: reduceRight(tail)(f)
  case _ => Seq.empty[B]
}

val list = List(1,2,3,4,5,6)

reduceLeft(list)(i => 2*i)
// => List(12, 10, 8, 6, 4, 2)

reduceRight(list)(i => 2*i)
// => List(2, 4, 6, 8, 10, 12)
```

These implementations don't attempt to construct the actual subclass of the input `Seq` for the output. The Scala collections implementations use the `CanBuildFrom` technique we discussed previously. Otherwise, they follow the classic model for implementing a left or right traversal using recursion.

You should learn these two patterns well enough to always remember the behaviors and trade-offs of left versus right traversal and recursion, even though in practice you'll almost always use Scala's built-in functions instead of writing your own.

Because we are processing a Seq, we should normally work with the elements left to right. It's true that Seq.apply(index: Int) returns the element at position index (counting from zero). However, for a linked list, this would require an *O(N)* traversal for each call to apply, yielding an *O(N²)* algorithm rather than *O(N)*, which we want. So, the implementation of foldRight "suspends" prefixing the value to the rest of the new Seq until the recursive invocation of foldRight returns. Hence, foldRight is not tail recursive.

For foldLeft, we use a nested function rl to implement the recursion. It carries along an accum argument that accumulates the new Seq[B]. When we no longer match on head +: tail, we've hit the empty tail Seq, at which point we return accum, which has the completed Seq[B] we'll return. When we make a recursive call to rl, it is the last thing we do (the tail call), because we prepend the new element to accum before passing its updated value to rl. Hence, foldLeft is tail recursive.

In contrast, when we hit the end of the input Seq in foldRight, we return an empty Seq[B] and *then* the new elements are prefixed to it as we pop the stack.

Finally, note the order of the output elements, which are different. It may surprise you at first that the left recursion returns a list that effectively reverses the input elements, but this is just an artifact of how sequences are constructed by prepending items to another sequence. Try rewriting both functions to work with Vectors (*http://bit.ly/ 1tozAI0*). You can use the same case match clauses, but append the elements to the new vector, rather than prepend them. The output vector from your new foldLeft will have the elements in the same order as the input, while the output of foldRight will now reverse the order.

So why have both kinds of recursion? If you're not worried about stack overflow, a right recursion might be the most natural fit for the operation you are doing. We saw that our foldRight for sequences keeps the elements in the same order. We could call re verse on the output of foldLeft, but that means two traversals of a collection, not just one. That could be expensive for very large collections.

However, there is one advantage of a right recursion over a left recursion. Consider the case where you have a potentially infinite stream of data coming in. You can't conceivably put all that data into a collection in memory, but perhaps you only need to process the first *N* elements, for some *N*, and then discard the rest. The library's Stream (*http:// bit.ly/1toy0G5*) type is designed for this purpose. Stream is *lazy*, which means that it only evaluates its tail on demand (but it evaluates the head eagerly, which is sometimes inconvenient).

By "evaluate," I mean that the only possible way to define an infinite stream in computing is to use some function that will produce values forever. That function could be reading from an input channel, like a socket, such as the Twitter "firehose," or a large file. Or it could be a function that generates a sequence of numbers. We'll see an example of the latter in a moment.

Now suppose we defined an infinite collection where the infinite function just generates random numbers. Most of Scala's collections are *strict* or *eager*, meaning that if we attempted to define a collection with this function, it would immediately consume all available memory while trying to build up this collection in memory.

On the other hand, a lazy stream would just call the random function once for the head, then wait until a client asked for subsequent values from the tail of the stream.

Let's consider an interesting example of an infinite `Stream` (*http://bit.ly/1toy0G5*) of numbers, the Fibonacci sequence.

Recall that a Fibonacci number `fib(n)` is defined as follows (ignoring negative numbers):

```
f(n) =
    0                   if n = 0
    1                   if n = 1
    f(n-1) + f(n-2)   otherwise
```

Like any good recursion, n equals 0 or 1 provides the termination condition we need, in which case `f(n) = n`. Otherwise, `f(n) = f(n-1) + f(n-2)`.

Now consider this definition using `Stream`s:

```
// src/main/scala/progscala2/fp/datastructs/fibonacci.sc

scala> import scala.math.BigInt

scala> val fibs: Stream[BigInt] =
     |   BigInt(0) #:: BigInt(1) #:: fibs.zip(fibs.tail).map (n => n._1 + n._2)

scala> fibs take 10 foreach (i => print(s"$i "))
0 1 1 2 3 5 8 13 21 34
```

Using the equivalent of the "cons" operation, `#::`, for `Stream`, we construct the first two values of the sequence eagerly for the special case of n equals 0 and 1, then we define the rest of the stream with a *recursive definition*. It is right-recursive, but we'll only take the first *n* elements and discard the rest.

Note that we are both defining `fibs` and defining the tail portion using `fibs` itself: `fibs.zip(fibs.tail).map(…)`. This tail expression pairs up all elements of `fibs` with the successor elements. For example, we have tuple elements like `(f(2), f(3))`, `(f(3), f(4))`, etc. going on to infinity, but we don't actually evaluate these expressions eagerly until the user asks for values. Note that the tuples are then mapped to an integer, the sum of their values, which is the next `f(n)` value!

The last line uses `take` to evaluate the first ten numbers in the sequence. (Eager collections also have the `take` method.) We must compute the tail eight times to get a total of ten numbers. Then we loop over them with `foreach` and print them, one per line.

This is a very clever and powerful definition of a recursive sequence, taken from the `Stream` Scaladoc (*http://bit.ly/1toy0G5*) page. Make sure you understand what it's doing. It helps to play with the pieces of the expression to understand what each one does and then work out the first several values by hand.

It's important to note that the structure of `fibs` is very similar to our implementation of `foldRight`, `f(0) + f(1) + tail`. Because it is effectively a right recursion, we can stop evaluating `tail` when we have as many head elements as we want. In contrast, trying to construct a left recursion that is also lazy is not possible, because it would look conceptually like this: `f(0 + f(1 + f(tail)))`. (Compare our implementation of `fol dLeft`). Hence, a right recursion lets us work with infinite, lazy streams, truncating them appropriately, while a left recursion does not.

 Left recursions are tail recursive. Right recursions can handle infinite, lazy streams with truncation.

However, note that some of the types that implement `foldRight` and `reduceRight` on sequences actually reverse the sequence first, then invoke `foldLeft` or `reduceLeft`, respectively. For example, `collection.TraversableOnce` (*http://bit.ly/1yMmXqG*) provides this implementation for most Seqs. This allows users to perform right-biased operations in a tail-recursive way, although with the extra overhead of reversing the sequence first.

Combinators: Software's Best Component Abstractions

When object-oriented programming went mainstream in the late '80s and early '90s, there was great hope that it would usher in an era of reusable software components, even an industry of component libraries. It didn't really work out that way, except in limited cases, like the windowing APIs of various platforms.

Why did this era of reusable components not materialize? There are certainly many factors, but the fundamental reason is that appropriate, *generative* source code or binary

---

interoperability protocols never materialized that would be the basis of these components. It's a paradox that the richness of object APIs actually undermined modularization into reusable components.

In the larger world, component models that succeeded are all based on very simple foundations. Digital integrated circuits (ICs) plug into buses with 2^n signaling wires, each of which is Boolean, either on or off. Upon the foundation of this extremely simple protocol, an industry was born with the most explosive growth of any industry in human history.

HTTP is another successful example of a "component model." Services interact through a narrow, well-defined interface, involving a handful of message types and a very simple standard for message content.

In both cases, higher-level protocols were built upon simple foundations, but these foundations enabled composition to create, to *generate*, more complex structures. In digital circuits, some binary patterns are interpreted as CPU instructions, others as memory addresses, and others as data values. REST, data formats like JSON, and other higher-level standards are built upon the foundation of HTTP.

When you look at a city, at first it looks like most buildings are unique, completely customized creations. In fact, standards are behind the unique veneers: electric power, water and sewage, standard conventions for room dimensions, standard furnishings, and these buildings are surrounded by standard roads holding cars that have their own hierarchy of standards.

Object-oriented programming never established fundamental, *generative* standards. Within each language community, the fundamental unit of composition is the object (with or without a class "template"). Yet objects are not fundamental enough. Every developer invents a new "standard" for a Customer type. No two teams can agree what fields and behaviors the Customer type should have, because each team needs different data and computations for scenarios related to customers. Something more fundamental than an object is needed.

Attempts to standardize components across language and process boundaries also came up short. Models like CORBA were far from simple. Most defined a binary (versus source) standard. This made interoperability very brittle, subject to *version hell*. It wasn't the choice of binary versus source standardization that was the problem. It was the complexity of the binary standard that led to failure.

In contrast, think about the examples we studied in this chapter. We started with a small set of collections, Lists, Vectors, Maps, etc., that all share a set of operations in common, most of which are defined on the Seq abstraction (trait). Most of our examples used Lists, but that was an arbitrary choice.

Except for the utility method `foreach`, the operations were all pure, higher-order functions. They had no side effects and they took other functions as arguments to do the custom work for filtering or transforming each element from the original collection. Such higher-order functions are related to the mathematical concept of *combinators* from *Combinatory Logic*.

We can sequence together these combinator functions to build up nontrivial behavior with relatively little code. We can separate data from the behavior we need to implement for particular problems. This is in opposition to the normal approach of object-oriented programming, which combines data and behavior. It's more typical to create ad hoc implementations of domain logic inside custom classes. We've seen a more productive way in this chapter. This is why the chapter started with the Alan J. Perlis quote.

Let's finish this discussion with a final example, a simplified payroll calculator:

```scala
// src/main/scala/progscala2/fp/combinators/payroll.sc

case class Employee (
  name: String,
  title: String,
  annualSalary: Double,
  taxRate: Double,
  insurancePremiumsPerWeek: Double)

val employees = List(
  Employee("Buck Trends", "CEO", 200000, 0.25, 100.0),
  Employee("Cindy Banks", "CFO", 170000, 0.22, 120.0),
  Employee("Joe Coder", "Developer", 130000, 0.20, 120.0))

// Calculate weekly payroll:
val netPay = employees map { e =>
  val net = (1.0 - e.taxRate) * (e.annualSalary / 52.0) -
    e.insurancePremiumsPerWeek
  (e, net)
}

// "Print" paychecks:
println("** Paychecks:")
netPay foreach {
  case (e, net) => println(f"  ${e.name+':'}%-16s ${net}%10.2f")
}

// Generate report:
val report = (netPay foldLeft (0.0, 0.0, 0.0)) {
  case ((totalSalary, totalNet, totalInsurance), (e, net)) =>
    (totalSalary + e.annualSalary/52.0,
      totalNet + net,
      totalInsurance + e.insurancePremiumsPerWeek)
}

println("\n** Report:")
```

```
println(f"  Total Salary:    ${report._1}%10.2f")
println(f"  Total Net:       ${report._2}%10.2f")
println(f"  Total Insurance: ${report._3}%10.2f")
```

This script prints the following:

```
** Paychecks:
   Buck Trends:      2784.62
   Cindy Banks:      2430.00
   Joe Coder:        1880.00

** Report:
   Total Salary:     9615.38
   Total Net:        7094.62
   Total Insurance:   340.00
```

We could have implemented this logic in many ways, but let's consider a few of the design choices.

First, although this section criticized object-oriented programming as a component model, OOP is still quite useful. We defined an Employee type to hold the fields for each employee. In a real application, we would load this data from a database.

Instead, what if we just use tuples instead of a custom type? You might try rewriting the code this way and compare the two versions. Using Employee and the names it provides for the different fields makes it easier to reason about the code. *Meaningful names* is an old principle of good software design. Although I've emphasized the virtues of fundamental collections, functional programming does not say that custom types are bad. As always, design trade-offs should be carefully considered.

However, Employee is *anemic*. It is a structure with minimal behavior. In classic object-oriented design, we might add a lot of behavior to Employee to help with the payroll calculation or other domain logic. I believe the design chosen here provides optimal *separation of concerns*. It's also so concise that the maintenance burden is small if the structure of Employee changes and this code has to change.

Note also that the logic was implemented using a small script, rather than a large application combining many classes defined over many files. Of course, this is a toy example, but hopefully you can see how nontrivial applications don't necessarily require large code bases.

There is a counterargument for using a dedicated type, the overhead of constructing instances. Here, this overhead is unimportant. What if we have *billions* of records? We'll return to this question when we explore *Big Data* in Chapter 18.

What About Making Copies?

Let's finish this chapter by considering a practical problem. Making copies of functional collections is necessary to preserve immutability, but suppose I have a Vector (*http://bit.ly/1tozAI0*) of 100,000 items and I need a copy with the item at index 8 replaced. It would be terribly inefficient to construct a completely new, 100,000-element Vector.

Fortunately, we don't have to pay this penalty, nor must we sacrifice immutability. The secret is to realize that 99,999 elements are not changing. If we can share the parts of the original Vector that aren't changing, while representing the change in some way, then creating the new vector can still be very efficient. This idea is called *structure sharing*.

If other code on a different thread is doing something different with the original vector, it is unaffected by the copy operation, because the original vector is not modified. In this way, a "history" of vectors is preserved, as long as there are references to one or more older versions. No version will be garbage-collected until there are no more references to it.

Because this history is maintained, a data structure that uses structure sharing is called a *persistent data structure*.

Our challenge is to select an implementation data structure that lets us expose Vector semantics (or the semantics of another data structure), while providing efficient operations that exploit structure sharing. Let's sketch the underlying data structure and how the copy operation works. We won't cover all the details in depth. For more information start with the Wikipedia page on *persistent data structures* (*http://bit.ly/1wO9wad*).

The tree data structure with a branching factor of 32 is used. The branching factor is the maximum number of child nodes each parent node is allowed to have and it means that search and modification operations are $O(log_{32}(N))$, effectively a constant for even large values of N!

Figure 6-2 shows an example for Vector(1,2,3,4,5). We'll use just two or three child nodes for legibility.

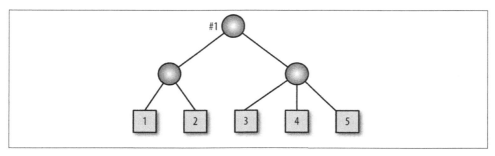

Figure 6-2. A Vector represented as a tree

When you reference the vector, you're actually referencing the root of this tree, marked by #1. As an exercise, you might work through how operations like accessing a particular element by its index, `map`, `flatMap`, etc., would work on a tree implementation of a Vector.

Now suppose we want to insert 2.5 between 2 and 3. To create a new copy, we don't mutate the original tree, but instead create a new tree. Figure 6-3 shows what happens when we add 2.5 between 2 and 3.

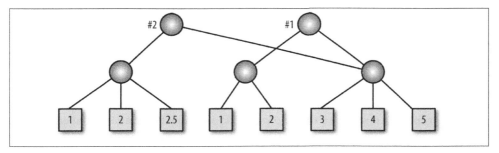

Figure 6-3. Two states of a Vector, before and after element insertion

Note that the original tree (#1) remains, but we have created a new root (#2) and new nodes between it and the child holding the new element. A new left subtree was created. With a branching factor of 32, we will have to copy up to 32 child references per level, but this number of copy operations is far less than the number required for all references in the original tree. Special handling is required when you need to add an element to a node that already has 32 elements.

Deletion and other operations work similarly. A good textbook on data structures will describe the standard algorithms for tree operations.

Therefore, it is possible to use large, immutable data structures, if their implementations support an efficient copy operation. There is extra overhead compared to a mutable vector, where you can simply modify an entry in place very quickly. Ironically, that doesn't mean that object-oriented and other *procedural* programs are necessarily simpler and faster.

Because of the dangers of mutability, it's common for classes to wrap collections they hold in accessor methods, which increase the code footprint, testing burden, etc. Worse, if the collection itself is exposed through a "getter" method, it's common to create defensive copies, where a copy of the collection is returned, rather than the original, so that a client can't modify the internal state of the object by modifying the collection outside the object's control. Because collection implementations in nonfunctional languages often have inefficient copy operations, the net effect can be less efficient programs than corresponding functional programs.

Immutable collections can not only be efficient, but they eliminate the need for all this extra code to defend against unwanted mutation.

There are other kinds of functional data structures that are optimized for efficient copying, optimized for modern hardware, such as minimizing cache misses, and other purposes. Many of these data structures were invented as alternatives to mutable data structures that are commonly discussed in classic textbooks on data structures and algorithms. For more on functional data structures, see *Purely Functional Data Structures* by Chris Okasaki and *Pearls of Functional Algorithm Design* by Richard Bird (both by Cambridge University Press), and *Algorithms: A Functional Programming Approach*, by Fethi Rabhi and Guy Lapalme (Addison-Wesley).

Recap and What's Next

We discussed the basic concepts of FP and argued for their importance for solving modern problems in software development. We saw how the fundamental collections and their common higher-order functions, *combinators*, yield concise, powerful, modular code.

Typical functional programs are built on this foundation. At the end of the day, *all* programs input data, perform transformations on it, then output the results. Much of the "ceremony" in typical programs just obscures this essential purpose.

Fortunately, traditional object-oriented languages have added many of these features. Most now support combinators on collections. Java 8 brings anonymous functions (called *lambdas*) to Java and the collections have been enhanced with higher-order functions.

For another, gentle introduction to FP aimed at programmers with OOP backgrounds, see *Functional Programming for the Object-Oriented Programmer* by Brian Marick (Leanpub). If you want to convince your Java developer friends that FP is worth their attention, consider my short *Introduction to Functional Programming for Java Developers* (O'Reilly).

Functional Programming in Scala, by Paul Chiusano and Rúnar Bjarnason (Manning Publications), is an excellent, in-depth introduction to functional programming using Scala.

To practice using combinators, see Phil Gold's "Ninety-Nine Scala Problems" webpage (*http://bit.ly/1nWgrMQ*).

Next, we'll return to `for` comprehensions and use our new knowledge of FP to understand how `for` comprehensions are implemented, how we can implement our own data types to exploit them, and how the combination of `for` comprehensions and combinator methods yield concise, powerful code. Along the way, we'll deepen our understanding of functional concepts.

We'll return to more advanced features of functional programming in Chapter 16 and we'll dive into more of the implementation details of Scala's collections in Chapter 12.

for Comprehensions in Depth

We described for comprehensions in "Scala for Comprehensions" on page 78. At this point, they look like a nice, more flexible version of the venerable for *loop*, but not much more. In fact, lots of sophistication lies below the surface, sophistication that has useful benefits for writing concise code with elegant solutions to a number of design problems.

In this chapter, we'll dive below the surface to really understand for comprehensions. We'll see how they are implemented in Scala and how your own container types can exploit them.

We'll finish with an examination of how many Scala container types use for comprehensions to address several common design problems, such as error handling during the execution of a sequence of processing steps. As a final step, we'll extract a well-known functional technique for a recurring idiom.

Recap: The Elements of for Comprehensions

for comprehensions contain one or more generator expressions, plus optional guard expressions (for filtering), and value definitions. The output can be "yielded" to create new collections or a side-effecting block of code can be executed on each pass, such as printing output. The following example demonstrates all these features. It removes blank lines from a text file:

```
// src/main/scala/progscala2/forcomps/RemoveBlanks.scala
package progscala2.forcomps

object RemoveBlanks {

  /**
   * Remove blank lines from the specified input file.
   */
  def apply(path: String, compressWhiteSpace: Boolean = false): Seq[String] =
```

```
      for {
        line <- scala.io.Source.fromFile(path).getLines.toSeq        // ❶
        if line.matches("""^\s*$""") == false                        // ❷
        line2 = if (compressWhiteSpace) line replaceAll ("\\s+", " ") // ❸
               else line
      } yield line2                                                   // ❹

  /**
   * Remove blank lines from the specified input files and echo the remaining
   * lines to standard output, one after the other.
   * @param args list of file paths. Prefix each with an optional "-" to
   *             compress remaining whitespace in the file.
   */
  def main(args: Array[String]) = for {
    path2 <- args                                                     // ❺
    (compress, path) = if (path2 startsWith "-") (true, path2.substring(1))
                       else (false, path2)                            // ❻
    line <- apply(path, compress)
  } println(line)                                                     // ❼
}
```

❶ Use scala.io.Source (*http://bit.ly/1tIcX1h*) to open the file and get the lines, where getLines returns a scala.collection.Iterator (*http://bit.ly/1q92kQc*), which we must convert to a sequence, because we can't return an Iterator from the for comprehension and the return type is determined by the initial generator.

❷ Filter for blank lines using a regular expression.

❸ Define a local variable, either each nonblank line unchanged, if whitespace compression is not enabled, or a new line with all whitespace compressed to single spaces.

❹ Use yield to return line, so the for comprehension constructs a Seq[String] (*http://bit.ly/1E8xLCt*) that apply returns. We'll return to the actual collection returned by apply in a moment.

❺ The main method also uses a for comprehension to process the argument list, where each argument is treated as a file path to process.

❻ If the file path starts with a - character, enable whitespace compression. Otherwise, only strip blank lines.

❼ Write all the processed lines together to stdout.

This file is compiled by sbt. Try running it at the sbt prompt on the source file itself. First, try it without the - prefix character. Here we show just a few of the lines of output:

```
> run-main progscala2.forcomps.RemoveBlanks \
  src/main/scala/progscala2/forcomps/RemoveBlanks.scala
[info] Running ...RemoveBlanks src/.../forcomps/RemoveBlanks.scala
// src/main/scala/progscala2/forcomps/RemoveBlanks.scala
```

```
package forcomps
object RemoveBlanks {
  /**
   * Remove blank lines from the specified input file.
   */
  def apply(path: String, compressWhiteSpace: Boolean = false): Seq[String] =
...
```

The blank lines in the original file are removed. Running with the - prefix yields this:

```
> run-main progscala2.forcomps.RemoveBlanks \
  -src/main/scala/progscala2/forcomps/RemoveBlanks.scala
[info] Running ...RemoveBlanks -src/.../forcomps/RemoveBlanks.scala
// src/main/scala/progscala2/forcomps/RemoveBlanks.scala
package forcomps
object RemoveBlanks {
  /**
  * Remove blank lines from the specified input file.
  */
  def apply(path: String, compressWhiteSpace: Boolean = false): Seq[String] =
...
```

Now runs of whitespace are compressed to single spaces.

You might try modifying this application to add more options, like prefixing with line numbers, writing the output back to separate files, calculating statistics, etc. How might you allow individual elements in the args array to be command-line options, like a typical Unix-style command line?

Let's return to the actual collection returned by the apply method. We can find out if we start the sbt console:

```
> console
Welcome to Scala version 2.11.2 (Java HotSpot(TM) ...).
...
scala> val lines = forcomps.RemoveBlanks.apply(
     |   "src/main/scala/progscala2/forcomps/RemoveBlanks.scala")
lines: Seq[String] = Stream(
// src/main/scala/progscala2/forcomps/RemoveBlanks.scala, ?)

scala> lines.head
res1: String = // src/main/scala/progscala2/forcomps/RemoveBlanks.scala

scala> lines take 5 foreach println
// src/main/scala/progscala2/forcomps/RemoveBlanks.scala
package forcomps
object RemoveBlanks {
  /**
   * Remove blank lines from the specified input file.
```

A lazy Stream (*http://bit.ly/1toy0G5*) is returned, which we introduced in "Tail Recursion Versus Traversals of Infinite Collections" on page 209. When the REPL printed the line after the definition of lines, the Stream.toString method computes the head of the stream (the comment line from the file) and it shows a question mark for the unevaluated tail.

We can ask for the head, then take the first five lines, which forces those lines to be evaluated, etc. Stream can be appropriate because we are processing files that could be very large, in which case storing the entire unfiltered contents in memory could consume too much memory. Unfortunately, if we actually do read the entire large data set, we'll still have it all in memory, because Stream remembers all the elements it evaluated. Note that each iteration of both for comprehensions (in apply and in main) are stateless, so we don't need to keep more than one line at a time in memory.

In fact, when you call toSeq on a scala.collection.Iterator (*http://bit.ly/1q92kQc*), the default implementation in the subtype scala.collection.TraversableOnce (*http://bit.ly/1pbs2bK*) returns a Stream (*http://bit.ly/1toy0G5*). Other types that subclass Iterator might return a strict collection.

for Comprehensions: Under the Hood

The for comprehension syntax is actually syntactic sugar provided by the compiler for calling the collection methods foreach, map, flatMap, and withFilter.

Why have a second way to invoke these methods? For nontrivial sequences, for comprehensions are much easier to read and write than involved expressions with the corresponding API calls.

The method withFilter is used for filtering elements just like the filter method that we saw previously. Scala will use filter if withFilter is not defined (with a compiler warning). However, unlike filter, it doesn't construct its own output collection. For better efficiency, it works with the other methods to combine filtering with their logic so that one less new collection is generated. Specifically, withFilter restricts the domain of the elements allowed to pass through subsequent combinators like map, flatMap, foreach, and other withFilter invocations.

To see what the for comprehension sugar encapsulates, let's walk through several informal comparisons first, then we'll discuss the details of the precise mapping.

Consider this simple for comprehension:

```
// src/main/scala/progscala2/forcomps/for-foreach.sc

val states = List("Alabama", "Alaska", "Virginia", "Wyoming")

for {
  s <- states
} println(s)
```

```
// Results:
// Alabama
// Alaska
// Virginia
// Wyoming

states foreach println
// Results the same as before.
```

The output is shown in the comments. (From this point on, I'll show REPL sessions less often. When I use code listings instead, I'll use comments to show important results.)

A single generator expression *without* a `yield` expression after the comprehension corresponds to an invocation of `foreach` on the collection.

What happens if we use `yield` instead?

```
// src/main/scala/progscala2/forcomps/for-map.sc

val states = List("Alabama", "Alaska", "Virginia", "Wyoming")

for {
  s <- states
} yield s.toUpperCase
// Results: List(ALABAMA, ALASKA, VIRGINIA, WYOMING)

states map (_.toUpperCase)
// Results: List(ALABAMA, ALASKA, VIRGINIA, WYOMING)
```

A single generator expression with a `yield` expression corresponds to an invocation of `map`. Note that when `yield` is used to construct a new container, the type of the first generator expression determines the final resulting collection. This makes sense when you look at that corresponding `map` expression. Try changing the input `List` to `Vector` and notice that a new `Vector` is generated.

What if we have more than one generator?

```
// src/main/scala/progscala2/forcomps/for-flatmap.sc

val states = List("Alabama", "Alaska", "Virginia", "Wyoming")

for {
  s <- states
  c <- s
} yield s"$c-${c.toUpper}"
// Results: List("A-A", "l-L", "a-A", "b-B", ...)

states flatMap (_.toSeq map (c => s"$c-${c.toUpper}"))
// Results: List("A-A", "l-L", "a-A", "b-B", ...)
```

The second generator iterates through each character in the string `s`. The contrived `yield` statement returns the character and its uppercase equivalent, separated by a dash.

When there are multiple generators, all but the last are converted to `flatMap` invocations. The last is a `map` invocation. Once again, a `List` is generated. Try using another input collection type.

What if we add a guard?

```
// src/main/scala/progscala2/forcomps/for-guard.sc

val states = List("Alabama", "Alaska", "Virginia", "Wyoming")

for {
  s <- states
  c <- s
  if c.isLower
} yield s"$c-${c.toUpper} "
// Results: List("l-L", "a-A", "b-B", ...)

states flatMap (_.toSeq withFilter (_.isLower) map (c => s"$c-${c.toUpper}"))
// Results: List("l-L", "a-A", "b-B", ...)
```

Note that the `withFilter` invocation is injected before the final `map` invocation.

Finally, defining a variable works like this:

```
// src/main/scala/progscala2/forcomps/for-variable.sc

val states = List("Alabama", "Alaska", "Virginia", "Wyoming")

for {
  s <- states
  c <- s
  if c.isLower
  c2 = s"$c-${c.toUpper} "
} yield c2
// Results: List("l-L", "a-A", "b-B", ...)

states flatMap (_.toSeq withFilter (_.isLower) map { c =>
  val c2 = s"$c-${c.toUpper} "
  c2
})
// Results: List("l-L", "a-A", "b-B", ...)
```

Translation Rules of for Comprehensions

Now that we have an intuitive understanding of how `for` comprehensions are translated to collection methods, let's define the details more precisely.

First, in a generator expression such as `pat <- expr`, `pat` is actually a pattern expression. For example, `(x, y) <- List((1,2),(3,4))`. Similarly, in a value definition `pat2 = expr`, `pat2` is also interpreted as a pattern.

The first step in the translation is to convert `pat <- expr` to the following:

```
// pat <- expr
pat <- expr.withFilter { case pat => true; case _ => false }
```

After this, the following translations are applied repeatedly until all comprehension expressions have been replaced. Note that some steps generate *new* for comprehensions that subsequent iterations will translate.

First, a for comprehension with one generator and a final `yield` expression:

```
// for ( pat <- expr1 ) yield expr2
expr map { case pat => expr2 }
```

A for *loop*, where `yield` isn't used, but side effects are performed:

```
// for ( pat <- expr1 ) expr2
expr foreach { case pat => expr2 }
```

A for comprehension with more than one generator:

```
// for ( pat1 <- expr1; pat2 <- expr2; ... ) yield exprN
expr1 flatMap { case pat1 => for (pat2 <- expr2 ...) yield exprN }
```

Note that the nested generators are translated to nested for comprehensions. The next cycle of applying the translation rules will convert them to method calls. The elided (…) expressions could be other generators, value definitions, or guards.

A for loop with more than one generator:

```
// for ( pat1 <- expr1; pat2 <- expr2; ... ) exprN
expr1 foreach { case pat1 => for (pat2 <- expr2 ...) yield exprN }
```

In the for comprehension examples we've seen before that had a guard expression, we wrote the guard on a separate line. In fact, a guard and the expression on the previous line can be written together on a single line, e.g., `pat1 <- expr1 if guard`.

A generator followed by a guard is translated as follows:

```
// pat1 <- expr1 if guard
pat1 <- expr1 withFilter ((arg1, arg2, ...) => guard)
```

Here, the `argN` variables are the arguments for the appropriate function passed to `with Filter`. For most collections, there will be a single argument.

A generator followed by a value definition has a surprisingly complex translation:

```
// pat1 <- expr1; pat2 = expr2
(pat1, pat2) <- for {                // ❶
  x1 @ pat1 <- expr1                 // ❷
} yield {
  val x2 @ pat2 = expr2              // ❸
  (x1, x2)                           // ❹
}
```

❶ We'll return a pair of the two patterns.

❷ x1 @ pat1 means assign to variable x1 the value corresponding to the whole expression that pat1 matches. Inside pat1, there might be other variables bound to the constituent parts. If pat1 is just an immutable variable name, the two assignments to x1 and pat1 are redundant.

❸ Assign to x2 the value of pat2.

❹ Return the tuple.

As an example of x @ pat = expr, consider the following REPL session:

```scala
scala> val z @ (x, y) = (1 -> 2)
z: (Int, Int) = (1,2)
x: Int = 1
y: Int = 2
```

The value z is the tuple (1,2), while x and y are the constituents of the pair.

The complete translation is hard to follow, so let's look at a concrete example:

```scala
// src/main/scala/progscala2/forcomps/for-variable-translated.sc

val map = Map("one" -> 1, "two" -> 2)

val list1 = for {
  (key, value) <- map    // How is this line and the next translated?
  i10 = value + 10
} yield (i10)
// Result: list1: scala.collection.immutable.Iterable[Int] = List(11, 12)

// Translation:
val list2 = for {
  (i, i10) <- for {
    x1 @ (key, value) <- map
  } yield {
    val x2 @ i10 = value + 10
    (x1, x2)
  }
} yield (i10)
// Result: list2: scala.collection.immutable.Iterable[Int] = List(11, 12)
```

Note how the two expressions inside the outer for {...} are translated. Even though we work with a pair (x1, x2) inside, only x2 (equivalent to i10) is actually returned. Also, recall that the elements of a Map (*http://bit.ly/15y3BGn*) are key-value pairs, so that's what we pattern match against in the generator shown, which iterates through the map.

This completes the translation rules. Whenever you encounter a for comprehension, you can apply these rules to translate it into method invocations on containers. You won't need to do this often, but sometimes it's a useful skill for debugging problems.

Let's look at one more example that uses pattern matching to parse a conventional properties file, with a key = value format:

```
// src/main/scala/progscala2/forcomps/for-patterns.sc

val ignoreRegex = """^\s*(#.*|\s*)$""".r                          // ❶
val kvRegex = """^\s*([^=]+)\s*=\s*([^#]+)\s*.*$""".r             // ❷

val properties = """
  |# Book properties
  |
  |book.name = Programming Scala, Second Edition # A comment
  |book.authors = Dean Wampler and Alex Payne
  |book.publisher = O'Reilly
  |book.publication-year = 2014
  |""".stripMargin                                                // ❸

val kvPairs = for {
  prop <- properties.split("\n")                                  // ❹
  if ignoreRegex.findFirstIn(prop) == None                        // ❺
  kvRegex(key, value) = prop                                      // ❻
} yield (key.trim, value.trim)                                    // ❼
// Returns: kvPairs: Array[(String, String)] = Array(
//   (book.name,Programming Scala, Second Edition),
//   (book.authors,Dean Wampler and Alex Payne),
//   (book.publisher,O'Reilly),
//   (book.publication-year,2014))
```

❶ A regular expression that looks for lines to "ignore," i.e., those that are blank or comments, where # is the comment marker and must be the first non-whitespace character on the line.

❷ A regular expression for key = value pairs, which handles arbitrary whitespace and optional trailing comments.

❸ An example multiline string of properties. Note the use of StringLike.strip Margin (*http://bit.ly/18bCByX*) to remove all leading characters on each line up to and including the |. This technique lets us indent those lines without having that whitespace interpreted as part of the string.

❹ Split the properties on line feeds.

❺ Filter for lines that we *don't* want to ignore.

❻ Use of a pattern expression on the lefthand side; extract the key and value from a valid property line, using the regular expression.

❼ Yield the resulting key-value pairs, trimming extraneous whitespace that remains.

An Array[(String,String)] is returned. It's an Array because the generator called String.split, which returns an Array.

See Section 6.19 in the *Scala Language Specification* (*http://bit.ly/1wNBOR8*) for more examples of for comprehensions and their translations.

Options and Other Container Types

We used Lists, Arrays, and Maps for our examples, but any types that implement foreach, map, flatMap, and withFilter can be used in for comprehensions and not just the obvious collection types. In other words, any type that can be considered a *container* could support these methods and allow us to use instances of the type in for comprehensions.

Let's consider several other container types. We'll see how exploiting for comprehensions can transform your code in unexpected ways.

Option as a Container

Option (*http://bit.ly/16yQhkp*) is a *binary* container. It has an item or it doesn't. It implements the four methods we need.

Here are the implementations for the methods we need in Option (from the Scala 2.11 library source code; some incidental details have been omitted or changed):

```scala
sealed abstract class Option[+T] { self =>                    // ❶
  ...
  def isEmpty: Boolean  // Implemented by Some and None.

  final def foreach[U](f: A => U): Unit =
    if (!isEmpty) f(this.get)

  final def map[B](f: A => B): Option[B] =
    if (isEmpty) None else Some(f(this.get))

  final def flatMap[B](f: A => Option[B]): Option[B] =
    if (isEmpty) None else f(this.get)

  final def filter(p: A => Boolean): Option[A] =
    if (isEmpty || p(this.get)) this else None

  final def withFilter(p: A => Boolean): WithFilter = new WithFilter(p)

  /** We need a whole WithFilter class to honor the "doesn't create a new
   * collection" contract even though it seems unlikely to matter much in a
   * collection with max size 1.
   */
  class WithFilter(p: A => Boolean) {
    def map[B](f: A => B): Option[B] = self filter p map f        // ❷
    def flatMap[B](f: A => Option[B]): Option[B] = self filter p flatMap f
    def foreach[U](f: A => U): Unit = self filter p foreach f
    def withFilter(q: A => Boolean): WithFilter =
```

```
        new WithFilter(x => p(x) && q(x))
    }
}
```

❶   The self => expression defines an alias for this for the Option instance. It is
    needed inside WithFilter later. See "Self-Type Annotations" on page 376 for more
    details.

❷   Use the self reference defined above to operate on the enclosing Option
    instance, rather than an instance of WithFilter. That is, if we used this, we
    would refer to the WithFilter instance.

The final keyword prevents subclasses from overriding the implementation. It might
be a little shocking to see a base class refer to derived classes. Normally, it would be
considered bad object-oriented design for base types to know anything about their derived types, if any.

However, recall from Chapter 2 that the sealed keyword means that the only allowed
subclasses must be defined in the same file. Options are either empty (None) or not
(Some). So, this code is robust, comprehensive (it covers all cases), concise, and entirely
reasonable.

The crucial feature about these Option methods is that the function arguments are only
applied if the Option isn't empty.

This feature allows us to address a common design problem in an elegant way. A common pattern in distributed computation is to break up a computation into smaller tasks,
distribute those tasks around a cluster, then gather the results together. For example,
Hadoop's MapReduce framework (*http://hadoop.apache.org*) uses this pattern. We
would like an elegant way to ignore the task results that are empty and just deal with
the nonempty results. For the moment, we'll ignore task errors.

First, let's assume that each task returns an Option, where None is returned for empty
results and Some wraps a nonempty result. We want to filter out the None results in the
most elegant way.

Consider the following example, where we have a list of three results, each of which is
an Option[Int]:

```
// src/main/scala/progscala2/forcomps/for-options-seq.sc

val results: Seq[Option[Int]] = Vector(Some(10), None, Some(20))

val results2 = for {
  Some(i) <- results
} yield (2 * i)
// Returns: Seq[Int] = Vector(20, 40)
```

`Some(i) <- list` pattern matches on the elements of `results`, removing the `None` values, and extracting the integers inside the `Some` values. We then yield the final expression we want. The output is `Vector(20, 40)`.

As an exercise, let's work through the translation rules. Here is the first step, where we apply the first rule for converting each `pat <- expr` expression to a `withFilter` expression:

```
// Translation step #1
val results2b = for {
  Some(i) <- results withFilter {
    case Some(i) => true
    case None => false
  }
} yield (2 * i)
// Returns: results2b: List[Int] = List(20, 40)
```

Finally, we convert the outer `for { x <- y} yield (z)` expression to a `map` call:

```
// Translation step #2
val results2c = results withFilter {
  case Some(i) => true
  case None => false
} map {
  case Some(i) => (2 * i)
}
// Returns: results2c: List[Int] = List(20, 40)
```

The `map` expression actually generates a compiler warning:

```
<console>:9: warning: match may not be exhaustive.
It would fail on the following input: None
        } map {
          ^
```

Normally, it would be dangerous if the partial function passed to `map` did not have a `case None => ...` clause. If a `None` showed up, a `MatchError` (*http://bit.ly/1udfTVy*) exception would be thrown. However, because the call to `withFilter` has already removed any `None` elements, the error won't happen.

Now let's consider another design problem. Instead of having independent tasks where we ignore the empty results and combine the nonempty results, consider the case where we run a sequence of dependent steps, and we want to stop the whole process as soon as we encounter a `None`.

Note that we have a limitation that using `None` means we receive no feedback about why the step returned nothing, such as a failure. We'll address this limitation in subsequent sections.

We could write tedious conditional logic that tries each case, one at a time, and checks the results,[1] but a for comprehension is better:

```scala
// src/main/scala/progscala2/forcomps/for-options-good.sc

def positive(i: Int): Option[Int] =
  if (i > 0) Some(i) else None

for {
  i1 <- positive(5)
  i2 <- positive(10 * i1)
  i3 <- positive(25 * i2)
  i4 <- positive(2  * i3)
} yield (i1 + i2 + i3 + i4)
// Returns: Option[Int] = Some(3805)

for {
  i1 <- positive(5)
  i2 <- positive(-1 * i1)      // ❶    EPIC FAIL!
  i3 <- positive(25 * i2)      // ❷
  i4 <- positive(-2 * i3)      // EPIC FAIL!
} yield (i1 + i2 + i3 + i4)
// Returns: Option[Int] = None
```

❶ None is returned. What happens with the left arrow?

❷ Is it okay to reference i2 here?

The positive function is our "worker" that returns an Option[Int], a Some(i) if the input i is positive, or a None, otherwise.

Note that the second and third expressions in the two for comprehensions use the previous values. As written, they appear to assume that the "happy path" will occur and it's safe to use the returned Int extracted from the Option[Int].

For the first for comprehension, the assumption works fine. For the second for comprehension, it *still* works fine! Once a None is returned, the subsequent expressions are effectively no-ops, because the function literals won't be evaluated when map or flat Map are called from that point forward.

Let's look at three more container types with the same properties, Either (*http://bit.ly/ 1sQZRtp*), Try (*http://bit.ly/1DDcSNz*), and a Validation (*http://bit.ly/10Fhgj8*) type in a popular, third-party library called *Scalaz*.

---

1. See the code example file *src/main/scala/progscala2/forcomps/for-options-bad.sc*.

Either: A Logical Extension to Option

We noted that the use of Option has the disadvantage that None carries no information that could tell us why no value is available, e.g., because an error occurred. Using Either (*http://bit.ly/1sQZRtp*) instead is one solution. As the name suggests, Either is a container that holds one and only one of two things. In other words, where Option handled the case of zero or one items, Either handles the case of one item or another.

Either is a parameterized type with two parameters, Either[+A, +B], where the A and B are the two possible types of the element contained in the Either. Recall that +A indicates that Either is *covariant* in the type parameter A and similarly for +B. This means that if you need a value of type Either[Any,Any] (for example, a method argument), you can use an instance of type Either[String,Int], because String and Int are subtypes of Any, therefore Either[String,Int] is a subtype of Either[Any,Any].

Either is also a sealed abstract class with two subclasses defined, Left[A] (*http://bit.ly/1zmtoDL*) and Right[B] (*http://bit.ly/13p4yWB*). That's how we distinguish between the two possible elements.

The concept of Either predates Scala. It has been used for a long time as an alternative to throwing exceptions. By historical convention, when used to hold either an error indicator or a value, the Left value is used to hold the error indicator, such as a message string or even an exception thrown by a lower-level library, and the normal return value is returned as a Right. To be clear, though, Either can be used for any scenario where you want to hold one object *or* another, possibly of different types.

Before we dive into some of the particulars of Either, let's just try porting our previous example. First, if you have a list of Either values and just want to discard the errors (Lefts), a simple for comprehension does the trick:

```scala
// src/main/scala/progscala2/forcomps/for-eithers-good.sc

def positive(i: Int): Either[String,Int] =
  if (i > 0) Right(i) else Left(s"nonpositive number $i")

for {
  i1 <- positive(5).right
  i2 <- positive(10 * i1).right
  i3 <- positive(25 * i2).right
  i4 <- positive(2  * i3).right
} yield (i1 + i2 + i3 + i4)
// Returns: scala.util.Either[String,Int] = Right(3805)

for {
  i1 <- positive(5).right
  i2 <- positive(-1 * i1).right    // EPIC FAIL!
  i3 <- positive(25 * i2).right
  i4 <- positive(-2 * i3).right    // EPIC FAIL!
```

```
} yield (i1 + i2 + i3 + i4)
// Returns: scala.util.Either[String,Int] = Left(nonpositive number -5)
```

This version is very similar to the implementation for Option, with the appropriate type changes. Like the Option implementation, we only see the first error. However, note that we have to call the right method on the values returned from positive. To understand why, let's discuss the purpose of the right and corresponding left methods.

Consider these simple examples of Either, Left, and Right adapted from the Scaladocs for Either:

```
scala> val l: Either[String, Int] = Left("boo")
l: Either[String,Int] = Left(boo)

scala> val r: Either[String, Int] = Right(12)
r: Either[String,Int] = Right(12)
```

We declare two Either[String, Int] values and assign a Left[String] to the first and a Right[Int] to the second.

By the way, you might recall from "unapply Method" on page 113 that you can use infix notation for type annotations when a type takes two parameters. So, we can declare l two ways:

```
scala> val l1: Either[String, Int] = Left("boo")
l1: Either[String,Int] = Left(boo)

scala> val l2: String Either Int = Left("boohoo")
l2: Either[String,Int] = Left(boohoo)
```

For this reason, I wish Either was named Or instead! If you *really* prefer Or you could use a type alias in your own code:

```
scala> type Or[A,B] = Either[A,B]
defined type alias Or

scala> val l3: String Or Int = Left("better?")
l3: Or[String,Int] = Left(better?)
```

Next, our combinator method friends map, fold, etc. aren't defined on Either itself. Instead, we have to call Either.left or Either.right. The reason is that our combinators take a single function argument, but we would need the ability to specify two functions, one to invoke if the value is a Left and one to invoke if the value is a Right. Instead, the left and right methods create "projections" that have the combinator methods:

```
scala> l.left
res0: scala.util.Either.LeftProjection[String,Int] = \
  LeftProjection(Left(boo))

scala> l.right
```

```
res1: scala.util.Either.RightProjection[String,Int] = \
  RightProjection(Left(boo))

scala> r.left
res2: scala.util.Either.LeftProjection[String,Int] = \
  LeftProjection(Right(12))

scala> r.right
res3: scala.util.Either.RightProjection[String,Int] = \
  RightProjection(Right(12))
```

Note that the Either.LeftProjection (*http://bit.ly/1rGFxuB*) values can hold either a Left or Right instance, and similarly for Either.RightProjection (*http://bit.ly/1rGFxuB*). Let's call map on these projections, passing in a single function:

```
scala> l.left.map(_.size)
res4: Either[Int,Int] = Left(3)

scala> r.left.map(_.size)
res5: Either[Int,Int] = Right(12)

scala> l.right.map(_.toDouble)
res6: Either[String,Double] = Left(boo)

scala> r.right.map(_.toDouble)
res7: Either[String,Double] = Right(12.0)
```

When you call LeftProjection.map and it holds a Left instance, it calls the function on the value held by the Left, analogous to how Option.map works with a Some. However, if you call LeftProjection.map and it holds a Right, it passes the Right instance through without modification, analogous to how Option.map works with None.

Similarly, calling RightProjection.map when it holds a Right instance means the function will be called on the value held by the Right, while nothing is changed if it actually holds a Left instance.

Note the return types. Because l.left.map(_.size) converts a String to an Int, the new Either is Either[Int,Int]. The second type parameter is not changed, because the function won't be applied to a Right[Int].

Similarly, r.right.map(_.toDouble) converts an Int to a Double, so an Either[String,Double] is returned. There is a "String.toDouble" method, which parses the string and returns a double or throws an exception if it can't. However, this method will never be called.

We can also use a for comprehension to compute the size of the String. Here is the previous expression and the equivalent for comprehension:

```
l.left map (_.size)            // Returns: Left(3)
for (s <- l.left) yield s.size // Returns: Left(3)
```

Throwing exceptions versus returning Either values

While Either has its charms, isn't it just easier to throw an exception when things go wrong? There are certainly times when an exception makes sense as a way to abandon a calculation, as long as some object on the call stack catches the exception and performs reasonable recovery.

However, throwing an exception breaks referential transparency. Consider this contrived example:

// src/main/scala/progscala2/forcomps/ref-transparency.sc

```
scala> def addInts(s1: String, s2: String): Int =
     |     s1.toInt + s2.toInt
addInts: (s1: String, s2: String)Int

scala> for {
     |   i <- 1 to 3
     |   j <- 1 to i
     | } println(s"$i+$j = ${addInts(i.toString,j.toString)}")
1+1 = 2
2+1 = 3
2+2 = 4
3+1 = 4
3+2 = 5
3+3 = 6

scala> addInts("0", "x")
java.lang.NumberFormatException: For input string: "x"
...
```

It appears that we can substitute invocations of addInts with values, rather than call the function. We might cache previous calls and return those instead. However, addInts throws an exception if we happen to pass a String that can't be parsed as an Int. Hence, we can't replace the function call with values that can be returned for all argument lists.

Even worse, the type signature of addInts provides no indication that trouble lurks. This is a contrived example of course, but parsing string input by end users is certainly a common source of exceptions.

It's true that Java's *checked exceptions* solve this particular problem. Method signatures indicate the possible error conditions in the form of thrown exceptions. However, for various reasons, checked exceptions hasn't worked well in practice. They aren't implemented by other languages, including Scala. Java programmers often avoid using them, throwing subclasses of the unchecked java.lang.RuntimeException (*http://bit.ly/108gaLU*) instead.

Using Either restores referential transparency and indicates through the type signature that errors can occur. Consider this rewrite of addInts:

// src/main/scala/progscala2/forcomps/ref-transparency.sc

```
scala> def addInts2(s1: String, s2: String): Either[NumberFormatException,Int]=
     |   try {
     |     Right(s1.toInt + s2.toInt)
     |   } catch {
     |     case nfe: NumberFormatException => Left(nfe)
     |   }
addInts2: (s1: String, s2: String)Either[NumberFormatException,Int]

scala> println(addInts2("1", "2"))
Right(3)

scala> println(addInts2("1", "x"))
Left(java.lang.NumberFormatException: For input string: "x")

scala> println(addInts2("x", "2"))
Left(java.lang.NumberFormatException: For input string: "x")
```

The type signature now indicates the possible failure "mode." Instead of grabbing control of the call stack by throwing the exception out of addInts2, we've *reified* the error by returning the exception as a value on the call stack.

Now, not only can you substitute values for the method invocations with valid strings, you could even substitute the appropriate Left[java.lang.NumberFormatExcep tion] values for invocations with invalid strings!

So, Either lets you assert control of call stack in the event of a wide class of failures. It also makes the behavior more explicit to users of your APIs.

Look at the implementation of addInts2 again. Throwing exceptions is quite common in Java and even Scala libraries, so we might find ourselves writing this try {...} catch {...} boilerplate a lot to wrap the good and bad results in an Either. For handling exceptions, maybe we should encapsulate this boilerplate with types and use names for these types that express more clearly when we have either a "failure" or a "success." The Try type does just that.

Try: When There Is No Do

scala.util.Try (*http://bit.ly/1DDcSNz*) is structurally similar to Either. It is a sealed abstract class with two subclasses, Success (*http://bit.ly/1E8xzmA*) and Failure (*http://bit.ly/1O8cqtD*).

Success is analogous to the conventional use of Right. It holds the normal return value. Failure is analogous to Left, but Failure always holds a Throwable.

Here are the signatures of these types (omitting some traits that aren't relevant to the discussion):

```
sealed abstract class Try[+T] extends AnyRef {...}
final case class Success[+T](value: T) extends Try[T] {...}
final case class Failure[+T](exception: Throwable) extends Try[T] {...}
```

Note that there is just one type parameter, Try[+T], compared to two for Either[+A, +B], because the equivalent of the Left type is now Throwable.

Also, Try is clearly asymmetric, unlike Either. There is only one "normal" type we care about (T) and a java.lang.Throwable (*http://bit.ly/1zmtxad*) for the error case. This means that Try can define combinator methods like map to apply to the T value when the Try is actually a Success.

Let's see how Try is used, again porting our previous example. First, if you have a list of Try values and just want to discard the Failures, a simple for comprehension does the trick:

```
// src/main/scala/progscala2/forcomps/for-tries-good.sc
import scala.util.{ Try, Success, Failure }

def positive(i: Int): Try[Int] = Try {
  assert (i > 0, s"nonpositive number $i")
  i
}

for {
  i1 <- positive(5)
  i2 <- positive(10 * i1)
  i3 <- positive(25 * i2)
  i4 <- positive(2  * i3)
} yield (i1 + i2 + i3 + i4)
// Returns: scala.util.Try[Int] = Success(3805)

for {
  i1 <- positive(5)
  i2 <- positive(-1 * i1)          // EPIC FAIL!
  i3 <- positive(25 * i2)
  i4 <- positive(-2 * i3)          // EPIC FAIL!
} yield (i1 + i2 + i3 + i4)
// Returns: scala.util.Try[Int] = Failure(
//   java.lang.AssertionError: assertion failed: nonpositive number -5)
```

Note the concise definition of positive. If the assertion fails, the Try block will return a Failure wrapping the thrown java.lang.AssertionError (*http://bit.ly/1wNb2HG*). Otherwise, the result of the Try expression is wrapped in a Success. A more explicit definition of positive showing the boilerplate is the following:

```
def positive(i: Int): Try[Int] =
  if (i > 0) Success(i)
  else Failure(new AssertionError("assertion failed"))
```

The `for` comprehensions look exactly like those for the original `Option` example. With type inference, there is very little boilerplate here, too. You can focus on the "happy path" logic and let `Try` capture errors.

Scalaz Validation

There is one scenario where all of the previous types aren't quite what we need. The combinators won't be called for subsequent expressions after an empty result (for `Option`) or failure. Effectively, we stop processing at the first error. However, what if we're performing several, independent steps and we would actually like to accumulate any and all errors as we go, then decide what to do? A classical scenario is validating user input, e.g., from a web form. You want to return any and all errors at once to the user.

The Scala standard library doesn't provide a type for this, but the popular, third-party library Scalaz (*http://bit.ly/1wOqLXV*) offers a Validation (*http://bit.ly/1OFhgj8*) type for this purpose:

```
// src/main/scala/progscala2/forcomps/for-validations-good.sc
import scalaz._, std.AllInstances._

def positive(i: Int): Validation[List[String], Int] = {
  if (i > 0) Success(i)                                        // ❶
  else Failure(List(s"Nonpositive integer $i"))
}

for {
  i1 <- positive(5)
  i2 <- positive(10 * i1)
  i3 <- positive(25 * i2)
  i4 <- positive(2  * i3)
} yield (i1 + i2 + i3 + i4)
// Returns: scalaz.Validation[List[String],Int] = Success(3805)

for {
  i1 <- positive(5)
  i2 <- positive(-1 * i1)            // EPIC FAIL!
  i3 <- positive(25 * i2)
  i4 <- positive(-2 * i3)            // EPIC FAIL!
} yield (i1 + i2 + i3 + i4)
// Returns: scalaz.Validation[List[String],Int] =
//   Failure(List(Nonpositive integer -5))                    // ❷

positive(5) +++ positive(10) +++ positive(25)                  // ❸
// Returns: scalaz.Validation[String,Int] = Success(40)

positive(5) +++ positive(-10) +++ positive(25) +++ positive(-30)   // ❹
// Returns: scalaz.Validation[String,Int] =
//   Failure(Nonpositive integer -10, Nonpositive integer -30)
```

❶ Success (*http://bit.ly/1rGFHSH*) and `Failure` (*http://bit.ly/1wO8l9E*) here are subclasses of `scalaz.Validation` (*http://bit.ly/1pbswyC*). They are not the `sca la.util.Try` (*http://bit.ly/1DDcSNz*) subtypes.

❷ Because we use a `for` comprehension, the evaluation is still short-circuited, so we don't see the last error for `i4`.

❸ However, in this and the following expressions, we evaluate all the calls to `pos itive`, then "add" the results or accumulate the errors.

❹ Both errors are reported.

Like `Either` (*http://bit.ly/1sQZRtp*), the first of the two type parameters is the type used to report errors. In this case, we use a `List[String]` so we can accumulate multiple errors. However, `String` or any other collection that supports appending values will also work. Scalaz handles the details of invoking the appropriate "concatenation" method.

The second type parameter is for the result returned if validation succeeds. Here we use an `Int`, but it could also be a collection type.

Note that the `for` comprehension still short-circuits the evaluation. That's still what we want, because each subsequent invocation of `positive` depends on a previous invocation.

However, we then see how to use the +++ "addition" operator[2] to perform *independent* evaluations, like you might do with web form input, and then aggregate together the results, if all of them validated successfully. Otherwise, all the errors are aggregated together as the result of this expression. We use a list of `Strings` for this purpose.

In a web form, you wouldn't be adding numbers together, but accumulating mixed fields. Let's adapt this example to be more realistic for form validation. We'll use as the success type `List[(String,Any)]`, which is a list of key-value tuples. If successful, we could call `toMap` on the `List` to create a `Map` to return to the caller.[3]

We'll validate a user's first name, last name, and age. The names must be nonempty and contain only alphabetic characters. The age, which will now start out as a string you might retrieve from a web form, must parse to a positive integer:

```
// src/main/scala/progscala2/forcomps/for-validations-good-form.sc
import scalaz._, std.AllInstances._

/** Validate a user's name; nonempty and alphabetic characters, only. */
```

2. This is one of several available techniques in Scalaz. See the Validation Scaladoc (*http://bit.ly/1pbswyC*) for a different example.

3. Why not just use `Map[String,Any]` instead? It appears that Scalaz doesn't support this choice.

```scala
def validName(key: String, name: String):
    Validation[List[String], List[(String,Any)]] = {
  val n = name.trim  // remove whitespace
  if (n.length > 0 && n.matches("""^\p{Alpha}$""")) Success(List(key -> n))
  else Failure(List(s"Invalid $key <$n>"))
}

/** Validate that the string is an integer and greater than zero. */
def positive(key: String, n: String):
    Validation[List[String], List[(String,Any)]] = {
  try {
    val i = n.toInt
    if (i > 0) Success(List(key -> i))
    else Failure(List(s"Invalid $key $i"))
  } catch {
    case _: java.lang.NumberFormatException =>
      Failure(List(s"$n is not an integer"))
  }
}

def validateForm(firstName: String, lastName: String, age: String):
    Validation[List[String], List[(String,Any)]] = {
  validName("first-name", firstName) +++ validName("last-name", lastName) +++
    positive("age", age)
}

validateForm("Dean", "Wampler", "29")
// Returns: Success(List((first-name,Dean), (last-name,Wampler), (age,29)))
validateForm("", "Wampler", "29")
// Returns: Failure(List(Invalid first-name <>))
validateForm("D e a n", "Wampler", "29")
// Returns: Failure(List(Invalid first-name <D e a n>))
validateForm("D1e2a3n_", "Wampler", "29")
// Returns: Failure(List(Invalid first-name <D1e2a3n_>))
validateForm("Dean", "", "29")
// Returns: Failure(List(Invalid last-name <>))
validateForm("Dean", "Wampler", "0")
// Returns: Failure(List(Invalid age 0))
validateForm("Dean", "Wampler", "xx")
// Returns: Failure(List(xx is not an integer))
validateForm("", "Wampler", "0")
// Returns: Failure(List(Invalid first-name <>, Invalid age 0))
validateForm("Dean", "", "0")
// Returns: Failure(List(Invalid last-name <>, Invalid age 0))
validateForm("D e a n", "", "29")
// Returns: Failure(List(Invalid first-name <D e a n>, Invalid last-name <>))
```

Using scalaz.Validation (*http://bit.ly/1pbswyC*) yields beautifully concise code for validating a set of independent values. It returns all the errors found, if there are any, or the values collected in a suitable data structure.

Recap and What's Next

`Either`, `Try`, and `Validation` express through types a fuller picture of how the program actually behaves. Both say that a valid value will (hopefully) be returned, but if not, they also encapsulate the failure information you'll need to know. Similarly, `Option` encapsulates the presence or absence of a value explicitly in the type signature.

By *reifying* the exception using one of these types,[4] we also solve an important problem in concurrency. Because asynchronous code isn't guaranteed to be running on the same thread as the "caller," the caller can't catch an exception thrown by the other code. However, by returning an exception the same way we return the normal result, the caller can get the exception. We'll explore the details in Chapter 17.

You probably expected this chapter to be a perfunctory explanation of Scala's fancy `for` *loops*. Instead, we broke through the facade to find a surprisingly powerful set of tools. We saw how a set of functions, `map`, `flatMap`, `foreach`, and `withFilter`, plug into `for` comprehensions to provide concise, flexible, yet powerful tools for building nontrivial application logic.

We saw how to use `for` comprehensions to work with collections, but we also saw how useful they are for other container types, specifically `Option` (*http://bit.ly/16yQhkp*), `util.Either` (*http://bit.ly/1sQZRtp*), `util.Try` (*http://bit.ly/1DDcSNz*), and `sca laz.Validation` (*http://bit.ly/1pbswyC*).

We've now finished our exploration of the essential parts of functional programming and their support in Scala. We'll learn more concepts when we discuss the type system in Chapter 14 and Chapter 15 and explore advanced concepts in Chapter 16.

Let's now turn to Scala's support for object-oriented programming. We've already covered many of the details in passing. Now we'll complete the picture.

---

4. The term *reify* means to make something concrete. We'll use it to mean encapsulating a concept into a "normal" instance, so it can be manipulated just like other instances.

## CHAPTER 8

Object-Oriented Programming in Scala

Scala is a functional programming language, but it is also an object-oriented programming language like Java, Python, Ruby, Smalltalk, and others. I've waited until now to explore Scala's "OO side" for two reasons.

First, I wanted to emphasize that functional programming has become an essential skill set for modern problems, a skill set that may be new to you. When you start with Scala, it's easy to use it as a "better Java," a better object-oriented language, and neglect the power of its functional side.

Second, a common architectural approach that Scala promotes is to use FP for *programming in the small* and OOP for *programming in the large*. Using FP for implementing algorithms, manipulating data, and managing state in a principled way is our best way to minimize bugs, the amount of code we write, and the risk of schedule delays. On the other hand, Scala's OO model provides tools for designing composable, reusable *modules*, which are essential for larger applications. Hence, Scala gives us the best of both worlds.

I've assumed you already understand the basics of object-oriented programming, such as Java's implementation. If you need a refresher, see Robert C. Martin's *Agile Software Development: Principles, Patterns, and Practices* or Bertrand Meyer's comprehensive introduction, *Object-Oriented Software Construction* (both by Prentice Hall). If you aren't familiar with *design patterns*, see *Design Patterns: Elements of Reusable Object-Oriented Software*, by Erich Gamma, Richard Helm, Ralph Johnson, and John Vlissides, known as the "Gang of Four" (Addison-Wesley).

In this chapter, we'll quickly review what we've already seen and fill in other details concerning Scala's terminology for OOP, including the mechanics of declaring classes and deriving one class from another, the notion of *value classes*, and how constructors work for Scala classes. The next chapter will dive into *traits* and then we'll spend a few chapters filling in additional details on Scala's object model and standard library.

Class and Object Basics

Classes are declared with the keyword `class`, while *singleton* objects are declared with the `object` keyword. For this reason, I use the term *instance* to refer to objects in general terms, even though *instance* and *object* are usually synonymous in most OO languages.

To prevent creation of *derived* classes from a class, prefix the declaration with the `final` keyword.

Use `abstract` to prevent instantiation of the class, such as when it contains or inherits member declarations (fields, methods, or types) without providing concrete definitions for them. Even when no members are undefined, `abstract` can still be used to prevent instantiation.

An instance can refer to itself using the `this` keyword. Although it's common to see `this` used in Java code, it's actually somewhat rare in Scala code. One reason is that constructor boilerplate is absent in Scala. Consider the following Java code:

```
// src/main/java/progscala2/basicoop/JPerson.java
package progscala2.basicoop;

public class JPerson {
  private String name;
  private int    age;

  public JPerson(String name, int age) {
    this.name = name;
    this.age  = age;
  }

  public void   setName(String name) { this.name = name; }
  public String getName()            { return this.name; }

  public void setAge(int age) { this.age = age;  }
  public int  getAge()        { return this.age; }
}
```

Now compare it with the following equivalent Scala declaration, in which all the boilerplate disappears:

```
class Person(var name: String, var age: Int)
```

Prefixing a constructor argument with a `var` makes it a mutable *field* of the class, also call an *instance variable* or *attribute* in different OO languages. Prefixing a constructor argument with a `val` makes it an immutable field. Using the `case` keyword infers the `val` keyword and also adds additional methods, as we've seen:

```
case class ImmutablePerson(name: String, age: Int)
```

Note that the state of an instance is the union of all the values currently represented by the instance's fields.

The term *method* refers to a function that is tied to an instance. In other words, its argument list has an "implied" this argument. Method definitions start with the def keyword. Scala will "lift" an applicable method into a function when a function argument is needed for another method or function.

Like most statically typed languages, Scala allows *overloaded methods*. Two or more methods can have the same name as long as their full *signatures* are unique. The signature includes the enclosing type name, method name, and the list of argument types (the names don't matter). In the JVM, different return types alone are not sufficient to distinguish methods.

However, recall from "Working Around Erasure" on page 142 that the JVM prevents some methods from being truly distinct, because of *type erasure* of the type parameters for *higher-kinded* types, i.e., types with type parameters, like List[A]. Consider the following example:

```scala
scala> object C {
     |    def m(seq: Seq[Int]): Unit = println(s"Seq[Int]: $seq")
     |    def m(seq: Seq[String]): Unit = println(s"Seq[String]: $seq")
     | }
<console>:9: error: double definition:
method m:(seq: Seq[String])Unit and
method m:(seq: Seq[Int])Unit at line 8
have same type after erasure: (seq: Seq)Unit
          def m(seq: Seq[String]): Unit = println(s"Seq[String]: $seq")
              ^
```

The type parameters Int and String are erased in the byte code.

Unlike Java, member *types* can be declared using the type keyword. These types provide a complementary mechanism to type parameterization, as we saw in "Abstract Types Versus Parameterized Types" on page 67. They are often used as aliases for more complex types, to aid readability. Are type members and parameterized types redundant mechanisms? No, but we'll have to wait until "Comparing Abstract Types and Parameterized Types" on page 374 to explore that question.

The term *member* refers to a field, method, or type in a generic way. Unlike in Java, a field and method can have the same name, but only if the method has an argument list:

```scala
scala> trait Foo {
     |    val x: Int
     |    def x: Int
     | }
<console>:9: error: value x is defined twice
  conflicting symbols both originated in file '<console>'
          def x: Int
              ^
```

```
scala> trait Foo {
     |     val x: Int
     |     def x(i: Int): Int
     | }
defined trait Foo
```

Type names must be unique.

Scala does not have *static* members, like Java. Instead, an `object` is used to hold members that span instances, such as constants.

If an `object` and a `class` have the same name and are defined in the same file, they are called *companions*.

Recall from Chapter 1, that when an `object` and a `class` have the same name *and* they are defined in the same file, they are *companions*. For case classes, the compiler automatically generates a companion object for you.

Reference Versus Value Types

Java syntax models how the JVM implements data. First, there is a set of special *primitives*: `short`, `int`, `long`, `float`, `double`, `boolean`, `char`, `byte`, and the keyword `void`. They are stored on the stack or CPU registers for better performance.

All other types are called *reference types*, because all instances of them are allocated on the heap and variables that refer to these instances actually refer to the corresponding heap locations. There are no "structural" types whose instances can live on the stack, as in C and C++, although this capability is being considered for a future version of Java. Hence the name *reference type* is used to distinguish these instances from primitive values. Instances of these types are created with the `new` keyword.

Scala has to obey the JVM's rules, of course, but Scala refines the clear distinction between primitives and reference types.

All reference types are subtypes of `AnyRef`. `AnyRef` is a subtype of `Any`, the root of the Scala type hierarchy. All value types are subtypes of `AnyVal`, which is also a subtype of `Any`. These are the only two subtypes of `Any`. Note that Java's root type, `Object` (*http://bit.ly/1E8xJKR*), is actually closest to `AnyRef`, not `Any`.

Instances of reference types are still created using the `new` keyword. Like other methods with no arguments, we can drop the parentheses when using a constructor that takes no arguments (called a *default constructor* in some languages).

Scala follows Java conventions for literal values of the number types and `Strings`. For example, `val name = "Programming Scala"` is equivalent to `val name = new String("Programming Scala")`. However, Scala also adds a literal syntax for tuples,

(1,2,3), which is equivalent to new Tuple3(1,2,3). We've also seen how language features make it easy to implement custom literal syntax conventions without compiler support, such as 1 :: 2 :: 3 :: Nil for Lists and Map("one" ->, "two" -> 2) for Maps.

It's common for instances of reference types to be created using objects with apply methods, which function as *factories*. (These methods must use new internally or an available literal syntax.) Because companion objects with such apply methods are generated automatically for case classes, instances of case classes are usually created this way.

The types Short, Int, Long, Float, Double, Boolean, Char, Byte, and Unit are called *value types*. They correspond to the JVM *primitives* short, int, long, float, double, boolean, char, byte, and the void keyword, respectively. All value types are subtypes of AnyVal in Scala's object model. AnyVal is the second of the two subtypes of Any.

"Instances" of value types are not created on the heap. Instead, the JVM primitive values are used instead and they are stored in registers or on the stack. Instances are always created using literal values, e.g., 1, 3.14, true. The literal value for Unit is (), but we rarely use that value explicitly.

In fact, there are no public constructors for these types, so an expression like val i = new Int(1) won't compile.

Why Is Unit's Literal Value ()?

Unit really behaves like a 0-tuple, a tuple with zero elements, written as (). The name "Unit" comes from the mathematics of multiplication, where any value that is multiplied by the unit value returns the original value. This is 1 for numbers, of course. Similarly for addition, 0 is the unit value. We'll revisit this concept in "Algebraic Data Types" on page 407.

Hence, Scala minimizes the use of "boxed" reference types, giving us the best of both worlds, the performance of primitives without boxing with object semantics in source code.

This uniformity of syntax allows us to declare parameterized collections of value types, like List[Int]. In contrast, Java requires the boxed types to be used, like List<Integer>. This complicates library code. It's common in Java *Big Data* libraries to have a long list of custom collection types specialized for each of the primitive types, or perhaps just long and double. You'll see a class dedicated to vectors of longs, a class dedicated to vectors of doubles, and so forth. The "footprint" of the library is larger and the implementation can't exploit code reuse as well. (There are still issues with boxing and collections that we'll explore in "Specialization for Value Types" on page 345.)

Value Classes

As we've seen, it's common for Scala to introduce wrapper types to implement *type classes*, also called *extension methods* (see "Type Class Pattern" on page 156). Unfortunately, wrappers around value types effectively turn them into reference types, defeating the performance optimization of using primitives.

Scala 2.10 introduced a solution, called *value classes*, and a tandem feature called *universal traits*. These types impose limits on what can be declared, but in exchange, they don't result in heap allocations for the wrappers:

```
// src/main/scala/progscala2/basicoop/ValueClassDollar.sc

class Dollar(val value: Float) extends AnyVal {
  override def toString = "$%.2f".format(value)
}

val benjamin = new Dollar(100)
// Result: benjamin: Dollar = $100.00
```

To be a valid value class, the following rules must be followed:

1. The value class has one and only one public `val` argument (as of Scala 2.11, the argument can also be nonpublic).

2. The type of the argument must not be a value class itself.

3. If the value class is parameterized, the `@specialized` (*http://bit.ly/1G2yWFq*) annotation can't be used.

4. The value class doesn't define secondary constructors.

5. The value class defines only methods, but no other `val`s and no `var`s.

6. However, the value class can't override `equals` and `hashCode`.

7. The value class defines no nested `trait`s, `class`es, or `object`s.

8. The value class cannot be subclassed.

9. The value class can only inherit from *universal traits*.

10. The value class must be a top-level type or a member of an object that can be referenced.[1]

---

1. Because of Scala's richer type system, not all types can be referenced in normal variable and method declarations like in Java. (However, all the examples we've seen so far work fine.) In Chapter 14, we'll explore new kinds of types and learn the rules for what it means to say that a type can or can't be referenced.

That's a long list, but the compiler provides good error messages when we break the rules.

At compile time the type is the outer type, `Dollar` in this example. The runtime type is the wrapped type, e.g., `Float`.

Usually the argument is one of the `AnyVal` types, but it doesn't have to be. If we wrap a reference type, we still benefit from not allocating the wrapper on the heap, as in the following implicit wrapper for `String`s that are phone numbers:

```scala
// src/main/scala/progscala2/basicoop/ValueClassPhoneNumber.sc

class USPhoneNumber(val s: String) extends AnyVal {

  override def toString = {
    val digs = digits(s)
    val areaCode  = digs.substring(0,3)
    val exchange  = digs.substring(3,6)
    val subnumber = digs.substring(6,10)  // "subscriber number"
    s"($areaCode) $exchange-$subnumber"
  }

  private def digits(str: String): String = str.replaceAll("""\D""", "")
}

val number = new USPhoneNumber("987-654-3210")
// Result: number: USPhoneNumber = (987) 654-3210
```

A value class can be a `case` class, but the many extra methods and the companion object generated are less likely to be used and hence more likely to waste space in the output class file.

A *universal trait* has the following properties:

1. It derives from `Any` (but not from other universal traits).
2. It defines only methods.
3. It does no initialization of its own.

Here a refined version of `USPhoneNumber` that mixes in two universal traits:

```scala
// src/main/scala/progscala2/basicoop/ValueClassUniversalTraits.sc

trait Digitizer extends Any {
  def digits(s: String): String = s.replaceAll("""\D""", "")       // ❶
}

trait Formatter extends Any {                                      // ❷
  def format(areaCode: String, exchange: String, subnumber: String): String =
    s"($areaCode) $exchange-$subnumber"
}
```

```
class USPhoneNumber(val s: String) extends AnyVal
    with Digitizer with Formatter {

  override def toString = {
    val digs = digits(s)
    val areaCode = digs.substring(0,3)
    val exchange = digs.substring(3,6)
    val subnumber  = digs.substring(6,10)
    format(areaCode, exchange, subnumber)                        // ❸
  }
}

val number = new USPhoneNumber("987-654-3210")
// Result: number: USPhoneNumber = (987) 654-3210
```

❶   Digitizer is a trait that contains the digits method we originally had in USPho neNumber.

❷   Formatter formats the phone number the way we want it.

❸   Use Formatter.format.

Formatter actually solves a design problem. We might like to specify a second argument to USPhoneNumber for a format string or some other mechanism for configuring the actual format produced by toString, because there are many popular format conventions. However, we're only allowed to pass one argument to USPhoneNumber, but we can mix in universal traits to do the configuration we want!

However, universal traits do sometimes trigger instantiation (i.e., heap allocation of an instance) by Scala, due to limitations of the JVM. Here's a summary of the circumstances requiring instantiation:

1. When a value class instance is passed to a function expecting a universal trait implemented by the instance. However, if a function expects an instance of the value class itself, instantiation isn't required.

2. A value class instance is assigned to an Array.

3. The type of a value class is used as a type parameter.

For example, when the following method is called with a USPhoneNumber, an instance of it will have to be allocated:

```
def toDigits(d: Digitizer, str: String) = d.digits(str)
...
val digs = toDigits(new USPhoneNumber("987-654-3210"), "123-Hello!-456")
// Result: digs: String = 123456
```

Also, when the following parameterized method is passed a USPhoneNumber, an instance of USPhoneNumber will have to be allocated:

```
def print[T](t: T) = println(t.toString)
print(new USPhoneNumber("987-654-3210"))
// Result: (987) 654-3210
```

To summarize, value classes provide a low-overhead technique for defining extension methods (type classes) and for defining types with meaningful domain names (like Dollar) that exploit the type safety of the underlying value.

 The term *value type* refers to the Short, Int, Long, Float, Double, Boolean, Char, Byte, and Unit types Scala has had for a long time. The term *value class* refers to the new construct for defining custom classes that derive from AnyVal.

For more information on the implementation details of value classes, see SIP-15: Value Classes (*http://bit.ly/1wNC0Qq*). *SIP* stands for *Scala Improvement Process*, the community mechanism for proposing new language and library features.

Parent Types

Derivation of *child* or *derived* types from a *parent* or *base* type is a core principle of most object-oriented languages. It's a mechanism for reuse, encapsulation, and polymorphic behavior (behavior that varies depending on the instance's actual type in a type hierarchy).

Like Java, Scala supports single inheritance, not multiple inheritance. A child (or derived) class can have one and only one parent (or base) class. The sole exception is the root of the Scala class hierarchy, Any, which has no parent.

We've already seen several examples of parent and child classes. Here are snippets of one of the first we saw, in "Abstract Types Versus Parameterized Types" on page 67, which demonstrates the use of type members. Here are the most important details again:

```
abstract class BulkReader {
  type In
  val source: In
  def read: String  // Read source and return a String
}

class StringBulkReader(val source: String) extends BulkReader {
  type In = String
  def read: String = source
}

class FileBulkReader(val source: java.io.File) extends BulkReader {
  type In = java.io.File
  def read: String = {...}
}
```

As in Java, the keyword `extends` indicates the parent class, in this case `BulkReader`. In Scala, `extends` is also used when a class inherits a trait as its parent (even when it mixes in other traits using the `with` keyword). Also, `extends` is used when one trait is the child of another trait or class. Yes, traits can inherit classes.

If we don't `extend` a parent class, the default parent is `AnyRef`.

Constructors in Scala

Scala distinguishes between a *primary constructor* and zero or more *auxiliary constructors*, also called *secondary constructors*. In Scala, the primary constructor is the entire body of the class. Any parameters that the constructor requires are listed after the class name. `StringBulkReader` and `FileBulkReader` are examples.

Let's revisit some simple case classes, `Address` and `Person`, that we saw in Chapter 5 and consider enhancements using secondary constructors:

```
// src/main/scala/progscala2/basicoop/PersonAuxConstructors.scala
package progscala2.basicoop

case class Address(street: String, city: String, state: String, zip: String) {

  def this(zip: String) =                                    // ❶
    this("[unknown]", Address.zipToCity(zip), Address.zipToState(zip), zip)
}

object Address {

  def zipToCity(zip: String)  = "Anytown"                    // ❷
  def zipToState(zip: String) = "CA"
}

case class Person(
    name: String, age: Option[Int], address: Option[Address]) {  // ❸

  def this(name: String) = this(name, None, None)            // ❹

  def this(name: String, age: Int) = this(name, Some(age), None)

  def this(name: String, age: Int, address: Address) =
    this(name, Some(age), Some(address))

  def this(name: String, address: Address) = this(name, None, Some(address))
}
```

❶ A secondary constructor that takes just a zip code argument. It calls helper methods to infer the city and state, but it can't infer the street.

❷ Helper functions that look up the city and state from the zip code (or at least they pretend to do that).

❸ Make the person's age and address optional.

❹ Provide convenient auxiliary constructors that let the user specify some or all of the values.

Note that an auxiliary constructor is named `this` and it must call the primary constructor or another auxiliary constructor as its first expression. The compiler also requires that the constructor called is one that appears *earlier* in the source code. So, we must order secondary constructors carefully in our code.

By forcing all construction to go through the primary constructor (eventually), code duplication is minimized and initialization logic for new instances is always uniformly applied.

The auxiliary constructor for `Address` is a good example of a method that does something nontrivial, rather than just provide convenient alternative invocations, like `Person`'s auxiliary constructors.

This file is compiled by **sbt**, so we can use the types in the following script:

```
// src/main/scala/progscala2/basicoop/PersonAuxConstructors.sc
import progscala2.basicoop.{Address, Person}

val a1 = new Address("1 Scala Lane", "Anytown", "CA", "98765")
// Result: Address(1 Scala Lane,Anytown,CA,98765)

val a2 = new Address("98765")
// Result: Address([unknown],Anytown,CA,98765)

new Person("Buck Trends1")
// Result: Person(Buck Trends1,None,None)

new Person("Buck Trends2", Some(20), Some(a1))
// Result: Person(Buck Trends2,Some(20),
//             Some(Address(1 Scala Lane,Anytown,CA,98765)))


new Person("Buck Trends3", 20, a2)
// Result: Person(Buck Trends3,Some(20),
//             Some(Address([unknown],Anytown,CA,98765)))

new Person("Buck Trends4", 20)
// Result: Person(Buck Trends4,Some(20),None)
```

This code works well enough, but actually there are a few issues with it. First, `Person` now has a lot of boilerplate for the auxiliary constructors. We already know that we can define method arguments with default values and the user can name the arguments when calling the methods.

Let's reconsider `Person`. First, let's add default values for `age` and `address` and assume that it's not "burdensome" for the user to specify `Some(…)` values:

```
// src/main/scala/progscala2/basicoop/PersonAuxConstructors2.sc
import progscala2.basicoop.Address

val a1 = new Address("1 Scala Lane", "Anytown", "CA", "98765")
val a2 = new Address("98765")

case class Person2(
  name: String,
  age: Option[Int] = None,
  address: Option[Address] = None)

new Person2("Buck Trends1")
// Result: Person2 = Person2(Buck Trends1,None,None)

new Person2("Buck Trends2", Some(20), Some(a1))
// Result: Person2(Buck Trends2,Some(20),
//          Some(Address(1 Scala Lane,Anytown,CA,98765)))

new Person2("Buck Trends3", Some(20))
// Result: Person2(Buck Trends3,Some(20),None)

new Person2("Buck Trends4", address = Some(a2))
// Result: Person2(Buck Trends4,None,
//          Some(Address([unknown],Anytown,CA,98765)))
```

The user of `Person` writes a little more code, but the reduced maintenance burden on the library developer is an important benefit. Trade-offs…

Let's decide we really prefer to maximize the user-friendly options. The second issue with our implementation is that the user has to create instances with `new`. Perhaps you noticed that the examples used `new` to construct instances.

Try removing the `new` keywords and see what happens. Unless you're invoking the primary constructor, you get a compiler error.

 The compiler does not automatically generate `apply` methods for secondary constructors in case classes.

However, if we overload `Person.apply` in the companion object, we can have our convenient "constructors" and avoid the requirement to use `new`. Here is our final implementation of `Person`, called `Person3`:

```
// src/main/scala/progscala2/basicoop/PersonAuxConstructors3.scala
package progscala2.basicoop3
```

```
import progscala2.basicoop.Address

case class Person3(
  name: String,
  age: Option[Int] = None,
  address: Option[Address] = None)

object Person3 {

  // Because we are overloading a normal method (as opposed to constructors),
  // we must specify the return type annotation, Person3 in this case.
  def apply(name: String): Person3 = new Person3(name)

  def apply(name: String, age: Int): Person3 = new Person3(name, Some(age))

  def apply(name: String, age: Int, address: Address): Person3 =
    new Person3(name, Some(age), Some(address))

  def apply(name: String, address: Address): Person3 =
    new Person3(name, address = Some(address))
}
```

Note that overloaded methods like apply that aren't constructors must have an explicit return type annotation.

Finally, here is a script that uses the final types:

```
// src/main/scala/progscala2/basicoop/PersonAuxConstructors3.sc
import progscala2.basicoop.Address
import progscala2.basicoop3.Person3

val a1 = new Address("1 Scala Lane", "Anytown", "CA", "98765")
val a2 = new Address("98765")

Person3("Buck Trends1")                              // Primary
// Result: Person3(Buck Trends1,None,None)

Person3("Buck Trends2", Some(20), Some(a1))          // Primary
// Result: Person3(Buck Trends2,Some(20),
//          Some(Address(1 Scala Lane,Anytown,CA,98765)))

Person3("Buck Trends3", 20, a1)
// Result: Person3(Buck Trends3,Some(20),
//          Some(Address(1 Scala Lane,Anytown,CA,98765)))

Person3("Buck Trends4", Some(20))                    // Primary
// Result: Person3(Buck Trends4,Some(20),None)

Person3("Buck Trends5", 20)
// Result: Person3(Buck Trends5,Some(20),None)

Person3("Buck Trends6", address = Some(a2))          // Primary
// Result: Person3(Buck Trends6,None,
```

```
//                Some(Address([unknown],Anytown,CA,98765)))

Person3("Buck Trends7", address = a2)
// Result: Person3(Buck Trends7,None,
//                Some(Address([unknown],Anytown,CA,98765)))
```

All examples with the `Primary` comment call the primary `apply` method generated automatically as part of the `case` class. The other examples without the comment call one of the other `apply` methods.

In fact, it's not all that common to define auxiliary constructors in Scala code, because alternative techniques generally work better for minimizing boilerplate while still providing users with flexible construction options. Instead, make judicious use of Scala's support for named and optional parameters, and use overloaded `apply` "factory" methods in objects.

Fields in Classes

We started the chapter with a reminder that the primary constructor arguments become instance fields if they are prefixed with the `val` or `var` keyword. For case classes, `val` is assumed. This convention greatly reduces source-code boilerplate, but how does it translate to byte code?

Actually, Scala just does implicitly what Java code does explicitly. There is a private field created internal to the class and the equivalent of "getter" and "setter" accessor methods are generated. Consider this simple Scala class:

```
class Name(var value: String)
```

Conceptually, it is equivalent to this code:

```
class Name(s: String) {
  private var _value: String = s                        // ❶

  def value: String = _value                            // ❷

  def value_=(newValue: String): Unit = _value = newValue // ❸
}
```

❶ Invisible field, declared mutable in this case.

❷ The "getter" or reader method.

❸ The "setter" or writer method.

Note the convention used for the `value_=` method name. When the compiler sees a method named like this, it will allow client code to drop the _, effectively enabling infix notation as if we were setting a bare field in the object:

```
scala> val name = new Name("Buck")
name: Name = Name@2aed6fc8

scala> name.value
res0: String = Buck

scala> name.value_=("Bubba")
name.value: String = Bubba

scala> name.value
res1: String = Bubba

scala> name.value = "Hank"
name.value: String = Hank

scala> name.value
res2: String = Hank
```

If we declare a field immutable with the `val` keyword, the writer method is not synthesized, only the reader method.

You can follow these conventions yourself, if you want to implement custom logic inside reader and writer methods.

We can pass constructor arguments to noncase classes that aren't intended to become fields. Just omit both the `val` and `var` keywords. For example, we might pass an argument needed to construct an instance, but we want to discard it afterwards.

Note that the value is still in the scope of the class body. As we saw in earlier examples of implicit conversion classes, they referred to the argument used to construct the instances, but most of them did not declare the argument to be a field of the instance. For example, recall our `Pipeline` example from "Phantom Types" on page 145:

```
object Pipeline {
  implicit class toPiped[V](value:V) {
    def |>[R] (f : V => R) = f(value)
  }
}
```

While `toPiped` refers to `value` in the `|>` method, `value` is not a field. Whether or not the constructor arguments are declared as fields with `val` or `var`, the arguments are visible in the entire class body. Hence they can be used by members of the type, such as methods. Compare with constructors as defined in Java and most other OO languages. Because the constructors themselves are methods, the arguments passed to them are not visible outside those methods. Hence, the arguments must be "saved" as fields, either public or hidden.

Why not just always make these arguments fields? A field is visible to clients of the type (that is, unless it's declared `private` or `protected`, as we'll discuss in Chapter 13). Unless these arguments are really part of the logical state exposed to users, they shouldn't be fields. Instead, they are effectively private to the class body.

The Uniform Access Principle

You might wonder why Scala doesn't follow the convention of the JavaBeans Specification (*http://bit.ly/1wNbg1E*) that reader and writer methods for a field `value` are named `getValue` and `setValue`, respectively. Instead, Scala chooses to follow the *Uniform Access Principle*.

As we saw in our `Name` example, it appears that clients can read and write the "bare" `value` field without going through accessor methods, but in fact they are calling methods. On the other hand, we could just declare a field in the class body with the default public visibility and then access it as a bare field:

```
class Name2(s: String) {
  var value: String = s
}
```

Now `value` is public and the accessor methods are gone.

Let's try it:

```
scala> val name2 = new Name2("Buck")
name2: Name2 = Name2@303becf6

scala> name2.value
res0: String = Buck

scala> name2.value_=("Bubba")
name2.value: String = Bubba

scala> name2.value
res1: String = Bubba
```

Note that user "experience" is identical. The user's code is agnostic about the implementation, so we are free to change the implementation from bare field access to accessor methods when necessary; for example, if we want to add some sort of validation on writes or lazily construct a result on reads, for efficiency. Conversely, we can replace accessor methods with public visibility of the field, to eliminate the overhead of a method call (though the JVM will probably eliminate that overhead anyway).

Therefore, the Uniform Access Principle has an important benefit in that it minimizes how much client code has to know about the internal implementation of a class. We can change that implementation without forcing client code changes, although a recompilation is required.

Scala implements this principle without sacrificing the benefits of access protections or the occasional need to perform additional logic besides just reading or writing a value.

Scala doesn't use Java-style getter and setter methods. Instead, it supports the Uniform Access Principle, where the syntax for reading and writing a "bare" field looks the same as the syntax for calling methods to read and write it, indirectly.

However, sometimes we need JavaBeans-style accessor methods for interoperability with Java libraries. We can annotate classes with the `scala.reflect.BeanProperty` (*http://bit.ly/1toozqm*) or the `BooleanBeanProperty` (*http://bit.ly/1u1960A*) annotation. See "JavaBean Properties" on page 499 for more details.

Unary Methods

We saw how the compiler lets us define an assignment method `foo_=` for field `foo`, then use it with the convenient syntax `myinstance.foo = value`. There's one other kind of operator we haven't seen how to implement, *unary operators*.

An example is negation. If we implement a complex number class, how would we support the negation of some instance c, i.e., `-c`? Here's how:

```
// src/main/scala/progscala2/basicoop/Complex.sc

case class Complex(real: Double, imag: Double) {
  def unary_- : Complex = Complex(-real, imag)                    // ❶
  def -(other: Complex) = Complex(real - other.real, imag - other.imag)
}

val c1 = Complex(1.1, 2.2)
val c2 = -c1                          // Complex(-1.1, 2.2)
val c3 = c1.unary_-                   // Complex(-1.1, 2.2)
val c4 = c1 - Complex(0.5, 1.0)       // Complex(0.6, 1.2)
```

❶ The method name is `unary_X`, where X is the operator character we want to use, - in this case. Note the space between the - and the :. This is necessary to tell the compiler that the method name ends with - and not :! For comparison, we also implement the usual minus operator.

Once we've defined a unary operator, we can place it *before* the instance, as we did when defining c2. We can also call it like any other method, as we did for c3.

Validating Input

What if we want to validate the input arguments to ensure that the resulting instances have a valid state? `Predef` (*http://bit.ly/1086O2z*) defines a useful set of overloaded methods called `require` that are useful for this purpose. Consider this class that encapsulates US zip codes. Two forms are allowed, a five-digit number and a "zip+4" form that adds an additional four digits. This form is usually written "12345-6789". Also, not all numbers correspond to real zip codes:

```scala
// src/main/scala/progscala2/basicoop/Zipcode.scala
package progscala2.basicoop

case class ZipCode(zip: Int, extension: Option[Int] = None) {
  require(valid(zip, extension),                                    // ❶
    s"Invalid Zip+4 specified: $toString")

  protected def valid(z: Int, e: Option[Int]): Boolean = {
    if (0 < z && z <= 99999) e match {
      case None    => validUSPS(z, 0)
      case Some(e) => 0 < e && e <= 9999 && validUSPS(z, e)
    }
    else false
  }

  /** Is it a real US Postal Service zip code? */
  protected def validUSPS(i: Int, e: Int): Boolean = true          // ❷

  override def toString =                                          // ❸
    if (extension != None) s"$zip-${extension.get}" else zip.toString
}
object ZipCode {
  def apply (zip: Int, extension: Int): ZipCode =
    new ZipCode(zip, Some(extension))
}
```

❶ Use the `require` method to validate input.

❷ A real implementation would check a USPS-sanctioned database to verify that the zip code actually exists.

❸ Override `toString` to return the format people expect for zip codes, with proper handling of the optional four-digit extension.

Here is a script that uses it:

```scala
// src/main/scala/progscala2/basicoop/Zipcode.sc
import progscala2.basicoop.ZipCode

ZipCode(12345)
// Result: ZipCode = 12345

ZipCode(12345, Some(6789))
// Result: ZipCode = 12345-6789

ZipCode(12345, 6789)
// Result: ZipCode = 12345-6789

try {
```

```
    ZipCode(0, 6789)  // Invalid Zip+4 specified: 0-6789
} catch {
    case e: java.lang.IllegalArgumentException => e
}

try {
    ZipCode(12345, 0)  // Invalid Zip+4 specified: 12345-0
} catch {
    case e: java.lang.IllegalArgumentException => e
}
```

One very good reason for defining domain-specific types like `ZipCode` is the ability to do validation of values once, during construction, so that users of `ZipCode` instances know that no further validation is required.

There are also `ensuring` and `assume` methods in `Predef` for similar purposes. We'll explore more uses for `require` and these two *assertion* methods in "Better Design with Design by Contract" on page 514.

Although we discussed validation in the context of construction, we can call these assertion methods inside any methods. However, an exception is the class bodies of value classes. The assertion checks can't be used there, otherwise a heap allocation would be required. However, `ZipCode` can't be a value class anyway, because it takes a second constructor argument.

Calling Parent Class Constructors (and Good Object-Oriented Design)

The primary constructor in a derived class must invoke one of the parent class constructors, either the primary constructor or an auxiliary constructor. In the following example, `Employee` is a subclass of `Person`:

```
// src/main/scala/progscala2/basicoop/EmployeeSubclass.sc
import progscala2.basicoop.Address

case class Person(     // This was Person2 previously, now renamed.
    name: String,
    age: Option[Int] = None,
    address: Option[Address] = None)

class Employee(                                                  // ❶
    name: String,
    age: Option[Int] = None,
    address: Option[Address] = None,
    val title: String = "[unknown]",                            // ❷
    val manager: Option[Employee] = None) extends Person(name, age, address) {

    override def toString =                                      // ❸
        s"Employee($name, $age, $address, $title, $manager)"
```

```
    }

val a1 = new Address("1 Scala Lane", "Anytown", "CA", "98765")
val a2 = new Address("98765")

val ceo = new Employee("Joe CEO", title = "CEO")
// Result: Employee(Joe CEO, None, None, CEO, None)

new Employee("Buck Trends1")
// Result: Employee(Buck Trends1, None, None, [unknown], None)

new Employee("Buck Trends2", Some(20), Some(a1))
// Result:  Employee(Buck Trends2, Some(20),
//             Some(Address(1 Scala Lane,Anytown,CA,98765)), [unknown], None)

new Employee("Buck Trends3", Some(20), Some(a1), "Zombie Dev")
// Result:  Employee(Buck Trends3, Some(20),
//             Some(Address(1 Scala Lane,Anytown,CA,98765)), Zombie Dev, None)

new Employee("Buck Trends4", Some(20), Some(a1), "Zombie Dev", Some(ceo))
// Result:  Employee(Buck Trends4, Some(20),
//             Some(Address(1 Scala Lane,Anytown,CA,98765)), Zombie Dev,
//             Some(Employee(Joe CEO, None, None, CEO, None)))
```

❶   Employee is declared a regular class, not a case class. We'll explain why in the
     next section.

❷   The new fields, title and manager, require the val keyword because Employ
     ee isn't a case class. The other arguments are already fields, from Person. Note
     that we also call Person's primary constructor.

❸   Override toString. Otherwise, Person.toString would be used.

In Java, we would define constructor methods and call super in them to invoke the
parent class initialization logic. In Scala, we implicitly invoke the parent class constructor through the ChildClass(…) extends ParentClass(…) syntax.

    Although super can be used to invoke overridden methods, as in Java,
                        it cannot be used to invoke a superclass constructor.

Good Object-Oriented Design: A Digression

This code *smells*. The declaration of Employee mixes val keywords or no keywords in
the argument list. But deeper problems lurk behind the source code.

We can derive a noncase class from a case class or the other way around, but we can't derive one case class from another. This is because the autogenerated implementations of `toString`, `equals`, and `hashCode` do not work properly for subclasses, meaning they ignore the possibility that an instance could actually be a derived type of the case class type.

This is actually by design; it reflects the problematic aspects of subclassing. For example, should an `Employee` instance and a `Person` instance be considered equal if both have the same name, age, and address? A more flexible interpretation of object equality would say yes, while a more restrictive version would say no. In fact, the mathematical definition of equality requires commutative behavior: `somePerson == someEmployee` should return the same result as `someEmployee == somePerson`. The more flexible interpretation would break associativity, because you would never expect an `Employee` instance to think it's equal to a `Person` instance that is not an `Employee`.

Actually, the problem of `equals` is even worse here, because `Employee` doesn't override the definitions of `equals` and `hashCode`. We're effectively treating all `Employee` instances as `Person` instances.

That's dangerous for small types like this. It's inevitable that someone will create a collection of employees, where they will try to sort the employees or use an employee as a key in a hash map. Because `Person.equals` and `Person.hashCode` will get used, respectively, anomalous behavior will occur when we have two people named John Smith, one of whom is the CEO while the other works in the mail room. The occasional confusion between the two will happen just often enough to be serious, but not often enough to be easily repeatable for finding and fixing the bug!

The real problem is that we are subclassing *state*. That is, we are using inheritance to add additional state contributions, `title` and `manager` in this case. In contrast, subclassing *behavior* with the *same* state fields is easier to implement robustly. It avoids the problems with `equals` and `hashCode` just described, for example.

Of course, these problems with inheritance have been known for a long time. Today, good object-oriented design favors *composition over inheritance*, where we compose units of functionality rather than build class hierarchies.

As we'll see in the next chapter, *traits* make composition far easier to use than Java interfaces, at least before Java 8. Hence, the examples in the book that aren't "toys" won't use inheritance that adds *state*. Such inheritance hierarchies are also very rare in production-quality Scala libraries, fortunately.

Hence, the Scala team could have made a choice to implement subclass-friendly versions of `equals`, `hashCode`, and `toString`, but that would have added extra complexity to support a bad design choice. Case classes provide convenient, simple domain types, with pattern matching and decomposition of instances of these types. Supporting inheritance hierarchies is not their purpose.

When inheritance is used, the following rules are recommended:

1. An abstract base class or trait is subclassed one level by concrete classes, including case classes.

2. Concrete classes are never subclassed, except for two cases:

    a. Classes that mix in other behaviors defined in `traits` (see Chapter 9). Ideally, those behaviors should be *orthogonal*, i.e., not overlapping.

    b. Test-only versions to promote automated unit testing.

3. When subclassing seems like the right approach, consider partitioning behaviors into traits and mix in those traits instead.

4. Never split logical state across parent-child type boundaries.

By "logical" state in the last bullet, I mean we might have some private, implementation-specific state that doesn't affect the externally visible, logical behavior of equality, hashing, etc. For example, our library might include special subtypes of our collections that add private fields to implement caching or logging behaviors (when a mixin trait for such features is not a good option).

So, what about `Employee`? If subclassing `Person` to create `Employee` is bad, what should we do instead? The answer really depends on the context of use. If we're implementing a Human Resources application, do we need a separate concept of `Person` or can `Employee` just be the base type, declared as a `case` class? Do we even need *any* types for this at all? If we're processing a result set from a database query, is it sufficient to use tuples or other containers to hold the fields returned from the query? Can we dispense with the "ceremony" of declaring a type altogether?

Let's just suppose we really need separate concepts of `Person` and `Employee`. Here's one way I would do it:

```scala
// src/main/scala/progscala2/basicoop/PersonEmployeeTraits.scala
package progscala2.basicoop2                              // ❶

case class Address(street: String, city: String, state: String, zip: String)

object Address {
  def apply(zip: String) =                                // ❷
    new Address(
      "[unknown]", Address.zipToCity(zip), Address.zipToState(zip), zip)

  def zipToCity(zip: String)  = "Anytown"
  def zipToState(zip: String) = "CA"
}
```

```scala
trait PersonState {                                  // ❸
  val name: String
  val age: Option[Int]
  val address: Option[Address]

  // Some common methods declared/defined here?
}
case class Person(                                   // ❹
  name: String,
  age: Option[Int] = None,
  address: Option[Address] = None) extends PersonState

trait EmployeeState {                                // ❺
  val title: String
  val manager: Option[Employee]
}
case class Employee(                                 // ❻
  name: String,
  age: Option[Int] = None,                           // ❼
  address: Option[Address] = None,
  title: String = "[unknown]",
  manager: Option[Employee] = None)
extends PersonState with EmployeeState
```

❶   Use a different package because earlier versions of some of these types are in package oop.

❷   Previously, Address had an auxiliary constructor. Now we use a second factory method.

❸   Define a trait for the state we *want* a person to have. You could pick a naming convention you like better than PersonState.

❹   When we just have Person instances, use this case class, which implements PersonState.

❺   Use the same technique for Employee, although it's less useful to declare a separate trait and case class for Employee. Still, consistency has its merits. The drawback is the extra "ceremony" we've introduced with separate traits and case classes.

❻   The Employee case class.

❼   Note that we have to define the default values twice for the fields shared between Person and Employee. That's a slight disadvantage (unless we actually need that flexibility).

Note that `Employee` is no longer a subclass of `Person`, but it is a subclass of `Person State`, because it mixes in that trait. Also, `EmployeeState` is not a subclass of `Person State`. Figure 8-1 is a class diagram to illustrate the relationships:

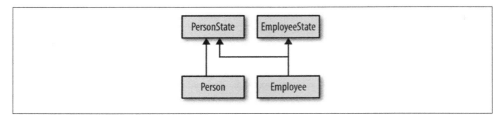

Figure 8-1. Class diagram for PersonState, Person, EmployeeState, and Employee

Note that both `Person` and `Employee` mix in traits, but `Employee` doesn't subclass another concrete class.

Let's try creating some objects:

```scala
// src/main/scala/progscala2/basicoop/PersonEmployeeTraits.sc
import progscala2.basicoop.{ Address, Person, Employee }

val ceoAddress  = Address("1 Scala Lane", "Anytown", "CA", "98765")
// Result: ceoAddress: oop2.Address = Address(1 Scala Lane,Anytown,CA,98765)

val buckAddress = Address("98765")
// Result: buckAddress: oop2.Address = Address([unknown],Anytown,CA,98765)

val ceo = Employee(
  name = "Joe CEO", title = "CEO", age = Some(50),
  address = Some(ceoAddress), manager = None)
// Result: ceo: oop2.Employee = Employee(Joe CEO,Some(50),
//            Some(Address(1 Scala Lane,Anytown,CA,98765)),CEO,None)

val ceoSpouse = Person("Jane Smith", address = Some(ceoAddress))
// Result: ceoSpouse: oop2.Person = Person(Jane Smith,None,
//            Some(Address(1 Scala Lane,Anytown,CA,98765)))

val buck = Employee(
  name = "Buck Trends", title = "Zombie Dev", age = Some(20),
  address = Some(buckAddress), manager = Some(ceo))
// Result: buck: oop2.Employee = Employee(Buck Trends,Some(20),
//            Some(Address([unknown],Anytown,CA,98765)),Zombie Dev,
//            Some(Employee(Joe CEO,Some(50),
//              Some(Address(1 Scala Lane,Anytown,CA,98765)),CEO,None)))

val buckSpouse = Person("Ann Collins", address = Some(buckAddress))
// Result: buckSpouse: oop2.Person = Person(Ann Collins,None,
//            Some(Address([unknown],Anytown,CA,98765)))
```

You'll notice I used named arguments for several declarations. When a constructor or other method takes a lot of arguments, I like using named arguments to make it clear what each argument means. It also helps avoid bugs when several arguments have the same type and it would be easy to switch values. Of course, you should try to avoid these risks by keeping the number of arguments small and making their types unique.

Now that I've whetted your appetite for traits, the next chapter explores them in depth. But first, we have one final topic to cover.

Nested Types

Scala lets us nest type declarations and definitions. For example, it's common to define type-specific exceptions and other useful types in an object. Here is a sketch of a possible database layer:

```scala
// src/main/scala/progscala2/basicoop/NestedTypes.scala

object Database {                                           // ❶
  case class ResultSet(/*...*/)                             // ❷
  case class Connection(/*...*/)                            // ❸

  case class DatabaseException(message: String, cause: Throwable) extends
    RuntimeException(message, cause)

  sealed trait Status                                        // ❹
  case object Disconnected extends Status
  case class  Connected(connection: Connection)  extends Status
  case class  QuerySucceeded(results: ResultSet) extends Status
  case class  QueryFailed(e: DatabaseException)  extends Status
}

class Database {
  import Database._

  def connect(server: String): Status = ???                 // ❺
  def disconnect(): Status = ???

  def query(/*...*/): Status = ???
}
```

❶ A simplified interface to databases.

❷ Encapsulate query *result sets*. We elided the details that we don't care about for this sketch.

❸ Encapsulate connection pools and other information.

❹ Use a sealed hierarchy for the status; all allowed values are defined here. Use case objects when instances don't actually carry any additional state information. These objects behave like "flags" indicating a state.

❺ The ??? is an actual method defined in `Predef`. It simply throws an exception. It is used to mark methods as unimplemented. It is a relatively recent introduction to the library.

Consider using `case object` when a case class doesn't have any fields representing additional state information.

The ??? method is very handy for providing a placeholder implementation of a method when code is under development. The code compiles, but you can't call the method!

There is one "hole" I've found with `case objects`. Consider this session:

```scala
scala> case object Foo
defined object Foo

scala> Foo.hashCode
res0: Int = 70822

scala> "Foo".hashCode
res1: Int = 70822
```

Apparently, the generated `hashCode` for the `case object` simply hashes the object's name. The object's package is ignored as are any fields in the object. This means that `case objects` are risky in contexts where a strong `hashCode` implementation is needed.

Avoid using `case objects` in contexts where a strong `hashCode` is required, such as keys for hash-based maps and sets.

Recap and What's Next

We filled in the details for the basics of Scala's object model, including constructors, inheritance, and nesting of types. We also digressed at times on the subject of good object-oriented design, in Scala or any language.

We also set the stage for diving into `traits`, Scala's enhancement to Java interfaces, which provide a powerful tool for composing behaviors from constituent parts, without resorting to inheritance and its drawbacks. In the next chapter we'll complete our understanding of traits and how to use them to solve various design problems.

## CHAPTER 9

Traits

In Java, a class can implement an arbitrary number of *interfaces*. This model is very useful for declaring that a class implements multiple abstractions. Unfortunately, it has one major drawback. For many interfaces, much of the functionality can be implemented with boilerplate code that will be valid for all classes that use the interface.

Often, an interface has members that are unrelated ("orthogonal") to the rest of the members in the implementating class. The term *mixin* is used for such focused and reusable state and behavior. Ideally, we would maintain this behavior independent of any concrete types that use it.

Before version 8, Java provided no built-in mechanism for defining and using such reusable code. Instead, Java programmers must use ad hoc conventions to reuse implementation code for a given interface. In the worst case, the developer just copies and pastes the same code into every class that needs it. A better, but imperfect solution has been to implement a separate class for the behavior, keep an instance of it in the original class, and then delegate method calls to the support class. This approach works, but it adds lots of needless overhead and error-prone boilerplate.

Interfaces in Java 8

Java 8 changes this picture. Interfaces can now *define* methods, called *defender methods* or just *default methods*. A class can still provide its own implementation, but if it doesn't the defender method is used. So, Java 8 interfaces behave more like Scala's traits.

However, one difference is that Java 8 interfaces are still limited to defining static fields, whereas Scala traits can define instance-level fields. This means that Java 8 interfaces can't manage any part of an instance's state. A class that implements the interface will have to supply fields for state. This also means that the defender methods have no state to access in their implementations, limiting what they can do.

In the discussion that follows, consider how you would implement the traits and classes presented using Java 8 interfaces and classes. What would port over easily to Java 8 and what would not?

Traits as Mixins

To consider the role of traits in modularizing Scala code, let's begin with the following code for a button in a graphical user interface (GUI) toolkit, which uses callbacks to notify clients when clicks occur:

```scala
// src/main/scala/progscala2/traits/ui/ButtonCallbacks.scala
package progscala2.traits.ui

class ButtonWithCallbacks(val label: String,
    val callbacks: List[() => Unit] = Nil) extends Widget {

  def click(): Unit = {
    updateUI()
    callbacks.foreach(f => f())
  }

  protected def updateUI(): Unit = { /* logic to change GUI appearance */ }
}

object ButtonWithCallbacks {

  def apply(label: String, callback: () => Unit) =
    new ButtonWithCallbacks(label, List(callback))

  def apply(label: String) =
    new ButtonWithCallbacks(label, Nil)
}
```

Widget is a "marker" trait we will expand later:

```scala
// src/main/scala/progscala2/traits/ui/Widget.scala
package progscala2.traits.ui

abstract class Widget
```

A list of callback functions of type () => Unit (pure side effects) are called when the button is clicked.

This class has two responsibilities: updating the visual appearance (which we've elided) and handling callback behavior, including the management of a list of callbacks and calling them whenever the button is clicked.

We should strive for *separation of concerns* in our types, as embodied in the *Single Responsibility Principle*, which says that every type should "do one thing" and not mix multiple responsibilities.

We would like to separate the button-specific logic from the callback logic, such that each part becomes simpler, more modular, easier to test and modify, and more reusable. The callback logic is a good candidate for a *mixin*.

Let's use traits to separate the callback handling from the button logic. We'll generalize our approach a little bit. Callbacks are really a special case of the *Observer Design Pattern*. So, let's create two traits that declare and partially implement the Subject and Observer logic from this pattern, then use them to handle callback behavior. To simplify things, we'll start with a single callback that counts the number of button clicks:

```scala
// src/main/scala/progscala2/traits/observer/Observer.scala
package progscala2.traits.observer

trait Observer[-State] {                                    // ❶
  def receiveUpdate(state: State): Unit
}

trait Subject[State] {                                      // ❷
  private var observers: List[Observer[State]] = Nil        // ❸

  def addObserver(observer:Observer[State]): Unit =         // ❹
    observers ::= observer                                  // ❺

  def notifyObservers(state: State): Unit =                 // ❻
    observers foreach (_.receiveUpdate(state))
}
```

❶ The trait for clients who want to be notified of state changes. They must implement the receiveUpdate message.

❷ The trait for subjects who will send notifications to observers.

❸ A list of observers to notify. It's mutable, so it's not thread-safe!

❹ A method to add observers.

❺ This expression means "prefix observer to observers and assign the result to observers."

❻ A method to notify observers of state changes.

Often, the most convenient choice for the State type parameter is just the type of the class mixing in Subject. Hence, when the notifyObservers method is called, the instance just passes itself, i.e., this.

Note that because Observer doesn't define the method it declares nor does it declare any other members, it is exactly equivalent to a pre-Java 8 interface at the byte code level. No abstract keyword is required, because the missing method body makes it clear. However, abstract classes, those with unimplemented method bodies, must be declared with the abstract keyword. For example:

```
trait PureAbstractTrait {
  def abstractMember(str: String): Int
}

abstract class AbstractClass {
  def concreteMember(str: String): Int = str.length
  def abstractMember(str: String): Int
}
```

 Traits with abstract members don't have to be declared abstract by adding the abstract keyword before the trait keyword. However, classes that are abstract, where one or more member is undefined, must be declared abstract.

To expand on the fifth note, because observers is mutable, the following two expressions are equivalent:

```
observers ::= observer
observers = observer :: observers
```

Now, let's define a simplified Button class:

```
// src/main/scala/progscala2/traits/ui/Button.scala
package progscala2.traits.ui

class Button(val label: String) extends Widget {

  def click(): Unit = updateUI()

  def updateUI(): Unit = { /* logic to change GUI appearance */ }
}
```

Button is considerably simpler. It has only one concern, handling clicks.

Let's put our Subject trait to use. Here is ObservableButton, which subclasses Button and mixes in Subject:

```
// src/main/scala/progscala2/traits/ui/ObservableButton.scala
package progscala2.traits.ui
import progscala2.traits.observer._

class ObservableButton(name: String)                          // ❶
    extends Button(name) with Subject[Button] {               // ❷

  override def click(): Unit = {                              // ❸
    super.click()                                             // ❹
    notifyObservers(this)                                     // ❺
  }
}
```

❶ A subclass of Button that mixes in observability.

❷ Extends `Button` and mixes in `Subject` and uses `Button` as the `Subject` type parameter, named `State` in the declaration of `Subject`.

❸ In order to notify observers, we have to override the `click` method. If there were other state-changing methods, all would require overrides.

❹ First, call the parent class `click` to perform the normal GUI update logic.

❺ Notify the observers, passing `this` as the `State`. In this case, there isn't any state other than the "event" that a button click occurred.

Let's try it with the following script:

```
// src/main/scala/progscala2/traits/ui/button-count-observer.sc
import progscala2.traits.ui._
import progscala2.traits.observer._

class ButtonCountObserver extends Observer[Button] {
  var count = 0
  def receiveUpdate(state: Button): Unit = count += 1
}

val button = new ObservableButton("Click Me!")
val bco1   = new ButtonCountObserver
val bco2   = new ButtonCountObserver

button addObserver bco1
button addObserver bco2

(1 to 5) foreach (_ => button.click())

assert(bco1.count == 5)
assert(bco2.count == 5)
```

The script declares an observer type, `ButtonCountObserver`, that counts clicks. Then it creates two instances and an `ObservableButton`, and it registers the two observers with the button. It clicks the button five times and then uses the `assert` method in `Predef` (*http://bit.ly/11QI0fF*) to verify the counts for each observer equals five.

Suppose we only need one instance of an `ObservableButton`. We don't need to declare a class that mixes in the traits we want. Instead, we can declare a `Button` and mix in the `Subject` trait "on the fly":

```
// src/main/scala/progscala2/traits/ui/button-count-observer2.sc
import progscala2.traits.ui._
import progscala2.traits.observer._

val button = new Button("Click Me!") with Subject[Button] {

  override def click(): Unit = {
    super.click()
```

```
      notifyObservers(this)
  }
}

class ButtonCountObserver extends Observer[Button] {
  var count = 0
  def receiveUpdate(state: Button): Unit = count += 1
}

val bco1    = new ButtonCountObserver
val bco2    = new ButtonCountObserver

button addObserver bco1
button addObserver bco2

(1 to 5) foreach (_ => button.click())

assert(bco1.count == 5)
assert(bco2.count == 5)
println("Success!")
```

We declared a `Button() with Subject[Button]` *instance*, without declaring a class first. This is similar to instantiating an anonymous class that implements an interface in Java, but Scala provides more flexibility.

 When declaring a class that only mixes in traits and doesn't extend another class, you must use the `extends` keyword anyway for the first trait listed and the `with` keyword for the rest of the traits. However, when instantiating a class and mixing in traits with the declaration, use the `with` keyword with all the traits.

In "Good Object-Oriented Design: A Digression" on page 264, I recommended stringent rules for subclassing. Have we broken those "rules"? Let's look at each one:

An abstract base class or trait is subclassed one level by concrete classes, including case classes

   We didn't use an abstract base class in this case.

Concrete classes are never subclassed, except for two cases: (1) classes that mix in other behaviors in traits

   Although `Button` and `ObservableButton`, its child, are both concrete, the latter only mixes in traits.

Concrete classes are never subclassed, except for two cases: (2) test-only versions to promote automated unit testing

   Not applicable.

When subclassing seems like the right approach, consider partitioning behaviors into traits and mix in those traits instead

We did!!

Never split logical state across parent-child type boundaries

The logical, visible state for buttons or other UI widgets is disjoint from the internal mechanism of state-change notification. So, UI state is still encapsulated in But ton, while the state associated with the *Observer* pattern, i.e., the list of observers, is encapsulated in the State trait.

Stackable Traits

There are several, further refinements we can do to improve the reusability of our code and to make it easier to use more than one trait at a time, i.e., to "stack" traits.

First, "clickability" is not limited to buttons in a GUI. We should abstract that logic, too. We could put it in Widget, the so-far empty parent type of Button, but it's not necessarily true that all GUI widgets will accept clicks. Instead, let's introduce another trait, Click able:

```
// src/main/scala/progscala2/traits/ui2/Clickable.scala
package progscala2.traits.ui2                                  // ❶

trait Clickable {
  def click(): Unit = updateUI()                               // ❷

  protected def updateUI(): Unit                               // ❸
}
```

❶   Use a new package because we're reimplementing types in traits.ui.

❷   The public method click is concrete. It delegates to updateUI.

❸   The updateUI method is protected and abstract. Implementing classes provide the appropriate logic.

Although this simple interface doesn't really need to follow the example of Button, where click delegates to a protected method, it was a useful idiom for separation of a public abstraction from an implementation detail, so we follow it here. It's a simple example of the *Template Method Pattern* described in the "Gang of Four" patterns book.

Here is the refactored button, which uses the trait:

```
// src/main/scala/progscala2/traits/ui2/Button.scala
package progscala2.traits.ui2
import progscala2.traits.ui.Widget

class Button(val label: String) extends Widget with Clickable {
```

```
    protected def updateUI(): Unit = { /* logic to change GUI appearance */ }
}
```

Observation should now be tied to `Clickable` and not `Button`, as it was before. When we refactor the code this way, it becomes clear that we don't really care about observing buttons. We really care about observing *events*, such as clicks. Here is a trait that focuses solely on observing `Clickable`:

```
// src/main/scala/progscala2/traits/ui2/ObservableClicks.scala
package progscala2.traits.ui2
import progscala2.traits.observer._

trait ObservableClicks extends Clickable with Subject[Clickable] {
  abstract override def click(): Unit = {          // ❶
    super.click()
    notifyObservers(this)
  }
}
```

❶   Note the `abstract override` keywords, discussed next.

The implementation is very similar to the previous `ObservableButton` example. The important difference is the `abstract` keyword. We had `override` before.

Look closely at this method. It calls `super.click()`, but what is `super` in this case? At this point, it could only appear to be `Clickable`, which *declares* but does not *define* the `click` method, or it could be `Subject`, which doesn't have a `click` method. So, `super` can't be bound to a real instance, at least not yet. This is why `abstract` is required here.

In fact, `super` will be bound when this trait is mixed into a concrete instance that defines the `click` method, such as `Button`. The `abstract` keyword tells the compiler (and the reader) that `click` is not yet fully implemented, even though `Observable Clicks.click` has a body.

The abstract keyword is only required on a method in a trait when the method *has* a body, but it invokes another method in super that doesn't have a concrete implementation in parents of the trait.

Let's use this trait with `Button` and its concrete `click` method:

```
// src/main/scala/progscala2/traits/ui2/click-count-observer.sc
import progscala2.traits.ui2._
import progscala2.traits.observer._

// No override of "click" in Button required.
val button = new Button("Click Me!") with ObservableClicks
```

```
class ClickCountObserver extends Observer[Clickable] {
  var count = 0
  def receiveUpdate(state: Clickable): Unit = count += 1
}

val bco1 = new ClickCountObserver
val bco2 = new ClickCountObserver

button addObserver bco1
button addObserver bco2

(1 to 5) foreach (_ => button.click())

assert(bco1.count == 5, s"bco1.count ${bco1.count} != 5")
assert(bco2.count == 5, s"bco2.count ${bco2.count} != 5")
println("Success!")
```

Note that we can now declare a `Button` instance and mix in `ObservableClicks` without having to override the `click` method. Not only that, even when we don't want to observe clicks, we can construct GUI objects that support clicking by mixing in `Clickable`.

This fine-grained composition through mixin traits is quite powerful, but it can be overused:

- Lots of traits slow down compile times, because the compiler has to do more work to synthesize the output byte code.
- Library users can find a long list of traits intimidating when looking at code or Scaladocs.

Let's finish our example by adding a second trait. The JavaBeans Specification (*http://bit.ly/1E8xIGM*) has the idea of "vetoable" events, where listeners for changes to a JavaBean can veto the change. Let's implement something similar with a trait that vetoes more than a set number of clicks. You could imagine implementing something similar to prevent users from accidentally clicking a button more than once that triggers a financial transaction. Here is our `VetoableClick` trait:

```
// src/main/scala/progscala2/traits/ui2/VetoableClicks.scala
package progscala2.traits.ui2
import progscala2.traits.observer._

trait VetoableClicks extends Clickable {                        // ❶
  // Default number of allowed clicks.
  val maxAllowed = 1                                            // ❷
  private var count = 0

  abstract override def click() = {
    if (count < maxAllowed) {                                   // ❸
      count += 1
      super.click()
```

```
        }
    }
}
```

❶ Also extends Clickable.

❷ The maximum number of allowed clicks. (A "reset" feature would be useful.)

❸ Once the number of clicks exceeds the allowed value (counting from zero), no
    further clicks are sent to super.

Note that maxAllowed is declared a val and the comment says it is the "default" value,
which implies it can be changed. How can that be if it's a val? The answer is that we can
override the value in a class or trait that mixes in this trait. In this use of both traits, we
reset the value to 2:

```
// src/main/scala/progscala2/traits/ui2/vetoable-click-count-observer.sc
import progscala2.traits.ui2._
import progscala2.traits.observer._

// No override of "click" in Button required.
val button =
    new Button("Click Me!") with ObservableClicks with VetoableClicks {
  override val maxAllowed = 2                                  // ❶
}

class ClickCountObserver extends Observer[Clickable] {          // ❷
  var count = 0
  def receiveUpdate(state: Clickable): Unit = count += 1
}

val bco1 = new ClickCountObserver
val bco2 = new ClickCountObserver

button addObserver bco1
button addObserver bco2

(1 to 5) foreach (_ => button.click())

assert(bco1.count == 2, s"bco1.count ${bco1.count} != 2")       // ❸
assert(bco2.count == 2, s"bco2.count ${bco2.count} != 2")
println("Success!")
```

❶ Override the value of maxAllowed to 2.

❷ Use the same ClickObserver as before.

❸ Note that the expected count is now 2, even though the actual number of button
    clicks is 5.

Try this experiment. Switch the order of the traits in the declaration of button to this:

```
val button = new Button("Click Me!") with VetoableClicks with ObservableClicks
```

What happens when you run this code now?

The assertions should now fail, claiming that the count observed is actually 5, not the expected 2.

We have three versions of click wrapped like an onion. The question is which version of click gets called first when we mix in VetoableClicks and ObservableClicks? The answer is the declaration order determines the order, from *right* to *left*.

Here is pseudocode for the effective call structure for each example:

```
// new Button("Click Me!") with VetoableClicks with ObservableClicks

def ObservableClicks.click() = {
  if (count < maxAllowed) {       // super.click => VetoableClicks.click
    count += 1
    {
      updateUI()                  // super.click => Clickable.click
    }
  }
  notifyObservers(this)
}

// new Button("Click Me!") with ObservableClicks with VetoableClicks

def VetoableClicks.click() = {
  if (count < maxAllowed) {
    count += 1
    {                             // super.click => ObservableClicks.click
      {
        updateUI()                // super.click => Clickable.click
      }
      notifyObservers(this)
    }
  }
}
```

In the first case, when ObservableClicks is last in the declaration order, the actual Clickable.click method is still vetoed, but the observers are notified for all clicks. You could interpret this is a bug if observers are expecting notification only when clicks are not vetoed.

In the second case, when VetoableClicks is last in the declaration order, the veto logic wraps all other click methods, so updateUI *and* notifyObservers are both called only when the click isn't vetoed.

A algorithm called *linearization* is used to resolve the priority of traits and classes in the inheritance tree for a concrete class. These two versions of button are straightforward.

The traits have priority order from right to left and the body of button, such as the version that overrides maxAllowed, is evaluated last.

We'll cover the full details of how linearization works for more complex declarations in "Linearization of an Object's Hierarchy" on page 326.

Constructing Traits

While the body of a trait functions as its primary constructor, traits don't support an argument list for the primary constructor, nor can you define auxiliary constructors.

We saw in the last section's examples that traits can extend other traits. They can also extend classes. However, there is no mechanism for a trait to pass arguments to the parent class constructor, even literal values. Therefore, traits can only extend classes that have a no-argument primary or auxiliary constructor.

However, like classes, the body of a trait is executed every time an instance is created that uses the trait, as demonstrated by the following script:

```scala
// src/main/scala/progscala2/traits/trait-construction.sc

trait T1 {
  println(s"  in T1: x = $x")
  val x=1
  println(s"  in T1: x = $x")
}

trait T2 {
  println(s"  in T2: y = $y")
  val y="T2"
  println(s"  in T2: y = $y")
}

class Base12 {
  println(s"  in Base12: b = $b")
  val b="Base12"
  println(s"  in Base12: b = $b")
}

class C12 extends Base12 with T1 with T2 {
  println(s"  in C12: c = $c")
  val c="C12"
  println(s"  in C12: c = $c")
}

println(s"Creating C12:")
new C12
println(s"After Creating C12")
```

Running this script yields the following output:

```
Creating C12:
  in Base12: b = null
  in Base12: b = Base12
  in T1: x = 0
  in T1: x = 1
  in T2: y = null
  in T2: y = T2
  in C12: c = null
  in C12: c = C12
After Creating C12
```

Here we have a base class `Base12` for C12. It is evaluated first, then the traits T1 and T2 (i.e., *left* to *right* in declaration order), and finally the body of C12.

The order of the `println` statements for T1 and T2 seem to be reversed compared to our `Clickable` example. Actually, this is consistent. Here we are tracking initialization order, which goes left to right.

When we declared `button` with traits in the order with `VetoableClicks` with `Observ ableClicks`, we first defined `click` as the method `VetoableClicks.click`. It called `super.click`, which wasn't resolved yet, at that moment. Then `ObservableClicks` was evaluated. It overrode `VetoableClicks.click` with its own version of `click`, but because it also called `super.click`, it will invoke `VetoableClicks.click`. Finally, because `ObservableClicks` extends `Clickable`, it provides a concrete `click` that `Vetoable Clicks.click` needs to call when it calls `super.click`.

So, while you can't pass construction parameters to traits, you can initialize fields, as well as methods and types, in the body of the trait. Subsequent traits or classes in the linearization can override these definitions. If a member is left abstract in the trait or abstract parent class where it is declared, a subsequent trait or class must define it. Concrete classes can't have any abstract members.

 Avoid concrete fields in traits that can't be initialized to suitable default values. Use abstract fields instead, or convert the trait to a class with a constructor. Of course, stateless traits don't have any issues with initialization.

Class or Trait?

When considering whether a "concept" should be a trait or a class, keep in mind that traits as mixins make the most sense for "adjunct" behavior. If you find that a particular trait is used most often as a parent of other classes, so that the child classes *behave as* the parent trait, then consider defining the trait as a class instead, to make this logical relationship more clear. (We said *behaves as*, rather than *is a*, because the former is the more precise definition of inheritance, based on the *Liskov Substitution Principle*.)

It's a general principle of good object-oriented design that an instance should always be in a known valid state, starting from the moment the construction process finishes.

Recap and What's Next

In this chapter, we learned how to use traits to encapsulate and share cross-cutting concerns between classes. We covered when and how to use traits, how to "stack" multiple traits, and the rules for initializing values within traits.

In the next few chapters, we explore Scala's object system and class hierarchy, with particular attention to the collections.

## CHAPTER 10

The Scala Object System, Part I

We've learned a lot about Scala's implementation of object-oriented programming. In this chapter, we'll discuss more details of the type hierarchy in the standard library, exploring some of those types in depth, such as Predef (*http://bit.ly/1086O2z*).

But first, let's discuss an important feature of the type system called *variance under inheritance*, which we'll need to understand before discussing several of the library types described later in this chapter.

We'll conclude with a discussion of object equality.

Parameterized Types: Variance Under Inheritance

An important difference between Java's and Scala's parameterized types (usually called *generics* in the Java literature) is how *variance under inheritance* works.

For example, suppose a method takes an argument of type List[AnyRef]. Can you pass a List[String] value? In other words, should a List[String] be considered a *subtype* of List[AnyRef]? If true, this kind of variance is called *covariance*, because the supertype-subtype relationship of the container (the parameterized type) "goes in the same direction" as the relationship between the type parameters.

We can also have types that are *contravariant*, where X[String] is a *supertype* of X[Any], for some type X.

If a parameterized type is neither covariant nor contravariant, it is called *invariant*. Conversely, some parameterized types can mix two or more of these behaviors.

Both Java and Scala support covariant, contravariant, and invariant types. However, in Scala, the variance behavior is defined as part of the type *declaration* using a so-called *variance annotation* on each type parameter, as appropriate. For covariant type parameters, + is used. For contravariant type parameters, - is used. No annotation is used for invariant type parameters. In other words, the type designer decides how the type should vary under inheritance.

Here are some example declarations (we'll see examples of real types shortly):

```
class W[+A] {...}      // covariant
class X[-A] {...}      // contravariant
class Y[A] {...}       // invariant
class Z[-A,B,+C] {...} // mixed
```

In contrast, Java parameterized type *definitions* do not define the variance behavior under inheritance. Instead, the variance behavior of a parameterized type is specified when the type is *used*, i.e., at the *call site*, when variables are declared.

The three kinds of variance notations for Java and Scala and their meanings are summarized in Table 10-1. T^{sup} is a *supertype* of T and T_{sub} is a *subtype* of T.

Table 10-1. Type variance annotations and their meanings

Scala	Java	Description
+T	? extends T	*Covariant* (e.g., $List[T_{sub}]$ is a subtype of List[T]).
-T	? super T	*Contravariant* (e.g., $X[T^{sup}]$ is a subtype of X[T]).
T	T	*Invariant* subclassing (e.g., can't substitute $Y[T^{sup}]$ or $Y[T_{sub}]$ for Y[T]).

Back to List—it is actually declared List[+A], which means that List[String] is a subclass of List[AnyRef], so Lists are covariant in the type parameter A. When a type like List has only one covariant type parameter, you'll often hear the shorthand expression "Lists are covariant" and similarly for contravariant types.

Covariant and invariant types are reasonably easy to understand. What about contravariant types?

Functions Under the Hood

The best example of contravariance is the set of traits FunctionN, such as scala.Function2 (*http://bit.ly/10Ft2tC*), where N is between 0 and 22, inclusive, and corresponds to the number of arguments that a function takes. Scala uses these traits to implement anonymous functions.

We've been using anonymous functions, also known as function literals, throughout the book. For example:

```
List(1, 2, 3, 4) map (i => i + 3)
// Result: List(4, 5, 6, 7)
```

The function expression i => i + 3 is actually *syntactic sugar* that the compiler converts to the following instantiation of an anonymous subclass of scala.Function1 (*http://bit.ly/13KD90C*):

```
val f: Int => Int = new Function1[Int,Int] {
  def apply(i: Int): Int = i + 3
}
List(1, 2, 3, 4) map (f)
// Result: List(4, 5, 6, 7)
```

The conventional name `apply` for the default method called when an object is followed by an argument list originated with the idea of *function application*. For example, once f is defined, we call it by applying an argument list to it, e.g., f(1), which is actually f.apply(1).

Historically, the JVM didn't allow "bare" functions in byte code. Everything had to be in an object wrapper. More recent versions of Java, especially Java 8, relax this restriction, but to enable Scala to work on older JVMs, the compiler has converted anonymous functions into anonymous subclasses of the appropriate FunctionN trait. You've probably written anonymous subclasses like this for Java interfaces many times in your Java projects.

The FunctionN traits are abstract, because the method `apply` is abstract. Note that we defined `apply` here. The compiler does this for us when we use the more concise literal syntax instead, i => i + 3. That function body is used to define `apply`.

Java 8 adds support for function literals, called *lambdas*. They use a different implementation than the one used by Scala, because Scala supports older JVMs.

Returning to contravariance, here is the declaration of scala.Function2 (*http://bit.ly/10Ft2tC*):

```
trait Function2[-T1, -T2, +R] extends AnyRef
```

The last type parameter, +R, the is the return type. It is *covariant*. The leading two type parameters are for the first and second function arguments, respectively. They are *contravariant*. For the other FunctionN traits, the type parameters corresponding to function arguments are contravariant.

Therefore, functions have mixed variance behavior under inheritance.

What does this really mean? Let's look at an example to understand the variance behavior:

```
// src/main/scala/progscala2/objectsystem/variance/func.scX

class CSuper                    { def msuper() = println("CSuper") }        // ❶
```

```
class C        extends CSuper { def m()    = println("C") }
class CSub     extends C     { def msub()  = println("CSub") }

var f: C => C = (c: C)      => new C          // ❷
    f         = (c: CSuper) => new CSub       // ❸
    f         = (c: CSuper) => new C          // ❹
    f         = (c: C)      => new CSub       // ❺
    f         = (c: CSub)   => new CSuper     // ❻ COMPILATION ERROR!
```

❶ Define a three-level inheritance hierarchy of classes.

❷ We define one function f as a var so we can keep assigning new functions to it. All valid function instances must be C => C (in other words, Function1[C,C]; note how we can use the literal syntax for the type, too). The values we assign must satisfy the constraints of variance under inheritance for functions. The first assignment is (c: C) => new C (it ignores the argument c).

❸ This function value, (c: CSuper) => new CSub, is valid, because the argument C is contravariant, so CSuper is a valid substitution, while the return value is covariant, so CSub is a valid replacement for C.

❹ Similar to the previous case, but we simply return a C.

❺ Similar to the previous cases, but we simply pass a C.

❻ An error! A function that takes a CSub argument is invalid, because of contravariance, and the return type CSuper is invalid due to covariance.

This script doesn't produce any output. If you run it, it will fail to compile on the last line, but the other statements will be valid.

Design by Contract (http://bit.ly/10FhJln) explains why these rules make sense. It is a formulation of the *Liskov Substitution Principle* and we'll discuss it briefly as a programming tool in "Better Design with Design by Contract" on page 514. For now, let's try to understand intuitively why these rules work.

The function variable f is of type C => C (that is, Function1[-C,+C]). The first assignment to f matches this type signature exactly.

Now we assign different anonymous function values to f. The whitespace makes the similarities and differences stand out when comparing the original declaration of f and the subsequent reassignments. We keep reassigning to f because we are testing what substitutions are valid for C => C.

The second assignment, (x:CSuper) => CSub, obeys the declaration for *contravariant* arguments and a *covariant* return type, but *why is this safe*?

The key insight is to recall how f will be used and what assumptions we can make about the actual function behind it. When we say its type is C => C, we are defining a <emphasis

role="keep-together">contract</emphasis>] that any valid C value can be passed to f and f will never return anything other than a C value.

So, if the actual function has the type (x:CSuper) => CSub, that function not only accepts any C value as an argument, it can also handle any instance of the parent type CSuper or another of its other subtypes, if any. Therefore, because we only pass C instances, we'll never pass an argument to f that is outside the range of values it promises to accept. In a sense, f is more "permissive" than it needs to be for this use.

Similarly, when it returns only CSub instances, that is also safe, because the caller can handle instances of C, so it can certainly always handle instances of CSub. In this sense, f is more "restrictive" than it needs to be for this use.

The last line in the example breaks both rules for input and output types. Let's consider what would happen if we allowed that substitution for f.

In this case, the actual f would only know how to handle CSub instances, but the caller would believe that any C instance can be passed to f, so a runtime failure is likely when f is "surprised," i.e., it tries to call some method that is only defined for CSub, not C. Similarly, if the actual f can return a CSuper, it will "surprise" the caller with an instance that is outside the range of expected return values, the allowed instances of C.

This is why function arguments must be contravariant and return values must be covariant.

Variance annotations only make sense on the type parameters for *types*, not for parameterized methods, because the annotations affect the behavior of subtyping. Methods aren't subtyped. For example, the simplified signature for the List.map method looks like this:

```
sealed abstract class List[+A] ... {  // mixin traits omitted
  ...
  def map[B](f: A => B): List[B] = {...}
  ...
}
```

There is no variance annotation on B and if you tried to add one, the compiler would throw an error.

 The + *variance annotation* means the parameterized type is *covariant* in the type parameter. The - variance annotation means the parameterized type is *contravariant* in the type parameter. No variance annotation means the parameterized type is *invariant* in the type parameter.

Finally, the compiler checks your use of variance annotations for invalid uses. Here's what happens if you attempt to define your own function with the wrong annotations:

```
scala> trait MyFunction2[+T1, +T2, -R] {
     |   def apply(v1:T1, v2:T2): R = ???
     | }
<console>:37: error: contravariant type R occurs in covariant position
in type (v1: T1, v2: T2)R of method apply
         def apply(v1:T1, v2:T2): R = ???
             ^
<console>:37: error: covariant type T1 occurs in contravariant position
in type T1 of value v1
         def apply(v1:T1, v2:T2): R = ???
             ^
<console>:37: error: covariant type T2 occurs in contravariant position
in type T2 of value v2
         def apply(v1:T1, v2:T2): R = ???
                   ^
```

Note the error messages. The compiler requires function arguments to behave *contravariantly* and return types to behave *covariantly*.

Variance of Mutable Types

All the parameterized types we've discussed so far have been immutable types. What about the variance behavior of mutable types? The short answer is that only *invariance* is allowed. Consider this example:

```
// src/main/scala/progscala2/objectsystem/variance/mutable-type-variance.scX

scala> class ContainerPlus[+A](var value: A)
<console>:34: error: covariant type A occurs in contravariant position
in type A of value value_=
       class ContainerPlus[+A](var value: A)
             ^

scala> class ContainerMinus[-A](var value: A)
<console>:34: error: contravariant type A occurs in covariant position
in type => A of method value
       class ContainerMinus[-A](var value: A)
             ^
```

The problem with a mutable field is that it behaves like a private field with public read *and* write accessor methods, even if the field is actually public and has no explicit accessor methods.

Recall from "Fields in Classes" on page 258 that def value_=(newA: A): Unit+ is the signature the compiler interprets as the setter for variable value. That is, we can write an expression myinstance.value = someA and this method will be called. Note that the first error message uses this method signature and complains that we're using covariant type A in a contravariant position.

The second error message mentions a method signature => A. That is, a function that takes no arguments and returns an A, just like the *by-name* parameters we first saw in "Call by Name, Call by Value" on page 87.

Here's another way to write the declaration using these methods explicitly, which looks more like traditional Java code:

```
class ContainerPlus[+A](var a: A) {
  private var _value: A = a
  def value_=(newA: A): Unit = _value = newA
  def value: A = _value
}
```

Why must the A passed to value_=(newA: A) be contravariant? This doesn't seem right, because we're assigning a new value to _value, but if the new value can be a supertype of A, then we'll get a type error, because _value must be of type A, right?

Actually, that's the wrong way to think about the situation. The covariant/contravariant rules apply to how subclasses behave relative to superclasses.

Assume for a moment that our declaration is valid. For example, we could instantiate ContainerPlus[C], using our C, CSub, and CSuper from before:

```
val cp = new ContainerPlus(new C)    // ❶
cp.value = new C                     // ❷
cp.value = new CSub                  // ❸
cp.value = new CSuper                // ❹
```

❶   Type parameter A is now C.

❷   Valid: we're just using the same type instance.

❸   Valid for the usual object-oriented reasons, since CSub is a subtype of C.

❹   Compilation error, because a CSuper instance can't be substituted for a C instance.

It's only when considering subtypes of ContainerPlus that trouble ensues:

```
val cp: ContainerPlus[C] = new ContainerPlus(new CSub)   // ❶
cp.value = new C              // ❷
cp.value = new CSub           // ❸
cp.value = new CSuper         // ❹
```

❶   Would be valid, if ContainerPlus[+A] were valid.

❷   From the declared type of c, this should be valid *and this is why the argument type must be contravariant*, but the actual value_= method for the instance can't accept a C instance, because its value field is of type CSub.

❸ OK.

❹ OK.

The expression labeled **❷** illustrates why the method argument needs to be contravariant. The user of c expects the instance to work with C instances. By looking at the actual implementation of value_=, we already know that we can't actually support contravariance, but let's ignore that for a moment and consider what happens if we change the variance annotation:

```scala
class ContainerMinus[-A](var a: A) {
  private var _value: A = a
  def value_=(newA: A): Unit = _value = newA
  def value: A = _value
}
```

We already know from the error messages at the beginning of this section that this is considered OK for the value_= method (even though it isn't actually OK), but now we get the second error we saw previously. The A is the return type for the value method, so A is in a covariant position.

Why must it be covariant? This is a little more intuitive. Again, the behavior of subtypes is the key. Once again, assume for a moment that the compiler allows us to instantiate ContainerMinus instances:

```scala
val cm: ContainerMinus[C] = new ContainerMinus(new CSuper)   // ❶
val c: C     = cm.value       // ❷
val c: CSuper = cm.value       // ❸
val c: CSub   = cm.value       // ❹
```

❶ Would be valid, if ContainerMinus[-A] were valid.

❷ cm thinks its value method returns a C, but the actual value method for the instance returns a CSuper. Oops...

❸ OK.

❹ Fails for the same reason in line **❷**.

So, if you think of a mutable field in terms of a getter and setter method, it appears in both covariant position when read and contravariant position when written. There is no such thing as a type parameter that is *both* contravariant and covariant, so the only option is for A to be invariant for the type of a *mutable* field.

Variance in Scala Versus Java

As we said, the variance behavior is defined in the *declaration* for Scala types, whereas it is defined when used, at the *call site*, in Java. The *client* of a type defines the variance behavior, defaulting to invariant. Java doesn't allow you to specify variance behavior at the definition site, although you can use expressions that look similar. Those expressions define *type bounds*, which we'll discuss shortly.

There are two drawbacks of Java's call-site variance specifications. First, it should be the library designer's job to understand the correct variance behavior and encode that behavior in the library itself. Instead, it's the library user who bears this burden. This leads to the second drawback. It's easy for a Java user to apply an incorrect annotation that results in unsafe code, like in the scenarios we just discussed.

Another problem in Java's type system is that Arrays are covariant in the type T. Consider this example:

```
// src/main/java/progscala2/objectsystem/JavaArrays.java
package progscala2.objectsystem;

public class JavaArrays {
  public static void main(String[] args) {
    Integer[] array1 = new Integer[] {
      new Integer(1), new Integer(2), new Integer(3) };
    Number[] array2 = array1;        // Compiles fine
    array2[2] = new Double(3.14);    // Compiles, but throws a runtime error!
  }
}
```

This file compiles without error. However, when you run it with SBT, hilarity ensues:

```
> run-main progscala2.objectsystem.JavaArrays
[info] Running progscala2.objectsystem.JavaArrays
[error] (run-main-4) java.lang.ArrayStoreException: java.lang.Double
java.lang.ArrayStoreException: java.lang.Double
  at progscala2.objectsystem.JavaArrays.main(JavaArrays.java:10)
  ...
```

What's wrong? We discussed previously that *mutable* collections must be invariant in the type parameter to be safe. Because Java arrays are covariant, we're allowed by the compiler to assign an Array[Integer] instance to an Array[Number] reference. Then the compiler thinks it's OK to assign *any* Number to elements of the array, but in fact, the array "knows" internally that it can only accept Integer values (including subtype instances, if any), so it throws a runtime exception, defeating the purpose of static type checking. Note that even though Scala wraps Java Arrays, the Scala class scala.Array (*http://bit.ly/1E8xJul*) is invariant in the type parameter, so it prevents this "hole."

See Maurice Naftalin and Philip Wadler, *Java Generics and Collections*, O'Reilly Media, 2006 for more details of Java's generics and arrays, from which the last example was adapted.

The Scala Type Hierarchy

We already know many of the types in Scala's type hierarchy. Let's look at the general structure of the hierarchy and fill in more details. Figure 10-1 shows the large-scale structure. Unless otherwise noted, all the types we'll discuss here are in the top-level `scala` package.

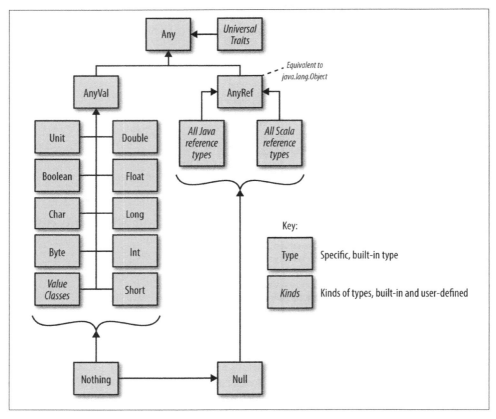

Figure 10-1. Scala's type hierarchy

At the root of the type hierarchy is `Any`. It has no parents and three children:

- `AnyVal`, the parent of value types and value classes
- `AnyRef`, the parent of all *reference* types
- *Universal Traits*, the newly introduced traits for the special uses we discussed in "Reference Versus Value Types" on page 248

AnyVal has nine concrete subtypes, called the *value types*. Seven are numeric value types: Byte (*http://bit.ly/1towT9A*), Char (*http://bit.ly/1tpoReU*), Short (*http://bit.ly/1wO4Ykf*), Int (*http://bit.ly/13p41nC*), Long (*http://bit.ly/1yMkigv*), Float (*http://bit.ly/1nWwcU6*), and Double (*http://bit.ly/1wl156h*). The remaining two are nonnumeric value types, Unit (*http://bit.ly/10Ftd8y*) and Boolean (*http://bit.ly/1voMvqd*).

In addition, Scala 2.10 introduced user-defined *value classes*, which extend AnyVal, as discussed in "Reference Versus Value Types" on page 248.

In contrast, all the other types are reference types. They are derived from AnyRef, which is the analog of java.lang.Object (*http://bit.ly/1E8xJKR*). Java's object model doesn't have a parent type of Object that encapsulates both primitives and reference types, because primitive types have special treatment.

 Before Scala 2.10, the compiler mixed into all instances of Scala reference types a "marker" trait named ScalaObject. The compiler no longer does this and the trait has been removed from Scala 2.11.

We have already learned about many of the reference types and we'll encounter more as we proceed. However, this is a good time to discuss a few of the widely used types.

Much Ado About Nothing (and Null)

Nothing (*http://bit.ly/1wNaLo6*) and Null (*http://bit.ly/1tIbUOQ*) are two unusual types at the bottom of the type system. Specifically, Nothing is a subtype of all other types, while Null is a subtype of all reference types.

Null is the familiar concept from most programming languages, although they don't usually define a Null *type*, just a keyword null that's "assigned" to a reference to indicate the reference actually has no assigned value. Null is implemented in the compiler as if it has the following declaration:

```
package scala
abstract final class Null extends AnyRef
```

How can it be both final and abstract? This declaration disallows subtyping and creating your own instances, but the runtime environment provides one instance, the familiar null we know and love (cough, cough, …).

Null is explicitly defined as a subtype of AnyRef, but it is also a subtype of all AnyRef types. This is the type system's formal way of allowing you to assign null to instances of any reference type. On the other hand, because Null is not a subtype of AnyVal, it is not possible to assign null to an Int, for example. Hence, Scala's null behaves exactly like Java's `null` behaves, as it must to coexist on the JVM. Otherwise, Scala could eliminate the concept of null and many potential bugs with it.

In contrast, `Nothing` has no analog in Java, but it fills a hole that exists in Java's type system. `Nothing` is implemented in the compiler as if it had the following declaration:

```
package scala
abstract final class Nothing extends Any
```

`Nothing` effectively extends `Any`. So, by construction in the type system, `Nothing` is a subclass of *all* other types, reference as well as value types. In other words, `Nothing` subclasses *everything*, as weird as that sounds.

Unlike `Null`, `Nothing` has no instances. Instead, it provides two capabilities in the type system that contribute to robust, type-safe design.

The first capability is best illustrated with our familiar `List[\+A]` (*http://bit.ly/1toub3N*) class. We now understand that `List` is *covariant* in A, so `List[String]` is a subtype of `List[Any]`, because `String` is a subtype of `Any`. Therefore, a `List[String]` instance can be assigned to a variable of type `List[Any]`.

Scala declares a type for the special case of an empty list, `Nil` (*http://bit.ly/1wN8LMz*). In Java, `Nil` would have to be a parameterized class like `List`, but this is unfortunate, because by definition, `Nil` never holds any elements, so a `Nil[String]` and a `Nil[Any]` would be different, but without distinction.

Scala solves this problem by having `Nothing`. `Nil` is actually declared like this:

```
package scala.collection.immutable
object Nil extends List[Nothing] with Product with Serializable
```

We'll discuss `Product` in the next section. `Serializable` is the familiar Java "marker" interface for objects that can be serialized using Java's built-in mechanism for this purpose.

Note that `Nil` is an `object` and it extends `List[Nothing]`. There is only one instance of it needed, because it carries no "state" (elements). Because `List` is covariant in the type parameter, `Nil` is a subtype of `List[A]` for *all* types A. Therefore, we don't need separate `Nil[A]` instances. One will do.

`Nothing` and `Null` are called *bottom* types, because they reside at the bottom of the type hierarchy, so they are subtypes of all (or most) other types.

The other use for `Nothing` is to represent expressions that terminate the program, such as by throwing an exception. Recall the special `???` method in `Predef` (*http://bit.ly/1O86O2z*) we saw in "Nested Types" on page 269. It can be called in a temporary method definition so the method is concrete, allowing an enclosing, concrete type to compile, but if the method is called, an exception is thrown. Here is the definition of `???`:

```scala
package scala
object Predef {
  ...
  def ??? : Nothing = throw new NotImplementedError
  ...
}
```

Because ??? "returns" Nothing, it can be called by any other function, no matter what type that function returns. Here is a pathological example:

```scala
scala> def m(l: List[Int]): List[Int] = l map (i => ???)
m: (l: List[Int])List[Int]

scala> m(List(1,2,3))
scala.NotImplementedError: an implementation is missing
  at scala.Predef$.$qmark$qmark$qmark(Predef.scala:252)
  ...
```

Note that m is still expected to return a List[Int] and the definition type checks, even though ??? "returns" Nothing.

More realistically, ??? is called by a method that has been declared, but not yet defined:

```scala
/** @return (mean, standard_deviation) */
def mean_stdDev(data: Seq[Double]): (Double, Double) = ???
```

For normal termination, the scala.sys (*http://bit.ly/1pbr6nI*) package defines an ex it method, analogous to the exit method in Java's System (*http://bit.ly/1s0NQ5n*). However, sys.exit returns Nothing.

This means that a method can declare that it returns a "normal" type, yet choose to call sys.exit if necessary, and still type check. A common example is the following idiom for processing command-line arguments, but exiting if an unrecognized option is provided:

```scala
// src/main/scala/progscala2/objectsystem/CommandArgs.scala
package progscala2.objectsystem

object CommandArgs {

  val help = """
  |usage: java ... objectsystem.CommandArgs arguments
  |where the allowed arguments are:
  |   -h | --help                  Show help
  |   -i | --in  | --input path    Path for input
  |   -o | --on  | --output path   Path for input
  |""".stripMargin

  def quit(message: String, status: Int): Nothing = {        // ❶
    if (message.length > 0) println(message)
    println(help)
    sys.exit(status)
```

```
    }

    case class Args(inputPath: String, outputPath: String)           // ❷

    def parseArgs(args: Array[String]): Args = {                      // ❸
      def pa(args2: List[String], result: Args): Args = args2 match { // ❹
        case Nil => result                                           // ❹
        case ("-h" | "--help") :: Nil => quit("", 0)                 // ❺
        case ("-i" | "--in" | "--input") :: path :: tail =>          // ❻
          pa(tail, result copy (inputPath = path))                   // ❼
        case ("-o" | "--out" | "--output") :: path :: tail =>        // ❽
          pa(tail, result copy (outputPath = path))
        case _ => quit(s"Unrecognized argument ${args2.head}", 1)    // ❾
      }
      val argz = pa(args.toList, Args("", ""))                       // ❿
      if (argz.inputPath == "" || argz.outputPath == "")            // ⓫
        quit("Must specify input and output paths.", 1)
      argz
    }

    def main(args: Array[String]) = {
      val argz = parseArgs(args)
      println(argz)
    }
}
```

❶ Print an optional message, then the help message, then exit with the specified error status. Following Unix conventions, 0 is used for normal exits and nonzero values are used for abnormal termination. Note that `quit` returns `Nothing`.

❷ A case class to hold the settings determined from the argument list.

❸ A nested, recursively invoked function to process the argument list. We use the idiom of passing an `Args` instance to accumulate new settings (but by making a copy of it).

❹ End of input, so return the accumulated settings.

❺ User asks for help.

❻ For the input argument, accept one of three variants for the option, `-i`, `--in`, or `--input`, followed by a path argument. Note that if the user doesn't provide a path (and there are no other arguments), the case won't match.

❼ Call `pa` on the tail with an updated result.

❽ Repeat for the output argument.

❾ Handle the error of an unrecognized argument.

❿ Call `pa` to process the arguments.

⓫ Verify that the input and output arguments were provided.

I find this example of pattern matching particularly elegant and concise.

This code is compiled when you build the project, so let's try it in `sbt`:

```
> run-main progscala2.objectsystem.CommandArgs -f
[info] Running progscala2.objectsystem.CommandArgs -f
Unrecognized argument -f

usage: java ... progscala2.objectsystem.CommandArgs arguments
where the allowed arguments are:
  -h | --help                Show help
  -i | --in | --input path   Path for input
  -o | --on | --output path  Path for input

Exception: sbt.TrapExitSecurityException thrown from the
  UncaughtExceptionHandler in thread "run-main-1"
  java.lang.RuntimeException: Nonzero exit code: 1
  at scala.sys.package$.error(package.scala:27)
[trace] Stack trace suppressed: run last compile:runMain for the full output.
[error] (compile:runMain) Nonzero exit code: 1
[error] ...

> run-main progscala2.objectsystem.CommandArgs -i foo -o bar
[info] Running progscala2.objectsystem.CommandArgs -i foo -o bar
Args(foo,bar)
[success] ...
```

We didn't throw an exception for the invalid argument, but `sbt` didn't like the fact that we called `exit`.

Products, Case Classes, and Tuples

Your case classes mix in the `scala.Product` (*http://bit.ly/1voMO4r*) trait, which provides a few generic methods for working with the fields of an instance, a `Person` instance, for example:

```
scala> case class Person(name: String, age: Int)
defined class Person

scala> val p: Product = Person("Dean", 29)
p: Product = Person(Dean,29)   //The case class instance is assignable to a Product variable.

scala> p.productArity
res0: Int = 2                  //The number of fields.

scala> p.productElement(0)
res1: Any = Dean               //Elements counted from zero.

scala> p.productElement(1)
res1: Any = 29
```

```
scala> p.productIterator foreach println
Dean
29
```

While having generic ways of accessing fields can be useful, its value is limited by the fact that Any is used for the fields' types, not their actual types.

There are also subtypes of Product for specific arities, up to 22 (for example, sca la.Product2 (*http://bit.ly/1zmsjMe*) for two-element products). These types add methods for selecting a particular field, with the correct type information preserved. For example, Product2[+T1,+T2] adds these methods:

```
package scala
trait Product2[+T1, +T2] extends Product {
  abstract def _1: T1
  abstract def _2: T2
  ...
}
```

These methods return the actual type of the field. The type parameters are covariant, because the ProductN traits are only used with immutable types, where reading the field with a method like _1 uses the corresponding type parameter, T1, in covariant position (i.e., only as a return type).

Recall that these methods are the same ones used to access the elements of tuples. In fact, all TupleN types extend the corresponding ProductN trait and provide concrete implementations for these _1 to _N methods, for _N up to and including 22:

```
scala> val t2 = ("Dean", 29)
t2: (String, Int) = (Dean,29)

scala> t2._1
res0: String = Dean

scala> t2._2
res2: Int = 29

scala> t2._3
<console>:36: error: value _3 is not a member of (String, Int)
              t2._3
                 ^
```

There is no third element nor a _3 method for Tuple2.

Why the upper limit of 22? It's really somewhat arbitrary and you could make the reasonable argument that having 22 elements in a tuple is way too many anyway.

That's true for human comprehension, but unfortunately, there is a common scenario where exceeding this limit would be useful: in holding the fields (or columns) of large data "records." It's not uncommon for SQL and NoSQL data sets to have schemas with

---

more than 22 elements. Tuples are useful, at least for smaller schemas, because they preserve the field (column) order and type. Hence, a 22-element limit is a problem.

It turns out that case classes in Scala 2.10 are also limited to 22 fields, but this implementation restriction has been eliminated in 2.11. Hence, data applications can use a case class for records with more than 22 elements.

 In Scala 2.10 and earlier, case classes are limited to 22 fields or less. This limitation is removed in Scala 2.11.

Hopefully, the 22-element limit for traits and products will be removed in a future release of Scala.

The Predef Object

For your convenience, whenever you compile code, the Scala compiler automatically imports the definitions in the top-level Scala package, called scala, as well as the definitions in the java.lang package (just like javac). Hence, many common Java and Scala types can be used without explicitly importing them or using fully qualified names. In addition, the compiler imports the definitions in the Predef (*http://bit.ly/1086O2z*) object that provides a number of useful definitions, many of which we've discussed previously.

Let's round out the features provided by Predef. Note that a number of changes are being introduced in the Scala 2.11 version of Predef, most of which are not visible. We'll discuss the 2.11 version.

Implicit Conversions

First, Predef defines many implicit conversions. One group of conversions includes wrappers around the AnyVal types:

```
@inline implicit def byteWrapper(x: Byte)       = new runtime.RichByte(x)
@inline implicit def shortWrapper(x: Short)     = new runtime.RichShort(x)
@inline implicit def intWrapper(x: Int)         = new runtime.RichInt(x)
@inline implicit def charWrapper(c: Char)       = new runtime.RichChar(c)
@inline implicit def longWrapper(x: Long)       = new runtime.RichLong(x)
@inline implicit def floatWrapper(x: Float)     = new runtime.RichFloat(x)
@inline implicit def doubleWrapper(x: Double)   = new runtime.RichDouble(x)
@inline implicit def booleanWrapper(x: Boolean) = new runtime.RichBoolean(x)
```

The Rich* types add additional methods, like comparison methods such as <= and compare. The @inline annotation encourages the compiler to "inline" the method call, i.e., eliminate it by inserting the new runtime.RichY(x) logic directly.

Why have two separate types for bytes, for example? Why not put all the methods in Byte itself? The reason is that the extra methods would force an instance to be allocated on the heap, due to implementation requirements for byte code. Byte instances, like the other AnyVal types, are not actually heap-allocated, but represented as Java's byte primitives. So, having separate Rich* types avoids the heap allocation except for those times when the extra methods are needed.

There are also methods for wrapping Java's mutable arrays in instances of scala.col lection.mutable.WrappedArray (*http://bit.ly/1OFtpV6*), which adds many of the collection methods we discussed in Chapter 6:

```
implicit def wrapIntArray(xs: Array[Int]): WrappedArray[Int]
implicit def wrapDoubleArray(xs: Array[Double]): WrappedArray[Double]
implicit def wrapLongArray(xs: Array[Long]): WrappedArray[Long]
implicit def wrapFloatArray(xs: Array[Float]): WrappedArray[Float]
implicit def wrapCharArray(xs: Array[Char]): WrappedArray[Char]
implicit def wrapByteArray(xs: Array[Byte]): WrappedArray[Byte]
implicit def wrapShortArray(xs: Array[Short]): WrappedArray[Short]
implicit def wrapBooleanArray(xs: Array[Boolean]): WrappedArray[Boolean]
implicit def wrapUnitArray(xs: Array[Unit]): WrappedArray[Unit]
```

Why are there separate methods for each AnyVal type? Each one uses a custom subclass of WrappedArray that exploits the fact that Java arrays of primitives are more efficient than arrays of boxed elements, so the less efficient, generic implementation for reference types is avoided.

There are similar methods for converting to scala.collection.mutable.ArrayOps (*http://bit.ly/1pbp9HU*). The only difference between WrappedArray and ArrayOps is that transformation functions for WrappedArray, such as filter, will return a new WrappedArray, while the corresponding functions in ArrayOps return Arrays.

Like WrappedArray and ArrayOps, there are analogous types for Strings, scala/ collection/immutable/WrappedString (*http://bit.ly/1wO5q1G*) and scala/collec tion/immutable/StringOps (*http://bit.ly/1bvlHxv*), which add collection methods to Strings, treating them like collections of Chars. Hence, Predef defines conversions between String and these types:

```
implicit def wrapString(s: String): WrappedString
implicit def unwrapString(ws: WrappedString): String

implicit def augmentString(x: String): StringOps
implicit def unaugmentString(x: StringOps): String
```

Having pairs of similar wrapper types, like WrappedArray/ArrayOps and WrappedString/StringOps, is a bit confusing, but fortunately the implicit conversions are invoked automatically, selecting the correct wrapper type for the method you need.

There are other methods for converting between Java's boxed types for primitives and Scala's AnyVal types. They make Java interoperability easier:

```
implicit def byte2Byte(x: Byte)        = java.lang.Byte.valueOf(x)
implicit def short2Short(x: Short)     = java.lang.Short.valueOf(x)
implicit def char2Character(x: Char)   = java.lang.Character.valueOf(x)
implicit def int2Integer(x: Int)       = java.lang.Integer.valueOf(x)
implicit def long2Long(x: Long)        = java.lang.Long.valueOf(x)
implicit def float2Float(x: Float)     = java.lang.Float.valueOf(x)
implicit def double2Double(x: Double)  = java.lang.Double.valueOf(x)
implicit def boolean2Boolean(x: Boolean) = java.lang.Boolean.valueOf(x)

implicit def Byte2byte(x: java.lang.Byte): Byte           = x.byteValue
implicit def Short2short(x: java.lang.Short): Short        = x.shortValue
implicit def Character2char(x: java.lang.Character): Char  = x.charValue
implicit def Integer2int(x: java.lang.Integer): Int       = x.intValue
implicit def Long2long(x: java.lang.Long): Long           = x.longValue
implicit def Float2float(x: java.lang.Float): Float        = x.floatValue
implicit def Double2double(x: java.lang.Double): Double    = x.doubleValue
implicit def Boolean2boolean(x: java.lang.Boolean): Boolean = x.booleanValue
```

Finally, in Scala 2.10, there is a group of implicit conversions that *prevent* null from being accepted as a value for an assignment. We'll just show one example, for Byte:

```
implicit def Byte2byteNullConflict(x: Null): Byte = sys.error("value error")
```

It triggers the following error:

```
scala> val b: Byte = null
<console>:23: error: type mismatch;
 found    : Null(null)
 required: Byte
Note that implicit conversions are not applicable because they are ambiguous:
 both method Byte2byteNullConflict in class LowPriorityImplicits of
 type (x: Null)Byte and method Byte2byte in object Predef of type (x: Byte)Byte
 are possible conversion functions from Null(null) to Byte
       val b: Byte = null
           ^
```

That works OK, but the error message isn't really that clear. It's complaining about ambiguous implicits, which the library deliberately introduced, but really it should just tell us more directly that we shouldn't assign null to anything.

Here's the error message produced by Scala 2.11:

```
scala> val b: Byte = null
<console>:7: error: an expression of type Null is ineligible for
  implicit conversion
       val b: Byte = null
                     ^
```

Scala 2.11 eliminates the conversion methods and provides a better, more concise error message.

Type Definitions

Predef defines several types and type aliases.

To encourage the use of immutable collections, Predef defines aliases for the most popular, immutable collection types:

```
type Map[A, +B]      = collection.immutable.Map[A, B]
type Set[A]          = collection.immutable.Set[A]
type Function[-A, +B] = Function1[A, B]
```

Two convenient aliases for two- and three-element tuples have been deprecated in 2.11, on the grounds that they aren't used enough and don't add enough value to justify their existence:

```
type Pair[+A, +B]      = Tuple2[A, B]
type Triple[+A, +B, +C] = Tuple3[A, B, C]
```

Other Predef type members support type inference:

final class ArrowAssoc[A] extends AnyVal
> Used to implement the a -> b literal syntax for creating two-element tuples. We discussed it in "Implicit Conversions" on page 149.

sealed abstract class <:<[-From, +To] extends (From) => To with Serializable
> *Witnesses* that type From is a subtype of type To. We discussed it in "Implicit Evidence" on page 140.

sealed abstract class =:=[-From, +To] extends (From) => To with Serializable
> *Witnesses* that types From and To are equal. We also mentioned it in "Implicit Evidence" on page 140.

type Manifest[T] = reflect.Manifest[T]
> Used to retain type information that's lost in the JVM's *type erasure*. There is a similar type OptManifest. We'll discuss them in "Class Tags, Type Tags, and Manifests" on page 526.

Other types, like scala.collection.immutable.List (*http://bit.ly/1toub3N*), are made visible through nested imports within Predef. Also, companion objects for some of the types are also made visible, such as `=:=` (*http://bit.ly/13p4bvs*), `Map` (*http://bit.ly/108flme*), and `Set` (*http://bit.ly/10FtE2s*).

Condition Checking Methods

Sometimes you want to assert a condition is true, perhaps to "fail fast" and especially during testing. `Predef` defines a number of methods that assist in this goal:

`def assert(assertion: Boolean)`
> Test that `assertion` is true. If not, throw a `java.lang.AssertionError` (*http://bit.ly/1wNb2HG*).

`def assert(assertion: Boolean, message: => Any)`
> Similar, but with an additional argument that's converted to a string message.

`def assume(assertion: Boolean)`
> Identical to `assert`, but conveys the meaning that the condition is assumed to be true when entering a block of code, such as a method.

`def assume(assertion: Boolean, message: => Any)`
> Similar, but with an additional argument that's converted to a string message.

`def require(requirement: Boolean)`
> Identical to `assume`, but the Scaladoc says it conveys the meaning that the caller failed to satisfy some requirement; it could also convey the meaning that an implementation could not achieve a required result.

`def require(requirement: Boolean, message: => Any)`
> Similar, but with an additional argument that's converted to a string message.

It's not shown, but all of these assertion methods are annotated with `@elidable(ASSERTION)`. The `@elidable` annotation tells the compiler not to generate byte code for a definition unless the argument to the annotation (`ASSERTION` in this case) is above a threshold that is specified during compilation. For example, `scalac -Xelide-below 2000` suppresses code generation for all annotated definitions with argument values below `2000`. `2000` happens to be the value defined for `ASSERTION` in the `elidable` (*http://bit.ly/1yMkBYF*) companion object. See the Scaladoc page (*http://bit.ly/1sRidKE*) for more information on `@elidable`.

Input and Output Methods

We've enjoyed the convenience of writing `println("foo")` instead of the more verbose Java equivalent, `System.out.println("foo"))`. `Predef` gives us four variants for writing strings to `stdout`:

```
def print(x: Any): Unit
```
Convert x to a String and write it to stdout, without adding a line feed at the end automatically.

```
def printf(format: String, xs: Any*): Unit
```
Format a printf-style string using format as the format and the rest of the arguments xs, then write the resulting String to stdout, without adding a line feed at the end automatically.

```
def println(x: Any): Unit
```
Like print, but appends a line feed at the end automatically.

```
def println(): Unit
```
Writes a blank line to stdout.

Predef in Scala 2.10 also defines several functions for reading input from stdin. However, these functions are deprecated in Scala 2.11. Instead, they are defined in a new scala.io.ReadStdin object that should be used instead. Otherwise, the method signatures and behaviors are the same:

```
def readBoolean(): Boolean
```
Reads a Boolean value from an entire line from stdin.

```
def readByte(): Byte
```
Reads a Byte value from an entire line from stdin.

```
def readChar(): Char
```
Reads a Char value from an entire line from stdin.

```
def readDouble(): Double
```
Reads a Double value from an entire line from stdin.

```
def readFloat(): Float
```
Reads a Float value from an entire line from stdin.

```
def readInt(): Int
```
Reads an Int value from an entire line from stdin.

```
def readLine(text: String, args: Any*): String
```
Prints formatted text to stdout and reads a full line from stdin.

```
def readLine(): String
```
Reads a full line from stdin.

```
def readLong(): Long
```
Reads a Long value from an entire line from stdin.

```
def readShort(): Short
```
Reads a Short value from an entire line from stdin.

```
def readf(format: String): List[Any]
```
Reads in structured input from stdin as specified by the format specifier.

```
def readf1(format: String): Any
```
Reads in structured input from stdin as specified by the format specifier, returning only the first value extracted, according to the format specification.

```
def readf2(format: String): (Any, Any)
```
Reads in structured input from stdin as specified by the format specifier, returning only the first two values extracted, according to the format specification.

```
def readf3(format: String): (Any, Any, Any)
```
Reads in structured input from stdin as specified by the format specifier, returning only the first three values extracted, according to the format specification.

 You can override the java.io.Reader (*http://bit.ly/1yMkDjd*) used for stdin or the java.io.OutputStreams (*http://bit.ly/1nWwU3D*) used for stdout or stderr using methods in scala.Console (*http://bit.ly/1aLWLEh*).

Miscellaneous Methods

Finally, there are a few more useful methods in Predef to highlight:

```
def ???: Nothing
```
Called in a method body for a method that is actually unimplemented. It provides a concrete definition for the method, allowing enclosing types to compile as concrete (as opposed to abstract). However, if called, the method throws a scala.NotImplementedError (*http://bit.ly/1G2zzia*). We first discussed it in "Nested Types" on page 269.

```
def identity[A](x: A): A
```
Simply returns the argument x. It is useful for passing to *combinator* methods when no change is required. For example, a work flow calls map to transform the elements of a collection, passing it a configurable function to do the transformation. Sometimes, no transformation is required, so you'll pass identity instead.

```
def implicitly[T](implicit e: T): T
```
Used when an implicit argument list is specified with the type shorthand [T : M], in which case the compiler adds an implicit argument list of the form (implicit arg: M[T]). (The actual name isn't arg, but something unique synthesized by the

compiler.) Calling `implicitly` returns the argument `arg`. Discussed previously in "Using implicitly" on page 133.

Now let's consider a very important topic in object-oriented design, checking the equality of objects.

Equality of Objects

Implementing a reliable equality test for instances is difficult to do correctly. Joshua Block's popular book, *Effective Java* (Addison-Wesley), and the *Scaladoc* page for Any-Ref.eq (*http://bit.ly/1yMkEDW*) describe the requirements for a good equality test.

Martin Odersky, Lex Spoon, and Bill Venners wrote a very good article on writing `equals` and `hashCode` methods, *How to Write an Equality Method in Java* (*http://bit.ly/13a2sBR*). Recall that these methods are created automatically for case classes.

In fact, I *never* write my own `equals` and `hashCode` methods. I find that any object that I use where I might need to test for equality or to use it as a `Map` key (where `hashCode` is used) *should* be a `case` class!

 Some of the equality methods have the same names as equality methods in other languages, but the semantics are sometimes different!

Let's look at the different methods used to test equality.

The equals Method

We'll use a case class to demonstrate how the different equality methods work:

```
// src/main/scala/progscala2/objectsystem/person-equality.sc

case class Person(firstName: String, lastName: String, age: Int)

val p1a = Person("Dean", "Wampler", 29)
val p1b = Person("Dean", "Wampler", 29)
val p2  = Person("Buck", "Trends",  30)
```

The `equals` method tests for *value* equality. That is, `obj1 equals obj2` is true if both `obj1` and `obj2` have the same value. They do not need to refer to the same instance:

```
p1a equals p1a    // = true
p1a equals p1b    // = true
p1a equals p2     // = false
p1a equals null   // = false
```

```
null equals p1a    // throws java.lang.NullPointerException
null equals null   // throws java.lang.NullPointerException
```

Hence, `equals` behaves like the `equals` method in Java and the `eql?` method in Ruby, for example.

The == and != Methods

Whereas == is an operator in many languages, it is a method in Scala. In Scala 2.10, == is defined as `final` in `Any` and it delegates to `equals`. A different implementation is used in 2.11, but the behavior is effectively the same:

```
p1a == p1a    // = true
p1a == p1b    // = true
p1a == p2     // = false
```

Hence, it behaves exactly like `equals`, namely it tests for *value* equality. The exception is the behavior when `null` is on the lefthand side:

```
p1a == null    // = false
null == p1a    // = false
null == null   // = true  (compiler warns that it's always true)
```

Should `null == null` be true? Actually, a warning is emitted:

```
<console>:8: warning: comparing values of types Null and Null using `=='
will always yield true
```

As you would expect, != is the negation, i.e., it is equivalent to `!(obj1 == obj2)`:

```
p1a != p1a    // = false
p1a != p1b    // = false
p1a != p2     // = true
p1a != null   // = true
null != p1a   // = true
null != null  // = false (compiler warns that it's always false.)
```

In Java, C++, and C#, the == operator tests for *reference*, not *value* equality. In contrast, Scala's == operator tests for *value* equality.

The eq and ne Methods

The `eq` method tests for *reference* equality. That is, `obj1 eq obj2` is true if both `obj1` and `obj2` point to the same location in memory. These methods are only defined for `AnyRef`:

```
p1a eq p1a    // = true
p1a eq p1b    // = false
```

```
p1a eq p2          // = false
p1a eq null        // = false
null eq p1a        // = false
null eq null       // = true  (compiler warns that it's always true.)
```

Just as the compiler issues a warning for `null == null`, it issues the same warning for `null eq null`.

Hence, eq behaves like the == operator in Java, C++, and C#.

The ne method is the negation of eq, i.e., it is equivalent to `!(obj1 eq obj2)`:

```
p1a ne p1a         // = false
p1a ne p1b         // = true
p1a ne p2          // = true
p1a ne null        // = true
null ne p1a        // = true
null ne null       // = false (compiler warns that it's always false.)
```

Array Equality and the sameElements Method

Comparing the contents of two Arrays doesn't have an obvious result in Scala:

```
Array(1, 2) == Array(1, 2)            // = false
```

That's a surprise! Thankfully, there's a simple solution in the form of the sameElements method:

```
Array(1, 2) sameElements Array(1, 2)    // = true
```

Actually, it's better to remember that Arrays are the mutable, raw Java arrays we know and love, which don't have the same methods we're accustomed to in the Scala collections library.

So, if you're tempted to compare arrays, consider whether or not it would be better to work with sequences instead (an argument for *not* using alternatives is when you really need the performance benefits of arrays).

In contrast, for example, Lists work as you would expect:

```
List(1, 2) == List(1, 2)              // = true
List(1, 2) sameElements List(1, 2)    // = true
```

Recap and What's Next

We discussed important topics in Scala's object system, such as the behavior under inheritance, the features in Predef, the fundamentals of the type hierarchy, and equality.

Next we'll complete our discussion of the object system by examining the behavior of member overriding and resolution rules.

## CHAPTER 11

The Scala Object System, Part II

We finish our discussion of Scala's object system by examining the rules for overriding members of classes and traits, including a discussion of the details of the *linearization* algorithm Scala uses for resolving member definitions and overrides in types that mix in traits and extend other types.

Overriding Members of Classes and Traits

Classes and traits can declare *abstract* members: *fields*, *methods*, and *types*. These members must be defined by a derived class or trait before an instance can be created. Most object-oriented languages support abstract methods, and some also support abstract fields and types.

 When overriding a concrete member, Scala requires the `override` keyword. It is optional when a subtype defines ("overrides") an abstract member. Conversely, it is an error to use `override` when you aren't actually overriding a member.

Requiring the `override` keyword has several benefits:

- It catches misspelled members that were intended to be overrides. The compiler will throw an error that the member doesn't override anything.

- It catches a subtle bug that can occur if a new member is added to a base class where the member's name collides with a preexisting member in a derived class, one which is unknown to the base class developer. That is, the derived-class member was never intended to override a base-class member. Because the derived-class member won't have the `override` keyword, the compiler will throw an error when the new base-class member is introduced.

- Having to add the keyword reminds you to consider what members should or should not be overridden.

Java has an optional @Override annotation for methods. It helps catch spelling errors, but it can't help with the subtle errors described in the second bullet item, because using the annotation is optional.

You can optionally use the override keyword when implementing an abstract member. Should you? Let's consider some arguments for and against.

Arguments in favor of always using the override keyword, in addition to those cited previously:

- It reminds the reader that a member defined in a parent class is being implemented (or overridden).
- If a parent class removes an abstract member that a child class defines, an error is reported.

Arguments against using the override keyword:

- Catching typos isn't actually necessary. A misdefined "override" means an undefined member still exists, so the derived class (or its concrete descendant classes) will fail to compile.
- If during the evolution of the code base, a developer maintaining the parent class abstract member decides to make it concrete, the change will go unnoticed when compiling the child class. Should the child class now call the super version of the method? The compiler will silently accept what is now a complete override of the new parent-class implementation.

Avoid Overriding Concrete Members

In other words, the arguments are somewhat subtle as to whether or not it's a good practice to use override for abstract members. This raises a larger question about override: should you *ever* override a concrete method? The correct answer is *almost never*.

The relationship between parent and child types is a *contract* and care is required to ensure that a child class does not break the implemented behaviors specified by the parent type.

When overriding concrete members, it is very easy to break this contract. Should an override of the foo method call super.foo? If so, then when should it be called within the child's implementation? Of course, the answers are different in each case.

A far more robust *contract* is the *Template Method Pattern* described in the famous "Gang of Four" Design Patterns book. In this pattern, the parent class provides a concrete implementation of a method, defining the outline of the required behavior. The method calls `protected`, *abstract* methods at the points where polymorphic behavior is needed. Then, subclasses *only* implement the `protected`, abstract members.

Here is an example, a sketch of a payroll calculator for a company based in the US:

```scala
// src/main/scala/progscala2/objectsystem/overrides/payroll-template-method.sc

case class Address(city: String, state: String, zip: String)
case class Employee(name: String, salary: Double, address: Address)

abstract class Payroll {
  def netPay(employee: Employee): Double = {                    // ❶
    val fedTaxes   = calcFedTaxes(employee.salary)
    val stateTaxes = calcStateTaxes(employee.salary, employee.address)
    employee.salary - fedTaxes -stateTaxes
  }

  def calcFedTaxes(salary: Double): Double                      // ❷
  def calcStateTaxes(salary: Double, address: Address): Double  // ❸
}

object Payroll2014 extends Payroll {
  val stateRate = Map(
    "XX" -> 0.05,
    "YY" -> 0.03,
    "ZZ" -> 0.0)

  def calcFedTaxes(salary: Double): Double = salary * 0.25      // ❹
  def calcStateTaxes(salary: Double, address: Address): Double = {
    // Assume the address.state is valid; it's found in the map!
    salary * stateRate(address.state)
  }
}

val tom  = Employee("Tom Jones", 100000.0, Address("MyTown", "XX", "12345"))
val jane = Employee("Jane Doe",  110000.0, Address("BigCity", "YY", "67890"))

Payroll2014.netPay(tom)     // Result: 70000.0
Payroll2014.netPay(jane)    // Result: 79200.0
```

❶ The `netPay` method uses the *Template Method Pattern*. It defines the protocol for calculating payroll, and delegates to abstract methods for details that change year over year, etc.

❷ The method for calculating federal taxes.

❸ The method for calculating state taxes.

❹ Concrete implementations of the abstract methods defined in the parent class.

Note that override is not used anywhere.

These days, when I see the override keyword in code, I see it as a potential *design smell*. Someone is overriding concrete behavior and subtle bugs might be lurking.

I can think of two exceptions to this rule. The first occurs when the parent-class implementation of a method does nothing useful. The toString, equals, and hashCode methods are examples. Unfortunately, overrides of the vacuous, default implementations of these methods are so ubiquitous that the practice has made us too comfortable with overriding concrete methods.

The second exception are those (rare?) occasions when you need to mix in non-overlapping behaviors. For example, you might override some critical method to add logging calls. In the child class override, when you invoke the logging calls versus the parent-class method, using super won't affect the external behavior (the contract) of the method, *as long as you correctly invoke the parent class method!*

 Don't override concrete members when you can avoid it, except for trivial cases like toString. Don't use the override keyword unless you're actually overriding a concrete member.

Attempting to Override final Declarations

If a declaration includes the final keyword, overriding the declaration is prohibited. In the following example, the fixedMethod is declared final in the parent class. Attempting to compile the example will result in a compilation error:

```
// src/main/scala/progscala2/objectsystem/overrides/final-member.scalaX
package progscala2.objectsystem.overrides

class NotFixed {
  final def fixedMethod = "fixed"
}

class Changeable2 extends NotFixed {
  override def fixedMethod = "not fixed"    // COMPILATION ERROR
}
```

This constraint applies to classes and traits as well as members. In this example, the class Fixed is declared final, so an attempt to derive a new type from it will also fail to compile:

```
// src/main/scala/progscala2/objectsystem/overrides/final-class.scalaX
package progscala2.objectsystem.overrides

final class Fixed {
```

```
    def doSomething = "Fixed did something!"
}

class Changeable1 extends Fixed      // COMPILATION ERROR
```

 Some of the types in the Scala library are final, including JDK classes like `String` and all the "value" types derived from `AnyVal` (see "The Scala Type Hierarchy" on page 294).

Overriding Abstract and Concrete Methods

For declarations that aren't final, let's examine the rules and behaviors for overriding, starting with methods.

Let's extend the `Widget` trait we introduced in "Traits as Mixins" on page 272 with an abstract method `draw`, to support "rendering" the widget to a display, web page, etc. We'll also override a concrete method familiar to any Java programmer, `toString()`, using an ad hoc format.

 Drawing is actually a *cross-cutting concern*. The state of a `Widget` is one thing; how it is rendered on different platforms—"fat" clients, web pages, mobile devices, etc.—is a separate issue. So, drawing is a very good candidate for a trait, especially if you want your GUI abstractions to be portable. However, to keep things simple, we will handle drawing in the `Widget` hierarchy itself.

Here is the revised `Widget` with `draw` and `toString` methods. We'll now make it an `abstract class`, only because it is a logical parent for all UI widgets, like buttons. However, we could continue to define it as a trait:

```
// src/main/scala/progscala2/objectsystem/ui/Widget.scala
package progscala2.objectsystem.ui

abstract class Widget {
  def draw(): Unit
  override def toString() = "(widget)"
}
```

The `draw` method is abstract because it has no body. Therefore, `Widget` has to be declared `abstract`. Each concrete subclass of `Widget` will have to implement `draw` or rely on a parent class that implements it, of course. We don't need to return anything from `draw`, so its return value is `Unit`, although some sort of "success" status could be returned.

The `toString()` method is straightforward. Because `AnyRef` defines `toString`, the `override` keyword is required for `Widget.toString`.

Here is the revised `Button` class, with `draw` and `toString` methods:

```
// src/main/scala/progscala2/objectsystem/ui/Button.scala
package progscala2.objectsystem.ui
import progscala2.traits.ui2.Clickable

class Button(val label: String) extends Widget with Clickable {

  // Simple hack for demonstration purposes:
  def draw(): Unit = println(s"Drawing: $this")

  // From Clickable:
  protected def updateUI(): Unit = println(s"$this clicked; updating UI")

  override def toString() = s"(button: label=$label, ${super.toString()})"
}
```

It also mixes in the `Clickable` trait we introduced in "Stackable Traits" on page 277. We'll exploit it shortly.

We could make it a case class, but as we'll see, we're going to subclass it for other button types and we want to avoid the previously discussed issues with case class inheritance.

`Button` implements the abstract method `draw`. The `override` keyword is optional here. `Button` also overrides `toString`, which requires the `override` keyword. Note that `su per.toString` is called.

 Should you use the `override` keyword when implementing an abstract method? I don't think so. Suppose in the future that the maintainer of `Widget` decides to provide a default implementation of `draw`, perhaps to log all calls to it. Now implementers should truly overwrite `draw` *and* call `Widget.draw`. If you've been "overriding" `draw` all this time, the compiler will silently accept that you are now *really* overriding a concrete method and you may never know of the change. However, if you leave off the `override` keyword, your code will fail to compile when the abstract `draw` method suddenly has an implementation. You'll know of the change.

The `super` keyword is analogous to `this`, but it binds to the parent type, which is the aggregation of the parent class and any mixed-in traits. The search for `super.to String` will find the "closest" parent type `toString`, as determined by the linearization process we'll discuss later in this chapter (see "Linearization of an Object's Hierarchy" on page 326). In this case, because `Clickable` doesn't define `toString`, `Widget.to String` will be called. We are reusing `Clickable` from "Stackable Traits" on page 277.

Overriding a concrete method should be done rarely, because it is error-prone. Should you invoke the parent method? If so, when? Do you call it before doing anything else, or afterward? While the writer of the parent method *might* document the overriding constraints for the method, it's difficult to ensure that the writer of a derived class will honor those constraints. A much more robust approach is the *Template Method Pattern*.

Here is a simple script that exercises `Button`:

```
// src/main/scala/progscala2/objectsystem/ui/button.sc
import progscala2.objectsystem.ui.Button

val b = new Button("Submit")
// Result: b: oop.ui.Button = (button: label=Submit, (widget))

b.draw()
// Result: Drawing: (button: label=Submit, (widget))
```

Overriding Abstract and Concrete Fields

Let's discuss overriding fields in traits and classes separately, because traits have some particular issues.

Overriding fields in traits

Consider this contrived example that uses an undefined field before it is properly initialized:

```
// src/main/scala/progscala2/objectsystem/overrides/trait-invalid-init-val.sc
// ERROR: "value" read before initialized.

trait AbstractT2 {
  println("In AbstractT2:")
  val value: Int
  val inverse = 1.0/value      // ❶
  println("AbstractT2: value = "+value+", inverse = "+inverse)
}

val obj = new AbstractT2 {
  println("In obj:")
  val value = 10
}
println("obj.value = "+obj.value+", inverse = "+obj.inverse)
```

❶ What is `value` when `inverse` is initialized?

Although it appears that we are creating an instance of the trait with `new AbstractT2` ..., we are actually using an anonymous class that implicitly extends the trait. Note the output that is produced if we run the script with the `scala` command ($ is the shell prompt):

```
$ scala src/main/scala/progscala2/objectsystem/overrides/trait-bad-init-val.sc
In AbstractT2:
AbstractT2: value = 0, inverse = Infinity
In obj:
obj.value = 10, inverse = Infinity
```

You get the results (with a few additional lines of output) if you use the REPL command `:load src/main/scala/progscala2/objectsystem/overrides/trait-bad-init-val.sc` or you paste the code into the REPL.

As you might expect, the `inverse` is calculated too early. Note that a divide-by-zero exception isn't thrown, but the compiler recognizes the value is infinite.

One way to detect this problem is to use the `scalac` compiler option `-Xcheckinit`, which will throw an exception when a field is referenced before it is initialized.

Scala provides two solutions to this problem. The first is *lazy values*, which we discussed in "lazy val" on page 91:

```
// src/main/scala/progscala2/objectsystem/overrides/trait-lazy-init-val.sc

trait AbstractT2 {
  println("In AbstractT2:")
  val value: Int
  lazy val inverse = 1.0/value        // ❶
  // println("AbstractT2: value = "+value+", inverse = "+inverse)
}

val obj = new AbstractT2 {
  println("In obj:")
  val value = 10
}
println("obj.value = "+obj.value+", inverse = "+obj.inverse)
```

❶   Added the keyword `lazy` *and* commented out the `println` statement.

Now `inverse` is initialized to a valid value:

```
In AbstractT2:
In obj:
obj.value = 10, inverse = 0.1
```

However, `lazy` only helps if the `println` statement is not used. If you remove the `//` and run it, you'll get `Infinity` again, because `lazy` only defers evaluation until the value is used. The `println` statement forces evaluation too soon.

If a val is lazy, make sure all uses of the val are also as lazy as possible.

The second solution, which is less commonly used, is *pre-initialized fields*. Consider this refined implementation:

```
// src/main/scala/progscala2/objectsystem/overrides/trait-pre-init-val.sc

trait AbstractT2 {
  println("In AbstractT2:")
  val value: Int
  val inverse = 1.0/value
  println("AbstractT2: value = "+value+", inverse = "+inverse)
}

val obj = new {
  // println("In obj:")      // ❶
  val value = 10
} with AbstractT2

println("obj.value = "+obj.value+", inverse = "+obj.inverse)
```

❶ Only type definitions and concrete field definitions are allowed in pre-initialization blocks. It would be a compilation error to use the println statement here, for example.

We instantiate an anonymous inner class, initializing the value field in the block, before the with AbstractT2 clause. This guarantees that value is initialized before the body of AbstractT2 is executed, as shown when you run the script:

```
In AbstractT2:
AbstractT2: value = 10, inverse = 0.1
obj.value = 10, inverse = 0.1
```

Even within the body of the trait, inverse is properly initialized.

Now let's consider the VetoableClicks trait we used in "Stackable Traits" on page 277. It defines a val named maxAllowed and initializes it to 1. We would like the ability to override the value in a class that mixes in this trait. Here it is again:

```
// src/main/scala/progscala2/traits/ui2/VetoableClicks.scala
package progscala2.traits.ui2
import progscala2.traits.observer._

trait VetoableClicks extends Clickable {              // ❶
  // Default number of allowed clicks.
  val maxAllowed = 1                                   // ❷
```

```scala
    private var count = 0

    abstract override def click() = {
      if (count < maxAllowed) {                                       // ❸
        count += 1
        super.click()
      }
    }
}
```

❶   Also extends `Clickable`.

❷   The maximum number of allowed clicks. (A "reset" feature would be useful.)

❸   Once the number of clicks exceeds the allowed value (counting from zero), no further clicks are sent to `super`.

It should be straightforward to implement an instance that mixes in this trait and overrides `maxAllowed` if we want. However, there are initialization issues we should review first.

To see those issues, let's first return to `VetoableClicks` and use it with `Button`. To see what happens, we'll also need to mix in the `ObservableClicks` trait that we also discussed in "Stackable Traits" on page 277:

```scala
// src/main/scala/progscala2/traits/ui2/ObservableClicks.scala
package progscala2.traits.ui2
import progscala2.traits.observer._

trait ObservableClicks extends Clickable with Subject[Clickable] {
  abstract override def click(): Unit = {          // ❶
    super.click()
    notifyObservers(this)
  }
}
```

❶   Note the `abstract override` keywords, discussed in "Stackable Traits" on page 277.

Here is a test script:

```scala
// src/main/scala/progscala2/objectsystem/ui/vetoable-clicks.sc
import progscala2.objectsystem.ui.Button
import progscala2.traits.ui2.{Clickable, ObservableClicks, VetoableClicks}
import progscala2.traits.observer._

val observableButton =                                               // ❶
  new Button("Okay") with ObservableClicks with VetoableClicks {
    override val maxAllowed: Int = 2                                 // ❷
  }

assert(observableButton.maxAllowed == 2,                             // ❸
```

```
      s"maxAllowed = ${observableButton.maxAllowed}")

class ClickCountObserver extends Observer[Clickable] {           // ❹
  var count = 0
  def receiveUpdate(state: Clickable): Unit = count += 1
}

val clickCountObserver = new ClickCountObserver                  // ❺
observableButton.addObserver(clickCountObserver)

val n = 5
for (i <- 1 to n) observableButton.click()                      // ❻

assert(clickCountObserver.count == 2,                           // ❼
  s"count = ${clickCountObserver.count}. Should be != $n")
```

❶ Construct an observable button by mixing in the required traits.

❷ The main point of this exercise is to override a val. Note that override and the full declaration of maxAllowed is required.

❸ Verify that we successfully changed maxAllowed.

❹ Define an observer to track the number of clicks that reach it.

❺ Instantiate an observer instance and "register" it with the button *Subject*.

❻ Click the button five times.

❼ Verify that the observer only saw two clicks; the other three were vetoed.

Recall that the mixin order of traits determines priority order, a subject that we'll finish exploring later in this chapter, in "Linearization of an Object's Hierarchy" on page 326.

Try switching the order of ObservableClicks and VetoableClicks in the line after the label ❶. What do you expect to happen now? You should see the final assertion test fail with a count of five instead of two. Why? Because ObservableClicks will now see each click *before* VetoableClicks sees it. In other words, VetoableClicks is now effectively doing nothing.

So, we see that we can override immutable field definitions. What if you want more dynamic control over maxAllowed, where it might vary during program execution? You can declare the field to be a mutable variable with var, then the declaration of observableButton changes to the following:

```
val observableButton =
  new Button("Okay") with ObservableClicks with VetoableClicks {
    maxAllowed = 2
  }
```

The previous override keyword with the full signature is no longer necessary.

I should mention that for logical consistency, you would need to decide what changing `maxAllowed` should mean for the state of the observer. If `maxAllowed` is decreased and the observer has already counted a larger number of clicks, should you add a mechanism to decrease the observer's count?

Now we can discuss the initialization issues we mentioned earlier. Because the body of the trait is executed before the body of the class using it, reassigning the field value happens *after* the initial assignment in the trait's body. Recall our previous pathological example of `inverse` using `value` before it was set. For `VetoableObserver`, suppose it initialized some sort of private array to save up to `maxAllowed` updates. The final assignment to `maxAllowed` would leave the object in an inconsistent state! You would need to avoid this problem manually, such as deferring the storage allocation until it's needed for the first updates, well after the initialization process has completed. Declaring `max Allowed` as a `val` doesn't eliminate this problem, although it does signal to users of the type that `VetoableClicks` makes assumptions about the state of the instance, namely that this part of the state won't change. Still, if you are the maintainer of `Vetoable Clicks`, you'll have to remember that users might override the value of `maxAllowed`, whether or not it is declared immutable!

Avoid var fields when possible (in classes as well as traits). Consider public var fields especially risky.

However, vals don't offer complete protection. A val in a trait can also be overridden during initialization of subclass instances, although it will remain immutable afterwards.

Overriding fields in classes

For members declared in classes, the behavior is essentially the same as for traits. For completeness, here is an example with both a `val` override and a `var` reassignment in a derived class:

```scala
// src/main/scala/progscala2/objectsystem/overrides/class-field.sc

class C1 {
  val name = "C1"
  var count = 0
}

class ClassWithC1 extends C1 {
  override val name = "ClassWithC1"
  count = 1
}

val c = new ClassWithC1()
println(c.name)
println(c.count)
```

The override keyword is required for the *concrete* val field name, but not for the var field count. This is because we are changing the initialization of a constant (val), which is a "special" operation.

If you run this script, the output is the following:

```
ClassWithC1
1
```

Both fields are overridden in the derived class, as expected. Here is the same example modified so that both the val and the var are abstract in the base class:

```
// src/main/scala/progscala2/objectsystem/overrides/class-abs-field.sc

abstract class AbstractC1 {
  val name: String
  var count: Int
}

class ClassWithAbstractC1 extends AbstractC1 {
  val name = "ClassWithAbstractC1"
  var count = 1
}

val c = new ClassWithAbstractC1()
println(c.name)
println(c.count)
```

The override keyword is not required for name in ClassWithAbstractC1, because the original declaration is abstract. The output of this script is the following:

```
ClassWithAbstractC1
1
```

It's important to emphasize that name and count are *abstract* fields, not concrete fields with default values. A similar-looking declaration of name in a Java class, String name, would declare a *concrete* field with the *default* value, null in this case. Java doesn't support abstract fields, only methods.

Overriding Abstract Types

We introduced abstract type declarations in "Abstract Types Versus Parameterized Types" on page 67, which Java doesn't support. Recall the BulkReader example from that section:

```
abstract class BulkReader {
  type In
  val source: In
  def read: String  // Read source and return a String
}
```

```
class StringBulkReader(val source: String) extends BulkReader {
  type In = String
  def read: String = source
}
...
```

The example shows how to declare an abstract type and how to define a concrete value in derived classes. BulkReader declares type In without initializing it. The concrete derived class StringBulkReader provides a concrete value using type In = String.

Unlike fields and methods, it is not possible to override a concrete type definition.

When Accessor Methods and Fields Are Indistinguishable: The Uniform Access Principle

Let's take one more look at maxAllowed in VetoableClick and discuss an interesting implication of mixing inheritance and the *Uniform Access Principle*, which we learned about in "The Uniform Access Principle" on page 260.

Here is a new version of VetoableClick, called VetoableClickUAP ("UAP" for uniform access principle) in a script that uses it:

```
// src/main/scala/progscala2/objectsystem/ui/vetoable-clicks-uap.sc
import progscala2.objectsystem.ui.Button
import progscala2.traits.ui2.{Clickable, ObservableClicks, VetoableClicks}
import progscala2.traits.observer._

trait VetoableClicksUAP extends Clickable {

  def maxAllowed: Int = 1                       // ❶

  private var count = 0

  abstract override def click() = {
    if (count < maxAllowed) {
      count += 1
      super.click()
    }
  }
}

val observableButton =
  new Button("Okay") with ObservableClicks with VetoableClicksUAP {
    override val maxAllowed: Int = 2            // ❷
  }

assert(observableButton.maxAllowed == 2,
  s"maxAllowed = ${observableButton.maxAllowed}")

class ClickCountObserver extends Observer[Clickable] {
  var count = 0
```

```
    def receiveUpdate(state: Clickable): Unit = count += 1
  }

  val clickCountObserver = new ClickCountObserver
  observableButton.addObserver(clickCountObserver)

  val n = 5
  for (i <- 1 to n) observableButton.click()

  assert(clickCountObserver.count == 2,
    s"count = ${clickCountObserver.count}. Should be != $n")
```

❶ maxAllowed is now a method that returns the default value of 1.

❷ Instead of overriding the method, use a value (val) definition.

The override keyword is required because the original method is defined. If the method is abstract in the trait, the override keyword is not required.

The output is the same as before, but we exploited the Uniform Access Principle to override the method definition with a value. Why is this allowed?

Using a method declaration supports the freedom to return a different value each time we call it, as long as the implementation does the necessary work. However, the declaration is consistent with the case where one and only one value is ever returned. Of course, this is preferred in functional programming, anyway. Ideally, a no-argument method should always return the same value in a pure functional world.

So, when we replace the method call with a value, we are exploiting *referential transparency* and not violating any rules about how the "method" implementation should behave.

For this reason, it's a common practice in Scala libraries for traits to declare no-argument methods instead of field values. Think of these methods as *property readers*, if you like. That gives implementers of types that use the trait complete freedom to provide an implementation for the method, perhaps to defer expensive initialization until necessary, or to simply use a value for implementation.

Overriding a method with a value in a subclass can also be handy when interoperating with Java code. For example, you can override a getter as a val by placing it in the constructor.

Consider the following example, in which a Scala Person class implements a hypothetical PersonInterface from some legacy Java library:

```
  class Person(val getName: String) extends PersonInterface
```

If you only need to override a few accessors in the Java code, this technique makes quick work of them.

What about overriding a parameterless method with a `var`, or overriding a `val` or `var` with a method? These are not permitted because they can't match the behaviors of the things they are overriding.

If you attempt to use a `var` to override a parameterless method, you get an error that the writer method, `override name_=`, is not overriding anything. For example, if an abstract method, `def name: String`, is declared in a trait and an implementing subclass attempts to use `override val name = "foo"`, this would be equivalent to overriding *two* methods, the original and `def name_=(…)`, but there is no such method.

If you could override a `val` with a method, there would be no way for Scala to guarantee that the method always returns the same value, consistent with `val` semantics.

Linearization of an Object's Hierarchy

Because of single inheritance, if we ignored mixed-in traits, the inheritance hierarchy would be linear, one ancestor after another. When traits are considered, each of which may be derived from other traits and classes, the inheritance hierarchy forms a directed, acyclic graph.

The term *linearization* refers to the algorithm used to "flatten" this graph for the purposes of resolving method lookup priorities, constructor invocation order, binding of `super`, etc.

Informally, we saw in "Stackable Traits" on page 277 that when an instance has more than one trait, they bind right to left, as declared. Consider the following example that demonstrates this straightforward linearization:

```
// src/main/scala/progscala2/objectsystem/linearization/linearization1.sc

class C1 {
  def m = print("C1 ")
}

trait T1 extends C1 {
  override def m = { print("T1 "); super.m }
}

trait T2 extends C1 {
  override def m = { print("T2 "); super.m }
}

trait T3 extends C1 {
  override def m = { print("T3 "); super.m }
}

class C2 extends T1 with T2 with T3 {
  override def m = { print("C2 "); super.m }
```

```
}
val c2 = new C2
c2.m
```

Running this script yields the following output:

```
C2 T3 T2 T1 C1
```

So, the m methods in the traits are called in the right-to-left order of the declaration of the traits. We'll also see why C1 is at the end of the list in a moment.

Next, let's see what the invocation sequence of the constructors looks like:

```
// src/main/scala/progscala2/objectsystem/linearization/linearization2.sc

class C1 {
  print("C1 ")
}

trait T1 extends C1 {
  print("T1 ")
}

trait T2 extends C1 {
  print("T2 ")
}

trait T3 extends C1 {
  print("T3 ")
}

class C2 extends T1 with T2 with T3 {
  println("C2 ")
}

val c2 = new C2
```

Running this script yields this output:

```
C1 T1 T2 T3 C2
```

So, the construction sequence is the reverse. This invocation order makes sense when you consider that the parent types need to be constructed before the derived types, because a derived type often uses fields and methods in the parent types during its construction process.

The output of the first linearization script is actually missing two types at the end. The full linearization for reference types actually ends with AnyRef and Any. So the linearization for C2 is actually the following:

```
C2 T3 T2 T1 C1 AnyRef Any
```

Prior to Scala 2.10, there was also a marker trait, ScalaObject, inserted in the hierarchy before AnyRef. Our output doesn't show AnyRef and Any because they don't have the print statements we used, of course.

In contrast, the value types, which subclass AnyVal, are all declared abstract final. The compiler manages instantiation of them. Because we can't subclass them, their linearizations are simple and straightforward.

What about the new value classes? Let's use a modified version of the USPhoneNumber we saw previously, where we have added the same m method we used earlier. The rules for value classes don't allow us to add the same print statements in the type bodies:

```
// src/main/scala/progscala2/basicoop/ValueClassPhoneNumber.sc

class USPhoneNumber(val s: String) extends AnyVal {

  override def toString = {
    val digs = digits(s)
    val areaCode  = digs.substring(0,3)
    val exchange  = digs.substring(3,6)
    val subnumber = digs.substring(6,10)  // "subscriber number"
    s"($areaCode) $exchange-$subnumber"
  }

  private def digits(str: String): String = str.replaceAll("""\D""", "")
}

val number = new USPhoneNumber("987-654-3210")
// Result: number: USPhoneNumber = (987) 654-3210
```

It prints the following when m is called:

```
USPhoneNumber Formatter Digitizer M
```

The output is consistent to what we saw for the C* class hierarchy. However, notice that the M trait is mixed into several other traits. Why does M show up last in the output, meaning its m method is the last in the lookup order? Let's examine linearization more closely.

We'll use our C* classes. All the classes and traits define the method m. The one in C2 is called first, because the instance is of that type. C2.m calls super.m, which resolves to T3.m. The search appears to be *breadth-first*, rather than *depth-first*. If it were depth-first, it would invoke C1.m after T3.m. Afterward, T3.m, T2.m, then T1.m, and finally C1.m are invoked. C1 is the parent of the three traits. From which of the traits did we traverse to C1? Actually, it is breadth-first, with "delayed" evaluation, as we will see. Let's modify our first example and see more explicitly how we got to C1:

```
// src/main/scala/progscala2/objectsystem/linearization/linearization3.sc

class C1 {
```

```
    def m(previous: String) = print(s"C1($previous)")
}

trait T1 extends C1 {
  override def m(p: String) = { super.m(s"T1($p)") }
}

trait T2 extends C1 {
  override def m(p: String) = { super.m(s"T2($p)") }
}

trait T3 extends C1 {
  override def m(p: String) = { super.m(s"T3($p)") }
}

class C2 extends T1 with T2 with T3 {
  override def m(p: String) = { super.m(s"C2($p)") }
}

val c2 = new C2
c2.m("")
```

Now we pass the name of the caller of super.m as a parameter, then C1 prints out who called it. Running this script yields the following output:

```
C1(T1(T2(T3(C2()))))
```

Here is the actual algorithm for calculating the linearization. A more formal definition is given in *The Scala Language Specification* (*http://bit.ly/1wNBOR8*).

Linearization Algorithm

1. Put the actual type of the instance as the first element.

2. Starting with the *rightmost* parent type and working *left*, compute the linearization of each type, appending its linearization to the cumulative linearization. (Ignore AnyRef and Any for now.)

3. Working from *left to right*, remove any type if it appears again to the *right* of the current position.

4. Append AnyRef and Any.

For value classes, replace AnyRef with AnyVal.

This explains how we got to C1 from T1 in the previous example. T3 and T2 also have it in their linearizations, but they come before T1, so the C1 terms they contributed were deleted. Similarly, the M trait in the USPhoneNumber example ends up at the righthand side of the list for the same reason.

Let's work through the algorithm using a slightly more involved example:

```
// src/main/scala/progscala2/objectsystem/linearization/linearization4.sc

class C1 {
  def m = print("C1 ")
}

trait T1 extends C1 {
  override def m = { print("T1 "); super.m }
}

trait T2 extends C1 {
  override def m = { print("T2 "); super.m }
}

trait T3 extends C1 {
  override def m = { print("T3 "); super.m }
}

class C2A extends T2 {
  override def m = { print("C2A " ); super.m }
}

class C2 extends C2A with T1 with T2 with T3 {
  override def m = { print("C2 "); super.m }
}

def calcLinearization(obj: C1, name: String) = {
  print(s"$name: ")
  obj.m
  print("AnyRef ")
  println("Any")
}

calcLinearization(new C2, "C2 ")
println("")
calcLinearization(new T3 {}, "T3 ")
calcLinearization(new T2 {}, "T2 ")
calcLinearization(new T1 {}, "T1 ")
calcLinearization(new C2A, "C2A")
calcLinearization(new C1, "C1 ")
```

The output is the following:

```
C2 : C2 T3 T1 C2A T2 C1 AnyRef Any

T3 : T3 C1 AnyRef Any
T2 : T2 C1 AnyRef Any
T1 : T1 C1 AnyRef Any
C2A: C2A T2 C1 AnyRef Any
C1 : C1 AnyRef Any
```

To help us along, we calculated the linearizations for the other types, and we also appended `AnyRef` and `Any` to remind ourselves that they should also be there.

So, let's work through the algorithm for `C2` and confirm our results. We'll suppress the
`AnyRef` and `Any` for clarity, until the end. See Table 11-1.

*Table 11-1. Hand calculation of C2 linearization: C2 extends C2A with T1 with T2
with T3 {...}*

#	Linearization	Description
1	C2	Add the type of the instance.
2	C2, T3, C1	Add the linearization for T3 (farthest on the right).
3	C2, T3, C1, T2, C1	Add the linearization for T2.
4	C2, T3, C1, T2, C1, T1, C1	Add the linearization for T1.
5	C2, T3, C1, T2, C1, T1, C1, C2A, T2, C1	Add the linearization for C2A.
6	C2, T3, T2, T1, C2A, T2, C1	Remove duplicates of C1; all but the *last* C1.
7	C2, T3, T1, C2A, T2, C1	Remove duplicates of T2; all but the *last* T2.
8	C2, T3, T1, C2A, T2, C1, AnyRef, Any	Finish!

What the algorithm does is push any shared types to the right until they come after *all*
the types that derive from them.

Try modifying the last script with different hierarchies and see if you can reproduce the
results using the algorithm.

> Overly complex type hierarchies can result in method lookup "sur-
> prises." If you have to work through this algorithm to figure out what's
> going on, try to simplify your code.

Recap and What's Next

We explored the fine points of overriding members in derived types, including the ability
to override (or implement abstract) no-argument methods with values. Finally, we
walked through the details of Scala's linearization algorithm for member lookup resolution.

In the next chapter, we'll learn about Scala's collections library.

## CHAPTER 12

The Scala Collections Library

With this chapter we finish our discussion of standard library topics by discussing the design of the collections library. The techniques used in this design solve particular problems that arise when designing collections that combine functional and object-oriented features, and address other concerns.

The collections library was significantly redesigned for Scala version 2.8. See the Scaladoc (*http://bit.ly/1bCEnM3*) for a detailed discussion of this redesign, which is still current.

Generic, Mutable, Immutable, Concurrent, and Parallel Collections, Oh My!

If you open the Scaladocs and type Map into the search box, you'll get five types! Fortunately, most are traits that declare or implement parts of the concrete Maps that you really care about. Most of the differences between those concrete types boil down to a few design questions you might have. Do you need mutability for performance (which you determined through profiling, of course)? Do you need concurrent access? Do you have operations that could be performed in parallel? Do you need the ability to iterate over the keys in sorted order, as well as perform the normal key-based lookup?

Table 12-1 lists the collection-related packages and their purposes. For the rest of this section, we'll drop the scala prefix, because you don't need it in import statements.

Table 12-1. The collection-related packages

Name	Description
collection (*http://bit.ly/1rGCORI*)	Defines the base traits and objects needed to use and extend Scala's collections library, including all definitions in subpackages. Most of the abstractions you'll work with are defined here.

Name	Description
collection.concurrent (*http://bit.ly/1pbpoTn*)	Defines a Map trait and TrieMap class with atomic, lock-free access operations.
collection.convert (*http://bit.ly/1wQupTN*)	Defines types for wrapping Scala collections with Java collection abstractions and wrapping Java collections with Scala collection abstractions.
collection.generic (*http://bit.ly/1tpnjSl*)	Defines reusable components used to build the specific mutable, immutable, etc. collections.
collection.immutable (*http://bit.ly/1u14Caq*)	Defines the immutable collections, the ones you'll use most frequently.
collection.mutable (*http://bit.ly/1udcgPt*)	Defines mutable collections. Most of the specific collection types are available in mutable and immutable forms, but not all.
collection.parallel (*http://bit.ly/1rGCUc6*)	Defines reusable components used to build specific mutable and immutable collections that distribute processing to parallel threads.
collection.parallel.immutable (*http://bit.ly/1nWuxOD*)	Defines parallel, immutable collections.
collection.parallel.mutable (*http://bit.ly/1yMjg47*)	Defines parallel, mutable collections.
collection.script (*http://bit.ly/13p3wKl*)	A deprecated package of tools for observing collection operations.

We won't discuss most of the types defined in these packages, but let's discuss the most important aspects of each package. We won't discuss the deprecated collection.script further.

The scala.collection Package

The types defined in collection declare and in some cases define the abstractions shared in common by the mutable and immutable sequential, mutable and immutable parallel, and concurrent collection types. That means, for example, that the destructive (mutation) operations that you'll find only in the mutable types aren't defined here. However, keep in mind that an actual collection instance at runtime might be mutable, where thread safety might be an issue.

Specifically, recall from "Sequences" on page 187 that the default Seq you get through Predef is collection.Seq (*http://bit.ly/1voJwOs*), while the other common types Predef exposes, such as List, Map, and Set, are specifically the collection.immutable variants. The reason Predef uses collection.Seq is so that Java arrays, which are mutable, can be treated uniformly as sequences. (Predef actually defines implicit conversions from Java arrays to collection.mutable.ArrayOps (*http://bit.ly/1E8xE9X*), which implements the sequence operations.) The plan is to change this in a future release of Scala to use the immutable Seq instead.

Unfortunately, for now, this also means that if a method declares that it returns an unqualified Seq, it might be returning a mutable instance. Similarly, if a method takes a Seq argument, a caller might pass a mutable instance to it.

If you prefer to use the safer immutable.Seq as the default, a common technique is to define a package object for your project with a type definition for Seq that effectively shadows the default definition in Predef, like the following:

```
// src/main/scala/progscala2/collections/safeseq/package.scala
package progscala2.collections
package object safeseq {
  type Seq[T] = collection.immutable.Seq[T]
}
```

Then, import its contents wherever needed. Note how the behavior changes for Seq in the following REPL session:

// src/main/scala/progscala2/collections/safeseq/safeseq.sc

```
scala> val mutableSeq1: Seq[Int] = List(1,2,3,4)
mutableSeq1: Seq[Int] = List(1, 2, 3, 4)

scala> val mutableSeq2: Seq[Int] = Array(1,2,3,4)
mutableSeq2: Seq[Int] = WrappedArray(1, 2, 3, 4)

scala> import progscala2.collections.safeseq._
import progscala2.collections.safeseq._

scala> val immutableSeq1: Seq[Int] = List(1,2,3,4)
immutableSeq1: safeseq.Seq[Int] = List(1, 2, 3, 4)

scala> val immutableSeq2: Seq[Int] = Array(1,2,3,4)
<console>:10: error: type mismatch;
 found    : Array[Int]
 required: safeseq.Seq[Int]
    (which expands to)  scala.collection.immutable.Seq[Int]
       val immutableSeq2: Seq[Int] = Array(1,2,3,4)
                                     ^
```

The first two Seq instances are the default collection.Seq exposed by Predef. The first references an immutable list and the second references a mutable (wrapped) Java array.

Then the new definition of Seq is imported, thereby shadowing the Predef definition.

Now the Seq type for the list is the safeseq.Seq alias, but we're not allowed to use it to reference an array, because the alias for immutable.Seq can't reference a mutable collection.

Either way, Seq is a convenient abstraction for any concrete collection where we just want the first few elements or we want to traverse from end to end.

The collection.concurrent Package

This package defines only two types, a `collection.concurrent.Map` (*http://bit.ly/ 1pbpB9b*) trait and a hash-trie `collection.concurrent.TrieMap` (*http://bit.ly/ 1u14SWH*) class that implements the trait.

`Map` extends `collection.mutable.Map` (*http://bit.ly/1tIa0hb*), but it makes the operations atomic, so they support thread-safe, concurrent access.

The one implementation of `collection.mutable.Map` is a hash-trie class `collec tion.concurrent.TrieMap`. It is a concurrent. *lock-free* implementation of a hash array mapped trie. It aims for scalable concurrent insert and remove operations and memory efficiency.

The collection.convert Package

The types defined in this package are used to implement implicit conversion methods to wrap Scala collections as Java collections and vice versa. We discussed them in "Scala's Built-in Implicits" on page 161.

The collection.generic Package

Whereas `collection` declares abstractions for all collections, `collection.generic` provides reusable components for implementing the specific mutable, immutable, parallel, and concurrent collections. Most of the types are only of interest to implementers of collections.

The collection.immutable Package

You'll work with collections defined in the `immutable` package most of the time. They provide single-threaded (as opposed to parallel) operations. Because they are immutable, they are thread-safe. Table 12-2 provides an alphabetical list of the most commonly used types in this package.

Table 12-2. Most commonly used immutable collections

Name	Description
BitSet (*http://bit.ly/1DDgSOb*)	Memory-efficient sets of nonnegative integers. The entries are represented as variable-size arrays of bits packed into 64-bit words. The largest entry determines the memory footprint of the set.
HashMap (*http://bit.ly/1sRf9yo*)	Maps implemented with hash trie for the keys.
HashSet (*http://bit.ly/ 13p3Ats*)	Sets implemented with a hash trie.

Name	Description
List (*http://bit.ly/1OFrqQC*)	A trait for linked lists, with *O(1)* head access and *O(n)* access to interior elements. The companion object has `apply` and other "factory" methods for constructing instances of implementing subclasses.
ListMap (*http://bit.ly/1zmrbsb*)	An immutable map backed by a list.
ListSet (*http://bit.ly/13p3ySx*)	An immutable set backed by a list.
Map (*http://bit.ly/1O8duhc*)	Trait for all key-value, immutable maps, with *O(1)* random access. The companion object has `apply` and other "factory" methods for constructing instances of implementing subclasses.
Nil (*http://bit.ly/1wQulOs*)	An object for empty lists.
NumericRange (*http://bit.ly/1G2y8A8*)	Generalizes ranges to arbitrary integral types. `NumericRange` is a more generic version of the Range class that works with arbitrary types. It must be supplied with an Integral implementation of the range type.
Queue (*http://bit.ly/1nWuSAv*)	An immutable FIFO (first-in, first-out) queue.
Seq (*http://bit.ly/1wO3lh1*)	A trait for immutable sequences. The companion object has `apply` and other "factory" methods for constructing instances of implementing subclasses.
Set (*http://bit.ly/1O8dA8A*)	A trait that declares the operations for immutable sets. The companion object has `apply` and other "factory" methods for constructing instances of implementing subclasses.
SortedMap (*http://bit.ly/1DDhOwT*)	The trait for immutable maps with an iterator that traverses the elements in sorted order. The companion object has `apply` and other "factory" methods for constructing instances of implementing subclasses.
SortedSet (*http://bit.ly/1nWuXEr*)	The trait for immutable sets with an iterator that traverses the elements in sorted order. The companion object has `apply` and other "factory" methods for constructing instances of implementing subclasses.
Stack (*http://bit.ly/1wN9UUA*)	An immutable LIFO (last-in, first-out) stack.
Stream (*http://bit.ly/1q8XiTl*)	A lazy list of values, thereby able to support a potentially infinite sequence of values.
TreeMap (*http://bit.ly/1G2ygjh*)	An immutable map with underlying red-black tree storage with *O(log(n))* operations.
TreeSet (*http://bit.ly/1tlamED*)	An immutable set with underlying red-black tree storage with *O(log(n))* operations.
Vector (*http://bit.ly/1wO3PZV*)	The default implementation of immutable, indexed sequences.

Bitsets are sets of nonnegative integers that are represented as variable-size arrays of bits packed into 64-bit words. The memory footprint of a bitset is determined by the largest number stored in it.

Vector is implemented using as a tree-based, *persistent data structure*, as discussed in "What About Making Copies?" on page 216. It provides excellent performance, with amortized *O(1))* operations.

It's worth looking at the source code for Map (*http://bit.ly/1rGRLTZ*), particularly the companion object. Notice that several implementations of Maps are declared for the special cases of zero to four key-value pairs. When you call Map.apply (defined in a parent trait), it tries to create an instance that's optimal for the actual data in the Map.

The scala.collection.mutable Package

There are times when you'll need a mutable collection with single-threaded operations. We've discussed how immutability should be the default choice. The mutation operations on these collections are *not* thread-safe. However, principled and careful use of mutable data can be appropriate for performance and other reasons. Table 12-3 provides an alphabetical list of the most commonly used collections in the mutable package.

Table 12-3. Most commonly used mutable collections

Name	Description
AnyRefMap (*http://bit.ly/1rGDmqL*)	Map for AnyRef keys that uses a hash table with open addressing. Most operations are generally faster than for HashMap (*http://bit.ly/1wN9Zre*).
ArrayBuffer (*http://bit.ly/1voKn1H*)	A buffer class that uses an array for internal storage. Append, update, and random access take *O(1)* (amortized) time. Prepends and removes are *O(n)*.
ArrayOps (*http://bit.ly/108dKwC*)	A wrapper class for Java arrays that implements the sequence operations.
ArrayStack (*http://bit.ly/1wQuXsB*)	A stack backed by an array. It's faster than the general-purpose Stack (*http://bit.ly/1u15Ke1*).
BitSet (*http://bit.ly/108dM7O*)	Memory-efficient sets of nonnegative integers. See the discussion of immutable.Bit Set in Table 12-2.
HashMap (*http://bit.ly/1wN9Zre*)	The mutable version of a hash-table based map.
HashSet (*http://bit.ly/1nWvdDl*)	The mutable version of a hash-table based set.
HashTable (*http://bit.ly/1tow40x*)	The trait used to implement mutable collections based on hash tables.
ListMap (*http://bit.ly/1zmrrr2*)	A mutable map backed by a list.
LinkedHashMap (*http://bit.ly/1zRy6dP*)	A hash-table based map where the elements can be traversed in their insertion order.
LinkedHashSet (*http://bit.ly/1nWvd6i*)	A hash-table based set where the elements can be traversed in their insertion order.
LongMap (*http://bit.ly/108dVIh*)	A mutable map backed by a hash table with open addressing where the keys are Longs. Most operations are substantially faster than for HashMap (*http://bit.ly/1wN9Zre*).
Map (*http://bit.ly/1tIaOhb*)	A trait for the mutable version of the Map abstraction. The companion object has ap ply and other "factory" methods for constructing instances of implementing subclasses.
MultiMap (*http://bit.ly/1OahnSr*)	The mutable Map where multiple values can be assigned to the same key.
PriorityQueue (*http://bit.ly/1wQv6MW*)	A heap-based, mutable priority queue. For the elements of type A, there must be an implicit Ordering[A] instance.

Name	Description
Queue (*http://bit.ly/1towgg3*)	A mutable FIFO (first-in, first-out) queue.
Seq (*http://bit.ly/1tpocKD*)	A trait for mutable sequences. The companion object has `apply` and other "factory" methods for constructing instances of implementing subclasses.
Set (*http://bit.ly/1voKYjX*)	A trait that declares the operations for mutable sets. The companion object has `apply` and other "factory" methods for constructing instances of implementing subclasses.
SortedSet (*http://bit.ly/1G2yzuz*)	The trait for mutable sets with an iterator that traverses the elements in sorted order. The companion object has `apply` and other "factory" methods for constructing instances of implementing subclasses.
Stack (*http://bit.ly/1u15Ke1*)	A mutable LIFO (last-in, first-out) stack.
TreeSet (*http://bit.ly/1E8xFuz*)	A mutable set with underlying red-black tree storage with *O(log(n))* operations.
WeakHashMap (*http://bit.ly/1wNad1w*)	A mutable hash map with references to entries that are weakly reachable. Entries are removed from this map when the key is no longer (strongly) referenced. This class wraps WeakHashMap (*http://bit.ly/1wQvcUF*).
WrappedArray (*http://bit.ly/1sRgpS9*)	A wrapper class for Java arrays that implements the sequence operations.

`WrappedArray` is almost identical to `ArrayOps`. The difference is in methods that return a new `Array`. For `ArrayOps`, those methods return a new `Array[T]`, while for `WrappedArray`, they return a new `WrappedArray[T]`. Hence, `ArrayOps` is better for contexts where the user is expecting an `Array`, but when the user doesn't care, a `WrappedArray` is more efficient if a sequence of transformations is required, because repeated "boxing" and "unboxing" of the `Array` in an `ArrayOps` (or `WrappedArray`) is avoided.

The scala.collection.parallel Package

The idea behind the parallel collections is to exploit modern multicore systems that provide parallel hardware threads. Any collection operations that can be performed in parallel could exploit this parallelism, in principle.

Specifically, the collection is split into pieces, combinator operations (e.g., `map`) are applied to the pieces, and then the results are combined to create the final result. That is, a *divide and conquer* strategy is used.

In practice, the parallel collections are not widely used, because the overhead of parallelization can overwhelm the advantages in many situations and not all operations can be parallelized. The overhead includes thread scheduling and the task of dividing the data into chunks, then combining results later on. Often, unless the collection is large, serial execution will be faster. So, be sure to profile real-world scenarios in your environment to determine whether your target collections are large enough and parallel operations perform fast enough to use a parallel collection.

For a concrete parallel collection, you can either construct an instance directly using the same idioms as for the nonparallel counterpart, or you can call the `par` method on the corresponding, nonparallel collection.

The parallel collections are organized like the nonparallel variants, as well. They have common traits and classes defined in the `scala.collection.parallel` (*http://bit.ly/10ahygG*) package, with immutable concrete collections in the `immutable` (*http://bit.ly/15iEXd9*) child package and mutable concrete collections in the `mutable` (*http://bit.ly/12GQ10p*) child package.

Finally, it's essential to understand that parallelization means that the order of nested operations is undefined. Consider the following example, where we combine the numbers from 1 to 10 into a string:

// src/main/scala/progscala2/collections/parallel.sc

```
scala> ((1 to 10) fold "") ((s1, s2) => s"$s1 - $s2")
res0: Any = " - 1 - 2 - 3 - 4 - 5 - 6 - 7 - 8 - 9 - 10"

scala> ((1 to 10) fold "") ((s1, s2) => s"$s1 - $s2")
res1: Any = " - 1 - 2 - 3 - 4 - 5 - 6 - 7 - 8 - 9 - 10"

scala> ((1 to 10).par fold "") ((s1, s2) => s"$s1 - $s2")
res2: Any = " - 1 -  - 2 -  - 3 - 4 - 5 -  - 6 -  - 7 -  - 8 -  - 9 -  - 10"

scala> ((1 to 10).par fold "") ((s1, s2) => s"$s1 - $s2")
res3: Any = " - 1 -  - 2 -  - 3 -  - 4 - 5 -  - 6 -  - 7 -  - 8 - 9 - 10"
```

For the nonparallel case, the same result is returned consistently, but *not* for repeated invocations when using a parallel collection!

However, addition works fine:

```
scala> ((1 to 10) fold 0) ((s1, s2) => s1 + s2)
res4: Int = 55

scala> ((1 to 10) fold 0) ((s1, s2) => s1 + s2)
res5: Int = 55

scala> ((1 to 10).par fold 0) ((s1, s2) => s1 + s2)
res6: Int = 55

scala> ((1 to 10).par fold 0) ((s1, s2) => s1 + s2)
res7: Int = 55
```

All runs yield the same result.

To be specific, the operation must be *associative* to yield predictable results for parallel operations. That is, `(a+b)+c == a+(b+c)` must always be true. The inconsistent spacing and "-" separators when building the strings in parallel indicate that the string composition operation used here isn't associative. In each run with the parallel collection, the collection is subdivided differently and somewhat unpredictably.

Addition is associative. It's also commutative, but that isn't necessary. Note that the string examples compose the elements in a predictable, left to right order, indicative of the fact that commutativity isn't required.

Because the parallel collections have nonparallel counterparts that we've already discussed, I won't list the specific types here. Instead, see the Scaladocs for the `parallel` (*http://bit.ly/10ahygG*), `parallel.immutable` (*http://bit.ly/15iEXd9*), and `parallel.mutable` (*http://bit.ly/12GQ10p*) packages. The Scaladocs also discuss other usage issues that we haven't discussed here.

Choosing a Collection

Aside from the decision to use a mutable versus immutable and nonparallel versus parallel collection, which collection type should you pick for a given situation?

Here are some informal criteria and options to consider. It's worth studying the *O(n)* performance of different operations for the collection types. See the Scaladoc (*http://bit.ly/13KECnF*) for an exhaustive list. There is also a useful StackOverflow discussion on choosing a collection (*http://bit.ly/1towvb6*).

I'll use the convention `immutable.List` (`mutable.LinkedList`) to indicate immutable and mutable options, when there are both.

Do you need ordered, traversable sequences? Consider an `immutable.List` (`mutable.LinkedList`), an `immutable.Vector`, or a `mutable.ArrayBuffer`.

`List`s provide *O(1)* prepending and reading of the head element, but *O(n)* appending and reading of internal elements.

Because `Vector` is a *persistent data structure* (as discussed previously), it is effectively *O(1)* for *all* operations.

`ArrayBuffer` is better if you need random access. Appending, updating, and random access all take *O(1)* (amortized) time, but prepending and deleting are *O(n)*.

So, when you need a sequence, you'll almost always use a `List`, when you mostly work with the head elements, and a `Vector` for more general access patterns. `Vector` is a powerful, general-purpose collection with excellent all-around performance. However, there are some situations where an `ArrayBuffer` will provide lower constant-time overhead and hence higher performance.

The other general scenario is the need for *O(1)*, key-based storage and retrieval, i.e., values stored by keys in an `immutable.Map` (`mutable.Map`). Similarly, `immutable.Set` (`mutable.Set`) is used to test for the existence of a value.

Design Idioms in the Collections Library

A number of *idioms* are used in the collections library to solve design problems and promote reuse. Let's discuss them and along the way, learn more about the "helper" types in the library that are used in the implementations.

Builder

I mentioned previously that the mutable collections are an appropriate compromise for performance when used carefully. In fact, the collections API uses them internally to build new output collections in operations like map. Implementations of the collection.mutable.Builder (*http://bit.ly/1u174xC*) trait are used internally to construct new instances during operations like map.

Builder has the following signature:

```
trait Builder[-Elem, +To] {
  def +=(elem: Elem): Builder.this.type
  def clear()
  def result(): To
  ... // Other methods derived from these three abstract methods.
}
```

The unusual Builder.this.type signature is a *singleton type*. It ensures that the += method can only return the Builder instance it was called on, i.e., this. If an implementation attempts to return a new instance of a Builder, for example, it won't type check! We'll study singleton types in "Singleton Types" on page 395.

Here is an example implementation of a builder for Lists:

```
// src/main/scala/progscala2/collections/ListBuilder.sc
import collection.mutable.Builder

class ListBuilder[T] extends Builder[T, List[T]] {

  private var storage = Vector.empty[T]

  def +=(elem: T) = {
    storage = storage :+ elem
    this
  }

  def clear(): Unit = { storage = Vector.empty[T] }

  def result(): List[T] = storage.toList
}

val lb = new ListBuilder[Int]
(1 to 3) foreach (i => lb += i)
```

```
lb.result
// Result: List(1, 2, 3)
```

A more efficient choice for the internal storage than Vector could be made, but it illustrates the point.

CanBuildFrom

Consider this simple example of mapping over a list of numbers:

```
scala> List(1, 2, 3, 4, 5) map (2 * _)
res0: List[Int] = List(2, 4, 6, 8, 10)
```

The *simplified* signature of this method in List (*http://bit.ly/1toub3N*) is the following:

```
map[B](f: (A) => B): List[B]
```

However, the standard library exploits reuse where possible. Recall from "Constraining Allowed Instances" on page 135 that map is actually defined in scala.collection.Tra versableLike (*http://bit.ly/1yMk4pK*), which is a mixin trait for List. The actual signature for map is the following:

```
trait TraversableLike[+A, +Repr] extends ... {
  ...
  def map[B, That](f: A => B)(
    implicit bf: CanBuildFrom[Repr, B, That]): That = {...}
}
```

Repr is the type of the collection used internally to store the items. B is the type of elements created by the function f. That is the type parameter of the target collection we want to create, which may or may not be the same as the original collection.

TraversableLike knows nothing of subtypes like List, but it can construct a new List to return because the implicit CanBuildFrom instance encapsulates the details.

CanBuildFrom is a trait for factories that create Builder instances, which do that actual incremental construct of new collections.

A drawback of using the CanBuildFrom technique is the extra complexity in the actual method signature. However, besides enabling object-oriented reuse of operations like map, CanBuildFrom modularizes and generalizes construction in other useful ways.

For example, a CanBuildFrom instance might instantiate Builders for a different concrete collection to be returned. Usually a new collection of the same type is returned, or perhaps a subtype that might be more efficient for the given elements.

For example, a Map with a lot of elements is best implemented by storing the keys in a hash table, providing amortized $O(1)$ storage and retrieval. However, for a small Map, it can be faster to simply store the elements in an array or list, where the $O(n)$ retrieval for small *n* is actually faster than the *O(1)* retrieval from a hash table, due to the larger constant factor overhead of the latter.

There are other cases where the input collection type can't be used for the output collection. Consider the following example:

```scala
scala> val set = collection.BitSet(1, 2, 3, 4, 5)
set: scala.collection.BitSet = BitSet(1, 2, 3, 4, 5)

scala> set map (_.toString)
res0: scala.collection.SortedSet[String] = TreeSet(1, 2, 3, 4, 5)
```

A BitSet (*http://bit.ly/1wO3JAt*) can only hold integers, so if we map it to a a set of strings, the implicit CanBuildFrom has to instantiate a different output collection, a SortedSet (*http://bit.ly/1nWuXEr*) in this case.

Similarly, for strings (sequences of characters), we encounter the following:

```scala
scala> "xyz" map (_.toInt)
res0: scala.collection.immutable.IndexedSeq[Int] = Vector(120, 121, 122)
```

Another benefit of CanBuildFrom is the ability of the instance to carry other context information that might not be known to the original collection or not suitable for it to carry around. For example, when working with a distributed computing API, special CanBuildFrom instances might be used for constructing collection instances that are optimal for serialization to remote processes.

Like Traits

We saw that Builder and CanBuildFrom take type parameters for the output collection. To support specifying these type parameters and to promote implementation reuse, most of the collections you know actually mix in corresponding ...Like traits that add the appropriate return-type parameter and provide implementations of common methods.

For example, here is how collection.immutable.Seq (*http://bit.ly/1wO3Ih1*) is declared:

```scala
trait Seq[+A] extends Iterable[A] with collection.Seq[A]
  with GenericTraversableTemplate[A, Seq] with SeqLike[A, Seq[A]]
  with Parallelizable[A, ParSeq[A]]
```

Note that collection.SeqLike (*http://bit.ly/1sRh2Ln*) is parameterized with both the element type A and Seq[A] itself. The latter parameter is used to constrain the allowed CanBuildFrom instances that can be used in methods like map. This trait also implements most of the familiar methods on Seq.

I encourage you to examine the Scaladoc entry for collection.immutable.Seq and some of the other common collection types we've discussed. Click the links to the other traits to see what they do. These traits and the traits they mix in form a nontrivial tree of types. Fortunately, most of these details are irrelevant for actually using the common concrete collection types.

To conclude, these are the three most important design idioms used in the collections:

1. `Builder` to abstract over construction
2. `CanBuildFrom` to provide implicit factories for constructing suitable `Builder` instances for a given context
3. `Like` traits that add the necessary return type parameter needed by `Builder` and `CanBuildFrom`, as well as providing most of the method implementations

If you build your own collections, you'll want to follow these idioms. Also, recall from Chapter 7 that if your collections implement `foreach`, `map`, `flatMap`, and `withFilter`, they can be used in `for` comprehensions, just like the built-in collections.

Specialization for Value Types

One benefit of Scala's uniform treatment of value types (e.g., `Int`, `Float`, etc.) and reference types is the ability to declare instances of parameterized types with the value types, e.g., `List[Int]`. In contrast, Java requires the boxed types to be used for containers, e.g., `List<Integer>`. Boxing requires extra memory per object and extra time for memory management. Also, primitive values that are contiguous in memory can improve cache hit ratios and therefore performance, for some algorithms.

Hence, it's common in data-centric Java libraries, like those libraries for *Big Data* applications, to have a long list of custom container types specialized for each of the primitive types, or perhaps just a few, like `long` and `double`. That is, you'll see a class dedicated to vectors of `longs`, a class dedicated to vectors of `doubles`, and so forth. So, the size of these libraries is much bigger than it would be if Java supported parameterized containers of primitives, but the performance of the custom primitive containers are often more than ten times better than the corresponding `Object`-based implementations.

Unfortunately, although Scala lets us declare instances of containers with value types, it doesn't actually solve this problem. Because of *type erasure*, the fact that the JVM doesn't retain information about the type of the container's elements, the elements are assumed to be `Objects` and a single implementation of the container is used for all element types. So, a `List[Double]` will still use boxed `Doubles`, for example.

Wouldn't it be great to have a mechanism to tell the compiler to generate "specialized" implementations of such containers that are optimized for desired primitives? In fact, Scala has a `@specialized` (*http://bit.ly/1G2yWFq*) annotation for this purpose. It tells the compiler to generate a custom implementation for the value types listed in the annotation call:

```
class SpecialVector[@specialized(Int, Double, Boolean) T] {...}
```

In this example, specialized versions of `SpecialVector` will be generated for `Int`, `Double`, and `Boolean`. If the list is omitted, specialized versions of the type will be generated for all the value types.

However, practical experience with `@specialized` since it was introduced has exposed some limitations. First, it can result in a lot of generated code, so injudicious use of `@specialized` can make a library excessively large.

Second, there are several design flaws in the implementation (see this recent presentation (*http://bit.ly/1tIqdD8*) for a more detailed discussion of the issues). If a field is declared of the generic type in the original container, it is not converted to a primitive field in the specialization. Rather, a *duplicate* field of the appropriate primitive type is created, leading to bugs. Another flaw is that the specialized containers are implemented as subclasses of the original generic container. This breaks when the generic container and a subtype are both specialized. The specialized versions should have the same inheritance relationship, but this can't be supported due to the JVM's single inheritance model.

So, because of these limitations, the Scala library makes limited use of `@specialized`. Most uses are for the `FunctionN`, `TupleN`, and `ProductN` types, plus a few collections.

Before we discuss an emerging alternative, note that there is also an `@unspecialized` (*http://bit.ly/1wNauBN*) annotation for methods. It is used when the type has the `@specialized` annotation, but you don't want a specialized version of the method generated. You might use this annotation when the performance benefit doesn't outweigh the extra code size.

Miniboxing

An alternative mechanism, called *miniboxing*, is under development. It attempts to remove the limitations of specialization. It will most likely appear in a future version of Scala, although it is available for experimentation now as a compiler plug-in (*http://scala-miniboxing.org*), so it's worth discussing now.

Once the plug-in is installed, it is used in essentially the same way as `@specialized`:

```
class SpecialVector[@miniboxed(Int, Double, Boolean) T] {...}
```

It reduces code bloat by converting a generic container into a trait with two subclasses, one to use for primitive values and one for reference (i.e., `AnyRef`) values. The primitive version exploits the observation that an 8-byte value can hold a value of any of the primitive types. A "tag" is added to indicate how the 8-byte value should be interpreted.

Hence, it behaves as a *tagged union*. Therefore, it's not necessary to have a separate instantiation for each primitive type. The reference implementation works as before.

By converting the original container to a trait, any preexisting inheritance relations are preserved in the two class instantiations. For example, if we have two parameterized containers class C[T] and D[T], with class D[T] extends C[T], and both are specialized, then the generated code looks conceptually like the following:

```
trait C[T]                                  // was class C[T]
class C_primitive[T] extends C[T]           // T is an AnyVal
class C_anyref[T] extends C[T]              // T is an AnyRef

trait D[T] extends C[T]                                      // was class D[T]
class D_primitive[T] extends C_primitive[T] with D[T]       // T is an AnyVal
class D_anyref[T] extends C_anyref[T] with D[T]            // T is an AnyRef
```

In the meantime, you can still use @specialized when you need the performance. Just be careful about the extra space required and the design limitations described earlier.

Recap and What's Next

We rounded out our understanding of the Scala collections library, including the distinctions between the mutable, immutable, and parallel variants, how to convert to and from Java collections, and the important, unfinished topic of enabling the collections to work efficiently with JVM primitive values, where the overhead of boxing is avoided.

Before we tackle the major topic of Scala's type system, the next chapter covers a topic you should know about, even though it won't be a daily "concern": Scala's rich support for fine-grained control over *visibility*. Scala goes well beyond Java's public, protect ed, private, and default package scoping capabilities.

## CHAPTER 13

Visibility Rules

Scala goes well beyond Java's four-tiered visibility rules: *public*, *protected*, *private*, and default package visibility. Visibility rules in object-oriented languages are designed to expose only the essential public abstraction of a type and encapsulate implementation information, hiding it from view.

This chapter covers the details in depth and to be honest, it's dry stuff. Superficially, they are just like Java's rules with the exception that *public* visibility is the default in Scala. Scala adds more sophisticated scoping rules, but you don't see them used a lot in every-day Scala code. So, consider skimming the first few sections of this chapter and the concluding section, "Final Thoughts on Visibility" on page 361. Save the rest of the chapter for when you need to know the particulars, especially when you start writing your own libraries.

Public Visibility: The Default

Unlike Java, but more like many other object-oriented languages, Scala uses *public* visibility by default. It's common to declare type members private, when you want to limit their visibility to the type only, or to declare them protected to limit visbility to subclasses. But Scala gives you more options. This chapter covers the details.

You'll want to use public visibility for anything that users of your objects should see and use. Keep in mind that the set of publicly visible members form the abstraction exposed by the type, along with the type's name itself.

The art of good object-oriented design includes defining minimal, clear, and cohesive public abstractions.

The conventional wisdom in object-oriented design is that fields should be private or protected. If access is required, it should happen through methods, but not everything should be accessible by default.

There are two reasons for this convention. The first is to prevent users from making modifications to mutable fields outside your control. However, using immutable values eliminates this concern. The second reason is that a particular field might be part of the implementation and not part of the public abstraction that you want to expose.

When access makes sense, the virtue of the *Uniform Access Principle* (see "The Uniform Access Principle" on page 260) is that we can give the user the semantics of public field access, but use either a method or actual direct access to the field, whichever is appropriate for the task. The user doesn't need to know which implementation is used. We can even change the implementation without forcing code changes on the user, although recompilation will be necessary.

There are two kinds of "users" of a type: derived types, and code that works with instances of the type. Derived types usually need more access to the members of their parent types than users of instances do.

Scala's visibility rules are similar to Java's, but tend to be both more consistently applied and more flexible. For example, in Java, if an inner class has a `private` member, the enclosing class can see it. In Scala, the enclosing class can't see a `private` member, but Scala provides another way to declare it visible to the enclosing class.

Visibility Keywords

As in Java and C#, the keywords that modify visibility, such as `private` and `protect ed`, appear at the beginning of declarations. You'll find them before the `class` or `trait` keywords for types, before the `val` or `var` for fields, and before the `def` for methods.

 You can also use an access modifier keyword on the primary constructor of a class. Put it after the type name and type parameters, if any, and before the argument list, as in this example: `class Restric ted[+A] private (name: String) {...}`.

Why do this? It forces users to call a factory method instead of instantiating types directly.

Table 13-1 summarizes the visibility scopes.

Table 13-1. Visibility scopes

Name	Keyword	Description
public	*none*	Public members and types are visible everywhere, across all boundaries.
protected	`protected`	Protected members are visible to the defining type, to derived types, and to nested types. Protected types are visible only within the same package and subpackages.
private	`private`	Private members are visible only within the defining type and nested types. Private types are visible only within the same package.
scoped protected	`protected[scope]`	Visibility is limited to `scope`, which can be a package, type, or `this` (meaning the same instance, when applied to members, or the enclosing package, when applied to types). See the following text for details.
scoped private	`private[scope]`	Synonymous with scoped protected visibility, except under inheritance (discussed in the following text).

Let's explore these visibility options in more detail. To keep things simple, we'll use fields for member examples. Method and type declarations behave the same way.

 Unfortunately, you can't apply any of the visibility modifiers to packages. Therefore, a package is always public, even when it contains no publicly visible types.

Public Visibility

Any declaration without a visibility keyword is "public," meaning it is visible everywhere. There is no `public` keyword in Scala. This is in contrast to Java, which defaults to public visibility only within the enclosing package (i.e., "package private"). Other object-oriented languages, like Ruby, also default to public visibility:

```
// src/main/scala/progscala2/visibility/public.scala

package scopeA {
  class PublicClass1 {
    val publicField = 1

    class Nested {
      val nestedField = 1
    }

    val nested = new Nested
  }

  class PublicClass2 extends PublicClass1 {
    val field2  = publicField + 1
    val nField2 = new Nested().nestedField
  }
```

```
  }

  package scopeB {
    class PublicClass1B extends scopeA.PublicClass1

    class UsingClass(val publicClass: scopeA.PublicClass1) {
      def method = "UsingClass:" +
        " field: " + publicClass.publicField +
        " nested field: " + publicClass.nested.nestedField
    }
  }
```

Everything is public in these packages and classes. Note that `scopeB.UsingClass` can access `scopeA.PublicClass1` and its members, including the instance of `Nested` and its public field.

Protected Visibility

Protected visibility is for the benefit of implementers of derived types, who need a little more access to the details of their parent types. Any member declared with the `pro tected` keyword is visible only to the defining type, including other instances of the same type and any derived types. When applied to a type, `protected` limits visibility to the enclosing package.

Java, in contrast, makes protected members visible throughout the enclosing package. Scala handles this case with scoped private and protected access:

```
// src/main/scala/progscala2/visibility/protected.scalaX
// WON'T COMPILE

package scopeA {
  class ProtectedClass1(protected val protectedField1: Int) {
    protected val protectedField2 = 1

    def equalFields(other: ProtectedClass1) =
      (protectedField1 == other.protectedField1) &&
      (protectedField1 == other.protectedField1) &&
      (nested == other.nested)

    class Nested {
      protected val nestedField = 1
    }

    protected val nested = new Nested
  }

  class ProtectedClass2 extends ProtectedClass1(1) {
    val field1 = protectedField1
    val field2 = protectedField2
    val nField = new Nested().nestedField  // ERROR
```

```
    }

    class ProtectedClass3 {
      val protectedClass1 = new ProtectedClass1(1)
      val protectedField1 = protectedClass1.protectedField1 // ERROR
      val protectedField2 = protectedClass1.protectedField2 // ERROR
      val protectedNField = protectedClass1.nested.nestedField // ERROR
    }

    protected class ProtectedClass4

    class ProtectedClass5 extends ProtectedClass4
    protected class ProtectedClass6 extends ProtectedClass4
  }

  package scopeB {
    class ProtectedClass4B extends scopeA.ProtectedClass4 // ERROR
  }
```

When you compile this file with `scalac`, you get five errors like the following, corresponding to the lines with the `// ERROR` comment:

```
.../visibility/protected.scalaX:23: error: value nestedField in class
Nested cannot be accessed in ProtectedClass2.this.Nested
 Access to protected value nestedField not permitted because
 enclosing class ProtectedClass2 in package scopeA is not a subclass of
 class Nested in class ProtectedClass1 where target is defined
    val nField = new Nested().nestedField  // ERROR
                              ^
...
5 errors found
```

`ProtectedClass2` can access protected members of `ProtectedClass1`, because it derives from it. However, it can't access the protected `nestedField` in `protected Class1.nested`. Also, `ProtectedClass3` can't access protected members of the `Protec tedClass1` instance it uses.

Finally, because `ProtectedClass4` is declared `protected`, it is not visible in the `scopeB` package.

Private Visibility

Private visibility completely hides implementation details, even from the implementers of derived classes. Any member declared with the `private` keyword is visible only to the defining type, including other instances of the same type. When applied to a type, `private` limits visibility to the enclosing package:

```
// src/main/scala/progscala2/visibility/private.scalaX
// WON'T COMPILE
```

```
package scopeA {
  class PrivateClass1(private val privateField1: Int) {
    private val privateField2 = 1

    def equalFields(other: PrivateClass1) =
      (privateField1 == other.privateField1) &&
      (privateField2 == other.privateField2) &&
      (nested == other.nested)

    class Nested {
      private val nestedField = 1
    }

    private val nested = new Nested
  }

  class PrivateClass2 extends PrivateClass1(1) {
    val field1 = privateField1  // ERROR
    val field2 = privateField2  // ERROR
    val nField = new Nested().nestedField // ERROR
  }

  class PrivateClass3 {
    val privateClass1 = new PrivateClass1(1)
    val privateField1 = privateClass1.privateField1 // ERROR
    val privateField2 = privateClass1.privateField2 // ERROR
    val privateNField = privateClass1.nested.nestedField // ERROR
  }

  private class PrivateClass4

  class PrivateClass5 extends PrivateClass4  // ERROR
  protected class PrivateClass6 extends PrivateClass4 // ERROR
  private class PrivateClass7 extends PrivateClass4
}

package scopeB {
  class PrivateClass4B extends scopeA.PrivateClass4  // ERROR
}
```

Compiling this file produces nine errors for the lines marked as errors.

Now, `PrivateClass2` can't access private members of its parent class `PrivateClass1`. They are completely invisible to the subclass, as indicated by the error messages. Nor can it access a private field in a `Nested` class.

Just as for the case of `protected` access, `PrivateClass3` can't access private members of the `PrivateClass1` instance it is using. Note, however, that the `equalFields` method can access private members of the `other` instance.

The declarations of `PrivateClass5` and `PrivateClass6` fail because, if allowed, they would enable `PrivateClass4` to "escape its defining scope." However, the declaration of `PrivateClass7` succeeds because it is also declared to be private. Curiously, our previous example was able to declare a public class that subclassed a protected class without a similar error.

Finally, just as for `protected` type declarations, the `private` types can't be subclassed outside the same package.

Scoped Private and Protected Visibility

Scala goes beyond most languages with an additional way of fine-tuning the scope of visibility; *scoped* `private` and `protected` visibility declarations. Note that using `private` or `protected` in a scoped declaration is interchangeable, because they behave identically, except under inheritance when applied to members.

 Although they behave nearly the same, it is a little more common to see `private[X]` rather than `protected[X]` used in Scala libraries. It's interesting to note that in the first version of this book, we noted that the Scala 2.7.X library used `private[X]` roughly five times more often than `protected[X]`. In Scala 2.11, the ratio is much closer, 5/3.

Let's begin by considering the only differences in behavior between scoped private and scoped protected—how they behave under inheritance when members have these scopes:

```
// src/main/scala/progscala2/visibility/scope-inheritance.scalaX
// WON'T COMPILE

package scopeA {
  class Class1 {
    private[scopeA]    val scopeA_privateField = 1
    protected[scopeA] val scopeA_protectedField = 2
    private[Class1]    val class1_privateField = 3
    protected[Class1] val class1_protectedField = 4
    private[this]      val this_privateField = 5
    protected[this]    val this_protectedField = 6
  }

  class Class2 extends Class1 {
    val field1 = scopeA_privateField
    val field2 = scopeA_protectedField
    val field3 = class1_privateField      // ERROR
    val field4 = class1_protectedField
    val field5 = this_privateField        // ERROR
    val field6 = this_protectedField
  }
```

```
    }

package scopeB {
  class Class2B extends scopeA.Class1 {
    val field1 = scopeA_privateField       // ERROR
    val field2 = scopeA_protectedField
    val field3 = class1_privateField       // ERROR
    val field4 = class1_protectedField
    val field5 = this_privateField         // ERROR
    val field6 = this_protectedField
  }
}
```

This file produces five compilation errors.

The first two errors, inside Class2, show us that a derived class inside the same package can't reference a member that is scoped private to the parent class or this, but it can reference a private member scoped to the package (or type) that encloses both Class1 and Class2.

In contrast, for a derived class outside the same package, it has no access to any of the scoped private members of Class1.

However, all the scoped protected members are visible in both derived classes.

We'll use scoped private declarations for the rest of our examples and discussion, because use of scoped private is a little more common in the Scala library than scoped protected, when the previous inheritance scenarios aren't a factor.

First, let's start with the most restrictive visibility, private[this], because it affects type members:

```
// src/main/scala/progscala2/visibility/private-this.scalaX
// WON'T COMPILE

package scopeA {
  class PrivateClass1(private[this] val privateField1: Int) {
    private[this] val privateField2 = 1

    def equalFields(other: PrivateClass1) =
      (privateField1 == other.privateField1) && // ERROR
      (privateField2 == other.privateField2) && // ERROR
      (nested == other.nested) // ERROR

    class Nested {
      private[this] val nestedField = 1
    }

    private[this] val nested = new Nested
  }

  class PrivateClass2 extends PrivateClass1(1) {
```

```
      val field1 = privateField1  // ERROR
      val field2 = privateField2  // ERROR
      val nField = new Nested().nestedField  // ERROR
    }

    class PrivateClass3 {
      val privateClass1 = new PrivateClass1(1)
      val privateField1 = privateClass1.privateField1  // ERROR
      val privateField2 = privateClass1.privateField2  // ERROR
      val privateNField = privateClass1.nested.nestedField // ERROR
    }
  }
```

Nine errors are reported by the compiler.

Lines 10 and 11 also won't parse. Because they are part of the expression that started on line 9, the compiler stopped after the first error.

The private[this] members are only visible to the same instance. An instance of the same class can't see private[this] members of another instance, so the equalFields method won't parse.

Otherwise, the visibility of class members is the same as private without a scope specifier.

When declaring a type with private[this], use of this effectively binds to the enclosing package, as shown here:

```
// src/main/scala/progscala2/visibility/private-this-pkg.scalaX
// WON'T COMPILE

package scopeA {
  private[this] class PrivateClass1

  package scopeA2 {
    private[this] class PrivateClass2
  }

  class PrivateClass3 extends PrivateClass1  // ERROR
  protected class PrivateClass4 extends PrivateClass1 // ERROR
  private class PrivateClass5 extends PrivateClass1
  private[this] class PrivateClass6 extends PrivateClass1

  private[this] class PrivateClass7 extends scopeA2.PrivateClass2 // ERROR
}

package scopeB {
  class PrivateClass1B extends scopeA.PrivateClass1 // ERROR
}
```

This produces four errors.

In the same package, attempting to declare a `public` or `protected` subclass fails. Only `private` and `private[this]` subclasses are allowed. Also, `PrivateClass2` is scoped to `scopeA2`, so you can't declare it outside `scopeA2`. Similarly, an attempt to declare a class in unrelated `scopeB` using `PrivateClass1` also fails.

Hence, when applied to types, `private[this]` is equivalent to Java's `package pri vate` visibility.

Next, let's examine type-level visibility, `private[T]`, where `T` is a type:

```scala
// src/main/scala/progscala2/visibility/private-type.scalaX
// WON'T COMPILE

package scopeA {
  class PrivateClass1(private[PrivateClass1] val privateField1: Int) {
    private[PrivateClass1] val privateField2 = 1

    def equalFields(other: PrivateClass1) =
      (privateField1 == other.privateField1) &&
      (privateField2 == other.privateField2) &&
      (nested    == other.nested)

    class Nested {
      private[Nested] val nestedField = 1
    }

    private[PrivateClass1] val nested = new Nested
    val nestedNested = nested.nestedField    // ERROR
  }

  class PrivateClass2 extends PrivateClass1(1) {
    val field1 = privateField1  // ERROR
    val field2 = privateField2  // ERROR
    val nField = new Nested().nestedField  // ERROR
  }

  class PrivateClass3 {
    val privateClass1 = new PrivateClass1(1)
    val privateField1 = privateClass1.privateField1  // ERROR
    val privateField2 = privateClass1.privateField2  // ERROR
    val privateNField = privateClass1.nested.nestedField // ERROR
  }
}
```

There are seven access errors in this file.

A `private[PrivateClass1]` member is visible to other instances, so the `equalFields` method now parses. Hence, `private[T]` is not as restrictive as `private[this]`. Note that `PrivateClass1` can't see `Nested.nestedField` because that field is declared `pri vate[Nested]`.

When members of T are declared `private[T]` the behavior is equivalent to `private`. It is not equivalent to `private[this]`, which is more restrictive.

What if we change the scope of `Nested.nestedField` to be `private[PrivateClass1]`? Let's see how `private[T]` affects nested types:

```scala
// src/main/scala/progscala2/visibility/private-type-nested.scalaX
// WON'T COMPILE

package scopeA {
  class PrivateClass1 {
    classNested {
      private[PrivateClass1] val nestedField = 1
    }

    private[PrivateClass1] val nested = new Nested
    val nestedNested = nested.nestedField
  }

  classPrivateClass2 extends PrivateClass1 {
    val nField = new Nested().nestedField   // ERROR
  }

  class PrivateClass3 {
    val privateClass1 = new PrivateClass1
    val privateNField = privateClass1.nested.nestedField // ERROR
  }
}
```

Two compilation errors occur.

Now `nestedField` is visible to `PrivateClass1`, but it is still invisible outside of `PrivateClass1`. This is how `private` works in Java.

Let's examine scoping using a package name:

```scala
// src/main/scala/progscala2/visibility/private-pkg-type.scalaX
// WON'T COMPILE

package scopeA {
  private[scopeA] class PrivateClass1

  package scopeA2 {
    private [scopeA2] class PrivateClass2
    private [scopeA]  class PrivateClass3
  }

  class PrivateClass4 extends PrivateClass1
```

```
    protected class PrivateClass5 extends PrivateClass1
    private class PrivateClass6 extends PrivateClass1
    private[this] class PrivateClass7 extends PrivateClass1

    private[this] class PrivateClass8 extends scopeA2.PrivateClass2 // ERROR
    private[this] class PrivateClass9 extends scopeA2.PrivateClass3
  }

  package scopeB {
    class PrivateClass1B extends scopeA.PrivateClass1 // ERROR
  }
```

Compiling this file also yields two errors.

Note that `PrivateClass2` can't be subclassed outside of `scopeA2`, but `PrivateClass3` can be subclassed in `scopeA`, because it is declared `private[scopeA]`.

Finally, let's look at the effect of package-level scoping of type members:

```
// src/main/scala/progscala2/visibility/private-pkg.scalaX
// WON'T COMPILE

package scopeA {
  class PrivateClass1 {
    private[scopeA] val privateField = 1

    class Nested {
      private[scopeA] val nestedField = 1
    }

    private[scopeA] val nested = new Nested
  }

  class PrivateClass2 extends PrivateClass1 {
    val field  = privateField
    val nField = new Nested().nestedField
  }

  class PrivateClass3 {
    val privateClass1 = new PrivateClass1
    val privateField  = privateClass1.privateField
    val privateNField = privateClass1.nested.nestedField
  }

  package scopeA2 {
    class PrivateClass4 {
      private[scopeA2] val field1 = 1
      private[scopeA]  val field2 = 2
    }
  }

  class PrivateClass5 {
    val privateClass4 = new scopeA2.PrivateClass4
```

```
      val field1 = privateClass4.field1   // ERROR
      val field2 = privateClass4.field2
    }
  }

  package scopeB {
    class PrivateClass1B extends scopeA.PrivateClass1 {
      val field1 = privateField     // ERROR
      val privateClass1 = new scopeA.PrivateClass1
      val field2 = privateClass1.privateField   // ERROR
    }
  }
```

This last file has three errors.

The only errors are when we attempt to access members scoped to scopeA from the unrelated package scopeB and when we attempt to access a member from a nested package scopeA2 that is scoped to that package.

> When a type or member is declared private[P], where P is the enclosing package, it is equivalent to Java's package private visibility.

Final Thoughts on Visibility

Scala visibility declarations are very flexible, and they behave consistently. They provide fine-grained control over visibility at all possible scopes, from the instance level (private[this]) up to package-level visibility (private[P], for a package P). For example, they make it easier to create reusable components with types exposed outside of the component's top-level package, while hiding implementation types and type members within the component's packages.

These fine-grained visibility controls are not widely used outside the standard library, but they should be. When you're writing your own libraries, consider which types and methods should be hidden from clients and apply the appropriate visibility rules to them.

Finally, we observed a potential "gotcha" with hidden members of traits—see the following tip.

> Be careful when choosing names for the members of traits. If two traits have a member of the same name and the traits are used in the same instance, a name collision will occur even if both members are private.

Fortunately, the compiler catches this problem.

Recap and What's Next

Scala's visibility rules offer fine-grained controls that allow us to limit visibility of features in precise ways. It's easy to be lazy and just use the default public visibility. However, good library design includes attention to what features are visible outside the library. Inside the library, limiting visibility between components helps ensure robustness and makes long-term maintenance easier.

Now we turn to a tour of Scala's type system. We already know quite a lot about it, but to really exploit the type system's power, we need a systematic understanding of it.

## CHAPTER 14

Scala's Type System, Part I

Scala is a statically typed language. Its type system is arguably the most sophisticated in any programming language, in part because it combines comprehensive ideas from functional programming and object-oriented programming. The type system tries to be logically comprehensive, complete, and consistent. It fixes several limitations in Java's type system.

Ideally, a type system would be expressive enough that you could prevent your program from ever "inhabiting" an invalid state. It would let you enforce these constraints at compile time, so runtime failures would never occur. In practice, we're far from that goal, but Scala's type system pushes the boundaries toward this long-term goal.

However, the type system can be intimidating at first. It is the most controversial feature of the language. When people claim that Scala is "complex," they usually have the type system in mind.

Fortunately, type inference hides many of the details. Mastery of the type system is not required to use Scala effectively, although you'll eventually need to be familiar with most constructs.

We've already learned a lot about the type system. This chapter ties these threads together and covers the remaining, widely used type system features that every new Scala developer should learn. The next chapter covers more advanced features that aren't as important to learn immediately if you're new to Scala. When we get to Chapter 24, we'll discuss type information in the context of reflection (runtime introspection) and macros.

We'll also discuss similarities with Java's type system, because it may be a familiar point of reference for you. Understanding the differences is also useful for interoperability with Java libraries.

In fact, some of the complexity in Scala's type system arises from features that represent idiosyncrasies in Java's type system. Scala needs to support these features for interoperability.

Now let's begin by revisiting familiar ground, *parameterized types*.

Parameterized Types

We have encountered parameterized types in several places already. In "Abstract Types Versus Parameterized Types" on page 67, we compared them to abstract types. In "Parameterized Types: Variance Under Inheritance" on page 285, we explored *variance* under subtyping.

In this section, we'll recap some of the details, then add additional information that you should know.

Variance Annotations

First, let's recall how *variance annotations* work. A declaration like List[+A] means that List is parameterized by a single type, represented by A. The + is a variance annotation and in this case it says that List is *covariant* in the type parameter, meaning that List[String] is considered a subtype of List[AnyRef], because String is a subtype of AnyRef.

Similarly, the - variance annotation indicates that the type is *contravariant* in the type parameter. One example is the types for the N arguments passed to FunctionN values. Consider Function2 (*http://bit.ly/1E8xyiz*), which has the type signature Function2[-T1, -T2, +R]. We saw in "Functions Under the Hood" on page 286 why the types for the function arguments must be contravariant.

Type Constructors

Sometimes you'll see the term *type constructor* used for a parameterized type. This reflects how the parameterized type is used to create *specific* types, in much the same way that an *instance constructor* for a class is used to construct instances of the class.

For example, List is the type constructor for List[String] and List[Int], which are different types. In fact, you could say that all classes are type constructors. Those without type parameters are effectively "parameterized types" with zero type parameter arguments.

Type Parameter Names

Consider using descriptive names for your type parameters. A complaint of new Scala developers is the terse names used for type parameters, like A and B, in the implementations and Scaladocs for methods like `List.+:`. On the other hand, you quickly learn how to interpret these symbols, which follow some simple rules:

1. Use single-letter or double-letter names like A, B, T1, T2, etc. for very generic type parameters, such as container elements. Note that the actual element types have no close connection to the containers. Lists work the same whether they are holding strings, numbers, other lists, etc. This decoupling makes "generic programming" possible.

2. Use more descriptive names for types that are closely associated with the underlying container. Perhaps `That` in the `List.+:` signature doesn't express an obvious meaning when you first encounter it, but it's sufficient for the job once you understand the collection design idioms that we discussed in "Design Idioms in the Collections Library" on page 342.

Type Bounds

When defining a parameterized type or method, it may be necessary to specify *bounds* on the type parameter. For example, a container might assume that certain methods exist on all types used for the type parameter.

Upper Type Bounds

Upper type bounds specify that a type must be a subtype of another type. For a motivating example, we saw in "Scala's Built-in Implicits" on page 161 that `Predef` (*http://bit.ly/11QI0fF*) defines implicit conversions to wrap instances of `Array` (*http://bit.ly/13p3phR*) (that is, a Java array) in a `collection.mutable.ArrayOps` (*http://bit.ly/1pbp9HU*) instance, where the latter provides the sequence operations we know and love.

There are several of these conversions defined. Most are for the specific `AnyVal` types, like `Long`, but one handles conversions of `Array[AnyRef]` instances:

```
implicit def refArrayOps[T <: AnyRef](xs: Array[T]): ArrayOps[T] =
  new ArrayOps.ofRef[T](xs)
implicit def longArrayOps(xs: Array[Long]): ArrayOps[Long] =
  new ArrayOps.ofLong(xs)
... // Methods for the other AnyVal types.
```

The type parameter `A <: AnyRef` means "any type A that is a *subtype* of `AnyRef`." Recall that a type is always a subtype and a supertype of itself, so A could also equal `AnyRef`. Hence, the `<:` operator indicates that the type to the left must be derived from the type to the right, or that they must be the same type. As we said in "Reserved Words" on page 51, this operator is actually a reserved word in the language.

By restricting the first method to apply only to subtypes of AnyRef, there is no ambiguity between this generic conversion method and the more specific conversion methods for Long, Int, etc.

These bounds are called *upper type bounds*, following the de facto convention that type hierarchies are drawn with subtypes below their supertypes. We followed this convention in the diagram shown in "The Scala Type Hierarchy" on page 294.

Type bounds and variance annotations cover unrelated issues. A type bound specifies constraints on allowed types that can be used for a type parameter in a parameterized type. For example T <: AnyRef limits T to be a subtype of AnyRef. A variance annotation specifies when an instance of a subtype of a parameterized type can be substituted where a supertype instance is expected. For example, because List[+T] is covariant in T, List[String] is a subtype of List[Any].

Lower Type Bounds

In contrast, a *lower type bound* expresses that one type must be a supertype (or the same type) as another. An example is the getOrElse method in Option (*http://bit.ly/16yQhkp*):

```
sealed abstract class Option[+A] extends Product with Serializable {
  ...
  @inline final def getOrElse[B >: A](default: => B): B = {...}
  ...
}
```

If the Option instance is Some[A], the value it contains is returned. Otherwise, the by-name parameter default is evaluated and returned. It is allowed to be a supertype of A. Why is that? In fact, why does Scala *require* that we declare the method this way? Let's consider an example that illustrates why this requirement is necessary (and poorly understood):

```
// src/main/scala/progscala2/typesystem/bounds/lower-bounds.sc

class Parent(val value: Int) {                        // ❶
  override def toString = s"${this.getClass.getName}($value)"
}
class Child(value: Int) extends Parent(value)

val op1: Option[Parent] = Option(new Child(1))        // ❷      Some(Child(1))
val p1: Parent = op1.getOrElse(new Parent(10))        // Result: Child(1)

val op2: Option[Parent] = Option[Parent](null)        // ❸      None
val p2a: Parent = op2.getOrElse(new Parent(10))       // Result: Parent(10)
val p2b: Parent = op2.getOrElse(new Child(100))       // Result: Child(100)
```

```
val op3: Option[Parent] = Option[Child](null)    // ❹     None
val p3a: Parent = op3.getOrElse(new Parent(20))  // Result: Parent(20)
val p3b: Parent = op3.getOrElse(new Child(200))  // Result: Child(200)
```

❶ A simple type hierarchy for demonstration purposes.

❷ The reference op1 only knows it's an Option[Parent], but it actually references
a (valid) subclass, Option[Child], because Option[+T] is covariant.

❸ Option[X](null) always returns None. In this case, the reference returned is
typed to Option[Parent].

❹ None again, but now the reference returned is typed to Option[Child], although
it is assigned to an Option[Parent] reference.

These two lines near the end illustrate the crucial point:

```
val op3: Option[Parent] = Option[Child](null)
val p3a: Parent = op3.getOrElse(new Parent(20))
```

The op3 line clearly shows that Option[Child](null) (i.e., None) is assigned to Op
tion[Parent], but what if instead that value came back from a "black-box" method call,
so we couldn't know what it really is? The crucial point in this example is that the calling
code only has references to Option[Parent], so it has the reasonable expectation that
a Parent value can be extracted from an Option[Parent], whether it has a None, in
which case the default Parent argument is returned, or it is a Some[Parent] or a
Some[Child], in which case the value in the Some is returned. All combinations return
a Parent value, as shown, although sometimes it is actually a Child subclass instance.

Suppose getOrElse had this declaration instead:

```
@inline final def getOrElse(default: => A): A = {...}
```

In this case, it would not type check to call op3.getOrElse(new Parent(20)), because
the object that op3 references is of type Option[Child], so it would expect a Child
instance to be passed to getOrElse.

This is why the compiler won't allow this simpler method signature and instead requires
the original signature with the [B >: A] bounds. To see this, let's sketch our own option
type, call it Opt, that uses this method declaration. For simplicity, we'll treat a null value
as the equivalent of None, for which getOrElse should return the default value:

```
// src/main/scala/progscala2/typesystem/bounds/lower-bounds2.sc
scala> case class Opt[+A](value: A = null) {
     |   def getOrElse(default: A) = if (value != null) value else default
     | }
<console>:8: error: covariant type A occurs in contravariant position
  in type A of value default
         def getOrElse(default: A) = if (value != null) value else default
                  ^
```

So, whenever you see the error message "covariant type A occurs in contravariant position…," it means that you have attempted to define a parameterized type that's covariant in the parameter, but you're also trying to define methods that accept instances of that type parameter, rather than a new supertype parameter, i.e., B >: A. This is disallowed for the reasons just outlined.

If this argument sounds vaguely familiar, it should. It's essentially the same behavior we discussed for function types in "Functions Under the Hood" on page 286 for the type parameters used for the function arguments. They must also be *contravariant*, e.g., Function2[-A1, -A2, +R], because those argument types occur in contravariant position in the apply methods used to implement instances of functions.

 When attempting to understand why variance annotations and type bounds work the way they do, remember to study what happens with instances of types from the perspective of code that uses them, where that code might have a reference to a parent type, but the actual instance is a child type.

Consider what happens if we change our *covariant* Opt[+A] to *invariant*, Opt[A]:

```
// src/main/scala/progscala2/typesystem/bounds/lower-bounds2.sc
scala> case class Opt[A](value: A = null) {
     |   def getOrElse(default: A) = if (value != null) value else default
     | }

scala> val p4: Parent = Opt(new Child(1)).getOrElse(new Parent(10))
<console>:11: error: type mismatch;
 found    : Parent
 required: Child
         val p4: Parent = Opt(new Child(1)).getOrElse(new Parent(10))
                                                          ^

scala> val p5: Parent = Opt[Parent](null).getOrElse(new Parent(10))
p5: Parent = Parent(10)

scala> val p6: Parent = Opt[Child](null).getOrElse(new Parent(10))
<console>:11: error: type mismatch;
 found    : Parent
 required: Child
         val p6: Parent = Opt[Child](null).getOrElse(new Parent(10))
                                                         ^
```

Only the p5 case works. We can no longer assign an Opt[Child] to an Opt[Parent] reference.

It's worth discussing the subtleties of another class of examples where parameterized types that are *covariant* in the type parameter must have *contravariant* behavior in some methods, when we add elements to an immutable collection to construct a new collection.

Consider the Seq.+: method for prepending an element to a sequence, creating a new sequence. We've used it before. It's typically used with operator notation, as in the following example:

```scala
scala> 1 +: Seq(2, 3)
res0: Seq[Int] = List(1, 2, 3)
```

In the Scaladocs, this method has a simplified signature, which assumes we're prepending elements of the same type (A), but the method's actual signature is more general. Here are both signatures:

```scala
def +:(elem: A): Seq[A] = {...}                              // ❶
def +:[B >: A, That](elem: B)(                               // ❷
  implicit bf: CanBuildFrom[Seq[A], B, That)]): That = {...}
```

❶   Simplified signature, which assumes the type parameter A stays the same.

❷   Actual signature, which supports prepending elements of an arbitrary new supertype and also includes the CanBuildFrom formalism we've discussed previously.

In the following example, we prepend a Double value to a Seq[Int]:

```scala
scala> 0.1 +: res0
<console>:9: warning: a type was inferred to be `AnyVal`; this may
  indicate a programming error.
            0.1 +: res0
                ^
res1: Seq[AnyVal] = List(0.1, 1, 2, 3)
```

You won't see this warning if you use a version of Scala before 2.11. I'll explain why in a moment.

The B type isn't the same as the new head value's type, Double in this case. Instead, B is inferred to be the *least upper bound* (LUB), i.e., the closest supertype of the original type A (Int) and the type of the new element (Double). Hence, B is inferred to be AnyVal.

For Option, B was inferred to be the same type as the default argument. If the object was a None, the default was returned and we could "forget about" the original A type.

In the case of a list, we are keeping the existing A-typed values and adding a new value of type B, so a LUB has to be inferred that is a parent of both A and B.

While convenient, inferring a broader, LUB type can be a surprise if you thought you were not changing from the original type parameter. That's why Scala 2.11 added a warning when an expression infers a broad LUB type.

The workaround is to explicitly declare the expected return type:

```
// Scala 2.11 workaround for warning.
scala> val l2: List[AnyVal] = 0.1 +: res0
l2: List[AnyVal] = List(0.1, 1, 2, 3)
```

Now the compiler knows that you want the broader LUB type.

To recap, there is an intimate relationship between parameterized types that are *covariant* in their parameters and *lower type bounds* in method arguments.

Finally, you can combine upper and lower type bounds:

```
class Upper
class Middle1 extends Upper
class Middle2 extends Middle1
class Lower extends Middle2
case class C[A >: Lower <: Upper](a: A)
// case class C2[A <: Upper >: Lower](a: A)   // Does not compile
```

The type parameter, A, must appear first. Note that the C2 case does *not* compile; the lower bound has to appear before the upper bound.

Context Bounds

We learned about *context bounds* and their uses in "Using implicitly" on page 133. Here is the example that we considered then:

```
// src/main/scala/progscala2/implicits/implicitly-args.sc
import math.Ordering

case class MyList[A](list: List[A]) {
  def sortBy1[B](f: A => B)(implicit ord: Ordering[B]): List[A] =
    list.sortBy(f)(ord)

  def sortBy2[B : Ordering](f: A => B): List[A] =
    list.sortBy(f)(implicitly[Ordering[B]])
}

val list = MyList(List(1,3,5,2,4))

list sortBy1 (i => -i)
list sortBy2 (i => -i)
```

Comparing the two versions of sortBy, note that the implicit parameter shown explicitly in sortBy1 and "hidden" in sortBy2 is a parameterized type. The type expression B : Ordering is equivalent to B with no modification and an implicit parameter of type Ordering[B]. This means that no particular type can be used for B unless there exists a corresponding Ordering[B].

A similar concept is *view bounds*.

View Bounds

View bounds look similar to context bounds and they can be considered a special case of context bounds. They can be declared in either of the following ways:

```
class C[A] {
  def m1[B](...)(implicit view: A => B): ReturnType = {...}
  def m2[A <% B](...): ReturnType = {...}
}
```

Contrast with the previous context bound case, where the implicit value for A : B had to be of type B[A]. Here, we need an implicit function that converts an A to a B. We say that "B is a view onto A." Also, contrast with a upper bound expression A <: B, which says that A *is* a subtype of B. A view bound is a looser requirement. It says that A must be convertable to B.

Here is a sketch of how this feature might be used. The Hadoop (*http://hadoop.apache.org*) Java API requires data values to be wrapped in custom serializers, which implement a so-called Writable (*http://bit.ly/1s0TMvi*) interface, for sending values to remote processes. Users of the API must work with these Writables explicitly, an inconvenience. We can use view bounds to handle this automatically (we'll use our own Writable for simplicity):

```
// src/main/scala/progscala2/typesystem/bounds/view-bounds.sc
import scala.language.implicitConversions

object Serialization {
  case class Writable(value: Any) {
    def serialized: String = s"-- $value --"             // ❶
  }

  implicit def fromInt(i: Int) = Writable(i)             // ❷
  implicit def fromFloat(f: Float) = Writable(f)
  implicit def fromString(s: String) = Writable(s)
}

import Serialization._

object RemoteConnection {                                // ❸
  def write[T <% Writable](t: T): Unit =                 // ❹
    println(t.serialized)  // Use stdout as the "remote connection"
}

RemoteConnection.write(100)       // Prints -- 100 --
RemoteConnection.write(3.14f)     // Prints -- 3.14 --
RemoteConnection.write("hello!")  // Prints -- hello! --
// RemoteConnection.write((1, 2))                        // ❺
```

❶ Use String as the "binary" format, for simplicity.

❷ Define a few implicit conversions. Note that we defined methods here, but we said that functions of type A => B are required. Recall that Scala will lift methods to functions when needed.

❸ Object that encapsulates writing to a "remote" connection.

❹ A method that accepts an instance of any type and writes it to the connection. It invokes the implicit conversion so the serialized method can be called on it.

❺ Can't use a tuple, because there is no implicit "view" available for it.

Note that we don't need Predef.implictly (*http://bit.ly/11QI0fF*) or something like it. The implicit conversion is invoked for us automatically by the compiler.

View bounds can be implemented with context bounds, which are more general, although view bounds provide a nice, shorthand syntax. Hence, there has been some discussion in the Scala community of deprecating view bounds. Here is the previous example reworked using context bounds:

```scala
// src/main/scala/progscala2/typesystem/bounds/view-to-context-bounds.sc
import scala.language.implicitConversions

object Serialization {
  case class Rem[A](value: A) {
    def serialized: String = s"-- $value --"
  }
  type Writable[A] = A => Rem[A]                                    // ❶
  implicit val fromInt: Writable[Int]       = (i: Int)    => Rem(i)
  implicit val fromFloat: Writable[Float]   = (f: Float)  => Rem(f)
  implicit val fromString: Writable[String] = (s: String) => Rem(s)
}

import Serialization._

object RemoteConnection {
  def write[T : Writable](t: T): Unit =                             // ❷
    println(t.serialized)  // Use stdout as the "remote connection"
}

RemoteConnection.write(100)      // Prints -- 100 --                ❸
RemoteConnection.write(3.14f)    // Prints -- 3.14 --
RemoteConnection.write("hello!") // Prints -- hello! --
// RemoteConnection.write((1, 2))
```

❶ A type alias that makes it more convenient to use context bounds, followed by the implicit definitions corresponding to the previous example.

❷ The write method now implemented with a context bound.

❸ The same calls to write from the previous example, producing the same results.

So, consider avoiding view bounds in your code, because they may be deprecated in the future.

Understanding Abstract Types

Parameterized types are common in statically typed, object-oriented languages. Scala also supports abstract types, which are common in some functional languages. We introduced abstract types in "Abstract Types Versus Parameterized Types" on page 67. These two approaches overlap somewhat, as we'll explore in a moment. First, let's discuss using abstract types:

```
// src/main/scala/progscala2/typesystem/abstracttypes/abstract-types-ex.sc

trait exampleTrait {
  type t1                  // t1 is unconstrained
  type t2 >: t3 <: t1      // t2 must be a supertype of t3 and a subtype of t1
  type t3 <: t1            // t3 must be a subtype of t1
  type t4 <: Seq[t1]       // t4 must be a subtype of Seq of t1
  // type t5 = +AnyRef      // ERROR: Can't use variance annotations

  val v1: t1               // Can't initialize until t1 defined.
  val v2: t2               // ditto...
  val v3: t3               // ...
  val v4: t4               // ...
}
```

The comments explain most of the details. The relationships between t1, t2, and t3 have some interesting points. First, the declaration of t2 says that it must be "between" t1 and t3. Whatever t1 becomes, it must be a superclass of t2 (or equal to it), and t3 must be a subclass of t2 (or equal to it).

Note the line that declares t3. It must specify that it is a subtype of t1 to be consistent with the declaration of t2. It would be an error to omit the type bound, because t3 <: t1 is implied by the previous declaration of t2. Trying t3 <: t2 triggers an error for an "illegal cyclic reference to t2" in the declaration type t2 >: t3 <: t1. We also can't omit the explicit declaration of t3 and assume its existence is "implied" somehow by the declaration for t2. Of course, this complex example is contrived to demonstrate the behaviors.

We can't use variance annotations on type members. Remember that the types are *members* of the enclosing type, not type parameters, as for parameterized types. The enclosing type may have an inheritance relationship with other types, but member types behave just like member methods and variables. They don't affect the inheritance relationships of their enclosing type. Like other members, member types can be declared abstract or concrete. However, they can also be refined in subtypes without being fully defined, unlike variables and methods. Of course, instances can only be created when the abstract types are given concrete definitions.

Let's define some traits and a class to test these types:

```
trait T1 { val name1: String }
trait T2 extends T1 { val name2: String }
case class C(name1: String, name2: String) extends T2
```

Finally, we can declare a concrete type that defines the abstract type members and initializes the values accordingly:

```
object example extends exampleTrait {
  type t1 = T1
  type t2 = T2
  type t3 = C
  type t4 = Vector[T1]

  val v1 = new T1 { val name1 = "T1"}
  val v2 = new T2 { val name1 = "T1"; val name2 = "T2" }
  val v3 = C("1", "2")
  val v4 = Vector(C("3", "4"))
}
```

Comparing Abstract Types and Parameterized Types

Technically, you could implement almost all the idioms that parameterized types support using abstract types and vice versa. However, in practice, each feature is a natural fit for different design problems.

Parameterized types work nicely for containers, like collections, where there is little connection between the types represented by the type parameter and the container itself. For example, a list works the same if it's a list of strings, a list of doubles, or a list of integers.

What about using type parameters instead? Consider the declaration of Some from the standard library:

```
case final class Some[+A](val value : A) { ... }
```

If we try to convert this to use abstract types, we might start with the following:

```
case final class Some(val value : ???) {
  type A
  ...
}
```

What should be the type of the argument value? We can't use A because it's not in scope at the point of the constructor argument. We could use Any, but that defeats the purpose of type safety.

Hence, parameterized types are the only good approach when arguments of the type are given to the constructor.

In contrast, abstract types tend to be most useful for type "families," types that are closely linked. Recall the example we saw in "Abstract Types Versus Parameterized Types" on page 67 (some unimportant details not repeated):

```scala
// src/main/scala/progscala2/typelessdomore/abstract-types.sc

import java.io._

abstract class BulkReader {
  type In
  val source: In
  def read: String  // Read and return a String
}

class StringBulkReader(val source: String) extends BulkReader {
  type In = String
  def read: String = source
}

class FileBulkReader(val source: File) extends BulkReader {
  type In = File
  def read: String = {...}
}
```

BulkReader declares the abstract type In with no type bounds. The subtypes String BulkReader and FileBulkReader define the type. Note that the user no longer specifies a type through a type parameter. Instead we have total control over the type member In and its enclosing class, so the implementation keeps them consistent.

Let's consider another example, a potential design approach for the *Observer Pattern* we've encountered before in "Traits as Mixins" on page 272 and again in "Overriding fields in traits" on page 317. Our first approach will fail, but we'll fix it in the next section on self-type annotations:

```scala
// src/main/scala/progscala2/typesystem/abstracttypes/SubjectObserver.scalaX
package progscala2.typesystem.abstracttypes

abstract class SubjectObserver {                                  // ❶
  type S <: Subject                                              // ❷
  type O <: Observer

  trait Subject {                                                // ❸
    private var observers = List[O]()

    def addObserver(observer: O) = observers ::= observer

    def notifyObservers() = observers.foreach(_.receiveUpdate(this)) // ❹
  }
```

```
trait Observer {                                            // ❺
  def receiveUpdate(subject: S)
}
```
}

❶   Encapsulate the subject-observer relationship in a single type.

❷   Declare abstract type members for the subject and observer types, bounded by the Subject and Observer traits declared here.

❸   The Subject trait, which maintains a list of observers.

❹   Notify the observers. This line *doesn't compile*.

❺   The Observer trait with a method for receiving updates.

Attempting to compile this file produces the following error:

```
em/abstracttypes/observer.scala:14: type mismatch;
[error]  found    : Subject.this.type (with underlying type
                    SubjectObserver.this.Subject)
[error]  required: SubjectObserver.this.S
[error]    def notifyObservers = observers foreach (_.receiveUpdate(this))
[error]                                                               ^
```

What we wanted to do is use bounded, abstract type members for the subject and observer, so that when we specify concrete types for them, especially the S type, our Observer.receiveUpdate(subject: S) will have the exact type for the subject, not the less useful parent type, Subject.

However, when we compile it, this is of type Subject when we pass it to receiveUpdate, not the more specific type S.

We can fix the problem with a self-type annotation.

Self-Type Annotations

You can use this in a method to refer to the enclosing instance, which is useful for referencing another member of the instance. Explicitly using this is not usually necessary for this purpose, but it's occasionally useful for disambiguating a reference when several items are in scope with the same name.

Self-type annotations support two objectives. First, they let you specify additional type expectations for this. Second, they can be used to create aliases for this.

To illustrate specifying additional type expectations, let's revisit our SubjectObserver class from the previous section. By specifying additional type expectations, we'll solve the compilation problem we encountered. Only two changes are required:

```
// src/main/scala/progscala2/typesystem/selftype/SubjectObserver.scala
package progscala2.typesystem.selftype

abstract class SubjectObserver {
  type S <: Subject
  type O <: Observer

  trait Subject {
    self: S =>                                           // ❶
    private var observers = List[O]()

    def addObserver(observer: O) = observers ::= observer

    def notifyObservers() = observers.foreach(_.receiveUpdate(self)) // ❷
  }

  trait Observer {
    def receiveUpdate(subject: S)
  }
}
```

❶ Declare a self-type annotation for Subject, which is self: S. This means that
    we can now "assume" that a Subject will really be an instance of the subtype S,
    which will be whatever concrete classes we define that mix in Subject.

❷ Pass self rather than this to receiveUpdate.

Now it compiles. Let's see how the types might be used to observe button clicks:

```
// src/main/scala/progscala2/typesystem/selftype/ButtonSubjectObserver.scala
package progscala2.typesystem.selftype

case class Button(label: String) {                       // ❶
  def click(): Unit = {}
}

object ButtonSubjectObserver extends SubjectObserver {    // ❷
  type S = ObservableButton
  type O = ButtonObserver

  class ObservableButton(label: String) extends Button(label) with Subject {
    override def click() = {
      super.click()
      notifyObservers()
    }
  }

  trait ButtonObserver extends Observer {
    def receiveUpdate(button: ObservableButton)
  }
}
```

```
import ButtonSubjectObserver._

class ButtonClickObserver extends ButtonObserver {          // ❸
  val clicks = new scala.collection.mutable.HashMap[String,Int]()

  def receiveUpdate(button: ObservableButton) = {
    val count = clicks.getOrElse(button.label, 0) + 1
    clicks.update(button.label, count)
  }
}
```

❶   A simple Button class.

❷   A concrete subtype of SubjectObserver for buttons, where Subject and Ob
server are both subtyped to the more specific types we want (note the type of
the value passed to ButtonObserver.receiveUpdate). ObservableButton
overrides Button.click to notify the observers after calling Button.click.

❸   Implement ButtonObserver to track the number of clicks for each button
in a UI.

The following script creates two ObservableButtons, attaches the same observer to
both, clicks them a few times, and prints the number of counts observed for each one:

```
// src/main/scala/progscala2/typesystem/selftype/ButtonSubjectObserver.sc
import progscala2.typesystem.selftype._

val buttons = Vector(new ObservableButton("one"), new ObservableButton("two"))
val observer = new ButtonClickObserver
buttons foreach (_.addObserver(observer))
for (i <- 0 to 2) buttons(0).click()
for (i <- 0 to 4) buttons(1).click()
println(observer.clicks)
// Map("one" -> 3, "two" -> 5)
```

So, we can use self-type annotations to solve a typing problem when using abstract type
members.

Another example is a pattern for specifying "modules" and wiring them together. Consider this example that sketches a three-tier application, with a persistence layer, middle
tier, and UI:

```
// src/main/scala/progscala2/typesystem/selftype/selftype-cake-pattern.sc

trait Persistence { def startPersistence(): Unit }          // ❶
trait Midtier { def startMidtier(): Unit }
trait UI { def startUI(): Unit }

trait Database extends Persistence {                         // ❷
  def startPersistence(): Unit = println("Starting Database")
}
trait BizLogic extends Midtier {
```

```
    def startMidtier(): Unit = println("Starting BizLogic")
  }
  trait WebUI extends UI {
    def startUI(): Unit = println("Starting WebUI")
  }

  trait App { self: Persistence with Midtier with UI =>            // ❸

    def run() = {
      startPersistence()
      startMidtier()
      startUI()
    }
  }

  object MyApp extends App with Database with BizLogic with WebUI   // ❹

  MyApp.run                                                         // ❺
```

❶　Define traits for the persistence, middle, and UI tiers of the application.

❷　Implement the "concrete" behaviors as traits.

❸　Define a trait (or it could be an abstract class) that defines the "skeleton" of how the tiers glue together. For this simple example, the run method just starts each tier. The self-type annotation is discussed in the following text.

❹　Define the MyApp object that extends App and mixes in the three concrete traits that implement the required behaviors.

❺　Run the application.

Running the script prints the following output from run:

```
Starting Database
Starting BizLogic
Starting WebUI
```

This script shows a schematic layout for an App (application) infrastructure supporting several tiers. Each abstract trait declares a start* method that does the work of initializing the tier. Each abstract tier is implemented by a corresponding concrete trait, not a class, so we can use each one as a mixin.

The App trait wires the tiers together. It's run method starts each tier. Note that no concrete implementations of these traits is specified here. A concrete application must be constructed by mixing in implementations of these traits.

The *self-type annotation* is the crucial point:

```
self: Persistence with Midtier with UI =>
```

When a type annotation is added to a self-type annotation, Persistence with Midtier with UI, in this case, it specifies that the trait or abstract class must be mixed with those traits or subtypes that implement any abstract members, in order to define a concrete instance. Because this assumption is made, the trait is allowed to access members of those traits, even though they are not yet part of the type. Here, App.run calls the start* methods from the other traits.

The concrete instance MyApp extends App and mixes in the traits that satisfy the dependencies expressed in the self type.

This picture of stacking layers leads to the name *Cake Pattern*, where modules are declared with traits and another abstract type is used to integrate the traits with a self-type annotation. A concrete object mixes in the actual implementation traits and extends an optional parent class (we'll discuss the implications of this pattern, pro and con, in more detail in "Traits as Modules" on page 508).

This use of self-type annotations is actually equivalent to using inheritance and mixins instead (with the exception that self would not be defined):

```scala
trait App extends Persistence with Midtier with UI {
  def run = { ... }
}
```

There are a few special cases where self-type annotations behave differently than inheritance, but in practice, the two approaches behave interchangeably.

However, they express different intent. The inheritance-based implementation just shown suggests that App is a subtype of Persistence, Midtier, and UI. In contrast, the self-type annotation expresses composition of behavior through mixins more explicitly.

Self-type annotations emphasize mixin composition. Inheritance can imply a subtype relationship.

That said, most Scala code tends to use the inheritance approach, rather than self-type annotations, unless integration of larger-scale "modules" (traits) is being done, where the self-type annotation conveys the design decisions more clearly.

Now let's consider the second usage of self-type annotations, aliasing this:

```scala
// src/main/scala/progscala2/typesystem/selftype/this-alias.sc

class C1 { self =>                                              // ❶
  def talk(message: String) = println("C1.talk: " + message)
  class C2 {
    class C3 {
      def talk(message: String) = self.talk("C3.talk: " + message)   // ❷
    }
    val c3 = new C3
```

```
  }
    val c2 = new C2
  }
  val c1 = new C1
  c1.talk("Hello")                                              // ❸
  c1.c2.c3.talk("World")                                        // ❹
```

❶   Define `self` to be an alias of `this` in the context of C1.

❷   Use `self` to call `C1.talk`.

❸   Call `C1.talk` via the `c1` instance.

❹   Call `C3.talk` via the `c1.c2.c3` instance, which will itself call `C1.talk`.

Note that the name `self` is arbitrary. It is not a keyword. Any name could be used. We could also define self-type annotations inside C2 and C3, if we needed them.

The script prints the following:

```
C1.talk: Hello
C1.talk: C3.talk: World
```

Without the self-type declaration, we can't invoke `C1.talk` directly from within `C3.talk`, because the latter shadows the former, since they share the same name. C3 is not a direct subtype of C1 either, so `super.talk` can't be used.

So, you can think of the self-type annotation in this context as a "generalized this" reference.

Structural Types

You can think of *structural types* as a type-safe approach to *duck typing*, the popular name for the way method resolution works in dynamically typed languages ("If it walks like a duck and talks like a duck, it must be a duck"). For example, in Ruby, when your code contains `starFighter.shootWeapons`, the runtime doesn't yet know if `shootWea pons` actually exists for the `starFighter` instance, but it follows various rules to locate the method to call or handle the failure if one isn't found.

Scala doesn't support this kind of runtime method resolution (an exception is discussed in Chapter 19). Instead, Scala supports a similar mechanism at compile time. Scala allows you to specify that an object must adhere to a certain *structure*: that it contains certain members (types, fields, or methods), without requiring a specific *named* type that encloses those members.

We normally use *nominal typing*, so called because we work with types that have names. In structural typing, we only consider the type's structure. It can be anonymous.

To see an example, let's examine how we might use structural types in the *Observer Pattern*. We'll start with the simpler implementation we saw in "Traits as Mixins" on page 272, as opposed to the one we considered previously in this chapter. First, here are the important details from that example:

```
trait Observer[-State] {
  def receiveUpdate(state: State): Unit
}
trait Subject[State] {
  private var observers: List[Observer[State]] = Nil
  ...
}
```

A drawback of this implementation is that any type that should watch for state changes in Subjects must implement the Observer trait. But really, the *true minimum* requirement is that they implement the receiveUpdate method.

So, here is a reimplementation of the example using a *structural type* for the Observer:

```
// src/main/scala/progscala2/typesystem/structuraltypes/Observer.scala
package progscala2.typesystem.structuraltypes

trait Subject {                                                 // ❶

  import scala.language.reflectiveCalls                          // ❷

  type State                                                     // ❸

  type Observer = { def receiveUpdate(state: Any): Unit }        // ❹

  private var observers: List[Observer] = Nil                    // ❺

  def addObserver(observer:Observer): Unit =
    observers ::= observer

  def notifyObservers(state: State): Unit =
    observers foreach (_.receiveUpdate(state))
}
```

❶ An unrelated change, but illustrative; remove the previous type parameter State and make it an abstract type instead.

❷ Enable the optional feature to allow reflective method calls (see the following text).

❸ The State abstract type.

❹ The type Observer is a *structural type*.

❺ The State type parameter was removed from Observer, as well.

The declaration type Observer = { def receiveUpdate(subject: Any): Unit } says that any object with this receiveUpdate method can be used as an observer. Unfortunately, Scala won't let a structural type refer to an abstract type or type parameter. So, we can't use State. We have to use a type that's already known, like Any. That means that the receiver may need to cast the instance to the correct type, a big drawback.

Another drawback is implied by the import statement. Because we don't have a type name to use to verify that a candidate observer instance implements the correct method, the compiler has to use reflection to confirm the method is present on the instance. This adds overhead, although it won't be noticeable unless observers are added frequently. Using reflection is considered an optional feature, hence the import statement.

This script tries the new implementation:

```
// src/main/scala/progscala2/typesystem/structuraltypes/Observer.sc
import progscala2.typesystem.structuraltypes.Subject
import scala.language.reflectiveCalls

object observer {                                             // ❶
  def receiveUpdate(state: Any): Unit = println("got one! "+state)
}

val subject = new Subject {                                  // ❷
  type State = Int
  protected var count = 0

  def increment(): Unit = {
    count += 1
    notifyObservers(count)
  }
}

subject.increment()
subject.increment()
subject.addObserver(observer)
subject.increment()
subject.increment()
```

❶   Declare an observer object with the correct method.

❷   Instantiate the State trait, providing a definition for the State abstract type and additional behavior.

Note that the observer is registered after two increments have occurred, so it will only print that it received the numbers 3 and 4.

Despite their disadvantages, structural types have the virtue of minimizing the coupling between two things. In this case, the coupling consists of only a single method signature, rather than a type, such as a shared trait.

Taking one last look at our example, we *still* couple to a particular *name*, the method receiveUpdate! In a sense, we've only moved the problem of coupling from a type name to a method name. This name is completely arbitrary, so we can push the decoupling to the next level; define the Observer type to be an alias for a one-argument function. Here is the final form of the example:

```
// src/main/scala/progscala2/typesystem/structuraltypes/SubjectFunc.scala
package progscala2.typesystem.structuraltypes

trait SubjectFunc {                                                      // ❶

  type State

  type Observer = State => Unit                                         // ❷

  private var observers: List[Observer] = Nil

  def addObserver(observer:Observer): Unit =
    observers ::= observer

  def notifyObservers(state: State): Unit =                             // ❸
    observers foreach (o => o(state))
}
```

❶ Use a new name for Subject. Rename the whole file, because the observer has faded into "insignificance"!

❷ Make Observer a type alias for a function State => Unit.

❸ Notifying each observer now means calling its apply method.

The test script is nearly the same. Here are the differences:

```
// src/main/scala/progscala2/typesystem/structuraltypes/SubjectFunc.sc

import progscala2.typeSystem.structuraltypes.SubjectFunc

val observer: Int => Unit = (state: Int) => println("got one! "+state)

val subject = new SubjectFunc { ... }
```

This is much better! All name-based coupling is gone, we eliminated the need for reflection calls, and we're able to use State again, rather than Any, as the function argument type.

This doesn't mean that structural typing is useless. Our example only needed a function to implement what we needed. In the general case, a structural type might have several members and an anonymous function might be insufficient for our needs.

Compound Types

When you declare an instance that combines several types, you get a *compound type*:

```
trait T1
trait T2
class C
val c = new C with T1 with T2   // c's type: C with T1 with T2
```

In this case, the type of c is `C with T1 with T2`. This is an alternative to declaring a type that extends C and mixes in T1 and T2. Note that c is considered a subtype of all three types:

```
val t1: T1 = c
val t2: T2 = c
val c2: C  = c
```

Type Refinements

Type refinements are an additional part of compound types. They are related to an idea you already know from Java, where it's common to provide an *anonymous inner class* that implements some interface, adding method implementations and optionally additional members.

For example, if you have a `java.util.List` (*http://bit.ly/1sRezAw*) of objects of type C, for some class C, you can sort the list in place using the static method, `java.util.Collections.sort` (*http://bit.ly/1wkYNnK*):

```
List<C> listOfC = ...
java.util.Collections.sort(listOfC, new Comparator<C>() {
  public int compare(C c1, C c2) {...}
  public boolean equals(Object obj) {...}
});
```

We "refine" the base type `Comparator` to create a new type. The JVM will give a unique synthetic name to this type in the byte code.

Scala takes this a step further. It synthesizes a new type that reflects our additions. For example, recall this type from the last section on structural typing and notice the type returned by the REPL (output wrapped to fit):

```
scala> val subject = new Subject {
     |     type State = Int
     |     protected var count = 0
     |     def increment(): Unit = {
     |       count += 1
     |       notifyObservers(count)
     |     }
     | }
subject: TypeSystem.structuraltypes.Subject{
  type State = Int; def increment(): Unit} = $anon$1@4e3d11db
```

The type signature adds the extra structural components.

Similarly, when we combine refinement with mixin traits as we instantiate an instance, a refined type is created. Consider this example where we mix in a logging trait (some details omitted):

```scala
scala> trait Logging {
     |    def log(message: String): Unit = println(s"Log: $message")
     | }

scala> val subject = new Subject with Logging {...}
subject: TypeSystem.structuraltypes.Subject with Logging{
  type State = Int; def increment(): Unit} = $anon$1@8b5d08e
```

To access the additional members added to the refinement from outside the instance, you would have to use the reflection API (see "Runtime Reflection" on page 524).

Existential Types

Existential types are a way of abstracting over types. They let you assert that some type "exists" without specifying exactly what it is, usually because you don't know what it is and you don't need to know it in the current context.

Existential types are particularly important for interfacing to Java's type system for three cases:

- The type parameters of generics are "erased" in JVM byte code (called *erasure*). For example, when a List[Int] is created, the Int type is not available in the byte code, so at runtime it's not possible to distinguish between a List[Int] and a List[String], based on the known type information.

- You might encounter "raw" types, such as pre-Java 5 libraries where collections had no type parameters. (All type parameters are effectively Object.)

- When Java uses wildcards in generics to express variance behavior when the generics are *used*, the actual type is unknown.

Consider the case of matching on Seq[A] objects. You might want to define two versions of a function double. One version takes a Seq[Int] and returns a new Seq[Int] with the elements doubled (multiplied by two). The other version takes a Seq[String], maps the String elements to Ints by calling toInt on them (assuming the strings represent integers) and then calls the version of double that takes a Seq[Int] argument:

```scala
object Doubler {
  def double(seq: Seq[String]): Seq[Int] = double(seq map (_.toInt))
  def double(seq: Seq[Int]): Seq[Int] = seq map (_*2)
}
```

You'll get a compilation error that the two methods "have the same type after erasure." A somewhat ugly workaround is to examine the elements of the lists individually:

```
// src/main/scala/progscala2/typesystem/existentials/type-erasure-workaround.sc

object Doubler {
  def double(seq: Seq[_]): Seq[Int] = seq match {
    case Nil => Nil
    case head +: tail => (toInt(head) * 2) +: double(tail)
  }

  private def toInt(x: Any): Int = x match {
    case i: Int => i
    case s: String => s.toInt
    case x => throw new RuntimeException(s"Unexpected list element $x")
  }
}
```

When used in a type context like this, the expression Seq[_] is actually shorthand for the *existential type*, Seq[T] forSome { type T }. This is the most general case. We're saying the type parameter for the list could be any type. Table 14-1 lists some other examples that demonstrate the use of type bounds.

Table 14-1. Existential type examples

Shorthand	Full	Description
Seq[_]	Seq[T] forSome {type T}	T can be any subtype of Any.
Seq[_ <: A]	Seq[T] forSome {type T <: A}	T can be any subtype of A (defined elsewhere).
Seq[_ >: Z <: A]	Seq[T] forSome {type T >: Z <: A}	T can be any subtype of A and supertype of Z.

If you think about how Scala syntax for generics is mapped to Java syntax, you might have noticed that an expression like java.util.List[_ <: A] is structurally similar to the Java variance expression java.util.List<? extends A>. In fact, they are the same declarations. Although we said that variance behavior in Scala is defined at the declaration site, you can use existential type expressions in Scala to define call-site variance behavior, although it is not usually done.

You'll see type signatures like Seq[_] frequently in Scala code, where the type parameter can't be specified more specifically. You won't see the full forSome existential type syntax very often.

Existential types exist primarily to support Java generics while preserving correctness in Scala's type system. Type inference hides the details from us in most contexts.

Recap and What's Next

This concludes a survey of the type system features you're most likely to encounter as you write Scala code and use libraries. Our primary focus was understanding the subtleties of object-oriented inheritance and why certain features like *variance* and *type bounds* are important. The next chapter continues the exploration with features that are less important to master as soon as possible.

If you would like a quick reference to type system and related concepts, bookmark "Scala's Types of Types" (*http://bit.ly/1s0LF1E*) by my Typesafe colleague Konrad Malawski.

## CHAPTER 15

Scala's Type System, Part II

This chapter continues the survey of the type system that we started in the previous chapter. The type features discussed here are the ones you'll encounter eventually, but you don't need to understand them right away if you're new to Scala. As you work on Scala projects and use third-party libraries, if you encounter a type system concept that you haven't seen before, you'll probably find it covered here. (For more depth than we can cover here, see *The Scala Language Specification* (*http://bit.ly/1wNBOR8*).) Still, I recommend you skim the chapter. For example, you'll see a few examples of *path-dependent* types in more advanced examples later in the book, although you won't need a "deep" understanding of them.

Path-Dependent Types

Scala, like Java before it, lets you nest types. You can access nested types using a *path* expression.

Consider the following example:

```
// src/main/scala/progscala2/typesystem/typepaths/type-path.scalaX
package progscala2.typesystem.typepaths

class Service {                                              // ❶
  class Logger {
    def log(message: String): Unit = println(s"log: $message")   // ❷
  }
  val logger: Logger = new Logger
}

val s1 = new Service
val s2 = new Service { override val logger = s1.logger }     // ERROR!  ❸
```

❶   Define a class `Service` with a nested class `Logger`.

❷ Use println for simplicitly.

❸ Compilation error!

Compiling this file produces the following error on the last line:

```
error: overriding value logger in class Service of type this.Logger;
  value logger has incompatible type
        val s2 = new Service { override val logger = s1.logger }
                                                      ^
```

Shouldn't the two Loggers' types be considered the same? No. The error message says it's expecting a logger of type this.Logger. In Scala, the type of each Service instance's logger is considered a different type. In other words, the actual type is *path-dependent*. Let's discuss the kinds of type paths.

C.this

For a class C1, you can use the familiar this inside the body to refer to the current instance, but this is actually a shorthand for C1.this in Scala:

```
// src/main/scala/progscala2/typesystem/typepaths/path-expressions.scala

class C1 {
  var x = "1"
  def setX1(x:String): Unit = this.x = x
  def setX2(x:String): Unit = C1.this.x = x
}
```

Inside a type body, but outside a method definition, this refers to the type itself:

```
trait T1 {
  class C
  val c1: C = new C
  val c2: C = new this.C
}
```

To be clear, the this in this.C refers to the trait T1.

C.super

You can refer to the parent of a type with super:

```
trait X {
  def setXX(x:String): Unit = {} // Do Nothing!
}
class C2 extends C1
class C3 extends C2 with X {
  def setX3(x:String): Unit = super.setX1(x)
  def setX4(x:String): Unit = C3.super.setX1(x)
  def setX5(x:String): Unit = C3.super[C2].setX1(x)
  def setX6(x:String): Unit = C3.super[X].setXX(x)
```

```
  // def setX7(x:String): Unit = C3.super[C1].setX1(x)    // ERROR
  // def setX8(x:String): Unit = C3.super.super.setX1(x)  // ERROR
}
```

`C3.super` is equivalent to `super` in this example. You can qualify which parent using [T], as shown for `setX5`, which selects C2, and `setX6`, which selects X. However, you can't refer to "grandparent" types (`setX7`). You can't chain `super`, either (`setX8`).

If you call `super` without qualification on a type with several ancestors, to which type does `super` bind? The rules of *linearization* determine the target of `super` (see "Linearization of an Object's Hierarchy" on page 326).

Just as for `this`, you can use `super` to refer to the parent type in a type body outside a method:

```
class C4 {
  class C5
}
class C6 extends C4 {
  val c5a: C5 = new C5
  val c5b: C5 = new super.C5
}
```

path.x

You can reach a nested type with a period-delimited path expression. All but the last elements of a type path must be *stable*, which roughly means they must be packages, singleton objects, or type declarations that alias the same. The last element in the path can be unstable, including classes, traits, and type members. Consider this example:

```
package P1 {
  object O1 {
    object O2 {
      val name = "name"
    }
    class C1 {
      val name = "name"
    }
  }
}
class C7 {
  val  name1 = P1.O1.O2.name    // Okay  - a reference to a field
  type C1    = P1.O1.C1         // Okay  - a reference to a "leaf" class
  val  c1    = new P1.O1.C1     // Okay  - same reason
  // val name2 = P1.O1.C1.name  // ERROR - P1.O1.C1 isn't stable.
}
```

The C7 members `name1`, `C1`, and `c1` all use stable elements until the last position, while `name2` has an unstable element (`C1`) before the last position.

You can see this if you uncomment the `name2` declaration, leading to the following compilation error:

```
[error] .../typepaths/path-expressions.scala:52: value C1 is not a member of
  object progscala2.typesystem.typepaths.P1.O1
[error]    val name2 = P1.O1.C1.name
[error]                        ^
```

Of course, avoiding complex paths in your code is a good idea.

Dependent Method Types

A new feature added in Scala 2.10 is *dependent method types*, a form of path-dependent typing that is useful for several design problems.

One application is the *Magnet Pattern*, where a single processing method takes an object, called a *magnet*, which ensures a compatible return type. For a detailed example of this technique, see the *spray.io* blog (*http://bit.ly/1tpmIQw*). Let's work through an example:

```
// src/main/scala/progscala2/typesystem/dependentmethodtypes/dep-method.sc

import scala.concurrent.{Await, Future}            // ❶
import scala.concurrent.duration._
import scala.concurrent.ExecutionContext.Implicits.global

case class LocalResponse(statusCode: Int)          // ❷
case class RemoteResponse(message: String)
...
```

❶ Import `scala.concurrent.Future` (*http://bit.ly/1xIkpsr*) and related classes for asynchronous computation.

❷ Define two case classes used to return a "response" from a computation, either a local (in-process) invocation or a remote service invocation. Note that they do not share a common supertype. They are completely distinct.

We'll explore the use of `Future`s (*http://bit.ly/1xIkpsr*) in depth in "Futures" on page 425. For now, we'll just sketch the details as needed. Continuing on:

```
sealed trait Computation {
  type Response
  val work: Future[Response]
}

case class LocalComputation(
    work: Future[LocalResponse]) extends Computation {
  type Response = LocalResponse
}
case class RemoteComputation(
    work: Future[RemoteResponse]) extends Computation {
  type Response = RemoteResponse
```

```
    }
    ...
```

A sealed hierarchy for `Computation` covers all the kinds of "computation" performed by our service, local and remote processing. Note that the `work` to be done is wrapped in a `Future`, so it runs asynchronously. Local processing returns a corresponding `LocalResponse` and remote processing returns a corresponding `RemoteResponse`:

```
object Service {
  def handle(computation: Computation): computation.Response = {
    val duration = Duration(2, SECONDS)
    Await.result(computation.work, duration)
  }
}

Service.handle(LocalComputation(Future(LocalResponse(0))))
// Result: LocalResponse = LocalResponse(0)
Service.handle(RemoteComputation(Future(RemoteResponse("remote call"))))
// Result: RemoteResponse = RemoteResponse(remote call)
```

Finally, a service is defined with a single entry point `handle`, which uses `scala.concur rent.Await` (*http://bit.ly/1tI8RGg*) to wait for the future to complete. `Await.result` returns the `LocalResponse` or `RemoteResponse`, corresponding to the input `Computation`.

Note that `handle` doesn't return an instance of a common superclass, because `LocalResponse` and `RemoteResponse` are unrelated. Instead, it returns a type dependent on the argument. It's also not possible for a `RemoteComputation` to return a `LocalResponse` and vice versa, because either combination won't type check.

Type Projections

Let's revisit our `Service` design problem in "Path-Dependent Types" on page 389. First, let's rewrite `Service` to extract some abstractions that would be more typical in real applications:

```
// src/main/scala/progscala2/typesystem/valuetypes/type-projection.scala
package progscala2.typesystem.valuetypes

trait Logger {                                            // ❶
  def log(message: String): Unit
}

class ConsoleLogger extends Logger {                      // ❷
  def log(message: String): Unit = println(s"log: $message")
}

trait Service {                                           // ❸
  type Log <: Logger
```

```
    val logger: Log
}

class Service1 extends Service {                                    // ❹
    type Log = ConsoleLogger
    val logger: ConsoleLogger = new ConsoleLogger
}
```

❶   A Logger trait.

❷   A concrete Logger that logs to the console, for simplicity.

❸   A Service trait that defines an abstract type alias for the Logger and declares a field for it.

❹   A concrete service that uses ConsoleLogger.

Suppose we want to "reuse" the Log type defined in Service1. Let's try a few possibilities in the REPL:

```
// src/main/scala/progscala2/typesystem/valuetypes/type-projection.sc

scala> import progscala2.typesystem.valuetypes._

scala> val l1: Service.Log    = new ConsoleLogger
<console>:10: error: not found: value Service
        val l1: Service.Log    = new ConsoleLogger
                ^

scala> val l2: Service1.Log   = new ConsoleLogger
<console>:10: error: not found: value Service1
        val l2: Service1.Log   = new ConsoleLogger
                ^

scala> val l3: Service#Log    = new ConsoleLogger
<console>:10: error: type mismatch;
 found    : progscala2.typesystem.valuetypes.ConsoleLogger
 required: progscala2.typesystem.valuetypes.Service#Log
        val l3: Service#Log    = new ConsoleLogger
                         ^

scala> val l4: Service1#Log   = new ConsoleLogger
l4: progscala2.typesystem.valuetypes.ConsoleLogger =
   progscala2.typesystem.valuetypes.ConsoleLogger@6376f152
```

Using Service.Log and Service1.Log means that Scala is looking for an *object* named Service and Service1, respectively, but these companion objects don't exist.

However, we can *project* the type we want with #. The first attempt doesn't type check. Although both Service.Log and ConsoleLogger are both subtypes of Logger, Service.Log is abstract so we don't yet know if it will actually be a supertype of Console

Logger. In other words, the final concrete definition could be another subtype of Logger that isn't compatible with ConsoleLogger.

The only one that works is val l4 = Service1#Log = new ConsoleLogger, because the types check statically.

Finally, all the simpler type specifications we write every day are called *type designators*. They are actually shorthand forms for type projections. Here are a few examples of designators and their longer projections, adapted from *The Scala Language Specification*, Section 3.2:

```
Int             // scala.type#Int
scala.Int       // scala.type#Int
package pkg {
  class MyClass {
    type t       // pkg.MyClass.type#t
  }
}
```

Singleton Types

We learned about *singleton objects* that are declared with the object keyword. There is also a concept called *singleton types*. Any instance v that is a subtype of AnyRef, including null, has a unique *singleton type*. You get it using the expression v.type, which can be used as types in declarations to narrow the allowed instances to *one*, the corresponding instance itself. Reusing our Logger and Service example from before:

```
// src/main/scala/progscala2/typesystem/valuetypes/type-types.sc

scala> val s11 = new Service1
scala> val s12 = new Service1

scala> val l1: Logger = s11.logger
l1: ...valuetypes.Logger = ...valuetypes.ConsoleLogger@3662093

scala> val l2: Logger = s12.logger
l2: ...valuetypes.Logger = ...valuetypes.ConsoleLogger@411c6639

scala> val l11: s11.logger.type = s11.logger
l11: s11.logger.type = progscala2.typesystem.valuetypes.ConsoleLogger@3662093

scala> val l12: s11.logger.type = s12.logger
<console>:12: error: type mismatch;
 found   : s12.logger.type (with underlying type ...valuetypes.ConsoleLogger)
 required: s11.logger.type
       val l12: s11.logger.type = s12.logger
                                  ^
```

The only possible assignment to l11 and l12 is s11.logger. The type of s12.logger is incompatible.

Singleton *objects* define both an instance and a corresponding type:

```
// src/main/scala/progscala2/typesystem/valuetypes/object-types.sc

case object Foo { override def toString = "Foo says Hello!" }
```

If you want to define methods that take arguments of this type, use Foo.type:

```
scala> def printFoo(foo: Foo.type) = println(foo)
printFoo: (foo: Foo.type)Unit

scala> printFoo(Foo)
Foo says Hello!
```

Types for Values

Every value has a type. The term *value types* refers to all the different forms these types may take, all of which we've encountered along the way.

In this section, we are using the term *value type* following the usage of the term in *The Scala Language Specification*. However, elsewhere in the book we use the term in the more conventional sense to refer to all subtypes of AnyVal.

For completeness, the value types are *parameterized types, singleton types, type projections, type designators, compound types, existential types, tuple types, function types,* and *infix types*. Let's review the last three types, because they provide convenient syntax alternatives to the conventional way of writing the types. We'll also cover a few details that we haven't seen already.

Tuple Types

We've learned that Scala allows you to write Tuple3[A,B,C] as (A,B,C), called a *tuple type*:

```
val t1: Tuple3[String, Int, Double] = ("one", 2, 3.14)
val t2: (String, Int, Double)       = ("one", 2, 3.14)
```

This is convenient for more complex types to reduce the number of nested brackets and it's a bit shorter because the TupleN is not present. In fact, it's rare to use the TupleN form of the type signature. Contrast List[Tuple2[Int,String]] with List[(Int,String)].

Function Types

We can write the type of a function, say a `Function2`, using the arrow syntax:

```
val f1: Function2[Int,Double,String] = (i,d) => s"int $i, double $d"
val f2: (Int,Double) => String = (i,d) => s"int $i, double $d"
```

Just as it's uncommon to use the `TupleN` syntax to specify a tuple, it's rare to use the `FunctionN` syntax.

Infix Types

A type that takes two type parameters can be written in infix notation. Consider these examples using `Either[A,B]`:

```
val left1:  Either[String,Int] = Left("hello")
val left2:  String Either Int  = Left("hello")
val right1: Either[String,Int] = Right(1)
val right2: String Either Int  = Right(2)
```

You can nest infix types. They are left-associative, unless the name ends in a colon (:), in which case they are right-associative, just like for terms (we haven't emphasized this, but if an expression isn't a type, it's called a *term*). You can override the default associativity using parentheses:

```
// src/main/scala/progscala2/typesystem/valuetypes/infix-types.sc

scala> val xll1:  Int Either Double  Either String  = Left(Left(1))
xll1: Either[Either[Int,Double],String] = Left(Left(1))

scala> val xll2: (Int Either Double) Either String  = Left(Left(1))
xll2: Either[Either[Int,Double],String] = Left(Left(1))


scala> val xlr1:  Int Either Double  Either String  = Left(Right(3.14))
xlr1: Either[Either[Int,Double],String] = Left(Right(3.14))

scala> val xlr2: (Int Either Double) Either String  = Left(Right(3.14))
xlr2: Either[Either[Int,Double],String] = Left(Right(3.14))


scala> val xr1:   Int Either Double  Either String  = Right("foo")
xr1: Either[Either[Int,Double],String] = Right(foo)

scala> val xr2:  (Int Either Double) Either String  = Right("foo")
xr2: Either[Either[Int,Double],String] = Right(foo)


scala> val xl:   Int Either (Double Either String)  = Left(1)
xl: Either[Int,Either[Double,String]] = Left(1)

scala> val xrl:  Int Either (Double Either String)  = Right(Left(3.14))
```

```
xrl: Either[Int,Either[Double,String]] = Right(Left(3.14))

scala> val xrr:  Int Either (Double Either String)  = Right(Right("bar"))
xrr: Either[Int,Either[Double,String]] = Right(Right(bar))
```

Obviously, it can become complicated quickly.

Now, let's move on to a big and important, if sometimes challenging topic, *higher-kinded types*.

Higher-Kinded Types

We're accustomed to writing methods like the following for Seq instances:

```
def sum(seq: Seq[Int]): Int = seq reduce (_ + _)

sum(Vector(1,2,3,4,5))   // Result: 15
```

First, let's generalize the notion of addition to a *type class* (recall "Type Class Pattern" on page 156), which allows us to generalize the element type:

```
// src/main/scala/progscala2/typesystem/higherkinded/Add.scala
package progscala2.typesystem.higherkinded

trait Add[T] {                                              // ❶
  def add(t1: T, T2: T): T
}

object Add {                                                // ❷
  implicit val addInt = new Add[Int] {
    def add(i1: Int, i2: Int): Int = i1 + i2
  }

  implicit val addIntIntPair = new Add[(Int,Int)] {
    def add(p1: (Int,Int), p2: (Int,Int)): (Int,Int) =
      (p1._1 + p2._1, p1._2 + p2._2)
  }
}
```

❶   A trait that defines addition as an abstraction.

❷   A companion object that defines instances of the trait as implicit values of Add for Ints and pairs of Ints.

Now, let's try it out:

```
// src/main/scala/progscala2/typesystem/higherkinded/add-seq.sc
import progscala2.typesystem.higherkinded.Add            // ❶
import progscala2.typesystem.higherkinded.Add._

def sumSeq[T : Add](seq: Seq[T]): T =                    // ❷
  seq reduce (implicitly[Add[T]].add(_,_))
```

```
sumSeq(Vector(1 -> 10, 2 -> 20, 3 -> 30))          // Result: (6,60)
sumSeq(1 to 10)                                     // Result: 55
sumSeq(Option(2))                                   // ❸ Error!
```

❶   Import the Add trait, followed by the implicits defined in the Add companion object.

❷   Use a *context bound* and implicitly (see "Using implicitly" on page 133) to "sum" the elements of a sequence.

❸   It's an error to pass an Option, because Option is not a subtype of Seq.

The sumSeq method can "sum" any sequence for which an implicit Add instance is defined.

However, sumSeq still only supports Seq subtypes. What if a container isn't a Seq subtype, but implements reduce? We would like a sum that's more generic.

Scala supports *higher-kinded types*, which let us abstract over parameterized types. Here's one possible way to use them:

```
// src/main/scala/progscala2/typesystem/higherkinded/Reduce.scala
package progscala2.typesystem.higherkinded
import scala.language.higherKinds                                   // ❶

trait Reduce[T, -M[T]] {                                            // ❷
  def reduce(m: M[T])(f: (T, T) => T): T
}

object Reduce {                                                     // ❸
  implicit def seqReduce[T] = new Reduce[T, Seq] {
    def reduce(seq: Seq[T])(f: (T, T) => T): T = seq reduce f
  }

  implicit def optionReduce[T] = new Reduce[T, Option] {
    def reduce(opt: Option[T])(f: (T, T) => T): T = opt reduce f
  }
}
```

❶   Higher-kinded types are considered an optional feature. A warning is issued unless you import the feature.

❷   A trait that defines "reduction" as an abstraction for higher-kinded types, M[T]. Using M as the name is an informal convention in many libraries.

❸   Define implicit instances for reducing Seq and Option values. For simplicity, we'll just use the reduce methods these types already provide.

Reduce is declared with M[T] *contravariant* (the - in front). Why? If we make it invariant (no + or -), implicit instances where M[T] is Seq won't get used for subtypes of Seq, such as Vector. (Try removing the -, then running the example that follows.) Note that the reduce method passes a container of type M[T] as an argument. As we saw in "Functions Under the Hood" on page 286 and again in "Lower Type Bounds" on page 366, arguments to methods are in *contravariant position*. So, we need Reduce to be *contravariant* in M[T].

Comparing to Add before, the implicits seqReduce and optionReduce are methods, rather than values, because we still have the type parameter T that needs to be inferred for specific instances. We can't use implicit vals like we could for Add.

Note that Seq is not given a type parameter in this expression, seqReduce[T] = new Reduce[T, Seq] {...} (and similarly for Option in optionReduce). The type parameter is inferred from the definition of Reduce. If you add it, e.g., … new Reduce[T, Seq[T]], you get a confusing error message, "Seq[T] takes no type parameters, expected: one."

Let's use sum2 to reduce Option and Seq instances:

```
// src/main/scala/progscala2/typesystem/higherkinded/add.sc
import scala.language.higherKinds
import progscala2.typesystem.higherkinded.{Add, Reduce}    // ❶
import progscala2.typesystem.higherkinded.Add._
import progscala2.typesystem.higherkinded.Reduce._

def sum[T : Add, M[T]](container: M[T])(                    // ❷
  implicit red: Reduce[T,M]): T =
    red.reduce(container)(implicitly[Add[T]].add(_,_))

sum(Vector(1 -> 10, 2 -> 20, 3 -> 30))                     // Result: (6,60)
sum(1 to 10)                                                // Result: 55
sum(Option(2))                                              // Result: 2
sum[Int,Option](None)                                       // ❸ ERROR!
```

❶   Import the Add and Reduce traits, followed by the implicits defined in their companion objects.

❷   Define a sum method that works with higher-kinded types (details to follow).

❸   It's an error to sum (reduce) an empty container. The type signature is added to the sum call to tell the compiler to interpret None as Option[Int]. Otherwise, we get a compilation error that it can't disambiguate between addInt and addIntIntPair for the T in Option[T]. With the explicit types, we get the real, runtime error we expect—that you can't call reduce on None (which is true for all empty containers).

The sum implementation is not trivial. We have the same context bound T : Add we had before. We would like to define a context bound for M[T], such as M[T] : Reduce, but we can't because Reduce takes two type parameters and context bounds only work for the case of one and only one parameter. Hence, we add a second argument list with an implicit Reduce parameter, which we use to call reduce on the input collection.

We can simplify the implementation a bit more. We can redefine Reduce with one type parameter, the higher-kinded type, allowing us to use it in a context bound like we wanted to do before:

```scala
// src/main/scala/progscala2/typesystem/higherkinded/Reduce1.scala
package progscala2.typesystem.higherkinded
import scala.language.higherKinds

trait Reduce1[-M[_]] {                                    // ❶
  def reduce[T](m: M[T])(f: (T, T) => T): T
}

object Reduce1 {                                          // ❷
  implicit val seqReduce = new Reduce1[Seq] {
    def reduce[T](seq: Seq[T])(f: (T, T) => T): T = seq reduce f
  }

  implicit val optionReduce = new Reduce1[Option] {
    def reduce[T](opt: Option[T])(f: (T, T) => T): T = opt reduce f
  }
}
```

❶ The Reduce1 abstraction with one type parameter, M, which is still contravariant, but the type parameter is not specified. Hence, it's an *existential type* (see "Existential Types" on page 386). Instead, the T parameter is moved to the re duce method.

❷ The seqReduce and optionReduce implicits are now values, rather than methods.

Whereas before we needed implicit methods so the type parameter T could be inferred, now we have just single instances that defer inference of T until reduce is called.

The updated sum method is simpler, too, and it produces the same results (not shown):

```scala
// src/main/scala/progscala2/typesystem/higherkinded/add1.sc
...

def sum[T : Add, M[_] : Reduce1](container: M[T]): T =
    implicitly[Reduce1[M]].reduce(container)(implicitly[Add[T]].add(_,_))
```

We now have two context bounds, one for Reduce1 and one for Add. The type parameters given on implicitly disambiguate between the two implicit values.

In fact, most uses of higher-kinded types you'll see will look more like this example, with M[_] instead of M[T].

Due to the extra abstraction and code sophistication that higher-kinded types introduce, should you use them? Libraries like Scalaz (*http://bit.ly/1wOqLXV*) and Shapeless (*http://bit.ly/1rGQfkG*) use them extensively to compose code in very concise and powerful ways. However, always consider the capabilities of your team members. Be wary of making code that's *so* abstract it's hard to learn, test, debug, evolve, etc.

Type Lambdas

A *type lambda* is analogous to a function nested within another function, only at the type level. They are used for situations where we need to use a parameterized type that has too many type parameters for the context. This is a coding idiom, rather than a specific feature of the type system.

Let's see an example using map, with a slightly different approach than we used for reduce in the previous section:

```
// src/main/scala/progscala2/typesystem/typelambdas/Functor.scala
package progscala2.typesystem.typelambdas
import scala.language.higherKinds

trait Functor[A,+M[_]] {                                          // ❶
  def map2[B](f: A => B): M[B]
}
object Functor {                                                  // ❷
  implicit class SeqFunctor[A](seq: Seq[A]) extends Functor[A,Seq] {
    def map2[B](f: A => B): Seq[B] = seq map f
  }
  implicit class OptionFunctor[A](opt: Option[A]) extends Functor[A,Option] {
    def map2[B](f: A => B): Option[B] = opt map f
  }

  implicit class MapFunctor[K,V1](mapKV1: Map[K,V1])              // ❸
      extends Functor[V1,({type λ[α] = Map[K,α]})#λ] {           // ❹
    def map2[V2](f: V1 => V2): Map[K,V2] = mapKV1 map {
      case (k,v) => (k,f(v))
    }
  }
}
```

❶   The name "Functor" is widely used for types with map operations. We'll discuss why in "The Functor Category" on page 412 in Chapter 16. Unlike our previous Reduce types, this one does not pass the collection as an argument to the method. Rather, we'll define implicit conversions to Functor classes that provide the map2 method. The "2" prevents confusion with the normal map method. This means we don't need M[T] to be contravariant and in fact it's useful to make it covariant now.

❷ Define implicit conversions for `Seq` and `Option` in the usual way. For simplicitly, just use their `map` methods in the implementations of `map2`. Because `Functor` is covariant in `M[T]`, the implicit conversion for `Seq` will get used for all subtypes, too.

❸ The core of the example: define a conversion for `Map`, where we have two type parameters, instead of one.

❹ Use a *type lambda* to handle the extra type parameter.

In `MapFunctor`, we "decide" that mapping over a `Map` means keeping the keys the same, but modifying the values. The actual `Map.map` (*http://bit.ly/1wkYedE*) method is more general, allowing you to modify both. (In fact, we're effectively implementing `Map.map Values` (*http://bit.ly/1wkYedE*)). The syntax of the *type lambda* idiom is somewhat verbose, making it hard to understand at first. Let's expand it to understand what it's doing:

```
... Functor[V1,             // ❶
     (                       // ❷
       {                     // ❸
         type λ[α] = Map[K,α]  // ❹
       }                     // ❺
     )#λ                     // ❻
   ]
```

❶ `V1` starts the list of type parameters, where `Functor` expects the second one to be a container that takes *one* type parameter.

❷ Open parenthesis for expression that's finished on line 6. It starts the definition of the second type parameter.

❸ Start defining a *structural type* (see "Structural Types" on page 381).

❹ Define a type member that aliases `Map`. The name λ is arbitrary (as always for type members), but it's widely used, giving this pattern its name.[1] The type has its own type parameter α (also an arbitrary name), used for the `Map` key type in this case.

❺ End the structural type definition.

❻ Close the expression started on line 2 with a type projection of the type λ out of the structural type (recall "Type Projections" on page 393). The λ is an alias for `Map` with an embedded type parameter that will be inferred in subsequent code.

Hence, the type lambda handles the extra type parameter required for `Map`, which `Functor` doesn't support. The α will be inferred in subsequent code. We won't need to reference λ or α explicitly again.

---

1. Of course, ASCII characters, like L, are easier to enter on most keyboards.

The following script verifies that the code works:

```
// src/main/scala/progscala2/typesystem/typelambdas/Functor.sc
import scala.language.higherKinds
import progscala2.typesystem.typelambdas.Functor._

List(1,2,3) map2 (_ * 2)                  // List(2, 4, 6)
Option(2) map2 (_ * 2)                    // Some(4)
val m = Map("one" -> 1, "two" -> 2, "three" -> 3)
m map2 (_ * 2)                            // Map(one -> 2, two -> 4, three -> 6)
```

You don't need the type lambda idiom often, but it's a useful technique for the problem described. A future release of Scala may provide a simpler syntax for this idiom.

Self-Recursive Types: F-Bounded Polymorphism

Self-recursive types, technically called *F-bounded polymorphic types*, are types that refer to themselves. A classic example is Java's Enum (*http://bit.ly/1wN98XJ*) abstract class, the basis for all Java enumerations. It has the following declaration:

```
public abstract class Enum<E extends Enum<E>>
extends Object
implements Comparable<E>, Serializable
```

Most Java developers are mystified by the Enum<E extends Enum<E>> syntax, but it has a few important benefits. You can see one in the signature for the compareTo method that Comparable<E> declares:

```
int compareTo(E obj)
```

It is a compilation error to pass an object to compareTo that isn't one of the enumeration values defined for the same type. Consider this example with two subtypes of Enum in the JDK, java.util.concurrent.TimeUnit (*http://bit.ly/108cKsx*) and java.net.Proxy.Type (*http://bit.ly/1yMiS5H*) (some details omitted):

```
scala> import java.util.concurrent.TimeUnit
scala> import java.net.Proxy.Type

scala> TimeUnit.MILLISECONDS compareTo TimeUnit.SECONDS
res0: Int = -1

scala> Type.HTTP compareTo Type.SOCKS
res1: Int = -1

scala> TimeUnit.MILLISECONDS compareTo Type.HTTP
<console>:11: error: type mismatch;
 found    : java.net.Proxy.Type(HTTP)
 required: java.util.concurrent.TimeUnit
            TimeUnit.MILLISECONDS compareTo Type.HTTP
                                            ^
```

In Scala, recursive types are also handy for defining methods whose return types are the same as the type of the caller, even in a type hierarchy. Consider this example where the make method should return an instance of the caller's type, not the Parent type that declares make:

```scala
// src/main/scala/progscala2/typesystem/recursivetypes/f-bound.sc

trait Parent[T <: Parent[T]] {                              // ❶
  def make: T
}

case class Child1(s: String) extends Parent[Child1] {       // ❷
  def make: Child1 = Child1(s"Child1: make: $s")
}

case class Child2(s: String) extends Parent[Child2] {
  def make: Child2 = Child2(s"Child2: make: $s")
}

val c1  = Child1("c1")        // c1: Child1 = Child1(c1)
val c2  = Child2("c2")        // c2: Child2 = Child2(c2)
val c11 = c1.make             // c11: Child1 = Child1(Child1: make: c1)
val c22 = c2.make             // c22: Child2 = Child2(Child2: make: c2)

val p1: Parent[Child1] = c1   // p1: Parent[Child1] = Child1(c1)
val p2: Parent[Child2] = c2   // p2: Parent[Child2] = Child2(c2)
val p11 = p1.make             // p11: Child1 = Child1(Child1: make: c1)
val p22 = p2.make             // p22: Child2 = Child2(Child2: make: c2)
```

❶ Parent has a recursive type. This syntax is the Scala equivalent of Java's syntax that we saw for Enum.

❷ Derived types must follow the signature idiom X extends Parent[X].

Note the type signatures shown in the comments of the values created at the end of the script. For example, p22 is of type Child2, even though we called make on a reference to a Parent.

Recap and What's Next

Perhaps the best example of a project that pushes the limits of the type system is Shapeless (*http://bit.ly/1rGQfkG*). Many advanced type concepts are also used extensively in Scalaz (*http://bit.ly/1wOqLXV*). They are worth studying as you master the type system and they provide many innovative tools for solving design problems.

It's important to remember that you don't have to master all the intricacies of Scala's rich type system to use Scala effectively. However, the better you understand the details of the type system, the easier it will be to exploit third-party libraries that use them. You'll also be able to build powerful, sophisticated libraries of your own.

Next we'll explore more advanced topics in functional programming.

## CHAPTER 16

Advanced Functional Programming

Let's return to functional programming and discuss some advanced concepts. You can skip this chapter if you're a beginner, but come back to it if you hear people using terms like *Algebraic Data Types*, *Category Theory*, and *Monads*.

The goal here is to give you a sense of what these concepts are and why they are useful without getting bogged down into too much theory and notation.

Algebraic Data Types

There are two common uses of the "ADT" acronym, *abstract data types* and *algebraic data types*, which is confusing. The former meaning is common in the object-oriented programming world. It includes our familiar friends like Seq, an abstraction for any of the sequential collections. In contrast, *algebraic data types* comes from the functional programming world. It may be less familiar, but it's equally important.

The term *algebraic data type* arises because the kinds of data types we'll discuss obey *algebraic*, i.e., mathematical properties. This is important because if we can prove properties about our types, it raises our confidence that they are bug-free and it promotes safe composition to create more complex data structures and algorithms.

Sum Types Versus Product Types

Scala types divide into *sum types* and *product types*.

Most of the classes you know are product types. When you define a case class, for example, how many unique instances can you have? Consider this simple example:

```
case class Person(name: Name, age: Age)
```

You can have as many instances of Person as the allowed Name instances *times* the allowed values for age. Let's say that Name encapsulates nonempty strings and disallows nonalphabetic characters (for some alphabet). There will effectively still be infinitely many values, but we'll say it's N. Similarly, Age limits integer values, let's say between 0 and 130. Why not use String and Int, respectively? We've been arguing all along that your types should express the allowed states and prevent invalid states, wherever possible.

Because we can combine any Name value with any Age value to create a Person, the number of possible Person instances is $131 * N$. For this reason, such types are called *product types*. Most of the types we're accustomed to using fall into this category.

It's also the source of the name for Scala's Product (*http://bit.ly/1G2wY7N*) type, a parent of all TupleN types and case classes, which we learned about in "Products, Case Classes, and Tuples" on page 299.

We learned in "Inferring Type Information" on page 46 that the single instance of Unit has the mysterious name (). This odd-looking name actually makes sense if we think of it as a zero-element tuple. Whereas a one-element tuple of Int values, (Int) or Tuple1[Int], can have 2^{32} values, one for each of the possible Int values, a no-element tuple can only have one instance, because it can't carry any state.

Consider what happens if we start with a two-element tuple, (Int, String), and construct a new type by appending Unit:

```
type unitTimesTuple2 = (Int, String, Unit)
```

How many instances does this type have? It's exactly the same as the number of types that (Int, String) has. In product terms, it's as if we *multiplied* the number of types by 1. Hence, this is the origin of the name Unit, just as one is the "unit" of multiplication and zero is the unit of addition.

Is there a zero for product types? We need a type with zero instances: scala.Nothing. Combining Nothing with any other type to construct a new type must have zero instances because we don't have an instance to "inhabit" the Nothing field.

An example of sum types is enumerations. Recall this example from Chapter 3:

```scala
// src/main/scala/progscala2/rounding/enumeration.sc

object Breed extends Enumeration {
  type Breed = Value
  val doberman = Value("Doberman Pinscher")
  val yorkie   = Value("Yorkshire Terrier")
  val scottie  = Value("Scottish Terrier")
  val dane     = Value("Great Dane")
  val portie   = Value("Portuguese Water Dog")
}
```

There are exactly five instances. Note that the values are mutually exclusive. We can't have combinations of them (ignoring the realities of actual dog procreation). The breed is one and only one of these values.

Another way to implement a sum type is to use a sealed hierarchy of objects:

```
sealed trait Breed { val name: String }
case object doberman extends Breed { val name = "Doberman Pinscher" }
case object yorkie   extends Breed { val name = "Yorkshire Terrier" }
case object scottie  extends Breed { val name = "Scottish Terrier" }
case object dane     extends Breed { val name = "Great Dane" }
case object portie   extends Breed { val name = "Portuguese Water Dog" }
```

 Use enumerations when you just need "flags" with an index and optional user-friendly strings. Use a sealed hierarchy of objects when they need to carry more state information.

Properties of Algebraic Data Types

In mathematics an *algebra* is defined by three aspects:

1. A set of *objects*: not to be confused with our the OO notion of objects. They could be numbers or almost anything.

2. A set of *operations*: how elements are combined to create new elements.

3. A set of *laws*: these are rules that define the relationships between operations and objects. For example, for numbers, $(x + (y + z)) == ((x + y) + z)$ (associativity law).

Let's consider product types first. The informal arguments we made about the numbers of instances are more formally described by operations and laws. Consider again the *operation* of "adding" Unit to (Int, String). We have a commutativity law:

```
Unit x (Int,String) == (Int,String) x Unit
```

This is true from the standpoint of the number of instances. It's analogous to $1 * N = N * 1$ for any number N. This generalizes to combinations with nonunit types:

```
Breeds x (Int,String) == (Int,String) x Breeds
```

Just like $M * N = N * M$ for any numbers M and N. Similarly, multiplication with "zero" (Nothing) commutes:

```
Nothing x (Int,String) == (Int,String) x Nothing
```

Turning to sum types, it's useful to recall that sets have unique members. Hence we could think of our allowed dog breeds as forming a set. That implies that adding Nothing to the set returns the same set. Adding Unit to the set would create a new set with all the original elements plus one, Unit. Similarly, if we added a nonunit type to the set, the new set would have all the instances of the additional type plus the original dog breeds. The same algebraic laws apply that we expect for addition:

```
Nothing + (doberman, yorkie, ...) == (doberman, yorkie, ...) + Nothing
Unit    + (doberman, yorkie, ...) == (doberman, yorkie, ...) + Unit
Person  + (doberman, yorkie, ...) == (doberman, yorkie, ...) + Person
```

There is even a *distributive law* of the form $x^*(a + b) = x^*a + x^*b$. I'll let you convince yourself that it actually works.

Final Thought on Algebraic Data Types

There are more properties we could explore, but I'll refer you to an excellent series of blog posts by Chris Taylor (*http://bit.ly/13oZm5l*) for more details.

What does all this have to do with programming? This kind of precise reasoning encourages us to examine our types. Do they have precise meanings? Do they constrain the allowed values to just those that make sense? Do they compose to create new types with precise behaviors?

My favorite example of "unexpected" precision is the List (*http://bit.ly/1toub3N*) type in Scala. It is an abstract class with exactly two concrete subtypes, Nil (*http://bit.ly/1wN8LMz*) and :: (*http://bit.ly/1zmq9fK*), the nonempty list. It might sound trivial to say a list is either empty or it isn't, but with these two types we can construct all lists and reason precisely about how all lists must behave.

Category Theory

Perhaps the most controversial debate in the Scala community is how much to embrace *Category Theory*, a branch of mathematics, as a source of what I'll argue are *Functional Design Patterns*. This section introduces you to the basic ideas of Category Theory and to a few of the actual *categories* most commonly used in functional programming. They are powerful tools, at least for those development teams willing to master them.

The use of Category Theory is controversial because of its intimidating mathematical foundation. Accessible documentation has been hard to find. Category Theory generalizes all of mathematics in ways that enable reasoning about global properties. Hence, it offers deep and far-reaching abstractions, but when applied to code, many developers struggle with extreme abstraction. It's easier for most of us to understand code with concrete, specific details, but we already know that abstractions are useful, as well. Striking a balance is key and where you feel comfortable striking that balance will determine whether or not Category Theory works for you.

However, Category Theory now occupies a central place in advanced functional programming. Its use was pioneered in Haskell to solve various design problems and to push the envelope of functional thinking. Implementations of the common categories are now available in most functional languages.

If you are an advanced Scala developer, you should learn the rudiments of Category Theory as applied to programming, then decide whether or not it is right for your team and project. Unfortunately, I've seen situations where libraries written by talented proponents of Category Theory have failed in their organizations, because the rest of the team found the libraries too difficult to understand and maintain. If you embrace Category Theory, make sure you consider the full life cycle of your code and the social aspects of development.

Scalaz (pronounced "Scala Zed") (*http://bit.ly/1wOqLXV*) is the primary library for Scala that implements categories. It is a good vehicle for learning and experimentation. We already used its `Validation` type in "Scalaz Validation" on page 240. I'll use simplified category implementations in this chapter to minimize what's new to learn.

In a sense, this section continues where "Higher-Kinded Types" on page 398 left off. There, we discussed abstracting over parameterized types. For example, if we have a method with `Seq[A]`, can we generalize it to `M[A]` instead, where `M` is a type parameter for any type that is itself parameterized by a single type parameter? Now we'll abstract over the functional *combinators*, `map`, `flatMap`, and so forth.

About Categories

Let's start with the general definition of a *category*, which contains three "entities" (recall our discussion of algebra):

1. A *class* consisting of a set of *objects*. These aren't the same terms from OOP, but they have similar implications.
2. A *class* of *morphisms*, also called *arrows*. A generalized notion of functions and written *f: A -> B* (`f: A => B` in Scala). For each morphism, *f*, one object is the *domain* of *f* and one is the *codomain*. It might seem strange to use the singular "object," but in some categories each *object* is itself a collection of values or another category.
3. A *binary operation* called *morphism composition* with the property that for *f: A -> B* and *g: B -> C*, the composition *g ∘ f: A -> C* exists.

Two axioms are satisfied by morphism composition:

1. Each object *x* has one and only one identity morphism, i.e., where the domain and codomain are the same, ID_x and composition with identity has the following property: $f \circ ID_x = ID_x \circ f$.
2. *Associativity*. For *f: A -> B, g: B -> C, h: C -> D, (f ∘ g) ∘ h = f ∘ (g ∘ h)*.

The categories we'll discuss next have these properties and laws. We'll look at just two categories that are used in software development (of the many categories known to mathematics), *Functor* and *Monad*. We'll also mention two more, *Applicative* and *Arrow*.

The Functor Category

Functor abstracts the map operation. We introduced it in "Type Lambdas" on page 402 to set up an example where a *type lambda* was necessary. We're going to implement it in a slightly different way here, first defining the abstraction and then implementing it for three concrete types, Seq, Option, and A => B:

```scala
// src/main/scala/progscala2/fp/categories/Functor.scala
package progscala2.fp.categories
import scala.language.higherKinds

trait Functor[F[_]] {                                          // ❶
  def map[A, B](fa: F[A])(f: A => B): F[B]                      // ❷
}

object SeqF extends Functor[Seq] {                             // ❸
  def map[A, B](seq: Seq[A])(f: A => B): Seq[B] = seq map f
}

object OptionF extends Functor[Option] {
  def map[A, B](opt: Option[A])(f: A => B): Option[B] = opt map f
}

object FunctionF {                                            // ❹
  def map[A,A2,B](func: A => A2)(f: A2 => B): A => B = {      // ❺
    val functor = new Functor[({type λ[β] = A => β})#λ] {     // ❻
      def map[A3,B](func: A => A3)(f: A3 => B): A => B = (a: A) => f(func(a))
    }
    functor.map(func)(f)                                      // ❼
  }
}
```

❶ In contrast to the previous version in "Type Lambdas" on page 402, this map method takes an instance of an F (which will be some kind of container) as an argument. Also, we don't use the name map2 here, like we did before.

❷ The map arguments are the functor F[A], a function A => B. An F[B] is returned.

❸ Define implementation objects for Seq and Option.

❹ Define an implementation object for mapping one function to another; not easy!

❺ FunctionF defines its own map method, constructed so invoking map has the same syntax for functions as it does for Seq, Option, and any other transformations we might implement. This map takes the initial function we're transforming and the function that does the transformation. Note the types: we're converting a A => A2 to A => B, which means the second function argument f is A2 => B. In other words, we're *chaining* functions.

❻ The implementation of map constructs a Functor with the correct types to do the transformation.

❼ Finally, FunctionF.map invokes the Functor. The return value of Func tionF.map is A => B.

FunctionF is nontrivial. To understand it, keep in mind that we aren't changing the initial type A, just chaining a second function call that takes the A2 output of func and calls f with it.

Let's try these types:

```
// src/main/scala/progscala2/fp/categories/Functor.sc
import progscala2.fp.categories._
import scala.language.higherKinds

val fii: Int => Int      = i => i * 2
val fid: Int => Double   = i => 2.1 * i
val fds: Double => String = d => d.toString

SeqF.map(List(1,2,3,4))(fii)              // Seq[Int]: List(2, 4, 6, 8)
SeqF.map(List.empty[Int])(fii)            // Seq[Int]: List()

OptionF.map(Some(2))(fii)                 // Option[Int]: Some(4)
OptionF.map(Option.empty[Int])(fii)       // Option[Int]: None

val fa = FunctionF.map(fid)(fds)                              // ❶
fa(2)                                     // String: 4.2

// val fb = FunctionF.map(fid)(fds)                           ❷
val fb = FunctionF.map[Int,Double,String](fid)(fds)
fb(2)

val fc = fds compose fid                                      // ❸
fc(2)                                     // String: 4.2
```

❶ Chain Int => Double and Double => String functions together, creating a new function, then call it on the next line.

❷ Unfortunately, the argument types can't be inferred, so explicit types are required in the function literals or on FunctionF.map.

❸ Note that FunctionF.map(f1)(f2) == f2 compose f1, not f1 compose f2!

So, why is the parameterized type with a map operation called a "Functor"? Let's look at the map declaration again. We'll redefine it with Seq for simplicity, then again with the argument lists switched:

```scala
scala> def map[A, B](seq: Seq[A])(f: A => B): Seq[B] = seq map f

scala> def map[A, B](f: A => B)(seq: Seq[A]): Seq[B] = seq map f
```

Now note the type of the new function returned when we use partial application on the second version:

```scala
scala> val fm = map((i: Int) => i * 2.1) _
fm: Seq[Int] => Seq[Double] = <function1>
```

So, this map method *lifts* a function A => B to Seq[A] => Seq[B]! In general, Func tor.map morphs A => B, for all types A and B, to F[A] => F[B] for many F (F has to be a category itself). Put another way, *Functor* allows us to apply a pure function (f: A => B) to a "context" holding one or more A values. We don't have to extract those values ourselves to apply f, then put the results into a new instance of the "context." The term *Functor* is meant to capture this abstraction of enabling the use of pure functions in this way.

In Category Theory terms, other categories are the objects and the morphisms are the mapping between categories. For example, List[Int] and List[String] would be two categories whose own objects are all possible lists of Ints and Strings, respectively.

Functor has two additional properties that fall out of the general properties and axioms for Category Theory:

1. A Functor F preserves identity. That is, the identity of the *domain* maps to the identity of the *codomain*.

2. A Functor F preserves composition. *F(f ∘ g) = F(f) ∘ F(g)*.

For an example of the first property, an empty list is the "unit" of lists; think of what happens when you concatenate it with another list. Mapping over an empty list always returns a new empty list, possibly with a different list element type.

Are the common and Functor-specific axioms satisfied? The following *ScalaCheck* property test verifies them:

```scala
// src/test/scala/progscala2/fp/categories/FunctorProperties.scala
package progscala2.fp.categories
import org.scalatest.FunSpec
import org.scalatest.prop.PropertyChecks

class FunctorProperties extends FunSpec with PropertyChecks {

  def id[A] = identity[A] _      // Lift identity method to a function
```

```scala
def testSeqMorphism(f2: Int => Int) = {                          // ❶
  val f1: Int => Int = _ * 2
  import SeqF._
  forAll { (l: List[Int]) =>
    assert( map(map(l)(f1))(f2) === map(l)(f2 compose f1) )
  }
}

def testFunctionMorphism(f2: Int => Int) = {                     // ❷
  val f1: Int => Int = _ * 2
  import FunctionF._
  forAll { (i: Int) =>
    assert( map(f1)(f2)(i) === (f2 compose f1)(i) )             // ❸
  }
}

describe ("Functor morphism composition") {                      // ❹
  it ("works for Sequence Functors") {
    testSeqMorphism(_ + 3)
  }
  it ("works for Function Functors") {
    testFunctionMorphism(_ + 3)
  }
}

describe ("Functor identity composed with a another function commutes") {
  it ("works for Sequence Functors") {                           // ❺
    testSeqMorphism(id[Int])
  }
  it ("works for Function Functors") {
    testFunctionMorphism(id)
  }
}

describe ("Functor identity maps between the identities of the categories") {
  it ("works for Sequence Functors") {                           // ❻
    val f1: Int => String = _.toString
    import SeqF._
    assert( map(List.empty[Int])(f1) === List.empty[String] )
  }
  it ("works for Function Functors") {
    val f1: Int => Int = _ * 2
    def id[A] = identity[A] _    // Lift method to a function
    import FunctionF._
    forAll { (i: Int) =>
      assert( map(id[Int])(f1)(i) === (f1 compose id[Int])(i) )
    }
  }
}

describe ("Functor morphism composition is associative") {
  it ("works for Sequence Functors") {                           // ❼
```

```
        val f1: Int => Int = _ * 2
        val f2: Int => Int = _ + 3
        val f3: Int => Int = _ * 5
        import SeqF._
        forAll { (l: List[Int]) =>
          val m12 = map(map(l)(f1))(f2)
          val m23 = (seq: Seq[Int]) => map(map(seq)(f2))(f3)
          assert( map(m12)(f3) === m23(map(l)(f1)) )
        }
      }
      it ("works for Function Functors") {
        val f1: Int => Int = _ * 2
        val f2: Int => Int = _ + 3
        val f3: Int => Int = _ * 5
        val f:  Int => Int = _ + 21
        import FunctionF._
        val m12 = map(map(f)(f1))(f2)
        val m23 = (g: Int => Int) => map(map(g)(f2))(f3)
        forAll { (i: Int) =>
          assert( map(m12)(f3)(i) === m23(map(f)(f1))(i) )
        }
      }
    }
  }
}
```

❶   A helper function that verifies morphism composition for SeqF. Essentially, does mapping the Functor object once with one function then mapping the output with the second function produce the same result as composing the functions and then mapping once?

❷   A similar helper function that verifies morphism composition for FunctionF.

❸   Note that we "morph" the functions, then verify they produce equivalent results by applying to a set of generated Int values.

❹   Verify morphism composition for both SeqF and FunctionF.

❺   Verify the identity property for both SeqF and FunctionF.

❻   Verify the Functor-specific axiom that identities are mapped to identities.

❼   Verify the Functor-specific axiom of associativity of morphisms.

Back to programming, is it of practical use to have a separate abstraction for map, given the sophistication of this code? In general, abstractions with mathematically provable properties enable us to reason about program structure and behavior. For example, once we had a generalized abstraction for mapping, we could apply it to many different data structures, even functions. This reasoning power of Category Theory is being applied in several areas of Computer Science research.

The Monad Category

If `Functor` is an abstraction for `map`, is there a corresponding abstraction for `flatMap`? Yes, *Monad*, which is named after the term *monas* used by the Pythagorean philosophers of ancient Greece that roughly translates "the Divinity from which all other things are generated."

Here is our definition of Monad:

```scala
// src/main/scala/progscala2/fp/categories/Monad.scala
package progscala2.fp.categories
import scala.language.higherKinds

trait Monad[M[_]] {                                               // ❶
  def flatMap[A, B](fa: M[A])(f: A => M[B]): M[B]                 // ❷
  def unit[A](a: => A): M[A]                                       // ❸

  // Some common aliases:                                          ❹
  def bind[A,B](fa: M[A])(f: A => M[B]): M[B] = flatMap(fa)(f)
  def >>=[A,B](fa: M[A])(f: A => M[B]): M[B] = flatMap(fa)(f)
  def pure[A](a: => A): M[A] = unit(a)
  def `return`[A](a: => A): M[A] = unit(a)     // backticks to avoid keyword
}

object SeqM extends Monad[Seq] {
  def flatMap[A, B](seq: Seq[A])(f: A => Seq[B]): Seq[B] = seq flatMap f
  def unit[A](a: => A): Seq[A] = Seq(a)
}

object OptionM extends Monad[Option] {
  def flatMap[A, B](opt: Option[A])(f: A => Option[B]):Option[B]= opt flatMap f
  def unit[A](a: => A): Option[A] = Option(a)
}
```

❶ Use `M[_]` for the type representing a data structure with "monadic" properties. As for `Functor`, it takes a single type parameter.

❷ Note that the function `f` passed to `flatMap` has the type `A => M[B]`, not `A => B`.

❸ Monad has a second function that takes a (by-name) value and returns it inside a Monad instance. In Scala, this is typically implemented with constructors and case class `apply` methods.

❹ Mathematics and other programming languages use different terms. The `>>=` and `return` names are the standard in Haskell. However, in Scala both names are problematic. The `=` at the end of `>>=` causes funny behavior due to the operator precedence of `=`. The name `return` collides with the keyword, unless escaped as shown.

Sometimes an abstraction with just `flatMap`, a.k.a. `bind`, is called *Bind*.

More commonly, an abstraction with just unit or pure is called *Applicative*. Note how unit resembles a case class apply method, where a value is passed in and an enclosing instance of a "wrapper" type is returned! Applicative is very interesting as an abstraction over construction. Recall from "Constraining Allowed Instances" on page 135 and "CanBuildFrom" on page 343 how CanBuildFrom is used in the collections library to construct new collection instances. Applicative is an alternative, if less flexible.

Let's try our Monad implementation:

```
// src/main/scala/progscala2/fp/categories/Monad.sc
import progscala2.fp.categories._
import scala.language.higherKinds

val seqf: Int => Seq[Int] = i => 1 to i
val optf: Int => Option[Int] = i => Option(i + 1)

SeqM.flatMap(List(1,2,3))(seqf)          // Seq[Int]: List(1,1,2,1,2,3)
SeqM.flatMap(List.empty[Int])(seqf)      // Seq[Int]: List()

OptionM.flatMap(Some(2))(optf)           // Option[Int]: Some(3)
OptionM.flatMap(Option.empty[Int])(optf) // Option[Int]: None
```

One way to describe flatMap is that it extracts an element of type A from the container on the left and *binds* it to a new kind of element in a new container instance, hence the alternative name. Like map, it removes the burden of knowing how to extract an element from M[A]. However, it looks like the function argument now has the burden of knowing how to construct a new M[B]. Actually, this is not an issue, because unit can be called to do this. In an OO language like Scala, the actual Monad type returned could be a subtype of M.

The *Monad Laws* are as follows.

unit behaves like an identity (so it's appropriately named):

```
flatMap(unit(x))(f) == f(x)        Where x is a value
flatMap(m)(unit) == m              Where m is a Monad instance
```

Like morphism composition for Functor, flat mapping with two functions in succession behaves the same as flat mapping over one function that is constructed from the two functions:

```
flatMap(flatMap(m)(f))(g) == flatMap(m)(x => flatMap(f(x))(g))
```

The code examples contain a property test to verify these properties (see *src/test/scala/progscala2/toolslibs/fp/MonadProperties.scala*).

The Importance of Monad

Ironically, Functor is more important to Category Theory than Monad, while its application to software is somewhat trivial compared to Monad's impact.

In essence, Monad is important because it gives us a principled way to wrap context information around a value, then propagate and evolve that context as the value evolves. Hence, it minimizes coupling between the values and contexts while the presence of the Monad wrapper informs the reader of the context's existence.

This "pattern" is used frequently in Scala, inspired by the pioneer usage in Haskell. We saw several examples in "Options and Other Container Types" on page 230, including Option (*http://bit.ly/16yQhkp*), Either (*http://bit.ly/1sQZRtp*), Try (*http://bit.ly/1DDcSNz*), and scalaz.Validation (*http://bit.ly/1OFhgj8*).

All are *monadic*, because they support flatMap and construction (case class apply methods instead of unit). All can be used in for comprehensions. All allow us to sequence operations and handle failures in different ways, usually through returning a subclass of the parent type.

Recall the simplified signature for flatMap in Try (*http://bit.ly/1DDcSNz*):

```
sealed abstract class Try[+A] {
  def flatMap[B](f: A => Try[B]): Try[B]
}
```

It's similar in the other types. Now consider processing a sequence of steps, where the previous outcome is fed into the next step, but we stop processing at the first failure:

```
// src/main/scala/progscala2/fp/categories/for-tries-steps.sc

import scala.util.{ Try, Success, Failure }

type Step = Int => Try[Int]                              // ❶

val successfulSteps: Seq[Step] = List(                   // ❷
  (i:Int) => Success(i + 5),
  (i:Int) => Success(i + 10),
  (i:Int) => Success(i + 25))
val partiallySuccessfulSteps: Seq[Step] = List(
  (i:Int) => Success(i + 5),
  (i:Int) => Failure(new RuntimeException("FAIL!")),
  (i:Int) => Success(i + 25))

def sumCounts(countSteps: Seq[Step]): Try[Int] = {       // ❸
  val zero: Try[Int] = Success(0)
  (countSteps foldLeft zero) {
    (sumTry, step) => sumTry flatMap (i => step(i))
  }
}

sumCounts(successfulSteps)
// Returns: scala.util.Try[Int] = Success(40)

sumCounts1(partiallySuccessfulSteps)
// Returns: scala.util.Try[Int] = Failure(java.lang.RuntimeException: FAIL!)
```

❶   Alias for "step" functions.

❷   Two sequences of steps, one successful, one with a failed step.

❸   A method that works through a step sequence, passing the result of a previous
     step to the next step.

The logic of sumCounts handles sequencing, while flatMap handles the Try (*http://bit.ly/1DDcSNz*) containers. Note that subtypes are actually returned, either Success (*http://bit.ly/1E8xzmA*) or Failure (*http://bit.ly/108cqtD*). We'll see that scala.concurrent.Future (*http://bit.ly/1xIkpsr*) is also monadic in "Futures" on page 425.

The use of Monad was pioneered in Haskell,[1] where functional purity is more strongly emphasized. For example, Monads are used to compartmentalize input and output (I/O) from pure code. The IO Monad handles this *separation of concerns*. Also, because it appears in the type signature of functions that use it, the reader and compiler know that the function isn't pure. Similarly, Reader and Writer Monads have been defined in many languages for the same purposes.

A generalization of Monad is *Arrow*. Whereas Monad lifts a *value* into a context, i.e., the function passed to flatMap is A => M[B], an *Arrow* lifts a function into a context, (A => B) => C[A => B]. Composition of Arrows makes it possible to reason about sequences of processing steps, i.e., A => B, then B => C, etc., in a referentially transparent way, outside the context of actual use. In contrast, a function passed to flatMap is explicitly aware of its context, as expressed in the return type!

Recap and What's Next

I hope this brief introduction to more advanced concepts was informative enough to help you understand a few ideas you'll hear people mention, and why they are powerful, if also challenging to understand.

Scala's standard library uses an object-oriented approach to add functions like map, flatMap, and unit, rather than implementing categories. However, with methods like flatMap, we get "monadic" behaviors that make for comprehensions so concise.

I've casually referred to *Monad, Functor, Applicative,* and *Arrow* as examples of *Functional Design Patterns*. While the term has a bad connotation for some functional programmers, overuse of patterns in the OOP world doesn't invalidate the core idea of reusable constructs, in whatever form they take.

---

1. Philip Wadler's home page (*http://bit.ly/1touA6s*) has many of his pioneering papers on Monad theory and applications.

Unfortunately, categories have been steeped in mystery because of the mathematical formalism and their names, which are often opaque to ordinary developers. But distilled to their essence, they are abstractions of familiar concepts, with powerful implications for program correctness, reasoning, concision, and expressiveness. Hopefully, these concepts will become more accessible to a wider range of developers.

Appendix A lists some books, papers, and blog posts that explore functional programming further. A few are worth highlighting here. Two other functional structures that you might investigate are *Lenses*, for getting or setting (with cloning) a value nested in an instance graph, and *Monad Transformers*, for composing Monads.

Functional Programming in Scala, by Paul Chiusano and Rúnar Bjarnason (Manning) is a great next step for pushing your FP knowledge further with lots of exercises in Scala. The authors are some of the main contributers to Scalaz (*https://github.com/scalaz*). Eugene Yokota wrote an excellent series of blog posts on learning Scalaz (*http://bit.ly/1u139AQ*).

Shapeless (*http://bit.ly/1rGQfkG*) also explores advanced constructs, especially in the type system. The aggregator site *http://typelevel.org* has some other instructive projects.

The next chapter returns to more practical grounds, the very important topic of writing concurrent software with Scala.

## CHAPTER 17

Tools for Concurrency

The *multicore problem* was a growing concern in the early 2000s as we hit the end of Moore's Law for single-core CPUs. We've continued to scale performance through increasing numbers of cores and servers, trading vertical scaling for horizontal scaling.

That's created a challenge for developers, because it has meant writing concurrent software. Concurrency isn't easy because it has traditionally required coordinated access to shared, mutable state, which means difficult multithreaded programming with tools like locks, mutexes, and semaphores. Failure to coordinate access correctly can result in the *spooky action at a distance* we mentioned in Chapter 2, where some mutable state you're using suddenly and unexpectedly changes, due to activity on another thread. Or it can mean race conditions and lock contention.

Functional programming started going mainstream when we learned that embracing immutability and purity largely bypasses these problems. We also saw a renaissance of older approaches to concurrency, like the actor model.

This chapter explores concurrency tools for Scala. You can certainly use any mechanism you've used with Java, including the multithreading APIs, message queues, etc. We'll just discuss Scala-specific tools, starting with an API for a very old approach: single-threaded processes that work together.

The scala.sys.process Package

In some cases, we can use small, synchronous processes that coordinate state through database transactions, message queues, or piping data from one process to another.

The `scala.sys.process` (*http://bit.ly/1xIm0hO*) package provides a DSL for running and managing operating system processes, including I/O. Here's a REPL session that demonstrates some of the features. Note that a Unix shell like `bash` is used for the commands:

```
// src/main/scala/progscala2/concurrency/process/processes.sc
scala> import scala.sys.process._
scala> import scala.language.postfixOps
scala> import java.net.URL
scala> import java.io.File

// Run the command, write to stdout.
scala> "ls -l src".!
total 0
drwxr-xr-x  4 deanwampler  staff  136 Dec 19  2013 main
drwxr-xr-x  4 deanwampler  staff  136 Dec 19  2013 test
res33: Int = 0

// Pass command tokens as a Seq, return a single string of the output.
scala> Seq("ls", "-l", "src").!!
res34: String =
"total 0
drwxr-xr-x  4 deanwampler  staff  136 Dec 19  2013 main
drwxr-xr-x  4 deanwampler  staff  136 Dec 19  2013 test
"
```

We can also connect processes. Consider these methods:

```
// Build a process to open a URL, redirect the output to "grep $filter",
// and append the output to file (not overwrite it).
def findURL(url: String, filter: String) =
  new URL(url) #> s"grep $filter" #>> new File(s"$filter.txt")

// Run ls -l on the file. If it exists, then count the lines.
def countLines(fileName: String) = s"ls -l $fileName" #&& s"wc -l $fileName"
```

The #> method in the DSL overwrites a file or pipes into stdin for a second process. The #>> method can only be used to overwrite a file. The #&& method only runs the process to its right if the process to its left succeeds, which means that it returns exit code zero. Both methods return a scala.sys.process.ProcessBuilder (*http://bit.ly/1nWnWU7*). They don't actually run the commands. For that we need to invoke their ! method:

```
scala> findURL("http://scala-lang.org", "scala") !
res0: Int = 0

scala> countLines("scala.txt") !
-rw-r--r--  1 deanwampler  staff  4111 Jul 31 22:35 scala.txt
      43 scala.txt
res1: Int = 0

scala> findURL("http://scala-lang.org", "scala") !
res2: Int = 0

scala> countLines("scala.txt") !
-rw-r--r--  1 deanwampler  staff  8222 Jul 31 22:35 scala.txt
```

```
     86 scala.txt
res3: Int = 0
```

Note that the file size doubled, because we appended new text for each run.

When it's an appropriate design solution, small, synchronous processes can be implemented in Scala or any other language, then *glued* together using the `process` package API.

Futures

For many needs, process boundaries are too course-grained. We need easy to use concurrency primitives within a single process. That is, we need a higher-level API than the traditional multithreading APIs, one that exposes reasonably intuitive building blocks.

Suppose you have units of work that you want to run asynchronously, so you don't block while they're running. They might need to do I/O, for example. The simplest mechanism is `scala.concurrent.Future` (*http://bit.ly/1xIkpsr*).

When you construct a `Future`, control returns immediately to the caller, but the value is not guaranteed to be available yet. The `Future` instance is a handle to an eventually available result. You can continue doing other work until the future completes, either successfully or unsuccessfully. There are different ways to handle this completion.[1]

We saw a simple example in "A Taste of Futures" on page 41, which we used to discuss implicit arguments, the `scala.concurrent.ExecutionContext` (*http://bit.ly/1s0FtqF*) required to manage and run futures. We used `ExecutionContext.global` (*http://bit.ly/1toqmM5*), which manages a thread pool using `java.util.concurrent.ForkJoin Pool` (*http://bit.ly/1nWo2uR*), which it uses to perform the work encapsulated in the `Futures`. As users, we don't need to care about how our asynchronous processing is executed, except for special circumstances, such as performance tuning. (While `Fork JoinPool` is part of JDK 7, because Scala currently supports JDK 6, it actually ships the original implementation by Doug Lea that was subsequently added to JDK 7.)

To explore `Futures`, first consider the case where we need to do ten things in parallel, then combine the results:

```
// src/main/scala/progscala2/concurrency/futures/future-fold.sc
import scala.concurrent.{Await, Future}
import scala.concurrent.duration.Duration
import scala.concurrent.ExecutionContext.Implicits.global
```

---

1. `Promise` (*http://bit.ly/1OFkdQJ*) is also useful for working with `Futures` in some cases. See the Scala documentation (*http://bit.ly/12STMkt*).

```
val futures = (0 to 9) map {                                    // ❶
  i => Future {
    val s = i.toString                                          // ❷
    print(s)
    s
  }
}

val f = Future.reduce(futures)((s1, s2) => s1 + s2)            // ❸

val n = Await.result(f, Duration.Inf)                          // ❹
```

❶ Create ten asynchronous futures, each performing some work.

❷ Future.apply takes two argument lists. The first has a single, by-name body to execute asynchronously. The second list has the implicit ExecutionContext. We're allowing the global implicit value to be used. Our body converts the integer to a string, prints it, then returns it. The type of futures is Indexed Seq[Future[String]]. In this contrived example, the Futures complete immediately.

❸ Reduce the sequence of Future instances into a single Future[String]. In this case, concatenate the strings.

❹ To block until the Future f completes, we use scala.concurrent.Await (*http:// bit.ly/1ud3W2c*). The Duration (*http://bit.ly/1xIm3Kw*) argument says to wait for *infinity*, if necessary. Using Await is the preferred way to block the current thread when you need to wait for a Future to complete.

Crucially, when the print statements in the Future body are called, the outputs will be out of order, e.g., 0214679538 and 0123467985 are the outputs of two of my runs. However, because fold walks through the Futures in the same order in which they were constructed, the string it produces always has the digits in strict numerical order, 0123456789.

Future.fold and similar methods (*http://bit.ly/1pbjSQR*) execute asynchronously themselves; they return a new Future. Our example only blocks when we called Await.result.

Often, we don't want to block on a result. Instead, we want a bit of code to be invoked when the Future completes. Registering a callback does the trick. For example, a simple web server might construct a Future to handle a request and use a callback to send the result back to the caller. The following example demonstrates the logic:

```
// src/main/scala/progscala2/concurrency/futures/future-callbacks.sc
import scala.concurrent.Future
import scala.concurrent.duration.Duration
import scala.concurrent.ExecutionContext.Implicits.global
```

```
case class ThatsOdd(i: Int) extends RuntimeException(          // ❶
  s"odd $i received!")

import scala.util.{Try, Success, Failure}                      // ❷

val doComplete: PartialFunction[Try[String],Unit] = {          // ❸
  case s @ Success(_) => println(s)                            // ❹
  case f @ Failure(_) => println(f)
}

val futures = (0 to 9) map {                                   // ❺
  case i if i % 2 == 0 => Future.successful(i.toString)
  case i => Future.failed(ThatsOdd(i))
}
futures map (_ onComplete doComplete)                          // ❻
```

❶ An exception we'll throw for odd integers.

❷ Import scala.util.Try (*http://bit.ly/1tI2jaD*) and its descendants, Success (*http://bit.ly/1rGy7aw*) and Failure (*http://bit.ly/1voyB7w*).

❸ Define a callback handler for both successful and failed results. Its type must be PartialFunction[Try[String],Unit], because the callback will be passed a Try[A], encapsulating success or failure. A will be String. The function's return type is Unit, because nothing can be returned from the handler, since it runs asynchronously. For a web server, it would send a response to the caller here.

❹ If the Future succeeds, the Success clause will match. Otherwise the Failure will match. We just print either result.

❺ Create the Futures where odd integers are "failures." We use two methods on the Future companion object for immediately completing the Future as a success or failure.

❻ Traverse over the futures to attach the callback, which will be called immediately since our Futures have already completed by this point.

Running the script produces output like the following, where the order varies from run to run:

```
Success(0)
Success(2)
Failure($line137.$read$$iw$$iw$ThatsOdd: odd 1 received!)      // ❶
Success(4)
Failure($line137.$read$$iw$$iw$ThatsOdd: odd 3 received!)
Success(6)
Success(8)
Failure($line137.$read$$iw$$iw$ThatsOdd: odd 5 received!)
Failure($line137.$read$$iw$$iw$ThatsOdd: odd 9 received!)
Failure($line137.$read$$iw$$iw$ThatsOdd: odd 7 received!)
```

❶   Ugly, synthesized name created when compiling ThatsOdd in the script.

We'll also see more examples of Future idioms in the next section.

Future (*http://bit.ly/1sR3rnc*) is "monadic" like Option, Try, Either, and the collections. We can use them in for comprehensions and manipulate the results with our combinator friends, map, flatMap, filter, and so forth.

Async

When working with Futures, excessive use of callbacks can get complicated quickly. So can composition of Futures to implement interdependent sequencing of tasks. A new scala.async.Async module is designed to make it easier to build such computations. It is described in SIP-22 (*http://bit.ly/1tpiwQL*), implemented for both Scala 2.10 and 2.11 on GitHub (*https://github.com/scala/async*), and distributed as an "optional module" (see Table 21-11 for the list of such modules for 2.11).

There are two fundamental methods used with an asynchronous block:

```
def async[T](body: => T): Future[T]          // ❶
def await[T](future: Future[T]): T           // ❷
```

❶   Start an asynchronous computation and return a Future for it immediately.

❷   Wait until a Future completes.

The following example simulates a sequence of asynchronous calls, first to determine if a "record" exists for an id and if so, to get the record. Otherwise, it returns an error record:

```
// src/main/scala/progscala2/concurrency/async/async.sc
import scala.concurrent.{Await, Future}
import scala.concurrent.duration.Duration
import scala.async.Async.{async, await}
import scala.concurrent.ExecutionContext.Implicits.global

object AsyncExample {
  def recordExists(id: Long): Boolean = {          // ❶
    println(s"recordExists($id)...")
    Thread.sleep(1)
    id > 0
  }

  def getRecord(id: Long): (Long, String) = {      // ❷
    println(s"getRecord($id)...")
    Thread.sleep(1)
    (id, s"record: $id")
  }
```

```
    def asyncGetRecord(id: Long): Future[(Long, String)] = async {      // ❸
      val exists = async { val b = recordExists(id); println(b); b }
      if (await(exists)) await(async { val r = getRecord(id); println(r); r })
      else (id, "Record not found!")
    }
  }

  (-1 to 1) foreach { id =>                                              // ❹
    val fut = AsyncExample.asyncGetRecord(id)
    println(Await.result(fut, Duration.Inf))
  }
```

❶ An expensive predicate to test for the existence of a record. It returns true if the
   id is greater than zero.

❷ Another expensive method, which retrieves the record for an id.

❸ A method that sequences asynchronous computations together. It first invokes
   recordExists asynchronously. It waits on the result and if true, it fetches the
   record asynchronously. Otherwise, it returns an error record.

❹ Try it with three indices.

It produces the following results (after a few seconds):

```
recordExists(-1)...
false
(-1,Record not found!)
recordExists(0)...
false
(0,Record not found!)
recordExists(1)...
true
getRecord(1)...
(1,record: 1)
(1,record: 1)
```

Note that getRecord is only called once, for the "valid" index 1.

Async code is cleaner than sequencing Futures; it's still not as transparent as truly synchronous code, but you get the benefits of asynchronous execution.

Using Futures, with or without Async, is a *tactic* for concurrency, but not a *strategy*. It
doesn't provide large-scale facilities for managing asynchronous processes, including
error handling, on an application-wide scale. For those needs, we have the actor model.

Robust, Scalable Concurrency with Actors

Actors were originally designed for use in Artificial Intelligence research. Carl Hewitt
and collaborators described them in a 1973 paper (the 2014 update is available at *ar-
xiv.org* (*http://bit.ly/1082H6P*)), and Gul Agha described the actor model theory in his

1987 book *Actors* (MIT Press). Actors are a core concept baked into the Erlang language and its virtual machine. In other languages, like Scala, actors are implemented as a library on top of other concurrency abstractions.

Fundamentally, an *actor* is an object that receives messages and takes action on those messages, one at a time and without preemption. The order in which messages arrive is unimportant in some actor systems, but not all. An actor might process a message internally, or it might forward the message or send a new message to another actor. An actor might create new actors as part of handling a message. An actor might change how it handles messages, in effect implementing a state transition in a state machine.

Unlike traditional object systems that use method calls, actor message sending is usually asynchronous, so the global order of actions is nondeterministic. Like traditional objects, an actor may control some state that it evolves in response to messages. A well-designed actor system will prevent any other code from accessing and mutating this state directly, or it will at least strongly discourage this practice.

These features allow actors to run in parallel, even across a cluster. They provide a *principled* approach to managing global state, largely (but not completely) avoiding the problems of traditional multithreaded concurrency.

Akka: Actors for Scala

In 2009 when the first edition of this book was written, Scala came with an actor library, which we used for the examples. However, a new, independent actor project called Akka (*http://akka.io*) had just started.

Today, the original actor library has been dropped from Scala and Akka is now the official library for actor-based concurrency in Scala. It remains a separate project. Both Scala and Akka are developed and supported by Typesafe (*http://typesafe.com*). Akka provides a comprehensive Java API, too.

In "A Taste of Concurrency" on page 19, we worked through a simple example using Akka. Now let's work through a more realistic example. You might find the Akka Scaladocs (*http://bit.ly/1zRtt3G*) useful as we go.

The two most important, production-ready implementations of the actor model are the Erlang implementation and Akka, which drew its inspiration from Erlang's implementation. Both implement an important innovation, a robust model of error handling and recovery.

Not only are actors created to do the routine work of the system, *supervisors* are created to watch the life cycle of one or more actors. Should an actor fail, perhaps because an exception is thrown, the supervisor follows a strategy for recovery that can include restarting, shutting down, ignoring the error, or delegating to its superior for handling.

When restarting, an *all-for-one* strategy is used when the failed actor is working closely with other actors, all under the same supervisor, and it's best to restart all of them. A *one-for-one* strategy is used when the managed actors are independent workers, where the failure of one has no impact on the others. Only the failed actor requires restarting.

This architecture cleanly separates error-handling logic from normal processing. It enables an architecture-wide strategy for error handling. Most importantly, it promotes a principle of *let it crash*.

Its common to mix error-handling logic with normal processing code, resulting in a complicated mess, which often fails to implement a complete, comprehensive strategy. Inevitably, some production scenarios will trigger a failed recovery that leaves the system in an inconsistent state. When the inevitable crash happens, service is compromised and diagnosing the real source of the problem proves difficult.

The example we'll use simulates a client interface invoking a service, which delegates work to workers. The client interface (and location of the `main` method) is called `Akka Client`. It passes user commands to a single `ServerActor`, which in turn delegates work to several `WorkerActors`, so that it never blocks. Each worker simulates a *sharded* data store. It maintains a map of keys (`Longs`) and values (`Strings`), and it supports CRUD (create, read, update, and delete) semantics.

`AkkaClient` constructs the `akka.actor.ActorSystem` (*http://bit.ly/1pbk2rd*) that controls everything. You'll have one or at most a few of those in any application. Then it constructs an instance of `ServerActor` and sends it a message to start processing. Finally, `AkkaClient` provides a simple command-line interface to the user.

Before walking through `AkkaClient`, let's look at `Messages`, which defines all the messages exchanged between our actors:

```
// src/main/scala/progscala2/concurrency/akka/Messages.scala
package progscala2.concurrency.akka
import scala.util.Try

object Messages {                                            // ❶
  sealed trait Request {                                     // ❷
    val key: Long
  }
  case class  Create(key: Long, value: String) extends Request    // ❸
  case class  Read(key: Long) extends Request                     // ❹
  case class  Update(key: Long, value: String) extends Request    // ❺
  case class  Delete(key: Long) extends Request                   // ❻

  case class  Response(result: Try[String])                       // ❼

  case class  Start(numberOfWorkers: Int = 1)                     // ❽
  case class  Crash(whichOne: Int)                                // ❾
  case class  Dump(whichOne: Int)                                 // ❿
```

```
      case object DumpAll
    }
```

❶   Use a `Messages` object to hold all the message types.

❷   Parent `trait` for all CRUD requests, all of which use a `Long` key.

❸   Create a new "record" with the specified key and value.

❹   Read the record for the given key.

❺   Update a record (or create it if it doesn't exist) with the new value for the given key.

❻   Delete a record for the given key or do nothing if it doesn't exist.

❼   Wrap responses in a common message. A `scala.util.Try` (*http://bit.ly/1tI2jaD*) wraps the result, indicating either success or failure.

❽   Start processing. This message is sent to the `ServerActor` and it tells it how many workers to create.

❾   Send a message to a worker to simulate a "crash."

❿   Send a message to "dump" the state of a single worker or all of them.

Now let's walk through `AkkaClient`:

```scala
// src/main/scala/progscala2/concurrency/akka/AkkaClient.scala
package progscala2.concurrency.akka
import akka.actor.{ActorRef, ActorSystem, Props}
import java.lang.{NumberFormatException => NFE}

object AkkaClient {                                         // ❶
  import Messages._

  private var system: Option[ActorSystem] = None           // ❷

  def main(args: Array[String]) = {                         // ❸
    processArgs(args)
    val sys = ActorSystem("AkkaClient")                     // ❹
    system = Some(sys)
    val server = ServerActor.make(sys)                      // ❺
    val numberOfWorkers =                                   // ❻
      sys.settings.config.getInt("server.number-workers")
    server ! Start(numberOfWorkers)                         // ❼
    processInput(server)                                    // ❽
  }

  private def processArgs(args: Seq[String]): Unit = args match {
    case Nil =>
    case ("-h" | "--help") +: tail => exit(help, 0)
    case head +: tail => exit(s"Unknown input $head!\n"+help, 1)
  }
  ...
```

❶ The client is an object so we can define main here.

❷ The single ActorSystem (*http://bit.ly/1pbk2rd*) is saved in an Option. We'll use it in the shutdown logic that we'll discuss in the following text. Note that the variable is private and mutable. Concurrent access to it won't be a concern, however, because the actor has total control over it.

❸ The main routine starts by processing the command-line arguments. The only one actually supported in processArgs is a help option.

❹ Create the ActorSystem and update the system option.

❺ Call a method on ServerActor's companion to construct an instance of it.

❻ Determine from the configuration how many workers to use.

❼ Send the Start message to the ServerActor to begin processing.

❽ Process command-line input from the user.

Akka uses Typesafe's Config library (*http://bit.ly/1DDoxMl*) for configuration values defined in files or programmatically. The configuration file we're using is the following:

```
// src/main/resources/application.conf
akka {                                             // ❶
  loggers  = [akka.event.slf4j.Slf4jLogger]        // ❷
  loglevel = debug

  actor {                                          // ❸
    debug {                                        // ❹
      unhandled = on
      lifecycle = on
    }
  }
}

server {                                           // ❺
  number-workers = 5
}
```

❶ Configure properties for the Akka system as a whole.

❷ Configure the logging module to use. The SBT build includes the akka-slf4j module that supports this interface. There is a corresponding logback.xml in the same directory that configures the logging (not shown). By default, all debug and higher messages are logged.

❸ Configure properties for every actor.

❹ Enable debug logging of occurrences when an actor receives a message it doesn't handle and any life cycle events.

❺   The `ServerActor` instance will be named `server`. This block configures settings for it. We have one custom setting, the number of workers to use.

Back to `AkkaClient`, processing user input is one long method:

```scala
...
private def processInput(server: ActorRef): Unit = {                    // ❶
  val blankRE = """^\s*#?\s*$""".r
  val badCrashRE = """^\s*[Cc][Rr][Aa][Ss][Hh]\s*$""".r
  val crashRE = """^\s*[Cc][Rr][Aa][Ss][Hh]\s+(\d+)\s*$""".r
  val dumpRE = """^\s*[Dd][Uu][Mm][Pp](\s+\d+)?\s*$""".r
  val charNumberRE = """^\s*(\w)\s+(\d+)\s*$""".r
  val charNumberStringRE = """^\s*(\w)\s+(\d+)\s+(.*)$""".r

  def prompt() = print(">> ")                                          // ❷
  def missingActorNumber() =
    println("Crash command requires an actor number.")
  def invalidInput(s: String) =
    println(s"Unrecognized command: $s")
  def invalidCommand(c: String): Unit =
    println(s"Expected 'c', 'r', 'u', or 'd'. Got $c")
  def invalidNumber(s: String): Unit =
    println(s"Expected a number. Got $s")
  def expectedString(): Unit =
    println("Expected a string after the command and number")
  def unexpectedString(c: String, n: Int): Unit =
    println(s"Extra arguments after command and number '$c $n'")
  def finished(): Nothing = exit("Goodbye!", 0)

  val handleLine: PartialFunction[String,Unit] = {                     // ❸
    case blankRE() =>   /* do nothing */
    case "h" | "help" => println(help)
    case dumpRE(n) =>                                                  // ❹
      server ! (if (n == null) DumpAll else Dump(n.trim.toInt))
    case badCrashRE() => missingActorNumber()                         // ❺
    case crashRE(n) => server ! Crash(n.toInt)
    case charNumberStringRE(c, n, s) => c match {                     // ❻
      case "c" | "C" => server ! Create(n.toInt, s)
      case "u" | "U" => server ! Update(n.toInt, s)
      case "r" | "R" => unexpectedString(c, n.toInt)
      case "d" | "D" => unexpectedString(c, n.toInt)
      case _ => invalidCommand(c)
    }
    case charNumberRE(c, n) => c match {                              // ❼
      case "r" | "R" => server ! Read(n.toInt)
      case "d" | "D" => server ! Delete(n.toInt)
      case "c" | "C" => expectedString
      case "u" | "U" => expectedString
      case _ => invalidCommand(c)
    }
    case "q" | "quit" | "exit" => finished()                         // ❽
    case string => invalidInput(string)                              // ❾
```

```
      }

      while (true) {
        prompt()                                                    // ❿
        Console.in.readLine() match {
          case null => finished()
          case line => handleLine(line)
        }
      }
    }
    ...
```

❶ Start with definitions of regular expressions to parse input.

❷ Define several nested methods for printing the prompt, for reporting errors, and to finish processing and shutdown.

❸ The main handler is a partial function, exploiting that convenient syntax. It starts with a matcher for blank lines (or "comments," lines where the first non-whitespace character is a #), which are ignored. Next it handles help requests (h or help).

❹ Ask one or all workers to dump their state, the "datastore" of key-value pairs.

❺ To demonstrate Akka supervision, handle a message to crash a worker. First, handle the case where the user forgot to specify an actor number. Second, handle the correct syntax, where a message is sent to the ServerActor.

❻ If the command contains a letter, number, and string, it must be a "create" or "update" command. If so, send it to the ServerActor. Otherwise, report an error.

❼ Similarly, if just a command letter and number are input, it must be a "read" or "delete" command.

❽ Three ways to quit the application (Ctrl-D also works).

❾ Treat all other input as an error.

❿ Print the initial prompt, then loop until there's no input, handling each line.

Note that we don't crash or exit on invalid user commands. Unfortunately, we aren't using a library like the Gnu *readline*, so backspaces aren't handled correctly.

To finish this file:

```
  ...
  private val help =                                              // ❶
  """Usage: AkkaClient [-h | --help]
    |Then, enter one of the following commands, one per line:
    |  h | help         Print this help message.
    |  c n string       Create "record" for key n for value string.
    |  r n              Read record for key n. It's an error if n isn't found.
    |  u n string       Update (or create) record for key n for value string.
    |  d n              Delete record for key n. It's an error if n isn't found.
```

```
          |   crash n        "Crash" worker n (to test recovery).
          |   dump [n]       Dump the state of all workers (default) or worker n.
          |   ^d | quit      Quit.
          |""".stripMargin

    private def exit(message: String, status: Int): Nothing = {          // ❷
      for (sys <- system) sys.shutdown()
      println(message)
      sys.exit(status)
    }
}
```

❶   A detailed help message.

❷   A helper function for exiting. It shuts the ActorSystem down, if it was initialized
    (if system is a Some), prints a message, and exits.

Next, let's look at ServerActor:

```
// src/main/scala/progscala2/concurrency/akka/ServerActor.scala
package progscala2.concurrency.akka
import scala.util.{Try, Success, Failure}
import scala.util.control.NonFatal
import scala.concurrent.duration._
import scala.concurrent.Future
import scala.concurrent.ExecutionContext.Implicits.global
import akka.actor.{Actor, ActorLogging, ActorRef,
  ActorSystem, Props, OneForOneStrategy, SupervisorStrategy}
import akka.pattern.ask
import akka.util.Timeout


class ServerActor extends Actor with ActorLogging {              // ❶
  import Messages._

  implicit val timeout = Timeout(1.seconds)

  override val supervisorStrategy: SupervisorStrategy = {        // ❷
    val decider: SupervisorStrategy.Decider = {
      case WorkerActor.CrashException => SupervisorStrategy.Restart
      case NonFatal(ex) => SupervisorStrategy.Resume
    }
    OneForOneStrategy()(decider orElse super.supervisorStrategy.decider)
  }

  var workers = Vector.empty[ActorRef]                           // ❸

  def receive = initial                                         // ❹

  val initial: Receive = {                                      // ❺
    case Start(numberOfWorkers) =>
      workers = ((1 to numberOfWorkers) map makeWorker).toVector
```

```
      context become processRequests                        // ❻
  }

  val processRequests: Receive = {                           // ❼
    case c @ Crash(n) => workers(n % workers.size) ! c
    case DumpAll =>                                          // ❽
      Future.fold(workers map (_ ? DumpAll))(Vector.empty[Any])(_ :+ _)
        .onComplete(askHandler("State of the workers"))
    case Dump(n) =>
      (workers(n % workers.size) ? DumpAll).map(Vector(_))
        .onComplete(askHandler(s"State of worker $n"))
    case request: Request =>
      val key = request.key.toInt
      val index = key % workers.size
      workers(index) ! request
    case Response(Success(message)) => printResult(message)
    case Response(Failure(ex)) => printResult(s"ERROR! $ex")
  }

  def askHandler(prefix: String): PartialFunction[Try[Any],Unit] = {
    case Success(suc) => suc match {
      case vect: Vector[_] =>
        printResult(s"$prefix:\n")
        vect foreach {
          case Response(Success(message)) =>
            printResult(s"$message")
          case Response(Failure(ex)) =>
            printResult(s"ERROR! Success received wrapping $ex")
        }
      case _ => printResult(s"BUG! Expected a vector, got $suc")
    }
    case Failure(ex) => printResult(s"ERROR! $ex")
  }

  protected def printResult(message: String) = {
    println(s"<< $message")
  }

  protected def makeWorker(i: Int) =
    context.actorOf(Props[WorkerActor], s"worker-$i")
}

object ServerActor {                                         // ❾
  def make(system: ActorSystem): ActorRef =
    system.actorOf(Props[ServerActor], "server")
}
```

❶ Mix in the ActorLogging (*http://bit.ly/13p1l9D*) trait, which adds a log field that can be used to log information.

❷ Override the default supervisor strategy with a custom `akka.actor.Supervi sorStrategy` (*http://bit.ly/1nWonhh*). If our simulated crash occurs, restart the actor. If another `NonFatal` (*http://bit.ly/1tI2D9y*) exception occurs, just continue (risky!!). Because these workers are considered independent, use the *one-for-one* strategy. If the `Decider` doesn't have an error, handling is delegated to the parent supervisor.

❸ Keep track of the worker actors through the `akka.actor.ActorRef` (*http://bit.ly/1tI2GSy*) instances that reference them.

❹ Define `receive` to be the `initial` request handler.

❺ `Receive` is a convenient type member of `Actor` (*http://bit.ly/1wNOjMI*) that aliases `PartialFunction[Any,Unit]`. This line declares the `Receive` that will be used to handle the initial `Start` message to the actor. Only `Start` is expected. If other messages are sent to the actor, they will remain in the actor's mailbox until they are explicitly handled. Think of this `Receive` as implementing the first state of a state machine for this actor.

❻ When `Start` is received, construct the workers and transition to the second state of the state machine, where message handling is done by `processRequests`.

❼ This `Receive` block handles the rest of the messages after `Start` is received. The first few case classes match on `Crash`, `DumpAll`, and `Dump` messages. The `re quest: Request` clause handles the CRUD commands. Finally, `Response` messages from workers are handled. Note that user-specified worker indices are converted modulo the number of actual workers to a valid index into the `work ers` vector. This actor prints the responses it receives from the workers.

❽ `DumpAll` needs to be forwarded to all workers and we would like to gather together all the responses from them and format a result message. We do that with the *ask pattern*. To use this feature, we must import `akka.pattern.ask` (at the top of the file). We use `?` to send a message, which returns a `Future` (*http://bit.ly/1sR3rnc*), instead of using `!`, which returns a `Unit`. Both message types are asynchronous, but in the ask pattern, a reply from the receiver is captured into the completion of the `Future`. We use `Future.fold` to join the sequence of `Futures` into a single `Future` wrapping a `Vector`. Then we use `onComplete` to register a callback, `askHandler`, to process the completed `Future`. You'll note that the nesting of types becomes complicated.

❾ The companion provides a convenient `make` method to construct the actor, following the required idiom for actor construction (discussed in the following text).

The `Actor.receive` method is *not* called every time a method is received. Instead, it is called *once*, when the actor is constructed to return a `Receive` (an alias to `PartialFunc` tion[Any,Unit]) that will be called repeatedly for each message. A message handler clause in this function can change the handling of all messages to a new Receive using Actor.become, as is done in the case clause for the Start message in initial. The Receive handler can be changed on every message, if desired, supporting the implementation of complex state machines. In this case, you can cut down on the boilerplate by mixing in the FSM (*http://bit.ly/1E8xj76*) (finite state machine) trait, which provides a convenient DSL for defining state machines.

ServerActor writes all worker replies to the console. It can't send them back to Akka Client, because the latter is not an actor! Hence, if ServerActor calls Actor.sender, the method that returns the original sender ActorRef, ActorSystem.deadLetters (*http://bit.ly/1pbk2rd*) is actually returned.

The idiom used to construct the ServerActor, system.actorOf(Props[ServerActor], "server"), is one of several possible variants. It solves two design problems. First, because actor instances are wrapped in ActorRefs, we can't simply call new ServerActor. Akka needs to properly wrap the instance and do other initialization steps.

Second, the Props (*http://bit.ly/1nWozgp*) singleton object exists primarily to solve an issue with how JVM byte code is generated. Actors need to be serializable, so they can be distributed remotely in clustered deployments; for details, see the Akka docs (*http://bit.ly/1zmn4MJ*). When actor instances are created inside other instances, the Scala compiler will close over the scope, as needed, for the instance. This could mean that an enclosing instance of some other class is captured in the serialized byte code. That instance might not be serializable, so the actor can't be transferred to another node, or perhaps worse, state in the enclosing instance might be encapsulated with the actor, potentially leading to inconsistent behavior on the remote node. The singleton Props effectively prevents this issue from happening.

Finally, here is WorkerActor:

```
// src/main/scala/progscala2/concurrency/akka/WorkerActor.scala
package progscala2.concurrency.akka
import scala.util.{Try, Success, Failure}
import akka.actor.{Actor, ActorLogging}

class WorkerActor extends Actor with ActorLogging {
  import Messages._

  private val datastore = collection.mutable.Map.empty[Long,String]  // ❶

  def receive = {
    case Create(key, value) =>                                       // ❷
      datastore += key -> value
      sender ! Response(Success(s"$key -> $value added"))
    case Read(key) =>                                                // ❸
      sender ! Response(Try(s"${datastore(key)} found for key = $key"))
```

```
      case Update(key, value) =>                             // ❹
        datastore += key -> value
        sender ! Response(Success(s"$key -> $value updated"))
      case Delete(key) =>                                    // ❺
        datastore -= key
        sender ! Response(Success(s"$key deleted"))
      case Crash(_) => throw WorkerActor.CrashException       // ❻
      case DumpAll =>                                         // ❼
        sender ! Response(Success(s"${self.path}: datastore = $datastore"))
  }
}

object WorkerActor {
  case object CrashException extends RuntimeException("Crash!")     // ❽
}
```

❶ Keep a *mutable* map of key-value pairs. Because the Receive handler is thread-safe (enforced by Akka itself) and this mutable state is private to the actor, it's safe to use a mutable object. Because sharing mutable state is dangerous, we'll *never* return this map to a caller through a message.

❷ Add a new key-value pair to the map. Send a response to the sender.

❸ Attempt to read a value for the given key. Wrapping the call to data store(key) in a Try (*http://bit.ly/12TttL0*) automatically captures into a Fail ure (*http://bit.ly/1xImqVs*) the exception that will be thrown if the key is not present. Otherwise, a Success (*http://bit.ly/1nWoER6*) is returned, wrapping the found value.

❹ Update an existing key with a new value (or create a new key-value pair).

❺ Delete a key-value pair. Effectively does nothing if the key isn't present.

❻ "Crash" the actor by throwing a CrashException. Recall that the WorkerActor supervision strategy is configured to restart the actor when this exception is thrown.

❼ Reply with the actor's state, namely a string built from the contents of the data store map.

❽ The special CrashException used to simulate actor crashes.

Let's run it at the sbt prompt:

```
run-main progscala2.concurrency.akka.AkkaClient
```

(Or you can use run and select the number from the list shown.) Enter h to see the list of commands and try several. Use quit to exit. There is also a file of commands that can run through the program using the following command from your shell or command window:

```
sbt "run-main progscala2.concurrency.akka.AkkaClient" < misc/run-akka-input.txt
```

Because the operation is inherently asynchronous, you'll see different results each time you run this script, and also if you copy and paste groups of input lines from the *misc/run-akka-input.txt* file.

Note that the data is lost when an actor is crashed. When this is unacceptable, the Akka Persistence module (*http://bit.ly/1toqYBf*) supports durable persistence of actor state so a restarted actor can recover the previous instance's state.

You might be concerned that the ServerActor's list of workers would become invalid when an actor crashes. This is why all access to an actor goes through a "handle," an ActorRef (*http://bit.ly/1tI2GSy*), and direct access to the Actor instance itself is prevented. (The exception is the special API for actor testing. See the akka.testkit (*http://bit.ly/1wNOSG9*) package.)

ActorRefs are very stable, so they make great *dependencies*. When a supervisor restarts an actor, it resets the ActorRef to point to the new instance. If the actor is not restarted nor resumed, all messages sent to the corresponding ActorRef are forwarded to the ActorSystem.deadLetters (*http://bit.ly/1pbk2rd*), which is the place where messages from dead actors go to die. Therefore, relationships between ActorRefs are stable and reliable.

Actors: Final Thoughts

Our application demonstrates a common pattern for handling a high volume of concurrent input traffic, delegating results to asynchronous workers, then returning the results (or just printing them in this case).

We only scratched the surface of what Akka offers. Still, you now have a sense for how a typical, nontrivial Akka application looks and works. Akka has excellent documentation at *http://akka.io*. Appendix A contains several books on Akka for more in-depth information, including the many patterns and idioms that have emerged for using Akka effectively.

Akka actors are lightweight, about 300 bytes per actor. Hence, you can easily create millions of them in a single, large JVM instance. Keeping track of that many autonomous actors would be a challenge, but if most of them are stateless workers, it can be managed, if necessary. Akka also supports clustering across thousands of nodes (*http://bit.ly/1wNP4FB*) for very high scalability and availability requirements.

A common criticism of the actor model, including Akka, is the loss of type safety. Recall that the Receive type alias is PartialFunction[Any,Unit], meaning it doesn't provide a way to narrow the type of messages an actor is allowed to receive. Therefore, if you send an unexpected message to an actor, you have to detect the problem at runtime. The compiler and the type system can't help enforce logical correctness. Similarly, all references between actors are ActorRefs, not specific Actor types.

Some attempts have been made to provide more restrictive typing, but without clear success so far. For most users, the loss of some type safety is compensated by the power and flexibility of the model.

It's also true that the actor model isn't a really a *functional programming* model. `Receive` returns `Unit`. Everything is done through side effects! Furthermore, the model embraces mutable state when useful, as in our `datastores`.

However, it's a strongly principled use of mutability, where the state is carefully encapsulated within an actor, whose manipulations of that state are guaranteed to be thread-safe. Messages between actors are expected to be immutable objects. Unfortunately, Scala and Akka can't enforce these principled constraints on mutability. It's up to you, but you have the tools to do it right.

It's interesting that the actor model is closely aligned with the vision of object-oriented programming espoused by Alan Kay, the coinventor of Smalltalk and the person who is believed to have cloned the term "object-oriented programming." He argued that objects should be autonomous encapsulations of state, which only communicate through message passing (*http://bit.ly/13p1udf*). In fact, invoking a method in Smalltalk was called *sending a message*.

Finally, the actor model is an example of a more general approach to large-scale, highly available, event-driven applications. But first, let's discuss two problems that arise when you distribute code between processes, along with two solutions for them, Pickling and Spores."

Pickling and Spores

A challenge of distributed programming is fast, controlled serialization and deserialization of data and code for movement around the cluster. This is an old problem and Java has had a built-in serialization mechanism since the beginning. However, far better performance is possible and the best choice involves balancing speed against other requirements. For example, does the format need to work with multiple languages, including non-JVM languages? Does it need to embed the schema and handle version changes?

The Scala Pickling library (*http://bit.ly/1pbCGzb*) aims to provide a serialization option with minimal boilerplate in source code and a pluggable architecture for different back-end formats.

We discussed a related problem earlier when describing the `Props` type in Akka, controlling what gets captured in a closure (function literal) when that closure will be distributed outside the process. The Spores project aims to solve this problem with an API that a developer uses to explicitly construct a "spore" (safe closure), where correctness is enforced by the API. More information about the project, with motivating examples, can be found at in the Scala docs (*http://bit.ly/1tI35ED*).

Both projects are currently under development and they may appear in a future release of Scala, possibly as separate libraries.

Reactive Programming

It's been recognized for a long time that large-scale applications must be *event driven* in some sense, meaning they need to respond to requests for service and send events (or messages) to other services when they need "help." The Internet is built on this premise. Such systems have been called *reactive*, because of their responsive nature, rather than attempting to drive how they work according to some internal logic.

A number of models have emerged that embrace this core principle in different ways. In addition to the actor model, here are two popular models, both of which embrace purity more than the actor model, which considers mutable state acceptable, as long as each example is localized within an actor:

Functional Reactive Programming (FRP)
> FRP (*http://bit.ly/13p1wBH*) is an early *dataflow* model developed first in Haskell by Conal Elliott and Paul Hudak for graphics applications, where time-oriented state updates need to propagate through a system. Rather than manually updating variables as the state they depend on changes, in FRP the dependencies between data elements are declared and the runtime manages state propagation for you. Hence, the user writes code using functional-style declarative and compositional idioms. More recently, FRP has been implemented in a language called *Elm* (*http://elm-lang.org*) by Evan Czaplicki, targeting JavaScript. The paper "Deprecating the Observer Pattern" (*http://bit.ly/1xImuEw*) examines a similar model in Scala.

Reactive Extensions (Rx)
> Rx (*https://rx.codeplex.com*) was developed by Erik Meijer and collaborators for .NET. It has since been ported to multiple languages, including Java (*http://bit.ly/10atK0M*) and Scala (Li Haoyi's project (*http://bit.ly/10FDMs8*)). Rx composes asynchronous programs using observable sequences representing event streams or other data sources, along with query operators (combinators) provided by a library called LINQ (language-integrated query).

Recently, the *Reactive Manifesto* (*http://reactivemanifesto.org*) was organized in an attempt to put some concrete definitions around what a "reactive" system should be. It defines four characteristics that scalable, resilient, reactive applications should support:

Message or Event Driven
> As a baseline, the system has to be designed to respond to messages or events (for some definition of those terms).

Elastically Scalable

The system has to scale to meet demand, which inevitably means horizontal scaling across processes, then cores, then nodes. Ideally, this process should happen dynamically in response to changing demand, both growing and shrinking. The characteristics of networks (such as performance and reliability) then become *first-class* concerns in the architecture of such systems. Services that maintain nontrivial state are hard to scale horizontally this way and it can be difficult to "shard" the state or replicate it reliably.

Resilient

Rare events become commonplace as the size of the system grows. Hence, failures must also be *first-class* concerns. The system must be engineered from the ground up to recover gracefully from failures.

Responsive

The system needs to be available to respond to service requests, even if *graceful degradation* is necessary in the face of failed components or extremely high traffic.

Actors, FRP, and Rx are all event-based. All have been scaled in various ways, although FRP and Rx are more oriented toward processing pipelines for individual streams of events, rather than networks of interacting components, like actors. Arguably, the actor model offers the strongest support for responsiveness, due to its robust error-handling strategy. Finally, these systems approach responsiveness in various ways, but all of them seek to minimize blocking.

Recap and What's Next

We learned how to build scalable, robust, concurrent applications using Akka actors for large-scale systems. We also learned about Scala's support for process management and futures. Finally, we discussed the general idea of *reactive* programming, of which actors are an example, and discussed two other popular models, FRP and Rx.

The next chapter examines one of the hottest areas of our industry today, *Big Data*, and why Scala has emerged as the de facto programming language in this field.

## CHAPTER 18

Scala for Big Data

I said in Chapter 17 that the need to write concurrent programs is driving adoption of FP. However, good concurrency models like actors make it easier for developers to continue using object-oriented programming techniques and avoid the effort of learning functional programming. So, perhaps the *multicore problem* isn't driving change as fast as many of us originally thought?

Now I think that *Big Data* will be a more compelling driver of FP adoption. While actor code still looks object-oriented, more or less, the difference between Big Data applications written in object-oriented Java versus functional Scala is striking. Functional *combinators*, e.g., `map`, `flatMap`, `filter`, `fold`, etc., have always been tools for working with data. Whether that data is in small, in-memory collections or spread across a petabyte-sized cluster, the same abstractions apply. Combinators generalize almost seamlessly across this scale. Once you know the Scala collections, you can pick up the Scala API of one of the popular Big Data tools very quickly. It's true that you'll eventually need to understand how these tools are implemented to write more performant applications, but you'll still be productive quickly.

I've spoken with many Java developers with Big Data experience and little prior interest in Scala. They light up when they see how concise their code could be if they made the switch. For this reason, Scala has emerged as the de facto programming language for Big Data applications, at least among developers like us. *Data Scientists* tend to stick with their favorite tools, such as R and Python.

Big Data: A Brief History

Big Data encompasses the tools and techniques that emerged over the past decade to address three growing challenges. The first was finding ways to work with extremely large data sets, far larger than conventional approaches could manage, like relational databases. The second challenge was the growing need for always-on availability, even when systems experience partial failures.

The early Internet giants like Amazon, eBay, Yahoo!, and Google were the first to face these challenges. They accumulated 100s of TB to several PB (petabytes) of data, far more than could be stored in any relational database and expensive file storage devices, even today. Furthermore, as Internet companies, they needed this data available 24x7. Even the "gold standard" availability of "5-9s" wasn't really good enough. Unfortunately, many early Internet companies experienced embarrassing and catastrophic outages, because they hadn't yet learned how to meet these challenges.

The successful companies attacked the problems from different angles. Amazon, for example, developed a database called *Dynamo* that eschewed the relational model in favor of a simple key-value storage model, with transaction support limited to single rows and sharding of the data around a cluster (described in the famous Dynamo research paper (*http://bit.ly/1yMfojJ*)). In exchange, they gained the ability to store much larger data sets by scaling horizontally, with much higher throughput for reads and writes, and with higher availability because node and rack failures would not result in data loss due to replication strategies. Many of the popular *NoSQL* databases today were inspired by Dynamo.

Google developed a clustered, virtualized filesystem, called *Google File System* (GFS) (*http://bit.ly/15IDCB4*), with similar scalability and availability characteristics. On top of GFS, they built a general-purpose computing engine that could distribute an analysis *job* over the cluster, with *tasks* running on many nodes, thereby exploiting parallelism to process the data far more quickly than a single-threaded program could process it. This computing engine, called *MapReduce* (*http://bit.ly/1zmz3Ke*), enabled a wide range of applications to be implemented, from SQL-like queries to machine-learning algorithms.

GFS and MapReduce inspired clone implementations that together came to be called *Hadoop* (*http://hadoop.apache.org*), which grew rapidly in popularity in the late 2000s as many other companies started using it to store and analyze their own, growing data sets. The file system is called HDFS: Hadoop Distributed File System.

Today, organizations with large data sets often deploy a mixture of Hadoop and NoSQL databases for a range of applications, from reduced-cost data warehousing and other "offline" analysis, to extremely large-scale transaction processing.

"Big Data" is also something of a misnomer because many data sets aren't *that* big, but organizations find the flexibility and low cost of the so-called Big Data tools to be useful for archiving, integrating, and analyzing data in a wide variety of formats and from a wide variety of sources.

For the rest of this chapter, we'll focus on the *computing engine* part of the story, how MapReduce-based tools have evolved and how MapReduce is slowly being replaced by improved successors, with Scala front and center in this evolution.

There are Scala APIs for most of the NoSQL databases, but for the most part, they are conventional APIs similar to Java APIs you might have used. Rather than spend time covering well-understood concepts with Scala veneers, we'll focus instead on more disruptive ideas, using functional programming to simplify and empower data-centric applications.

Improving MapReduce with Scala

The MapReduce Java API is very low level and difficult to use, requiring special expertise to implement nontrivial algorithms and to obtain good performance. The model combines a *map* step, where files are read and the data is converted to key-value pairs as needed for the algorithm. The key-value pairs are shuffled over the cluster to bring together identical keys and then perform final processing in the *reduce* step. Many algorithms require several map-reduce "jobs" sequenced together. Unfortunately, MapReduce flushes data to disk after each job, even when the next job in the sequence will read the data back into memory. The round-trip disk I/O is a major source of inefficiency in MapReduce jobs over massive data sets.

In MapReduce, *map* really means *flat map*, because for every input (say a line from a text file), zero to many output key-value pairs will be generated. *Reduce* has the usual meaning. However, imagine if the Scala containers only had these two combinators, `flatMap` and `reduce`? Many transforms you would like to do would be awkward to implement. Plus, you would need to understand how to do this *efficiently* over large data sets. The upshot is this: while in principle you can implement almost any algorithm in MapReduce, in practice it requires special expertise and challenging programming.

Cascading (*http://cascading.org*) is the best known Java API that promotes a range of useful abstractions for typical data problems on top of Hadoop MapReduce and it hides many of the low-level MapReduce details (note that as I write this, a replacement backend that eliminates MapReduce is being implemented). Twitter invented *Scalding* (*http://bit.ly/1wNnkzG*), a Scala API on top of Cascading that has become very popular.

Let's examine a classic algorithm, *Word Count*. It is the "Hello World" of Hadoop, because it's conceptually easy to understand, so you can focus on learning an API. In Word Count, a corpus of documents are read in by parallel *map* tasks (usually one task per file). The text is tokenized into words and each map task outputs a sequence of *(word, count)* pairs with the *count* of each *word* found in the document. In the simplest implementation, the mapper just writes *(word, 1)* every time *word* is encountered, but a performance optimization is to only emit one *(word, count)* pair, thereby reducing the number of key-value pairs that get shuffled over the cluster to reducers. The *word* functions as a key in this algorithm.

The shuffling process brings all the same *word* tuples together to the *reducer* tasks, where a final count is done and the tallies are written back to disk. This is why it's logically equivalent to write 10 *(Foo, 1)* tuples or 1 *(Foo, 10)* tuple. Addition is *associative*; it doesn't matter where we add the 10 *Foos*.

Let's compare implementing Word Count in the three APIs: Java MapReduce, Cascading, and Scalding.

 Because these examples would require quite a few additional dependencies to build and run, and some of the toolkits don't yet support Scala 2.11, all of the files have the "X" extension so sbt doesn't attempt to compile them. Instead, see the footnotes for each example for information on building and using them.

To save space, I'll just show part of the Hadoop MapReduce version. The full source is available in the downloadable code examples for the book at the location shown in the comment:[1]

```
// src/main/java/progscala2/bigdata/HadoopWordCount.javaX
...
class WordCountMapper extends MapReduceBase
    implements Mapper<IntWritable, Text, Text, IntWritable> {

  static final IntWritable one  = new IntWritable(1);
  static final Text word = new Text;

  @Override public void map(IntWritable key, Text valueDocContents,
      OutputCollector<Text, IntWritable> output, Reporter reporter) {
    String[] tokens = valueDocContents.toString.split("\\s+");        // ❶
    for (String wordString: tokens) {
      if (wordString.length > 0) {
        word.set(wordString.toLowerCase);
        output.collect(word, one);
      }
    }
  }
}

class WordCountReduce extends MapReduceBase
    implements Reducer<Text, IntWritable, Text, IntWritable> {
```

---

1. See the Hadoop tutorial (*http://bit.ly/1OFjLBZ*) for another implementation and for instructions on building and running Hadoop applications. See also *Hadoop: The Definitive Guide, Third Edition*, by Tom White (O'Reilly).

```
public void reduce(Text keyWord, java.util.Iterator<IntWritable> counts,
    OutputCollector<Text, IntWritable> output, Reporter reporter) {
  int totalCount = 0;
  while (counts.hasNext) {                                          // ❷
    totalCount += counts.next.get;
  }
  output.collect(keyWord, new IntWritable(totalCount));
  }
}
```

❶   The actual work of the map step. The text is tokenized and for each *word* found, it is written to the output as the key and a count of one is written as the value.

❷   The actual work of the reduce step. For each *word* key, a collection of counts is summed. The word and the final count are written to the output, which will go to files.

This code reminds me of the original EJB 1.X API. Highly invasive and inflexible. Framework boilerplate abounds. You have to wrap all fields in Writable (*http://bit.ly/1s0TMvi*), a serialization format, because Hadoop won't do that for you. You have tedious Java idioms. Not shown is the class that provides the main routine, which adds another 12 or so lines of setup code. I won't explain all the API details, but hopefully you get the main point that the API requires attention to a lot of details that are unrelated to the trivial algorithm.

Minus import statements and comments, this version is about 60 lines of code. That's not huge. MapReduce jobs tend to be smaller than general-purpose IT applications, but this is also a very simple algorithm. Implementing more sophisticated algorithms raises the complexity level considerably. For example, consider a common SQL query you might write on the output, assuming it's in a table named wordcount:

```
SELECT word, count FROM wordcount ORDER BY word ASC, count DESC;
```

Simple. Now search the Internet for *secondary sort mapreduce* and marvel at the complexity of the MapReduce implementations you find.

Cascading provides an intuitive model of *pipes* that are joined into *flows*, where the sources and sinks for data are *taps*. Here is the *full* program (imports elided) for the equivalent Cascading implementation:[2]

```
// src/main/java/progscala2/bigdata/CascadingWordCount.javaX
package impatient;

import ...;
```

---

2. Adapted from *Cascading for the Impatient*, Part 2 (*http://docs.cascading.org/impatient*), © 2007-2013 Concurrent, Inc. All Rights Reserved.

```
public class CascadingWordCount {
  public static void main( String[] args ) {
    String input  = args[0];
    String output = args[1];

    Properties properties = new Properties();                    // ❶
    AppProps.setApplicationJarClass( properties, Main.class );
    HadoopFlowConnector flowConnector = new HadoopFlowConnector( properties );

    Tap docTap = new Hfs( new TextDelimited( true, "\t" ), input );  // ❷
    Tap wcTap = new Hfs( new TextDelimited( true, "\t" ), output );

    Fields token = new Fields( "token" );                        // ❸
    Fields text = new Fields( "text" );
    RegexSplitGenerator splitter =
        new RegexSplitGenerator( token, "[ \\[\\]\\(\\),.]" );
    Pipe docPipe =                                               // ❹
      new Each( "token", text, splitter, Fields.RESULTS );

    Pipe wcPipe = new Pipe( "wc", docPipe );                     // ❺
    wcPipe = new GroupBy( wcPipe, token );
    wcPipe = new Every( wcPipe, Fields.ALL, new Count(), Fields.ALL );

    // Connect the taps, pipes, etc., into a flow.
    FlowDef flowDef = FlowDef.flowDef()                          // ❻
     .setName( "wc" )
     .addSource( docPipe, docTap )
     .addTailSink( wcPipe, wcTap );

    // Run the flow.
    Flow wcFlow = flowConnector.connect( flowDef );             // ❼
    wcFlow.complete();
  }
}
```

❶ A small amount of setup code, including configuration for running in Hadoop.

❷ Read and write data using *taps* for HDFS.

❸ Name two *fields* in the tuples representing records. Use a regular expression to split the text into a token stream.

❹ Create a pipe that iterates over the input text and outputs just the words.

❺ Connect a new pipe that performs a group-by operation with the words as the grouping keys. Then append a pipe that counts the sizes of each group.

❻ Create the flow that connects the input and output taps to the pipeline.

❼ Run it.

The Cascading version is about 30 lines without the imports. Even without knowing much about this API, the real algorithm emerges. After we tokenize the corpus into words, we want to *group by* those words and then size each group. That's really all this algorithm does. If we had the "raw words" in a table, the SQL query would be this:

```
SELECT word, COUNT(*) as count FROM raw_words GROUP BY word;
```

Cascading offers an elegant API that has become popular. It is hampered by the relative verbosity of Java and the lack of anonymous functions in pre-Java 8, when the API was created. For example, the `Each`, `GroupBy`, and `Every` objects should be higher-order functions. They are in Scalding.

Here's the Scalding version:[3]

```
// src/main/scala/progscala2/bigdata/WordCountScalding.scalaX

import com.twitter.scalding._                              // ❶

class WordCount(args : Args) extends Job(args) {

  TextLine(args("input"))                                   // ❷
    .read
    .flatMap('line -> 'word) {                              // ❸
      line: String => line.trim.toLowerCase.split("""\s+""")
    }
    .groupBy('word){ group => group.size('count) }          // ❹
    .write(Tsv(args("output")))                             // ❺
}
```

❶   Just one import statement.

❷   Read text files where each line is a "record." `TextLine` abstracts over the local filesystem, HDFS, S3, etc. How you run a Scalding job determines how filesystem paths are interpreted, whereas Cascading requires you to make this choice in the source code. Each line will have the field name 'line, where Scalding uses Scala symbols to specify fields by name. The expression `args("input")` means grab the *path* from the command-line option - -input *path*.

❸   Take each 'line and tokenize it into words, using `flatMap`. The syntax ('line -> 'word) means that we select a single input field (there is only one at this point) and the single output field will be called 'word.

❹   Group by the words and count the group sizes. The output schema of these records will be ('word, 'count).

❺   Write the output as tab-separated values to the *path* given on the command line with - -output *path*.

---

3. Adapted from the scalding-workshop example on GitHub (*https://github.com/deanwampler/scalding-workshop*).

The Scalding version is a dozen lines, with the single import statement! Now, almost all the framework details have receded into the background. It's pure algorithm. You *already* know what `flatMap` and `groupBy` are doing, even though Scalding adds an extra argument list to most *combinators* for field selection.

We evolved from a lengthy, tedious *program* to a simple *script*. The whole software development process is changed when you can write such concise programs.

Moving Beyond MapReduce

A growing trend is the need to process events in "real time." MapReduce is only usable for batch-mode jobs. HDFS only recently added support for incremental updates to files. Most Hadoop tools don't support this feature yet.

This trend has led to the creation of new tools, such as *Storm* (*http://bit.ly/13p9UBh*), a clustered event processing system.

Other growing concerns are the MapReduce performance limitations, such as the excessive disk I/O mentioned previously, and the difficulties of the programming API and underlying model.

Most first-generation technologies have limitations that eventually lead to replacements. The major Hadoop vendors recently embraced a MapReduce replacement called *Spark* (*http://spark.apache.org*), which supports both a batch-mode and streaming model. Spark is written in Scala and it provides excellent performance compared to MapReduce, in part because it caches data in memory between processing steps. Perhaps most important, Spark provides the sort of intuitive API that Scalding provides—incredibly concise, yet expressive.

Where Scalding and Cascading use a pipe metaphor, Spark uses a *Resilient, Distributed Dataset* (RDD), an in-memory data structure distributed over the cluster. It's resilient in the sense that if a node goes down, Spark knows how to reconstruct the missing piece from the source data.

Here is one Spark implementation of Word Count:[4]

```
// src/main/scala/progscala2/bigdata/WordCountSpark.scalaX
package bigdata

import org.apache.spark.SparkContext
import org.apache.spark.SparkContext._

object SparkWordCount {
  def main(args: Array[String]) = {
    val sc = new SparkContext("local", "Word Count")      // ❶
```

---

4. Adapted from the spark-workshop example on GitHub (*https://github.com/deanwampler/spark-workshop*).

```
      val input = sc.textFile(args(0)).map(_.toLowerCase)                    // ❷
      input
        .flatMap(line => line.split("""\W+"""))                              // ❸
        .map(word => (word, 1))                                              // ❹
        .reduceByKey((count1, count2) => count1 + count2)                    // ❺
        .saveAsTextFile(args(1))                                             // ❻
      sc.stop()                                                              // ❼
    }
  }
```

❶   Start with a `SparkContext`. The first argument specifies the "master." In this case, we run locally. The second argument is an arbitrary name for the job.

❷   Load one or more text files from the path specified with the first command-line argument (in Hadoop, directory paths are given and all files in them are read) and convert the strings to lowercase, returning an RDD.

❸   Split on nonalphanumeric sequences of characters, flat-mapping from lines to words.

❹   Map each word to the tuple (`word, 1`). Recall the output of the Hadoop map tasks for Word Count discussed earlier.

❺   Use `reduceByKey`, which functions like a SQL `GROUP BY` followed by a *reduction*, in this case summing the values in the tuples, the 1s. In Spark, the first element of a tuple is the default *key* for operations like this and the rest of the tuple is the *value*.

❻   Write the results to the path specified as the second input argument. Spark follows Hadoop conventions and actually treats the path as a directory to which it writes one "partition" file per final task (with naming convention `part-n`, where n is a five-digit number, counting form `00000`).

❼   Shut down the context and stop.

Like the Scalding example, this program is about a dozen lines of code.

Whether you use more mature, but still growing tools like Scalding or up and coming tools like Spark, I hope it's clear that Scala APIs have a unique advantage over Java-based APIs. The functional combinators we already know are the ideal basis for thinking about data analytics, both for users of these tools and also for implementers.

Categories for Mathematics

We discussed *categories* in Chapter 16. A category we didn't discuss that's becoming popular in Big Data is *Monoid*. If you skipped that chapter, just think of *categories* as mathematically oriented *design patterns*.

Monoid is the abstraction for *addition*. It has these properties:

---

1. A single, associative, binary operation
2. An identity element

Addition of numbers satisfies these properties. We have associativity, *(1.1 + 2.2) + 3.3 == 1.1 + (2.2 + 3.3)*, and *0* is the identity element. Multiplication works, too, with *1* as the identity. Addition and multiplication of numbers are also commutative, *1.1 + 2.2 == 2.2 + 1.1*, but that's *not* required for a Monoid.

What's the big deal? It turns out a *lot* of data structures satisfy these properties, so if you generalize code to work with Monoids, it can be highly reusable (see the list on Wikipedia (*http://bit.ly/1tphZ15*)).

Examples include string concatenation, matrix addition and multiplication, computing maxima and minima, and approximation algorithms like HyperLogLog for finding unique values, Min-hash for set similarity, and Bloom filters for set membership (see Avi Bryant's great "Add ALL The Things!" talk (*http://bit.ly/1wQpFNV*)).

Some of these data structures also commute. All can be implemented with parallel execution for high performance over large data sets. The approximation algorithms listed trade off better space efficiency for less accuracy.

You'll see *Monoid* implemented in a number of mathematics packages, including those in the next section.

A List of Scala-Based Data Tools

Besides the Hadoop platform and Scala APIs for databases, a number of tools have emerged for related problems, like general mathematics and Machine Learning. Table 18-1 list some of the active projects you might investigate, including the ones we discussed previously, for completeness.

Table 18-1. Data and mathematics libraries

Option	URL	Description
Algebird	*http://bit.ly/10Fk2F7*	Twitter's API for abstract algebra that can be used with almost any Big Data API.
Factorie	*http://factorie.cs.umass.edu/*	A toolkit for deployable *probabilistic modeling*, with a succinct language for creating relational factor graphs, estimating parameters, and performing inference.
Figaro	*http://bit.ly/1nWnQf4*	A toolkit for *probabilistic programming*.
H2O	*http://bit.ly/1G2rfz5*	A high-performance, in-memory distributed compute engine for data analytics. Written in Java with Scala and R APIs.
Relate	*http://bit.ly/13p17zp*	A thin database access layer focused on performance.

Option	URL	Description
ScalaNLP	*http://www.scalanlp.org/*	A suite of Machine Learning and numerical computing libraries. It is an umbrella project for several libraries, including Breeze (*http://bit.ly/1q8K1uq*), for machine learning and numerical computing, and Epic (*http://bit.ly/1wNX2iJ*), for statistical parsing and structured prediction.
ScalaStorm	*http://bit.ly/10aaroq*	A Scala API for Storm.
Scalding	*https://github.com/twitter/scalding*	Twitter's Scala API around Cascading (*http://cascading.org*) that popularized Scala as a language for Hadoop programming.
Scoobi	*https://github.com/nicta/scoobi*	A Scala abstraction layer on top of MapReduce with an API that's similar to Scalding's and Spark's.
Slick	*http://slick.typesafe.com/*	A database access layer developed by Typesafe.
Spark	*http://spark.apache.org/*	The emerging standard for distributed computation in Hadoop environments, as well in Mesos clusters (*http://mesos.apache.org*) and on single machines ("local" mode).
Spire	*https://github.com/non/spire*	A numerics library that is intended to be generic, fast, and precise.
Summingbird	*https://github.com/twitter/summingbird*	Twitter's API that abstracts computation over Scalding (batch mode) and Storm (event streaming).

While the Hadoop environment gets a lot of attention, general-purpose tools like Spark, Scalding/Cascading, and H2O also support smaller deployments, when a large Hadoop cluster is unnecessary.

Recap and What's Next

Few segments of our industry make the case for Scala more strongly than *Big Data*. The way that Scalding and Spark improve upon the Java MapReduce API is striking, even disruptive. Both have made Scala the obvious choice for data-centric application development.

Normally we think of Scala as a statically typed language, like Java. However, the standard library contains a special trait for creating types with more dynamic behavior, like you find in languages such as Ruby and Python, as we'll see in the next chapter. This feature is one tool for building *domain-specific languages* (DSLs), which we'll explore in the chapter after that.

## CHAPTER 19

Dynamic Invocation in Scala

Most of the time, Scala's static typing is a virtue. It adds safety constraints that are useful for ensuring correctness at runtime and easier comprehension when browsing code. These benefits are especially useful in large-scale systems.

Occasionally, you might miss the benefits of dynamic typing, however, such as allowing method calls that don't exist at compile time! The popular *Ruby on Rails* web framework (*http://rubyonrails.org*) uses this technique very effectively in its ActiveRecord API. Let's see how we might implement the same technique in Scala.

A Motivating Example: ActiveRecord in Ruby on Rails

ActiveRecord is the original object-relational mapping (ORM) library integrated with Rails. Most of the details don't concern us here,[1] but one of the useful features it offers is a DSL for composing queries that consist of chained method calls on a domain object.

However, the "methods" aren't actually defined. Instead, invocations are routed to Ruby's catch-all for undefined methods, method_missing. Normally, this method throws an exception, but it can be overridden in classes to do something else. ActiveRecord does this to interpret the "missing method" as a directive for constructing a SQL query.

Suppose we have a simple database table of states in the United States (for some dialect of SQL):

```
CREATE TABLE states (
  name      TEXT,     -- Name of the state.
  capital   TEXT,     -- Name of the capital city.
  statehood INTEGER   -- Year the state was admitted to the union.
);
```

---

1. See the Active Record Basics RailsGuide (*http://bit.ly/1wQpq5r*) for more information.

With `ActiveRecord` you can construct queries as follows, where the Ruby domain object `State` is the analog of the table `states`:

```
# Find all states named "Alaska"
State.find_by_name("Alaska")
# Find all states named "Alaska" that entered the union in 1959
State.find_by_name_and_statehood("Alaska", 1959)
...
```

For a table with lots of columns, defining all permutations of the `find_by_*` methods would be unworkable. However, the *protocol* defined by the naming convention is easy to automate, so no explicit definitions are required. `ActiveRecord` automates all the boilerplate needed to parse the name, generate the corresponding SQL query, and construct in-memory objects for the results.

Note that `ActiveRecord` implements an *embedded* or *internal* DSL, where the language is an idiomatic dialect of the host language Ruby, rather than an alternative language that requires its own grammar and parser.

Dynamic Invocation in Scala with the Dynamic Trait

It might be useful to implement a similar DSL in Scala, but normally Scala expects all such methods to be defined explicitly. Fortunately, Scala version 2.9 added the `scala.Dynamic` (*http://bit.ly/1pbhB8b*) trait to support the dynamic resolution behavior we just described.

The `Dynamic` trait is a marker trait; it has no method definitions. Instead, the compiler sees this trait and follows a protocol for handling uses of it. The protocol is summarized in the trait's Scaladoc page (*http://bit.ly/1pbhB8b*), using the following example for some instance `foo` of a class `Foo` that extends `Dynamic`:

```
foo.method("blah")       ~~> foo.applyDynamic("method")("blah")
foo.method(x = "blah")   ~~> foo.applyDynamicNamed("method")(("x", "blah"))
foo.method(x = 1, 2)     ~~> foo.applyDynamicNamed("method")(("x", 1), ("", 2))
foo.field                ~~> foo.selectDynamic("field")
foo.varia = 10           ~~> foo.updateDynamic("varia")(10)
foo.arr(10) = 13         ~~> foo.selectDynamic("arr").update(10, 13)
foo.arr(10)              ~~> foo.applyDynamic("arr")(10)
```

`Foo` must implement any of the *Dynamic* methods that might be called. The `applyDynamic` method is used for calls that don't use named parameters. If the user names any of the parameters, `applyDynamicNamed` is called. Note that the first argument list has a single argument for the method name invoked. The second argument list has the actual arguments passed to the method.

You can declare these second argument lists to allow a variable number of arguments if you want or you can declare a specific set of typed arguments. It all depends on how you expect users to call the methods.

The methods `selectDynamic` and `updateDynamic` are for reading and writing fields that aren't arrays. The second to last example shows the special form used for writing array elements. For reading array elements, the invocation is indistinguishable from a method call with a single argument. So, for this case, `applyDynamic` has to be used.

Let's create a simple query DSL in Scala using `Dynamic`. Actually, our example is closer to a query DSL in .NET languages called LINQ (*http://bit.ly/ms-linq*) (language-integrated query). LINQ enables SQL-like queries to be embedded into .NET programs and used with collections, database tables, etc. LINQ is one inspiration for *Slick* (*http://slick.typesafe.com*), a Scala *functional-relational mapping* (FRM) library.

We'll implement just a few possible operators, so we'll call it CLINQ, for *cheap language-integrated query*. We'll define a case class with that name and yes, it's meant to sound silly.

We'll assume we want to query in-memory data structures, specifically a sequence of maps (key-value pairs) with a SQL-inspired DSL. The implementation is compiled with the code examples, so let's first try the script that both demonstrates the syntax we want and verifies that the implementation works:

```
// src/main/scala/progscala2/dynamic/clinq-example.sc

scala> import progscala2.dynamic.CLINQ
import progscala2.dynamic.CLINQ

scala> def makeMap(name: String, capital: String, statehood: Int) =
     |   Map("name" -> name, "capital" -> capital, "statehood" -> statehood)

// "Records" for Five of the states in the U.S.A.
scala> val states = CLINQ(
     |   List(
     |     makeMap("Alaska",     "Juneau",      1959),
     |     makeMap("California", "Sacramento",  1850),
     |     makeMap("Illinois",   "Springfield", 1818),
     |     makeMap("Virginia",   "Richmond",    1788),
     |     makeMap("Washington", "Olympia",     1889)))
states: dynamic.CLINQ[Any] =
Map(name -> Alaska, capital -> Juneau, statehood -> 1959)
Map(name -> California, capital -> Sacramento, statehood -> 1850)
Map(name -> Illinois, capital -> Springfield, statehood -> 1818)
Map(name -> Virginia, capital -> Richmond, statehood -> 1788)
Map(name -> Washington, capital -> Olympia, statehood -> 1889)
```

We import the `dynamic.CLINQ` case class that we'll study in a moment. Then we create an instance with a sequence of maps, where each map is a "record."

In contrast to the `ActiveRecord` example, we'll use the `n_and_m` to simply project out the fields we want, like a SQL `SELECT` statement, where `all` will correspond to `SELECT *` (some of the output elided):

```
scala> states.name
res0: dynamic.CLINQ[Any] =
Map(name -> Alaska)
Map(name -> California)
Map(name -> Illinois)
Map(name -> Virginia)
Map(name -> Washington)

scala> states.capital
res1: dynamic.CLINQ[Any] =
Map(capital -> Juneau)
Map(capital -> Sacramento)
...

scala> states.statehood
res2: dynamic.CLINQ[Any] =
Map(statehood -> 1959)
Map(statehood -> 1850)
...

scala> states.name_and_capital
res3: dynamic.CLINQ[Any] =
Map(name -> Alaska, capital -> Juneau)
Map(name -> California, capital -> Sacramento)
...

scala> states.name_and_statehood
res4: dynamic.CLINQ[Any] =
Map(name -> Alaska, statehood -> 1959)
Map(name -> California, statehood -> 1850)
...

scala> states.capital_and_statehood
res5: dynamic.CLINQ[Any] =
Map(capital -> Juneau, statehood -> 1959)
Map(capital -> Sacramento, statehood -> 1850)
...

scala> states.all
res6: dynamic.CLINQ[Any] =
Map(name -> Alaska, capital -> Juneau, statehood -> 1959)
Map(name -> California, capital -> Sacramento, statehood -> 1850)
...
```

Finally, how about some WHERE clauses?

```
scala> states.all.where("name").NE("Alaska")
res7: dynamic.CLINQ[Any] =
Map(name -> California, capital -> Sacramento, statehood -> 1850)
Map(name -> Illinois, capital -> Springfield, statehood -> 1818)
Map(name -> Virginia, capital -> Richmond, statehood -> 1788)
Map(name -> Washington, capital -> Olympia, statehood -> 1889)
```

```
scala> states.all.where("statehood").EQ(1889)
res8: dynamic.CLINQ[Any] =
Map(name -> Washington, capital -> Olympia, statehood -> 1889)

scala> states.name_and_statehood.where("statehood").NE(1850)
res9: dynamic.CLINQ[Any] =
Map(name -> Alaska, statehood -> 1959)
Map(name -> Illinois, statehood -> 1818)
Map(name -> Virginia, statehood -> 1788)
Map(name -> Washington, statehood -> 1889)
```

CLINQ knows nothing about the keys in the maps, but the Dynamic trait allows us to support methods constructed from them. Here is CLINQ:

```
// src/main/scala/progscala2/dynamic/CLINQ.scala
package progscala2.dynamic
import scala.language.dynamics                                    // ❶

case class CLINQ[T](records: Seq[Map[String,T]]) extends Dynamic {

  def selectDynamic(name: String): CLINQ[T] =                     // ❷
    if (name == "all" || records.length == 0) this                // ❸
    else {
      val fields = name.split("_and_")                            // ❹
      val seed = Seq.empty[Map[String,T]]
      val newRecords = (records foldLeft seed) {
        (results, record) =>
          val projection = record filter {                        // ❺
            case (key, value) => fields contains key
          }
          // Drop records with no projection.
          if (projection.size > 0) results :+ projection
          else results
      }
      CLINQ(newRecords)                                           // ❻
    }

  def applyDynamic(name: String)(field: String): Where = name match {
    case "where" => new Where(field)                              // ❼
    case _ => throw CLINQ.BadOperation(field, """Expected "where".""")
  }

  protected class Where(field: String) extends Dynamic {          // ❽
    def filter(value: T)(op: (T,T) => Boolean): CLINQ[T] = {      // ❾
      val newRecords = records filter {
        _ exists {
          case (k, v) => field == k && op(value, v)
        }
      }
      CLINQ(newRecords)
    }

    def applyDynamic(op: String)(value: T): CLINQ[T] = op match {
```

```
        case "EQ" => filter(value)(_ == _)                          // ⑩
        case "NE" => filter(value)(_ != _)                          // ⑪
        case _ => throw CLINQ.BadOperation(field, """Expected "EQ" or "NE".""")
      }
    }

    override def toString: String = records mkString "\n"            // ⑫
  }

  object CLINQ {                                                     // ⑬
    case class BadOperation(name: String, msg: String) extends RuntimeException(
      s"Unrecognized operation $name. $msg")
  }
```

❶ Dynamic is an optional language feature, so we import it to enable it.

❷ We'll use selectDynamic for the *projections* of fields.

❸ Return all the fields for the "keyword" all or for no records.

❹ Two or more fields are joined by _and_, so split the name into an array of field names.

❺ Filter the maps to return just the named fields.

❻ Construct a new CLINQ to return.

❼ Use applyDynamic for operators that follow projections. We will only implement where for the equivalent of SQL WHERE clauses. A new Where instance is returned, which also extends Dynamic. Note that the *same* set of records will be in scope for this instance, so we don't need to construct the new object with them! If another SQL-like keyword is used, it is an error.

❽ The Where class used to filter the records for particular values of the field named field.

❾ A helper method that filters the in-scope records for those maps that have a key-value pair with the name specified by field and a corresponding value v such that op(value, v) returns true.

❿ If EQ is the operator, call filter to return only records where the value for the given field is equal to the user-specified value.

⑪ Support the not equals case. Note that supporting greater than, less than, etc. would require more careful handling of the types, because not all possible value types support such expressions.

⑫ Create strings for the records that are easier to read.

⑬ Define the BadOperation exception in the companion object.

CLINQ is definitely "cheap" in several ways. It doesn't implement other useful operations from SQL, like the equivalent of GROUP BY. Nor does it implement other WHERE-clause operators like greater than, less than, etc. They are actually tricky to support, but not impossible, because not all possible value types support them.

DSL Considerations

The `Dynamic` trait is one of Scala's many tools for implementing *embedded* or *internal* DSLs. We'll explore them in depth in the next chapter. For now, note a few things.

First, the implementation is not easy to understand, which means it's hard to maintain, debug, and extend. It's very tempting to use a "cool" tool like this and live to regret the effort you've taken on. So, use `Dynamic`, as well as any DSL feature, judiciously.

Second, a related challenge that plagues all DSLs is the need to provide meaningful, helpful error messages to users. Try experimenting with the examples we used in the previous section and you'll easily write something the compiler can't parse and the error messages won't be very helpful. (Hint: try using infix notation, where some periods and parentheses are removed.)

Third, a good DSL should prevent the user from writing something that's logically invalid. This simple example doesn't really have that problem, but it becomes a challenge for more advanced DSLs.

Recap and What's Next

We explored Scala's "hook" for writing code with dynamically defined methods and values, which are familiar to users of dynamically typed languages like Ruby. We used it to implement a query DSL that "magically" offered methods based on data values!

However, we also summarized some of the challenges of writing DSLs with features like this. Fortunately, we have many tools at our disposal for writing DSLs, as we'll explore in the next chapter.

## CHAPTER 20

Domain-Specific Languages in Scala

A *domain-specific language* (DSL) is a programming language that mimics the terms, idioms, and expressions used among experts in the targeted domain. Code written in a DSL reads like structured prose for the domain. Ideally, a domain expert with little experience in programming can read, understand, and validate this code, if not also write code in the DSL.

We will just scratch the surface of this large topic and Scala's support for it. For more in-depth coverage, see the DSL references in Appendix A.

Well-crafted DSLs offer several benefits:

Encapsulation
> A DSL hides implementation details and exposes only those abstractions relevant to the domain.

Productivity
> Because implementation details are encapsulated, a DSL optimizes the effort required to write or modify code for application features.

Communication
> A DSL helps developers understand the domain and domain experts to verify that the implementation meets the requirements.

However, DSLs also have several drawbacks:

DSLs are difficult to create
> Although writing a DSL is "cool," the effort shouldn't be underestimated. First, the implementation techniques can be nontrivial (see the following example). Second, good DSLs are harder to design than traditional APIs. The latter tend to follow language idioms for API design, where uniformity is important and easy to follow.

In contrast, because each DSL is a unique language, we are free to create idioms that reflect the unique features of the target domain. The greater latitude makes it harder to find the best abstractions.

DSLs are hard to maintain

DSLs can require more maintenance over the long term as the domain changes, because of the nontrivial implementation techniques used. Implementation simplicity is often sacrificed for a better user experience.

However, a well-designed DSL can be a powerful tool for building flexible and robust applications, *if* it will be used frequently.

From the implementation point of view, DSLs are classified as *internal* and *external*.

An *internal* (or *embedded*) DSL is an idiomatic way of writing code in a general-purpose programming language, like Scala. No special-purpose parser is needed. In contrast, an *external* DSL is a custom language with its own custom grammar and parser.

Internal DSLs can be easier to create because they don't require a special-purpose parser. On the other hand, the constraints of the underlying language limit the options for expressing domain concepts. External DSLs remove this constraint. You can design the language any way you want, as long as you can write a reliable parser for it. Using a custom parser can be challenging, too. Returning good error messages to the user has always been a challenge for parser writers.

Examples: XML and JSON DSLs for Scala

A decade ago, XML was the *lingua franca* of machine-to-machine communication on the Internet. JSON has been usurping that role more recently. Scala's XML support is implemented partly as a library, with some built-in syntax support. Both are now moving toward deprecation, to simplify the language and to make it easier for third-party libraries to be used instead. In Scala 2.11, the XML support was extracted into a separate module from the rest of the library (see the Scaladocs (*http://bit.ly/1wNWn0P*).) Our sbt build includes this module in its dependencies, so we can use it in this section.

Let's briefly explore working with XML in Scala to see the DSL it implements. The main types we'll see are scala.xml.Elem (*http://bit.ly/1yMf7gL*) and scala.xml.Node (*http://bit.ly/1voxdBR*):

```
// src/main/scala/progscala2/dsls/xml/reading.sc
import scala.xml._                                        // ❶

val xmlAsString = "<sammich>...</sammich>"                // ❷
val xml1 = XML.loadString(xmlAsString)

val xml2 =                                                // ❸
<sammich>
```

```
      <bread>wheat</bread>
      <meat>salami</meat>
      <condiments>
        <condiment expired="true">mayo</condiment>
        <condiment expired="false">mustard</condiment>
      </condiments>
    </sammich>

    for {                                                      // ❹
      condiment <- (xml2 \\ "condiment")
      if (condiment \ "@expired").text == "true"
    } println(s"the ${condiment.text} has expired!")

    def isExpired(condiment: Node): String =                   // ❺
      condiment.attribute("expired") match {
        case Some(Nil) | None => "unknown!"
        case Some(nodes) => nodes.head.text
      }

    xml2 match {                                               // ❻
      case <sammich>{ingredients @ _*}</sammich> => {
        for {
          condiments @ <condiments>{_*}</condiments> <- ingredients
          cond <- condiments \ "condiment"
        } println(s"  condiment: ${cond.text} is expired? ${isExpired(cond)}")
      }
    }
```

❶ Import the public API declarations from the scala.xml (*http://bit.ly/
1voxeWe*) package.

❷ Define a string containing XML and parse it into a scala.xml.Elem. The XML
(*http://bit.ly/1rGxcqG*) object can read from a variety of sources, including
URLs.

❸ Use an *XML literal* to define a scala.xml.Elem.

❹ Iterate through the XML and extract fields. The xml \ "foo" only matches on
child nodes, while the xml \\ "foo" operator traverses deeper in the tree of
nodes, if necessary. XPath expressions (*http://www.w3.org/TR/xpath20*) are
supported, such as the @expired expression that finds attributes with that name.

❺ A helper method to find all occurrences of the attribute expired in the condi
ment node. If an empty sequence or None is returned, return "unknown!"
Otherwise, grab the first one in the sequence and return its text, which should
be "true" or "false."

❻ Pattern match with XML literals. This expression extracts the ingredients, then
a sequence of the condiment tags, then it extracts each condiment and prints
data about it.

The XML object supports a few ways to save XML to a file or to a `java.io.Writer` (*http://bit.ly/1tphCna*):

```
// src/main/scala/progscala2/dsls/xml/writing.sc

XML.save("sammich.xml", xml2, "UTF-8")                                    // ❶
```

❶ Write the XML starting at the `xml2` node to the file `sammich.xml` in this directory, using UTF-8 encoding.

Scala added limited support for JSON parsing in its *parser combinator* library, which we'll explore in "External DSLs with Parser Combinators" on page 473. There are now many excellent JSON libraries for Scala, as well as for Java, so the built-in JSON support should only be considered for limited needs. So, which alternative should you use? If you're using a major framework already, consult the documentation for its preferred choice. Otherwise, because the landscape is changing rapidly, your best bet is to search for options that seem right for your needs.

Internal DSLs

Several features of Scala syntax support creation of *internal* (embedded) DSLs:

Flexible rules for names
> Because you can use almost any characters in a name, it's easy to create names that fit the domain, like algebraic symbols for types with corresponding properties. For example, if you have a `Matrix` type, you can implement matrix multiplication with a * method.

Infix and postfix notation
> Defining a * method wouldn't make much sense if you couldn't use infix notation, e.g., `matrix1 * matrix2`. Postfix notation, e.g., `1 minute`, is also useful.

Implicit arguments and default argument values
> Both features reduce boilerplate and hide complex details, such as a context that has to be passed to every method in the DSL, but can be handled instead with an implicit value. Recall that many `Future` (*http://bit.ly/1sR3rnc*) methods take an implicit `ExecutionContext` (*http://bit.ly/1s0FtqF*).

Type classes
> A related use of implicits are conversions to "add" methods to existing types. For example, the `scala.concurrent.duration` (*http://bit.ly/10884Ty*) package has implicit conversions for numbers that allow you to write `1.25 minutes`, which returns a `FiniteDuration` (*http://bit.ly/1nWnnJN*) instance equal to 75 seconds.

Dynamic method invocation

As we discussed in Chapter 19, the `Dynamic` (*http://bit.ly/1DDdSBj*) trait makes it possible for an object to accept almost any apparent method or field invocation, even when the type has no method or field defined with that name.

Higher-order functions and by-name parameters

Both enable custom DSLs to look like native control constructs, like the `contin ue` example we saw in "Call by Name, Call by Value" on page 87.

Self-type annotations

Nested parts of a DSL implementation can refer to an instance in an enclosing scope if the latter has a self-type annotation visible to the nested parts. This could be used to update a state object in the enclosing scope, for example.

Macros

Some advanced scenarios can be implemented using the new *macros* facility, which we'll learn about in Chapter 24.

Let's create an internal DSL for a payroll application that computes an employee's paycheck every pay period (two weeks). The DSL will compute the *net* salary, by subtracting the *deductions* from the *gross* salary, such as taxes, insurance premiums, retirement fund contributions, etc.

Let's begin with some common types we'll use in both the internal and external DSLs:

```scala
// src/main/scala/progscala2/dsls/payroll/common.scala
package progscala2.dsls.payroll

object common {
  sealed trait Amount { def amount: Double }              // ❶

  case class Percentage(amount: Double) extends Amount {
    override def toString = s"$amount%"
  }

  case class Dollars(amount: Double) extends Amount {
    override def toString = s"$$$amount"
  }

  implicit class Units(amount: Double) {                  // ❷
    def percent = Percentage(amount)
    def dollars = Dollars(amount)
  }

  case class Deduction(name: String, amount: Amount) {    // ❸
    override def toString = s"$name: $amount"
  }

  case class Deductions(                                  // ❹
    name: String,
```

```
    divisorFromAnnualPay: Double = 1.0,
    var deductions: Vector[Deduction] = Vector.empty) {

  def gross(annualSalary: Double): Double =                        // ❺
    annualSalary / divisorFromAnnualPay

  def net(annualSalary: Double): Double = {
    val g = gross(annualSalary)
    (deductions foldLeft g) {
      case (total, Deduction(deduction, amount)) => amount match {
        case Percentage(value) => total - (g * value / 100.0)
        case Dollars(value) => total - value
      }
    }
  }

  override def toString =                                          // ❻
    s"$name Deductions:" + deductions.mkString("\n  ", "\n  ", "")
  }
}
```

❶   A small sealed type hierarchy that encapsulates a deduction "amount" that is either a percentage deduction from the gross or a fixed dollar amount.

❷   An implicit class that handles conversion from Double to the correct Amount subtype. It is only used in the internal DSL.

❸   A type for a single deduction with a name and an amount.

❹   A type for all the deductions. It also holds a name (e.g., "Biweekly") and a "divisor" used to calculate the period's gross pay from the annual gross pay.

❺   Once the deductions are constructed, return the gross and net for the pay period.

❻   Most of the toString methods are overridden to return the format we want.

Here is the start of the internal DSL, including a main that demonstrates the DSL syntax:

```
// src/main/scala/progscala2/dsls/payroll/internal/dsl.scala
package progscala2.dsls.payroll.internal
import scala.language.postfixOps                                  // ❶
import progscala2.dsls.payroll.common._

object Payroll {                                                  // ❷

  import dsl._                                                    // ❸

  def main(args: Array[String]) = {
    val biweeklyDeductions = biweekly { deduct =>                 // ❹
      deduct federal_tax        (25.0  percent)
      deduct state_tax          (5.0   percent)
      deduct insurance_premiums (500.0 dollars)
      deduct retirement_savings (10.0  percent)
```

```
    }
    println(biweeklyDeductions)                                    // ❺
    val annualGross = 100000.0
    val gross = biweeklyDeductions.gross(annualGross)
    val net   = biweeklyDeductions.net(annualGross)
    print(f"Biweekly pay (annual: $$${annualGross}%.2f): ")
    println(f"Gross: $$${gross}%.2f, Net: $$${net}%.2f")
  }
}
```

❶ We want to use postfix expressions, e.g., `20.0 dollars`.

❷ Object to test the DSL.

❸ Import the DSL, which we'll see in a moment.

❹ The DSL in action. Hopefully a business stakeholder can easily understand the rules expressed here and perhaps even edit them. To be clear, *this is Scala syntax.*

❺ Print the deductions, then compute the net pay for the biweekly payroll.

The output of this program is as follows (the test `progscala2.dsls.payroll.inter nal.DSLSpec` uses *ScalaCheck* for more exhaustive verification):

```
Biweekly Deductions:
  federal taxes: 25.0%
  state taxes: 5.0%
  insurance premiums: $500.0
  retirement savings: 10.0%
Biweekly pay (annual: $100000.00): Gross: $3846.15, Net: $1807.69
```

Now let's see how it's implemented:

```
object dsl {                                                       // ❶

  def biweekly(f: DeductionsBuilder => Deductions) =               // ❷
    f(new DeductionsBuilder("Biweekly", 26.0))

  class DeductionsBuilder(                                         // ❸
    name: String,
    divisor: Double = 1.0,
    deducts: Vector[Deduction] = Vector.empty) extends Deductions(
      name, divisor, deducts) {

    def federal_tax(amount: Amount): DeductionsBuilder = {         // ❹
      deductions = deductions :+ Deduction("federal taxes", amount)
      this
    }

    def state_tax(amount: Amount): DeductionsBuilder = {
      deductions = deductions :+ Deduction("state taxes", amount)
      this
    }
```

```
      def insurance_premiums(amount: Amount): DeductionsBuilder = {
        deductions = deductions :+ Deduction("insurance premiums", amount)
        this
      }

      def retirement_savings(amount: Amount): DeductionsBuilder = {
        deductions = deductions :+ Deduction("retirement savings", amount)
        this
      }
    }
  }
}
```

❶ Wrap the public DSL pieces in an object.

❷ The method biweekly is the entry point for defining deductions. It constructs an empty DeductionsBuilder object that will be mutated in place (the easiest design choice) to add new Deduction instances.

❸ Build the Deductions, which it subclasses for convenience. The end user only sees the Deductions object, but the builder has extra methods for sequencing expressions.

❹ The first of the four kinds of deductions supported. Note how it updates the Deductions instance in place.

The DSL works as written, but I would argue that it's far from perfect. Here are some issues:

It relies heavily on Scala syntax tricks
It exploits infix notation, function literals, etc. to provide the DSL, but it would be easy for a user to break the code by adding periods, parentheses, and other changes that seem harmless.

The syntax uses arbitrary conventions
Why are the curly braces and parentheses where they are? Why is the deduct argument needed in the anonymous function?

Poor error messages
If the user enters invalid syntax, Scala error messages are presented, not domain-centric error messages.

The DSL doesn't prevent the user from doing the wrong thing
Ideally, the DSL would not let the user invoke any construct in the wrong context. Here, too many constructs are visible in the dsl object. Nothing prevents the user from calling things out of order, constructing instances of implementation constructs (like Percentage), etc.

It uses mutable instances

Maybe this isn't so bad, unless you're a purist. A DSL like this is not designed to be high performance nor would you run it in a multithreading context. The mutability simplifies the implementation without serious compromises.

Most of these issues could be be fixed with more effort.

Some of my favorite examples of internal DSLs are the popular Scala testing libraries, *ScalaTest* (*http://scalatest.org*), *Specs2* (*http://bit.ly/1vovYm2*), and *ScalaCheck* (*http://scalacheck.org*). They provide great examples of DSLs that work well for developers, making the effort of creating these DSLs justified.

External DSLs with Parser Combinators

When you write a parser for an external DSL, you can use a parser generator tool like Antlr (*http://www.antlr.org*). However, the Scala library includes a *parser combinator* library that can be used for parsing most external DSLs that have a context-free grammar. An attractive feature of this library is the way it defines an internal DSL that makes parser definitions look very similar to familiar grammar notations, like Extended Backus-Naur Form (EBNF).

Scala 2.11 moved the parser combinators to a separate JAR file, so it's now optional. There are other libraries that often provide better performance, such as Parboiled 2 (*http://bit.ly/1sRz2Fk*). We'll use Scala's library for our example. Other libraries offer similar DSLs.

We have included the parser combinators library in the sbt build dependencies (see the Scaladocs (*http://bit.ly/1wQprq9*)).

About Parser Combinators

Just as the collection combinators we already know construct data transformations, parser combinators are building blocks for parsers. Parsers that handle specific bits of input, such as floating-point numbers, integers, etc., are combined together to form parsers for larger expressions. A good parser library supports sequential and alternative cases, repetition, optional terms, etc.

A Payroll External DSL

We'll reuse the previous example, but with a simpler grammar, because our external DSL does not have to be valid Scala syntax. Other changes will make parser construction easier, such as adding commas between each deduction declaration.

As before, let's start with the imports and main routine:

```
// src/main/scala/progscala2/dsls/payroll/parsercomb/dsl.scala
package progscala2.dsls.payroll.parsercomb
import scala.util.parsing.combinator._
import progscala2.dsls.payroll.common._                          // ❶

object Payroll {

  import dsl.PayrollParser                                        // ❷

  def main(args: Array[String]) = {
    val input = """biweekly {                                     // ❸
      federal tax          20.0  percent,
      state tax            3.0   percent,
      insurance premiums   250.0 dollars,
      retirement savings   15.0  percent
    }"""
    val parser = new PayrollParser                                // ❹
    val biweeklyDeductions = parser.parseAll(parser.biweekly, input).get

    println(biweeklyDeductions)                                   // ❺
    val annualGross = 100000.0
    val gross = biweeklyDeductions.gross(annualGross)
    val net   = biweeklyDeductions.net(annualGross)
    print(f"Biweekly pay (annual: $$${annualGross}%.2f): ")
    println(f"Gross: $$${gross}%.2f, Net: $$${net}%.2f")
  }
}
```

❶ Use some of the common types again.

❷ Use the "root" parser for deductions.

❸ The input. Note that this time the input is a String, not an idiomatic Scala expression.

❹ Create a parser instance and use it by calling biweekly, which returns a parser for the entire DSL. The parseAll method returns a Parsers.ParseResult (*http://bit.ly/1topI19*). To get the Deductions, we have to call get.

❺ Print the output just like the previous example. The deduction numbers are different from before. Hence the *net* will be different.

Here is the parser definition:

```
object dsl {

  class PayrollParser extends JavaTokenParsers {                 // ❶

    /** @return Parser[(Deductions)] */
    def biweekly = "biweekly" ~> "{" ~> deductions <~ "}" ^^ { ds => // ❷
      Deductions("Biweekly", 26.0, ds)
    }
```

```
/** @return Parser[Vector[Deduction]] */
def deductions = repsep(deduction, ",") ^^ { ds =>          // ❸
  ds.foldLeft(Vector.empty[Deduction]) (_ :+ _)
}

/** @return Parser[Deduction] */
def deduction = federal_tax | state_tax | insurance | retirement // ❹

/** @return Parser[Deduction] */
def federal_tax = parseDeduction("federal", "tax")          // ❺
def state_tax   = parseDeduction("state", "tax")
def insurance   = parseDeduction("insurance", "premiums")
def retirement  = parseDeduction("retirement", "savings")

private def parseDeduction(word1: String, word2: String) =   // ❻
  word1 ~> word2 ~> amount ^^ {
    amount => Deduction(s"${word1} ${word2}", amount)
  }

/** @return Parser[Amount] */
def amount = dollars | percentage                            // ❼

/** @return Parser[Dollars] */
def dollars = doubleNumber <~ "dollars" ^^ { d => Dollars(d) }

/** @return Parser[Percentage] */
def percentage = doubleNumber <~ "percent" ^^ { d => Percentage(d) }

def doubleNumber = floatingPointNumber ^^ (_.toDouble)
  }
}
```

❶ The class defining the grammar and parser, through methods.

❷ The top-level parser, created by building up smaller parsers. The entry method biweekly returns a Parser[Deductions], which is a parser capability of parsing a string for a complete deductions specification. It returns a Deductions object. We'll discuss the syntax in a moment.

❸ Parse a comma-separated list of deductions. Adding the requirement to use a comma simplifies the parser implementation. The repsep method parses an arbitrary number of deduction expressions.

❹ Recognize four possible deductions.

❺ Call a helper function to construct the four deduction parsers.

❻ The helper method for the four deductions.

❼ Parse the amount, a double literal followed by dollars or percent. A corresponding Amount instance is constructed.

Let's look at biweekly more closely. Here it is rewritten a bit to aid the discussion:

```
"biweekly" ~> "{" ~> deductions <~ "}"                    // ❶
  ^^ { ds => Deductions("Biweekly", 26.0, ds) }           // ❷
```

❶ Find three *terminal tokens*, biweekly, {, and }, with the results of evaluating the deductions *production* between the {…}. The arrow-like operators (actually methods, as always), ~> and <~, mean drop the token on the side of the ~. So the literals are dropped and only the result of deductions is retained.

❷ The ^^ separates the left side (*reduction tokens*) from the right side (*grammar rule*) for the production. The *grammar rule* takes as arguments the tokens retained. If there is more than one, a partial function literal is used of the form { case t1 ~ t2 ~ t2 => ... }, for example. In our case, ds is a Vector of Deduction instances, which is used to construct a Deductions instance.

Note that DeductionsBuilder in the internal DSL is not needed here. See the test progscala2.dsls.payroll.parsercomb.DSLSpec, which uses *ScalaCheck*, for exhaustive verification.

Internal Versus External DSLs: Final Thoughts

Let's compare the internal and external DSLs the user writes. Here is the internal DSL again:

```
val biweeklyDeductions = biweekly { deduct =>
  deduct federal_tax          (25.0  percent)
  deduct state_tax            (5.0   percent)
  deduct insurance_premiums   (500.0 dollars)
  deduct retirement_savings   (10.0  percent)
}
```

Here is the external DSL again:

```
val input = """biweekly {
  federal tax          20.0  percent,
  state tax            3.0   percent,
  insurance premiums   250.0 dollars,
  retirement savings   15.0  percent
}"""
```

The external DSL is simpler, but the user must embed the DSL in strings. Hence, code completion, refactoring, color coding, and other IDE features aren't available.

On the other hand, the external DSL is easier (and actually more fun) to implement. It should have less fragility from reliance on Scala parsing tricks.

You'll have to weigh which trade-offs make the most sense for your situation. If the DSL is "close-enough" that it can be implemented internally with reasonable effort and robustness, the user experience will generally be better. It's clearly the best choice for the test libraries mentioned earlier. If the DSL is too far removed from Scala syntax, perhaps

---

because it's a well-known language, like SQL, using an external DSL with quoted strings is probably best.

Recall that we can implement our own string interpolators (see "Build Your Own String Interpolator" on page 153). This is a useful way to encapsulate a parser built with combinators behind a slightly easier syntax. For example, if you implement a SQL parser of some sort, let the user invoke it with `sql"SELECT * FROM table WHERE …;"`, rather than having to use the parser API calls explicitly like we did.

Recap and What's Next

It's tempting to create DSLs with abandon. DSLs in Scala can be quite fun to work with, but don't underestimate the effort required to create robust DSLs that meet your clients' usability needs, while at the same time requiring reasonable effort for long-term maintenance and support.

In the next chapter, we'll explore the Scala tools and and libraries.

## CHAPTER 21

Scala Tools and Libraries

This chapter fills in some details about the Scala tools we've already used, such as the compiler `scalac` and the REPL `scala`. We'll discuss build tool options and IDE and text editor integration, and look at testing libraries for Scala. Finally, we'll list some of the popular third-party Scala libraries you might find useful.

Command-Line Tools

Even if you do most of your work with IDEs or the SBT REPL, understanding how the command-line tools work gives you additional flexibility, as well as a fallback should the graphical tools fail you. Most of the time, you'll configure compiler flags through your SBT build files or IDE settings, and you'll invoke the REPL through your SBT session, using the `console` command.

"Installing Scala" on page 3 described how to install the command-line tools. All of them are located in the *SCALA_HOME/bin* directory, where *SCALA_HOME* is the directory where you installed Scala.

You can read more information about the command-line tools at *http://www.scala-lang.org/documentation/*.

scalac Command-Line Tool

The `scalac` command compiles Scala source files and generates JVM class files.

The `scalac` command is just a shell-script wrapper around the `java` command, passing it the name of the Scala compiler's `Main` object. It adds Scala JAR files to the CLASS PATH and it defines several Scala-related system properties.

You invoke `scalac` like this:

```
scalac <options> <source files>
```

Recall from "A Taste of Scala" on page 9 that source file names don't have to match the public class name in the file. In fact, you can define multiple public classes in a file. Similarly, package declarations don't have to match the directory structure.

However, in order to conform to JVM requirements, a separate class file will be generated for each type with a name that corresponds to the type's name. Also, the class files will be written to directories corresponding to the package declarations.

Table 21-1 shows the list of the `scalac` options as reported by `scalac -help` for the 2.11.2 compiler (edited slightly).

Table 21-1. The scalac command options

Option	Description
`-Dproperty=value`	Pass `-Dproperty=value` directly to the runtime system.
`-Jflag`	Pass Java flag directly to the runtime system.
`-Pplugin:opt`	Pass an option to a compiler plug-in.
`-X`	Print a synopsis of advanced options (Table 21-3 discusses these advanced options).
`-bootclasspath path`	Override location of bootstrap class files.
`-classpath path`	Specify where to find user class files.
`-d directory or jar`	Destination for generated class files.
`-dependencyfile file`	Specify the file in which dependencies are tracked.
`-deprecation`	Output source locations where deprecated APIs are used.
`-encoding encoding`	Specify character encoding used by source files.
`-explaintypes`	Explain type errors in more detail.
`-extdirs dirs`	Override location of installed compiler extensions.
`-feature`	Emit warning and location for usages of features that should be imported explicitly.
`-g:level`	Specify `level` of generated debugging info: `none`, `source`, `line`, `vars` (default), `notailcalls`.
`-help`	Print a synopsis of standard options.
`-javabootclasspath path`	Override the Java boot classpath.
`-javaextdirs path`	Override the Java `extdirs` classpath.
`-language:feature`	Enable one or more language features: `dynamics`, `postfixOps`, `reflective Calls`, `implicitConversions`, `higherKinds`, `existentials`, and `experi mental.macros` (comma-separated list, with no spaces).
`-no-specialization`	Ignore occurrences of the `@specialize` annotations.
`-nobootcp`	Do not use the boot classpath for the Scala JARs.
`-nowarn`	Generate no warnings.
`-optimise`	Generate faster byte code by applying optimizations to the program.
`-print`	Print program with all Scala-specific features removed.
`-sourcepath path`	Specify where to find input source files.

Option	Description
-target:*target*	Target platform for object files: jvm-1.5 (deprecated), jvm-1.6 (default), jvm-1.7.
-toolcp *path*	Add to the runner classpath.
-unchecked	Enable additional warnings where generated code depends on assumptions.
-uniqid	Uniquely tag all identifiers in debugging output.
-usejavacp	Utilize the java.class.path in classpath resolution.
-usemanifestcp	Utilize the manifest in classpath resolution.
-verbose	Output messages about what the compiler is doing.
-version	Print product version and exit.
@*file*	A text file containing compiler arguments (options and source files).

Let's discuss a few of these options.

Use -encoding UTF8 if you use non-ASCII characters in names or the allowed symbols, such as ⇒ (Unicode \u21D2) instead of =>.

Use -explaintypes when you need a more complete explanation for a type error.

Starting with Scala 2.10, some more advanced language features have been made optional, so that teams can selectively enable the ones they want to use. This is part of an ongoing effort to address complexity concerns about Scala, while still allowing advanced constructs to be used when desired. Use -feature to emit a warning and the source location for any usage of these features when the corresponding import statement is missing in the source code and the corresponding -language:*feature* compiler flag wasn't used.

The list of optional language features is defined by values in the scala.language (*http:// bit.ly/10a8xnZ*) object. Its Scaladoc (*http://bit.ly/10a8xnZ*) page also explains why these features are optional. Table 21-2 lists the features.

Table 21-2. The optional language features

Name	Description
dynamics	Enables the Dynamic trait (see Chapter 19).
postfixOps	Enables postfix operators (e.g., 100 toString).
reflectiveCalls	Enables using structural types (see "Reflecting on Types" on page 525).
implicitConversions	Enables defining implicit methods and members (see "Implicit Conversions" on page 149).
higherKinds	Enables writing higher-kinded types (see "Higher-Kinded Types" on page 398).
existentials	Enables writing existential types (see "Existential Types" on page 386).
experimental	Contains newer features that have not yet been tested in production. Macros are the only experimental feature in Scala at this time (see "Macros" on page 532).

The advanced -X options (printed by `scalac -X` and `scala -X`) control verbose diagnostic output, fine-tune the compiler behavior, control use of experimental extensions and plug-ins, etc. Table 21-3 discusses a few of these options.

Table 21-3. Some of the -X advanced options

Option	Description
-Xcheckinit	Wrap field accessors to throw an exception on uninitialized access (see "Overriding fields in traits" on page 317).
-Xdisable-assertions	Generate no assertions or assumptions.
-Xexperimental	Enable experimental extensions.
-Xfatal-warnings	Fail the compilation if there are any warnings.
-Xfuture	Turn on "future" language features (if any for a particular release).
-Xlint	Enable recommended additional warnings.
-Xlog-implicit-conversions	Print a message whenever an implicit conversion is inserted.
-Xlog-implicits	Show more detail on why some implicits are not applicable.
-Xmain-class *path*	Specify the class to use for the `Main-Class` entry in the JAR file's manifest. Only useful with `-d` *jar* option.
-Xmigration:*v*	Warn about constructs whose behavior may have changed since version *v* of Scala.
-Xscript *object*	Treat the source file as a script and wrap it in a main method.
-Y	Print a synopsis of *private* options, which are used by implementers of new language features.

To see an example of the extra warnings provided by -Xlint, consider the following, where we first start the REPL with the -Xlint option:

```
$ scala -Xlint
Welcome to Scala version 2.11.2 ...
...
scala> def hello = println("hello!")
<console>:7: warning: side-effecting nullary methods are discouraged:
  suggest defining as `def hello()` instead
       def hello = println("hello!")
            ^
hello: Unit
```

Any function that returns Unit can only perform side effects. In this case, we write output. It's a common convention in Scala code to only use *nullary* methods, those with no argument list, for functions without side effects. Hence, this warning.

The -Xscript option is useful when you want to compile a script file as if it were a regular Scala source file, usually to eliminate the startup overhead of compiling the script repeatedly.

I recommend routine use of the -deprecation, -unchecked, feature, and -Xlint options. (The -Xlint option may throw too many warnings for some code bases.) They help prevent some bugs and encourage you to eliminate use of obsolete libraries. We use these flags, as well as a few others, in the *build.sbt* file in the code examples.

The scala Command-Line Tool

The scala command runs the program, if given. Otherwise, it starts the REPL. It is also a shell script, like scalac. You invoke scala like this:

```
scala <options> [<script|class|object|jar> <arguments>]
```

The same options accepted by scalac apply here, plus the additional options shown in Table 21-4.

Table 21-4. The additional scala command options

Option	Description
-howtorun	What to run, a script, object, jar, or make a guess (default).
-i file	Preload the contents of file before starting the REPL.
-e string	Execute string as if it were entered in the REPL.
-save	Save the compiled script in a JAR file for future use, thereby avoiding the overhead of recompilation.
-nc	Don't run the compilation daemon, fsc, the offline compiler that is otherwise started automatically to avoid the overhead of restarting the compiler each time.

The first nonoption argument is interpreted as the program to run. If nothing is specified, the REPL is started. When specifying a program, any arguments after the program argument will be passed to it in the args array we've used previously in various examples.

Unless you specify the -howtorun option, scala will infer the nature of the program. If it is a file of Scala source code, it will be executed as a script. If it is class file with a main routine or a JAR file with a valid Main-Class attribute, it will be executed as a typical Java program.

Use the -i file option in the interactive mode when you want to preload a file before typing commands. Once in the REPL, you can also load a file using the command :load filename. Such a file is useful when you find yourself repeating the same commands when you start a REPL.

When using the REPL, you have several commands at your disposal. Enter :help to see a list of them with brief descriptions. Table 21-5 lists the available commands for Scala 2.11.2, edited slightly.

Table 21-5. Commands available within the Scala REPL

Command	Description
:cp *path*	Add a JAR or directory to the classpath.
:edit *id or line*	Edit the input history.
:help *[command]*	Print this summary or command-specific help.
:history *[num]*	Show the history (optional *num* is the number of commands to show).
:h? *string*	Search the history.
:imports *[name name …]*	Show the import history, identifying sources of names.
:implicits [-v]	Show the implicits in scope (optional -v for more verbose output).
:javap *path or class*	Disassemble a file or class name.
:line *id or line*	Place lines at the end of history.
:load *path*	Interpret lines in a file given by *path*.
:paste [-raw] *[path]*	Enter paste mode or paste a file.
:power	Enable power user mode (see the text that follows).
:quit	Exit the interpreter (or use Ctrl-D).
:replay	Reset execution and replay all previous commands.
:reset	Reset the REPL to its initial state, forgetting all session entries.
:save *path*	Save the session to a file for replaying later.
:sh *command line*	Run a shell command (result is implicitly ⇒ List[String]).
:settings *[+ or -]options*	Enable (+)/disable(-) flags, set compiler options.
:silent	Disable/enable automatic printing of results.
:type [-v] *expr*	Display the type of an expression without evaluating it.
:kind [-v] *expr*	Display the kind of an expression's type.
:warnings	Show the suppressed warnings from the most recent line that had any warnings.

The "power user mode" enabled by :power adds additional commands for viewing in-memory data, such as the abstract syntax tree and interpreter properties, and for manipulating the compiler.

Invoking scripts with scala is tedious when you use these scripts frequently. On Windows and Unix-like systems, you can create standalone Scala scripts that don't require you to use the scala *script-file-name* invocation.

For Unix-like systems, the following example demonstrates how to make an executable script. Remember that you have to make the permissions executable, e.g., chmod +x secho:

```
#!/bin/sh
# src/main/scala/progscala2/toolslibs/secho
exec scala "$0" "$@"
```

```
!#
print("You entered: ")
args.toList foreach { s => printf("%s ", s) }
println
```

Here is how you might use it:

```
$ secho Hello World
You entered: Hello World
```

Similarly, here is an example Windows `.bat` command:

```
::#!
@echo off
call scala %0 %*
goto :eof
::!#
print("You entered: ")
args.toList foreach { s => printf("%s ", s) }
println
```

Limitations of scala versus scalac

There are some limitations when running a source file with `scala` versus compiling it with `scalac`.

A script executed with `scala` is wrapped in an anonymous `object` that looks more or less like the following example:

```
object Script {
  def main(args: Array[String]): Unit = {
    new AnyRef {
      // Your script code is inserted here.
    }
  }
}
```

Scala `objects` cannot embed package declarations, which means you can't declare packages in scripts. This is why the examples in this book that declare packages must be compiled and executed separately.

Conversely, there are valid scripts that can't be compiled with `scalac`, unless the `-Xscript` *object* option is used, where *object* will be the name of the compiled object, replacing the word `Script` in the previous example. In other words, this compiler option creates the same wrapper that the REPL does implicitly.

An object wrapper is required for compilation because function definitions and function invocations outside of types are not allowed. The following example runs fine with `scala` as a script:

```
// src/main/scala/progscala2/toolslibs/example.sc
```

```
case class Message(name: String)

def printMessage(msg: Message) = println(msg)

printMessage(new Message("This works fine with the REPL"))
```

However, if you try to compile the script with scalac without the -Xscript option, you get the following errors:

```
example.sc:3: error: expected class or object definition
def printMessage(msg: Message) = println(msg)
^
example.sc:5: error: expected class or object definition
printMessage(new Message("This works fine with the REPL"))
^
two errors found
```

Instead, compile it and run it this way:

```
scalac -Xscript MessagePrinter src/main/scala/progscala2/toolslibs/example.sc
scala  -classpath . MessagePrinter
```

Because the script effectively uses the default package, the generated class files will be in the current directory:

```
MessagePrinter$$anon$1$Message$.class
MessagePrinter$$anon$1$Message.class
MessagePrinter$$anon$1.class
MessagePrinter$.class
MessagePrinter.class
```

Try running javap -private (discussed in the next section) on each of these files to see the declarations they contain. The -p flag tells it to show all members, including private and protected members (use javap -help to see all the options). Omit the .class, e.g., javap MessagePrinter$$anon1Message$.

MessagePrinter and MessagePrinter$ are wrappers generated by scalac to provide the entry point for the script as an "application." MessagePrinter has the static main method we need.

MessagePrinter$$anon$1 is the generated Java class that wraps the whole script. The printMessage method in the script is a *private* method in this class.

MessagePrinter$$anon1Message is the Message class.

MessagePrinter$$anon1Message$ is the Message companion object.

The scalap and javap Command-Line Tools

Decompilers are useful when you want to understand how Scala constructs are implemented in JVM byte code. They help you understand how Scala names are *mangled* into JVM-compatible names, when necessary.

The venerable `javap` comes with the JDK. It outputs declarations as they would appear in Java source code, even for class files that were compiled from Scala code by `scalac`. Therefore, running `javap` on these class files is a good way to see how Scala definitions are mapped to valid byte code.

The Scala distribution comes with `scalap`, which outputs declarations as they would appear in Scala source code. However, the Scala 2.11.0 and 2.11.1 distributions omitted `scalap` by mistake. You can download the 2.11.1 JAR file here (*http://bit.ly/1sR1x6i*). Just copy it to the *lib* directory of your installation. Version 2.11.2 includes `scalap`.

Using *MessagePrinter.class* from the previous section, run `scalap -cp . Message Printer`. You should get the following output (reformatted to fit the page):

```
object MessagePrinter extends scala.AnyRef {
  def this() = { /* compiled code */ }
  def main(args : scala.Array[scala.Predef.String]) : scala.Unit = {
    /* compiled code */
  }
}
```

Compare this output with the output from `javap -cp . MessagePrinter`:

```
Compiled from "example.sc"
public final class MessagePrinter {
  public static void main(java.lang.String[]);
}
```

Now we see the declaration of `main` as we would typically see it in a Java source file.

Both these tools have a `-help` option that describes the invocation options they support.

As an exercise, try decompiling the class files generated from *progscala2/toolslibs/ Complex.scala*, which implements `Complex` numbers. It has already been compiled by SBT. Try running `scalap` and `javap` on the resulting class files. Note how the declared package name `toolslibs` is specified. The class file built with Scala 2.11 can be decompiled as follows with `javap`:

```
javap -cp target/scala-2.11/classes toolslibs.Complex
```

How are the + and - method names encoded? What are the names of the "getter" methods for the `real` and `imaginary` fields? What Java types are used for these fields? What is the output produced by `scalap` and `javap`?

The scaladoc Command-Line Tool

The `scaladoc` command is analogous to `javadoc`. It is used to generate documentation from Scala source files, called Scaladocs. The `scaladoc` parser supports the same @ annotations that `javadoc` supports, such as `@author`, `@param`, etc.

The easiest way to use `scaladoc` for your project is to run the doc task in SBT.

The fsc Command-Line Tool

The *fast scala compiler* runs as a daemon process to enable faster invocations of the compiler, mostly by eliminating the startup overhead. It is particularly useful when running scripts repeatedly (for example, when rerunning a test suite until a bug can be reproduced). In fact, `fsc` is invoked automatically by the `scala` command. You can also invoke it directly.

Build Tools

Most new projects use SBT (*http://www.scala-sbt.org/*) as their build tool, so we'll focus our discussion on it. However, Scala plug-ins have been implemented for several other build tools, including Ant (*http://ant.apache.org/*), Maven (mvn) (*http://maven.apache.org/*), and Gradle (*http://www.gradle.org/*).

SBT, the Standard Build Tool for Scala

is a sophisticated tool for building Scala and Java projects. It has lots of configuration options and plug-in capabilities. We've been using it all along for the code examples. Let's look at its features in a bit more detail, including the structure of the actual build file for the code. However, we'll just scratch the surface (see the SBT documentation (*http://bit.ly/13p0B4r*) and *SBT in Action*, by Joshua Suereth and Matthew Farwell (Manning) for more details).

By now you've installed SBT (*http://www.scala-sbt.org/*). If you do JVM-based web development, see also the new `sbt-web` project (*https://github.com/sbt/sbt-web$$*), which adds plug-ins for building and managing web assets such as HTML pages and CSS files from template languages.

 The *fastest* way to get started with SBT is to copy and edit an existing build. For example, start with the build files in one of the Activator Templates (*http://bit.ly/1G2pLF0*).

SBT is similar to Maven in the sense that many of the tasks you'll need to do, like compiling and automated testing, are already built in, along with suitable dependencies between tasks, like compiling before testing. The build files in SBT are used to define project metadata, such as the name and version for releases, define dependencies using the Maven conventions and repositories (but using Ivy (*http://ant.apache.org/ivy*) as the dependency resolution tool), and perform other customizations. A Scala-based DSL is used as the language.

SBT builds are defined by one or more build files, depending on the sophistication and customization required for your project. For the book's code examples, the *project* is relatively simple, although supporting two versions of Scala adds a little complexity.

The main build file is in the root directory of the code examples. It is named *build.sbt*. There are two additional files in the *project* subdirectory: *build.properties*, which defines the version of SBT we want to use, and *plugins.sbt*, which adds SBT plug-ins for generating Eclipse project files. (IntelliJ IDEA can import SBT projects directly.) It's also common to put *build.sbt* in the *project* directory.

Let's look at a simplified version of our *build.sbt*, starting with some definitions:

```
name := "Programming Scala, Second Edition: Code examples"

version := "2.0"

organization := "org.programming-scala"

scalaVersion := "2.11.2"
```

Definitions like `name := "Programming Scala, …"` define variables. The DSL currently requires a blank line between each definition, to make it easier to infer the end of the definition. If you forget a blank line, you'll get an error message that suggests the mistake.

Here are the dependencies defined in the file (many are elided):

```
libraryDependencies ++= Seq(
  "com.typesafe.akka"  %% "akka-actor"  % "2.3.4",
  "org.scalatest"      %% "scalatest"   % "2.2.1" % "test",
  "org.scalacheck"     %% "scalacheck"  % "1.11.5" % "test",
  ...
)
```

Sometimes a sequence, `Seq`, is required for a definition, such as the list of dependencies we need, the *Akka actor* library, version 2.3.4, *ScalaTest* and *ScalaCheck* (see "Test-Driven Development in Scala" on page 492), as well as many others we've elided.

Not shown in this file are definitions of Maven-compatible repositories on the Internet to find these dependencies. SBT already knows a list of standard locations, but you can define custom ones, too. There are examples of repository specifications in the *project/ plugins.sbt* file. See the definition of `resolvers`.

The rest of this definition of libraryDependencies, of which a few of the actual definitions, are shown here.

Finally, compiler flags are defined for scalac and javac:

```
scalacOptions = Seq(
  "-encoding", "UTF-8", "-optimise",
  "-deprecation", "-unchecked", "-feature", "-Xlint", "-Ywarn-infer-any")

javacOptions  ++= Seq("-Xlint:unchecked", "-Xlint:deprecation")
```

Not used in our file, but useful to know, is the ability to define multiple statements that are executed automatically when the REPL starts console, for example:

```
initialCommands in console := """
  |import foo.bar._
  |import foo.bar.baz._
  |""".stripMargin
```

These are analogous to the -i file option for scala discussed earlier. There are two other variants of console. The first is consoleQuick (you can also type console-quick), which does not compile your code first. This is useful when you want to try out something but the code isn't currently building (or it will take a long time).

The other variant is consoleProject (or console-project), which ignores your code, but loads with the SBT and build definition on the CLASSPATH, along with some useful imports.

The initialCommands in console also apply to consoleQuick, but you can also define a custom value. In contrast, the initialCommands in console are not used for consoleProject, but you can define a custom value:

```
initialCommands in console := """println("Hello from console")"""
initialCommands in consoleQuick := """println("Hello from consoleQuick")"""
initialCommands in consoleProject := """println("Hello from consoleProject")"""
```

There are corresponding cleanupCommands, too, which are useful for automated cleanup of resources you might always use, e.g., database sessions.

Other Build Tools

The plug-ins for other build tools all exploit the same incremental compilation available in SBT, so build times should be roughly the same, independent of the build tool.

The Scala distribution's *lib/scala-compiler.jar* file includes Ant tasks for scalac, fsc, and scaladoc. They are used very much like the corresponding Java Ant tasks. The *build.xml* configuration required is described at the Scala Ant Tasks page (*http://bit.ly/1wQotKr*), which is old but still valid.

A Scala Maven plug-in is available on the GitHub (*http://bit.ly/1E8x6AW*). It does not require Scala to be installed, because it will download Scala for you.

You can also use the integrated Maven support in Eclipse or IntelliJ.

If you prefer Gradle, details on the Gradle plug-in can be found on Gradle (*http://bit.ly/1q8GQ5O*).

Integration with IDEs and Text Editors

If you come from a Java background, you are probably a little bit spoiled by the rich features of today's Java IDEs. Scala IDE plug-ins have come a long way since the first edition of this book and many professional teams now work exclusively with these tools. Scala support is still not as mature as comparable Java support, but all the essential pieces are there. Most of the IDE Scala plug-ins integrate with SBT or Maven for builds, and provide syntax highlighting, some automated refactorings, and a new *worksheet* feature that is a very nice alternative to the command-line REPL.

If you use Eclipse, see the *Scala IDE* project (*http://scala-ide.org*) for details on installing and using the Scala plug-in into Eclipse. You can also download a complete Eclipse package with the plug-in already configured.

If you prefer Maven over SBT, see this link for details on using Maven for Scala builds within Eclipse (*http://bit.ly/1xIl3WQ*).

Working with the Scala plug-in is very similar to working with the Java tooling in Eclipse. You can create Scala projects and files, run SBT builds and tests, and navigate and refactor code, all within the IDE.

The Eclipse plug-in pioneered a feature not found in the venerable Java plug-in, a *worksheet* that combines the interactivity of the REPL with the convenience of a text editor.

If you have a Scala project open, right-click the top-level project folder to invoke the pop-up menu, then navigate to New → Other. In the "Select a wizard" dialog, open the Scala Wizards folder and select Scala Worksheet. Give it a name and location. The corresponding file will be given the extension *.sc*. The worksheet opens populated with a default `object` definition containing a single `println` statement. You can rename the object and delete the `println` statement if you want.

Now enter statements as you see fit. Every time you save the file, the contents will be evaluated and the results will be shown on the righthand side of the panel. Make some changes and save again. The worksheet behaves like a "window-oriented" REPL. It's particularly nice for experimenting with code snippets and APIs, including Java APIs!

If you use IntelliJ IDEA, open the Plugins preferences and search for the Scala plug-in to install. It offers comparable features to the Eclipse plug-in, including its own version of the worksheet feature.

Finally, NetBeans has a Scala plug-in with an *Interactive Console* feature that is similar to the worksheet feature in Eclipse and IntelliJ IDEA. See SourceForge (*http://bit.ly/1tooTVZ*) for information about the NetBeans plug-in.

Text Editors

While IDEs are popular with Scala developers, you'll also find that many of them prefer using a text editor, like Emacs (*http://www.gnu.org/software/emacs*), Vim (*http://www.vim.org*), and SublimeText (*http://www.sublimetext.com*).

Consult the official documentation and community forums for your favorite editor to find the available plug-ins and configuration options for Scala development. Several editor plug-ins can use the ENSIME plug-in (*https://github.com/ensime*), originally designed for Emacs, which provides some "IDE-like" capabilities, such as navigation and some refactorings.

Test-Driven Development in Scala

Test-driven development (TDD) is an established practice in software development with the goal of driving the design of code through tests. A test for a bit of functionality is written *first*, then the code that makes the test pass is written *afterwards*.

However, TDD is more popular among object-oriented programmers. Functional programmers tend to use the REPL to work out types and algorithms, *then* write the code. This has the disadvantage of not creating a permanent, automated "verifier" suite, like TDD produces, but it's true that functional code is less likely to break over time if it is *pure*. As compensation, many functional programmers will write some tests *after* the code is written, to provide a regression-testing suite.

However you write tests, ScalaTest (*http://www.scalatest.org*) and Specs2 (*http://bit.ly/1vovYm2*) provide DSLs for various testing styles. ScalaTest in particular lets you pick from a variety of styles by mixing in different traits.

In functional languages with rich type systems, like Scala, specifying the types is also seen as a regression-testing capability, one that's exercised every time the compiler is invoked. The goal is to define types that eliminate the possibility of invalid states, when possible.

These types should have well-defined properties. *Property-based testing* or *type-based property-based testing* is another angle on testing popularized by Haskell's Quick-Check (*http://bit.ly/1E8x9Na*) and now ported to many languages. Conditions for a type are specified that should be true for all instances of the type. Recall our discussion in

"Algebraic Data Types" on page 407. A property-based testing tool tries the conditions using a representative sample of instances that are automatically generated. It verifies that the conditions are satisfied for all the instances (in some cases, combinations of them). In contrast, with a conventional TDD tool, it would be up to the test writer to generate a representative set of example instances and try all possibilities.

ScalaCheck (*http://scalacheck.org*) is a Scala port of QuickCheck. Both ScalaTest and Specs2 can drive ScalaCheck property tests. Also, both can be used with JUnit (*http://junit.org*) and TestNG (*http://testng.org*), making it easy to mix Java and Scala testing.

If you work in a Java-only shop and you are interested in trying Scala with minimal risk, consider introducing one or more of these Scala testing tools to test-drive your Java code. It's a low-risk, if limited way to try Scala.

Similarly, all three tools are now supported by the SBT and the plug-ins for Ant, Maven, and Gradle.

The tests provided with the code examples are written in ScalaTest and ScalaCheck, with some JUnit tests to demonstrate Java-Scala interoperability.

All three tools provide excellent examples of Scala *internal* DSLs. Study them for ideas when you want to write your own DSLs. Study the implementations to learn tricks of the trade.

Third-Party Libraries

Since the first edition of this book, the number of third-party libraries written in Scala has grown enormously. Some widely used libraries today didn't exist at that time and some of the libraries that were popular then have waned. This trend will certainly continue, so consider this section to be a snapshot in time. It is also not intended to be comprehensive. Use it as a starting point, then search the Web to see what options exist for your needs.

A good place to start is *http://typelevel.org*, which aggregates a variety of powerful libraries for different purposes.

Of course you can use any JVM library written in another language, too. I won't cover those options.

Let's start with "full stack" libraries and frameworks for building web-based applications. By "full stack," I mean everything from backend services to template engines for HTML,

JavaScript, and CSS. Others are more limited in their scope, focusing on specific tasks. Table 21-6 summarizes the most popular, currently available options.

Table 21-6. Libraries for web-based applications

Name	URL	Description
Play	*http://www.playframework.com/*	Typesafe-supported, full-stack framework with Scala and Java APIs. It is also integrated with Akka.
Lift	*http://liftweb.net/*	The first, and still-popular, full-stack framework.

Table 21-7 describes libraries that are oriented toward backend services.

Table 21-7. Libraries for services

Name	URL	Description
Akka	*http://akka.io*	Comprehensive, actor-based, distributed computing system. Discussed in "Robust, Scalable Concurrency with Actors" on page 429.
Finagle	*http://bit.ly/1vowyQ0*	An extensible system for building JVM services based on functional abstractions. Developed at Twitter, it is used to construct many of their services.[a]
Unfiltered	*http://bit.ly/1s0F5s3*	A toolkit for servicing HTTP requests that provides a consistent API in front of various backend services.
Dispatch	*http://bit.ly/1087FQQ*	API for asynchronous HTTP.

[a] See the Functional Systems report (*http://bit.ly/13pON3l*) for a recent talk describing Finagle and its design philosophy.

Table 21-8 describes various advanced libraries that explore features of the type system, implement functional programming constructs, etc.

Table 21-8. Advanced libraries

Name	URL	Description
Scalaz	*http://bit.ly/1ud2bC9*	The library that pioneered Category Theory concepts in Scala. It also provides handy tools for many design problems. Discussed in "Scalaz Validation" on page 240 and "Category Theory" on page 410.
Shapeless	*http://bit.ly/1rGQfkG*	A library that explores generic programming using type classes and dependent types.

These two libraries are listed at typelevel. Other libraries described there also explore advanced language features.

The *scala.io* (*http://bit.ly/1s0Fef2*) package provides limited capabilities for I/O and the Java APIs are hard to use. Two third-party projects listed in Table 21-9 seek to fill the gap.

Table 21-9. I/O libraries

Name	URL	Description
Scala I/O	*http://bit.ly/1nWmZeh*	A full-featured and popular I/O library.
Rapture I/O	*http://rapture.io/*	A wrapper for `java.io` with a better API.

Table 21-10 describes miscellaneous libraries for particular design problems.

Table 21-10. Miscellaneous libraries

Name	URL	Description
scopt	*https://github.com/scopt/scopt*	A library for command-line parsing.
Typesafe Config	*https://github.com/typesafehub/config*	A configuration library (Java API).
ScalaARM	*http://bit.ly/13oZkdG*	Joshua Suereth's library for automatic resource management.
Typesafe Activator	*https://github.com/typesafehub/activator*	A tool for managing sample Scala projects. Hosted at *http://typesafe.com/activator*.

See Table 18-1 in Chapter 18 for a list of libraries for *Big Data* and mathematics.

Finally, recall from the Preface that we said the Scala 2.11 release has modularized the library to decompose it into smaller JAR files, so library components that are less frequently used are made optional. Table 21-11 describes them. You can find them at the Maven repository (*http://bit.ly/1tI0UB3*).

Table 21-11. Scala 2.11 optional modules

Name	Artifact Name	Description
XML	scala-xml	XML parsing and construction.
Parser Combinators	scala-parser-combinators	Library of combinators for building parsers.
Swing	scala-swing	A Swing library.
Async	scala-async	An asynchronous programming facility for Scala that offers a direct API for working with Futures.
Partest	scala-partest	Testing framework for the Scala compiler and library.
Partest Interface	scala-partest-interface	Testing framework for the Scala compiler and library.

For a comprehensive list of current, third-party libraries, see the Awesome Scala list on GitHub (*https://github.com/lauris/awesome-scala*). Also, *http://ls.implicit.ly/* aggregates many Scala libraries.

Recap and What's Next

This chapter filled in details about the Scala tools you'll use daily. Next, we'll look at how Java and Scala code interoperate with each other.

## CHAPTER 22

Java Interoperability

Of all the alternative JVM languages, Scala's interoperability with Java source code is among the most seamless. This chapter begins with a discussion of interoperability with code written in Java.

Because Scala syntax is primarily a superset of Java syntax, invoking Java code from Scala is usually straightforward. Going the other direction requires that you understand how some Scala features are encoded in byte code while still satisfying the JVM specification. We discuss several of the interoperability issues here.

Using Java Names in Scala Code

Java's rules for type, method, field, and variable names are more restrictive than Scala's rules. So, in *almost* all cases, you can just use the Java names in Scala code. You can create new instances of Java types, call Java methods, and use Java variables and instance fields.

The exception is when a Java name is actually a Scala keyword. As we saw in "Reserved Words" on page 51, "escape" the name with single back ticks. For example, consider the match keyword in Scala and the match method on java.util.Scanner (*http://bit.ly/10a8fgA*). Call the latter with myScanner.`match`.

Java and Scala Generics

All along, we've been using Java types in Scala code, like java.lang.String. You can even use Java *generic* classes, such as Java collections in Scala.

What about using Scala parameterized types in Java? Consider the following JUnit 4 test, which uses scala.collection.mutable.LinkedHashMap (*http://bit.ly/190DOMw*) and scala.Option (*http://bit.ly/12uGdb2*). It shows some of the idiosyncrasies you might encounter:

```
// src/test/java/progscala2/javainterop/SMapTest.java
import org.junit.*;
import org.junit.runner.RunWith;
import org.junit.runners.JUnit4;
import static org.junit.Assert.*;
import scala.*;
import scala.collection.mutable.LinkedHashMap;

public class SMapTest extends org.scalatest.junit.JUnitSuite {        // ❶
  static class Name {
    public String firstName;
    public String lastName;

    public Name(String firstName, String lastName) {
      this.firstName = firstName;
      this.lastName  = lastName;
    }
  }

  LinkedHashMap<Integer, Name> map;

  @Before
  public void setup() {
    map = new LinkedHashMap<Integer, Name>();
    map.update(1, new Name("Dean", "Wampler"));
  }

  @Test
  public void usingMapGetWithOptionName() {                           // ❷
    assertEquals(1, map.size());
    Option<Name> n1 = map.get(1);   // Note: Option<Name>
    assertTrue(n1.isDefined());
    assertEquals("Dean", n1.get().firstName);
  }

  @Test
  public void usingMapGetWithOptionExistential() {                    // ❸
    assertEquals(1, map.size());
    Option<?> n1 = map.get(1);      // Note: Option<?>
    assertTrue(n1.isDefined());
    assertEquals("Dean", ((Name) n1.get()).firstName);
  }
}
```

❶ This JUnit test will be executed by ScalaTest if JUnitSuite is mixed in.

❷ A test using typed values.

❸ A test using existential types for the values.

You can also use Scala's tuple types, although you can't exploit Scala's syntactic sugar, e.g., ("someString", 101):

```
// src/test/java/progscala2/javainterop/ScalaTuples.java
package progscala2.javainterop;
import scala.Tuple2;

public class ScalaTuples {
  public static void main(String[] args) {
    Tuple2 stringInteger = new Tuple2<String,Integer>("one", 2);

    System.out.println(stringInteger);
  }
}
```

However, the FunctionN types are very difficult to use from Java due to "hidden" members that the compiler synthesizes automatically. For example, attempting to compile the following code will fail:

```
// src/test/java/progscala2/javainterop/ScalaFunctions.javaX
package progscala2.javainterop;
import scala.Function1;

public class ScalaFunctions {
  public static void main(String[] args) {
    // Fails to compile, due to missing methods the Scala compiler would add.
    Function1 stringToInteger = new Function1<String,Integer>() {
      public Integer apply(String s) {
        Integer.parseInt(s);
      }
    };

    System.out.println(stringToInteger("101"));
  }
}
```

The compiler will complain that the abstract method apply$mcVJ$sp(long) is undefined. The Scala compiler would generate this for us.

This severely limits the ability to call the higher-order functions in Scala's collections from Java code. You might try to pass a Java 8 *lambda* where a scala.FunctionN is expected, but they are incompatible. (The plan for Scala 2.12 is to unify Scala Functions and Java lambdas, eliminating this incompatibility.)

Hence, if you want to call a Scala API from Java, you can't call *higher-order* methods, those that take functions arguments or return functions.

JavaBean Properties

We saw in Chapter 8 that Scala does not follow the *JavaBeans* conventions for field reader and writer methods, in order to support the more useful *Uniform Access Principle*.

However, there are times when you need JavaBeans accessor methods. For example, some *dependency injection* frameworks exploit them. Also, JavaBeans accessor methods are used by IDEs that support bean "introspection."

Scala solves this problem with an annotation that you can apply to a field, @sca la.beans.BeanProperty (*http://bit.ly/1toozqm*), which tells the compiler to generate JavaBeans-style getter and setter methods. The scala.beans (*http://bit.ly/1G2pzpb*) package also contains other annotations for configuring bean properties, etc.

For Scala 2.10 and earlier, the package name is actually scala.reflect for the JavaBeans annotations.

For example, we can annotate the fields of the Complex class we saw previously:

```
// src/main/scala/progscala2/javainterop/ComplexBean.scala
package progscala2.javainterop

// Scala 2.11. For Scala 2.10 and earlier, use scala.reflect.BeanProperty.
case class ComplexBean(
  @scala.beans.BeanProperty real: Double,
  @scala.beans.BeanProperty imaginary: Double) {

  def +(that: ComplexBean) =
    new ComplexBean(real + that.real, imaginary + that.imaginary)
  def -(that: ComplexBean) =
    new ComplexBean(real - that.real, imaginary - that.imaginary)
}
```

This class has already been compiled by SBT. If you decompile the *ComplexBean.class* file, you'll see the following methods in the output:

```
$ javap -cp target/scala-2.11/classes javainterop.ComplexBean
...
  public double real();
  public double imaginary();
  ...
  public double getReal();
  public double getImaginary();
  ...
}
```

No setters are shown, because the fields are immutable. In contrast, decompiling the original Complex reveals only the real() and imaginary() methods. Hence, even when you use the BeanProperty annotation, you still get the normal field reader and optionally writer methods.

AnyVal Types and Java Primitives

Notice also in the previous `Complex` example that the `Double` fields are compiled to Java primitive `doubles`. All the `AnyVal` types are converted to their corresponding Java primitives. In particular, `Unit` is mapped to `void`.

Scala Names in Java Code

Scala allows more flexible identifiers, e.g., *operator characters* like *, <, etc., which aren't allowed in byte-code identifiers. Hence, these characters are encoded (or "mangled") to satisfy the JVM constraints. They are translated as shown in Table 22-1.

Table 22-1. Encoding of operator characters

Operator	Encoding	Operator	Encoding	Operator	Encoding	Operator	Encoding
=	$eq	>	$greater	<	$less		
+	$plus	-	$minus	*	$times	/	$div
\	$bslash	|	$bar	!	$bang	?	$qmark
:	$colon	%	$percent	^	$up	&	$amp

Recap and What's Next

An important benefit of Scala is that you can continue using existing Java code. Calling Java from Scala is easy (with a few exceptions).

Our next chapter covers application design considerations essential for truly succeeding with Scala.

## CHAPTER 23

Application Design

Until now, we've mostly discussed language features. The applications we've written have been very small, even in Chapter 18. That's a very good thing. Drastic reduction in code size means all the problems of *software development* diminish in significance.

Not all applications can be small, however. This chapter considers the concerns of large applications. We'll discuss a few language and API features that we haven't covered yet, consider a few design patterns and idioms, and discuss architecture approaches, such as the notion of *traits* as *modules* and balancing object-oriented versus functional design techniques.

Recap of What We Already Know

Let's recap a few of the concepts we've covered already that make small design problems easier to solve and thereby provide a stable foundation for applications.

Functional containers

> Most of the book examples have been tiny in large part because we've used the concise, powerful *combinators* provided by collections and other containers. They allow us to implement logic with a minimum amount of code.

Types

> Types enforce constraints. Ideally, they express as much information as possible about the behavior of our programs. For example, using Option (*http://bit.ly/12uGdb2*) can eliminate the use of nulls. See also *Error handling strategies* later in the list. Parameterized types and abstract type members are tools for abstraction and code reuse, such as the *family polymorphism* (or *covariant specialization*) example of a Reader abstraction in "Abstract Types Versus Parameterized Types" on page 67.

Mixin traits
> Traits enable modularized and composable behaviors (see "Traits: Interfaces and "Mixins" in Scala" on page 96 and Chapter 9).

`for` *comprehensions*
> `for` comprehensions provide a convenient "DSL" for working with containers using `flatMap`, `map`, and `filter/withFilter` (Chapter 7).

Pattern matching
> Pattern matching makes quick work of data extraction for processing (Chapter 4).

Implicits
> Implicits solve many design problems, including boilerplate reduction, threading context through method calls, implicit conversions, even some type constraints (Chapter 5).

Fine-grained visibility rules
> Scala's fine-grained visibility rules enable precise control over the visibility of implementation details in APIs, only exposing the public abstractions that clients should use. It takes discipline to do this, but it's worth the effort to prevent avoidable coupling to the API internals, which makes evolution more difficult (Chapter 13).

Package objects
> An alternative to fine-grained visibility controls is putting all implementation constructs in a protected package, then using a top-level package object to expose only the appropriate public abstractions. For example, type members can alias types that would otherwise be hidden (see "Package Objects" on page 66).

Error handling strategies
> `Option` (*http://bit.ly/16yQhkp*), `Either` (*http://bit.ly/1sQZRtp*), `Try` (*http://bit.ly/1DDcSNz*), and Scalaz's `Validation` (*http://bit.ly/10Fhgj8*) types *reify* exceptions and other errors, making them part of the "normal" result returned from functions. The type signature also tells the user what successful or error results to expect (see "Options and Other Container Types" on page 230).
>
> `Future` (*http://bit.ly/1xIkpsr*) exploits `Try` for the same purpose. The actor model implemented in Akka (*http://akka.io*) has a robust, strategic model for supervision of actors and handling failures (Chapter 17).

Let's consider other application-level concerns, starting with *annotations*.

Annotations

Annotations are a technique for tagging declarations with *metadata*, used in many languages. Some Scala annotations provide directives to the compiler. They have been used with object-relational mapping (ORM) frameworks to define persistence mapping information for types. They have been used for *dependency injection*, i.e., wiring components together (for example, see Martin Fowler's blog post (*http://bit.ly/1zmlaf1*)). We've used a few annotations already, such as `scala.annotation.tailrec` (*http://bit.ly/1wkPggo*) to catch the error of thinking a recursive function is tail-recursive when it actually isn't.

Annotations aren't used as often in Scala as they are in Java, but they are still useful. Some Java keywords are implemented as annotations in Scala (e.g., `strictfp`, `native`). Java annotations can be used in Scala code, for example, if you want to use annotations for dependency injection with the Spring Framework (*http://spring.io*) or Guice (*https://github.com/google/guice*).

Scala's annotations are derived from `scala.annotation.Annotation` (*http://bit.ly/1pbhnOm*). Annotations that subclass this abstract class directly are not preserved for the type checker to use nor are they available at runtime. There are two principle subtypes (traits) that remove these limitations. Annotations that extend `scala.annotation.ClassfileAnnotation` (*http://bit.ly/1OFhsPb*) are retained as Java annotations in class files. Annotations that extend `scala.annotation.StaticAnnotation` (*http://bit.ly/1wNImze*) are available to the type checker, even across compilation units.

Table 23-1 lists the annotations that derive from `Annotation` directly (including `ClassfileAnnotation` and `StaticAnnotation`).

Table 23-1. Scala annotations derived from Annotation

Name	Java equivalent	Description
`ClassfileAnnotation`	Annotate with `@Retention(RetentionPolicy.RUNTIME)`	The parent trait for annotations that are stored as Java annotations in the class file for runtime access.
`BeanDescription`	`BeanDescriptor` (class)	An annotation for *JavaBean* types or members that associates a short description (provided as the annotation argument) that will be included when generating bean information.
`BeanDisplayName`	`BeanDescriptor` (class)	An annotation for *JavaBean* types or members that associates a name (provided as the annotation argument) that will be included when generating bean information.
`BeanInfo`	`BeanInfo` (class)	A marker that indicates that a `BeanInfo` class should be generated for the marked Scala class. A `val` becomes a read-only property. A `var` becomes a read-write property. A `def` becomes a method.
`BeanInfoSkip`	*N.A.*	A marker that indicates that bean information should not be generated for the annotated member.
`StaticAnnotation`	Static fields, `@Target(ElementType.TYPE)`	The parent trait of annotations that should be visible across compilation units and define "static" metadata.

Name	Java equivalent	Description
TypeCon straint	N.A.	An annotation trait that can be applied to other annotations that define constraints on a type, relying only on information defined within the type itself, as opposed to external context information where the type is defined or used. The compiler can exploit this restriction to rewrite the constraint.
unchecked	Similar to @Suppress Warnings("un checked")	A marker annotation for the selector in a match statement (e.g., the x in x match {...}) that suppresses a compiler warning if the case clauses are not "exhaustive." You can still have a runtime MatchError occur if a value of x fails to match any of the case clauses. See the upcoming example.

Table 23-2 lists the subtypes of StaticAnnotation, except for those defined in the scala.annotation.meta package, which are listed separately in Table 23-3.

Table 23-2. Scala annotations derived from StaticAnnotation[a]

Name	Java equivalent	Description
BeanProperty	*JavaBean* convention	A marker for a field (including a constructor argument with the val or var keyword) that tells the compiler to generate a JavaBean-style "getter" and "setter" method. The setter is only generated for var declarations. See the discussion in "JavaBean Properties" on page 499.
BooleanBean Property	*same*	Like BeanProperty but the getter method name is isX instead of getX.
cloneable	java.lang.Cloneable (interface)	A class marker indicating that a class can be cloned.
compileTimeOn ly	N.A.	The annotated item won't be visible after compile time. For example, it is used in macros and will disappear after expansion.
deprecated	java.lang.Deprecat ed	A marker for any definition indicating that the defined "item" is obsolete. The compiler will issue a warning when the item is used.
deprecatedName	N.A.	A marker for a parameter name as obsolete. This is needed because calling code can use the parameter name, e.g., val x = foo(y = 1).
elidable	N.A.	Used to suppress code generation, e.g., for unneeded log messages.
implicitNot Found	N.A.	Customize the error message when an implicit value can't be found.
inline	N.A.	A method marker telling the compiler that it should try "especially hard" to inline the method.
native	native (keyword)	A method marker indicating the method is implemented as "native" code. The method body will not be generated by the compiler, but usage of the method will be type checked.
noinline	N.A.	A method marker that prevents the compiler from inlining the method, even when it appears to be safe to do so.
remote	java.rmi.Remote (interface)	A class marker indicating that the class can be invoked from a remote JVM.

Name	Java equivalent	Description
specialized	*N.A.*	An annotation applied to type parameters in parameterized types and methods. It tells the compiler to generate optimized versions of the type or method for the `AnyVal` types corresponding to platform primitive types. Optionally, you can limit the `AnyVal` types for which specialized implementations will be generated.
strictfp	strictfp (keyword)	Turn on strict floating point.
switch	*N.A.*	An annotation to be applied to a match expression, e.g., `(x: @switch) match {...}`. When present, the compiler will verify that the match has been compiled to a table-based or lookup-based `switch` statement. If not, it will issue an error if it instead compiles into a series of conditional expressions, which are less efficient.
tailrec	*N.A.*	A method annotation that tells the compiler to verify that the method will be compiled with *tail-call optimization*. If it is present, the compiler will issue an error if the method cannot be optimized into a loop. This can also happen when a method is overridable, because it isn't `private` or `final`.
throws	throws (keyword)	Indicates which exceptions are thrown by the annotated method. See the upcoming discussion.
transient	transient (keyword)	Marks a field as "transient."
unchecked	*N.A.*	Limit compiler checks, such as looking for exhaustive match expressions.
uncheckedStable	*N.A.*	A marker for a value that is assumed to be stable even though its type is volatile.
uncheckedVariance	*N.A.*	A marker for a type argument that is volatile, when it is used in a parameterized type, to suppress variance checking.
unspecialized	*N.A.*	Limit generation of specialized forms.
varargs	*N.A.*	For a method with repeated parameters, generate a Java-style varargs method for interoperability.
volatile	volatile (keyword, for fields only)	A marker for an individual field or a whole type, which affects all fields, indicating that the field may be modified by a separate thread.

[a] Except for the `annotation.meta` annotations, which are listed in the next table.

There are additional `StaticAnnotations` defined in `annotation.meta` (*http://bit.ly/1G2p0vB*) for fine-grained control of annotation application in byte code.

Table 23-3. Scala meta annotations

Name	Description
beanGetter	Retrict an annotation given with `@BeanProperty` to just appear on the generated getter method (e.g., `getX` for field x).
beanSetter	Retrict an annotation given with `@BeanProperty` to just appear on the generated setter method.
companionClass	The Scala compiler creates an implicit conversion method for the corresponding implicit class.
companionMethod	Like `companionClass`, but also apply the annotation to the conversion method generated.

Name	Description
companionObject	Unused. Intended for case classes where a companion object is automatically generated.
field	Applied to the definition of an annotation to specify its default target, a field in this case. The default can be overridden using the previous annotations in this table.
getter	Like field, but for getter methods.
languageFeature	Used for language features in scala.language (*http://bit.ly/1nWlrkz*).
param	Like field, but for param methods.
setter	Like field, but for setter methods.

Finally, Table 23-4 lists the single subtype of ClassfileAnnotation.

Table 23-4. Scala annotations derived from ClassfileAnnotation

Name	Java equivalent	Description
SerialVersionUID	serialVersionUID *static* field in a class	Defines a globally unique ID for serialization purposes. The annotation's constructor takes a Long argument for the UID.

Declaring an annotation in Scala doesn't require a special syntax as in Java. Here is the definition of implicitNotFound (*http://bit.ly/1toohzB*):

```
package scala.annotation

final class implicitNotFound(msg: String) extends StaticAnnotation {}
```

Traits as Modules

Java offers classes and packages as units of modularity, with JAR files being the most coarse-grained *component* abstraction. A problem with packages has always been the limited visibility controls. It just hasn't been practical enough to hide implementation types from public visibility, so few people have done it. Scala makes this possible with its richer visibility rules, but they aren't widely used. Package objects are another way to define what clients should use versus what they shouldn't.

The other important goal of modularity is to enable composition. Scala's traits provide excellent support for mixin components, as we've seen. In fact, Scala embraces traits, rather than classes, as the mechanism for defining modules.

We sketched an example in "Self-Type Annotations" on page 376 using the *Cake Pattern*. Here are the important parts of that example:

```
// src/main/scala/progscala2/typesystem/selftype/selftype-cake-pattern.sc

trait Persistence { def startPersistence(): Unit }    // ❶
trait Midtier { def startMidtier(): Unit }
trait UI { def startUI(): Unit }
```

```
trait Database extends Persistence {                          // ❷
  def startPersistence(): Unit = println("Starting Database")
}
trait BizLogic extends Midtier {
  def startMidtier(): Unit = println("Starting BizLogic")
}
trait WebUI extends UI {
  def startUI(): Unit = println("Starting WebUI")
}

trait App { self: Persistence with Midtier with UI =>        // ❸
  def run() = {
    startPersistence()
    startMidtier()
    startUI()
  }
}

object MyApp extends App with Database with BizLogic with WebUI  // ❹
```

❶   Define traits for the persistence, middle, and UI tiers of the application.

❷   Implement the "concrete" behaviors as traits.

❸   Define a trait (or it could be an abstract class) that defines the "skeleton" of how the tiers glue together. For this simple example, the run method just starts each tier.

❹   Define the MyApp object that extends App and mixes in the three concrete traits that implement the required behaviors.

Each trait—Persistence, Midtier, and UI—functions as a *module* abstraction. The concrete implementations are cleanly separated from them. They are composed to build the application. The self-type annotation specifies the wiring.

The Cake Pattern has been used as an alternative to dependency injection mechanisms (*http://bit.ly/1tHZ8Qd*). It has been used to construct the Scala compiler itself (Martin Odersky and Matthias Zenger, Scalable Component Abstractions, *OOPSLA '05*).

However, there are drawbacks. Nontrivial dependency graphs in "cakes" frequently lead to problems with initialization order of the dependencies. Workarounds include lazy vals and using methods rather than fields, both of which defer initialization until a dependent is (hopefully) initialized.

The net effect has been less emphasis in the use of the Cake Pattern in many applications, including the compiler. The pattern is still useful, but use it wisely.

Design Patterns

Design patterns have taken a beating lately. Critics dismiss them as workarounds for missing language features. Indeed, some of the *Gang of Four* patterns[1] are not really needed in Scala, because native features provide better alternatives. Other patterns are part of the language itself, so no special coding is needed. Of course, patterns are frequently misused or overused, becoming a panacea for every design problem, but that's not the fault of the patterns themselves.

Design patterns document recurring, widely useful ideas. Patterns become a useful part of the vocabulary that developers use to communicate. I argued in "Category Theory" on page 410 that *categories* are design patterns adopted from mathematics into functional programming.

Let's list the *Gang of Four* patterns and discuss the particular implications for Scala and toolkits like Akka, such as specific examples of this pattern in action (whether the pattern name is used or not). I'll follow the categories in the book: *creational*, *structural*, and *behavioral* patterns.

Creational Patterns

Abstract Factory

> An abstraction for constructing instances from a type family without explicitly specifying the types. The `apply` methods in `objects` can be used for this purpose, where they instantiate an instance of an appropriate type based on the arguments to the method. The functions passed to `Monad.flatMap` and the `apply` method defined by *Applicative* also abstract over construction.

Builder

> Separates construction of a complex object from its representation so the same process can be used for different representations. A classic Scala example is `collection.generic.CanBuildFrom` (*http://bit.ly/1zRqZC9*), used to allow combinator methods like `map` to build a new collection of the same type as the input collection.

Factory Method

> Define a method that subtypes override (or implement) to decide what type to instantiate and how. `CanBuildFrom.apply` is an abstract method for constructing a builder that can construct an instance. Subtypes and particular instances provide the details. `Applicative.apply` provides a similar abstraction.

---

1. See Erich Gamma et al., *Design Patterns: Elements of Reusable Object-Oriented Software*, Addison-Wesley, 1995.

Prototype

Start with a prototypical instance and copy it with optional modifications to construct new instances. Case class `copy` methods are a great example, where the user can clone an instance while specifying arguments for changes. We mentioned, but didn't cover *Lenses* in "Category Theory" on page 410. They provide an alternative technique for getting or setting (with copying) a value nested in an arbitrarily deep graph.

Singleton

Ensure a type has only one instance and all users of the type can access that instance. Scala implemented this pattern as a first-class feature of the language with `objects`.

Structural Patterns

Adapter

Create an interface a client expects around another abstraction, so the latter can be used by the client. In "Traits as Mixins" on page 272 and later in "Structural Types" on page 381, we discussed the trade-offs of several possible implementations of the *Observer* pattern, specifically the coupling between the abstraction and potential observers. We started with a trait that the observer was expected to implement. Then we replaced it with a *structural type* to reduce the dependency, effectively saying a potential observer didn't have to implement a trait, just provide a specific method. Finally, we noted that we could completely decouple the observer if we used an anonymous function. This function is an *adapter*. It is called by the subject, but internally it can invoke any observer logic necessary.

Bridge

Decouple an abstraction from its implementation, so they can vary independently. *Type classes* provide an interesting example that takes this principle to a logical extreme. Not only is the abstraction removed from types that might need it, only to be added back in when needed, but the implementation of a type class abstraction for a given type can also be defined separately.

Composite

Tree structures of instances that represent part-whole hierarchies with uniform treatment of individual instances or composites. Functional code tends to avoid ad hoc hierarchies of types, preferring to use generic structures like trees instead, providing uniform access and the full suite of combinators for manipulation of the tree. *Lenses* are a tool for working with nontrivial composites.

Decorator

Attach additional responsibilities to an object "dynamically." Type classes do this at compile time, without modifying the original source code of the type. For true runtime flexibility, the `Dynamic` (*http://bit.ly/1pbhB8b*) trait might be useful. *Monads* and *Applicatives* are also useful for "decorating" a value or computation, respectively.

Facade

Provide a uniform interface to a set of interfaces in a subsystem, making the subsystem easier to use. Package objects support this pattern. They can expose only the types and behaviors that should be public.

Flyweight

Use sharing to support a large number of fine-grained objects efficiently. The emphasis on immutability in functional programming makes this straightforward to implement. An important set of examples are the *persistent data structures*, like `Vector` (*http://bit.ly/1bgKyXi*).

Proxy

Provide a surrogate to another instance to control access to it. Package objects support this goal at a course-grained level. Note that immutable instances are not at risk of corruption by clients, so the need for control is reduced.

Behavioral Patterns

Chain of Responsibility

Avoid coupling a sender and receiver. Allow a sequence of potential receivers to try handling the request until the first one succeeds. This is exactly how pattern matching works. The description is even more apt in the context of Akka `receive` blocks, where "sender" and "receiver" aren't just metaphors.

Command

Reify a request for service. This enables requests to be queued, supports undo, replay, etc. This is explicitly how Akka works, although undo and replay are not supported, but could be in principle. A classic use for *Monad* is an extension of this problem, sequencing "command" steps in a predictable order (important for languages that are lazy by default) with careful management of state transitions.

Interpreter

Define a language and a way of interpreting expressions in the language. The term *DSL* emerged after the *Gang of Four* book. We discussed several approaches in Chapter 20.

Iterator

Allow traversal through a collection without exposing implementation details. Almost all work with functional containers is done this way.

Mediator

Avoid having instances interact directly by using a mediator to implement the interaction, allowing that interaction to evolve separately. ExecutionContext (*http://bit.ly/1q8FoQZ*) could be considered an example of a mediator, because it is used to handle coordination of asynchronous computations, e.g., in Futures, without the latter having to know any of the mechanics of coordination. Similarly, messages between Akka actors are mediated by the runtime system with minimal connections between the actors. While a specific ActorRef (*http://bit.ly/1u0MFIS*) is needed to send a message, it can be determined through means like name lookup, without having to hardcode dependencies programmatically, and it provides a level of indirection between actors.

Momento

Capture an instance's state so it can be stored and used to restore the state later. *Memoization* is made easier by pure functions. A *Decorator* could be used to add memoization, with the additional benefit that reinvocation of the function can be avoided if it's called with arguments previously used; the *memo* is returned instead.

Observer

Set up a one-to-many dependency between a *subject* and *observers* of its state. When state changes occur, notify the observers. We discussed this pattern for *Adapter* in the previous section.

State

Allow an instance to alter its behavior when its state changes. When values are immutable, new instances are constructed to represent the new state. In principle, the new instance could exhibit different behaviors, although usually these changes are carefully constrained by a common supertype abstraction. The more general case is a *state machine*. We saw in "Robust, Scalable Concurrency with Actors" on page 429 that Akka actors and the actor model in general can implement state machines.

Strategy

Reify a family of related algorithms so that they can be used interchangeably. Higher-order functions make this easy. For example, when calling map, the actual "algorithm" used to transform each element is a caller's choice.

Template Method

Define the skeleton of an algorithm as a final method, with calls to other methods that can be overridden in subclasses to customize the behavior. This is one of my favorite patterns, because it is far more principled and safe than overriding concrete methods, as I discussed in "Avoid Overriding Concrete Members" on page 312. Note that an alternative to defining abstract methods for overriding is to make the template method a higher-order function and then pass in functions to do the customization.

Visitor

Insert a protocol into an instance so that other code can access the internals for operations that aren't supported by the type. This is a terrible pattern because it hacks the public interface and complicates the implementation. Fortunately, we have far better options. Defining an `unapply` or `unapplySeq` method lets the type designer define a low-overhead protocol for exposing only the internal state that's appropriate. Pattern matching uses this feature to extract these values and implement new functionality. Type classes are another way of adding new behaviors to existing types, although they don't provide access to internals that might be needed in special cases. Of course, needing such access to internal state is a serious *design smell*.

Better Design with Design by Contract

Our types make statements about allowed states for our programs. We use test-driven development (TDD) or other test approaches to verify behaviors that our types can't specify. Well before TDD and functional programming went mainstream, Bertrand Meyer described an approach called *Design by Contract* (DbC), which he implemented in the Eiffel language (*http://bit.ly/1OFhJln*). The idea has fallen out of favor, but there are new incarnations built around the idea of *contracts* between clients and services. This is a very useful metaphor for thinking about design. We'll mostly use DbC terminology.

A "contract" of a module can specify three types of conditions:

1. What constraints exist for inputs passed to a module, in order for it to successfully perform a service? These constraints are called *preconditions*. If the service doesn't behave as a "pure" function, the constraints might also cover system requirements and external data. Preconditions constrain what clients can do.

2. What constraints exist for the results the module guarantees to deliver, assuming the preconditions were satisfied? These are *postconditions* and they constrain the service.

3. What *invariants* must be true before *and* after an invocation of a service?

In addition, Design by Contract requires that these contractual constraints must be specified as executable code, so they can be enforced automatically at runtime. If a condition fails, the system terminates immediately, forcing you to find and fix the underlying cause immediately. (I once worked on a project that used DbC successfully until the team leadership decided that abrupt termination was "inconvenient." Within a few months, the logs were full of contract failures that nobody bothered fixing anymore.)

It's been conventional to only test the conditions during testing, but not production, both to remove the extra overhead and to avoid crashing in production if a condition fails. Note that the *let it crash* philosophy of the actor model turns this on its head. If a condition fails at runtime, *shouldn't it crash and let the runtime trigger recovery*?

Scala doesn't provide explicit support for Design by Contract, but there are several methods in `Predef` (*http://bit.ly/1086O2z*) that can be used for this purpose: `assert`, `assume`, `require`. The following example shows how to use `require` and `assert` for contract enforcement:

```
// src/main/scala/progscala2/appdesign/dbc/BankAccount.sc

case class Money(val amount: Double) {                        // ❶
  require(amount >= 0.0, s"Negative amount $amount not allowed")

  def +  (m: Money): Money = Money(amount + m.amount)
  def -  (m: Money): Money = Money(amount - m.amount)
  def >= (m: Money): Boolean = amount >= m.amount
}

case class BankAccount(balance: Money) {

  def debit(amount: Money) = {                                // ❷
    assert(balance >= amount,
      s"Overdrafts are not permitted, balance = $balance, debit = $amount")
    new BankAccount(balance - amount)
  }

  def credit(amount: Money) = {                               // ❸
    new BankAccount(balance + amount)
  }
}
```

❶ Encapsulate money, only allowing positive amounts using `require`, a precondition. (See the following discussion about production runs.)

❷ Don't allow the balance to go negative. This is really an invariant condition of `BankAccount`, which is why I used `assert` instead of `require`.

❸ No contract violations are expected to occur, at least in this simple example without transactions, etc.

We can try it with the following script:

```
import scala.util.Try

Seq(-10, 0, 10) foreach (i => println(f"$i%3d: ${Try(Money(i))}"))
```

```
val ba1 = BankAccount(Money(10.0))
val ba2 = ba1.credit(Money(5.0))
val ba3 = ba2.debit(Money(8.5))
val ba4 = Try(ba3.debit(Money(10.0)))

println(s"""
  |Initial state: $ba1
  |After credit of $$5.0: $ba2
  |After debit of $$8.5: $ba3
  |After debit of $$10.0: $ba4""".stripMargin)
```

The `println` output is the following:

```
-10: Failure(java.lang.IllegalArgumentException:
       requirement failed: Negative amount -10.0 not allowed)
  0: Success($0.0)
 10: Success($10.0)

Initial state: BankAccount($10.0)
After credit of $5.0: BankAccount($15.0)
After debit of $8.5: BankAccount($6.5)
After debit of $10.0: Failure(java.lang.AssertionError:
  assertion failed: Overdrafts are not permitted, balance = $6.5, debit = $10.0)
```

Each of the `assert`, `assume`, and `require` methods have two overloaded versions, like this pair for `assert`:

```
final def assert(assertion: Boolean): Unit
final def assert(assertion: Boolean, message: => Any): Unit
```

If the predicate argument is false, the message is used as part of the failure message in the second version. Otherwise a default message is used.

The `assert` and `assume` methods behave identically. The names signal different intent. Both throw `AssertionError` on failure and both can be completely removed from the byte code if you compile with the option `-Xelide-below ASSERTION` (or a higher value).

The `require` methods are intended for testing method arguments (including constructors). They throw `IllegalArgumentException` on failure and their code generation is *not* affected by the `-Xelide-below` option. Therefore, in our `Money` type, the `require` check will never be turned off, even in a production build that turns off `assert` and `assume`. If that's not what you want, use one of the latter two methods instead.

Type system enforcing is ideal, when you can achieve it, but the Scala type system can't enforce all constraints we might like. Hence, TDD (or variants) and assertion checks inspired by Design by Contract will remain useful tools for building correct software.

The Parthenon Architecture

The most seductive idea in object-oriented programming has been called *the ubiquitous language*, meaning that all team members, from business stakeholders to QA, use the same domain language to promote effective communication (the term was coined by Eric Evans in his book *Domain Driven Design*, Prentice-Hall, 2003). In practical terms, this means that all domain concepts are implemented as types with ad hoc behaviors, and they are used liberally in the code.

Functional code doesn't look like this. You'll see relatively few "atomic" data types and containers, all with precise algebraic properties. The code is concise and precise, important benefits for meeting schedule and quality demands.

The problem with *implementing* many real-world domain concepts is their inherent *contextual* nature. Your idea of a `Taxpayer` is different from mine, because you have different use cases (or user stories or requirements or whatever term you prefer) to implement than I do. If we boil our problems down to their essence, we have a bunch of numbers that we need to ingest from a data store, process them arithmetically according to some specific rules governed by tax law, and then report the results. *All programs are CRUD* (create, read, update, and delete)…I'm exaggerating, but only a little bit.

The rules I follow for deciding whether or not to implement a domain concept in code are the following:

- Compared to using generic types like tuples or maps:
  - The concept improves encapsulation significantly.
  - The concept clarifies human understanding of the code.
- The concept has well-defined, mathematical properties.
- The concept improves correctness, such as restricting the allowed values compared to more general types.

Should *money* be its own type? Yes, because it has well-defined properties. With a `Money` type, I can do algebra and enforce rules that the enclosed `Double` or `BigDecimal` is nonnegative, that rounding to the nearest penny is done according to standard accounting rules, and so forth.

Even `USZipCode` has well-defined properties. You don't do arithmetic with zip codes, but the allowed values can be constrained to the five or five plus four digits recognized by the US Postal Service.

I'll use value classes (subtypes of `AnyVal`) for these types when I can, for efficiency.

However, for `Taxpayer` and other vague concepts, I'll use key-value maps, collections, or tuples with just the data fields I need for the use case I'm implementing.

But is there more we can do to gain the benefits of *ubiquitous language* without the drawbacks? I've been thinking about an architectural style that tries to do just that.

 The following discussion is a sketch of an idea that is mostly theoretical and untested.

It combines four layers:

A DSL for the ubiquitous language
> It is used to declare use cases. The UI (user interface) design is here, too, because it is also a tool for communication and hence a language.

A library for the DSL
> The implementation of the DSL, including the types implemented for some domain concepts, the UI, etc.

Use case logic
> Functional code that implements each use case. It remains as focused and concise as possible, relying primarily on standard library types, and a bare minimum of the domain-oriented types. Because this code is so concise, most of the code for each use case is a *single vertical slice through the system*.

Core libraries
> The Scala standard library, Akka, Play, APIs for logging, database access, etc., plus any reusable code extracted from the use case implementations.

The picture that emerges reminds me of classical Greek temples, because of the columns of code that implement each use case. So, I'll be pretentious and call it *The Parthenon Architecture* (see Figure 23-1).

The temple foundation represents the core libraries. The columns represent the use case implementations. The *entablature* represents the domain-support library, including the DSL implementation and UI. The *pediment* at the top represents the DSL code written by users to implement each use case. For more on temple terms, see the Wikipedia page (*http://bit.ly/1xIkJHH*).

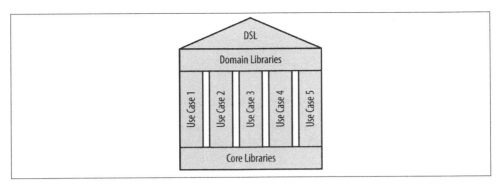

Figure 23-1. The Parthenon Architecture

What's new and potentially controversial about this idea is the columns of use case code that appear to reject reuse. There is a reusable library of domain-centric code on the top and various libraries on the bottom, but it looks like the *Stovepipe* antipattern (*http:// bit.ly/1s0EuXt*).

However, every design choice has advantages and disadvantages. The advantage of reuse is the removal of duplication, but the disadvantage, especially in object-oriented systems, is the tendency to create choke points, where many code paths flow through the same reusable objects. This becomes a problem if they contain evolving state. It becomes difficult to separate the logic of one use case from another, which makes independent development harder and limits the ability of horizontal scaling by splitting use cases across multiple processes.

Also, the functional code for each use case should be very small, like many of the examples in this book, so that trivial duplication is not worth the cost of removal. Instead, the simple, in-place data flow logic is easy to understand, test, and evolve.

Let's sketch an example using the payroll external DSL from "External DSLs with Parser Combinators" on page 473. It will be a little convoluted, because we're going to read comma-separated data for a list of employees, create strings from it in the DSL, parse the strings to create the data structures we need, and finally proceed to implement two use cases: a report with each employee's pay check and a report showing the totals for the pay period. Using intermediate strings like this doesn't make sense for a real application, but it lets us reuse the previous DSL without modification and it illustrates the points:

```
// src/main/scala/progscala2/appdesign/parthenon/PayrollUseCases.scala
package progscala2.appdesign.parthenon
import progscala2.dsls.payroll.parsercomb.dsl.PayrollParser
import progscala2.dsls.payroll.common._

object PayrollParthenon {                                          // ❶
  val dsl = """biweekly {
```

```
    federal tax          %f   percent,
    state tax            %f   percent,
    insurance premiums   %f   dollars,
    retirement savings   %f   percent
  }"""
                                                            // ❷
private def readData(inputFileName: String): Seq[(String, Money, String)] =
  for {
    line <- scala.io.Source.fromFile(inputFileName).getLines.toVector
    if line.matches("\\s*#.*") == false   // skip comments
  } yield toRule(line)

private def toRule(line: String): (String, Money, String) = {    // ❸
  val Array(name, salary, fedTax, stateTax, insurance, retirement) =
    line.split("""\s*,\s*""")
  val ruleString = dsl.format(
    fedTax.toDouble, stateTax.toDouble,
    insurance.toDouble, retirement.toDouble)
  (name, Money(salary.toDouble), ruleString)
}

private val parser = new PayrollParser                      // ❹

private def toDeduction(rule: String) =
  parser.parseAll(parser.biweekly, rule).get

private type EmployeeData = (String, Money, Deductions)      // ❺
                                                            // ❻
private def processRules(inputFileName: String): Seq[EmployeeData] = {
  val data = readData(inputFileName)
  for {
    (name, salary, rule) <- data
    deductions       = toDeduction(rule)
  } yield (name, salary, toDeduction(rule))
}
                                                            // ❼
def biweeklyPayrollPerEmployeeReportUseCase(data: Seq[EmployeeData]): Unit ={
  val fmt  = "%-10s %6.2f  %5.2f  %5.2f\n"
  val head = "%-10s %-7s  %-5s     %s\n"
  println("\nBiweekly Payroll:")
  printf(head, "Name", "Gross", "Net", "Deductions")
  printf(head, "----", "-----", "---", "----------")
  for {
    (name, salary, deductions) <- data
    gross = deductions.gross(salary.amount)
    net   = deductions.net(salary.amount)
  } printf(fmt, name, gross, net, gross - net)
}
                                                            // ❽
def biweeklyPayrollTotalsReportUseCase(data: Seq[EmployeeData]): Unit = {
  val (gross, net) = (data foldLeft (0.0, 0.0)) {
    case ((gross, net), (name, salary, deductions)) =>
```

```
      val g = deductions.gross(salary.amount)
      val n = deductions.net(salary.amount)
      (gross + g, net + n)
    }
    printf("\nBiweekly Totals: Gross %7.2f, Net %6.2f, Deductions: %6.2f\n",
      gross, net, gross - net)
  }

  def main(args: Array[String]) = {
    val inputFileName =
      if (args.length > 0) args(0) else "misc/parthenon-payroll.txt"
    val data = processRules(inputFileName)

    biweeklyPayrollTotalsReportUseCase(data)
    biweeklyPayrollPerEmployeeReportUseCase(data)
  }
}
```

❶ Now use the DSL to define a format string, where the actual numbers will be loaded at runtime.

❷ Read the data from an input file, remove comment lines (those that start with optional whitespace followed by the # character), and then convert each employee record to a rule using the DSL. We're ignoring error handling throughout for simplicity and we're reusing the Money class we used in the Design by Contract discussion (not shown).

❸ Split each record into fields, convert the numbers to Doubles, and format the rule string for each employee. Return the employee name, salary, and rule.

❹ Construct a DSL parser and use it to parse the rule string, like before.

❺ Define a type alias to improve code readability, an economical solution that we only need internally.

❻ Read the data file and extract the name, salary, and the Deductions per employee.

❼ Use case: report on each employee's gross salary, net salary, and deductions for the biweekly pay period.

❽ Use case: report on the total gross salary, net salary, and deductions for all employees for the biweekly pay period.

By default, it loads a data file in the *misc* directory. If you run it in sbt with the command run-main progscala2.appdesign.parthenon.PayrollParthenon, you get the following output for the two use cases invoked in main:

```
Biweekly Totals: Gross 19230.77, Net 12723.08, Deductions: 6507.69

Biweekly Payroll:
Name       Gross    Net    Deductions
----       -----    ---    ----------
```

```
Joe CEO      7692.31  5184.62  2507.69
Jane CFO     6923.08  4457.69  2465.38
Phil Coder   4615.38  3080.77  1534.62
```

Though there is plenty of room for refinement, this rough sketch illustrates how the actual use case implementations (methods) can be small, independent "columns" of code. They use a few, choice domain concepts from the "top" library, and the core infrastructure provided by the Scala API from the "bottom" library.

Recap and What's Next

We discussed several pragmatic issues for application development, including design patterns and Design by Contract. We explored an architecture model I've been considering, which I pretentiously called the Parthenon Architecture.

We've come to our last chapter, a look at Scala's facilities for reflection and metaprogramming.

## CHAPTER 24

Metaprogramming: Macros and Reflection

Metaprogramming is programming that manipulates programs, rather than data. In some languages, the difference between *programming* and *metaprogramming* isn't all that significant. Lisp dialects, for example, use the same *S-expression* representation for code and data, a property called *homoiconicity*. So, manipulating code is straightforward and not uncommon. In statically typed languages like Java and Scala, metaprogramming is less common, but it's still useful for solving many design problems.

The word *reflection* is also sometimes used to mean metaprogramming in general. That is the sense of the term for the Scala reflection library. However, sometimes the term has the narrower meaning of runtime "introspection" of code with limited or no modifications.

In languages like Scala where code is compiled and then run, versus being interpreted "on the fly" like many dynamically typed languages, there is a distinction between compile-time and runtime metaprogramming. In compile-time metaprogramming, any invocations occur just before or during compilation. The classic C-language preprocessor is an example of processing that transforms the *source code* before it's compiled.

Scala's metaprogramming support happens at compile time using a *macro* facility. Macros work more like constrained compiler plug-ins, because they manipulate the *abstract syntax tree* (AST) produced from the parsed source code. Macros are invoked to manipulate the AST before the final compilation phases leading to byte-code generation.

The Java reflection library and Scala's expanded library offer runtime reflection.

Scala's reflection API, which includes the macro support, is the most rapidly evolving part of Scala. Because it's a fast-moving target, we'll focus on the most stable parts: runtime reflection and a macro tool called *quasiquotes*. However, we'll end with a full macro example using the current macro API.

A next-generation macro facility is being developed. The project is called *Scala Meta* (*http://scalameta.org*). At the time of this writing, a preview release is forthcoming. You should look there for the latest information about macros as they will appear in a subsequent release of Scala. For the current macro implementation for Scala 2.10 and 2.11, see *http://scalamacros.org* and Macro Paradise (*http://bit.ly/1xIibcu*), the incubator project for the current macro system.

We'll begin with some useful REPL tools for understanding the types of expressions, then explore runtime reflection, followed by quasiquotes with a final macro example.

Tools for Understanding Types

The REPL has a `:type` command for printing type information:

```
scala> if (true) false else 11.1
res0: AnyVal = false

scala> :type if (true) false else 11.1
AnyVal

scala> :type -v if (true) false else 11.1
// Type signature
AnyVal

// Internal Type structure
TypeRef(TypeSymbol(abstract class AnyVal extends Any))
```

The `:type` command just shows the type. Usually the REPL echoes the type anyway. However, the `-v` (verbose) option also shows the "internal type structure." The `scala.reflect.api.Types.TypeRef` (*http://bit.ly/1xIibJp*) and `scala.reflect.api.Symbols.TypeSymbol` (*http://bit.ly/1rGtvkG*) types are defined in the reflection API, which is now a separate library from the core standard library. The *Scaladocs* can be found at *http://bit.ly/1wQkYDN*.

Runtime Reflection

Whereas compile-time reflection is used for manipulating code, runtime reflection is used primarily to "tweak" language semantics (within limits) and to load code that isn't known at compile time, so-called *extreme late binding*.

For example, which instance to use for a particular feature might be specified dynamically through properties or command-line arguments. The reflection API is used to locate the corresponding types in the available byte code found on the CLASSPATH, and if found, construct instances. Tools like IDEs can use reflection to discover and load plug-ins. IDEs often use reflection to learn about code in projects and libraries, to support code completion, type checking, etc. Byte-code tools might use reflection to look for security vulnerabilities and other problems.

Reflecting on Types

You can use Java's reflection API, such as methods in java.lang.Class (*http://bit.ly/1ucWSml*):

```
// src/main/scala/progscala2/metaprogramming/reflect.sc

scala> import scala.language.existentials
import scala.language.existentials

scala> trait T[A] {
     |    val vT: A
     |    def mT = vT
     | }
defined trait T

scala> class C(foo: Int) extends T[String] {
     |    val vT = "T"
     |    val vC = "C"
     |    def mC = vC
     |
     |    class C2
     | }
defined class C

scala> val c = new C(3)
c: C = $anon$1@5a58e6a4

scala> val clazz = classOf[C]              // Scala method: classOf[C]
clazz: Class[C] = class C

scala> val clazz2 = c.getClass             // Method from java.lang.Object
clazz2: Class[_ <: C] = class $anon$1

scala> val name  = clazz.getName
name: String = C

scala> val methods = clazz.getMethods
methods: Array[java.lang.reflect.Method] =
  Array(public java.lang.String C.mC(), public java.lang.Object C.vT(), ...)

scala> val ctors = clazz.getConstructors
ctors: Array[java.lang.reflect.Constructor[_]] = Array(public C(int))

scala> val fields = clazz.getFields
fields: Array[java.lang.reflect.Field] = Array()

scala> val annos = clazz.getAnnotations
```

```
annos: Array[java.lang.annotation.Annotation] = Array()

scala> val parentInterfaces = clazz.getInterfaces
parentInterfaces: Array[Class[_]] = Array(interface T)

scala> val superClass = clazz.getSuperclass
superClass: Class[_ >: C] = class java.lang.Object

scala> val typeParams = clazz.getTypeParameters
typeParams: Array[java.lang.reflect.TypeVariable[Class[C]]] = Array()
```

These methods are only available on subtypes of AnyRef. Note that getFields does *not* appear to recognize the fields in C for Scala types!

Predef defines methods for testing whether an object matches a type and for casting an object to a type:

```
scala> c.isInstanceOf[String]
<console>:13: warning: fruitless type test: a value of type C cannot
  also be a String (the underlying of String)
              c.isInstanceOf[String]
                      ^
res0: Boolean = false

scala> c.isInstanceOf[C]
res1: Boolean = true

scala> c.asInstanceOf[T[AnyRef]]
res2: T[AnyRef] = C@499a497b
```

Java uses operators that are language keywords for these tasks. The Scala method names are deliberately verbose to discourage their use! Other language features, especially pattern matching, are better alternatives.

Class Tags, Type Tags, and Manifests

The core Scala 2.11 library has a small reflection API, while the more advanced reflection features are in the separate library. Let's investigate ClassTag (*http://bit.ly/1tHWxpq*) in the core library, which is a tool for retaining some information that is otherwise lost to *type erasure*, the "feature" of the JVM where it doesn't retain the values used for type parameters when instantiating parameterized types.

We saw in "More on Type Matching" on page 122 that erasure prevents us from pattern matching on the types used as type parameters in parameterized types. We used an ugly workaround then, where we first matched on the collection and then on the types within it. We also can't overload methods where the only difference between them is the type parameter for a parameterized type used in the signatures.

ClassTag provides a better workaround that we'll now examine:

```
// src/main/scala/progscala2/metaprogramming/match-types.sc
import scala.reflect.ClassTag

def useClassTag[T : ClassTag](seq: Seq[T]): String = seq match { // ❶
  case Nil => "Nothing"
  case head +: _ => implicitly(seq.head).getClass.toString        // ❷
}

def check(seq: Seq[_]): String =                                   // ❸
  s"Seq: ${useClassTag(seq)}"

Seq(Seq(5.5,5.6,5.7), Seq("a", "b"),                               // ❹
    Seq(1, "two", 3.14), Nil) foreach {
  case seq: Seq[_] => println("%20s:  %s".format(seq, check(seq)))
  case x           => println("%20s:  %s".format(x, "unknown!"))
}
```

❶   Use a context bound with `ClassTag`.

❷   If we have a nonempty list, use `implicitly` to get the implicit `ClassTag` instance
    and call its `apply` method on `seq.head` to determine its type. The flaw of this
    method is that it returns the first element's type, but if a sequence of mixed types
    is passed in, a *least upper bound* supertype is actually the correct type to return.
    We'll fix this bug shortly.

❸   A helper method to try both functions.

❹   Test the implementation with some examples.

The output is the following, where now we know the type of each sequence's elements:

```
 List(5.5, 5.6, 5.7):  Seq: class java.lang.Double
         List(a, b):  Seq: class java.lang.String
  List(1, two, 3.14):  Seq: class java.lang.Integer
            List():  Seq: Nothing
```

However, as mentioned, it's not accurate for `Seq[Any]` with mixed elements, the second
to last example.

The compiler exploits the type information it knows to construct the implicit `Class
Tag`. However, when given previously constructed lists, the crucial type information is
already lost. This is an issue if you're passing collections around and somewhere deep
in the stack some method wants to use a `ClassTag` for introspection. You'll need to
construct the collection *and* a corresponding `ClassTag` in the same scope, then pass
them together somehow, perhaps through an implicit argument for the `ClassTag` in
subsequent method calls. We'll come back to this issue a little later.

Hence, `ClassTag`s can't "resurrect" type information from byte code, but they can be
used to capture and exploit type information before it is erased.

ClassTag is actually a weaker version of scala.reflect.api.TypeTags#TypeTag (*http://bit.ly/1083R1Y*), found in the separate API. The latter retains the full compile-time information (we'll use it shortly), whereas ClassTag only returns the runtime information. Finally, there is a scala.reflect.api.TypeTags#WeakTypeTag (*http://bit.ly/1wNDoCw*) for abstract types. See the detailed descriptions in the Scala docs (*http://bit.ly/1wNSvwT*).

Note that there are older types in the reflect package called Manifests that were used for the same purpose before Scala 2.10 introduced TypeTag, ClassTag, etc. These types are being deprecated. You'll see them in older source code. However, you should use the newer features.

Another important usage for ClassTag is to construct Java Arrays of the correct Any Ref subtype. Here is an example adapted from the Scaladoc (*http://bit.ly/1tHWxpq*) page for ClassTag:

```
// src/main/scala/progscala2/metaprogramming/mkArray.sc
scala> import scala.reflect.ClassTag
import scala.reflect.ClassTag

scala> def mkArray[T : ClassTag](elems: T*) = Array[T](elems: _*)
mkArray: [T](elems: T*)(implicit evidence$1: scala.reflect.ClassTag[T])Array[T]

scala> mkArray(1, 2, 3)
res0: Array[Int] = Array(1, 2, 3)

scala> mkArray("one", "two", "three")
res1: Array[String] = Array(one, two, three)

scala> mkArray(1, "two", 3.14)
<console>:10: warning: a type was inferred to be `Any`;
  this may indicate a programming error.
              mkArray(1, "two", 3.14)
                      ^
res2: Array[Any] = Array(1, two, 3.14)
```

It uses the Array.apply (*http://bit.ly/1wN2lNE*) method for AnyRefs, which has a second argument list with a single implicit ClassTag argument.

Scala's Advanced Runtime Reflection API

The rest of the reflection API supports richer runtime reflection as well as the compile-time macros. It includes types that represent abstract syntax trees and other contexts. It is distributed as a separate JAR file, for which we included a dependency in the sbt build. The full details of this API are described at in the Scala docs (*http://bit.ly/1vorYlD*). We'll discuss the core ideas of this very large API and a few examples for a common task, runtime introspection of types:

```
// src/main/scala/progscala2/metaprogramming/match-type-tags.sc

import scala.reflect.runtime.universe._                           // ❶

def toType2[T](t: T)(implicit tag: TypeTag[T]): Type = tag.tpe    // ❷
def toType[T : TypeTag](t: T): Type = typeOf[T]                   // ❸
```

❶ Import the definitions defined in the runtime "universe," which is of type sca
   la.reflect.api.JavaUniverse (*http://bit.ly/1tomZEK*). It exposes the types
   reflecting language elements and convenience methods for the target platform.

❷ Use an implicit argument for a TypeTag[T] (*http://bit.ly/1G2nqd2*), then ask it
   for its type.

❸ More convenient alternative using a context bound. The typeOf[T] method is
   a shortcut for implicitly[TypeTag[T]].tpe.

Recall that TypeTag retains the full compile-time type information while ClassTag only
retains the runtime type information.

Let's try these methods with a few types:

```
scala> toType(1)
res1: reflect.runtime.universe.Type = Int

scala> toType(true)
res2: reflect.runtime.universe.Type = Boolean

scala> toType(Seq(1, true, 3.14))
<console>:12: warning: a type was inferred to be `AnyVal`;
   this may indicate a programming error.
              toType(Seq(1, true, 3.14))
                    ^
res3: reflect.runtime.universe.Type = Seq[AnyVal]

scala> toType((i: Int) => i.toString)
res4: reflect.runtime.universe.Type = Int => java.lang.String
```

Note that the types for the parameterized type parameters are correctly determined,
fixing the bug we had in useClassTag. We'll omit the AnyVal warnings from now on.

We can compare types for equality or parent-child relationships:

```
toType(1) =:= typeOf[AnyVal]          // false
toType(1) =:= toType(1)               // true
toType(1) =:= toType(true)            // false

toType(1) <:< typeOf[AnyVal]          // true
toType(1) <:< toType(1)               // true
toType(1) <:< toType(true)            // false
```

```
typeOf[Seq[Int]] =:= typeOf[Seq[Any]]        // false
typeOf[Seq[Int]] <:< typeOf[Seq[Any]]        // true
```

We've been calling the `tpe` method to get the Type (*http://bit.ly/1u0JfG4*) from the TypeTag (*http://bit.ly/1083R1Y*). You can also get the latter directory with the helper function `typeTag`:

```
typeTag[Int]          // reflect.runtime.universe.TypeTag[Int] = TypeTag[Int]
typeTag[Seq[Int]]     // ...TypeTag[Seq[Int]] = TypeTag[scala.Seq[Int]]
```

Recall in "Functions Under the Hood" on page 286, we discussed covariance and contravariance of functions. Let's revisit those details using these new tools:

```
// src/main/scala/progscala2/metaprogramming/func.sc

class CSuper                { def msuper() = println("CSuper") }
class C        extends CSuper { def m()     = println("C") }
class CSub     extends C     { def msub()  = println("CSub") }

typeOf[C      => C      ] =:= typeOf[C => C]    // true   ❶
typeOf[CSuper => CSub   ] =:= typeOf[C => C]    // false
typeOf[CSub   => CSuper] =:= typeOf[C => C]    // false

typeOf[C      => C      ] <:< typeOf[C => C]    // true   ❷
typeOf[CSuper => CSub   ] <:< typeOf[C => C]    // true   ❸
typeOf[CSub   => CSuper] <:< typeOf[C => C]    // false  ❹
```

❶   None of the pairs is equal except for an exact match.

❷   A type is its own subtype, so this should be true.

❸   True because the argument is a supertype of C, satisfying contravariance for arguments, and the return type is a subtype of C, satisfying covariance of return types.

❹   Breaks both rules for argument types and return types.

 Can't remember the rules for when one type is a subtype of another? Use `typeOf` or our `toType` method and `<:<` to figure it out.

Now consider some of the information we can learn from the types. First, the Type returned is an instance of TypeRef (*http://bit.ly/13oZSjD*), so we use an extractor to determine the "prefix," the symbol for the type (its name), and any type parameters it takes:

```
def toTypeRefInfo[T : TypeTag](x: T): (Type, Symbol, Seq[Type]) = {
  val TypeRef(pre, typName, parems) = toType(x)
```

```
    (pre, typName, parems)
}
```

The `Type` and `Symbol` types in the tuple are both defined in `reflect.runtime.uni`verse, not to be confused with `scala.Symbol`.

```
toTypeRefInfo(1)                      // (scala.type, class Int, List())
toTypeRefInfo(true)                   // (scala.type, class Boolean, List())
toTypeRefInfo(Seq(1, true, 3.14))     // (scala.collection.type, trait Seq,
                                      //    List(AnyVal))
toTypeRefInfo((i: Int) => i.toString) // (scala.type, trait Function1,
                                      //    List(Int, java.lang.String))
```

Note the different `scala.collection.type` "prefix" for Seq versus `scala.type` for the other examples. Both `Seq` and `Function1` have nonempty type parameter lists, as we would expect.

We get even more information with `TypeApi` (*http://bit.ly/1tHXBcY*). Let's try it with Seq in the REPL, to see the types returned. We'll elide long output:

```
scala> val ts = toType(Seq(1, true, 3.14))
ts: reflect.runtime.universe.Type = Seq[AnyVal]

scala> ts.typeSymbol
res0: reflect.runtime.universe.Symbol = trait Seq

scala> ts.erasure
res1: reflect.runtime.universe.Type = Seq[Any]

scala> ts.typeArgs
res2: List[reflect.runtime.universe.Type] = List(AnyVal)

scala> ts.baseClasses
res4: List[reflect.runtime.universe.Symbol] =
  List(trait Seq, trait SeqLike, trait GenSeq, trait GenSeqLike, ...)

scala> ts.companion
res5: reflect.runtime.universe.Type = scala.collection.Seq.type

scala> ts.decls
res6: reflect.runtime.universe.MemberScope = SynchronizedOps(
  method $init$, method companion, method seq)

scala> ts.members
res7: reflect.runtime.universe.MemberScope = Scopes(
  method seq, method companion, method $init$, method toString, ...)
```

Most of these are self-explanatory. The `companion` method returns the type of the companion type, `decls` returns the declarations in `Seq` itself, while `members` returns all declarations that are inherited, too.

You'll find more examples in the overview (*http://bit.ly/1vorYlD*) and the reflection Scaladocs (*http://bit.ly/1wQkYDN*).

Macros

Scala's current macro system has been used to implement clever solutions to difficult design problems in many advanced toolkits. However, to use it requires understanding compiler internals, such as the abstract syntax tree (AST) representation used by the compiler. So, a principle goal of the *Scala Meta* project (*http://scalameta.org*) is to implement a new macro system that avoids this coupling to compiler details and the learning burden for users. It will also apply various lessons learned from work on the first system

Because *Scala Meta* is not yet available and the current system will eventually go away, we won't discuss it in detail, but we will end our discussion with an example. However, one feature is expected to remain relatively unchanged in *Scala Meta*, namely *quasiquotes*, which is a tool for manipulating ASTs much more easily, using interpolated strings. It eliminates much of the boilerplate and detailed knowledge required to write macros in the old API. The quasiquote documentation can be found in the Scala docs (*http://bit.ly/1G2nABb*).

Note that the remaining examples for this chapter only work with Scala 2.11, although they use just a few changes in the API since 2.10. Specifically, a `showCode` helper method we'll see shortly is new and an API change was made that we'll mention in the macro example later.

Let's work through some of the features:

```
// src/main/scala/progscala2/metaprogramming/quasiquotes.sc

import reflect.runtime.universe._                        // ❶

import reflect.runtime.currentMirror                     // ❷
import tools.reflect.ToolBox
val toolbox = currentMirror.mkToolBox()
```

❶ Import the `universe` features needed for quasiquotes.

❷ Bring in the convenient "toolbox."

There are several ways to construct quasiquotes, depending on the type of AST tree you're building. We'll use the general form q"..." and tq"..." for type expressions. The full list of options with examples can be found at in the Scala documentation (*http://bit.ly/1sQY5bO*).

```
scala> val C = q"case class C(s: String)"
C: reflect.runtime.universe.ClassDef =
case class C extends scala.Product with scala.Serializable {
```

```
  <caseaccessor> <paramaccessor> val s: String = _;
  def <init>(s: String) = {
    super.<init>();
    ()
  }
}

scala> showCode(C)
res0: String = case class C(s: String)

scala> showRaw(C)
res1: String = ClassDef(Modifiers(CASE), TypeName("C"), List(), ...)
```

The showCode method prints a string similar to the original Scala syntax of the decla-ration (exactly the same in this simple example), and showRaw prints the types corre-sponding to the actual AST tree.

Whereas q is used for general quasiquotes, tq is used to construct trees for types, specifically:

```
scala> val  q =  q"List[String]"
q: reflect.runtime.universe.Tree = List[String]

scala> val tq = tq"List[String]"
tq: reflect.runtime.universe.Tree = List[String]

scala> showRaw(q)
res2: String = TypeApply(Ident(TermName("List")),
  List(Ident(TypeName("String"))))

scala> showRaw(tq)
res2: String = AppliedTypeTree(Ident(TypeName("List")),
  List(Ident(TypeName("String"))))

scala> q equalsStructure tq
res4: Boolean = false
```

We need to use showRaw to see that they are actually different. The Scaladoc page for scala.reflect.api.Trees#TypeApplyExtractor (*http://bit.ly/1084PeH*) explains the difference. TypeApply (*http://bit.ly/1pbfyRp*) corresponds to a type specification that appears in a *term*, such as foo[T] in def foo[T](t: T) = ..., and AppliedType Tree (*http://bit.ly/1vossbl*) is used for type declarations, like T in val t: T.

To test equality, use equalsStructure.

You can expand other quasiquotes into a quasiquote using string interpolation ${…}, called "unquoting":

```
scala> Seq(tq"Int", tq"String") map { param =>
     |     q"case class C(s: $param)"
     | } foreach { q =>
     |     println(showCode(q))
```

```
    |  }
case class C(s: Int)
case class C(s: String)
```

Hence we can parameterize code generation! Note that we used type quasiquotes (tq"...") because the "param" function argument is used for a type declaration. Try replacing showCode with showRaw, then compare the output when you replace tq quasiquotes with q or just a string, e.g., "Int".

In some cases, normal values are "lifted" to quasiquotes when interpolated:

```
scala> val list = Seq(1,2,3,4)
scala> val fmt = "%d, %d, %d, %d"
scala> val printq = q"println($fmt, ..$list)"
```

The ..$list syntax expands the list into comma-separated values. (There is also a ...$list for sequences of sequences.) Here we use it to generate a call to a variable-argument function, println. The reverse process is "unlifting," commonly used with pattern matching on quasiquoted strings.

```
scala> val q"${i: Int} + ${d: Double}" = q"1 + 3.14"
i: Int = 1
d: Double = 3.14
```

There are a few other kinds of quasiquotes: cq generates trees for case clauses, fq generates trees for for comprehensions, and pq generates trees for pattern-match expressions. See the Scala docs (*http://bit.ly/1sQY5bO*) for detailed examples.

A Macro Example: Enforcing Invariants

When we discussed *Design by Contract* in "Better Design with Design by Contract" on page 514, we mentioned one aspect of a contract is the *invariants* that should be true before *and* after every method invocation and state change. Let's implement a macro that enforces invariants.

Recall that we said that macros are a limited form of compiler plug-in, invoked in an intermediate phase of the compilation process. This leads to a requirement for macros that they must be compiled separately and ahead of time from the code that uses them. We'll implement the macro in a source file and use it in a *ScalaTest* test file to meet this requirement. This works because sbt compiles tests separately from the main code. Also, macro implementations follow certain idioms, which we'll also see. Here is the source for the macro invariant:

```
// src/main/scala/progscala2/metaprogramming/invariant.scala
package metaprogramming
import reflect.runtime.universe._                              // ❶
import scala.language.experimental.macros
import scala.reflect.macros.blackbox.Context                   // ❷
```

```
/**
 * A Macro written using the current macro syntax along with quasiquotes.
 * Requires a predicate for an invariant to be true before each expression
 * is evaluated.
 */
object invariant {                                              // ❸
  case class InvariantFailure(msg: String) extends RuntimeException(msg)

  def apply[T](predicate: => Boolean)(block: => T): T = macro impl   // ❹

  def impl(c: Context)(predicate: c.Tree)(block: c.Tree) = {    // ❺
    import c.universe._                                         // ❻
    val predStr = showCode(predicate)                          // ❼
    val q"..$stmts" = block                                    // ❽
    val invariantStmts = stmts.flatMap { stmt =>               // ❾
      val msg = s"FAILURE! $predStr == false, for statement: " + showCode(stmt)
      val tif = q"throw new metaprogramming.invariant.InvariantFailure($msg)"
      val predq2 = q"if (false == $predicate) $tif"
      List(q"{ val tmp = $stmt; $predq2; tmp };")
    }
    val tif = q"throw new metaprogramming.invariant.InvariantFailure($predStr)"
    val predq = q"if (false == $predicate) $tif"
    q"$predq; ..$invariantStmts"                               // ❿
  }
}
```

❶ Import the reflection and macro features required. We are building a "blackbox" macro; it won't change the type signature of the expression it encloses (see the docs (*http://bit.ly/1u0JZuI*) for details).

❷ For 2.10, use `scala.reflect.macros.Context` instead.

❸ The `invariant.apply` method is used to wrap the expressions for which we want to enforce invariants. If a failure occurs, `InvariantFailure` is thrown.

❹ Macros always start with a public method that is invoked in client code, with a body that contains `macro impl`. In this case, `invariant` is passed two arguments: a predicate to test around each statement in the second argument, and a `block` of code to evaluate.

❺ The implementation method `impl` takes arguments corresponding to those for `apply`, where each one is the corresponding abstract syntax tree generated from the expression. The type `c.Tree` is a path-dependent type in the `Context` (*http://bit.ly/1wNTqNJ*) object, the first argument to `impl`.

❻ We must use the universe corresponding to the context, so we import its members.

❼ Create a string for the `predicate` that will be used in failure messages.

❽ Convert the `block` into a sequence of statements, using pattern matching.

⑨ Flat map over the statements, modifying each one to capture its return value, then check the predicate (throwing an `InvariantFailure` on failure), and then finish with the return value.

⑩ Rejoin the statements, prefixed with an initial test of the predicate, and return the modified AST.

Without quasiquotes, this implementation would be much harder to write, because we would have to know details of the AST implementation and how to manipulate AST trees.

Let's see an example and try it in the following ScalaTest, where we'll use a class `Variable` with two mutable fields and we'll impose the invariant that the s field, a string, is never changed:

```scala
// src/test/scala/progscala2/metaprogramming/InvariantSpec.scala
package metaprogramming
import reflect.runtime.universe._
import org.scalatest.FunSpec

class InvariantSpec extends FunSpec {
  case class Variable(var i: Int, var s: String)

  describe ("invariant.apply") {
    def succeed() = {                              // ❶
      val v = Variable(0, "Hello!")
      val i1 = invariant(v.s == "Hello!") {        // ❷
        v.i += 1
        v.i += 1
        v.i
      }
      assert (i1 === 2)
    }

    it ("should not fail if the invariant holds") { succeed() }

    it ("should return the value returned by the expressions") { succeed() }

    it ("should fail if the invariant is broken") {
      intercept[invariant.InvariantFailure] {      // ❸
        val v = Variable(0, "Hello!")
        invariant(v.s == "Hello!") {
          v.i += 1
          v.s = "Goodbye!"
          v.i += 1
        }
      }
    }
  }
}
```

❶   Helper method to check cases where the invariant holds.

❷   Require the string field to remain the same while executing the statements in the block.

❸   Expect `InvariantFailure` because the string is modified.

It's instructive to comment out the `intercept[...]` line and the corresponding closing brace. The test fails with the following error message:

```
[info] - should fail if the invariant is broken *** FAILED ***
[info]    metaprogramming.invariant$InvariantFailure:
    FAILURE! v.s.==("Hello!") == false, for statement: v.`s_=`("Goodbye!")
```

A powerful feature is our ability to show a readable message for the predicate that failed and the statement that triggered the failure. The whole implementation is just a few dozen lines of code, demonstrating the power of macros.

If you wrote all the code by hand, the first test in `InvariantSpec` might look schematically like the following, where I converted a few statements in the loop to a helper method `fail`, to reduce boilerplate:

```
def fail[T](predStr: String, stmtStr: String): Nothing = {
  val msg = s"FAILURE! $predStr == false, for statement: $stmtStr"
  throw new metaprogramming.invariant.InvariantFailure(msg)
}
val v = Variable(0, "Hello!")
val i1 = {
  if (v.s != "Hello!") fail("v.s == \"Hello!\"", "")
  val tmp1 = v.i += 1
  if (v.s != "Hello!") fail("v.s == \"Hello!\"", "v.i += 1")
  val tmp2 = v.i += 1
  if (v.s != "Hello!") fail("v.s == \"Hello!\"", "v.i += 1")
  val tmp3 = v.i
  if (v.s != "Hello!") fail("v.s == \"Hello!\"", "v.i")
  tmp3
}
```

The quasiquotes documentation has other useful examples, such as printing debug statements before each statement in a block is executed.

Final Thoughts on Macros

The power of macros is quite seductive, but developing, debugging, and maintaining them is challenging. You can find many examples of their use in third-party libraries. Also keep in mind that the whole reflection API, especially the macros package, is considered experimental and it will continue to evolve rapidly.

Wrapping Up and Looking Ahead

If you've read this far in *Programming Scala, Second Edition*, you have learned about all the major features of the language and how best to use them. I hope you'll find the code examples useful as templates for your own projects. For a more extensive collection of examples for different kinds of applications and toolkits, see the *Activator* project on the Typesafe website (*http://typesafe.com/activator*). Typesafe also offers developer and production subscriptions for Scala, Akka, Play, and a growing list of other tools. Typesafe provides training and consulting, too.

How will Scala change in the next few years? It's been five years since the first edition of this book. The changes have been enormous, both in the maturity of the language and in industry adoption. I expect brisk adoption to continue, especially in the *Big Data* space. Evolution of Scala itself is stabilizing. Even macros will stabilize in a year or two. Much of the work on Scala and the larger ecosystem now aims to improve performance, reduce bugs, deprecate language "warts," and improve tooling around Scala, like IDE support.

Martin Odersky is also working on a new Scala-like language based on a new type system called *DOT*, for *dependent object typing*, which may become Scala 3.0 (see the DOT slideshow (*http://bit.ly/1wQmW72*) and PDF (*http://bit.ly/1E8x3Ff*) for more).

DOT is based on *dependent typing*, the state of the art in type theory that will allow you to express concepts like "an array of three elements" as a type. Currently, the type systems of most languages can't express the size constraint as part of a type. Why does this matter? It pushes us closer to the ultimate goal of provably correct programs, where the types are theorems and the programs are proofs (see the Wikipedia page (*http://bit.ly/1rGuO jy*)).

The new language will also simplify the type system in other ways and remove other language warts. It is several years away, at least.

In the meantime, you can use Scala now to improve how you create applications, while leveraging the richness of the mature Java ecosystem and going forward, the vibrant JavaScript ecosystem with the new port of Scala to JavaScript, scala.js (*http://www.scala-js.org*). I hope that *Programming Scala, Second Edition* will help you be successful as you go.

References

Abelson, Harold, Gerald Jay Sussman, and Julie Sussman, *Structure and Interpretation of Computer Programs*. The MIT Press, 1996.

Agha, Gul, *Actors*. The MIT Press, 1987.

"Akka: Build powerful concurrent & distributed applications more easily," *http://akka.io*.

Alexander, Alvin, *Scala Cookbook: Recipes for Object-Oriented and Functional Programming*. O'Reilly Media, 2013.

Algebird (*https://github.com/twitter/algebird*)

Allen, Jamie, *Effective Akka*. O'Reilly Media, 2013.

Antlr (*http://www.antlr.org/*)

Barr, Michael and Charles Wells, "Category Theory for Computing Science" (*http://bit.ly/1wMZX9G*), 1998.

Behavior-Driven Development (*http://behaviour-driven.org/*)

Bloch, Joshua, *Effective Java (Second Edition)*. Addison-Wesley, 2008.

Bird, Richard, *Pearls of Functional Algorithm Design*. Cambridge University Press, 2010.

Bjarnason, Rúnar Óli, "Stackless Scala and Free Monads" (*http://bit.ly/1yMbuY2*).

Bonér, Jonas, "Real-World Scala: Dependency Injection (DI)" (*http://bit.ly/10FcguX*).

Bruce, Kim, Martin Odersky, and Philip Wadler, "A Statically Safe Alternative to Virtual Types," *Proc. ECOOP '98*, E. Jul (Ed.), LNCS 1445, pp. 523–549, Springer-Verlag, 1998.

"Building bug-free O-O software: An introduction to Design by Contract" (*http://bit.ly/1tpbvPM*).

Chiusano, Paul and Rúnar Bjarnason, *Functional Programming in Scala*. Manning Publications, 2013.

Dean, Jeffrey and Sanjay Ghemawat, "MapReduce: Simplified Data Processing on Large Clusters" (*http://bit.ly/mapreduce-pdf*).

Dzilums, Lauris, "Awesome Scala" (*https://github.com/lauris/awesome-scala*).

Easterbrook, Steve, "An introduction to Category Theory for Software Engineers" (*http://bit.ly/1s0AvtM*).

Eiffel Software (*http://eiffel.com*)

Effective Scala (*http://twitter.github.io/effectivescala/*)

Evans, Eric, *Domain Driven Design*. Prentice-Hall, 2003.

Extension Methods (C# Programming Guide) (*http://bit.ly/1xIhCj0*)

Finagle (*https://twitter.github.io/finagle/*)

Ford, Bryan, "The Packrat Parsing and Parsing Expression Grammars Page" (*http://bit.ly/1s0ACWi*).

Fowler, Martin, *Domain-Specific Languages*. Addison-Wesley, 2010.

Ghosh, Debasish, *DSLs in Action*. Manning Press, 2010.

Gamma, Erich, Richard Helm, Ralph Johnson, and John Vlissides ("Gang of Four"), *Design Patterns: Elements of Reusable Object-Oriented Software*. Addison-Wesley, 1995.

Gradle (*http://www.gradle.org/*)

Guice (*http://code.google.com/p/google-guice/*)

Hadoop (*http://hadoop.apache.org*)

Haller, Philipp and Martin Odersky, "Actors That Unify Threads and Events" (*http://bit.ly/1vooxv3*).

Hewitt, Carl, Peter Bishop, and Richard Steiger, "A Universal Modular Actor Formalism for Artificial Intelligence," *IJCAI '73*, August 20-23, 1973, Stanford, California, USA.

Hewitt, Carl, "Actor Model of Computation" (*http://bit.ly/1082H6P*), 2014.

Hoare, Tony, "Null References: The Billion Dollar Mistake," *http://bit.ly/null-refs-th*.

Hofer, Christian, Klaus Ostermann, Tillmann Rendel, and Adriaan Moors, "Polymorphic Embedding of DSLs" (*http://bit.ly/1sQUgmU*), GPCE '08, October 19–23, 2008, Nashville, Tennessee.

Hypertext Transfer Protocol — HTTP/1.1 (*http://bit.ly/rfc-http*).

Hunt, Andrew and Dave Thomas, *The Pragmatic Programmer*. Addison-Wesley, 2000.

Introducing Spring Scala (*http://bit.ly/1pbd7P1*)

Iry, James, "Phantom Types in Haskell and Scala" (*http://bit.ly/1tHUsdb*).

Java Platform SE 8 API (*http://bit.ly/1rGsadG*)

The Java Tutorials. Lesson: Java Regular Expressions (*http://bit.ly/1tol9Uz*).

Laddad, Ramnivas, *AspectJ in Action (Second Edition)*. Manning Press, 2009.

Lawvere, F. William and Stephen H. Schanuel, *Conceptual Mathematics, A First Introduction to Categories*. Cambridge University Press, 2009.

Lipovaca, Miran, *Learn You a Haskell for Great Good!* No Starch Press, 2011.

Liskov Substitution Principle (*http://bit.ly/1DDaMgy*).

Malawski, Konrad, "Scala's Types of Types" (*http://bit.ly/1pbddpG*).

Marick, Brian, *Functional Programming for the Object-Oriented Programmer*. Leanpub, 2012.

Martin, Robert C., *Agile Software Development: Principles, Patterns, and Practices*. Prentice Hall, 2003.

Meyer, Bertrand, *Object-Oriented Software Construction (Second Edition)*. Prentice Hall, 1997.

Naftalin, Maurice and Philip Wadler, *Java Generics and Collections*. O'Reilly Media, 2006.

Nilsson, Rickard, *ScalaCheck: The Definitive Guide*. Artima Press, 2013.

Odersky, Martin and Matthias Zenger, "Scalable Component Abstractions," *OOPSLA '05*, October 16–20, 2005, San Diego, California, USA.

Odersky, Martin, Lex Spoon, and Bill Venners, "How to Write an Equality Method in Java" (*http://bit.ly/13a2sBR*).

Odersky, Martin, Lex Spoon, and Bill Venners, *Programming in Scala, Second Edition*. Artima Press, 2010.

Okasaki, Chris, *Purely Functional Data Structures*. Cambridge University Press, 1998.

O'Sullivan, Bryan, John Goerzen, and Don Steward, *Real World Haskell*. O'Reilly Media, 2009.

Parsing Expression Grammar (*http://bit.ly/1wkLnrW*)

Paul, Thomas, "Working with Money in Java" (*http://bit.ly/1rGsiKi*).

Phillips, Andrew and Nermin Serifovic, *Scala Puzzlers*. Artima Press, 2014.

Pierce, Benjamin C., *Types and Programming Languages*. The MIT Press, 2002.

Rabhi, Fethi and Guy Lapalme, *Algorithms: A Functional Programming Approach.* Addison-Wesley, 1999.

Roestenburg, Raymond, Rob Bakker, and Rob Williams, *Akka in Action.* Manning, 2014.

S-99: Ninety-Nine Scala Problems (*http://bit.ly/1nWgrMQ*)

Sargent, Will, "Error Handling in Scala" (*http://bit.ly/10FcXnT*)

Scala Automatic Resource Management (*http://bit.ly/13oZkdG*)

ScalaCheck (*http://scalacheck.org/*)

The Scala Language Specification (*http://bit.ly/1wNBOR8*)

The Scala Library (*http://www.scala-lang.org/api/current/*)

The Scala Programming Language (*http://www.scala-lang.org/*)

ScalaTest (*http://www.scalatest.org/*)

Scalaz (*https://github.com/scalaz/scalaz*)

Scalding (*https://github.com/twitter/scalding*)

Shapeless: Generic Programming for Scala (*https://github.com/milessabin/shapeless*)

Simple Build Tool (*http://www.scala-sbt.org*)

SIP-15: Value Classes (*http://bit.ly/1wNC0Qq*)

Spark (*http://spark.apache.org*)

Specs2 (*http://bit.ly/1tpceR3*)

Spiewak, Daniel, "What is Hindley-Milner? (and why is it cool?)" (*http://bit.ly/1zmiWMF*).

Spiewak, Daniel, "Interop Between Java and Scala" (*http://bit.ly/1tpci3p*).

Spiewak, Daniel, "The Magic Behind Parser Combinators" (*http://bit.ly/10a3jZd*).

The Spring Framework (*http://spring.io*)

Suereth, Joshua, *Scala in Depth.* Manning Press, 2012.

Suereth, Joshua and Matthew Farwell, *SBT in Action.* Manning Press, 2013.

Szyperski, Clemens, *Component Software: Beyond Object-Oriented Programming.* Addison-Wesley Longman Limited, 1998.

Taylor, Chris, "The Algebra of Algebraic Data Types" (*http://bit.ly/13oZm5l*).

Turbak, Franklyn, David Gifford, and Mark A. Sheldon, *Design Concepts of Programming Languages.* The MIT Press, 2008.

Typesafe, Inc. (*http://typesafe.com*)

Van Roy, Peter and Seif Haridi, *Concepts, Techniques, and Models of Computer Programming*. The MIT Press, 2004.

Wadler, Philip, "The Expression Problem" (*http://bit.ly/1ucWnbN*).

Walters, R.F.C., *Categories and Computer Science*. Cambridge University Press, 1992.

Wampler, Dean, *Introduction to Functional Programming for Java Developers*. O'Reilly Media, 2011.

Theoretical Computer Science: "What's new in purely functional data structures since Okasaki?" (*http://bit.ly/1wQkSMm*).

White, Tom, *Hadoop: The Definitive Guide, Third Edition*. O'Reilly Media, 2012.

Wirfs-Brock, Rebecca and Alan McKean, *Object Design: Roles, Responsibilities, and Collaborations*. Pearson Education, 2003.

Wyatt, Derek, *Akka Concurrency*. Artima Press, 2013.

Index

We'd like to hear your suggestions for improving our indexes. Send email to index@oreilly.com.

generic classes, 497–499
generics, 2, 67
GFS (Google File System), 446
Gradle, 491
guards, 79, 92
    in case clauses, 111

H

H2O, 454
Hadoop, 446
Hash (see maps)
higher-kinded types, 398–402, 411
higher-order functions, 23, 171

I

identifiers
    characters allowed in, 13
    rules summary for, 72–73
IDEs (integrated development environments), 9,
    10, 525
if statements, 52, 77
    pattern matching and, 126
immutable variables, 10, 34, 171–174
immutable variants, 336–338
implicit keyword, 41–43, 52, 131, 150
implicits, 504
    built-in, 161–168
    implicit arguments, 131–148
        with capabilities, 135
        for constraining allowed instances, 135–
            140
        error messages, 144
        in execution contexts, 134
        implicit evidence, 140–141
        implicitly method, 133–134
        phantom types, 145–148
        rules for, 148–148
        type erasure, 142–144
    implicit conversions, 52, 139, 149–156, 301–
        304
        and the Expression Problem, 155–156
        string interpolation, 153–155
    implicit resolution rules, 160–161
    overview, 131
    technical issues with, 158–160
    and the Type Class Pattern, 156–158
    wise use of, 168
import keyword, 52

import statements, 65–67
    package objects, 66–67
    relative imports, 66
infix notation, 27
infix types, 397–398
inheritance, 253–254, 264
instances, 246–248
integer literals, 54–55
interfaces (see traits)
internal DSLs, 77
interpolated strings, 23, 94–96, 153–155
Interpreter pattern, 512
invariance, 285
invariants, 514
Iterator pattern, 512

J

Java, 1
    composable mixins, 3
    interoperability with, 497–501
        AnyVal types and Java primitives, 501
        Java and Scala generics, 497–499
        JavaBean properties, 499–500
        Scala names in Java code, 501
        using Java names in Scala code, 497
    Java 8, 3, 271, 287
    javap, 487
    reflection API, 525–526
    variance in, versus Scala, 292–293
    Virtual Machine (see JVM (Java Virtual Machine))
JSON, 466–468
JVM (Java Virtual Machine), 1

L

lambdas, 3, 176, 287
lazy evaluation, 52, 173
lazy values, 91, 318
least upper-bound variance, 369
least-upper bound values, 78
let it crash, 431, 515
libraries, third-party, 493–495
lifting, 177, 187
Like traits, 344–345
linearization, 281, 326–331
LINQ, 459
Liskov Substitution Principle, 288

query DSL, 459

R

ranges, 36–37
Reactive Extensions (Rx), 443
Reactive Manifesto, 443
reactive programming, 443–444
recursion, 44–46
    in functional programming, 178–179
    in sequence matching, 106–110
    tail recursion, 209–212
    tail-call self-recursion, 179–181
reduce function, 175
reducing, 201–205
reference equality, 309
reference types, 248–250
referential transparancy, 170–171
reflection, 523, 524–531
    Class Tags, 526–528
    Manifests, 528
    Scala advanced runtime reflection API, 528–532
    Type Tags, 528
    types, 525–526
regexes, 120
regular expressions, 120–121
Relate, 454
relative imports, 66
REPL (read, evaluate, print, loop), 8–10
    paste mode, 34
    tools for understanding types, 524
requires keyword, 52
reserved keywords, 51–53
return keyword, 52
return type for methods, 45–51
    required explicit declarations of, 47
Ruby on Rails, 457
runtime reflection, 524–531

S

SBT (standard build tool), 4, 5–6, 488–490
Scala
    advanced runtime reflection API, 528–532
    code examples, 11
    collections library (see collections library)
    installing, 3–9
    introduction to, 1–3
    reflection library, 526–528

    reserved keywords list, 51–53
    type hierarchy, 294–295
scala command, 7
scala command-line tool, 483–485
Scala Meta, 524, 532
Scala reflection API, 523
scala.sys process package, 423–425
scalac, 479–483, 485–486
Scaladocs, 5, 9, 67, 488
ScalaNLP, 454
scalap, 12, 487
ScalaStorm, 455
Scalaz, 240–242, 402, 411
Scalding, 447, 451, 455
Schönfinkel, Moses, 183
Scoobi, 455
sealed class hierarchies, 62, 123–125
sealed keyword, 52, 62, 231
self expression, 231
self-recursive types, 404–405
self-type annotations, 376–381
separation of concerns, 272, 420
sequences, 106–110, 187–192
sets, 194
Shapeless, 402
Single Responsibility Principle, 155, 272
singleton objects, 396
Singleton pattern, 15, 511
singleton types, 342, 395–396
Slick, 455
some class, 60–62
Spark, 452–453, 455
Spire, 455
Spores project, 442
stackable traits, 277–282
State pattern, 513
static typing, 1
statics, 15
Strategy pattern, 513
Stream, 211, 223–224
strict evaluation, 174
string argument, 14
string interpolation, 94–96, 153–155
string literals, 56
structural types, 381–384
structure sharing, 216–218
subtype polymorphism, 155, 158
subtype polymorphism versus pattern matching, 28

About the Authors

Dean Wampler, Ph.D., is the Architect for Big Data Products at Typesafe. He has been a vocal advocate for Scala and Functional Programming as the ideal tools for big data applications. Dean is the coauthor of *Programming Hive* and the author of *Functional Programming for Java Developers* from O'Reilly. Dean contributes to several open source projects and is the co-organizer of several technology conferences and Chicago-based user groups. Dean can be found on Twitter as @deanwampler.

Alex Payne is a programmer, writer, and angel investor working primarily with early-stage companies. He has deployed Scala as CTO of the online banking service Simple and as Platform Lead at Twitter. Alex organizes the annual Emerging Languages conference, a showcase for new programming languages and developer tools. He is a regular speaker at technology and business conferences. You can find him on Twitter as @al3x or on his website, *https://al3x.net*.

Colophon

The animal on the cover of *Programming Scala* is a Malayan tapir (*Tapirus indicus*), also called an Asian tapir. It is a black-and-white hoofed mammal with a round, stocky body similar to that of a pig. At 6–8 feet long and 550–700 pounds, the Malayan is the largest of the four tapir species. It lives in tropical rain forests in Southeast Asia.

The Malayan tapir's appearance is striking: its front half and hind legs are solid black, and its midsection is marked with a white saddle. This pattern provides perfect camouflage for the tapir in a moonlit jungle. Other physical characteristics include a thick hide, a stumpy tail, and a short, flexible snout. Despite its body shape, the Malayan tapir is an agile climber and a fast runner.

The tapir is a solitary and mainly nocturnal animal. It tends to have very poor vision, so it relies on smell and hearing as it roams large territories in search of food, tracking other tapirs' scents and communicating via high-pitched whistles. The Malayan tapir's predators are tigers, leopards, and humans, and it is considered endangered due to habitat destruction and overhunting.

The cover image is from the Dover Pictorial Archive. The cover fonts are URW Typewriter and Guardian Sans. The text font is Adobe Minion Pro; the heading font is Adobe Myriad Condensed; and the code font is Dalton Maag's Ubuntu Mono.

Get even more for your money.

Join the O'Reilly Community, and register the O'Reilly books you own. It's free, and you'll get:

- $4.99 ebook upgrade offer
- 40% upgrade offer on O'Reilly print books
- Membership discounts on books and events
- Free lifetime updates to ebooks and videos
- Multiple ebook formats, DRM FREE
- Participation in the O'Reilly community
- Newsletters
- Account management
- 100% Satisfaction Guarantee

Signing up is easy:

1. Go to: oreilly.com/go/register
2. Create an O'Reilly login.
3. Provide your address.
4. Register your books.

Note: English-language books only

To order books online:
oreilly.com/store

For questions about products or an order:
orders@oreilly.com

To sign up to get topic-specific email announcements and/or news about upcoming books, conferences, special offers, and new technologies:
elists@oreilly.com

For technical questions about book content:
booktech@oreilly.com

To submit new book proposals to our editors:
proposals@oreilly.com

O'Reilly books are available in multiple DRM-free ebook formats. For more information:
oreilly.com/ebooks

O'REILLY®

Have it your way.

Lightning Source UK Ltd.
Milton Keynes UK
UKOW06f1957020215

245516UK00003B/20/P